Visual
Basic® 6

Rob Thayer

SAMS

Unleashed

Visual Basic 6 Unleashed

Copyright © 1998 by Sams Publishing

International Standard Book Number: 0-672-31309-X

Library of Congress Catalog Card Number: 98-84091

Printed in the United States of America

First Printing: September 1998

00 99   4   3   2

Trademarks

Warning and Disclaimer

EXECUTIVE EDITOR
Chris Denny

AQUISITIONS EDITOR
Sharon Cox

DEVELOPMENT EDITOR
Tony Amico

MANAGING EDITOR
Jodi Jensen

SENIOR EDITOR
Susan Ross Moore

COPY EDITORS
Sara Bosin
Kelli M. Brooks
Molly Schaller

INDEXER
C.J. East

TECHNICAL EDITOR
Sakher Youness

SOFTWARE DEVELOPMENT SPECIALIST
John Warriner

TEAM COORDINATOR
Carol Ackerman

PRODUCTION
Marcia DeBoy
Jenny Earhart
Cynthia Fields
Susan Geiselman

COVER DESIGNER
Aren Howell

INTERIOR DESIGNER
Gary Adair

Overview

Introduction

PART I   VISUAL BASIC 6

Chapter 1   The VB5 Programmer's Guide To VB6

Chapter 2   New ActiveX Controls

Chapter 3   New Add-Ins and Utilities

PART II   CREATING COMPONENTS IN VB6

Chapter 4   An Overview of ActiveX Programming

Chapter 5   Creating ActiveX Controls

Chapter 6   Deploying ActiveX Controls

Chapter 7   ActiveX Scripting with VBScript

Chapter 8   Data Consumers and Data Sources

Chapter 9   Apartment Model Threading

Chapter 10   Object-Oriented Programming in Visual Basic

Chapter 11   Creating and Using Class Modules

Part III   Database Programming

Chapter 12   An Overview of Database Programming in VB6

Chapter 13   The ADO Data Control

Chapter 14   Working in the Data Environment

Chapter 15   Using the Data Report Utility

Chapter 16   Database Tools and Utilities

Chapter 17   Advanced Data Controls

Chapter 18   SQL and the T-SQL Debugger

PART IV   INTERNET PROGRAMMING

Chapter 19   Creating ActiveX Documents

Chapter 20   Creating DHTML Applications

Chapter 21 Mail-Enabling Your Applications with MAPI

Chapter 22 Using the Internet Transfer Control

Chapter 23 Client/Server Programming with Winsock

PART V ADVANCED PROGRAMMING TOPICS

Chapter 24 Using Office 97 Components with Visual Basic

Chapter 25 Using Windows API Functions

Chapter 26 Useful API Functions

Chapter 27 Creating Telephony Applications with TAPI

Chapter 28 Adding Speech Recognition with SAPI

Chapter 29 Creating Your Own Add-Ins

Chapter 30 Accessing the System Registry

Chapter 31 Creating Online Help Systems

Chapter 32 Debugging and Testing Techniques

Chapter 33 Dynamic Control Creation and Indexing

Chapter 34 Implementing OLE Drag and Drop Capabilities

Chapter 35 Tuning and Optimizing Your Application

Chapter 36 Algorithms for VB Programmers

Chapter 37 Differences Between VBA and VB6

Chapter 38 Programming for Microsoft Transaction Server

Chapter 39 Visual SourceSafe: A Necessity for Serious Developers

INDEX

Contents

INTRODUCTION   **1**

PART I   VISUAL BASIC 6   **5**

1   THE VB5 PROGRAMMER'S GUIDE TO VB6   **7**

New Language Features 9

    New Functions..10

New Wizards..13

    The Add-In Designer...14

    The Application Wizard...14

    The Package and Deployment Wizard 14

    The Toolbar Wizard...16

Other Changes and Enhancements 16

    New and Enhanced Controls 16

    Internet Features 17

    Component Creation 18

Summary...18

2   NEW ACTIVEX CONTROLS   **19**

The `Coolbar` Control..20

    The `Band` Object and the `Bands` Collection 21

    `Coolbar` Properties...23

    `Coolbar` Events 24

    The `Coolbar` In Action...24

The `ImageCombo` Control...32

    The `ComboItem` Object 33

    `ImageCombo` Properties, Methods, and Events 34

    The `ImageCombo` In Action..35

The `MonthView` Control..37

    `MonthView` Properties..38

    `MonthView` Methods 40

    `MonthView` Events 42

The `DateTimePicker` Control (`DTPicker`)......................................42

    `DTPicker` Properties and Events 43

    `DTPicker Formats` 44

The `FlatScrollbar` Control 46

    Properties..47

Summary...47

3 NEW ADD-INS AND UTILITIES 49

The API Viewer...50

The VB6 Resource Editor..51

Visual Modeler 56

The Visual Component Manager 59

The VB6 Template Manager...62

Summary..64

PART II   CREATING COMPONENTS IN VB6   65

4 AN OVERVIEW OF ACTIVEX PROGRAMMING 67

A Brief History of ActiveX 68

DDE and OLE 1.0..68

OLE 2.0 and COM 69

VBXes and OCXes 75

ActiveX Controls and Visual Basic..75

The Basics of ActiveX Control Creation..76

New ActiveX Control Concepts 77

Other ActiveX Projects In Visual Basic 77

Summary..79

5 CREATING ACTIVEX CONTROLS 81

Think First, Code Later 82

The Power of ActiveX Controls 83

The Birth of an ActiveX Control..83

The Three Paths of Control Creation 85

Using Constituent Controls 86

Passing Along Properties..87

Down to the Basics 87

Control Containers..89

Ambient Objects 90

Putting It All Together: The Interface 90

Creating the Control 92

Assembling the Control..93

Adding the Code 96

A Few Problems with the LightButton Control............................104

The Property Bag...109

Trying Out the LightButton Control... Again 111

The Life of a Control Instance 112

Adding More Properties to the LightButton Control...................116

Initializing, Reading, and Writing Properties 124

All Systems Go! 127

One More Property: Enabled...128

Expanding on the Control's Interface 130

    Adding Events to the Sample Control.....................................131

    Creating Custom Events 135

    A Few Last Words on Events 138

Adding Methods to the Sample Control..139

    The Refresh Method 139

    The Flash Method 139

    Odds and Ends..141

Summary 147

6   DEPLOYING ACTIVEX CONTROLS   149

Compiling the Control 150

    Creating an .OCX File..150

    Using the Control in Visual Basic...154

    Using the Control on a Web Page 155

The Package and Deployment Wizard 155

Deploying .CAB Files 156

Summary 157

7   ACTIVEX SCRIPTING WITH VBSCRIPT   159

Down-and-Dirty VBScript 160

    The Main Differences Between VB and VBScript 161

    Objects in VBScript..161

    Using Procedures in VBScript..162

    A Sample Script..163

More VBScript 167

    Operators 167

    Functions 167

    Statements 173

Summary 174

8   DATA CONSUMERS AND DATA SOURCES   175

Introduction to Data Sources and Data Consumers 176

Creating a Data Source..176

    Building the Control's User Interface 178

    Adding Properties 180

    Trying Out the Control 185

    Implementing Database Functionality...186

    Adding Methods 190

    The Finished Product..191

Creating a Data Consumer 192

Summary 193

9   APARTMENT MODEL THREADING   195

Introduction to Multithreaded Development 196
   Defining a Thread 196
   Understanding Concurrency 197
   The ActiveX/COM+ Approach 198
Multithreaded Development in Visual Basic 6....................................198
   Understanding Apartment-Model Threading 199
   Re-Entrancy 200
   Serialization...201
   Thread Aggregation 201
   Benefit of the Round-Robin Threading Model 203
   Thread Control...203
Thread Safety 203
Implementing Multithreaded Systems 205
   Advice for Implementing Multiple Threads
      of Execution 205
   When Not to Use Multithreaded Development..............................206
Instantiating Externally Creatable Classes 207
Issues in Recording Apartment Events..208
Tips on Testing and Debugging Multithreaded Systems 208
   Out-of-Process Components 209
   In-Process Components 209
   Using a Native Code Debugger..209
   Analyzing Debug Messages 210
Multithreading Single-Use Objects 210
The Meaning of `SingleUse`..211
   Out of Process Components and Multiple `SingleUse` Classes 211
   Internal and External Creation of `SingleUse` Class Instances 212
Summary..212

10   OBJECT-ORIENTED PROGRAMMING IN VISUAL BASIC   213

Migrating from Legacy Programming Practices 215
From OTFP to OOP 216
A Primer on Classes 217
   The Visual Basic Class 217
   An Example of Class Identities..219
Creating VB Classes 220
Building Classes With the Class Builder 221
   The Menus..223
   The Properties, Methods, and Events Pane....................................224
Understanding the Difference Between Collections and Aggregations of
   Objects 227

Understanding How Objects Talk to Each Other 228
Understanding Subsystems 229
    Understanding Application Subsystems 229
    Understanding How Subsystems Talk to Each Other 230
Summary 230

11 CREATING AND USING CLASS MODULES   233

Realizing the Importance of Using Analysis Methods.......................234
Building the Foundation for Object-Oriented Analysis 235
    The Requirements Gatherer...235
    The Object-Oriented Analyst..236
    The Architect 238
Implementing the Use-Case Methodology for Your Environment......239
    The Problem Statement 240
    The Use-Case Model 245
    The Sequence Diagram 247
    The First Sequence Diagram 248
    The Analysis Class Model..253
Summary 254

PART III   DATABASE PROGRAMMING   257

12 AN OVERVIEW OF DATABASE PROGRAMMING IN VB6   259

Database Access Methods in VB6 260
    DAO...261
    RDO...262
    ADO...263
The Data View Window 264
The Data Environment Designer 264
Database Controls 266
The Future of Data Access in VB..266
Summary 267

13 THE ADO DATA CONTROL   269

ADO: An Overview 270
A Review of Relational Databases 270
    Tables...271
    Primary Keys 271
    Understanding Data Normalization..272
    Using Foreign Keys 273
    Referential Integrity...275

Indexes...275
Views...276
Examining the Use of Client/Server Design 276
Two-Tiered Client/Server Applications...............................277
Multi-Tiered Client/Server Applications.............................277
Understanding Thin Clients Versus Thick Clients 277
Using the ADO Data Control and Libraries.............................279
ADO Object Model..280
Creating an OLE DB Data Source 290
Creating an ADO Database Front End 292
Remoting of ADO Recordsets 295
Summary..296

14   WORKING IN THE DATA ENVIRONMENT   299
Introduction to the Data Environment 300
Defining the Connection 301
Using the SQL Query Designer 303
Child Commands..308
Using the Data Environment to Access the Database 311
Summary..314

15   USING THE DATA REPORT UTILITY   315
Introduction to the Data Report Utility 316
Creating a Report 316
Adding and Setting Up a Data Environment............................317
Designing the Report..321
Previewing the Report...328
Printing the Report 331
Exporting the Report 332
The Data Report Utility and Crystal Reports: How They Compare ..334
Summary..334

16   DATABASE TOOLS AND UTILITIES   337
The Data View Window 338
The SQL Editor..339
Stored Procedures 339
Setting Triggers 340
The Query Designer 341
Creating Data Objects Using the Data Object Wizard.................342
Creating a Class Object...342
Creating the Custom Data Control 347
Using the New Control Object 348
Using the Data Form Wizard 349
Summary...354

17 ADVANCED DATA CONTROLS 357

The `DataList` Control 358

The `DataCombo` Control 361

The `DataGrid` Control 363

`DataGrid` Properties 364

`DataGrid` Methods 368

`DataGrid` Events 370

Using the `DataGrid` Control 370

The Hierarchical `FlexGrid` Control (`MSHFlexGrid`) 374

`MSHFlexGrid` Properties 376

`MSHFlexGrid` Methods 384

`MSHFlexGrid` Events..385

Using the `MSHFlexGrid` Control....................................386

Summary 389

18 SQL AND THE T-SQL DEBUGGER 391

Working with Standard SQL 392

Retrieving Data 394

Inserting Data 403

Deleting Data...405

Updating Data 406

Grouping SQL Statements into Transactions 407

Altering the Database Structure with Data Definition Statements 409

Using the T-SQL Debugger 412

Installing the T-SQL Debugger 412

Using the T-SQL Debugger..414

T-SQL Debugger Options 421

Summary 423

PART IV INTERNET PROGRAMMING 425

19 CREATING ACTIVEX DOCUMENTS 427

Understanding ActiveX Documents 428

What Is an ActiveX Document? 428

Understanding the Advantages of ActiveX Documents 429

Exploring the `UserDocument` Object 430

Key Events and Properties...430

Creating and Storing Properties for a `UserDocument` 431

Asynchronous Downloading of Controls 432

Using the `Hyperlink` Object 434

ActiveX Document DLLs Versus ActiveX Document EXEs..............436

Creating Your First ActiveX Document 437

Starting an ActiveX Document Project 438
Creating the Interface for the Document.........................439
Adding Code to the Document 440
Testing Your ActiveX Document...441
Compiling Your Document 441
Menu Design for ActiveX Documents 442
Adding Forms and Documents to ActiveX Documents 445
Adding Additional Documents 445
Deploying an ActiveX Document in Internet Explorer 447
Using the ActiveX Document Migration Wizard 448
Running the ActiveX Document Migration Wizard 449
Viewing the Wizard's Work...451
Summary 452

20 CREATING DHTML APPLICATIONS   453
An Overview of Dynamic HTML 454
DHTML Applications: What Are They? 455
Understanding the DHTML Object Model 457
Dynamic HTML Objects..457
Dynamic HTML Events 459
Understanding the DHTML Project Type 463
Using the Page Designer 464
Designing Pages for DHTML 464
Using DHTML to Maintain State 470
Implementing DHTML Applications 473
Debugging DHTML Applications..474
Compiling Your Application 474
Deploying DHTML Applications...476
Installing the Package and Deployment Wizard 477
Using the Package and Deployment Wizard...............................477
Summary 482

21 MAIL-ENABLING YOUR APPLICATIONS WITH MAPI   483
Understanding the MAPI Specification 484
MAPI Service Providers 486
The MAPI Spooler 488
Using the MAPI Controls: MAPISession and MAPIMessages 488
Creating MAPI Programs with Visual Basic 493
Creating Mail-Enabled Applications 494
Creating E-Mail Applications 505
Summary 518

22   USING THE INTERNET TRANSFER CONTROL   519

Properties, Methods, and Events 521

Properties 521

Methods 524

Events 528

Using the Internet Transfer Control with a Proxy Server 529

Accessing Files and Documents with the OpenURL Method...............530

Accessing FTP Servers with the Execute Method............................531

Summary...533

23   CLIENT/SERVER PROGRAMMING WITH WINSOCK   535

TCP/IP Fundamentals..536

How Does It Work?..537

A Word About Clients and Servers 538

Domain Names and IP Addresses 538

Understanding Ports 539

Using the Microsoft Winsock Control 539

Winsock Operating Modes 540

TCP Basics 540

UDP Basics 540

Properties of the Winsock Control 541

Methods of the Winsock Control 543

Events 545

Creating the Price Lookup Example..547

Creating the Client..547

Creating the Server 549

Running the Example 553

Enhancements to the Price Lookup Example 555

Summary...556

PART V   ADVANCED PROGRAMMING TOPICS   565

24   USING OFFICE 97 COMPONENTS WITH VISUAL BASIC   559

OLE...560

The OLE Control 561

OLE Control Properties and Methods...568

OLE Automation..569

Using OLE Automation..572

Summary...577

25   USING WINDOWS API FUNCTIONS   579

The Windows API Library Files 580
    USER32.DLL 581
    GDI32.DLL 582
    KERNEL32.DLL 582
Declaring a Windows API Function 583
Passing Arguments by Value and by Reference 585
Declare Statement Argument Data Types 586
    Using Aliases 588
    Using Ordinal Numbers as Function Names 588
The API Text Viewer 589
Using Windows API Functions in Your Applications 592
How to Use Windows API Callbacks 594
Summary 595

26   USEFUL API FUNCTIONS   597

Graphics and Display Functions 599
    Copying Images: BitBlt& and StretchBlt& 599
    Draw a Rectangle with Rounded Corners 603
    Rotating Text 604
System Functions 607
    Wait for a Child Process 608
    Exit Windows 612
    Stop Ctrl+Alt+Del and Ctrl+Tab 613
    Find the Windows and System Directories 614
Summary 615

27   CREATING TELEPHONY APPLICATIONS WITH TAPI   617

How It Works 619
    Types of TAPI Applications 620
Creating a TAPI Application 620
    What You Need 621
    A Sample Program 621
Other TAPI Functions 625
Summary 626

28   ADDING SPEECH RECOGNITION WITH SAPI   627

Overview of SAPI 4.0..628
Creating a Speech Recognition Application 629
    Setting up the Microphone 630
    Using the Direct Speech Control..631
    Properties and Methods of the Direct Speech Control 634

Creating a Text-to-Speech Application...635
    Creating the Text-to-Speech Project 635
    Properties and Methods of the `Text-to-Speech` Control 638
Summary 641

29   CREATING YOUR OWN ADD-INS   643
Understanding the Extensibility Model 644
Assessing the Extensibility Object Model 644
Understanding the Core Objects Package 645
    The `Root` Object..645
    The `IDTExtensibility` Interface Object................................649
    The Visual Basic Instance Variable 651
Understanding the Form Manipulation Package 651
    The `CommandBar` Object 651
    The `CodePane` Object 652
Understanding the Event Response Package 652
Understanding the Add-In Management Package 652
    Understanding the Project and Component Manipulation
        Package 653
    Understanding the Code Manipulation Package 653
Implementing the Extensibility Model in a Practical Way.................654
Understanding What Makes a Wizard 661
    Determining When a Wizard is Needed 661
    Effective Wizard Design 662
Planning the Computer Wizard...662
Using the Wizard Manager 665
    Creating the Template 666
    Building the Wizard from the Template 667
    Using the Template 668
Modifying the Code 675
    Providing Exception Handling 678
    Controlling the Flow 680
Using the Wizard Resource File 683
Summary 687

30   ACCESSING THE SYSTEM REGISTRY   689
INI Files 691
    Accessing INI Files With the Windows API...............................692
    Creating an INI File Editor 697
The System Registry..715
    Accessing the Registry With VB Functions 718
    Accessing the Registry With the Windows API 720
    Creating a System Registry Editor 725
Summary 735

31   CREATING ONLINE HELP SYSTEMS   737

Building a Help System 738
   Building a Topics File 739
   Labeling the Topics 744
Creating a Standard Help Project 747
   Using the Help Topics Dialog Box 751
   Enhancing the Standard Help File..758
   Using Secondary Window Formats 759
   Linking to the Internet..761
   Adding Multimedia 761
Moving to HTML Help 762
   Using the HTML Help Workshop...765
   Converting from Older Help Projects 772
   Using Advanced HTML Help Features..773
   Linking to the Internet..774
   Adding Multimedia 775
Accessing Help from a Visual Basic Application.................................775
   The Windows Common Dialog Control 775
   Context-Sensitive Help 777
Summary..779

32   DEBUGGING AND TESTING TECHNIQUES   781

Starting at the Beginning 782
Error Handling 783
Avoiding Program Errors 783
Debugging Programs in Visual Basic...784
   Stepping Through Code..785
   Special Debugging Windows...787
Summary..791

33   DYNAMIC CONTROL CREATION AND INDEXING   793

Creating Control Arrays 794
   Pros and Cons of Using Control Arrays 795
   Using a Control Array 796
Designing Event Handlers for Control Arrays 800
Creating Controls Dynamically 801
Instantiating Forms at Runtime 803
Using Control Array Properties 805
   The Count Property 805
   The Item Property 806
   The LBound and UBound Properties 806
Creating Data Controls Dynamically 807
Summary..808

34   IMPLEMENTING OLE DRAG-AND-DROP CAPABILITIES   809

An Overview of OLE Drag and Drop 810

What Is OLE Drag and Drop? 810

How Does OLE Drag and Drop Work? 811

Beginning the Drag 812

Going Over the Target...812

Completing the Drag 813

Automatic or Manual Processing? 813

Using Automatic OLE Drag and Drop 814

Controlling the Manual Process 817

The `DataObject` Object 818

The `OLEDrag` Method 819

The `OLEStartDrag` Event 820

The `OLEDragOver` Event 821

Providing Customized Visual Feedback 822

The `OLEGiveFeedback` Event 822

The `OLEDragDrop` Event..824

The `OLECompleteDrag` Event 825

Enhancing Visual Basic Applications with OLE Drag and Drop........826

Summary 829

35   TUNING AND OPTIMIZING YOUR APPLICATION   831

Optimizing and Tuning with Visual Basic 832

Understanding the Art of Optimizing and Tuning 832

Using Proper Software Designs When Creating Applications 833

Testing on the Designated Platform or Environment 834

Knowing What to Optimize...834

Testing Compiled Versions 835

Optimizing and Tuning During the Entire Development

Process 835

Avoiding Over-Optimizing 835

Commenting Your Code Like a Maintenance Programmer 836

Creating and Using Templates to Perform Code Benchmarking........836

Reviewing Performance Tips and Tricks 841

Using the Visual Basic Compiler to Tune and Optimize 841

Sorting Strings with a List Box..843

Using the Windows API 843

Using Data Controls to Conserve SQL Server User

Connections...843

Understanding Visual Basics Limitations 845

Reducing the Dots When Using Objects.......................................845

Using Method Parameters with Out-of-Process or Distributed
Components 846
Increasing Perceived Speed with Splash Screens and Progress
Indicators..846
Using Early Object Binding Versus Late Binding 846
Optimizing Display Speed...847
Optimizing Data Types 847
Optimizing File I/O Operations...847
Optimizing Memory 848
Avoiding Calling Functions and Procedures in Different
Modules...848
Selecting the Proper Component Type 848
Optimizing Web-Based Components 849
Multithreaded or Single-Threaded Components 849
Using the Visual Basic Code Profiler 850
Installing the Visual Basic Code Profiler 851
Using the Visual Basic Code Profiler 852
Summary..856

36   ALGORITHMS FOR VB PROGRAMMERS   857
Algorithms 858
Sorting 858
Data Encryption/Decryption 863
Data Compression/Decompression 867
Summary..874

37   DIFFERENCES BETWEEN VBA AND VB6   875
An Overview of VBA 876
What VBA Is and Is Not 876
The VBA Development Environment 877
Programming Differences 879
Summary..888

38   PROGRAMMING FOR MICROSOFT TRANSACTION SERVER   889
Understanding Distributed Transaction Processing 890
Transaction Monitors..891
Object Request Brokers..892
Introducing Microsoft Transaction Server 893
Managing Database Connections 894
Managing Distributed Objects..895
Transaction Coordination 895
Integrating Visual Basic Classes with Transaction Server 896
Initializing the Visual Basic Project 896

Stateless Objects 898
Transaction Context...899
Registering Visual Basic DLLs with Transaction Server 903
Calling Transaction Server Objects from Visual Basic 908
Setting the Product ID..910
Calling the Transaction Server Object 912
Summary...913

39 VISUAL SOURCESAFE: A NECESSITY FOR SERIOUS DEVELOPERS 915
Understanding Source Control 916
Introducing Visual SourceSafe 917
Understanding How VSS Can Help You 917
Installing the VSS Server 918
Administering the VSS Environment 919
Understanding Project-Oriented Programming 922
Using Projects in Visual SourceSafe.............................922
Checking the Files Back Into Visual SourceSafe 925
Adding Files to the SourceSafe Project 926
Tracking Different Versions of Your Project.....................926
Using Visual SourceSafe from Visual Basic 6 927
VSS Options 927
Using an Existing Visual Basic Project..........................929
Creating New Visual Basic Projects 931
Summary...932

INDEX 933

About the Authors

Robert Thayer is the President of Thayer Technologies, Inc., a Phoenix-based company that specializes in the design and creation of Windows applications and client/server systems. He can be reached at rob@thayertech.com or via TTI's Web site at http://www.thayertech.com.

John D. Conley III is President and Chief System Architect of Samsona Software Co. Inc., a firm that specializes in developing custom software for organizations and creating development tools. He is the co-author of several books, including *Visual Basic 5.0 Development Unleashed*, *Visual Basic 5.0 Fundamentals Unleashed*, *Special Edition Using Oracle Web Application Server 3.0*, and *Working with Cartridges*. A graduate of the University of Oklahoma and former student of U.C. Berkeley, he has over 11 years of professional software development experience and 17 years total. He can be reached at samsona@dallas.net, http://www.samsona.com, or 972-394-3983.

Loren D. Eidahl is the President of Cornerstone Technology Systems (CTS), an Internet consulting firm specializing in providing complete Internet business solutions, ranging from Internet access to total integrated solutions. Loren has been involved with computers since the early days of the PC when 16KB was a lot of RAM, and BASIC was definitely not Visual. Over the past ten years he has been a consultant to a wide range of industries, including a national retail chain and several large financial institutions. Loren can be reached via email at leidahl@cornerstonetech.com or on the Web at http://www.cornerstonetech.com.

Lowell Mauer has been a programmer and instructor for 20 years. He has taught programming at Montclair State College in New Jersey and has developed and marketed a Visual Basic application for airplane pilots and is involved in creating several corporate Web site applications. As a manager of technical support, he has attended seminars and training sessions in several countries and is an expert is more than six computer languages. He currently is a Senior Business Analyst at Cognos Corporation in New York City, N.Y., where he helps in the implementation and use of several PC-based computer products.

Dedication

This book is dedicated to Danielle Bird, who got me roped into writing these books in the first place.

—Rob Thayer

Acknowledgments

I should start by thanking all of the other authors who have contributed material to this book. Their expertise and dedication to this project is greatly valued.

I'd also like to thank Sharon Cox, the Acquisitions Editor for this title, and all of the others who have worked hard to get this book on the shelf: Tony Amico, Susan Ross Moore, Chris Denny, and everyone else who was involved. Thanks also to Valda Hilley, always a source of wisdom and insight.

On a personal note, I'd like to thank my friends and family for all their help during this project. Mom, Dad, Tracy, Vince, Vicki, Kevin, David, Fe, and Steve, thanks for being there. To Joe Miano, Chuck Seifert, Gary Moore, Kevin Twiggs, Peter Stutsman, Mike and Debby Freeman, Frank Newkirk, and all my good friends, all I can say is that I deeply value your friendship. An extra special thanks goes to David and Ellen Adams (www.fallenwall.org), who have always been there when I needed them.

Rob Thayer

Tell Us What You Think!

As the reader of this book, *you* are our most important critic and commentator. We value your opinion and want to know what we're doing right, what we could do better, what areas you'd like to see us publish in, and any other words of wisdom you're willing to pass our way.

As the Executive Editor for the Visual Basic Programming team at Macmillan Computer Publishing, I welcome your comments. You can fax, e-mail, or write me directly to let me know what you did or didn't like about this book—as well as what we can do to make our books stronger.

Please note that I cannot help you with technical problems related to the topic of this book, and that due to the high volume of mail I receive, I might not be able to reply to every message.

When you write, please be sure to include this book's title and author as well as your name and phone or fax number. I will carefully review your comments and share them with the author and editors who worked on the book.

> Fax: 317-817-7070
>
> E-mail: vb@mcp.com
>
> Mail: Chris Denny
>   Executive Editor
>   Visual Basic Programming Team
>   Macmillan Computer Publishing
>   201 West 103rd Street
>   Indianapolis, IN 46290 USA

Introduction

It's amazing how far Visual Basic has come since its initial release. Originally considered nothing more than a hobbyist's language, VB is now the number one development tool for Windows applications. Even though it has gone through a large number of changes and enhancements over the years, it's still an easy-to-learn, easy-to-use language.

Visual Basic has done a remarkable job of keeping up with the times. As the Internet gained in popularity, VB was right in there with controls and project types that could be used to exploit the availability of global communications. In some cases, Visual Basic has been the technology leader, implementing new ways of doing things before any other development tool. In other cases, VB wasn't the first to support a new technology but it was certainly the easiest. The creation of ActiveX controls, for example, was done exclusively by C++ programmers—that is, until VB5 and its freeware cousin, VB5 Control Creation Edition, were released. Now, ActiveX control creation can be accomplished by even beginning programmers.

Despite the fact that Visual Basic has matured so quickly, it's only been in recent years that VB has gotten its due as a viable tool for software development. This is primarily because the area of data access was neglected for quite some time, and you simply cannot have a serious development tool without extensive database support. It wasn't until VB3 came along that support for Microsoft's Jet database engine was added, and even that wasn't enough to allow VB to compete with the likes of C++. Subsequent releases of the product added support for ODBC and RDO data access methods, bringing VB into the realm of the serious development tools.

The latest release of Visual Basic brings several changes in the area of database access, adding the ActiveX Data Objects (ADO) access method. ADO, the successor to DAO and RDO, is destined to become the one-size-fits-all data access method for Windows development. VB6 supports the still immature ADO in a big way, with half a dozen new controls optimized specifically for use with ADO databases. The Data Environment, a way of exploiting ADO's hierarchical database organization, has also been added to Visual Basic 6. Add in the Data Report Utility, a built-in tool for generating reports using the structure of the Data Environment, and you can see that VB6 is truly centered around ADO.

In addition to extensive support for ADO, there is a long list of other changes that have been made to this latest release of Visual Basic. You can consider this book to be a guide to many of the more important new features as well as some of the technologies that have been implemented in previous versions.

Part I, "Visual Basic 6," offers a brief introduction to some of VB6's new features, controls, and utilities. Chapter 1, "The VB5 Programmer's Guide To VB6," gives you the low-down on what's new in this version. It's highly recommended that you read this chapter if you have just starting using VB6. In addition to describing all of VB6's new features, it also includes information on some of the new string-handling statements and functions that have been added to the Visual Basic language. Chapter 2, "New ActiveX Controls," introduces you to all of the new additions to VB's Toolbox. Chapter 3, "New Add-Ins and Utilities," discusses some of VB6's new built-in utilities.

Part II, "Creating Components In VB6," helps you get started in creating powerful reusable components, such as ActiveX controls and class modules. Chapter 4, "An Overview of ActiveX Programming," provides a general overview of ActiveX component creation in VB6. The next chapter, "Creating ActiveX Controls," actually shows you how to create a useful control, and Chapter 6, "Deploying ActiveX Controls," shows you how to deploy your controls in other programs or on the Internet.

Chapter 7, "ActiveX Scripting with VBScript," tells you what you need to know to use VBScript for using ActiveX controls on Web pages. This chapter is designed specifically for Visual Basic programmers who want to learn more about VBScript, and it points out the differences between the two development tools.

Chapter 8, "Data Consumers and Data Sources," shows you how you can create an ActiveX control that works as a data source (such as VB's Data control). It also tells you how to create data consumers that can be bound to such data sources. In Chapter 9, "Apartment Model Threading," you'll see an example of a multi-threaded component that uses apartment model threading.

Object-oriented programming is a hot topic, and Chapter 10, "Object-Oriented Programming In Visual Basic," tells you what you need to know to follow OOP principles in VB. Chapter 11, "Creating and Using Class Modules," provides an introduction to the powerful but often misused class modules.

Part III of this book, "Database Programming," covers all of the new database features in VB6. This area has received quite a bit of attention from Microsoft with this release of Visual Basic, and this book also gives it the attention it deserves. In Chapter 12, "An Overview of Database Programming In VB6," you'll see how databases are now supported in Visual Basic as well as what the future holds.

Chapter 13, "The ADO Data Control," shows you how to use the new ADO Data control for accessing databases. Chapter 14, "Working In the Data Environment," discusses the new Data Environment for utilizing the hierarchical organization of the ADO model.

Chapter 15, "Using the Data Report Utility," discusses the new utility for generating reports from ADO data sources. Other new tools and utilities for working with databases can be found in Chapter 16, "Database Tools and Utilities." VB6 also adds a number of new ActiveX controls for working with ADO data sources. These new controls are covered in Chapter 17, "Advanced Data Controls." Finally, the Enterprise Edition's T-SQL Debugger utility is discussed in Chapter 18, "SQL and the T-SQL Debugger."

Developing applications for the Internet has become a hot topic of discussion among VB programmers, and Part IV, "Internet Programming," will provide you with the information you need for effective Internet/intranet programming. Chapter 19, "Creating ActiveX Documents," illustrates how to create and implement ActiveX documents. Chapter 20, "Creating DHTML Applications," covers one of the more exciting new project types in VB6, the Dynamic HTML application. VB6 also adds support for creating server-side applications for Microsoft's Internet Information Server (IIS).

For developers creating applications that run under Windows but interact with the Internet, there are Chapters 21, 22, and 23. Chapter 21, "Mail-Enabling Your Applications With MAPI," shows you how to use VB's MAPI ActiveX controls to send and receive electronic mail. Chapter 22, "Using the Internet Transfer Control," illustrates the use of VB's Inet control for accessing files and documents via the HTTP and FTP protocols. Finally, Chapter 23, "Client/Server Programming With Winsock," shows how to use the Winsock control for low-level Internet communication.

Part V of this book, "Advanced Programming Topics," is a hodge-podge of information for more advanced developers. It's here that you can learn more about using the Windows API as well as Microsoft's TAPI and SAPI libraries. You can also find more information about using Office 97 components via OLE automation, how to access the System Registry, creating online Help systems, how to program for the Microsoft Transaction Server, and many other topics.

This book is not designed to be a step-by-step tutorial for beginning programmers, but rather as a kind of quick-start guide for intermediate and advanced programmers. The chapters contained herein are meant to be a way of introducing key concepts in the areas you want to learn more about. For example, you may want to know more about how to use VB6's new Data Report Utility. If you read Chapter 15 ("Using the Data Report Utility"), you'll gain a much better understanding of how that particular utility works. The chapter won't tell you everything there is to know about the Data Report Utility; that is not the intention. What it will tell you are the basics, providing you with enough information so you can easily learn more just by using the utility.

I sincerely believe that this book will help you master many of the more complex aspects of Visual Basic programming, as well as introduce you to some of the more interesting new features of VB6. I wish you luck in your programming endeavors!

Rob Thayer

Visual Basic 6

IN THIS PART

- The VB5 Programmer's Guide To VB6   7
- New ActiveX Controls   19
- New Add-Ins and Utilities   49

CHAPTER 1

The VB5 Programmer's Guide To VB6

by Rob Thayer

IN THIS CHAPTER

- New Language Features *9*
- New Wizards *13*
- Other Changes and Enhancements *16*

When a new version of Visual Basic is released, the first thing every VB programmer wants to know is, "What's new, and how can I use it to my benefit?" This entire book is geared toward answering that important question, and this chapter will provide you with brief descriptions of some of the new features of VB6. However, before we get into the details of how Visual Basic 6 differs from VB5, let's go back and quickly recap the major changes that have been introduced with prior releases of the product.

The original version of Visual Basic was rather limited, and was by no stretch of the imagination a tool for serious development. However, it was a landmark product in that it brought a graphical design environment to the world of Windows development. It was neat, but it was also seen by the majority of programmers as a "toy" language.

The subsequent version of the product, VB2, didn't really do much to enhance Visual Basic's position in the development world because it still lacked native database support. However, Access 1.0 was released shortly after VB2, and the beginnings of a marriage between the two started to take hold.

It wasn't until VB3 was released that Visual Basic really started to gain support from the development community. Among other innovations, the new version added the Jet database engine, giving VB the built-in database support that it so desperately needed. VB3 also added support for VBX modules, the 16-bit predecessors to the OCX components used in later versions of the product.

Third-party support for Visual Basic really started to increase with the release of VB3. It was also about this time that VB was starting to gain recognition as a viable development environment. It still had a long way to go, but VB was finally starting to take shape as a powerful and flexible programming language.

VB4 was something of a "stepping stone" designed primarily for easing the transition between 16-bit and 32-bit development. In fact, VB4 actually consisted of two separate development environments: one for 16-bit applications and one for 32-bit applications. Because of the support for 32-bit development, it was in VB4 that we first saw the 32-bit OCX controls that are now so commonplace.

VB4 added some other important new features, such as the ability to create OLE custom controls and DLLs. Because Access 2.0 was released after VB3, VB4 also addressed compatibility issues between the Jet engine and the newer version of Access.

Although VB4 brought quite a few changes to the Visual Basic environment, the next version really gave it a boost. VB5 added a slew of new project types, including ActiveX controls, ActiveX DLLs, and ActiveX documents. VB's compiler received an overhaul as well, so that VB could support native code compilation in addition to pseudocode (P-Code) compilation.

This brings us to the current version of Visual Basic, VB6, and that same question, "What's new?". The paradoxical answer: a little and a lot. On one hand, there are few major changes that have been made, and VB6 is really not very different from VB5. On the other hand, VB6 has a long list of minor changes, ranging from new language features to a re-vamping of the Setup Wizard (now called the Package and Deployment Wizard).

Like VB4, VB6 seems to be a stepping stone rather than a major overhaul of the development environment. In VB4, the move was towards 32-bit application development. This time, Microsoft is easing Visual Basic programmers into a new database accessing method (ADO) that is destined to eventually take the place of other accessing methods such as DAO and ODBC. Therefore, it should be no surprise that many of the new features found in VB6 are in the area of data access.

ADO, or ActiveX Data Objects, has been implemented in VB6 as an ActiveX control (the `ADO Data` control). This control is discussed in great detail in Chapter 13, "The ADO Data Control". Because data access methods are in a state of flux with this version of Visual Basic, Chapter 12, "An Overview of Database Programming In VB6", provides a brief discussion of the ways in which databases can currently be used from within VB. It also gives a hint of what the future will hold for Visual Basic data access.

In addition to the new `ADO Data` control, VB6 now comes with an enhanced array of database manipulation and reporting tools. These are detailed in Chapters 15, "Using the Data Report Utility," and 16, "Database Tools and Utilities." Several new data-aware controls have also been added to VB6's Toolbox; they are covered in Chapter 17, "Advanced Data Controls." Many other changes have been made concerning data access. See Chapter 12 for more information.

Aside from the changes in the data access area and the move towards ADO, VB6 has been enhanced in many other ways. Although we won't be going into any of these changes in detail, the rest of this chapter will at least make you aware of what's new and what has been improved.

New Language Features

Like all of the versions that preceded it, Visual Basic 6 brings changes to the core of its development environment, the language itself. Several new string functions have been added, and certain data types now offer more flexibility when being used with public properties, methods, or functions.

Public properties and methods can now use UDTs (user-defined types) as arguments or return value types. Likewise, function and property procedures can return arrays. This will no doubt come as good news to those who have found VB to be too limited in the types of data that can be passed to and from procedures.

Object creation has also been enhanced in VB6, specifically in the `CreateObject` function. In addition to creating local objects, you can now specify an optional machine name and create objects on remote systems.

The `StrConv` function, which can perform several different conversions on strings, has been extended with an optional argument called `LCID`. The `LCID` argument enables you to specify a LocaleID for a string different than the local system's LocaleID.

Several new object types have been added to VB6. Called the File System Objects, or FSO. These objects include a set of methods that can make working with files and directories easier and faster. The FSO group may be familiar to VBScript programmers because these objects originated from scripting languages.

Under certain conditions, VB6 will now enable you to assign the contents of one array to another. Although the array that is being copied can be of either a variable- or fixed-size, only variable-sized arrays can be on the left side of the assignment.

New Functions

A total of fourteen new functions have been added to Visual Basic's already impressive repertoire of built-in commands and procedures. Either by coincidence or by design, they all have to do with strings in some fashion.

The new functions are described briefly in the following sections. If you want to find more specific information about a particular function, consult VB's online Help system or the Visual Basic reference manual.

CallByName Function

This function enables you to use string values to specify the names of properties or methods at runtime, rather than hard-coding the names into the code. For example, if you wanted to set the `Visible` property of the `txtInfo` TextBox control, you would have to hardcode it like this in previous versions of Visual Basic:

```
txtInfo.Visible = True
```

With the new `CallByName` function, you can use strings to specify the property name:

```
CallByName txtInfo, "Visible", vbLet, True
```

You can also read property settings or execute methods with the `CallByName` function. However, you cannot use a string value to specify the name of the object that has the property or method.

Filter Function

The `Filter` function, when passed a one-dimensional array, will return a subset of that array that includes only those items that contain a given search string. Alternatively, the subset array can include items that *don't* contain the given search string. Strings can be compared using either a binary or textual comparison method, or the setting of the `Option Compare` statement can be used.

FormatCurrency Function

Programmers who routinely need to display monetary values will find the new `FormatCurrency` function a welcome addition. Simply put, the `FormatCurrency` function converts a given expression into a currency format. The parameters of the function enable you to specify how many digit positions there will be after the decimal point, whether or not a leading zero is displayed for fractional values, whether or not negative values should be placed within parentheses, and whether or not digits should be grouped together where appropriate.

The way in which numbers are formatted depends a lot on the regional settings for the machine on which the `FormatCurrency` function is used. In the United States, for example, the number would likely be displayed with a preceding dollar sign, and digit grouping (if enabled) would use commas (such as "$32,768.00").

FormatDateTime Function

This function returns an expression that is formatted as a date and/or time value when given a valid date expression. You can choose to display long ("Friday, February 06, 1998") or short ("2/6/98") date values, and you can display time using 12-hour or 24-hour formats. Regional settings for the computer on which the `FormatDateTime` function is used will influence the way in which dates and times are formatted.

FormatNumber Function

The `FormatNumber` function is almost identical to the `FormatCurrency` function, except the formatted number that is returned does not include a preceding monetary symbol (such as a dollar sign). Again, a computer's regional settings will dictate how a number is formatted by this function.

FormatPercent Function

The `FormatPercent` function returns the formatted percentage value for a given expression. For example, passing a value of .75 to this function might result in a formatted value of "75%." All of the same parameters that are found in the `FormatCurrency` and `FormatNumber` functions can also be applied to the `FormatPercent` function, so you can specify things such as a fixed number of digits after the decimal point (if any).

InstrRev Function

The InstrRev function performs the same task as the regular Instr function: It returns the character position of a given search string within a second string. The difference is that the InstrRev function works in reverse and starts searching from the *end* of the second string rather than from the beginning.

Join Function

The Join function is passed a one-dimensional array and returns a string that contains the items of the array concatenated (joined) together. You can specify that the array items be delimited by a given string character, or you can specify a zero-length string (" ") so no delimiters are used.

MonthName Function

The MonthName function is very simple: pass it a number from 1 to 12 and it will return the name of the corresponding month ("January", "February", and so forth). You can also specify that short month names ("Jan", "Feb") be returned instead.

Replace Function

The Replace function acts as a simple search and replace operation. Pass it the string to search, the string to find and another string with which to substitute it, and the Replace function does the rest. You can optionally specify how many times to perform the string substitution and whether strings should be compared using a binary or textual comparison method.

Round Function

This is one simple function that should have been added to Visual Basic a long time ago. The Round function returns the value of a given expression, rounded off to a specified number of decimal places.

Split Function

The Split function performs the opposite of the new Join function. Rather than concatenate elements of an array into a single string, the Split function divides up a string into separate items and returns them as a one-dimensional array. A delimiter character can be specified so the Split function knows where items in the string start and stop. If no delimiter character is provided, Split uses the space character as the delimiter. Among other uses, this function can come in handy when you need to parse a sentence into individual words.

StrReverse Function

The `StrReverse` function returns a given string in reverse order. Therefore, the string "Visual Basic" would be returned by the `StrReverse` function as "cisaB lausiV".

WeekdayName Function

To convert a numeric value of 1 to 7 into the corresponding day of the week (1 = "Sunday", 2 = "Monday", an so on), use the `WeekdayName` function. Though the full day name is returned by this function, you can optionally specify that the `WeekdayName` function returns the abbreviated name (such as "Sun", "Mon") instead. If your numbering system for days of the week does not begin with Sunday, you can specify a different day as being the first weekday.

New Wizards

One of Visual Basic's strong points is its collection of wizards, which serve to automate complicated or mundane development tasks. For example, the Setup Wizard (renamed in VB6 to the Package and Deployment Wizard) enables you to quickly and easily create setup programs and archives for the distribution of applications and components. How time-consuming and dull this chore would be without the wizard—thank you, VB!

Other versions of Visual Basic have seen new wizards being added and others enhanced, and VB6 is no exception. Several changes and additions have been made to VB's stock of helpful wizards. Although we will only cover a few of them in detail in this book, that should be of no consequence. Wizards are, for the most part, embarrassingly easy to use. Experienced programmers should have no trouble at all in figuring them out.

Though simple to use, some wizards do deserve a closer look. The Class Builder Utility, which has been enhanced in VB6, is covered in Chapter 11, "Creating and Using Class Modules."

In the area of database access, one wizard has been added and another has been enhanced. The new Data Object Generator Wizard enables you to easily create middle-tier objects that are bound to UserControls and the Data Environment. The Data Form Wizard has been updated so you can now build code-only forms with no bound controls, and it also has the ability of producing DAO or RDO code. These two wizards are covered in Chapter 16, "Database Tools and Utilities."

Two more utilities have also been added to VB6: the Add-In Designer and the Toolbar Wizard. They are discussed briefly in the following sections. Changes to the Package and Deployment Wizard (formerly the Setup Wizard) and the Application Wizard are also discussed in the following sections.

The Add-In Designer

The Add-In Designer can't technically be considered a wizard, but it's close. Actually, it's a class that can be added to a project to facilitate the development process for an add-in. It enables you to set properties that determine the Add-In's name, description, target application and version, initial load behavior, and other pertinent pieces of information. The Add-In Designer then provides code for the add-in's DLL or EXE file to ensure that the add-in registers correctly with its target application.

The Application Wizard

The Application Wizard hasn't changed too drastically from the version that shipped with VB5. However, some new options have been added that make this already powerful wizard even more flexible.

To begin with, you are given much greater control over the creation of menus and sub-menus (see Figure 1.1). You can also launch the Data Form and Toolbar Wizards from within the Application Wizard if they are pertinent to the application you are creating.

FIGURE 1.1

The Application Wizard gives you greater control over the creation of menus and sub-menus.

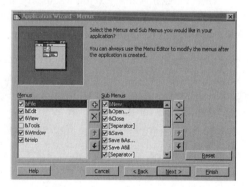

If you find yourself creating the same type of applications over and over again with the wizard, you can save your choices as a profile. When invoked, the first thing the wizard will prompt you for is the name of an existing profile. If you have one you want to use, all of the options you chose for that profile will be loaded in and you can step through the wizard and make any necessary changes.

The Package and Deployment Wizard

Formerly called the Setup Wizard, the Package and Deployment Wizard (see Figure 1.2) has gotten more than just a name change and a facelift. For starters, it now supports a wider range of data access formats, including ADO, DAO, ODBC, OLE DB, and RDO.

What's more, the wizard can be run as an add-in from within Visual Basic or as a stand-alone utility.

FIGURE 1.2

The Package and Deployment Wizard, formerly called the Setup Wizard.

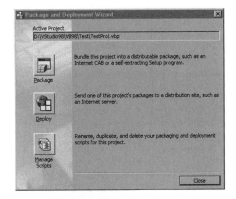

The "package" part of the wizard refers to the bundling of a Visual Basic project into a distributable package, either a compressed CAB file or an executable Setup program. Of course, you can still optionally create multiple CAB files, broken down into one of five selectable sizes—small enough to fit on a standard 1.44MB diskette, for example.

> **NOTE**
>
> CAB (short for "cabinet") files are Microsoft's answer to ZIP files. CABs are archive files that can contain one or more files and are compressed to save space and download time.

The new wizard gives you control over the Start menu groups and items that are created by a Setup program. You can also specify that one or more distribution files be installed as shared files.

Once a package has been created, it can then be "deployed" to a distribution site, such as an Internet server. Various deployment options are available, including FTP and HTTP. When the wizard is complete, it will attempt to send the package to the server that was specified. If you don't want to deploy the package to a server, you can choose to move the package to a local or network folder instead.

After going through the necessary steps for packaging and deployment, the wizard enables you to save your options as a script. That way, if you ever need to repeat the process, you can use the script instead of having to go through all of the motions again. Don't worry if you start growing a large collection of scripts—the wizard includes options for handling (renaming, duplicating, and deleting) any scripts you might have created.

The Toolbar Wizard

The new Toolbar Wizard (see Figure 1.3) makes it easy to add toolbars to a Form, UserDocument, UserControl, or Property Page. Although the wizard provides dozens of pre-existing icons, you can also use any other icons you may have available as long as they're stored as .BMP or .ICO files.

FIGURE 1.3.

The Toolbar Wizard makes the creation of tool- bars a snap.

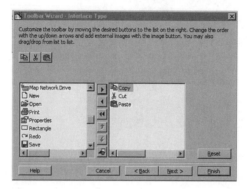

Although this wizard can be used separately, it can also be launched from within the newly enhanced Application Wizard.

Other Changes and Enhancements

In addition to the changes and enhancements made to the Visual Basic language and wizards discussed earlier, VB6 brings changes in many other areas. For example, several new ActiveX controls have been added and others have been enhanced. Control creation has received quite a bit of attention from Microsoft. Internet-related features in VB have also been affected. We'll discuss some of the more important changes that have been made to these three areas in turn.

New and Enhanced Controls

New ActiveX controls include `Coolbar`, `DateTimePicker`, `FlatScrollbar`, `ImageCombo`, and `MonthView`. Four new data-bound controls, `DataGrid`, `DataList`, `DataCombo`, and `MSHFlexGrid`, , have also been added. Chapter 2, "New ActiveX Controls," covers the first set of controls. Chapter 17, covers the new database controls. The `DataRepeater` control, which lets you use repeating sets of bound controls within a single container, is another new component in VB6.

A number of existing ActiveX controls have been enhanced in VB6. These include: `ImageList`, `ListView`, `MSChart`, `ProgressBar`, `Slider`, `TabStrip`, `Toolbar`, and

`TreeView`. In addition, many controls have been updated in the areas of focus and data binding. See the "What's New in Controls?" topic in the MSDN Library for specific information about new properties, events, and methods that have been added to the existing ActiveX controls.

On a more general level, VB6 now enables you to dynamically add or remove controls to and from a form at runtime. This is accomplished using the `Add` method and `Remove` method of a form's `Controls` collection. No doubt, this is a feature for which many VB programmers have been waiting. When you're dealing with a form that includes a large number of controls that are not always needed, this feature enables you to quickly load the form, and then add the necessary controls afterwards. This can improve the application's performance considerably.

The `LoadPicture` method, which is included in controls such as `Image` or `PictureBox`, has also been updated. Picture size and color depth can now be specified as optional parameters to the method.

The new `ValidateControls` method can be called before exiting a form so the contents of the last control on the form can be validated.

Internet Features

With the popularity of the Internet, it's no surprise that VB6 builds on the Internet features introduced in VB5. However, there really haven't been as many changes in this area as might be expected. VB6 does add support for server-side IIS (Internet Information Server) applications to handle Web browser requests and other tasks.

Another Internet-related feature that has been improved is the `AsyncRead` method of the UserControl (ActiveX control) and UserDocument (ActiveX document) objects. `AsyncRead` has been enhanced to provide more information about the status of a read operation. For example, you can now determine how many bytes have been read, as well as the total number of bytes to be read.

Visual Basic 6 also adds a new project type for use on the Internet—the DHTML (Dynamic HTML) application. DHTML application projects use a combination of Dynamic HTML and Visual Basic code, resulting in an interactive application that can be run from within a Web browser. The DHTML application can respond to actions the user performs with the Web browser. For example, it can extract data from the Web page and use it perform a database query. The information returned from the database could then be displayed on the Web page.

Component Creation

The area of component creation has also received quite a bit of attention from Microsoft. As the concept of reusable components becomes more and more engrained within the minds of VB programmers, it makes sense that the tools to create and use those components continue to evolve and improve.

To begin with, ActiveX controls can now be much more flexible in their design. Creating data consumers and data sources—that is, controls that use or supply information from a database—is now possible. Chapter 8, "Data Consumers and Data Sources," shows you how to do just that.

Lightweight UserControls, those that are windowless or transparent, can also be created. In addition, apartment-model threading can now be used so procedures run asynchronously on separate threads. Lightweight controls are discussed in Chapter 4, "An Overview of ActiveX Programming," and an example of apartment model threading is shown in Chapter 9, "Apartment Model Threading."

When debugging and testing ActiveX controls written in VB, you can now choose to run the control in a Web browser or another program instead of on a Visual Basic form. This makes it much easier to ensure that the controls you are developing will work well in the environments for which they are intended. The testing of ActiveX controls is covered in Chapter 5, "Creating ActiveX Controls."

Creating and using classes in Visual Basic has never been easier. Persistent class properties, support for managing ClassIDs between projects, and enhancements to the Class Builder utility all add up to greatly improved class development. Chapter 11, "Creating and Using Class Modules," contains everything you need to know about using classes in VB6.

Summary

Without a doubt, the new version of Visual Basic brings many changes. Some are quite simple, such as minor syntax changes to existing statements and functions; others are more profound, like the new way of accessing databases using ADO.

It seems that VB6 has modified or improved just about every area in some way. There have been changes to VB's Internet features, component creation, the language itself, and data access. This chapter should have provided you with a brief introduction to these many changes. It should also have helped you determine where in this book to turn when you desire more information about specific topics.

New ActiveX Controls

by Rob Thayer

IN THIS CHAPTER

- The `Coolbar` Control *20*
- The `ImageCombo` Control *32*
- The `MonthView` Control *37*
- The `DateTimePicker` Control (`DTPicker`) *42*
- The `FlatScrollBar` Control *46*

CHAPTER 2

The last four versions of Visual Basic have brought changes to the Toolbox, with new controls appearing and others disappearing. VB6 is no exception, with Microsoft adding quite a few new ActiveX controls to the Visual Basic developer's palette.

Some of these new controls are covered in other chapters of this book. For example, four new database-specific controls are discussed in Chapter 17, "Advanced Data Controls." Also, the new ADO Data control is detailed completely in Chapter 13, "The ADO Data Control."

This chapter covers the five new general-purpose controls in VB6: `Coolbar`, `DateTimePicker`, `FlatScrollbar`, `ImageCombo`, and `MonthView`. In addition to the specifics for each control (properties, methods, and events), some sample applications will also be provided so you can see the new controls in action.

> **NOTE**
>
> Only the unique properties, events, and methods for the controls will be discussed. Standard properties like `Name`, `Enabled`, or `DragIcon` will not be covered. To see a complete list of the properties, events, and methods for a control class, use VB's Object Browser.

The `Coolbar` Control

Although the `Coolbar` control has been available for free download from Microsoft's Web site for some time now, VB6 is the first version to include the control in its Toolbox right out of the box.

`Coolbar` is a container control that enables you to add "sliding" toolbars to your applications. These toolbars consist of one or more *bands*, with the bands existing on the same row or starting a new row.

This description of the `Coolbar` control leaves a lot to be desired because you really have to see a `Coolbar` in action to understand how it works. One of the best examples of `Coolbar` usage can be found in Microsoft's Internet Explorer Web browser. Figure 2.1 shows IE with a `Coolbar` that consists of three rows and a total of five bands. The first row contains two bands—the menu items and the Internet Explorer logo. The next row has only one band and contains icons for different program functions, such as Back, Forward, and Stop. The third and final row contains an Address combo box in one band and a Links toolbar. The Links toolbar is at its minimum width and only the caption is showing. However, the size of the toolbar can be adjusted by clicking on and dragging the band's "move handle," the vertical line that can be found on the left-most side of each `Coolbar` band.

FIGURE 2.1.

Internet Explorer is one popular application that makes effective use of the Coolbar *control.*

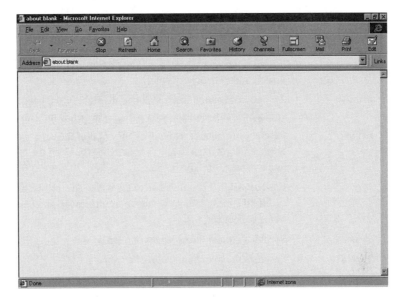

Because the Coolbar control acts primarily as a container, its bands can include just about any kind of control. The IE example is a good one because its Coolbar bands contain menu items, an image, buttons, and a combo box.

Now that you have a basic idea of what the Coolbar control does, it's time to look at the details of how to use it. But before discussing the various properties, events, and methods of the Coolbar control, it is necessary to first talk about two object types that are used with the control: the Band object and the Bands collection.

The Band Object and the Bands Collection

As stated earlier, a Coolbar control consists of one or more separate sections called *bands*. These Band objects form the Bands collection.

The Bands collection has the same properties and methods as any other collection in Visual Basic. There is a Count property and Add, Clear, Item, and Remove methods. There are no events.

The Band object has its own unique set of properties, with no events or methods. Most of the Band object's properties are used to specify how and where the band will appear in the Coolbar control. Table 2.1 lists the unique properties for the Band object and includes a description of each.

TABLE 2.1. THE UNIQUE PROPERTIES OF THE Coolbar CONTROL'S BAND OBJECT

Property	Description
AllowVertical	Specifies whether the band will be displayed if the Coolbar's orientation is vertical rather than horizontal.
Caption	An optional caption that appears to the right of the band's move handle. For vertical Coolbars, the caption will appear below the band's move handle.
Child	References a control that will be the child of the Band object. For example, to contain a combo box within a band, you would set the band's Child property to the name of the combo box.
Key	Used to assign a unique name to the band. This can be used later in code to specify the band without having to use the index number of the band in the Bands collection.
MinHeight	Specifies the minimum height of a band.
MinWidth	Specifies the minimum width of a band.
NewRow	Specifies whether the band will begin on a new row in the Coolbar. This is how you can arrange the bands in a Coolbar, with some bands being in the same row and others starting a new row.
Position	Returns the numerical position of a Band object within the Coolbar control. For horizontal Coolbars, bands are numbered from left to right and from top to bottom.
Style	Specifies whether a band is to remain a fixed size or if it can be resized.

In addition to the properties listed in Table 2.1, the Band object also has some properties that deal with the background image and the foreground and background colors of the band. If desired, these details can be "inherited" from the Coolbar control itself. The UseCoolbarColors and UseCoolbarPicture properties are used to specify that the colors and background image for the band are to be taken directly from the Coolbar control. If the UseCoolbarPicture property is set to True, then the Coolbar's background image is used. In that case, the FixedBackground property can specify whether the image remains fixed if the band is resized or rearranged.

A band's background image can be different than that of its Coolbar control. To use a different background image for a band, set its UseCoolbarPicture property to False and set its Picture property to the background image desired. The same goes for foreground and background text colors. Set its UseCoolbarColors to False and then set its ForeColor and BackColor properties appropriately.

The Band object's Image property can be used to insert an image directly to the right of the band's move handle. If the band has a caption, the image will appear between the move handle and the caption. Before using the Image property, you must first set the

`Coolbar` control's `ImageList` property to the name of an existing `ImageList` control. The value assigned to the `Band` object's `Image` property specifies the index number of the image in the `ImageList`.

Individual `Band` objects within a `Bands` collection are accessed either by index number or key name. For example, assuming that the name of the `Coolbar` control that contains the bands is called `cbrTest` and the `Key` property for the second band in the collection has been assigned the value `SecondBand`, either one of the following lines of code can be used to set that band's `NewRow` property:

```
cbrTest.Bands(2).NewRow = True
```

```
cbrTest.Bands.Item("SecondBand").NewRow = True
```

In the first line of code, the index number of the `Band` object is specified. In the next line, the `Item` property is used to access the `Band` object by giving its key name. Although the second method is longer, it enables the `Band` object to be accessed without knowing its position in the `Bands` collection. It also makes the code easier to follow because the name of the band is given.

Coolbar Properties

Although many of the aspects of how a `Coolbar` control appears are specified by the properties of its individual `Band` objects, there are also some properties for the `Coolbar` itself that determine how the control looks and acts.

To begin with, the orientation of the `Coolbar` can be specified by the `Orientation` property. The default value of 0 (`cc3OrientationHorizontal`) is used for a horizontal `Coolbar`, and a value of 1 (`cc3OrientationVertical`) is used for a vertical `Coolbar`. Of course, the value of this property directly affects the control's bands because they always have the same orientation as the `Coolbar` control.

Other `Coolbar` properties also affect the bands directly. The `Picture` property can be used to specify a background image for the overall `Coolbar` control. The bands can also use this image by setting their `UseCoolbarPicture` property to True as discussed in the previous section.

The `ImageList` property is used to specify the name of an `ImageList` control that contains images that can be displayed next to the bands' move handles. This was also discussed earlier.

The `BandBorders` property specifies whether or not the borders between the bands should be displayed. The default value of True indicates that the border lines should be shown. The border around the `Coolbar` control itself cannot be hidden.

Individual bands contain different kinds of objects. In the Internet Explorer example given earlier, the size of the bands varied based on the content of the bands themselves. However, you can choose to make all of the bands in a `Coolbar` control the same height by setting the `VariantHeight` property to False. In that case, the height of the bands will be based on the largest `MinHeight` property of all the bands. The default value for this property is True, indicating that the height of the bands should be variable, based on the largest `MinHeight` property of the bands in each row.

`Coolbar` bands can contain a variety of different objects or controls, but the rule is that each object must expose a Windows handle. Lightweight controls like the `Label` control don't expose their Windows handle, so they cannot be used in a `Coolbar` band. Some of the controls that can be used include (but are not limited to) the following: `CheckBox`, `ComboBox`, `CommandButton`, `Frame`, `ListBox`, `ListView`, `MaskedEdit`, `MCI`, `OptionButton`, `PictureBox`, `ProgressBar`, `RichTextBox`, `Slider`, `StatusBar`, `TextBox`, and `UpDown`.

You might not want your users to be able to re-arrange the order of the bands in the `Coolbar` control at runtime. To prevent this, set the `FixedOrder` property to True. The default value is False.

Rather than calculating and setting the `Top`, `Left`, `Height`, and `Width` properties for a `Coolbar` control, you can sometimes use the `Align` property to automatically move and resize the `Coolbar` to a specific area of the `Coolbar`'s container object (usually a `Form`). Values for this property include `vbAlignTop` (1), `vbAlignBottom` (2), `vbAlignLeft` (3), and `vbAlignRight` (4). When these values are used, the `Coolbar` cannot be moved from its current position. To be able to move the `Coolbar` again, set the `Align` property to `vbAlignNone` (0). Note that setting the `Align` property to `vbAlignLeft` or `vbAlignRight` does not automatically change the `Coolbar`'s orientation to vertical.

If you want to give the `Coolbar`'s background image an embossed look, you can use the `EmbossPicture` property. Set it to True and then use the `EmbossHighlight` and `EmbossShadow` properties to specify the colors for the highlight and shadow.

Coolbar Events

Other than standard events such as `Click` or `MouseMove`, the `Coolbar` control has only one unique event. The `HeightChanged` event is triggered when the user changes the height of the control. It is also triggered when bands are rearranged by the user or the band height is changed in code. The new height is passed as an argument to the event.

The Coolbar In Action

To show how the `Coolbar` control can be used, a very simple text editor will be constructed. The `Coolbar` will consist of three bands. The first will contain icons for opening, saving, and creating new files. The second will contain icons for copy, cut, and paste operations. The final band will contain a command button that is used to exit the program. All of the bands will be included in a single row.

To begin creating the program, first design its user interface. Use Table 2.2 and Figure 2.2 as a guide. Note that Figure 2.2 shows the program's two `Toolbar` controls containing sets of icons. These come from the two `ImageList` controls. The icons will be added in just a moment. Also, don't worry about the placement of the controls. That will be changed in the program's code.

TABLE 2.2. THE CONTROLS AND PROPERTIES FOR THE SAMPLE COOLBAR PROGRAM

Control Type	Property	Value
Form	Name	frmCBTest
	Caption	Coolbar Test
	Height	4620
	StartUpPosition	2 - CenterScreen
	Width	6495
Coolbar	Name	cbrMain
	Align	1 - Align Top
TextBox	Name	txtWorkspace
	Height	3735
	Left	120
	MultiLine	True
	Top	960
	Width	6255
ImageList	Name	ilsEditIcons
	Left	720
	Top	2880
ImageList	Name	ilsFileIcons
	Left	2760
	Top	2880
Toolbar	Name	tbrEdit
	Height	585
	ImageList	ilsEditIcons
	Left	240

continues

TABLE 2.2. CONTINUED

Control Type	Property	Value
	Top	3600
	Width	1695
Toolbar	Name	tbrFile
	Height	585
	ImageList	ilsFileIcons
	Left	2160
	Top	3600
	Width	1815
CommonDialog	Name	dlgFileOps
	Filter	*.txt
	Left	4200
	Top	3600
CommandButton	Name	cmdExit
	Height	600
	Left	5040
	Top	3600
	Width	1215

FIGURE 2.2.

The user interface for the Coolbar *sample program (design mode).*

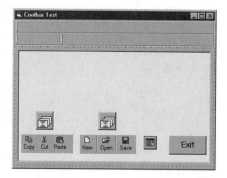

The ImageList controls need images assigned to them. All of the images shown in the Toolbars in Figure 2.2 can be found on the Visual Basic or Visual Studio CD-ROM. On the Visual Studio 98 CD, they are located in the directory \COMMON\ GRAPHICS\BITMAPS\TLBR_W95.

Use the ImageList controls' Custom Properties dialog box to assign the graphics to the controls. For the ilsEditIcons control, assign it the following graphics (in order): COPY.BMP, CUT.BMP, and PASTE.BMP. For the ilsFileIcons, assign the following graphics (in order): NEW.BMP, OPEN.BMP, and SAVE.BMP.

The next step is to assign the images in the `ImageList` controls to the buttons in the two `Toolbar` controls. Start with the `tbrEdit` toolbar. Use the control's Custom Properties dialog box to set up the buttons. Use Table 2.3 as a guide for modifying the properties:

TABLE 2.3. THE SETTINGS FOR THE BUTTONS IN THE TBREDIT TOOLBAR CONTROL

Style	Caption	Key	ToolTipText	ImageIndex
0 - tbrDefault	Copy	btnCopy	Copy	1
0 - tbrDefault	Cut	btnCut	Cut	2
0 - tbrDefault	Paste	btnPaste	Paste	3

Do the same for the `tbrFile` control, using Table 2.4 as a guide for setting the properties of the various buttons. Note that two "separators" are included in the list. These are nothing more than vertical lines that separate the buttons. They don't require values for their `Caption`, `Key`, `ToolTipText`, or `ImageIndex` properties.

TABLE 2.4. THE SETTINGS FOR THE BUTTONS IN THE TBRFILE TOOLBAR CONTROL

Style	Caption	Key	ToolTipText	ImageIndex
0 - tbrDefault	New	btnNew	New File	1
3 - tbrSeparator	-	-	-	-
0 - tbrDefault	Open	btnOpen	Open File	2
3 - tbrSeparator	-	-	-	-
0 - tbrDefault	Save	btnSave	Save File	3

Now that the program's user interface elements have been assembled, the code can be added. The first procedure is the `Form_Load` event (see Listing 2.1), which sets the properties of the three bands of the `Coolbar` control.

LISTING 2.1. CH02-01.TXT—THE COOLBAR SAMPLE PROGRAM'S Form_Load EVENT, WHICH SETS UP PROPERTIES OF THE COOLBAR CONTROL'S BANDS

```
Private Sub Form_Load()

' Set up the properties for the individual Bands
' of the Coolbar control (cbrMain).
'   Band 1 ("FileBand"):
With cbrMain.Bands(1)
    .Key = "FileBand"
    .Style = cc3BandNormal
    .Width = 0
End With
```

continues

LISTING 2.1. CONTINUED.

```
'    Band 2 ("EditBand"):
With cbrMain.Bands(2)
    .Key = "EditBand"
    .NewRow = False
    .Style = cc3BandNormal
    .Width = 0
End With
'    Band 3 ("ExitBand"):
With cbrMain.Bands(3)
    .Key = "ExitBand"
    .MinHeight = 600
    .MinWidth = 1215
    .NewRow = False
    .Style = cc3BandFixedSize
End With

' Make the cbrMain Coolbar control the container
' for tbrFile, and assign that control as a child
' of the Coolbar control's "FileBand" Band.
Set tbrFile.Container = cbrMain
Set cbrMain.Bands.Item("FileBand").Child = tbrFile
' Set the minimum height and width of the "FileBand"
' Band to the height and width of the Toolbar.
cbrMain.Bands.Item("FileBand").MinWidth = tbrFile.Width
cbrMain.Bands.Item("FileBand").MinHeight = tbrFile.Height

' Make the cbrMain Coolbar control the container
' for tbrEdit, and assign that control as a child
' of the Coolbar control's "EditBand" Band.
Set tbrEdit.Container = cbrMain
Set cbrMain.Bands.Item("EditBand").Child = tbrEdit
' Set the minimum height and width of the "EditBand"
' Band to the height and width of the Toolbar.
cbrMain.Bands.Item("EditBand").MinWidth = tbrEdit.Width
cbrMain.Bands.Item("EditBand").MinHeight = tbrEdit.Height

' Make the cbrMain Coolbar control the container
' for cmdExit, and assign that control as a child
' of the Coolbar control's "ExitBand" Band.
Set cmdExit.Container = cbrMain
Set cbrMain.Bands.Item("ExitBand").Child = cmdExit

End Sub
```

The Form_Load procedure contains all of the code that pertains to the Coolbar control (cbrMain). First, several properties for the three bands are set. Note that the first two bands are of the normal style and the last (the Exit button) is fixed size.

Next, the bands are assigned child objects. The "FileBand" band is assigned the `tbrFile` toolbar as its child. Likewise, the `tbrFile` control's `Container` property is set to the `Coolbar` control, `cbrMain`. The "FileBand" band's `MinWidth` and `MinHeight` properties are set so the user cannot resize the band any smaller than the original size of the `tbrFile` toolbar that it contains.

The "EditBand" band is assigned the `tbrEdit` toolbar as its child, and `tbrEdit`'s `Container` property is also set to `cbrMain`. The `MinWidth` and `MinHeight` properties for the "EditBand" band are also set to the size of the `tbrEdit` toolbar.

The "ExitBand" band and the `cmdExit` command button are set up as container and child just like the other bands. The `MinWidth` and `MinHeight` properties don't have to be set for this band, however, because the band is of a fixed size.

The next procedure to add is the `tbrEdit_ButtonClick` event (see Listing 2.2). This event is triggered whenever the user clicks on one of the buttons in the `tbrEdit` control, which is a child of the `Coolbar` control's "EditBand" band. It contains simple code that performs copy, cut, and paste operations in the text box (`txtWorkspace`).

LISTING 2.2. CH02-02.TXT—THE `tbrEdit_ButtonClick` EVENT, WHICH IS USED TO PERFORM TASKS WHEN THE BUTTONS ON THE EDIT TOOLBAR (CONTAINED BY THE "EDITBAND" BAND OF THE COOLBAR CONTROL) ARE PRESSED.

```
Private Sub tbrEdit_ButtonClick(ByVal Button As ComctlLib.Button)

' This procedure is used to act on the Edit buttons
' in the Coolbar control's "EditBand" Band. The
' Toolbar control tbrEdit, a child of the Coolbar
' band, actually contains the buttons. Which item
' was clicked on is determined by looking at the
' Key property of the Button object that is passed
' to this event procedure.

Select Case Button.Key
    Case "btnCopy":
        ' Copy - Copy the selected text in the
        ' text box to the Clipboard.
        Clipboard.Clear
        Clipboard.SetText txtWorkspace.SelText
    Case "btnCut":
        ' Cut - Copy the selected text in the
        ' text box to the Clipboard, then erase
        ' the selected text.
        Clipboard.Clear
        Clipboard.SetText txtWorkspace.SelText
```

continues

LISTING 2.2. CONTINUED

```
        txtWorkspace.SelText = ""
    Case "btnPaste":
        ' Paste - Paste the contents of the
        ' Clipboard to the text box.
        txtWorkspace.SelText = Clipboard.GetText()
End Select

End Sub
```

The next procedure, tbrFile_ButtonClick, is similar to the last. It is triggered when the user clicks on the buttons in the tbrFile toolbar, which is a child of the Coolbar's "FileBand" band. It performs operations to open, save, or create new text files. The procedures SaveTextFile and LoadTextFile are used to actually read and write files. All three procedures—tbrFile_ButtonClick, SaveTextFile, and LoadTextFile—are shown in Listing 2.3.

LISTING 2.3. CH02-03.TXT—THE tbrFile_ButtonClick EVENT, IS USED TO PERFORM TASKS WHEN THE BUTTONS ON THE FILE TOOLBAR (CONTAINED BY THE "FILEBAND" BAND OF THE COOLBAR CONTROL) ARE PRESSED. THE SaveTextFile AND LoadTextFile PROCEDURES ARE ALSO INCLUDED IN THIS LISTING.

```
Private Sub tbrFile_ButtonClick(ByVal Button As ComctlLib.Button)

' This procedure is used to act on the File buttons
' in the Coolbar control's "FileBand" Band. The
' Toolbar control tbrFile, a child of the Coolbar
' band, actually containsn the buttons. Which item
' was clicked on is determined by looking at the
' Key property of the Button object that is passed
' to this event procedure.

Dim lonStatus As Long

Select Case Button.Key
    Case "btnNew":
        ' New File - Blank out the text box.
        txtWorkspace.Text = ""
    Case "btnOpen":
        ' Open File - Get a file name using the
        ' CommonDialog control (dlgFileOps) and
        ' use the LoadTextFile procedure to read
        ' the file into the text box.
        dlgFileOps.ShowOpen
        If dlgFileOps.FileName <> "" Then
            LoadTextFile
        End If
    Case "btnSave":
```

```
            ' Save File - If necessary, get a file name
            ' using the dlgFileOps control, then use
            ' the SaveTextFile procedure to save the
            ' text box contents to the file.
            If dlgFileOps.FileName = "" Then
                dlgFileOps.ShowSave
                If dlgFileOps.FileName <> "" Then
                    SaveTextFile
                End If
            Else
                SaveTextFile
            End If
End Select

End Sub

Private Sub SaveTextFile()

' This procedure writes the contents of the text
' box (txtWorkspace) to a file.

Dim intFileNum As Integer

intFileNum = FreeFile
Open dlgFileOps.FileName For Output As #intFileNum
Print #intFileNum, txtWorkspace.Text
Close #intFileNum

End Sub


Private Sub LoadTextFile()

' This procedure reads the contents of a file and
' places it in the text box (txtWorkspace).

Dim intFileNum As Integer

txtWorkspace.Text = ""

intFileNum = FreeFile
Open dlgFileOps.FileName For Input As #intFileNum
While Not EOF(intFileNum)
    Line Input #intFileNum, strDataIn
    txtWorkspace.Text = txtWorkspace.Text _
        & strDataIn & vbCrLf
Wend
Close #intFileNum

End Sub
```

The final bit of code to add is the `cmdExit_Click` procedure (Listing 2.4), which is called when the user clicks on the `Exit` button. The button is a child of the `Coolbar`'s "ExitBand" band.

LISTING 2.4. CH02-04.TXT—THE `cmdExit_Click` EVENT PROCEDURE, WHICH EXITS THE PROGRAM.

```
Private Sub cmdExit_Click()

' Exit the program.

Unload Me
End

End Sub
```

After all of the code has been added, try out the program. You'll see that the two toolbars (tbrEdit and tbrFile) are now a part of the cbrMain Coolbar control. The cmdExit button is also part of cbrMain. Figure 2.3 shows the program at runtime.

FIGURE 2.3.

The Coolbar program in action. Note that the Coolbar *control (at the top of the program) consists of three bands.*

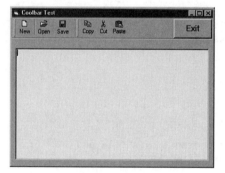

Try resizing the Coolbar's bands. You'll find that the second band will only slide to the right until its minimum width has been reached. Sliding the second band back to the left will also be stopped when the first band is at its minimum width. The third band is fixed and cannot be resized at all. In fact, it doesn't even have a move handle.

The ImageCombo Control

The `ImageCombo` control is an enhanced version of the standard combo control. However, there are some differences between the two controls, both inside and out.

To begin with, the `ImageCombo` control enables you to display images next to the items in a drop-down list. You can actually assign each item two images, one for when the item is not selected and one for when it is selected. The selected image also appears next to the item's caption at the top of the `ImageCombo` in the text box section. All images come from a single `ImageList` control.

The `ImageCombo` control also enables you to indent items in the list. This means that you can arrange the items into a hierarchy format if desired.

The `ImageCombo` control is also much different internally than the `ComboBox` control. Each of the items in an `ImageCombo` list is a separate `ComboItem` object, and together they make the `ComboItems` collection. This makes the management of list items a lot easier and more flexible. It also means that you do not add and remove items from an `ImageCombo` the way you would from a `ComboBox`. The `AddItem` and `RemoveItem` methods are not used with `ImageCombo` controls. Instead, you use the `ComboItems` collection's `Add` and `Remove` methods.

Using an `ImageCombo` control is easy, especially if you are used to dealing with collections. The next section describes some of the important properties, methods, and events of the `ImageCombo` control. A familiarity with the standard `ComboBox` control is assumed because there are still many parallels between the `ComboBox` and `ImageCombo` controls.

The `ComboItem` Object

As stated earlier, the items in an `ImageCombo` control are actually individual `ComboItem` objects. The `ComboItem` objects have their own properties. In addition to the standard `Index` and `Key` properties typically used with collection objects, you can also access other properties of the `ComboItem` object that specify information about the list item. For example, the `Text` property is used to specify the caption for the list item.

You can also control how far an item is indented by setting a `ComboItem` object's `Indentation` property. A value of 0 indicates that the item is to be left-justified in the list. Other values indent the item by a factor of 10 pixels. Therefore, a value of 2 would cause the item to be indented 20 pixels.

To assign images to `ComboItem` objects, you'll need to use an `ImageList` control. Load the `ImageList` with the graphics desired, then set the `ImageCombo` control's `ImageList` property to the name of the `ImageList` control. You can then assign specific images to each item in the `ImageCombo`'s `ComboItems` collection by setting a `ComboItem` object's `Image` and `SelImage` properties to the index number of the desired graphics in the `ImageList` control.

To determine whether a particular list item is selected, you can examine the `ComboItem` object's `Selected` property. A value of True indicates that the item is selected, and False indicates that it is not.

Because the `ImageCombo` control's list items are contained within the `ComboItems` collection, the only way to add new items is by using the `Add` method. The `Add` method has the following syntax:

```
Add([Index], [Key], [Text], [Image], [SelImage], [Indentation])
```

The arguments of the `Add` method correspond to the properties of the `ImageCombo` item, and each argument is optional. Therefore, you can set all of the necessary properties for a list item (an `ImageCombo` object) simply by using the `Add` method.

To remove an item from the `ComboItems` collection, use the collection's `Remove` method. The only argument is the index number of the item to be removed. To remove all items from the collection use the `Clear` method, which has no arguments.

ImageCombo Properties, Methods, and Events

Much of the manipulation performed on an `ImageCombo` control is actually done via the `ComboItem` objects in the `ComboItems` collection, as discussed in the last section. However, there are a few properties and methods of the `ImageCombo` control of which you need to be aware.

The `ImageCombo` control's `ImageList` property contains a reference to the `ImageList` control that contains the graphics that will be used with the list items. The `Indentation` property can be used to specify a default indentation factor for any `ComboItem` objects that are added to the control's `ComboItems` collection.

Like the standard `ComboBox` control, the `ImageCombo` control has `SelLength`, `SelStart`, and `SelText` properties for working with the list item that has been selected. In addition, the `SelectedItem` property returns a reference to the actual `ComboItem` object that was selected.

The `ImageCombo` control also has `GetFirstVisible` and `SetFirstVisible` methods that are used to determine or set the first item visible in the control's list box. These methods work the same as those of the `ListView` control.

The `Change` and `Validate` events are present in the `ImageCombo` control just as they are in the `ComboBox` control. However, the `Scroll` event is not available for the `ImageCombo`.

The `ImageCombo` In Action

To show how the `ImageCombo` control can be used, a short example program will be constructed. The program will consist of nothing more than an `ImageCombo` control and an `ImageList` control. The `ImageCombo` will be used to select a country or region from a list. Each country on the list will have a flag displayed next to it, and the names of regions will have a globe graphic next to them.

Build the program's user interface by using Table 2.5 and Figure 2.4 as a guide.

TABLE 2.5. THE CONTROLS, PROPERTIES, AND THEIR VALUES FOR THE `ImageCombo` EXAMPLE PROGRAM.

Control Type	Property	Value
Form	Name	`frmICTest`
	Height	1995
	StartUpPosition	2 - CenterScreen
	Width	4680
ImageList	Name	`ilsFlags`
	Left	3840
	Top	1080
ImageCombo	Name	`imcCountry`
	Font	MS Sans Serif 12pt Bold
	Height	570
	ImageList	`ilsFlags`
	Left	120
	Text	Choose a country or region
	Top	360
	Width	4335

FIGURE 2.4.

The ImageCombo example program's user interface (design mode).

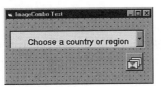

Before adding the program's code, you'll need to assign the images that the `ImageCombo` control will use into the `ImageList` control, `ilsFlags`. All of the graphics for this can be found on the Visual Basic and Visual Studio CD-ROMs. On the Visual Studio 98 CD, the first six images can be found in the subdirectory \COMMON\GRAPHICS\ICONS\FLAGS and the last image can be found in \COMMON\GRAPHICS\ICONS\ELEMENTS.

Use the ImageList control's Custom Properties dialog box to load the following image files, in this order: FLGASTRL.ICO, FLGCAN.ICO, FLGGERM.ICO, FLGJAPAN.ICO, FLGUK.ICO, FLGUSA02.ICO, and EARTH.ICO.

After the images have been assigned, you can add the program's code, which consists of only one procedure (see Listing 2.5):

LISTING 2.5. CH02-05.TXT—THE Form_Load PROCEDURE, WHICH SETS UP THE ITEMS IN THE ImageCombo CONTROL imcCountry.

```
Private Sub Form_Load()

Dim objNewItem As ComboItem

Set objNewItem = imcCountry.ComboItems.Add(1, _
    "R1", "Region 1 - Australia/Asia", 7, 7, 1)
Set objNewItem = imcCountry.ComboItems.Add(2, _
    "AUS", "Australia", 1, 1, 4)
Set objNewItem = imcCountry.ComboItems.Add(3, _
    "JPN", "Japan", 4, 4, 4)
Set objNewItem = imcCountry.ComboItems.Add(4, _
    "R2", "Region 2 - Europe", 7, 7, 1)
Set objNewItem = imcCountry.ComboItems.Add(5, _
    "GER", "Germany", 3, 3, 4)
Set objNewItem = imcCountry.ComboItems.Add(6, _
    "UK", "United Kingdom", 5, 5, 4)
Set objNewItem = imcCountry.ComboItems.Add(7, _
    "R3", "Region 3 - North America", 7, 7, 1)
Set objNewItem = imcCountry.ComboItems.Add(8, _
    "CAN", "Canada", 2, 2, 4)
Set objNewItem = imcCountry.ComboItems.Add(9, _
    "USA", "United States", 6, 6, 4)

End Sub
```

The Form_Load procedure sets up the ImageCombo control by adding ComboItem objects to its ComboItems collection. This is accomplished via the collection's Add method. The first argument to the Add method is the index number of the item. Next is a key name. In this example, all of the items have been assigned short two- or three-character key names ("R1" for Region 1, "AUS" for Australia, and so on). The next argument is the item's caption.

The fourth and fifth arguments are the index numbers of the images in the `ImageList` control that is referenced by the `ImageCombo`'s `ImageList` property. The first index number specifies the image to be used when the item is not selected and the second number specifies the image to be used when the item is selected. To simplify things, the same index is used for both selected and non-selected item states. Visual Basic will highlight the image when it is selected, as you'll soon see.

The final argument to the `Add` method is the indentation number for the item. Regional items are given an indentation number of 0, indicating that they are to be left-justified. Specific countries within the regions are given an indentation number of 3, which indents them 30 pixels from the left side of the list box.

When you run the program, you'll see that the items in the `ImageCombo` control's drop-down list have icons next to them and are arranged in a simple hierarchy of regions and countries (see Figure 2.5). Notice how the selected item's graphic is highlighted by Visual Basic.

FIGURE 2.5.

The `ImageCombo` *example program in action. Each item in the* `ImageCombo`'s *drop-down list has a graphic next to it and the items are arranged in a simple hierarchy.*

The `MonthView` Control

One of the more interesting new components in VB6 is the `MonthView` control. In a nutshell, this control displays a calendar that shows one or more months. The user can move from month to month and select a date (or several dates). The selected date or dates can be read from one of the control's properties.

In its default state, the `MonthView` control (see Figure 2.6) shows a single month. At the top of the control, the month and year are displayed. There are also two navigation buttons so the user can move to the previous or next month.

FIGURE 2.6.

The MonthView *control.*

The current date is always circled in red. The selected date (or dates) have a grey background. By default, the current month is shown and the current date is selected. The current date is also shown at the bottom of the control, but that can be suppressed if desired.

The DateTimePicker control, which will be discussed next, is similar to the MonthView control. However, MonthView gives you more control over how date values are displayed and selected. On the other side of the coin, the DateTimePicker control enables a much wider range of values types to be entered, including date and time values.

MonthView Properties

MonthView gives you a fair amount of control over how its calendar portion is displayed. For example, you are not stuck with displaying a single month at a time. You can choose the number of rows and columns that are displayed using the MonthRows and MonthColumns properties. If you want to display three months at a time, side by side, you would set MonthRows to 1 and MonthColumns to 3. Or you could show an entire year at a time by setting MonthRows to 3 and MonthColumns to 4 (see Figure 2.7). MonthView limits you to displaying a maximum of 12 months at a time, though not all of the months have to be in the same year. For example, the MonthView control could show 4 months from one year and 8 months from the next year.

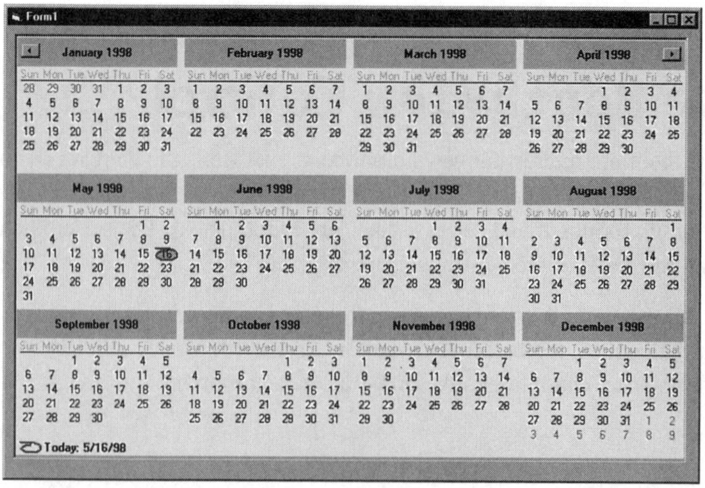

FIGURE 2.7.

The MonthView *control, expanded to show an entire year.*

No matter how many months are displayed, the buttons to move to the previous or next month are always included at the top of the control. By default, these buttons will move back or forth a single month. However, you can change this by setting the ScrollRate property. A value of 2, for example, will cause the control to skip two months forward or backward when the navigation buttons are used.

You can limit the range of months that are displayed and selectable by the MonthView control using the MinDate and MaxDate properties. So if you want to limit the months to the year 1998, set MinDate to "1/1/98" and MaxDate to "12/31/98".

Various properties are used to specify the colors of the different parts of the MonthView control. The ForeColor property controls the color of the date numbers that belong to the current month. Strangely, the BackColor property doesn't really change much other than a thin line at the bottom of the control. To change the background color of the calendar, use the MonthBackColor property.

The title portion of the control, which displays the month and year, has its colors changed via the TitleBackColor and TitleForeColor properties. Finally, the color for the date numbers for next or previous months can be changed with the TrailingForeColor property. If you don't want these numbers displayed, set TrailingForeColor to the same color value as MonthBackColor.

By default, the current date is displayed at the bottom of the MonthView control. You can disable the current date display by setting the ShowToday property to False.

Another default of the MonthView control is to have weeks starting with Sundays. However, you can specify a new starting day by changing the StartOfWeek property. This will be reflected by the way the calendar is displayed, with the day you specify occupying the first column of the calendar.

For certain applications, you might want the week number to be displayed next to each row of dates shown on the monthly calendar. Weeks are numbered starting with the first full week of the year; that is, the week that contains the first Sunday (or date specified by the StartOfWeek property) in January will be week 1. To display week numbers, set the ShowWeekNumbers property to True.

The MonthView control also enables you to specify how dates are selected. You can choose to have the user select only a single date, or you can allow a range of dates to be selected. You cannot, however, have non-consecutive dates selected.

MonthView defaults to a single date selection. If you want to enable the user to select a date range, set the MultiSelect property to True. To limit the maximum number of days that can be selected, use the MaxSelCount property.

2

NEW ACTIVEX
CONTROLS

When the user selects a date, it is placed in the MonthView control's Value property. You can also determine the various parts of the selected date using the Month, Day, and Year properties. The DayOfWeek and Week properties provide even more information about the selected date. If you want to have a date other than the current date initially displayed when the MonthView control is shown, you can set one or more of these properties to specify the default selected date. For example, if you set the Week property to 3, the control will show the month that contains the third week of the year. Unless the DayOfWeek and Year properties are also set, they will come from the current date. So if the current date happens to be a Tuesday in 1998, the initially displayed and selected date would be January 20, 1998, the Tuesday of week 3 in 1998. Of course, you could also set the Value property to "1/20/98" and specify the exact date that way.

When multiple dates are selected, the Value, Month, Day, Year, DayOfWeek, and Week properties all reflect the first selected date. The SelStart property will contain the date of the first date selected, and the SelEnd property will contain the last date.

The last two properties to be discussed are DayBold and VisibleDays. Though each serves a completely different function, they can sometimes be used together.

The VisibleDays property is actually an array, and it contains the dates that are displayed on the MonthView calendar. The date in the upper left corner of the calendar corresponds to VisibleDays(1). This is not necessarily the first day of the month, since the dates of previous months are often displayed when the first of the month does not happen to fall on the first day of the week.

The DayBold property is also an array. It contains Boolean values that correspond to the VisibleDays dates and indicate whether or not the date should be displayed in a bold font. For example, if you wanted to use the DayBold property to show the fifth visible date on the MonthView1 calendar in bold, you might use a line of code such as:

```
MonthView1.DayBold(MonthView1.VisibleDays(5)) = True
```

In this example, the date value returned by the VisibleDays property for array element 5 is used as the index for the DayBold property.

MonthView Methods

The MonthView control has two unique methods that need to be noted, ComputeControlSize and HitTest.

The ComputeControlSize method enables you determine the height and width of a MonthView control, given its number of rows and columns. MonthView controls can get pretty large when displaying multiple months. By using the ComputeControlSize method before changing the `MonthColumns` and `MonthRows` properties, you can ensure that the control will fit on your form. The syntax of the `ComputeControlSize` method is:

```
ComputeControlSize(rows, columns, width, height)
```

You specify the *rows* and *columns* arguments before calling the method, then examine the variables passed as the *width* and *height* arguments. The *rows* and *columns* arguments are of type Integer, and width and height are of type Single.

The second unique method of the `MonthView` control is `HitTest`. `HitTest` is used to determine the part of the MonthView control that the mouse pointer is positioned on as well as the date that corresponds to the pointer's position (if any). The syntax for the HitTest method is:

```
ctrlpart = HitTest(x, y, date)
```

The value returned by the `HitTest` method (*ctrlpart*) specifies the part of the control in which the mouse cursor is positioned. This value corresponds to the `MonthViewHitTestAreas` Enum (see Table 2.6). The *x* and *y* arguments are the mouse pointer's coordinates, and the Date variable specified by the *date* argument will contain the date that is under the mouse pointer, if any.

TABLE 2.6. THE VALUES OF THE `MonthViewHitTestAreas` Enum.

Enum Member	Value
mvwCalendarBack	0
mvwCalendarDate	1
mvwCalendarDateNext	2
mvwCalendarDatePrev	3
mvwCalendarDay	4
mvwCalendarWeekNum	5
mvwNoWhere	6
mvwTitleBack	7
mvwTitleBtnNext	8
mvwTitleBtnPrev	9
mvwTitleMonth	10
mvwTitleYear	11
mvwTitleTodayLink	12

MonthView Events

When the user double-clicks on a date, the DateDblClick event is fired. However, when the date is clicked on, first the SelChange event is triggered and then the DateClick event fires. This sequence also occurs if the user selects a range of dates. Note that when dates are clicked on, the MonthView control's Click event is not triggered as well.

When the user moves to a previous or later month, or when the control is initially displayed, the GetDayBold event occurs. The name of this event refers to the fact that this is the procedure to be used when you want to change the appearance of certain dates, such as making them bold.

The DateTimePicker Control (DTPicker)

Although the DTPicker control sometimes uses a calendar display that is very similar to that of the MonthView control, these two components are not the same. The DTPicker control provides a greater range of values that can be selected, including time values.

The DTPicker control has four different formats for values that it will accept. These are long date, short date, time, and custom. Figure 2.8 shows the different formats of the DTPicker control.

FIGURE 2.8.

The formats of the DTPicker *control.*

When working with dates, the DTPicker control can utilize a drop-down calendar (see Figure 2.9). This is where DTPicker is similar to MonthView. However, you do not have the same amount of control over the way the calendar is displayed that you do with MonthView.

FIGURE 2.9.

The DTPicker *control features a drop-down calendar similar to the one used in the* MonthView *control.*

In addition to supporting a number of different time and date formats, the DTPicker control also lets you create your own formats. You'll see how to do this later in this chapter.

DTPicker Properties and Events

When dealing with dates, the DTPicker control uses a drop-down calendar by default. You can change only a few things about how the calendar is displayed, specifically the colors for the different parts of the calendar.

The CalendarBackColor property controls the background color of the calendar, and the CalendarForeColor property controls the color of the dates in the currently displayed month. The color of dates from previous or trailing months can be changed with the CalendarTrailingForeColor property. The colors of the title bar that shows the month and year for the calendar can be controlled with the CalendarTitleForeColor and CalendarTitleBackColor properties.

Like the MonthView control, you can specify the starting day of the week with the DayOfWeek property. You can also set the minimum and maximum dates to be displayed or selected with the MinDate and MaxDate properties.

Rather than use a drop-down calendar to select dates, the DTPicker control can use up and down arrows like those that are used to select time values (refer to Figure 2.8). To use arrows instead of the drop-down calendar, set the UpDown property to True.

You can add a checkbox to the DTPicker control by setting the CheckBox property to True. When a date is selected by the user, the box becomes checked. If no date is selected, the box is unchecked. You can use this feature when a date value is optional.

To retrieve date or time values entered via the DTPicker control, you can use the Value property. You can also get other information on the control's value by using the Month, Day, Year, Hour, Minute, and Second properties. Like the MonthView control, you can also use any of these properties to set the control's initial value.

DTPicker Formats

The Format property is used to determine the date or time format that the DTPicker control will use. Figure 2.8 shows the different values possible for the Format property and how the control will look when each value is used.

If the Format property is set to dtpCustom (3), you can create your own format for the date or time. You can specify the format in the CustomFormat property. The format string uses codes that specify certain pieces of information. Table 2.7 lists the codes that can be used with the CustomFormat property:

TABLE 2.7. THE FORMAT CODES THAT CAN BE USED IN THE CustomFormat PROPERTY.

Code	Description	Example
d	One- or two-digit day	2
dd	Two-digit day	02
ddd	Day-of-week abbreviation	Tue
dddd	Day-of-week name	Tuesday
h	One- or two-digit hour, 12-hour format	9
hh	Two-digit hour, 12-hour format	09
H	One- or two-digit hour, 24-hour format	6
HH	Two-digit hour, 24-hour format	14
m	One- or two-digit minute	8
mm	Two-digit minute	08
M	One- or two-digit month number	1
MM	Two-digit month number	01
MMM	Month abbreviation	Jan
MMMM	Month name	January
s	One- or two-digit second	7
ss	Two-digit second	07
t	One-letter AM/PM abbreviation	a
tt	Two-letter AM/PM abbreviation	am
y	One-digit year	8
yy	Two-digit year	98
yyy	Full year	1998
X	Callback field (see text)	

2

If you were to use a format string of "HH:DD:MM", the DTPicker control would display a time value in 24-hour time format. Therefore, 3:45pm would be shown as "15:45:00".

The "X" format code is used for creating your own formats. Suppose for example that you wanted to display "TGIF!" if the day of the week of the date that is selected by the user is a Friday. You want to display the day of the week for any day other than Friday.

To accomplish this, you might set the CustomFormat property to "XX" and the Format property to dtpCustom. You would then have to use the DTPicker control's FormatSize and Format events to handle the custom format.

The FormatSize event is called each time the DTPicker's value changes and it encounters an "X" code in the format string. You can use this event to specify how large the string value that you will be inserting in place of the "X" code will be. Because the largest value that you will be inserting is "Wednesday," the maximum size of the insertion string is 9. The code for the FormatSize event might look like this:

```
Private Sub dtpPickDate_FormatSize(ByVal CallbackField _
    As String, Size As Integer)

    If CallbackField = "XX" Then
        Size = 9
    End If

End Sub
```

The CallbackField parameter of the FormatSize event is the format code. Remember, you used a code of "XX" in the CustomFormat property, so you test to see if the callback field is "XX". You can use as many format codes in your format string as you'd like, it's just that they have to be of different lengths so they can be differentiated between one another. For example, you can use "XX," "XXX," "XXXX," and so on.

Now that you've specified the size of the insertion string, you have to actually have the correct value inserted into the format string in place of the "XX" code. This is done in the Format event:

```
Private Sub dtpPickDate_Format(ByVal CallbackField As String, _
    FormattedString As String)

    If CallbackField = "XX" Then
        Select Case dtpPickDate.DayOfWeek
            Case 0:    FormattedString = "Sunday"
            Case 1:    FormattedString = "Monday"
            Case 2:    FormattedString = "Tuesday"
            Case 3:    FormattedString = "Wednesday"
            Case 4:    FormattedString = "Thursday"
            Case 5:    FormattedString = "TGIF!"
```

```
        Case 6:    FormattedString = "Saturday"
      End Select
   End If

End Sub
```

Once again, the `CallbackField` parameter is examined to see if it is "XX". Then the `DTPicker` control's `DayOfWeek` property is used to assign the correct string value to the `FormattedString` property. This value is then used to replace the "XX" code.

The FlatScrollbar Control

There's really not too much to get excited about with the `FlatScrollbar` control. Basically, it's little more than an enhanced version of the `HScrollBar` and `VScrollBar` controls Visual Basic programmers have been using all along. Both horizontal and vertical scrollbars are supported, and you have more options available to you when it comes to how the scrollbars appear and how they react to users' actions.

The `FlatScrollbar` is the same type of scrollbar used in Microsoft's Internet Explorer. Rather than remaining static, the components of the `FlatScrollbar` are more interactive; that is, they change appearance when the mouse cursor is positioned over them. Move the mouse cursor over the "thumb" and it changes color. Click on the scroll arrows and they too change color. This is how the control reacts when it is in its default 2D mode.

Another mode enables the thumb and scroll arrows of the `FlatScrollbar` control to become 3D (beveled) when they are under the mouse pointer. Yet another mode turns the `FlatScrollbar` into a clone of the `HScrollBar` and `VScrollBar` controls. Perhaps Microsoft has plans to eventually replace the two older scrollbar controls with the single, more flexible `FlatScrollbar` control. You can see an example of all four of the `FlatScrollBar`'s modes in Figure 2.10.

FIGURE 2.10.

The different modes of the FlatScrollBar *control at runtime.*

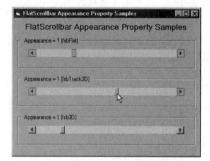

One other perk that comes with the FlatScrollbar is the ability to have its scroll arrows disabled. If a scrollbar has reached its minimum or maximum value, you can disable the appropriate scroll arrow to give the user a visual cue that he or she has reached the scrollbar's limits.

Properties

The FlatScrollbar control works almost identically to the HScrollbar and VScrollbar controls. You still have the Max, Min, LargeChange, aznd SmallChange properties for specifying the range of values and by how much the current value is increased or decreased based on a user's actions. In addition, the current value of the scrollbar is still read or set with the Value property.

The way in which the FlatScrollbar control appears and reacts to users' actions is dictated by the value of the Appearance property. The default value of 1 (fsbFlat) gives the scrollbar a 2D appearance, with the thumb and scroll arrows changing color when the mouse pointer is positioned over them. A value of 2 (fsbTrack3D) also maintains the scrollbar's initial 2D appearance, but the thumb and scroll arrows become 3D when the mouse cursor points at them. Assigning the Appearance property a value of 0 (fsb3D) gives the FlatScrollbar control the 3D appearance of the standard HScrollbar and VScrollbar controls. Figure 2.10 shows the effects of the different Appearance property values.

The Orientation property lets you specify whether the scrollbar will be horizontal (sldHorizontal or 0) or vertical (sldVertical or 1). The FlatScrollbar control is in a horizontal configuration as the default.

The Arrows property specifies which scroll arrows will be enabled. By default, both arrows are enabled and the Arrows property has a value of 0 (fsbBoth). To enable only the left or up scroll arrow, set Arrows to 1 (fsbLeftUp). To enable only the right or down scroll arrow, set Arrows to 2 (fsbRightDown).

Summary

Visual Basic 6 has added some new components to VB's already impressive Toolbox. Five new general-purpose controls have been added: Coolbar, ImageCombo, MonthView, DateTimePicker, and FlatScrollBar.

This chapter introduced you to each of these controls. The unique properties, methods, and events of each control were discussed thoroughly. In some cases, sample programs were also given that illustrated how you could actually implement the controls.

2

NEW ACTIVEX CONTROLS

New Add-Ins and Utilities

by Rob Thayer

IN THIS CHAPTER

- **The API Viewer   50**
- **The VB6 Resource Editor   51**
- **Visual Modeler   56**
- **The Visual Component Manager   59**
- **The VB6 Template Manager   62s**

Visual Basic 6 comes with some new or updated add-ins and standalone utilities. Some, such as Microsoft's Visual Modeler, are only available with the Enterprise Edition of Visual Basic or Visual Studio.

This chapter introduces you to VB's newest utilities. It covers the API Viewer add-in, which lets you cut and paste declarations, constants, and type definitions for Win32 API functions into your program; the VB6 Resource Editor, which allows you to easily create resource files that can be used for localization of your applications; the Visual Modeler, a complex modeling tool for application architecture; the Visual Component Manager, an add-in for tracking components such as ActiveX controls, templates, and classes; and the Template Manager, an add-in that lets you easily add pre-existing code snippets, menus, and control sets to your projects.

The API Viewer

The API Viewer is not new to VB6, but this is the first version of Visual Basic that implements the utility as an add-in instead of as a standalone program. The API Viewer does still exist as a standalone utility, however, and can also be used outside of Visual Basic.

For those who are unfamiliar with this utility, the API Viewer is used to extract declarations, constants, and type definitions for the Win32 API functions. You can copy these items to the Clipboard, then paste them into your program where needed. For example, you might find several function declaration statements for the API routines that you will be using, copy them to the Clipboard, and then paste them into a module.

Figure 3.1 shows the API Viewer being used as a Visual Basic add-in. The API functions `BitBlt` and `StretchBlt` have been selected from the API Viewer's Available Items list box, and the appropriate Visual Basic `Declare` statements for the two functions appear in the Selected Items text box. The `Declare` statements can be copied to the Clipboard by clicking the Copy button. Basically, the API Viewer saves you from a lot of typing and prevents you from using invalid function declarations or misspelled constant and type definitions.

Before adding items to the Selected Items text box, you can specify their scope by choosing either the Public or Private option button. This is really just a frill, and you can always change the scope of a declaration or type definition after it has been pasted into your program.

FIGURE 3.1.

The API Viewer being used as an add-in from within Visual Basic.

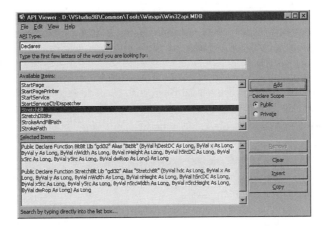

Typically, all of the function declarations, constants, and type definitions used by the API Viewer come from the WIN32API.TXT file that is included with Visual Basic. However, you can also create your own text files that contain such declarations and definitions and use them with the API Viewer. You might want to consider doing this if you create a component such as a DLL that contains a number of different functions. If you distribute the DLL to other programmers, make sure to also distribute the text file containing the function declarations so they can also use it with the API Viewer on their system. For another example of a file that contains function declarations, constants, and type definitions, see the MAPI32.TXT file that is included with VB. This file is designed to be used with Microsoft's Messaging API (MAPI), which enables you to add electronic mail functionality to your programs.

The API Viewer provides an option for converting function declaration text files such as WIN32API.TXT into a database format. Organizing the information into a database simply allows the API Viewer to work more efficiently. To convert a text file to a database, use the Convert Text to Database option on the API Viewer's File menu.

The API Viewer is an extremely easy-to-use utility and you should have no trouble using it. However, if you'd like more information on this utility and how to use Win32 API functions in your applications, see Chapter 25, "Using Windows API Functions."

The VB6 Resource Editor

Resource files are nothing new to Visual Basic, but the Resource Editor (ResEdit) add-in is. Prior to ResEdit, resource files had to be created manually or by using a program such as Visual C++'s AppStudio program. They then had to be compiled using the Resource Compiler utility located on the Visual Basic CD-ROM.

3

NEW ADD-INS
AND UTILITIES

In a nutshell, resource files store data, such as strings or icons, that would normally be hard-coded into your program or stored in a database. Although this may seem an unnecessary step, it does make a lot of sense for certain applications. You'll see why in just a moment.

To use the Resource Editor from Visual Basic, use the Add-In Manager to ensure that it is loaded. Then, click the Resource Editor icon that is added to VB's toolbar. You should then see the ResEdit Add-In's dockable window (see Figure 3.2).

FIGURE 3.2.

The Resource Editor add-in's window.

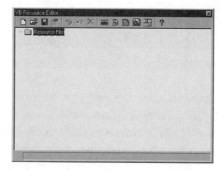

The ResEdit utility is very easy to use. You can use the icons on its toolbar to create, open, and save resource files. Other icons allow you to add data to the resource file you're currently using. There are five different types of data that can be stored in resource files: strings, cursors, icons, bitmaps, and custom resources. Custom resources include any kind of binary data, such as sounds (WAVs) or videos (AVIs).

As you can see, resource files can contain a wide variety of data types. But this brings us back to the question of why this data would be stored in a separate resource file rather than being hard-coded into the program or, more likely, accessed from a database.

Resource files are typically used in applications that are to be distributed in foreign countries. The resource file can contain strings and other data that are designed specifically for the country in which the application is used. For example, you could use a resource file to contain all of the strings that are displayed by a program. String resources are given a numeric identifier, and each identifier can have one or more language-specific strings associated with it: one for English, one for Spanish, one for French, and so on. This is referred to as *localization* because the computer's locale ID (LCID) is used to determine which string to use. That way, you can have a single program that will automatically utilize the languages of different countries and you don't have to create separate versions for English, Spanish, French, and so on.

To better illustrate how resource files are used for localization, look at Figure 3.3. It shows the Resource Editor being used to hold three different language versions (English, French, and Spanish) of the numbers one through ten and zero. Each of the three languages are stored in separate tables. The numbers along the left side indicate the identifier of the string.

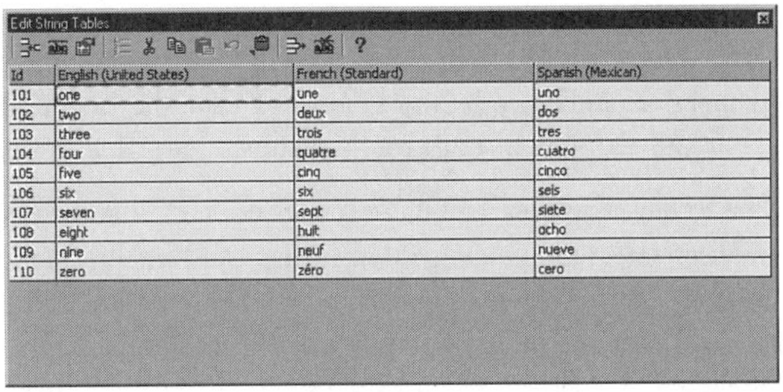

FIGURE 3.3.

The Resource Editor can be used for localization, the storing of data that is specific to certain languages or dialects.

Id	English (United States)	French (Standard)	Spanish (Mexican)
101	one	une	uno
102	two	deux	dos
103	three	trois	tres
104	four	quatre	cuatro
105	five	cinq	cinco
106	six	six	seis
107	seven	sept	siete
108	eight	huit	ocho
109	nine	neuf	nueve
110	zero	zéro	cero

To create these string tables, you would click the Edit String Table icon in the Resource Editor's toolbar. You can then add rows and tables to the matrix of strings. Each numeric identifier has its own row, and each row can have one or more tables (which appear as columns in the Resource Editor). Each table has a single property, which can be selected from the drop-down list box at the top of the table. It allows you to select the language or dialect for the table. When the program that utilizes the resource file is run, the system's LCID is used to determine which table to use. If no match is found, the first table is used as the default. In Figure 3.3, there are ten rows (using the identifiers 101 through 110) and three tables (or columns) in each row: English (United States), French (Standard), and Spanish (Mexican). If the program that utilizes such a resource file was run on a computer that is designated as using the French language, the second table would automatically be used.

You can add or delete tables and rows using the toolbar icons along the top of the Edit String Tables window. To edit the contents of each table entry, simply select the item and type in a string value. You can also change the numeric identifiers to whatever you like.

After you've created a string table, you need to be able to extract the strings that correspond to the numeric identifiers from within your program. This is done using VB's `LoadResString` function. Simply pass the function the string's identifier number and it will return the string. For example, if you had a Label control called `lblNumber` on a form and were using the string table shown in Figure 3.3 to display the word for the number 5 in the native language of the computer on which the program was running, you might code it like this:

```
lblNumber.Caption = LoadResString(105)
```

If the system's LCID indicates that the system uses U.S. English as its standard language, then lblNumber.Caption will be assigned the string value "five". If the system uses Standard French, lblNumber.Caption will be assigned "cinq". Finally, if the system uses Mexican Spanish, lblNumber.Caption will be assigned "cinco". If none of these three languages are indicated by the system's LCID, the first table (U.S. English) is used as the default and lblNumber.Caption is assigned the value "five".

What if you want to have multiple language strings contained in the resource file and want to have the user select the language that is displayed rather than relying on the system's LCID? In that case, you have to use a single table to contain all of the strings and programatically determine the numeric identifiers to use. For example, if you were to store the values shown in Figure 3.3 in a single table, the U.S. English strings might be stored in identifiers 101 through 110. The Standard French strings would be stored following them, in identifiers 111 through 120. The Mexican Spanish strings would come next, in identifiers 121 through 130. You could then use a section of code similar to the one shown below to extract and display the correct strings:

```
' The integer value intLanguage specifies the
' language to be used (1=English, 2=French,
' 3=Spanish).
Select Case intLanguage
    Case 1:  lblNumber.Caption = LoadResString(105)
    Case 2:  lblNumber.Caption = LoadResString(115)
    Case 3:  lblNumber.Caption = LoadResString(125)
End Select
```

Like the previous example, this would assign the string for the number 5 into the lblNumber.Caption property. Based on the value of the intLanguage variable, the string that is used would be either English, French, or Spanish.

You can store data types other than strings in resource files. The Resource Editor also lets you add cursors, icons, bitmaps, and custom resources such as binary files. The only restriction is that the files can be a maximum of 64KB each. To add any of these data items, you need only click the appropriate icon in the Resource Editor's toolbar. You'll then be presented with a File dialog box, and you can specify the file that contains the item you want to add to the resource file. Figure 3.4 shows the Resource Editor with multiple string tables, cursors, icons, bitmaps, and custom resources being used.

FIGURE 3.4.

Resource files can include string tables, cursors, icons, bitmaps, and custom resources.

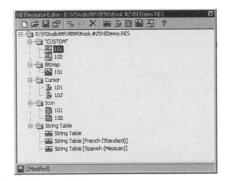

Note that the items for each data type are grouped together and the identifier numbers for one data type are independent of another. For example, a bitmap can have an identifier of 101 and a string table can also use the same identifier. These items are not related, so having duplicate identifiers is not a problem.

To extract a bitmap, icon, or cursor from a resource file, you have to use VB's `LoadResPicture` function. This function is used in a way similar to the `LoadResString` function, but you have to pass it the data format as well as the identifier. Use the constants `vbResBitmap` (0), `vbResIcon` (1), and `vbResCursor` (2) to specify the data format of the item to be retrieved. For example, to load a bitmap from the resource file and assign it to the `Picture` property of a control called `picLocalOffice`, you might use a line of code such as

```
Set picLocalOffice.Picture = LoadResPicture(101, vbResBitmap)
```

In this example, the bitmap that is used corresponds to the bitmap in the resource file with the identifier 101.

If you want to load in a string that contains the actual bits of a bitmap, icon, or cursor resource, or if you are accessing a custom resource, you will need to use the `LoadResData` function. `LoadResData` is used just like the `LoadResPicture` function, except the values for specifying the data format are different and there are more of them. Table 3.1 lists the possible values.

TABLE 3.1. THE POSSIBLE VALUES FOR SPECIFYING THE DATA FORMAT WHEN USING THE `LoadResData` FUNCTION.

Resource Data Type	Value
Cursor	1
Bitmap	2

continues

TABLE 3.1. CONTINUED

Resource Data Type	Value
Icon	3
Menu	4
Dialog Box	5
String	6
Font Directory	7
Font	8
Accelerator Table	9
User-Defined Resource	10
Group Cursor	12
Group Icon	14

When you add custom resources to the resource file with ResEdit, you should right-click on the item and change its properties. Change the item's Type to indicate the type of data item that it is. For example, if you're adding a WAV audio file, change its Type to "WAV". This will create a new group in the ResEdit window for data items of type **WAV**. You can then access the items in the group by passing the name of the data type rather than one of the values shown in Table 3.1. For example, you could use a line of code like the following to access the resource corresponding to the identifier 200 in the WAV resource group:

```
strWavData = LoadResData(200, "WAV")
```

This makes the code a lot easier to understand because you are in effect specifying the type of resource you are accessing.

When you are done adding resources with the Resource Editor, you need to save them into a resource file. The Resource Editor automatically compiles the resources for you, and you no longer have to use a separate utility such as the Resource Compiler. Projects can have only one resource file loaded in at any given time, but you can reuse resource files again and again by loading them into other projects.

Visual Modeler

One of the more complex utilities included with the Enterprise Edition of Visual Basic (and Visual Studio) is Microsoft's Visual Modeler 2.0. This tool uses a graphic user interface to facilitate object-oriented design and development. Visual Modeler was created jointly by Microsoft and Rational Software, the company that makes the popular modeling tool Rational Rose.

Visual Modeler lets you look at the "big picture" of an application's development, showing how components relate and interact with one another. Instead of working at the level of the application's source code, you can see the overall architecture of the application. Under most circumstances, programs are quite simple in their design and can be easily understood without a tool like Visual Modeler. Where Visual Modeler shines is when the application being designed is very large and uses many different components and data sources.

Visual Modeler applies a three-tier approach to the architecture of applications. The first tier is User Services and consists of visual interfaces such as forms that are used for gathering data and presenting information. The second tier, Business Services, consists of components such as classes that respond to requests from the user or perform tasks. Data Services, the third tier, work with databases to maintain, access, and update data. The middle tier, Business Services, acts as a bridge between the User Services and the Data Services tiers. The presentation of an application's components divided into these three tiers is referred to as the *Three-Tiered Service Model*. One of the main goals of a three-tier architecture model is to have the Business Services tier take care of most of the application's business logic. An example of this model is shown in Figure 3.5.

3

NEW ADD-INS AND UTILITIES

FIGURE 3.5.

The Visual Modeler utility, showing the Three-Tiered Service Model for a sample application.

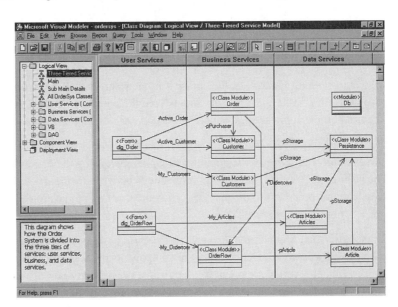

Visual Modeler has three different views, or levels of abstraction, for an application: logical view, component view, and deployment view. The Three-Tiered Service Model falls under the logical view category because it shows the logical structure of the application, including the relationships between its components. The component view has a broader scope, showing the physical structure of the application, such as the EXE and DLL files that it uses. An example of the component view is shown in Figure 3.6.

FIGURE 3.6.

The Visual Modeler in component view, showing the actual EXE and DLL files that the sample application uses.

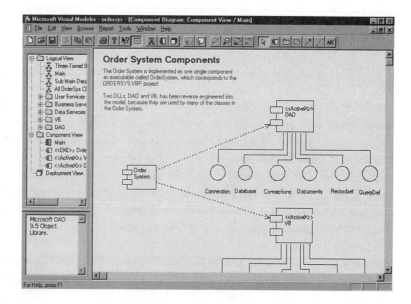

As you can see in Figure 3.6, the component view shows that the sample application uses two DLL files, DAO and VB. You can also see the objects from the DAO DLL file that are used by the application: Connection, Database, Connections, Documents, Recordset, and QueryDef.

An even broader scope of the application can be seen using the deployment view. This view shows the system's nodes, the connections between them, and the allocation of the application's processes to those nodes. Of course, not all applications use nodes, so this view is not always needed.

Although Visual Modeler makes viewing the entirety of a complex application easier, it also provides a way of documenting the components of the application and how they work together. Every component can be given a description that tells what it does and how it is used. Visual Modeler also lets you delve into the details of each component, showing its various interface elements, relations, and other information. Figure 3.7 shows the specifications for one of the class modules in a sample application.

FIGURE 3.7.

The specifications for one of the class modules in a sample application.

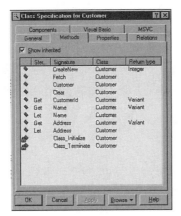

In addition to the graphic modeling of applications, Visual Modeler can generate Visual Basic code automatically, using the design model that has been created. It also supports *reverse engineering*, meaning that the model of the application can be automatically created or updated whenever changes have been made to the application's code. By utilizing this feature, you can have Visual Modeler create a model for an existing application that does not already have one—an easy way to get an overview of a complex project that you know little about. The combination of modeling, code generation, and reverse engineering is referred to as *round-trip engineering*.

Because of the complexity of the Visual Modeler, it is beyond the scope of this chapter. If you want to learn more about how to use this utility for application modeling, consult Visual Modeler's online Help system. You can also find more information on the MSDN Library CD-ROM, including a step-by-step tutorial that uses a sample ordering system application.

The Visual Component Manager

Creating solid components and reusing them again and again in different projects is a good idea, but not always so easy to implement. The biggest problem is that these components are not always located in one place. Trying to find what you need—or even knowing what you have—can sometimes be a daunting task.

The Visual Component Manager, a VB add-in, makes the cataloging of components much easier. It stores such components in a repository database, along with attributes and search keywords. If you need to find a component, you need only search the repository via the Component Manager. What's more, you can use a local repository for the components that exist on your system as well as a network repository that can be shared by

3

NEW ADD-INS
AND UTILITIES

other programmers in your organization. Why re-invent the wheel by creating a new component if someone else has already done the work for you?

> **NOTE**
>
> The Visual Component Manager can use only two database formats: Microsoft Access and SQL Server.

A huge variety of component types can be tracked with the Visual Component Manager. A basic rule of thumb is that if you can add it to a Visual Basic project, you can track it with the Component Manager. The repository database can include information on Active documents, ActiveX controls, COM servers, documents, HTML files, and templates. In VB, the templates category is broad and includes the following:

- Classes
- Code procedures
- Control sets
- Forms
- MDI Forms
- Menus
- Modules
- Project templates
- Property pages
- User controls
- User documents

When you first use the Visual Component Manager, it includes many of the components that are installed with Visual Basic, such as form templates. Figure 3.8 shows the form templates that the Visual Component Manager includes by default. Note that specific information for each form template is included.

As you can see by Figure 3.8, the component types tracked by the Visual Component Manager are grouped together into folders and organized into a hierarchy for easy navigation. You can also search for a specific component by using the Find Item(s) icon on the Component Manager's toolbar.

FIGURE 3.8.

The Visual Component Manager includes many of the components that are installed with VB in its repository database.

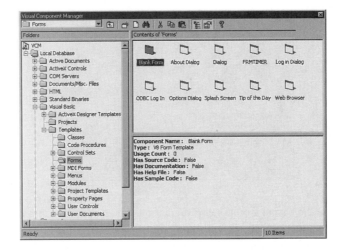

When you add a new component to the repository, you are *publishing* it, because it is made available to anyone who has access to the repository. The Visual Component Manager makes adding components easy by providing the Publish Wizard (see Figure 3.9). To invoke the wizard, right-click on the folder you want to add the component to and select the New Component option. Then simply enter in information about the component—name, filename, author, description, keywords, and whether or not it is a COM object that needs to be registered—and it will be added to the repository. Before adding a component, make sure that the folder you want it added to is selected. For instance, if you want to add a new form component, first make sure that the Form folder is selected in the component hierarchy. If necessary, you can create a new folder in the hierarchy by right-clicking on its parent folder and choosing the New Folder option.

You can also create an entirely new repository database by right-clicking on the root node of the component hierarchy (called VCM) and choosing the Repository option; then choose the New option. Or if you want to access an existing repository database, such as one on a network, select the Repository option and then the Open option.

In addition to the components used in Visual Basic, you can also use the Visual Component Manager to track the components used in other Visual Studio products, such as Visual InterDev or Visual C++. If you use the Visual Modeler utility discussed earlier in this chapter, you can publish classes and logical packages from that tool directly into the repository database. Simply choose the Publish to VCM option from Visual Modeler's Tools menu. All published components will then appear in the Component Manager's Visual Modeler folder.

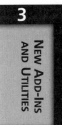

FIGURE 3.9.

The Publish Wizard makes it easy to add, or "publish," components to the repository database.

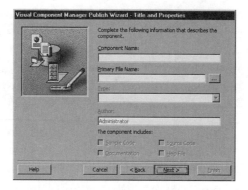

When you use the Visual Component Manager to find a specific component that you want to use in your application, you need only right-click on the component and select the Add to Project option. It will be instantly added to the current VB project.

If you're a professional developer who has created hundreds or even thousands of components, adding them to the repository database can be a big job. But if you ever spend time trying to track down a pre-existing component for use in a project, it will be well worth the time to have your components organized in a central database. If you're working with other VB programmers, using the Visual Component Manager makes even more sense because you can share the components that have been developed with your colleagues, and vice versa.

The VB6 Template Manager

The Template Manager is oddly named because it is not a utility like other Manager add-ins in VB, such as the Visual Component Manager or the Visual Data Manager. Instead, loading the Template Manager adds three new options to VB's Tools menu item: Add Code Snippet, Add Menu, and Add Control Set. Each option allows you to add pre-existing components to your project, just the way you would add a pre-existing form or class module.

The Add Code Snippet option displays a dialog box like the one shown in Figure 3.10. VB comes with two pre-defined code snippets: Load Resources and Registry Access. The Load Resources code snippet adds code to your project for accessing items in a resource file (see the discussion of the Resource Editor earlier in this chapter). The Registry Access code snippet adds code for accessing the system Registry. In both cases, the code is added to the currently selected form or module.

FIGURE 3.10.

The Template Manager's Add Code Snippet option (on VB's Tools menu) lets you paste code into the currently selected form or module.

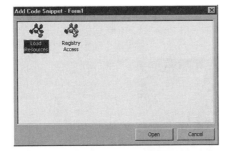

Code snippets are really nothing more than .BAS files that contain VB code. You can easily create your own code snippets by saving whatever code you want to use in a .BAS file and saving it in VB's `Template\Code` subdirectory. Note that even though they share the same file extensions, code snippets and modules are not used in the same way. A module is added to a project as a separate component. Code snippets are simply pasted into the current form or module and do not add new components to the project.

The Add Menu option is used to add menu items and the corresponding code to the currently selected form. VB comes with several pre-built menu items including File, Edit, View, Window, Help, and Explorer File. To create your own menus that can be used with this option, start with a blank form and add the menu items you want to include to the form. Then add some skeleton code for the menu items' Click events. Save the form to VB's `Template\Menus` subdirectory. Make sure you save the file with a .FRM extension. You can choose to save a single menu item (such as File) or an entire menu bar (File, Edit, and so on). Saving single menu items is usually preferred because it gives you greater control over how you can put together the menu bar for an application.

The Add Control Set option is used to add to a form ActiveX controls that often work together. They also include any necessary code for the controls. The control sets included with VB are Button ListBox, Mover ListBox, and TreeView ListView Splitter. Button ListBox adds a ListBox control and four buttons for Add, Delete, Up, and Down functions (see Figure 3.11).

The Mover ListBox control set adds two ListBox controls and buttons that allow you to add items from the first ListBox to the second and remove items from the second ListBox back to the first. This control set is useful when creating setup programs, letting users choose the options they want to install by selecting them from the first ListBox and showing their selections in the second ListBox.

The TreeView ListView Splitter control set adds a TreeView control and a ListView control. When a node is selected on the TreeView control, any items it contains are shown in

3

NEW ADD-INS AND UTILITIES

the ListView control. This control set can be handy when working with databases or the system Registry.

FIGURE 3.11.

The Button ListBox control set adds a ListBox control and four CommandButton controls to the currently selected form. Code is also added that enables the controls to work together.

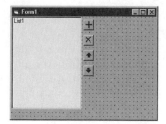

If you want to create your own control set, all you need to do is add the necessary controls and skeleton code to a form, then save it to VB's `Templates\Controls` subdirectory. Make sure that you give it a .FRM extension.

You may be wondering if the functions of the Template Manager can also be accomplished via the Visual Component Manager. The answer is yes. The Component Manager does let you track code snippets, menus, and control sets. You can add them to your project the same way you would add other components.

Summary

Visual Basic 6 has added or updated several add-ins and standalone utilities. Many of these deal directly or indirectly with the concept of component reuse. For example, the VB6 Resource Editor lets you create resource files, which are components that can be reused in different projects. The Visual Component Manager lets you track all of the components on your system (or on a network) by storing information about each component in a repository database. The Template Manager lets you add existing code snippet, menu, or control set components to your projects.

Other add-ins and utilities discussed in this chapter are the API Viewer add-in and Microsoft's Visual Modeler. The API Viewer lets you cut and paste declarations, constants, and type definitions for the Win32 API functions. The Visual Modeler is a complex utility that allows you to create abstract views of your applications so you can see how the various components that make up the application relate to one another.

Creating Components in VB6

PART

II

IN THIS PART

- An Overview of ActiveX Programming   *67*
- Creating ActiveX Controls   *81*
- Deploying ActiveX Controls   *149*
- ActiveX Scripting with VBScript   *159*
- Data Consumers and Data Sources   *175*
- Apartment Model Threading   *195*
- Object-Oriented Programming In Visual Basic   *213*
- Creating and Using Class Modules   *233*

An Overview of ActiveX Programming

by Rob Thayer

IN THIS CHAPTER

- A Brief History of ActiveX *68*

CHAPTER 4

One of the hottest buzzwords to hit the VB development community is ActiveX. It's no wonder; the last version of Visual Basic had the term plastered just about everywhere. There were ActiveX controls, ActiveX documents, ActiveX DLLs, and ActiveX EXEs. Microsoft has made it abundantly clear: Visual Basic is centered around ActiveX technology.

But what can ActiveX really do for us, and why should we be so excited about it? Is ActiveX mainly an Internet technology? And, perhaps most importantly, how will ActiveX affect the way we program?

To answer these questions, it's necessary to learn a little more about what ActiveX is (and is not). You may be surprised to find that ActiveX really isn't a new technology at all. In a nutshell, ActiveX equals OLE, the same OLE that we've been using for years. Microsoft seems to have played a fast one on us, labeling old technology with a slick sounding name and touting it as the wave of the future. The name change may have been a marketing ploy, but Microsoft is right. ActiveX *is* the wave of the future—at least for Visual Basic programmers. And although the Internet does play into the picture in some ways, ActiveX is a whole lot more.

A Brief History of ActiveX

Programmers are not historians. They don't like to read lengthy histories about a specific technology; they just want to learn how to use it. But when talking about a technology as all-encompassing as ActiveX, knowing a little about its previous history is a must. Before you can understand where ActiveX is going, you first need to know where it came from.

DDE and OLE 1.0

ActiveX can trace its roots all the way back to Dynamic Data Exchange (DDE), a way of passing data and commands between applications. Though DDE is still supported by Visual Basic to maintain backward compatibility, it is seldom used.

Out of DDE evolved OLE 1.0, Object Linking and Embedding. True to its name, OLE brought the ability to link objects to one another or to embed one object inside another. The classic example of using OLE is the word processor/spreadsheet combination. A reference to a spreadsheet file can be added to a word processing document. If the user was to click on the reference, the spreadsheet program that is used to edit the spreadsheet would be automatically loaded and changes could be made. In this way, the spreadsheet is *linked* to the word processing document. With OLE, the spreadsheet can also be *embedded* into the word processing document. A window that shows the contents of the spreadsheet would be contained within the document. Changes to the spreadsheet can then be made inside that window. The spreadsheet program is still used to make the changes, but this is transparent to the user. He or she never has to leave the word processor to make changes to the spreadsheet.

DDE and OLE 1.0 are technologies that were designed to change the way we use computers. They bridged the gap between *application-centric* use and *data-centric* use. In application-centric computing, to work on a certain kind of file (such as a word processing document, a graphic image, or a spreadsheet), you would call up whichever program was used to edit that kind of file. To work on a word processing document, you might invoke Microsoft Word. With data-centric computing, it's the other way around. If you want to work on a word processing document, you need only click on the document itself. The operating system then determines which application is associated with that file type and loads it, along with the document.

Although the concept of data-centric computing sounds like it does nothing more than make things easier for the user, it goes far beyond that. It also facilitates the embedding of different object types within other objects. A Web browser, for example, can display an HTML document that contains many different object types: images, sounds, videos, animation, and others. If the Web browser does not natively support the object type, the external program (typically, a "plug-in" for Netscape browsers or an ActiveX control in Internet Explorer) that is associated with the object type can be used to display the object within the page. Again, this is transparent to the user.

OLE 2.0 and COM

Although OLE 1.0 did a lot to advance the concept of data-centric computing, OLE 2.0 did even more. OLE 2.0 brings together several technologies to create a standard way of using objects. The basis for this is a technology called COM.

COM, or *component object model*, provides the fundamental ability for multiple applications or software components to cooperate and communicate with one another. It doesn't matter in what language the components were written or who programmed them. It doesn't even matter if the components are running on different computers or different operating systems. COM and a similar technology called DCOM (*distributed component object model*) provide an elegant way for everything to work together.

The component object model defines a set of standards that all objects (commonly referred to as *component objects*) must follow. These standards are what enable an application to utilize objects without knowing the details of the object itself. It is the principles of COM that enable Visual Basic programs to use ActiveX controls (objects) simply by adding the controls to the Toolbox.

While standardizing components, COM also promotes the concepts of object-oriented programming. Under the COM method, objects (software components) can be re-used and expanded upon while still providing backward compatibility with applications that have been programmed to use previous versions.

COM In Action

COM encompasses many different concepts such as client/server, versioning, and GUIDs. The best way to explain these concepts is with a theoretical example that utilizes the elements of COM.

To explain how COM works, take a look at a sample application (PICVIEW.EXE). The PICVIEW program enables the user to view images that are in GIF87a format. To save some coding, PICVIEW's programmer utilized an object (SEEGIF.OCX) that provided the capability to decode and view GIF files. Figure 4.1 shows how COM is used to facilitate the interaction between PICVIEW.EXE (a *client* object) and SEEGIF.OCX (a *server* object). Note that in this context, a server is a software component that "serves" the requests of its clients.

FIGURE 4.1

COM establishes an interface between the client application and the object server, allowing the client to communicate with the server.

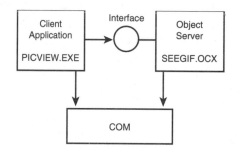

PICVIEW does not initially interact directly with SEEGIF. It goes through COM first, and COM gives PICVIEW an *interface pointer* by which it can communicate with SEEGIF. After the connection between PICVIEW and SEEGIF has been established, COM is no longer used as a middleman for communication.

All interaction between clients and object servers is done via interface pointers, and a client never has direct access to an object in its entirety. An interface is a clearly-defined contract between a client and a server that specifies how the two objects will work together.

> **NOTE**
>
> Although this example uses an .OCX file, server objects can be of several different file types, including .DLLs and .EXEs.

When PICVIEW attempts to gain access to SEEGIF through COM, it is given an interface pointer to SEEGIF's IUnknown interface. All server objects have an IUnknown interface. IUnknown enables the client to do two things and two things only:

To partially control the lifetime of the object (using *reference counting,* which will be covered later)

To invoke the objectís QueryInterface function

The QueryInterface function enables a client to ask an object if it supports the functionality that it desires. In this example, PICVIEW would use QueryInterface to ask SEEGIF if it supports the capability to view GIF87a images. SEEGIF then has the option of denying or accepting the request (based on security issues or user permissions). If SEEGIF does not have the functionality that PICVIEW needs or denies the request for other reasons, the client has the opportunity to accommodate for that situation in its code. If SEEGIF does have the desired functionality, it returns to PICVIEW a new pointer to the requested interface.

This is somewhat confusing, so let's expand on our example to better illustrate this concept. Say that a new version of SEEGIF has been released, and it has been enhanced to accommodate the GIF89a file specification as well as GIF87a. The programmer of PICVIEW knows that SEEGIF now supports both GIF87a and GIF89a images, but he's not sure which version of SEEGIF the user of PICVIEW will have on his system. He would like to be able to accommodate both so his program works with any version of the SEEGIF.OCX. Figure 4.2 shows how PICVIEW uses SEEGIF's QueryInterface function to obtain a new interface pointer.

FIGURE 4.2

The client uses the server's QueryInterface function to obtain a pointer to a new interface.

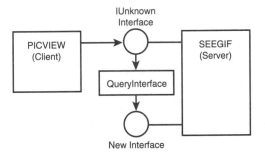

SEEGIF's QueryInterface provides PICVIEW with a pointer to a new interface. The PICVIEW client begins by using COM to obtain the initial interface pointer to SEEGIF, as shown in the earlier example. It then uses SEEGIF's QueryInterface to see if an interface for GIF89a (SEEGIF version 2) is available. If it is, then PICVIEW knows that it can provide support for viewing GIF89a images. If an interface is not available, then PICVIEW can compensate for that in its code and support only GIF87a image formats

(SEEGIF version 1). In effect, `QueryInterface` enables a client to be written that can take advantage of as much of an objectís functionality as it would ideally like to use instead of being limited to the lowest common denominator. Figure 4.3 shows how a server can have multiple interfaces, and how the `QueryInterface` function can be used to point a client to one or more of those interfaces.

FIGURE 4.3

SEEGIF's QueryInterface function is used to point PICVIEW to the different interfaces that are available to it.

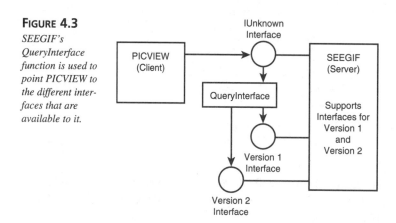

Versioning

What happens if the user of PICVIEW obtains the new version of SEEGIF? The PICVIEW application is then immediately able to provide support for GIF89a images even though that application has not been replaced or updated. If a third version of SEEGIF comes out and the PICVIEW user obtains that also, then what happens? PICVIEW continues to work as it always has, but it does not take advantage of any of SEEGIF's new functionality. That is, until an upgrade is made to the PICVIEW program to accommodate the new features of SEEGIF!

This brings up the topic of *versioning*. Under COM, multiple versions of an object are contained in a single object module. Instead of changing the objectís interface to accommodate newer versions, additional interfaces are added to the object. This way, a single object module can provide backward compatibility and can support multiple versions, even though one version might be drastically different from those previous. In the following example, SEEGIF.OCX contains two different versions in one object module.

GUIDs

You might be wondering how a client identifies the particular interface for which it is looking. After all, an OCX that provides the same functionality as SEEGIF will not necessarily be called SEEGIF, and its interfaces might go by different names than those used in the SEEGIF object. How does a client know what is available on the current system?

Interfaces are not identified by COM using names—names are simply a programming convenience. COM uses Globally Unique Identifiers (*GUIDs,* pronounced "goo-Ids" or "gwids") exclusively to reference interfaces. A client specifies the class of an object that it requires. Locator services, which are a part of the COM Library, are used by COM to determine from the class identifier which server object implements that class and where on the system the object can be located. A catalog of all available GUIDs on a system can be found in the System Registry in Windows 95 and Windows NT.

GUIDs are 128-bit integers that are used to identify every interface and every object class. Because of their size, each GUID is virtually guaranteed to be unique, even on systems or networks that contain thousands or millions of objects. If human-readable names were used rather than GUIDs, a conflict would be imminent.

Reference Counting

Earlier in this chapter, the process of reference counting was briefly mentioned. Reference counting is a way for a server object to keep track of how many clients are currently using it.

Unlike the operating systems of the past, new operating systems can only load an object into memory once, no matter how many applications are using it. This solves the problem of a single object being loaded into memory multiple times and hogging valuable system resources, but it raises another problem: how does an object know when its clients are done with it?

Knowing when an object is no longer needed is accomplished by reference counting. An object is responsible for keeping track of the clients that use it. It doesn't care *which* clients are using it, only how many. When a client is finished using an object, the object is notified. After an object is no longer being used by any clients, it removes itself from memory. Problem solved! Of course, an object is reloaded whenever another client requests it and the process starts all over again.

Location Transparency and Marshaling

Much has been discussed about COM, but not much has been mentioned yet about DCOM (Distributed Component Object Model). What's the difference between COM and DCOM? DCOM is simply a version of COM that facilitates COM's functionality over a network. In fact, DCOM was previously referred to as Network OLE.

One of COM/DCOM's more interesting features is its provision for *location transparency.* Location transparency refers to COM/DCOM's capability to use a local or not-local object in the exact same way; that is, an object server can exist on the same system that also houses its client, or it can exist on a completely separate system that is connected via a network.

With location transparency, objects might also be running in-process (in the same address space as its client) or out-of-process. No matter where an object exists—locally (either in-process or out-of-process) or on another system—COM/DCOM serves it to the client in the same way. No special coding is required by the client for using out-of-process objects.

However, there are times when an object needs to make special considerations when it is being used over a network. Usually, they are based on performance concerns. An object designer can choose to support a process called *custom marshaling* in his objects. Custom marshaling enables an object to take special action if it is being accessed via a network. Of course, this is all done transparently to the client, and objects do not need to support this process.

The good news is that you really don't need to know the specifics of how COM objects work in order to create them with Visual Basic. However, a good understanding of the basic behind-the-scenes workings of these objects will help you fully grasp the role that ActiveX controls and other project types play.

Other Features of OLE and COM

Those who are well-versed in the aspects of Visual Basic programming are no doubt aware that one of OLE's strongest features is *drag-and-drop*. Although drag-and-drop has been around since the first version of OLE, OLE 2.0 improved on this feature by enabling drag-and-drop operations to be performed between applications and the operating system. A full discussion of utilizing drag-and-drop functions from Visual Basic can be found in Chapter 34, "Implementing OLE Drag and Drop Capabilities".

OLE also brings the capability of direct control of one application from another, called *OLE automation* or *ActiveX automation*. With OLE automation, you can execute commands that affect one application from within another application (including Visual Basic programs). For example, you could open a Microsoft Word session from within a program. OLE automation is discussed in Chapter 24, "Using Office 97 Components with Visual Basic."

Earlier in this chapter, the concept of embedded and linked objects was covered. An example was given where a spreadsheet is embedded into a word processing document. OLE provides the capability for the linking and embedding of objects. But it is also OLE that enables a *container* (in this case, the word processing program) to store a document that consists of various objects and data. This is referred to as *OLE Structured Storage*, and such a document is called a *compound document*.

Compound documents are internally organized into a hierarchy system that contains *storages* and *streams*. Storages typically contain one or more streams, which in turn contain some type of data. You can liken this organization scheme to a disk file system, where a storage is a directory and a stream is a file.

VBXes and OCXes

Using the principles set forth by the component object model, it is possible to create reusable objects that follow a standard format. However, for Visual Basic programmers it wasn't until VB4 that this concept really came into play.

The original controls that came with Visual Basic, introduced in VB1, had .VBX extensions. They were not based on the COM standard, but instead utilized their own proprietary format. These controls were also only 16-bit, whereas COM objects are 32-bit. These 32-bit controls use the .OCX extension and were introduced with VB4.

One of the major purposes of VB4 was to ease the transition between 16-bit VBX controls and 32-bit OCX controls, which were built on the COM standard. This wasn't always an easy transition, however, because it required giving up any third-party VBX controls that may have already been purchased and buying new 32-bit versions.

In addition to introducing 32-bit OCX controls, VB4 also brought a complete redesign of Visual Basic's core. Rather than use an old 16-bit language engine, VB4 was built on a new 32-bit engine called Object Basic. This later became known as VBA, or Visual Basic for Applications. This is an interesting point to note, because like the 32-bit OCX controls, VBA is also based on COM.

The next version of Visual Basic, VB5, used 32-bit OCX controls—by then being referred to as ActiveX controls—exclusively. It also provided the ability to easily create ActiveX controls from within Visual Basic itself. VB6 continues with the 32-bit control tradition and expands on the flexibility of VB-created controls. The creation of ActiveX controls is the subject of Chapter 5, "Creating ActiveX Controls."

ActiveX Controls and Visual Basic

Ever since VB5 was released, ActiveX has become the hottest topic among Visual Basic programmers. And although Microsoft would like us to believe that ActiveX equals the Internet, that is not really the whole story.

Although its true that ActiveX controls can be created in Visual Basic and then implemented on Web pages, the scope of these components should not be limited to one particular medium. Instead, the development of ActiveX controls should be viewed as a way of creating reusable components that can be used in regular Visual Basic applications. If your desire is to design an ActiveX control for use on the Internet, that's fine. Just keep in mind that ActiveX controls can be used as more than just as bells and whistles for Web pages.

The Basics of ActiveX Control Creation

ActiveX controls are created using the appropriately-named ActiveX Control project type. This project type starts you out with a `UserControl` object, which is similar in some ways to a `Form` object. In fact, some aspects of ActiveX control development in VB parallel the development of regular applications. For example, you can choose to design a control's interface just like you would design a program's interface, by utilizing other controls from the Toolbox. Instead of placing the controls on a `Form`, you place them on a `UserControl` object.

Not all ActiveX controls are designed this way, however. In fact, there are three different models for control creation. The first is enhancing an existing control. For example, you may want to expand on the `TextBox` control in some way. Rather than re-invent the wheel and design a whole new `TextBox`, you could simply use the existing control and add the functionality that you desire. The properties, methods, and events of the original `TextBox` control would be exposed by the new control, and other properties, events, and methods could be added if desired. This new `TextBox` could then be compiled into an entirely separate control.

Another way of creating an ActiveX control is again by using other controls from the Toolbox, called *constituent controls*. However, instead of enhancing or expanding on a single control, you use one or more constituent controls to build a new control. For example, you could use a `PictureBox` control and some `CommandButtons` controls to create a "slide show" control. The properties, events, and methods that you expose for the new control can be mapped to the constituent controls, and you can add your own interface elements as well.

You might want to create a control that is so unique that it has to be built from scratch instead of by using constituent controls. These are called *user-drawn controls*, because you have to "draw" the control's interface yourself. As you might imagine, these are some of the hardest controls to create because you cannot use existing components. You also have to create many of your own properties, events, and methods because there are no constituent controls to which they can be mapped. On the other hand, user-drawn controls offer unlimited flexibility in their design.

As you'll see in Chapter 5, ActiveX controls have a life-cycle that is much different than applications. Controls are constantly being destroyed and re-created. To top it off, controls act differently at design time than they do at runtime. This is often confusing, and it does take some time to get used to.

Chapters 5 and 6, "Deploying ActiveX Controls," show you how to create a simple ActiveX control that uses constituent controls. You'll learn how to expose select properties, events, and methods of the constituent controls as well as how to create your own unique properties, events, and methods.

For those who wish to use their ActiveX controls on Web pages, it is helpful to know the basics of VBScript. VBScript is the scripting language that is built into Microsoft's Internet Explorer Web browser. You can use VBScript code, which is in many ways identical to Visual Basic code, to enable your ActiveX controls to interact with one another and with the user. VBScript is discussed in Chapter 7, "ActiveX Scripting With VBScript."

New ActiveX Control Concepts

In Visual Basic 6, the flexibility of ActiveX controls has been greatly improved. VB-written ActiveX controls can now act as *data consumers* and *data sources*, so you can design your own database components. These types of controls are discussed in Chapter 8, "Data Consumers and Data Sources."

You can also implement a technique known *as apartment model threading* into your controls so two or more "threads" can be executed simultaneously. This concept is explained in Chapter 9, "Apartment Model Threading."

Other ActiveX Projects In Visual Basic

Aside from the ActiveX Control project, Visual Basic also includes several other project types that contain the ActiveX label. There are ActiveX EXEs, ActiveX DLLs, ActiveX Document EXEs, and ActiveX Document DLLs. All are based on the component object model (COM), which is why they are given the ActiveX designation.

ActiveX EXE

Although similar in name, ActiveX EXEs bear little resemblance to Standard EXEs, and they serve an entirely different purpose. Whereas Standard EXEs are used primarily to create executable applications, ActiveX EXEs are used to create out-of-process components.

In-process components are those that run in the same address space of an application (also called a *client*). In-process components can be thought of as parts of the application itself, even though they might actually exist in a separate file or library. For example, if your Visual Basic program calls a function that exists in a Dynamic Link Library (DLL), that function is linked to your application when the application is executed. It becomes a part of the application (its client) and runs in the same address space, thus it is an in-process component.

Out-of-process components, on the other hand, do not run in the same address space of their client but instead run in their own address space. An application (a client) can use out-of-process components the same way they use in-process components. However, out-of-process components offer an important benefit. Since they run in their own address space, the code for the out-of-process component can execute simultaneously with its client. Therefore, a client can tell an out-of-process component to do something without having to wait for it to finish. When the component's task is done, it can notify its client by using *asynchronous notification*, a way of passing messages back to the client.

As mentioned earlier, ActiveX EXEs contain one or more out-of-process components in the form of class modules. You can create reusable components and compile them into an ActiveX EXE and use them in your Visual Basic applications. To create a project type like this, you should be familiar with creating and using class modules, as well as how to implement asynchronous notification.

When deciding whether to create a component as in-process or out-of-process, speed and the use of system resources are the major considerations. Since in-process components exist within the same memory space as their client, they are more efficient than out-of-process components. However, an out-of-process component can be used by more than one client simultaneously, cutting down on the amount of system resources that are used.

ActiveX DLL

ActiveX DLLs differ from ActiveX EXEs in that they are in-process components instead of out-of-process components. Like ActiveX EXEs, ActiveX DLLs contain reusable components in the form of class modules. However, they are linked to their client applications when the application is executed, and they run in the client's address space.

When a client application asks an in-process component to perform a task, control of the program is given to the component. The client application has to wait until the component is done performing the task before it can continue with its own processing.

ActiveX Document EXE

Before getting into the uses of this project type, an explanation of ActiveX documents is necessary. Simply said, ActiveX documents are reusable applications that can be housed within a container application. The forerunner of the ActiveX document can be seen in Office 95's Binder application, which can act as a container for documents created by the Office suite of programs.

When you think of documents, you probably think of Microsoft Word files or something similar. And, in some ways, ActiveX documents are like Word documents. In fact, the common analogy for explaining ActiveX documents is to compare them to Word documents.

Word documents can be loaded and viewed using a *container* application, such as Microsoft Word. Likewise, ActiveX documents can be loaded, viewed, and used within a container application, such as Internet Explorer. What this means is that you can create a completely separate and self-contained application and have it loaded into a Web browser (or some other such container) where it can be used just as if it was a self-running program.

In Visual Basic, the creation of ActiveX documents is based on the UserDocument object. The UserDocument object is very similar to a form; you can place controls on it and add code to it the same way. You can also add forms, class modules, and other objects to an ActiveX document project. When the project is compiled (either as a DLL or an EXE), a .vbd (Visual Basic Document) file is created. This is the main file for ActiveX documents created in Visual Basic, and will be the one that is accessed by the document's container application. You'll also need the compiled DLL or EXE file to use the ActiveX document, but the .vbd file acts as the starting point, just as a .vbp file is used to indicate the components of a VB project so Visual Basic knows what to include when the project is loaded.

Like ActiveX EXEs, ActiveX documents are out-of-process components. When an ActiveX Document EXE is used in a container application, it runs in its own address space. This can cause some problems. If two instances of Internet Explorer (the container application) are both using the same ActiveX document, only one copy of the ActiveX document is actually loaded into memory (in its own address space). Because there is only one set of global variables for the ActiveX document, one container application might cause the variables to be set in such a way that would affect the other container application using the ActiveX document. Therefore, ActiveX Document DLLs are safer and faster to use.

ActiveX Document DLL

ActiveX Document DLLs are the same as ActiveX Document EXEs, except they run in-process with their client (a container application) instead of out-of-process. Although they can take up more resources than their EXE counterparts if multiple instances of the same ActiveX document are being used by different container applications, ActiveX Document DLLs are safer to use and execute slightly faster than ActiveX Document EXEs.

Summary

Visual Basic is centered around ActiveX technology, which is really nothing more than a new name for OLE. Though the term ActiveX is often brandied about when discussing the Internet, it is no way an exclusively Internet technology.

4

AN OVERVIEW OF
ACTIVEX
PROGRAMMING

Almost every aspect of Visual Basic is built on COM, the component object model. COM defines a standard way for objects to communicate with one another. It also facilitates the concepts of reusable component design.

Those who are unsure of the roles that ActiveX and COM play in Visual Basic development are at a disadvantage. Because so much of VB is based on COM, including ActiveX controls and other project types, knowledge of how COM works and how ActiveX fits into the big picture is a must.

This chapter introduced you to COM and ActiveX. With an understanding of these concepts, you are better prepared for learning more about how to create ActiveX controls in Visual Basic.

Creating ActiveX Controls

by Rob Thayer

IN THIS CHAPTER

- Think First, Code Later *82*
- Creating the Control *92*
- Expanding on the Control's Interface *130*
- Adding Methods to the Sample Control *139*

Now that you've been introduced to DCOM and some of the design considerations important to ActiveX control creation, it's time to get down to business and start developing some ActiveX controls. In this chapter, you'll create a versatile but simple control that you can use in your own applications or on your own Web pages.

The first part of this chapter discusses the importance of good design techniques. You'll learn how to design your own controls so that they will be flexible but sturdy. We'll also plan the details of the sample control.

The second part of this chapter will begin to guide you through the creation of the sample control while easing you into the finer details of ActiveX control creation. Bit by bit, the sample control will be expanded on until it fits all the specifications that are a part of its original design.

Think First, Code Later

If you're like most programmers (myself included), you're tempted to dive into a programming project without giving much thought to design. An astonishing number of programs have been created with the idea that they will "design themselves" as they are being developed. As new features are added to the program, code gets rewritten and changed around until it bears only a vague resemblance to its original concept. The worst part is that bad design (or *no* design) often leads to the programmer being burdened with supporting a tangled mess of code that is difficult for him to comprehend—even when he is the original author! Be honest—how many times have you decided to rewrite some or all of a program after having to make modifications to it long after the programming was supposedly "done?"

Many programming problems are the result of poor design caused by little thought being put into the entire project from start to finish. When creating ActiveX controls, good design is an even bigger issue than when creating applications. Not only are you designing a component that should work with the project it was initially designed for, you should also be thinking ahead to the future when your control may be needed again. And if you're creating something that will be distributed to other programmers for their own use, your control needs to be even more flexible. After all, you never know what kind of crazy functionality *other* programmers may require!

To put it another way, what would the chapter of this book be like if it was written with no predefined outline of instruction in mind? First off, it's a sure bet that Sams would never have let me write it! But if they did, it's doubtful that you would read very far into it, and it probably wouldn't be much use to you. Instead of following a fairly straight path that attempts to gradually guide you through the finer points of control design, it would be filled with random thoughts and ideas. You would likely be so confused that you would give up in disgust before finishing the first page. Luckily, some thought was put into assembling a complete and orderly flow of information, and I've tried to cover all the issues important to the topic of creating ActiveX controls.

It's difficult to overestimate the virtues of good design techniques. Just a bit of foresight and careful thought before coding can save you literally hours of programming time later. As the old saying goes, "an ounce of prevention is worth a pound of cure." Nowhere is that adage truer than in computer programming—Visual Basic programming included!

The Power of ActiveX Controls

ActiveX controls can be powerful—provided that they're designed correctly. Generally, the hottest-selling third-party controls all have two important things in common. They are all flexible, and they all have good interfaces. Great care was taken in their creation, and it paid off handsomely for their developers. It can pay off for you, too.

To illustrate just how powerful a control can be, take a look at Microsoft's Internet Explorer Web browser. Would you believe that entire program consists primarily of two ActiveX controls? It's true, and you can use the same controls (SHDOCVW.OCX and HTMLCTL.OCX) to implement a fully functional Web browser (complete with support for VBScript, JavaScript, and all the rest of IE's goodies) into your own applications. Now *that's* power!

Another important factor of good design is standardization. Certain standards for interface elements—properties, events, and methods—are often desired if not expected. It is in the control designer's best interest to have as many interface elements as possible follow certain standards. For example, the background color of an object is best represented by a property named BackColor rather than BGColor, Background, or BkgrndColor. Programmers are already familiar with the BackColor property because it is used in many other controls. If your control adheres to certain standards, it will be easier and more intuitive to use.

Like properties, there are certain methods and events that your control may be expected to provide, depending on its type. For example, if your control is some mutation of the standard CommandButton, it would be downright bizarre if it didn't include a Click event or a Move method.

The Birth of an ActiveX Control

Controls start out as an idea. You probably have several ideas for ActiveX controls already floating around in your head. If so, that's great! But give them a little time to mature before trying to crank out some code.

In this chapter, we're going to build a new ActiveX control from start to finish. Without further ado, here's the start: an idea of what the control will do and how it will look.

Our sample control will look similar to the standard `Label` control (and will use that control in its construction), but it will act more like a `CommandButton`. The idea is to have a button that will automatically "light up" whenever the cursor is on it. When the cursor is moved off it, the button "darkens" to its original state. Most likely, it will be used as part of an array of controls that present a menu of options that give the user a visual cue (the control lighting up) as to when an option is ready to be selected. It's a simple but versatile control that can be used again and again in all kinds of applications.

Of course, the first impulse is to fire up Visual Basic and get down to coding the thing. But let's hang on for just a minute and think about this just a little longer.

One good way to generate some ideas for expanding on the original idea is to visualize the control—or similar controls—being used in many different applications. Think about the neatest CD-ROM program you've ever seen. How could its developers have used the control? And what would they have added to it to make it fit in with the rest of their program? The goal here is not to make your control the end-all be-all of controls but to think up ways its functionality can be increased with some simple tweaks and maybe a little extra coding time.

The current version of our sample control would be versatile, but admittedly it wouldn't exactly knock your socks off in terms of visual appeal. Really snazzy programs would probably have a high-res graphic for their option buttons that would change to another high-res graphic when selected, or "on." Wait a minute…we could do that with our control. We wouldn't want to scrap the original idea though because there are times when high-res graphics are either not appropriate or just aren't desired. To make the control really flexible, we'll offer the developer (that is, the person using it in her application) two options: one for a quick-and-dirty text-only implementation and one where images can be specified.

Using the first option, the developer need only specify a caption and some colors (or use the defaults), and the control will be ready to go. The second option would require the creation of some graphic images, but it would look much slicker. For example, the "unselected" image could be a beveled picture with some text centered on it, and the "selected" image could be the same thing with the text "glowing." When the user moves the cursor on the image, the text appears to glow—a neat effect with absolutely no programming required by the developer.

The beauty of all this is that adding the support for the graphic images option would be minimal in terms of coding the control. The meat of the control will be in determining whether the cursor is on it, which will be the exact same no matter which of the two options is used. With a few extra lines of code, an otherwise good control can often become a potentially great control.

We undoubtedly could add many other features to our sample control to beef it up. Maybe you have a few of your own already. But for the sake of brevity, we're going to move along and start thinking about the design of the control's interface. Under other circumstances, a lot more thought would definitely be a good idea.

Here are a few other ways to get your brain neurons firing and come up with some ideas of how you can enhance your control:

- Get away from the computer for a while and do something else. Sometimes ideas will come from out of nowhere even when you're not consciously thinking about the control.

- Look at other similar controls. There's no use in programming an exact copy of a control that's already available somewhere else because you would probably be better off just buying or downloading a copy of it. Instead, look at the features that other controls provide (or don't provide). Maybe you'll see something that can be improved upon.

- Sleep on it. You may wake up with some new ideas.

- Draw your control on paper. Actually seeing what the control will look like may make you realize that it's lacking something. It's better to realize it now than after you've spent a lot of time getting the control to look "just so."

The Three Paths of Control Creation

There are three ways you can go about creating a new control. But no matter which path you decide to take in designing your control, you will always start out with a UserControl object. Just as you start designing an application with a blank Form object, you start designing a control with a blank UserControl object. You can then use one of the three basic design methods detailed in the following paragraphs to expand on the UserControl object.

The first method involves expanding on an already existing control. For example, you could take VB's PictureBox control, add a few new properties and methods to it, and you would have a whole new control class. However, there may be some ethical (and legal) considerations involved in doing so. You couldn't, for example, purchase a third-party control, make a few changes to it, and remarket it as your own. You could, however, make modifications to the control for use in your own application—provided, of course, that you've purchased the control.

The second method of control creation is similar to the first: using one or more other controls (such as those in VB's toolbox) to build your own control. For example, you could use the TextBox control together with a few CommandButton controls to create something of a mini word processor. This is the easiest way to create a new control because it's almost like building a small application. It's also the method we'll use to create our sample control.

The final method is to start completely from scratch. If you have something in mind that is completely unlike any other control you've ever seen before, this is the method you'll use to create it. Because you have to draw the control entirely on your own, controls created in this fashion are referred to as *user-drawn controls*. Obviously, this is the most difficult way to create a control because you're not using prewritten objects to build it—you have to do everything yourself. On the other side of the coin, this method gives you the most freedom in design.

Whichever method you select for creating your controls is entirely up to you. Of course, it will also depend in a large part on the type of control you're creating.

Using Constituent Controls

Preexisting controls used to build your new control are called *constituent controls*. Although this is the fastest path to creating controls, you need to watch out for some pitfalls. For example, this method requires some overhead in terms of distributing your control because you also need to distribute copies of any constituent controls. In terms of difficulty, this is not too large of an issue because you can use the Setup Wizard to quickly create a setup program for your control that will seamlessly handle the installation (and registration) of all constituent controls. A bigger problem comes in the form of licensing issues. If you have licensed third-party components that you use as constituent controls, whomever you distribute your new control to must also have licenses for those components.

The good news is that you have carte blanche for using many of the objects in VB's toolbox as constituent controls. Some of the control objects included in the Professional Edition of Visual Basic, however, may need to be licensed by the end-user before being used on his or her system. The list of "safe" VB controls include (but are not limited to) the following: CheckBox, ComboBox, CommandButton, Data, DirListBox, DriveListBox, FileListBox, Frame, HScrollBar, Image, Label, Line, ListBox, OptionButton, PictureBox, Shape, TextBox, Timer, and VScrollBar.

Licensing of controls may seem like a nuisance, but it is required to protect the developers of controls—which may in fact be you, if you're planning to market your control to other VB programmers. For example, say that you create a new control called SuperWidget and sell it to Joe for use in his own applications. Joe in turn uses the control as a constituent control for his own ActiveX control, `MegaWidget`. If he sells or gives away copies of `MegaWidget`, he would also be indirectly selling or giving away copies of the `SuperWidget` control. Pretty soon, many programmers would have a working copy of `SuperWidget`, and it's doubtful that they would want to buy another copy of it from you. Thus, licensing is important for protecting developers.

We're not going to be using any constituent controls that are affected by licensing issues in our sample control. Using only the standard VB control objects, you can still create an incredible number of unique and interesting ActiveX controls.

Passing Along Properties

When using constituent controls, you can often "pass along" the properties of those controls to the interface of the new control. For example, because we'll be using the `Label` control as one of the constituent controls in our sample control, we can utilize several of its properties when creating the new control's interface, including its `ForeColor` and `Font` properties. When the developer using the new control changes its `Font` property, he is in effect changing the `Font` property of the Label constituent control. This is all transparent to him, but the code for our sample control is simplified because the addition of a new `Font` property (and all the code that it would require) is not needed—it's already provided by the `Label` control.

One of the first things you want to do when designing your control's interface is determine which constituent control properties you want to make available to developers (that is, the users of your control, including yourself). After all, there's no use in reinventing the wheel, so you might as well utilize as much of the power of your constituent controls as you can.

The same thing goes for events and methods. You can pass along the events of constituent controls using the `RaiseEvent` statement, and you can of course call the methods of other controls quite easily within the methods of your control that you make available to developers. Events and methods are discussed in more detail later in this chapter.

Down to the Basics

As I stated earlier, developers will expect certain basics or standards from your control. If your control has some text or a caption of some sort, they will instinctively use the `ForeColor` property to change the color of that text. And when they click the cursor on your control, they will expect it to raise a `Click` event. By following certain guidelines, you can make your control as intuitive as possible.

If at all possible (and applicable), your control should provide the properties in Table 5.1 as a part of its interface. Note that some of these properties are automatically provided

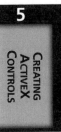

by the control's container object. More information is available in the following section, "Control Containers."

TABLE 5.1. STANDARD PROPERTIES THAT SHOULD BE INCLUDED IN A CONTROL'S INTERFACE, IF APPLICABLE.

Property	Used to Specify
BackColor	The color of the control's background
BackStyle	The opaqueness or transparency of the control's background (if applicable)
BorderStyle	The type of border around the control (if any)
Caption	The text on a button or label (if applicable)
Enabled	The availability of a control for receiving focus
Font	The text or caption's font type, attributes, and size
ForeColor	The color of any foreground objects, including text
Height	The vertical size of the control
Left	The X coordinate of the control on the screen
Name	The name by which the control is referenced
Text	The text in a text box (if applicable)
Top	The Y coordinate of the control on the screen
Visible	The visual state of the control on the screen
Width	The horizontal size of the control

Like properties, certain standard events also should be included in your control's interface. They are listed in Table 5.2.

TABLE 5.2. STANDARD EVENTS THAT SHOULD BE INCLUDED IN A CONTROL'S INTERFACE, IF APPLICABLE.

Event	Triggered When
Click	The user clicks the mouse cursor on the control
DblClick	The user double-clicks the mouse cursor on the control
KeyDown	The user holds down a key on the keyboard
KeyPress	The user presses (and releases) a key on the keyboard
KeyUp	The user releases a key on the keyboard that was held down
MouseDown	The user holds down the mouse button
MouseMove	The user moves the mouse cursor within the control
MouseUp	The user releases the mouse button

Note that the `KeyDown`, `KeyPress`, and `KeyUp` events are only triggered for the control if it has the focus.

Last but not least, your control's interface should include certain methods. They are listed in Table 5.3. Some of them are automatically provided for you by the control's container, which we'll talk about in just a moment.

TABLE 5.3. STANDARD METHODS THAT SHOULD BE INCLUDED IN A CONTROL'S INTERFACE, IF APPLICABLE.

Method	Does the Following
Move	Changes the position of the control on the screen
Refresh	Redraws the control if it is visible on the screen

Control Containers

Certain properties, methods, and events are provided by the control's *container*. A control cannot exist by itself and must always be contained by some other object. If you're going to use the control in an application, the container is likely to be a form. If you're using the control on an HTML page, the container is the page itself.

The properties furnished by the container object are called *extender properties* because the container "extends" them to the control. A control's `Top` and `Left` properties are actually extender properties because they relate to the control's position within its container. There is no way that you could code the `Top` and `Left` properties in your control because you have no idea where (or on what kind of container) the control will be used. Even if you did attempt to add a `Top` or `Left` property, the extender properties of the same name would take precedence over your custom properties. If the developer sets the `Left` property of your control using conventional methods, only the extender property would be altered.

The `Left`, `Name`, `Top`, and `Visible` properties are all provided by the container, which means that you don't have to add any code to include those properties in your control's interface. This is certainly good news because it helps shave off some of the time it takes to develop a control.

You may be wondering why the `Name` property would originate from the container rather than the control itself. You could set the name of your control (for example, `UltraWingding`) in the control's code, but then every instance of your control would have the same name—which is, of course, unacceptable. Instead, the container automatically assigns a name to a control instance using its class name and a sequential number: `UltraWingding1`, `UltraWingding2`, and so on.

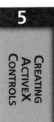

5

CREATING
ACTIVEX
CONTROLS

If you want, your control can also function as a container. You don't need to do anything special to add this capability, only set the `UserControl`'s `ControlContainer` property to `True`. Your control would then automatically provide extender properties to its constituent controls.

Ambient Objects

There may be times when your control will require some information about its container. Certain properties, such as its background and foreground colors, are furnished by `Ambient` object, and they are appropriately referred to as *ambient properties*. If, for example, you want the font used by your control to match that of its container object, your control can do so by checking the Ambient object's `Font` property and then setting its own `Font` property to match it.

Other commonly used ambient properties include `LocaleID` (or LCID), which is used to determine the version of Visual Basic that the object was compiled in, allowing controls to be *localized*, or modified on-the-fly for different international flavors of VB; `DisplayName`, which can be used in design time error-trapping routines to indicate exactly which instance of the control caused the error; and `DisplayAsDefault`, which indicates to your control whether it is the default button for the container object.

Another important ambient property is `UserMode`. By checking the `UserMode` property, your control can determine whether it is being used at design time or runtime. This comes in handy if you want to disable certain properties or functionality from a runtime instance of your control. We'll use the `UserMode` property in the development of our sample control later in this chapter.

If any ambient properties change, the `UserControl`'s `AmbientChanged` event is triggered. If you use ambient properties in some way to alter your control's appearance, you'll want to add code in that event to automatically have any changes applied to your control also.

Putting It All Together: The Interface

The properties, events, and methods that your control exposes to developers make up its interface. When designing a control's interface, your main goal is to get it right the first time. After the interface is defined, it's set in stone and should not be changed. This is one of the major stipulations of ActiveX controls: Control interfaces must not change. If you do need to make some changes to an interface (perhaps due to some additional functionality being added to the control), you need to define a new interface and still maintain all the properties, events, and methods of the old one. Your control will then contain multiple interfaces and will still maintain compatibility with applications that rely on the previous interface.

This is why good design is so important when it comes to the creation of ActiveX controls. If great care isn't taken in designing the control, it's likely that some important element of its interface will be missing. You simply cannot make a change—even a minor one—to the interface of a control that has been distributed or used in other applications. If you do, you risk the likely possibility of someone receiving a new copy of the control that suddenly won't work with applications that relied on its previous interface. This is not to say that you cannot *add* to a control's interface, such as by supporting new properties or methods. It's only when you make changes that break the control's backward compatibility that you have to worry. For example, you cannot remove a property or change the syntax of a method unless the original syntax is also supported.

Before we get into the actual coding of our sample control, it is a good idea to list all the properties, events, and methods that will comprise its interface. Table 5.4 lists each element, including its type (property, event, or method) and its source (the control itself or extender properties). Properties also show value type (Long integer, String, and so on) and default value.

TABLE 5.4. THE ELEMENTS THAT WILL MAKE UP THE SAMPLE CONTROL'S INTERFACE.

Element	Type	Source	Value Type	Default Value
			Properties	
BackColor	Property	Control	OLE_COLOR	&H00FFFFFF
BorderStyle	Property	Control	Integer	1
ButtonMode	Property	Control	Integer	0
Caption	Property	Control	String	Control Name
Enabled	Property	Control	Boolean	True
Font	Property	Control	StdFont	Arial Bold 20 point
ForeColor	Property	Control	OLE_COLOR	&H80000008
Height	Property	Control	Long	*Varies*
Left	Property	Extender	Long	*Varies*
Name	Property	Extender	String	*Assigned by container*
Picture	Property	Control	StdPicture	*None*
SelColor	Property	Control	OLE_COLOR	&H0080FFFF
SelPicture	Property	Control	StdPicture	*None*
Top	Property	Extender	Long	*Varies*
Visible	Property	Extender	Boolean	True
Width	Property	Control	Long	*Varies*

5

CREATING
ACTIVEX
CONTROLS

continues

TABLE 5.4. CONTINUED

Element	Type	Source	Value Type	Default Value
			Events	
Click	Event	Control		
DblClick	Event	Control		
KeyDown	Event	Control		
KeyPress	Event	Control		
KeyUp	Event	Control		
MouseDown	Event	Control		
MouseMove	Event	Control		
MouseUp	Event	Control		
			Methods	
Move	Method	Extender		
Refresh	Method	Control		

You may notice that certain properties listed as "standard" in Table 5.1 have been omitted from this list. For example, the BackStyle property is not applicable because if the background was transparent, we would never know whether the control was selected. Remember that the control will be changing the background color to indicate a "lighted" (or selected) condition. A transparent background would always be the same, so by default the BackStyle property *must* be set to 0 - Opaque.

Four new properties have also been added to the list: ButtonMode, Picture, SelColor, and SelPicture. ButtonMode will be used to specify which of the control's modes should be used (text-only or images). Picture and SelPicture will specify which graphic images to use for the button's selected or deselected states (these two properties will be ignored if the control is in text-only mode). The SelColor property indicates which color to use for the background when the control is selected.

The control will also have several additional events that are not listed because they are hidden from the user of the control. These events are specific to the UserControl object and are used to read and set property values and so on.

Now that the control's interface has been completely planned, we're finally ready to start coding. So bring up Visual Basic 6 and let's get started!

Creating the Control

Our sample control will be called LightButton because it "lights up" whenever the cursor is on it. Rather than present you with all the code for the control at one time, I'll give it to you a little at a time. First, we'll create a basic version that will only support the text-only mode. Then we'll add to the control little by little until it is built up into the final product. As new sections of code are added and existing parts are modified, you'll learn more about the details of creating ActiveX controls.

Assembling the Control

When you start up Visual Basic 6, you're presented with a screen similar to the one shown in Figure 5.1. You are given many different project types from which to choose. To create a new ActiveX control, double-click the ActiveX Control icon.

FIGURE 5.1.
Visual Basic 6 prompts you to select a project type when it starts up.

After Visual Basic loads in a few components, you'll see a blank Design window (see Figure 5.2). Although this looks suspiciously like a standard VB form, it's not. It's actually an instance of a UserControl object, which is the basis for designing controls in Visual Basic.

NOTE

Some controls may not make full use of the UserControl object. Those controls that do not require a graphical user interface may only display an icon during design mode and become invisible at runtime. For example, an enhanced version of the Timer control would show an icon at design time (using the UserControl object's Picture property) and would always be a fixed size. At runtime, the control would become invisible by setting the UserControl object's Visible property to False.

FIGURE 5.2.

*A blank ActiveX
Control project.*

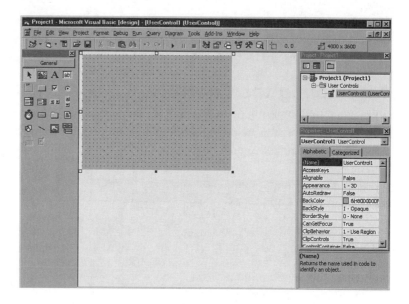

When you resize the UserControl object, you're changing the default size of your control. The default size specifies how big new instances of the control will be when they are first created, so you don't want it any bigger than necessary. To resize the control, simply use its drag handles to make it smaller or larger. Notice that the left and top sides of the UserControl object are flush against the Design window, and that the sizing handles on those sides are hollow. You can resize the UserControl, but you cannot *move* it. You really don't need to. Remember, it's not a form. Screen position is not relevant with UserControl objects at this point because their true positions will not be known until they are placed on their container objects.

The top of VB's IDE window shows the project name (currently, the default name of Project1), the name of the control (UserControl1), and the control's class name (UserControl). The class name will always be the same, even after you've changed the name of the control. No matter what kind or how many changes you make to the control, it is still an instance of the UserControl class while you're in design mode. But when the control is in run mode, it becomes a class of its own. We'll talk more about the state of a control's class later in this chapter.

The first thing we want to do in the creation of our control is give it a name. In the Properties window, change UserControl1's Name property to LightButton. As soon as you make the change, you'll see that the name of the control has been changed at the top of the IDE window. By changing the control's name, you've also changed the name of its class, although this won't be apparent until later.

Several other changes need to be made to the `UserControl` (now called `LightButton`) control's properties. Make the changes to the properties listed in Table 5.5 by altering the corresponding values in the Properties window.

TABLE 5.5. THE PROPERTIES THAT NEED TO BE CHANGED FOR THE `UserControl` OBJECT.

Property	*Change to*
Appearance	0 - Flat
BackColor	&H00FFFFFF&
BorderStyle	1 - Fixed Single

Now we need to add two objects from VB's toolbox to the `LightButton` control. These are the constituent controls that will be used to build our new control. Add a `Label` object and a `Timer` object to the `LightButton` control, as shown in Figure 5.3. The exact sizes of the objects are not important because the `Label` object's size and position will be modified in the control's code, and the `Timer` object is invisible anyway. But try to make your control look similar to the one shown in Figure 5.3.

FIGURE 5.3.

A `Label` *object and a* `Timer` *object are added to the control.*

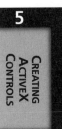

Change the property values for the Label object (Label1) to those listed in Table 5.6. Then change the property values for the Timer object (Timer1) to those in Table 5.7.

TABLE 5.6. THE PROPERTIES THAT NEED TO BE CHANGED FOR THE Label OBJECT.

Property	Change to
Alignment	2 - Center
Appearance	0 - Flat
AutoSize	True
BackStyle	0 - Transparent
Font	Arial Bold 20 point
ForeColor	&H80000008&
Name	lblCaption

TABLE 5.7. THE PROPERTIES THAT NEED TO BE CHANGED FOR THE Timer OBJECT.

Property	Change to
Interval	250
Name	tmrChkStatus

NOTE

Throughout this chapter, the names of objects from VB's toolbox will be pre-fixed with a three-character mnemonic indicating a class type: txt for objects of the TextBox class, pic for objects of the PictureBox class, and so on. Using such mnemonics is a good programming practice because it makes it easy to tell the type of object being referenced in your code.

Adding the Code

Now that the control's external appearance is finished, it's time to fill in the code that will bring the control to life. We need to declare some Windows API functions, and that requires a global code module. To add one to the current project, choose Project | Add Module from the menu. This will bring up the Add Module dialog box. Double-click the Module icon to add a new module to the project. The Project Explorer window should now show that Project1 contains two parts: LightButton (the control itself) and Module1 (the global code module you just added).

Bring up the Code window for Module1 by double-clicking its name in the Project Explorer window. Add the code in Listing 5.1 to the General Declarations section.

LISTING 5.1. CODE THAT SHOULD BE ADDED TO Module1's General Declarations SECTION.

```
Type POINTAPI
     X As Long
     Y As Long
End Type

Declare Function GetCursorPos& Lib "user32" (lpPoint As POINTAPI)
Declare Function WindowFromPoint& Lib "user32" (ByVal lpPointX As Long, _
     ByVal lpPointY As Long)
```

To know whether the cursor is on the control, two Windows API functions (GetCursorPos and WindowFromPoint) are required. The purpose of those two functions will be explained shortly.

Next, add the code in Listing 5.2 to LightButton's General Declarations section.

LISTING 5.2. CODE THAT SHOULD BE ADDED TO UserControl's General Declarations SECTION.

```
Private mbooButtonLighted As Boolean
Private molcBackColor As OLE_COLOR
Private mpoiCursorPos As POINTAPI
```

The two Private statements declare variables that will be used later. By declaring them as Private variables, they are not exposed outside the control but can be used in any subroutine or function of the LightButton control.

You may think the names used for these variables look a little strange because they are prefixed with mnemonics mboo and mpoi. However, there is a method behind the madness. The naming convention used (both here and throughout the rest of this chapter) allows the name to relay some basic information about the variable. The first character (m) signifies that the variable is defined as module-level as opposed to procedure-level. The next three characters indicate the variable type: boo for Boolean and poi for the POINTAPI structure. When these variable names are used in the control's code, you can instantly tell their type.

The next section of code that needs to be added will go into UserControl's Initialize event. The Initialize event is triggered whenever an instance of the control is created. Add the code in Listing 5.3 to UserControl's Initialize event.

LISTING 5.3. CODE THAT SHOULD BE ADDED TO UserControl's Initialize EVENT.

```
Private Sub UserControl_Initialize()

    ' When the control initializes, the button is
    ' not "lighted".
    mbooButtonLighted = False

    ' Since UserControl's BackColor property will
    ' be changed if the control is "selected", its
    ' initial value must be stored in a temporary
    ' variable.
    molcBackColor = UserControl.BackColor

End Sub
```

The first thing that the control needs to do when it is initialized is set the ButtonLighted flag to False, indicating that the button is not currently selected. It also needs to keep the default value of the control's BackColor property because that property will change later when the control is selected, and its original value will be lost. The default color is what the control's background will be changed back to if the control is unselected.

Note that even though the name of the UserControl object was changed to LightButton, the control's event procedure names still reference it as UserControl. Like the events for Form objects, a UserControl's event procedure names do not change and will always reference the control as UserControl no matter what its name is. When referencing the control's properties and methods, the same rule applies. Listing 5.4 includes several references to UserControl's properties.

The next section of code goes into tmrChkStatus's Timer event. This is where all the real work is done. The Timer event (which is triggered approximately four times a second) determines whether the cursor is on the control and takes the appropriate action to indicate the control's status. Add the code in Listing 5.4 to tmrChkStatus's Timer event.

LISTING 5.4. CODE THAT SHOULD BE ADDED TO tmrChkStatus's Timer EVENT.

```
Private Sub tmrChkStatus_Timer()

    ' This event will fire about 4 times per second,
    ' and is used to see if the control's status
    ' changes from selected ("lighted") to
    ' un-selected, and vice-versa.

    Dim lonCStat As Long
    Dim lonCurrhWnd As Long

    ' Disable the timer temporarily.
    tmrChkStatus.Enabled = False
```

```
    ' Using two Windows API functions, determine the
    ' handle of the window that the cursor is
    ' currently positioned on.
    lonCStat = GetCursorPos&(mpoiCursorPos)
    lonCurrhWnd = WindowFromPoint(mpoiCursorPos.X, _
        mpoiCursorPos.Y)

    If mbooButtonLighted = False Then
        ' If the control is not currently "lighted",
        ' and it matches the handle of the window that
        ' the cursor is on, light it up.
        If lonCurrhWnd = UserControl.hWnd Then
            mbooButtonLighted = True
            UserControl.BackColor = &H0080FFFF
        End If
    Else
        ' If the control is "lit", and it no longer
        ' matches the handle of the window that the
        ' cursor is on, un-light it.
        If lonCurrhWnd <> UserControl.hWnd Then
            mbooButtonLighted = False
            UserControl.BackColor = molcBackColor
        End If
    End If

    ' Re-enable the timer.
    tmrChkStatus.Enabled = True

End Sub
```

The Timer event uses the two Windows API functions we defined earlier to check on the status of the mouse cursor. In a nutshell, this is accomplished by comparing the control's handle with the handle of whatever object the cursor is currently on. If the two handles match, then the cursor is on the control.

Just about every object that you see on the screen has its own handle, a unique number that is used to identify the object to the Windows operating system. Our control is no exception, and every instance of the control is assigned its own handle when it's created.

The Timer event is, as stated earlier, triggered about four times each second (you can shorten or lengthen the amount of time between firings by changing tmrChkStatus's Interval property). When the event is triggered, it calls the GetCursorPos API function to fetch the mouse cursor's X and Y coordinates. Those coordinates are then fed into the WindowFromPoint API function, which returns the handle (hWnd) of whichever window (or object) currently occupies those coordinates. By comparing the value returned by the WindowFromPoint function with the handle of our control (UserControl.hWnd), we can tell whether the cursor is currently on it. It's a simple but effective method.

You may be wondering why we didn't simply use UserControl's MouseMove event to determine whether the cursor was on the control. The MouseMove event is triggered only when the cursor is within the boundaries of the control. When the cursor moves off the object, the MouseMove event is no longer triggered. Unfortunately, MouseMove can only do half the job for us, and that's just not enough.

There's only one more section of code to add before we can try out the control, and it will be added to UserControl's Resize event (see Listing 5.5). The control needs to reposition the Label object whenever it is resized so that it will always be centered. Because the Resize event is triggered when a new instance of the control is created, there's no need to duplicate this code in UserControl's Initialize event.

LISTING 5.5. CODE THAT SHOULD BE ADDED TO UserControl's Resize EVENT.

```
Private Sub UserControl_Resize()

    ' Reposition the Label constituent control so it
    ' is centered within the UserControl.
    lblCaption.Top = (Height - lblCaption.Height) /
    lblCaption.Left = (Width - lblCaption.Width) /

End Sub
```

Because the Label object's AutoSize property is set to True, it will automatically be set to the smallest size possible whenever its Caption or Font properties change. Therefore, all that needs to be done in the Resize event is to center the Label object on the control.

There is a slight problem with the Resize event. If the Label object is larger than the size of UserControl, it will still be centered, but its left and right sides will be truncated. Under other circumstances, it would probably be a good idea to change the size of UserControl to match the size of the Label object. However, that would not be feasible here. Keep in mind that the control will offer the capability of displaying graphic images to indicate a selected or unselected state. In that case, the developer using the control will undoubtedly set its Height and Width properties to match the exact size of the graphic images. Changing the Height and Width of the control to accommodate the entire Label object would then cause a gap between the images and the control's border—and that would be unsightly. It's better to just truncate the Label caption.

Now that all the code has been added, it would be a good idea to save the control project. Use Table 5.8 as a guide for saving the three files that make up the project.

TABLE 5.8. THE NAMES THAT SHOULD BE GIVEN TO THE PROJECT FILES WHEN THEY ARE BEING SAVED.

Project File	Save As...	Save As Type
Module1	LightButton	Basic Files (*.BAS)
LightButton	LightButton	User Defined Control Files (*.CTL)
Project1	TestControl1	Project Files (*.VBP)

You're probably eager to try out the sample control, but there's still one step left. Because controls cannot run by themselves, we need a test form that will act as a container for the control. We can't simply add a form to the TestControl1 project because the form would become a part of the control, which would put us back to square one. Instead, we need to create a whole new project that will act as the testing grounds for the new control.

To add a new project, choose File | Add Project from the menu. This will bring up the Add Project dialog box. Double-click the Standard Exeicon to create the kind of project that we can use for testing purposes.

If you look in the Project Explorer window, you should see that Project2 has been added, as shown in Figure 5.4. One of the handier features of VB is the capability to work on more than one project simultaneously in the Visual Basic environment. This allows you to test out controls without having to compile them—an incredible time-saver. If you could work on only one project at a time (as versions of Visual Basic prior to VB5 mandated), you would have to edit your control, save it, compile it, load in a test project, test the control, and then load in the control project again to make any necessary changes. The entire edit-and-test process would then begin anew. With the later versions of VB, you can easily switch between project modules by double-clicking their names in the Project Explorer window or by choosing a module name from VB's Window menu.

NOTE

If your Project Explorer window doesn't look like the one in Figure 5.4, try clicking the small icon that looks like a folder at the top of the Project Explorer. This toggles between the two different project views.

To set Project2 as the Startup project, you have to right-click on Project2 in the Project Explorer and select Set As Startup from the pop-up menu. Its name will then appear in bold, indicating its status as the Startup project for the project group.

FIGURE 5.4.

The Project Explorer window, which shows that two projects (LightButton and Project2) are being worked on simultaneously.

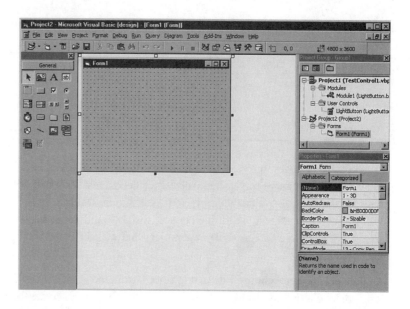

You may wonder why VB would not automatically choose Project2 as the Startup project when Project1 cannot be run by itself. In VB5, this was the case. But in VB6, running an ActiveX control project brings up a dialog box like the one shown in Figure 5.5. Instead of using a test form, you can use the control in some other container such as a Web browser. If that is the environment that you are designing the control to be primarily used in, then it makes sense to test the control in that environment. For this project, however, we'll be using a form as the test container. If you want to try running the control in Internet Explorer or some other container, then by all means give it a shot.

FIGURE 5.5.

When you try to run an ActiveX control project in VB6, you get a dialog box that lets you specify a container (such as a Web browser) for the control.

With the new project (Project2) added, you now have a test form on which you can try out the control. The test form is ready to go, but how do you create an instance of the control on the form? After all, there is no icon for it in the toolbox. That's true, but it's only because the control is still in design mode. For it to be available for use in other projects, it has to be taken out of design mode and put into run mode.

To put the control into run mode, go back to the control by double-clicking its name (LightButton) in the Project Explorer window. You should then see the LightButton control's Design window. By closing its Design window, you immediately switch the control from design mode to run mode. To close the Design window, click on the Close Window icon (as indicated in Figure 5.6).

FIGURE 5.6.

The Close Window icon, which closes the Design window, is located at the top right of the Visual Basic IDE.

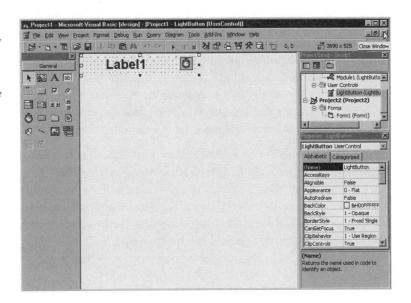

After you've closed LightButton's Design window, display Project2's Form1 by double-clicking on it in the Project Explorer window. Note that an icon for the LightButton control now appears in the toolbox. If you position the mouse cursor on the icon, a ToolTip window will appear with the name of the control: LightButton.

Double-click the LightButton control icon to create an instance of it on the test form. Note that its size is the same as it was in LightButton's Design window. Remember, whatever size you make the control in the Design window is its default size. The test form should now look similar to the one shown in Figure 5.7.

Now for the neat part. Position the cursor anywhere on the control. When you do, the control's background changes from white to yellow. Move the cursor off the control, and the background color changes back to white. Congratulations, you've just created your first working control!

FIGURE 5.7.

*The test form,
complete with a
new instance of
the* LightButton
control.

Try resizing the control. When you do, its caption (currently, Label1) is automatically centered. This is because of the code we added to the control's Resize event.

Select the control by clicking it, then look at the Properties window. You'll notice that the name of this instance of the control has appropriately been named LightButton1. That name originated from the control's container, which in this case is Project2's Form1. As stated earlier in this chapter in the section titled "Control Containers," the container uses a control's class name and a sequential number to name instances of a control. Thus, we get LightButton1 as the default name for our control.

Look at the properties for LightButton1. As you can see, there aren't many available. In fact, all the properties listed have been automatically provided by the control's container (Form1). When you create a control, you have a great deal of power over which properties it will expose; that's the good news. The bad news is that you have to add code to accommodate each property that is to be exposed. We'll add several properties to the sample control later in this chapter. But before we do, we'll take a look at the runtime version of our control to see whether there are any immediate ways in which it can be improved.

A Few Problems with the LightButton Control

You may have already noticed that VB's title bar has developed something of a twitch. This is caused by LightButton's Timer event, which is triggering four times each second. To prevent this, we should disable LightButton's Timer object if the control's container is in design mode and only enable it when the container has been put into run mode.

Another problem is that the default caption for the control is Label1, which is derived from the default name of LightButton's Label object. A better default caption would be the name assigned to the instance of the LightButton control, which in this case would be LightButton1.

To make these changes, the LightButton control has to be switched back into design mode. To do so, double-click LightButton's name in the Project Explorer window. Note that when `LightButton` returns to design mode, its icon is disabled in the toolbox. Because the control is no longer in run mode, it is not currently available for use in other projects.

To verify this, double-click `Project2`'s `Form1` in the Project Explorer window. When the form appears, you should see its instance of the `LightButton` control filled with diagonal lines (see Figure 5.8). This indicates that the control cannot be displayed because it is not in run mode. Double-click `LightButton`'s name again in the Project Explorer window to switch back to the control project.

FIGURE 5.8.

Form1's instance of the `LightButton` *control cannot be displayed when the control is in design mode.*

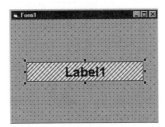

To take care of the first problem (the `Timer` event triggering while its container, the test form, is still in design mode), modify `UserControl`'s `InitProperties` and `ReadProperties` events as shown in Listing 5.6.

LISTING 5.6. MODIFICATIONS TO THE `InitProperties` AND `ReadProperties` EVENTS NEED TO BE MADE TO DISABLE THE CONTROL'S `Timer` WHEN ITS CONTAINER IS IN DESIGN MODE.

```
Private Sub UserControl_InitProperties()

    ' If the control's container is in design mode,
    ' disable the Timer, which causes the control to
    ' not function.
    tmrChkStatus.Enabled = Ambient.UserMode

    ' Set the default values for some properties.

    ' The Caption property defaults to the name
    ' assigned to the control by its container.
    Caption = Ambient.DisplayName


End Sub


Private Sub UserControl_ReadProperties(PropBag As PropertyBag)

    ' If the control's container is in design mode,
```

continues

LISTING 5.6. CONTINUED

```
' disable the Timer, which causes the control to
' not function.
tmrChkStatus.Enabled = Ambient.UserMode

End Sub
```

The InitProperties event contains a line of code that assigns a default value to the Caption property that we'll be adding in just a moment. Right now, we're more concerned with the line that sets tmrChkStatus's Enabled property.

If you're wondering why the same line of code was added to both the InitProperties event and the ReadProperties event, that will become apparent when you understand the sequence of events triggered for UserControl objects. That topic will be discussed in just a moment. For now, just add the same line of code to both events.

You may also be wondering why tmrChkStatus's Enabled property was changed in the InitProperties event rather than the Initialize event. There's a good reason for this. Ambient properties and extender properties cannot be referenced in a control's Initialize event because at that point, the control has not yet been *sited* on its container. That is, the control has no idea what container it is in until it has already been initialized. Ambient and Extender objects are examples of *late bound* objects, meaning that any information about them is not available when the control is compiled. On the other hand, an *early bound* object—for example, the Label object that was used in the creation of the sample control—has all information about it available to the control when the control is compiled.

The second problem (the caption not accurately reflecting the name assigned to the control as a default) is best solved by adding a Caption property to the control. Make sure that the control's Code window is displayed; then choose Tools | Add Procedure from the menu. This will bring up the Add Procedure dialog box. For the Name, enter **Caption**. Make sure that Property is selected as the procedure Type, and Public is selected for Scope. Click OK to add the necessary property procedures.

Two new empty procedures have been added to UserControl's Code window: one that retrieves the value of the property (the Get procedure) and one that stores the value of the property (the Let procedure). The procedures should appear as they do in Listing 5.7. These procedures are provided only as a starting point and require some modifications before they will work properly.

LISTING 5.7. TWO NEW Property PROCEDURES ARE ADDED TO EXPOSE THE CONTROL'S Caption PROPERTY.

```
Public Property Get Caption() As Variant

End Property


Public Property Let Caption(ByVal vNewValue As Variant)

End Property
```

The first thing that needs to be changed is the type of variable used by these procedures to reference the property. By default, the Variant variable type is used because it can accommodate any kind of value. Even though the procedures could be used as-is, using Variant variable types is inefficient. Because the Caption property is a string, all variable types should be changed from Variant to String. Don't forget to change the default argument of vNewValue (indicating a Variant) to NewValue. Some code also needs to be added to each procedure to facilitate the actual storing or retrieving of the property's value. Use Listing 5.8 as a guide for modifying the two Property procedures.

LISTING 5.8. ADDING CODE TO THE Property PROCEDURES HANDLES THE STORING AND RETRIEVING OF THE CONTROL'S Caption PROPERTY.

```
Public Property Get Caption() As String

    ' The Caption property comes directly from
    ' lblCaption's Caption property.
    Caption = lblCaption.Caption

End Property


Public Property Let Caption(ByVal NewValue As String)

    ' Caption's new value is passed directly to
    ' lblCaption's Caption property.
    lblCaption.Caption = NewValue
    UserControl.PropertyChanged "Caption"

End Property
```

Property procedures are similar to Sub or Function procedures. A Property Get procedure returns a value when it is called, much like a Function. The value returned is the value of the property. A Property Let procedure, on the other hand, does not return a value but instead requires that a value be passed to it. The value passed to it indicates what the property should be changed to.

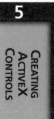

For example, the following line of code would cause the `Property Get Caption` procedure to be triggered:

```
TestCaption = LightButton1.Caption
```

When the procedure is triggered, the value for `Caption` (a string variable) is obtained from `lblCaption`'s `Caption` property.

The `Property Let Caption` procedure would be triggered with a line of code such as the following:

```
LightButton1.Caption = "Put Cursor Here"
```

When the `Property Let` procedure is triggered, the string `"Put Cursor Here"` is passed to the routine in its `NewValue` argument. That string is in turn stored in the `lblCaption` object's `Caption` property.

When the control is initialized, the `Caption` property receives the default value of the `Ambient` object's `DisplayName` for the control. This has already been taken care of in `UserControl`'s `InitProperties` event (refer to Listing 5.6).

> **NOTE**
>
> Some properties have a `Property Set` procedure rather than a `Property Let` procedure. The two work in the same way, except that `Property Set` is used for properties that reference objects rather than variables. For example, a property that references a string value (a variable) such as the `Caption` property above would have a `Property Let` procedure. A property that references a picture (an object) would have a `Property Set` procedure.

`Property Let` or `Property Set` procedures should call `UserControl`'s `PropertyChanged` if any changes are made to the property, as shown earlier in Listing 5.8. The name of the property is passed to `PropertyChanged` so that the event can tell exactly which property has been modified. Calling `PropertyChanged` is not mandatory, but it is a good idea because it lets Visual Basic know that the property has been changed.

In the preceding `Property Get` and `Property Let` procedures, the `lblCaption` object's `Caption` property is passed to `LightButton`'s `Caption` property, and vice versa. This is an example of passing a control's properties directly to and from constituent controls. In this case, the `Caption` property that is exposed by the `LightButton` control is really nothing more than a middleman for changing and reading the `lblCaption` object's `Caption` property.

The Property Bag

We're not out of the woods just yet. We still need a way of saving and retrieving the Caption property to and from memory. But why do we need to do this? After all, the control's caption value is stored in the lblCaption object's Caption property, right? Yes, that's true, but we still need a way to save the value between instances of the control. Remember, control instances have a violent life and get destroyed and re-created again and again (as you'll soon see).

The saving and retrieving of property values is done in UserControl's WriteProperties and ReadProperties events. Add the code to those events as shown in Listing 5.9.

LISTING 5.9. THE CODE THAT NEEDS TO BE ADDED TO UserControl's WriteProperties AND ReadProperties EVENTS TO SAVE AND RETRIEVE THE Caption PROPERTY FROM MEMORY.

```
Private Sub UserControl_WriteProperties(PropBag As PropertyBag)

    ' Write properties to the property bag.
    PropBag.WriteProperty "Caption", Caption, Ambient.DisplayName

End Sub


Private Sub UserControl_ReadProperties(PropBag As PropertyBag)

    ' If the control's container is in design mode,
    ' disable the Timer, which causes the control to
    ' not function.
    tmrChkStatus.Enabled = Ambient.UserMode

    ' Read properties from the property bag.
    Caption = PropBag.ReadProperty("Caption", Ambient.DisplayName)

End Sub
```

To facilitate the easy saving and retrieving of property values, Visual Basic provides a nifty little item called the *property bag*. The property bag is a phantom spot in memory that temporarily stores property values. You can put property values into the bag, and you can take them out of the bag by using the property bag's methods WriteProperty and ReadProperty, respectively. This is exactly what we've done in the preceding events.

When you call the WriteProperty method to put a value into the property bag, you need to specify the property name (in this case, "Caption"), the variable name (Caption), and a default name. It seems odd to specify a default name when storing a value, but Visual Basic uses the default to see whether the value needs to be saved. If the current property

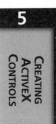

value is the same as the default value, VB won't save it in the property bag because it doesn't need to.

When retrieving properties with the `ReadProperty` method, you must specify the property name (again, `"Caption"`) and the default value. If you try to read a property value that is not in the property bag, the `ReadProperty` method returns the default value.

Every reference to a property by the `WriteProperty` method invokes the property's `Property Let` (or `Property Set`) procedure. Likewise, a reference to a property by the `ReadProperty` method invokes the property's `Property Get` procedure.

There is actually a simple way of adding properties to controls with only a single line of code. Consider the following line of code:

```
Public EasyProperty As String
```

That single line of code, placed into `UserControl`'s `General Declarations` section, is enough to create a property called `EasyProperty` that can be set from within other objects (such as a form). The property does not need to be written to the property bag, and it does not require a `Property Get` or `Property Let` procedure. So why bother with all the overhead of `Property Get`, `Property Let`, `WriteProperties`, and `ReadProperties`?

Even though this method is easy to use, it has some serious drawbacks. For one, it gives you absolutely no control over validation of property values—using a `Property Let` (or `Property Set`) procedure does. Using a public variable, any value that can be stored by the variable's value type can be assigned to the property. You also have no control over whether the property will be read-only or write-only. All Public variables can be read or changed freely.

Another problem is that there is no way to notify Visual Basic that the property has been changed, as you can by calling `UserControl`'s `PropertyChanged` event in a `Property Let` or `Property Set` procedure. If the property is to be passed to a constituent control, you must use `Property` procedures so that you are aware of when the property changes.

If you want to implement a property that does not affect constituent controls and can accept any value for its type, you can use this shortcut method if you want. However, I recommend sticking with the `Property Get`/`Property Let`/`ReadProperties`/`WriteProperties` combination. It means a little more work, but it's worth it for the extra control that you get over your properties.

In a nutshell, for every property that you include in your control's interface, you'll follow these four basic steps:

1. Add a `Property Get` procedure. Modify the procedure's declaration statement to reflect the type of value or object that the property references. Add code to the

procedure to assign the property's value to the variable or object indicated in the procedure's declaration. If the control is designed for use on a Web page, you will want to make all properties of the Variant type since VBScript only supports Variants. *This step does not need to be done if the property is write-only; that is, it can be changed but not read. Write-only properties are rarely used.*

2. Add a `Property Let` (or `Property Set`) procedure. Modify the procedure's declaration statement to reflect the type of value or object that the property references. Add code to the procedure to check the value that was passed to the procedure to ensure that it is valid. If it is valid, assign that value to whatever variable, object, or property is being used to hold the property's value; then call `UserControl`'s `PropertyChanged` event. If it is not valid, raise an error indicating that an invalid property value was specified. *This step does not need to be done if the property is read-only and should not be modified.*

3. Add a call to the property bag's `ReadProperty` method in `UserControl`'s `ReadProperties` event. *If no `Property Get` procedure was included (indicating a write-only property), this step can be skipped.*

4. Add a call to the property bag's `WriteProperty` method in `UserControl`'s `WriteProperties` event. If no `Property Let` or `Property Set` procedure was included (indicating a read-only property), this step can be skipped.

Don't worry, it sounds like much more work than it really is. Many properties can be added in just minutes by using the Add Property dialog box, making some minor modifications to the `Property` procedure declarations, and adding a few lines of code. It gets much easier with only a little bit of practice.

Trying Out the `LightButton` Control... Again

It's time to try out the changes that have been made to the `LightButton` control. But first, make sure that you save all the files in the project group by choosing File | Save Project Group from the menu. You'll be prompted for the names of the files in `Project2` as well as the name of the project group. Use the information in Table 5.9 as a guide for naming the files.

TABLE 5.9. THE NAMES THAT SHOULD BE GIVEN TO THE NEW PROJECT GROUPS FILES WHEN THEY ARE BEING SAVED.

Project File	Save As...	Save As Type
Form1	LBTestForm	Form files (*.FRM)
Project2	LBTestProj	Project files (*.VBP)
LightButton	LBTest	Project Group files (*.VBG)

Now switch the control back into run mode by closing its Code window and its Design window. When both windows have been closed, the icon for the LightButton control will reappear in the toolbox, and you'll see the test form with an instance of the sample control on it.

Move the cursor onto the control. It no longer lights up because the test project and the test form are still in design mode. If you run the test project by pressing F5 or clicking the Run button in Visual Basic's toolbar, you'll see that the control now functions as expected. That's because the test form (the control's container) is in run mode. The LightButton control's Ambient.UserMode property is now True, which enables the Timer object that allows the control to do its thing.

When you stop the test project, an interesting thing happens. The Ambient.UserMode property changes to False, and the Timer object is disabled. But how can this happen when the code to change the Timer object's Enabled property is in the InitProperties and ReadProperties events? These events happen at the beginning of a control instance's lifetime, not at the end. So why are those events triggered again, causing the Timer object to be disabled based on the new status of the Ambient.UserMode property?

When the test project stops running, the instance of the LightButton control on the test form is destroyed and a new one is created in its place, thereby triggering the ReadProperties event again. Objects—especially controls—are constantly being destroyed and re-created. The sequence of events that occur during a control's lifetime may seem a little strange, but they must be understood if you are to go any further in designing controls.

The Life of a Control Instance

A control can be thought of as having two different modes *in regards to its container object*: design-time and runtime. *Design time* begins when you place an instance of the control on the container object. *Runtime* begins when you run the project that contains the control's container object, either from within Visual Basic or as a compiled executable file that runs outside VB. To better illustrate just what happens to an instance of a control when it is in these different modes, I'll list the exact sequence of events for each.

As stated before, design-time mode occurs when an instance of the control is placed on a container object (usually a form). A control is also in design-time mode when changes are being made to the control's project or to the control itself. Design-time mode only happens within the Visual Basic environment.

When changes are made to a control and the *control* is taken out of design mode, its *container* is still in design-time mode. Any instances of a control on the container are destroyed and immediately re-created when the control is put into run mode. This occurs all the time, though there is no obvious indication that it is happening.

The following list shows the sequence of events that occurs when a design-time instance of a control is created:

```
Initialize
InitProperties
Resize/Paint
```

Note that this is the only time that the `InitProperties` event is ever triggered, with one important exception that will be covered in a moment. The `InitProperties` event sets all the control instance's properties to their default values.

The `Resize` and `Paint` events may or may not be triggered, depending on how the control itself was created. If the control utilizes constituent controls, then the `Resize` event will occur so that the size and locations of any constituent controls can be adjusted based on the control's default property settings (which, of course, were just initialized in the `InitProperties` event). In this case, the `Paint` event will not occur.

If, however, the control was created from scratch and does not use constituent controls (that is, it's a user-drawn control), then the `Paint` event is triggered, but the `Resize` event is not. User-drawn controls always re-create their appearance in their `Paint` event rather than in their `Resize` event.

Either the `Resize` event or the `Paint` event is also triggered when the size of the control instance is altered, either from within code or by dragging its grab handles. These events do not occur when the control instance is moved on the form because the actual appearance of the instance does not change.

When a container that includes an instance of a control is run from within the Visual Basic environment, the design-time instance of the control is destroyed, and a runtime instance is created in its place. But before the design-time instance is destroyed, two events occur:

```
WriteProperties
Terminate
```

The `WriteProperties` event gives the design-time instance of the control a chance to save any changes that were made to its properties. They are saved to the copy of the form that is in memory but not to the .FRM file that is saved on disk.

By the time the `Terminate` event is triggered, the control instance is no longer displayed on the form. This is the last step before the instance is destroyed completely.

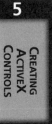

Now, a new runtime instance of the control is created. The events that occur at this point are similar to the sequence of events that occurred when the design-time instance was first created:

```
Initialize
ReadProperties
Resize/Paint
```

The only difference is that the `InitProperties` event has been replaced with the `ReadProperties` event. Because it's likely that changes were made to the control instance's properties during design time, triggering the `InitProperties` event and resetting all the instance's default property values wouldn't make much sense—the control would lose all its changes. Instead, the `ReadProperties` event occurs, so any property changes that were made (and that were recently saved in memory using the `WriteProperties` event) can be restored and applied to the new instance of the control.

Note also that the `Resize` and `Paint` events follow the same rules as they did earlier, with the `Resize` event only occurring for controls that utilize constituent controls and the `Paint` event only occurring for user-drawn controls.

When the project stops running, the runtime instance of the control is destroyed, and a new design-time instance is created. Control instances are constantly getting destroyed and re-created!

The only event that occurs before creating a new design-time instance is the `Terminate` event. You may be wondering why the `WriteProperties` event doesn't also get triggered. It's because runtime changes to properties are never saved. When the design-time instance is re-created, you want its properties to be exactly the same as the last design-time instance you were working on. Otherwise, things would really get confusing.

Now the new design-time instance of the control is ready to be created. The events that occur are the same as they were for the previous runtime instance:

```
Initialize
ReadProperties
Resize/Paint
```

The design-time instance's properties have been restored, and the control instance has been redisplayed. `Resize` and `Paint` are still following the rules mentioned earlier.

Going back to the changes made to the sample control earlier in this chapter, remember that we had to check the `Ambient` object's `UserMode` property (to enable or disable the control's `Timer` event) in both the `InitProperties` event and the `ReadProperties` event. Remember also that we couldn't check the `UserMode` property in the control's `Initialize` event because the `Ambient` object's properties are not yet available during that event. When the control instance is created on the form for the first time, the `InitProperties` event is triggered, but the `ReadProperties` event is not. And when a new design-time instance is created, the `ReadProperties` event is triggered, but the `InitProperties` event is not. Therefore, the `UserMode` check has to be in both to cover all the bases.

Event sequences are tricky when using controls within the Visual Basic environment because controls are constantly alternating between design-time and runtime modes. But when a control is executed as part of an executable (.EXE) file or is included on a Web page, things get much simpler. Here's what happens when a control instance is used as part of a compiled application:

```
Initialize
ReadProperties
Resize/Paint
- Other events -
Terminate
```

Again, note that the `Resize` event only occurs for controls that use constituent controls, and the `Paint` event only occurs for user-drawn controls.

The `Terminate` event does not occur until the container housing the instance of the control is unloaded or destroyed. Also, several other events are likely to happen between the initial `Resize` or `Paint` event and the `Terminate` event: `GotFocus`, `LostFocus`, `Click`, `DblClick`, and so on.

You may notice that there is no `WriteProperties` event. That's because there is nowhere for the control to write its properties. It can't modify the contents of the executable file to save the properties, nor would you want it to—then the control's properties would not be properly initialized the next time the application was run. Any changes to a control's properties during runtime are lost, just as they were when the runtime instance was destroyed to create a new design-time instance of the control in our previous example.

Controls used on Web pages act a little differently from those used in applications. This is because HTML pages have no way of saving property values. Because the controls exist on their own and not as a part of a form, an HTML page acts as if the control instance is being created for the first time no matter how many times the page is loaded and displayed:

```
Initialize
InitProperties
Resize/Paint
- Other events -
Terminate
```

The sequence of events is basically the same as it is for a control used in an executable file, but the ReadProperties event has been replaced with our old friend, the InitProperties event. Because there is no form from which it can read property settings, they are instead initialized to their default values every time the Web page is loaded. However, property values *can* be changed using the <PARAM> tag that is part of HTML's <OBJECT> tag. Implementing ActiveX controls on Web pages is discussed in Chapter 6, "Deploying ActiveX Controls." For now, it's important to understand the basic sequence of events that occur in the life of a control instance, no matter what mode it may happen to be in.

Adding More Properties to the LightButton Control

Part one of the LightButton control is working pretty well, but we still need to add the capability to use graphic images to indicate a selected or deselected button status. To do that, we're going to need to add some properties. Delete the instance of the LightButton control on the test form, then switch back to the control's code window.

Before adding more properties, a few variables, types, and objects need to be defined in UserControl's General Declarations section. Change that section to reflect the code shown in Listing 5.10.

LISTING 5.10. CHANGES TO UserControl's General Declarations SECTION.

```
Public Enum lbModeTypes
    [Text Only Mode] =
    [Image Mode]
End Enum

Public Enum lbBorderStyleTypes
    None =
    [Fixed Single]
End Enum

Private mbooButtonLighted As Boolean
Private mfonFont As StdFont
Private mmodButtonMode As lbModeTypes
Private molcBackColor As OLE_COLOR
Private molcSelColor As OLE_COLOR
Private mpicPicture As New StdPicture
Private mpicSelPicture As New StdPicture
Private mpoiCursorPos As POINTAPI
```

You can either type in the code in Listing 5.11 verbatim, complete with the Property procedure declarations, or you can choose Tools|Add Procedure from the menu as a shortcut. If you use the second method, add all the procedures listed in Table 5.10, making sure that you type the name of the procedure in the Name box, select Property for Type, and select Public for Scope. Then use Listing 5.11 to add the code for each Property procedure.

No matter which method you decide to use, be sure that the code in your sample control matches the code in Listing 5.11. Be careful—there are some subtle differences in the Property procedure declaration lines that vary from procedure to procedure. For example, note that although most properties use a Property Let declaration, the Picture property uses a Property Set declaration instead. Also, don't forget to change the Property Let procedure's vNewValue argument to NewValue.

TABLE 5.10. ADD Property PROCEDURES FOR THE FOLLOWING PROPERTIES.

Property Name	Type	Scope
BackColor	Property	Public
BorderStyle	Property	Public
ButtonMode	Property	Public
Font	Property	Public
ForeColor	Property	Public
Picture	Property	Public
SelColor	Property	Public
SelPicture	Property	Public

LISTING 5.11. ADDING THE FOLLOWING Property PROCEDURES CODE TO YOUR CONTROL, MAKING SURE THAT YOU PAY CLOSE ATTENTION TO DETAILS.

```
Public Property Get BackColor() As OLE_COLOR

        ' The control's BackColor property is "stored" in
        ' the UserControl object's BackColor property.
        BackColor = UserControl.BackColor

End Property


Public Property Let BackColor(ByVal NewValue As OLE_COLOR)

        ' The control's new BackColor value is passed
        ' directly to the UserControl object's BackColor
        ' property.
        UserControl.BackColor = NewValue
        UserControl.PropertyChanged "BackColor"
```

5

CREATING
ACTIVEX
CONTROLS

continues

LISTING 5.11. CONTINUED

```
    ' Store the new BackColor value in a "holding"
    ' variable for later use.
    molcBackColor = NewValue

End Property


Public Property Get BorderStyle() As lbBorderStyleTypes

    ' The control's BorderStyle property is "stored" in
    ' the UserControl object's BorderStyle property.
    BorderStyle = UserControl.BorderStyle

End Property


Public Property Let BorderStyle(ByVal NewValue As lbBorderStyleTypes)

    ' Make sure that the value being assigned to the
    ' BorderStyle property is valid.
    If NewValue = None Or NewValue = [Fixed Single] Then
            ' The control's new BorderStyle value is passed
            ' directly to the UserControl object's BorderStyle
            ' property.
            UserControl.BorderStyle = NewValue
            UserControl.PropertyChanged "BorderStyle"
    Else
            ' Invalid BorderStyle value - raise an error.
            Err.Raise Number:=vbObjectError + 32112, _
                Description:="Invalid BorderStyle value (0 or 1 only)"
    End If

End Property


Public Property Get ButtonMode() As lbModeTypes

    ' The ButtonMode property is stored in a "holding"
    ' variable, mmodButtonMode.
    ButtonMode = mmodButtonMode

End Property


Public Property Let ButtonMode(ByVal NewValue As lbModeTypes)

    ' Don't let a new value be assigned to
    ' mmodButtonMode (ButtonMode's "holding" variable)
    ' unless it is valid.
```

```
        If NewValue = [Text Only Mode] Or NewValue = [Image Mode] Then
            mmodButtonMode = NewValue
            ' If ButtonMode is Text Only Mode (0), show
            ' the lblCaption object. If ButtonMode is
            ' Image Mode (1), hide the lblCaption object.
            If mmodButtonMode = [Text Only Mode] Then lblCaption.Visible = True
            If mmodButtonMode = [Image Mode] Then lblCaption.Visible = False
            UserControl.PropertyChanged "ButtonMode"
        Else
            ' Invalid ButtonMode value - raise an error.
            Err.Raise Number:=vbObjectError + 32113, _
                Description:="Invalid ButtonMode value (0 or 1 only)"
        End If

End Property


Public Property Get Font() As StdFont

    ' The value for the control's Font property is
    ' "stored" in the lblCaption object's Font property.
    Set Font = lblCaption.Font

End Property


Public Property Set Font(ByVal NewValue As StdFont)

    ' Store the control's new Font value in the
    ' lblCaption object's Font property.
    Set lblCaption.Font = NewValue
    UserControl.PropertyChanged "Font"

End Property


Public Property Get ForeColor() As OLE_COLOR

    ' The control's ForeColor property is "stored" in
    ' lblCaption's ForeColor property.
    ForeColor = lblCaption.ForeColor

End Property


Public Property Let ForeColor(ByVal NewValue As OLE_COLOR)

    ' The control's new ForeColor value is passed
    ' directly to lblCaption's ForeColor property.
    lblCaption.ForeColor = NewValue
```

continues

5

CREATING
ACTIVEX
CONTROLS

LISTING **5.11.** CONTINUED

```
    UserControl.PropertyChanged "ForeColor"

End Property


Public Property Get Picture() As StdPicture

    ' The control's Picture property is "stored" in
    ' the UserControl object's Picture property.
    Set Picture = UserControl.Picture

End Property


Public Property Set Picture(ByVal NewValue As StdPicture)

    ' First, change UserControl's Picture property to
    ' display the image selected.
    Set UserControl.Picture = NewValue

    ' Then store the new image in a "holding" picture
    ' object.
    Set mpicPicture = NewValue

    ' If Picture's image is Nothing, set the ButtonMode
    ' property back to Text Only Mode (0). If Picture
    ' does contain an image, set the ButtonMode
    ' property to Image Mode (1).
    If NewValue Is Nothing Then
        ButtonMode = [Text Only Mode]
    Else
        ButtonMode = [Image Mode]
    End If

    UserControl.PropertyChanged "Picture"

End Property


Public Property Get SelColor() As OLE_COLOR

    ' The control's SelColor property is stored in a
    ' "holding" variable, molcSelColor.
    SelColor = molcSelColor

End Property


Public Property Let SelColor(ByVal NewValue As OLE_COLOR)
```

```
        ' Store SelColor's new value in a "holding"
        ' variable, molcSelColor.
        molcSelColor = NewValue
        UserControl.PropertyChanged "SelColor"

End Property


Public Property Get SelPicture() As StdPicture

        ' SelPicture's image is retrieved from a "holding"
        ' picture object, mpicSelPicture.
        Set SelPicture = mpicSelPicture

End Property


Public Property Set SelPicture(ByVal NewValue As StdPicture)

        ' Store SelPicture's new value in a "holding"
        ' picture object, mpicSelPicture.
        Set mpicSelPicture = NewValue
        UserControl.PropertyChanged "SelPicture"

End Property
```

There are many things going on in these Property procedures, so I'll go through them on a property-by-property basis and explain what's happening.

BackColor

BackColor is used just like any other control's BackColor property: it specifies the control's background color.

Because the lblCaption object is transparent (as defined earlier), changing the UserControl object's BackColor property essentially changes the background color of the control as a whole. Thus, we can store the control's BackColor property value directly in UserControl's BackColor property.

Whenever the BackColor property changes (and its Property Let procedure is invoked), the new value is passed directly to UserControl.BackColor, which creates an immediate change in the control's appearance. The new value is also stored in a "holding" variable because UserControl's BackColor property will change when the control is selected, and its original contents will be lost. The holding variable, molcBackColor, is used to save the original value.

Properties such as BackColor that specify color values use OLE_COLOR in their procedure declarations.

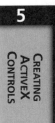

BorderStyle

The BorderStyle property is another example of passing values directly to other objects. UserControl's BorderStyle property is used to store BorderStyle's value. Changing UserControl.BorderStyle also modifies the appearance of the control.

The BorderStyle property is defined as lbBorderStyleTypes, an enumeration that was added to UserControl's General Declarations section. The items in the enumeration (None and Fixed Single) will become the options that can be selected for the BorderStyle property in the Properties window for an instance of the LightButton control.

BorderStyle's Property Let procedure keeps values other than those in the enumeration from being assigned to the property. If an invalid value is detected, an error is raised.

ButtonMode

The ButtonMode property cannot be directly passed to another object's property because no other object has a ButtonMode property—we made it up! If you remember correctly, ButtonMode specifies how the control will work. If it's set to Text Only Mode (0), the control uses a "text-only" display and changes its background color to indicate a selected or unselected state. If it's set to Image Mode (1), images (specified by the Picture and SelPicture properties) will be used instead.

In ButtonMode's case, a module-level integer variable (mmodButtonMode) is used to hold its value. Note that code has been added to ButtonMode's Property Let procedure to ensure that only the values Text Only Mode (0) and Image Mode (1) will be accepted. If anything other than 0 or 1 is passed to the Property Let procedure, an error message is displayed.

After the property's value has been validated, lblCaption's Visible property is set accordingly. If the control is in Text Only Mode (ButtonMode = 0), then the label should be displayed. However, if the control is in Image Mode (ButtonMode = 1), the label is hidden so that it doesn't display on top of the images.

Font

Here's another example of passing values directly to constituent controls. The Font property is stored in (and retrieved from) lblCaption.Font. Thus, whenever the Font property is modified, the change is automatically reflected in the control's appearance.

Font properties use StdFont in their procedure declarations. StdFont is a special object type that contains the font type, size, and attributes in one package. And because the Font property refers to an object (StdFont), it uses a Property Set procedure rather than a Property Let procedure.

ForeColor

`ForeColor` works similarly to the `BackColor` property and is passed directly to the `lblCaption` object. However, a copy of `ForeColor`'s value does not need to be copied to a "holding" variable because the control's `ForeColor` property does not change when the control goes from a selected to a nonselected state and vice versa.

Because the `ForeColor` property specifies a color, it also uses `OLE_COLOR` in its procedure declarations.

Picture

The `Picture` property is used to specify the image that should be displayed if the control is in a nonselected state. This image is also used as the default image; that is, the image that will be showing when the control is initially displayed.

Any value passed to the `Picture` property goes directly into `UserControl`'s `Picture` property, altering the appearance of the control. But the value also goes into a "holding" object, `mpicPicture`. But why both?

Consider what happens when the control changes from a nonselected to a selected state. The image that currently resides in `UserControl.Picture` will be replaced with the image (specified by the `SelPicture` property) that indicates that the control is selected. The original image would be lost. Therefore, a copy of it is stored in `mpicPicture` just in case it needs to be recalled later.

The value assigned to the `Picture` property is in the form of a `StdPicture` object. The `StdPicture` object dictates that the property uses a `Property Set` procedure rather than a `Property Let` procedure. Also, notice that whenever values are assigned to the `Picture` property (or its holding object, `mpicPicture`), Visual Basic's `Set` command must be used. The rule is that if the property requires a `Set` command to assign it a value, a `Property Set` procedure must be used in lieu of `Property Let`.

If the control's `Picture` property is altered, the `Property Set` procedure also modifies the value of the `ButtonMode` property. After all, if an image is specified for the `Picture` property, the control should automatically switch out of `Text Only` Mode into `Image` Mode (`ButtonMode = 1`). However, a little extra logic is needed to determine whether the `Picture` property's new value is indeed an image. This is done by checking to see whether the new value is `Nothing`.

If `NewValue` is anything other than `Nothing`, `NewValue` should contain an image, and the `ButtonMode` property can be switched to `Image` Mode (`1`). If it is `Nothing`, then `NewValue` does not contain an image, and the `ButtonMode` property should be set back to `Text Only` Mode (`0`).

SelColor

The `SelColor` property is used to specify which color the control's background will be changed to in order to indicate a selected state for the control. This property is really meaningless unless the control is in `Text Only Mode` (ButtonMode = 0).

`SelColor`'s value is stored in `molcSelColor`, a module-level variable defined as type `OLE_COLOR`.

SelPicture

The `SelPicture` property specifies the image that will be used to indicate a selected state for the control when it is in image mode (ButtonMode = 1). Like the `Picture` property, it is of the `StdPicture` type and requires a `Property Set` procedure rather than a `Property Let` procedure.

Initializing, Reading, and Writing Properties

Even though we've added several new properties that influence how the control looks or works, they wouldn't do much good if they couldn't be stored and retrieved as instances of the control are destroyed or re-created. Also, some properties need to be assigned default values when the control is initially created. To accomplish the initialization, reading, and writing of properties, we need to make some modifications to `UserControl`'s `InitProperties`, `ReadProperties`, and `WriteProperties` events. Use Listing 5.12 as a guide to making changes to those events.

LISTING 5.12. CHANGES THAT NEED TO BE MADE TO `UserControl`'s `InitProperties`, `ReadProperties`, AND `WriteProperties` EVENTS SO THAT THE CONTROL'S PROPERTIES CAN BE INITIALIZED, STORED, AND RETRIEVED.

```
Private Sub UserControl_InitProperties()

    ' If the control's container is in design mode,
    ' disable the Timer, which causes the control to
    ' not function.
    tmrChkStatus.Enabled = Ambient.UserMode

    ' Set the default values for some properties.

    ' The Caption property defaults to the name
    ' assigned to the control by its container.
    Caption = Ambient.DisplayName

    ' The SelColor property defaults to the color
    ' yellow.
    SelColor = &H80FFFF
```

```
    ' The ButtonMode property defaults to
    ' Text Only Mode (0).
    ButtonMode = [Text Only Mode]

End Sub


Private Sub UserControl_ReadProperties(PropBag As PropertyBag)

    ' If the control's container is in design mode,
    ' disable the Timer, which causes the control to
    ' not function.
    tmrChkStatus.Enabled = Ambient.UserMode

    ' Get properties from the property bag.

    BackColor = PropBag.ReadProperty("BackColor", &HFFFFFF)
    BorderStyle = PropBag.ReadProperty("BorderStyle", 1)
    ButtonMode = PropBag.ReadProperty("ButtonMode", mmodButtonMode)
    Caption = PropBag.ReadProperty("Caption", Ambient.DisplayName)
    ForeColor = PropBag.ReadProperty("ForeColor", &H80000008)
    SelColor = PropBag.ReadProperty("SelColor", &H80FFFF)

    Set Font = PropBag.ReadProperty("Font", mfonFont)
    Set Picture = PropBag.ReadProperty("Picture", Nothing)
    Set SelPicture = PropBag.ReadProperty("SelPicture", Nothing)

End Sub


Private Sub UserControl_WriteProperties(PropBag As PropertyBag)

    ' Save properties to the property bag.

    PropBag.WriteProperty "BackColor", BackColor, &HFFFFFF
    PropBag.WriteProperty "BorderStyle", BorderStyle,
    PropBag.WriteProperty "ButtonMode", ButtonMode, mmodButtonMode
    PropBag.WriteProperty "Caption", Caption, Ambient.DisplayName
    PropBag.WriteProperty "ForeColor", ForeColor, &H80000008
    PropBag.WriteProperty "SelColor", SelColor, &H80FFFF

    PropBag.WriteProperty "Font", Font, mfonFont
    PropBag.WriteProperty "Picture", Picture, Nothing
    PropBag.WriteProperty "SelPicture", SelPicture, Nothing

End Sub
```

Code has been added to the InitProperties event to assign default values to the SelColor and ButtonMode properties, neither of which are held in the properties of constituent controls.

The ReadProperties and WriteProperties events now contain all the code necessary to read and write the control's new properties from and to the property bag. Any values that are assigned to the properties will now "stick" as new instances of the control are created (and old ones are destroyed).

You may be wondering exactly how to go about determining what a property's default value should be for the WriteProperty and ReadProperty methods. As a rule of thumb, it should be whatever value the property initially contains when a new instance of the control is created. And you must make sure that the default value used in the WriteProperty method is the same as the one used in the ReadProperty method. Otherwise, you may get unpredictable results.

Only one more change needs to be made before the control can be tested again. Right now, the tmrChkStatus object's Timer event is only set up to change the background color. But because the ButtonMode property has been added and the control can be in either Text Only Mode or Image Mode, the Timer event has to differentiate between the two modes and take the appropriate action.

Listing 5.13 shows the new tmrChkStatus_Timer event. The only part that needs to be changed is the large If...End If block at the end of the event's code. However, the entire section of code has been included here to avoid any confusion about the changes that need to be made.

LISTING 5.13. THE NEW tmrChkStatus_Timer EVENT CODE.

```
Private Sub tmrChkStatus_Timer()

    ' This event will fire about 4 times per second,
    ' and is used to see if the control's status
    ' changes from selected ("lighted") to
    ' un-selected, and vice-versa.

    Dim lonCStat As Long
    Dim lonCurrhWnd As Long

    ' Disable the timer temporarily.
    tmrChkStatus.Enabled = False

    ' Using two Windows API functions, determine the
    ' handle of the window that the cursor is
    ' currently positioned on.
    lonCStat = GetCursorPos&(mpoiCursorPos)
    lonCurrhWnd = WindowFromPoint(mpoiCursorPos.X, _
        mpoiCursorPos.Y)

    If mbooButtonLighted = False Then
        ' If the control is not currently "lighted",
```

```
' and it matches the handle of the window that
' the cursor is on, either light it up (if
' ButtonMode = Text Only Mode) or switch its
' background image to the one that indicates
' that the button is selected.
If lonCurrhWnd = UserControl.hWnd Then
        mbooButtonLighted = True
        If mmodButtonMode = [Text Only Mode] Then
            UserControl.BackColor = molcSelColor
        Else
            Set UserControl.Picture = mpicSelPicture
        End If
    End If
Else
    ' If the control is "lit", and it no longer
    ' matches the handle of the window that the
    ' cursor is on, either un-light it (if
    ' ButtonMode = Text Only Mode) or switch its
    ' background image to the one that indicates
    ' that the button is not selected.
    If lonCurrhWnd <> UserControl.hWnd Then
        mbooButtonLighted = False
        If mmodButtonMode = [Text Only Mode] Then
            UserControl.BackColor = molcBackColor
        Else
            Set UserControl.Picture = mpicPicture
        End If
    End If
End If

' Re-enable the timer.
tmrChkStatus.Enabled = True
```

```
End Sub
```

All Systems Go!

Now that all the proper changes have been made to the control, it's finally time to test it again. Save your changes to the Project Group and then switch back to the test project.

Delete the previous instance of the LightButton control and create a new one. It should appear labeled as "LightButton1".

In the control's Properties window, you'll see all the new properties that we've added: BackColor, ButtonMode, Caption, Font, ForeColor, Picture, SelColor, and SelPicture. Experiment by changing any of the properties, and you'll see that they work just like the properties of any other control. Don't change the Picture or SelPicture properties just yet because we're going to try them out in a moment.

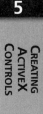

Try running `Project2` and moving the cursor on and off the control. When the cursor is on the control, the background color should change to whatever color was specified by the `SelColor` property. When the cursor is off the control, the background color should be whatever the `BackColor` property specifies. Stop the program so that you can make some more changes to the control's properties.

Try setting the control's `Width` property to 3000 and its `Height` property to 900. Then use the two image files (`TEST-OFF.BMP` and `TEST-ON.BMP` located in the `\SOURCE\CHAP05` directory) that are included on the CD-ROM as the values for the `Picture` and `SelPicture` properties, respectively. Notice that when a picture value is assigned to the `Picture` property, `ButtonMode` automatically switches to `Image Mode`.

Run `Project2` again to try the control in `Image Mode`. When the control is initially displayed, it shows the `TEST-OFF.BMP` image (see Figure 5.9) as the default. When the cursor is moved onto the control, the `TEST-ON.BMP` image is displayed (see Figure 5.10), and the text appears to "light up" to indicate a selected status. Because any two images can be used with the `LightButton` control, the possibilities for what it can do are endless!

FIGURE 5.9.

The `LightButton` *control, running in* `Image Mode`, *initially shows the* `TEST-OFF.BMP` *image.*

FIGURE 5.10.

The `LightButton` *control shows the* `TEST-ON.BMP` *image to indicate a selected state.*

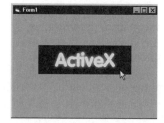

One More Property: `Enabled`

One more property needs to be added to the `LightButton` control: the `Enabled` property. Some special considerations need to be taken with this property, so I wanted to discuss it separately from the rest.

To begin with, the `Property Get` and `Property Let` statements can be added for the `Enabled` property just like any of the others. Get back into the control's design mode and add the `Property` procedures shown in Listing 5.14.

LISTING 5.14. THE `Property` PROCEDURES FOR THE `Enabled` PROPERTY.

```
Public Property Get Enabled() As Boolean

    Enabled = UserControl.Enabled

End Property


Public Property Let Enabled(ByVal NewValue As Boolean)

    UserControl.Enabled = NewValue
    UserControl.PropertyChanged "Enabled"

End Property
```

Next, add the following line of code to `UserControl`'s `WriteProperties` event:

```
PropBag.WriteProperty "Enabled", Enabled, True
```

Finally, add the following line to `UserControl`'s `ReadProperties` event:

```
Enabled = PropBag.ReadProperty("Enabled", True)
```

Nothing new here. Any new value assigned to the `Enabled` property is passed directly to the `UserControl` object's `Enabled` property, and any time the `Enabled` property's value is read, it is taken directly from `UserControl.Enabled`. Also, the `WriteProperty` and `ReadProperty` events don't look any different from those of the other properties. So what's the big deal?

The `Enabled` property will not work correctly as it is. If the control's container becomes disabled, it is supposed to disable all the controls that it contains; that is, none of the controls can have their events triggered. However, the controls still need to be able to redraw themselves if required. Therefore, the control needs to *think* it's enabled when in fact it is not.

There is a way to get around this quirky problem, but to do so the container needs to know the *procedure ID* of the control's `Enabled` property. If it knows the procedure ID, the container can set the `Enabled` property of the control to `False` without actually calling the `Enabled` property procedures.

Assigning the correct procedure ID to the control's `Enabled` property is done using the Procedure Attributes dialog box. To access it, choose Tools | Procedure Attributes from the menu. This will bring up a dialog box similar to the one shown in Figure 5.11.

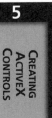

FIGURE 5.11.
*The Procedure
Attributes dialog
box, which is used
to set the* Enabled
*property's proce-
dure ID.*

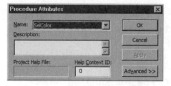

In the Name box, select the Enabled property. Click the Advanced button, and then select Enabled in the Procedure ID box. Click OK.

That's all there is to it. The Enabled property should now work correctly.

Expanding on the Control's Interface

Now that all the properties defined in the control's interface have been added, it's time to add the events and methods that were also a part of the interface. Table 5.11 shows the elements of the control's interface that still need to be implemented.

TABLE 5.11. THE EVENTS AND METHODS DEFINED IN THE LightButton CONTROL'S INTERFACE THAT HAVE NOT YET BEEN IMPLEMENTED.

Element	Type
Click	Event
DblClick	Event
KeyDown	Event
KeyPress	Event
KeyUp	Event
MouseDown	Event
MouseMove	Event
MouseUp	Event
StatusChanged	Event
Flash	Method
Refresh	Method

If you compare Table 5.11 to Table 5.4, which lists all the control's interface elements, you'll see that several methods (Drag, Move, SetFocus, ShowWhatsThis, and Zorder) have been omitted from this list. They're still a part of the control's interface, but they have already been implemented—furnished automatically by the control's container object. Remember, certain elements that appear to be part of a control are actually provided for and controlled by the container itself. The same thing goes for properties. Many are automatically provided by the control's container or the `Ambient` object, including `DragIcon`, `DragMode`, `Height`, `HelpContextID`, `Index`, `Left`, `Object`, `Parent`, `TabIndex`, `TabStop`, `Tag`, `ToolTipText`, `Top`, `WhatsThisHelpID`, and `Width`. As you can see, much of a control's base functionality is already built in.

Four events (`DragDrop`, `DragOver`, `GotFocus`, and `LostFocus`) are also missing from Table 5.11 because they too are provided by the control's container. So right off the bat, your control has four events, five methods, and more than 15 different properties that are a part of its interface but don't require a single line of code on your part. Not bad!

Almost all the events and methods listed in Table 5.11 that *will* require some coding will originate from the control's `UserControl` object. Just as the properties of constituent controls can be "passed" to the control's interface, so it goes with events and methods. There's no need to reinvent the wheel; the functionality required is already provided by the constituent controls.

Only one event (`StatusChanged`) and one method (`Flash`) will need to be custom created. Don't worry, adding events and methods (even custom ones) is easy to do, as you'll see in the next few pages.

Adding Events to the Sample Control

We'll begin by adding the events that originate from the control's `UserControl` object: `Click`, `DblClick`, `KeyDown`, `KeyPress`, `KeyUp`, `MouseDown`, `MouseMove`, and `MouseUp`.

Events raised by a control's constituent controls or the `UserControl` object give you, the control's developer, an opportunity to react to those events and, if desired, expose them as a part of your control's interface. However, the events of constituent controls are unavailable to the user of the control unless the events have been purposely exposed. For example, if the user clicks the mouse cursor on an instance of the `LightButton` control, the `UserControl` object's `Click` event will be raised. You might also expect that `LightButton`'s `Click` event would also be raised automatically, but it is not. You need to *expose* `UserControl`'s `Click` event *as* `LightButton`'s `Click` event. The developer using the control won't know the difference—just as he would be unaware that `LightButton`'s `Caption` property is in reality the same thing as the `Caption` property of `LightButton`'s constituent control `lblCaption`.

To expose a constituent control's event, only two lines of code are needed. The first line needs to be added to the end of `UserControl`'s General Declarations section as follows:

```
Public Event Click()
```

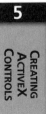

As you've probably already surmised, this adds a public Click event to the control. Declaring the event as public *exposes* it, allowing it to be available to other objects.

The other line of code required to expose UserControl's Click event appropriately goes into UserControl_Click:

RaiseEvent Click

This will raise LightButton's Click event (which was defined by the Public Event statement earlier) whenever UserControl's Click event is triggered. If you want, you could also include code in UserControl_Click to do something special (such as making a clicking sound) before raising the control's Click event. The developer using the control can in turn put his own code in the LightButton_Click event, which has now been made available to him.

As you can see, exposing the events of constituent controls is easy. With only two lines of code required, it makes sense to expose as many events as possible to provide your control with the greatest functionality.

To expose the rest of UserControl's events, first use Listing 5.15 as a guide for making changes to LightButton's General Declarations section. Then use Listing 5.16 to make the necessary changes to the appropriate UserControl event procedures.

LISTING 5.15. LightButton's General Declarations SECTION, WITH LINES ADDED TO FACILITATE THE EXPOSURE OF THE UserControl OBJECT'S EVENTS.

```
Public Enum lbModeTypes
    [Text Only Mode] =
    [Image Mode]
End Enum

Public Enum lbBorderStyleTypes
    None =
    [Fixed Single]
End Enum

' Expose the control's events as a part of its
' interface.
Public Event Click()
Public Event DblClick()
Public Event KeyDown(KeyCode As Integer, Shift As Integer)
Public Event KeyPress(KeyAscii As Integer)
Public Event KeyUp(KeyCode As Integer, Shift As Integer)
Public Event MouseDown(Button As Integer, Shift As Integer, _
    X As Single, Y As Single)
Public Event MouseMove(Button As Integer, Shift As Integer, _
    X As Single, Y As Single)
Public Event MouseUp(Button As Integer, Shift As Integer, _
```

```
    X As Single, Y As Single)

Private mbooButtonLighted As Boolean
Private mfonFont As StdFont
Private mmodButtonMode As lbModeTypes
Private molcBackColor As OLE_COLOR
Private molcSelColor As OLE_COLOR
Private mpicPicture As New StdPicture
Private mpicSelPicture As New StdPicture
Private mpoiCursorPos As POINTAPI
```

LISTING 5.16. UserControl's EVENT PROCEDURES, WHICH, WHEN TRIGGERED, RAISE THE
LightButton EVENTS DEFINED IN THE General Declarations SECTION.

```
Private Sub UserControl_Click()

    ' If UserControl's Click event is triggered,
    ' LightButton's Click event is in turn raised.
    RaiseEvent Click

End Sub


Private Sub UserControl_DblClick()

    ' If UserControl's DblClick event is triggered,
    ' LightButton's DblClick event is in turn raised.
    RaiseEvent DblClick

End Sub


Private Sub UserControl_KeyDown(KeyCode As Integer, _
    Shift As Integer)

    ' If UserControl's KeyDown event is triggered,
    ' LightButton's KeyDown event is in turn raised,
    ' and the KeyCode and Shift arguments are passed
    ' to that event.
    RaiseEvent KeyDown(KeyCode, Shift)

End Sub


Private Sub UserControl_KeyPress(KeyAscii As Integer)

    ' If UserControl's KeyPress event is triggered,
    ' LightButton's KeyPress event is in turn raised,
    ' and the KeyAscii argument is passed to that
    ' event.
    RaiseEvent KeyPress(KeyAscii)
```

5

**CREATING
ACTIVEX
CONTROLS**

continues

LISTING 5.16. CONTINUED

```vb
End Sub


Private Sub UserControl_KeyUp(KeyCode As Integer, _
    Shift As Integer)

    ' If UserControl's KeyUp event is triggered,
    ' LightButton's KeyUp event is in turn raised,
    ' and the KeyCode and Shift arguments are
    ' passed to that event.
    RaiseEvent KeyUp(KeyCode, Shift)

End Sub


Private Sub UserControl_MouseDown(Button As Integer, _
    Shift As Integer, X As Single, Y As Single)

    ' If UserControl's MouseDown event is triggered,
    ' LightButton's MouseDown event is in turn raised,
    ' and the Button, Shift, X and Y arguments are
    ' passed to that event.
    RaiseEvent MouseDown(Button, Shift, X, Y)

End Sub


Private Sub UserControl_MouseMove(Button As Integer, _
    Shift As Integer, X As Single, Y As Single)

    ' If UserControl's MouseMove event is triggered,
    ' LightButton's MouseMove event is in turn raised,
    ' and the Button, Shift, X and Y arguments are
    ' passed to that event.
    RaiseEvent MouseMove(Button, Shift, X, Y)

End Sub


Private Sub UserControl_MouseUp(Button As Integer, _
    Shift As Integer, X As Single, Y As Single)

    ' If UserControl's MouseUp event is triggered,
    ' LightButton's MouseUp event is in turn raised,
    ' and the Button, Shift, X and Y arguments are
    ' passed to that event.
    RaiseEvent MouseUp(Button, Shift, X, Y)

End Sub
```

Although the `Click` and `DblClick` events are straightforward, the others require that information obtained when the original event is triggered be passed along when the corresponding control event is raised. This requires declaring the types of arguments for the event in its `Public Event` declaration and listing the arguments in the appropriate `RaiseEvent` command, as you can see in Listings 5.15 and 5.16.

If you want to test the passing of events from constituent controls to the `LightButton` control, here's a simple test. Add two `Label` objects (`Label1` and `Label2`) to the test form of the project. Then add the following lines of code to the `LightButton1_MouseMove` event:

```
Label1.Caption = CStr(X)
Label2.Caption = CStr(Y)
```

Now run the test project. When you move the mouse cursor anywhere on the `LightButton` control, its coordinates will be displayed in `Label1` and `Label2` (and, of course, the control will indicate a selected state). When you move the cursor off the control, the cursor's coordinates are no longer updated. That's because the `MouseMove` event, which actually originated as `UserControl_MouseMove`, only fires when the cursor is on the control (or, more specifically, when it is on the `UserControl` object). When you're finished with this test, remove the code from the `LightButton1_MouseMove` event and delete the two `Label` objects.

Creating Custom Events

There isn't much difference between using the events of constituent controls and creating events of your own design. You still need to declare the event using a `Public Event` statement just as you did before. And you need to add a `RaiseEvent` statement just like the ones that you added to the constituent controls' event procedures. The only difference is that now you need to decide *where* to put the `RaiseEvent` statement or statements so that the event will be properly triggered.

The last event that needs to be implemented in `LightButton`'s interface is the `StatusChanged` event. It is to be triggered whenever a change occurs to the status of the `LightButton` control. Therefore, the event will be raised when the control becomes selected and when it becomes deselected. This gives the developer using the control the opportunity to take some action when the control's state changes. For instance, he may want to pop up a small help window when the cursor is on the control and then remove it when the control becomes unselected. Using `LightButton`'s `StatusChanged` event, he can do just that.

To add the `StatusChanged` event, it first needs to be declared with the `Public Event` command. Add the following line of code to the rest of the `Public Event` declarations in `LightButton`'s `General Declarations` section:

```
Public Event StatusChanged(NewStatus As Integer)
```

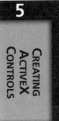

This will add the StatusChanged event to the control's interface. The event uses a single argument, which will indicate the control's new status (0 = Not selected, 1 = Selected).

Now, to actually raise the StatusChanged event, change the code in the tmrChkStatus_Timer event to what is shown in Listing 5.17. Pay close attention to the position of the two newly added RaiseEvent commands.

LISTING 5.17. THE tmrChkStatus_Timer EVENT, WITH TWO NEW LINES OF CODE ADDED TO RAISE THE CONTROL'S StatusChanged EVENT AT THE APPROPRIATE TIMES.

```
Private Sub tmrChkStatus_Timer()

    ' This event will fire about 4 times per second,
    ' and is used to see if the control's status
    ' changes from selected ("lighted") to
    ' unselected, and vice versa.

    Dim lonCStat As Long
    Dim lonCurrhWnd As Long

    ' Disable the timer temporarily.
    tmrChkStatus.Enabled = False

    ' Using two Windows API functions, determine the
    ' handle of the window that the cursor is
    ' currently positioned on.
    lonCStat = GetCursorPos&(mpoiCursorPos)
    lonCurrhWnd = WindowFromPoint(mpoiCursorPos.X, _
        mpoiCursorPos.Y)

    If mbooButtonLighted = False Then
        ' If the control is not currently "lighted",
        ' and it matches the handle of the window that
        ' the cursor is on, either light it up (if
        ' ButtonMode = Text Only Mode) or switch its
        ' background image to the one that indicates
        ' that the button is selected.
        If lonCurrhWnd = UserControl.hWnd Then
            mbooButtonLighted = True
            If mmodButtonMode = [Text Only Mode] Then
                UserControl.BackColor = molcSelColor
            Else
                Set UserControl.Picture = mpicSelPicture
            End If
            RaiseEvent StatusChanged(1)
        End If
    Else
        ' If the control is "lit", and it no longer
        ' matches the handle of the window that the
        ' cursor is on, either un-light it (if
        ' ButtonMode = Text Only Mode) or switch its
```

```
    ' background image to the one that indicates
    ' that the button is not selected.
    If lonCurrhWnd <> UserControl.hWnd Then
        mbooButtonLighted = False
        If mmodButtonMode = [Text Only Mode] Then
            UserControl.BackColor = molcBackColor
        Else
            Set UserControl.Picture = mpicPicture
        End If
        RaiseEvent StatusChanged(0)
    End If
End If

    ' Re-enable the timer.
    tmrChkStatus.Enabled = True

End Sub
```

The two `RaiseEvent` commands have been strategically placed to trigger the `StatusChanged` event only when the control's status actually changes. You must be careful not to place a `RaiseEvent` command where it will be constantly triggered—unless, of course, that is your intent. Also, in most cases, you will want to handle any special processing *before* raising the event. In Listing 5.17, you can see that the `StatusChanged` event is raised only *after* the appearance of the control has been changed.

When the control changes from an unselected to a selected state, the `RaiseEvent` is called with a 1 as its argument. When the reverse happens and the control's state changes from selected to unselected, `RaiseEvent` uses a 0 as its argument. The value of the argument can be tested by code added to `LightButton`'s `StatusChanged` event to see what the control's new status is.

There is still one more place where a `RaiseEvent` statement should be added. It makes sense that whenever the control's status changes, the `StatusChanged` event should be triggered. But it also stands to reason that the event should also fire whenever the control's status is initialized. The status is initialized (appropriately enough) in `UserControl`'s Initialize event, so that's where the last `RaiseEvent` statement needs to be added. Change `UserControl_Initialize` as shown in Listing 5.18.

LISTING 5.18. THE LAST `RaiseEvent` COMMAND NEEDS TO BE ADDED TO THE `UserControl_Initialize` EVENT, WHERE THE CONTROL'S STATUS IS INITIALIZED.

```
Private Sub UserControl_Initialize()

    ' When the control initializes, the button is
    ' not "lighted".
```

5

CREATING
ACTIVEX
CONTROLS

continues

LISTING 5.18. CONTINUED

```
mbooButtonLighted = False

' Since the control's status has just been
' initialized, the StatusChanged event should
' be raised.
RaiseEvent StatusChanged(0)

' Since UserControl's BackColor property will
' be changed if the control is "selected", its
' initial value must be stored in a temporary
' variable.
molcBackColor = UserControl.BackColor

End Sub
```

The StatusChanged event is initially raised to indicate an unselected state because that is the control's default status.

As you can see, adding events to your controls is simple. When you design your control's interface and determine all the custom events that you would like to include, you may want to keep them in mind when you are working out the logic of your control's code. That way, it will be easier to figure out exactly where and when you should raise the events.

A Few Last Words on Events

It's important that you choose a descriptive name for your custom events. For example, the StatusChanged event name clearly indicates when and why the event is triggered. If you choose cryptic names for your events, developers that use them may not be aware of their exact function. If, for example, the name StatChg were used rather than StatusChanged, would you have known right away what event it was supposed to represent? It's unlikely that you would.

Another little frill that you may want to include in your control is the selection of a default event—the event that will be shown when you double-click an instance of the control in VB's design mode. For example, when you double-click an instance of a CommandButton control, the CommandButton_Click event appears, ready to be edited. This makes sense because that is the event that will most likely be modified for that particular object class.

To make the StatusChanged event the default event for the LightButton control, you'll need to bring up the Procedure Attributes dialog box—the same tool that was used to change the Enabled property's Procedure ID earlier in this chapter.

To display the Procedures Attribute dialog box, choose Tools | Procedure Attributes from VB's menu. Make sure that the StatusChanged event is selected in the Name box; then click the Advanced button. Click the User Interface Default box so that it is checked; then click OK. The StatusChanged event will now be the control's default event.

Adding Methods to the Sample Control

If adding events to a control is easy, then adding methods is even easier. Basically, methods are Public procedures that can be called from outside the control. In this section, we will add two new methods (Refresh and Flash) to the LightButton control.

The Refresh Method

Unless your control is of the invisible kind (for example, a variation on the Timer object), it is wise to include a Refresh method. The Refresh method redraws the control whenever requested. Actually, all you need to add to the control's Refresh method is a call to UserControl.Refresh, so all the work is already done for you!

Add the procedure shown in Listing 5.19 to the LightButton control's code.

LISTING 5.19. LightButton's Refresh METHOD, A Public PROCEDURE, WHICH CONSISTS OF A CALL TO UserControl.Refresh.

```
Public Sub Refresh()

      UserControl.Refresh

End Sub
```

It doesn't get much easier than that! If your control is of the user-drawn variety, UserControl.Refresh will in turn raise UserControl's Paint event so that the control is redrawn. If your control uses constituent controls, each control's Resize event will be raised by UserControl.Refresh. Either way, all bases will be covered, and you don't have to worry about adding complex code to redraw your control.

Adding the Refresh method is simple. Adding the Flash method takes only marginally more effort.

The Flash Method

The Flash method is, to be honest, nothing more than a frill added to the LightButton control to illustrate the addition of custom methods. It does serve a function, however, by letting the developer "flash" the control (that is, quickly switch it from a selected to an unselected state) a specified number of times. Among other things, the Flash method could be used to draw attention to the control.

Like the Refresh method, the Flash method consists of a single Public procedure that is added to the LightButton control's code. Use Listing 5.20 to add that procedure.

LISTING 5.20. THE Public PROCEDURE THAT FACILITATES THE Flash METHOD.

```
Public Sub Flash(NumTimes As Integer)

    Dim booButtonLighted As Boolean
    Dim intFlashLoop As Integer
    Dim sinOldTimer As Single

    ' If an invalid argument was passed to the
    ' method, exit now.
    If NumTimes <= 0 Then Exit Sub

    booButtonLighted = mbooButtonLighted

    For intFlashLoop = 1 To (NumTimes * 2)
        ' Switch the button's status.
        booButtonLighted = Not booButtonLighted
        If booButtonLighted = True Then
            ' Change the control's background color or
            ' image to reflect a "selected" state.
            If mmodButtonMode = [Text Only Mode] Then
                UserControl.BackColor = molcSelColor
            Else
                Set UserControl.Picture = mpicSelPicture
            End If
        Else
            ' Change the control's background color or
            ' image to reflect an "unselected" state.
            If mmodButtonMode = [Text Only Mode] Then
                UserControl.BackColor = molcBackColor
            Else
                Set UserControl.Picture = mpicPicture
            End If
        End If
        ' Wait a short amount of time before changing the
        ' control's status again.
        sinOldTimer = Timer
        Do
            DoEvents
        Loop Until (Timer >= sinOldTimer + 0.5)
    Next intFlashLoop

End Sub
```

The Flash method first checks to make sure that it was not passed an invalid argument. Although anything greater than zero will be considered valid as the code is now, you may want to specify an upper range for the `NumTimes` argument as well. For example, to make sure that the control flashes no more than ten times, change the method's first `If...Then` statement to the following:

```
If NumTimes <= 0 Or NumTimes > 10 Then Exit Sub
```

Of course, you can change the validation process for the `NumTimes` argument to use whatever rules you want.

After the `NumTimes` argument has been tested, the current value of `mbooButtonLighted` (the Boolean variable that keeps track of the control's selected or unselected status) is stored in `booButtonLighted`. A `For...Next` loop is then performed twice as many times as indicated by the `NumTimes` argument—one time to select the control and another time to unselect it, although not necessarily in that order.

Every time the loop is executed, the control's status is flip-flopped, or changed from a selected to an unselected status or vice versa. This is easily accomplished by the following line of code:

```
booButtonLighted = Not booButtonLighted
```

Because the `booButtonLighted` variable is of type Boolean, its value is changed to its opposite whenever this statement is executed. Thus, it changes from True to False, or from False to True.

The same code that was used in `tmrChkStatus`'s `Timer` event is used in the `For...Next` loop to change the control's appearance. But before the next pass through the loop, a short period of time must pass; otherwise, the flashing will happen too quickly. A few lines of code have been added to pause for half a second—though you can change the amount of time from .5 second to whatever you think is appropriate. A `DoEvents` statement is executed again and again until the allotted amount of time has passed because we wouldn't want to tie up the system while the control is busy flashing.

When the `For...Next` loop is finished, the control's status will have been switched back to whatever it was before the `Flash` method was called because the loop always executes an even number of times.

So there you have it—two new methods added to the `LightButton` control, accomplished using nothing more than two `Public` procedures. The control's interface can now be called complete. However, you can still add a few more things to the `LightButton` control that will help to round it out, as you'll see in the next section.

Odds and Ends

When you've completed all the design and coding for your control, there are a few odds and ends that you can take care of to give it more of a professional look. For example,

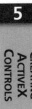

you may want to add an About box to your control to relay copyright or author information, especially if you plan on distributing the control to other developers.

Other frills that you can add to your control include assigning it a toolbox bitmap to replace the standard `UserControl` icon. Believe me, if you create several ActiveX controls in Visual Basic and add them to the toolbox, you'll be unable to tell one from the other if they all use the same icon!

You can also group your control's properties together by type (Appearance, Font, and so on) and add short descriptions that describe their use. Doing so is easy and requires absolutely no coding, but it may be helpful to any developers who use your control—including yourself!

None of these odds and ends are really necessary, and you do not need to add them to your controls if you don't want to. But if you plan on distributing your controls to other developers, your goal should be to make your control as easy to use as possible. Taking a few minutes to add these last few polishes will help advance you towards that goal.

Adding an About Box

Adding an About box to your control allows you to convey important information about the control to the developer using it. It can show the control's copyright notice, an email address for support, or even your company's logo. You can put whatever you want in your control's About box.

The first step in adding an About box is to add a form to the control's project. To do so, right-click on `Project1` in the Project Explorer window, then select Add | Form from the pop-up menu. When the dialog box with all of the forms is displayed, you can choose a regular form to design your About box from scratch or you can use the Aboutb form type, which provides you with a pre-built About box form that you can modify.

No matter what kind of form you use, you are free to change it however you want. You can add objects from the toolbox to the form, change its properties, or even assign a bitmap image to the form's `Picture` property to display a custom-created graphic as the About box. Just remember that anything you add to the form will increase the size of your control—an important consideration when implementing controls on the Internet. My advice is to keep it as simple as possible while still conveying all the information desired.

For the `LightButton` control, I used the About form type to create a familiar-looking About box. All I had to do was fill in the blanks and rearrange the form's controls a bit. Figure 5.12 shows the result.

FIGURE 5.12.

The LightButton
control's About
box.

Adding an About box does require a little coding, but it's not much. To begin with, a Public procedure needs to be added to LightButton's code (*not* the form's code) to actually display the About box when it is called for. Listing 5.21 shows such a procedure.

LISTING 5.21. A PUBLIC PROCEDURE THAT WILL DISPLAY THE ABOUT BOX FORM WHEN REQUESTED. THE PROCEDURE SHOULD BE ADDED TO THE LightButton CONTROL'S CODE, NOT TO THE FORM'S CODE.

```
Public Sub DisplayAboutBox()

    frmAbout.Show vbModal

End Sub
```

In Listing 5.21, the procedure is named DisplayAboutBox, but you can call it whatever you like.

Next, we need to hide the form (and clear it out of memory) when its Done button is clicked. The code to do that goes into the Click event of the Form's CommandButton object. If you used the Aboutb form type, this is already done for you. If you created an About box from scratch, you'll need to add code like that shown in Listing 5.22. Of course, you'll have to change the name of the CommandButton to reflect the name you used on your About box form.

LISTING 5.22. THE ABOUT BOX FORM IS UNLOADED AND REMOVED FROM MEMORY WHEN ITS DONE BUTTON IS CLICKED.

```
Private Sub cmdDone_Click()

    Unload frmAbout
    Set frmAbout = Nothing

End Sub
```

The only thing left to do is to use our old friend, the Procedure Attributes dialog box, to assign the DisplayAboutBox procedure to the correct Procedure ID. To bring up the

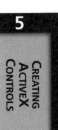

dialog box, make sure that the LightButton control is displayed in the Design window and that the UserControl object is selected. Then choose Tools | Procedure Attributes from the menu.

Select the DisplayAboutBox procedure (or whatever you called it) in the Name box; then click the Advanced button. Select AboutBox in the Procedure ID box; then click OK. That's all there is to it!

Before testing the About box, be sure to close the form's Design and Code windows. Also close the LightButton control's Design and Code windows, if necessary. Then display the test form by double-clicking its name in the Project Explorer window.

Click once on the instance of the LightButton control so that its properties are displayed in the Properties window. Click the About property; then click on the ... button. The About box that you created should pop up. When you're finished viewing it, click the Done button and the box will disappear.

Your About box forms do not need to be like the one shown here, with only a few lines of text and a Done button. You can get as creative as you want. Just keep the size of your control in mind.

Property Grouping and Descriptions

The Procedure Attributes dialog box is also used to group properties into general categories and add short descriptions. You can put your control's properties into one of the default categories (Appearance, Behavior, Data, DDE, Font, List, Misc, Position, Scale, and Text), or you can add your own category.

Admittedly, the process of describing properties and grouping them into categories can be tedious. Thankfully, it doesn't take too long—and it is worth the effort.

To call up the Procedure Attributes dialog box, first make sure that the control's Code or Design window is displayed. Then choose Tools | Procedure Attributes from VB's menu. Click on the dialog box's Advanced button to display the advanced options.

Select a property in the Name box. To add a description to the selected property, simply type in as much or as little text as you want in the Description box.

To select a category for the property, choose one from the Property Category drop-down list box. If you want to add the property to a category other than those provided in the list box, type in the category name in the Property Category text box. When you've finished making changes to the property, click the Apply button.

To maintain consistency, it's a good idea to group properties into the categories that they would be assigned to in other controls. A list of the standard properties often included in the interfaces of custom controls is shown in Table 5.12, along with the category that they are usually assigned to. You can use this table as a guide for grouping properties into categories.

TABLE 5.12. THE CATEGORIES THAT THE STANDARD PROPERTIES ARE USUALLY ASSIGNED TO.

Property	Category
BackColor	Appearance
BorderStyle	Appearance
Caption	Appearance
DragIcon	Behavior
DragMode	Behavior
Enabled	Behavior
Font	Font
ForeColor	Appearance
Height	Location
HelpContextID	Misc
Index	Misc
Left	Location
Name	Misc
Picture	Appearance
TabIndex	Behavior
TabStop	Behavior
Tag	Misc
ToolTipText	Misc
Top	Location
Visible	Behavior
WhatsThisHelpID	Misc
Width	Location

Group the `SelPicture` and `SelColor` properties into the Appearance category and the `ButtonMode` property into the Behavior category. If you're not sure which group a property should belong to, put it in the Miscellaneous (Misc) category.

After the properties have been assigned categories, it's time to give them descriptions. The good news is that many of your control's properties will already have default descriptions assigned to them. This includes any properties provided by the control's container or `Ambient` object. Only the properties that have been added to the control with the `Property Get`/`Property Let` procedures will require descriptions. For the

LightButton control, this leaves only the BackColor, BorderStyle, ButtonMode, Caption, Font, ForeColor, Picture, SelColor, and SelPicture properties left to describe.

If you want to skip the assigning of descriptions to all the remaining properties, that's okay. But I suggest that you add descriptions for the BackColor, ButtonMode, Picture, SelColor, and SelPicture properties. Some of those properties are unique to the LightButton control, and their uses may not be readily transparent. Also, the BackColor and Picture properties are used slightly differently than they are in other controls. This should be pointed out to whomever uses the LightButton control.

Table 5.13 lists the descriptions that I used for the remaining properties. You can use the same ones, or you can come up with your own descriptions.

TABLE 5.13. THE DESCRIPTIONS GIVEN TO EACH OF LightButton's PROPERTIES.

Property	Description
BackColor	Specifies the control's background color. Only used if the ButtonMode property is set to Text Only Mode (0).
BorderStyle	Specifies the type of border the control should have (0=None, 1=Fixed Single).
ButtonMode	Determines how the control will function. Text Only Mode (0) uses the background color to indicate the control's state, and Image Mode (1) uses images to indicate state.
Caption	The text that is displayed on the control. Only used if the ButtonMode property is set to Text Only Mode (0).
Font	The font used to display the control's caption.
ForeColor	The color of the control's caption. Only used if the ButtonMode property is set to Text Only Mode (0).
Picture	The image displayed when the control is in an unselected state. Only used if the ButtonMode property is set to Image Mode (1).
SelColor	The background color used to indicate that the control is in a selected state. Only used if the ButtonMode property is set to Text Only Mode (0).
SelPicture	The image displayed when the control is in a selected state. Only used if the ButtonMode property is set to Image Mode (1).

You may notice when you're adding the property descriptions that the control's events and methods are also listed in the Name box. You can add descriptions to them, too. If you do, they will be displayed in the Object Browser when the control's class is viewed. If you have added any events or methods unique to your control, I suggest that you assign short descriptions to them.

Because the StatusChanged event and the Flash method are unique to the LightButton control, I've added descriptions to them, too. The descriptions I used are listed in Table 5.14.

TABLE 5.14. DESCRIPTIONS FOR THE LightButton CONTROL'S StatusChanged EVENT AND Flash METHOD.

Event/Method	Description
StatusChanged	Triggered if the control's status changes from selected to unselected, or vice versa.
Flash	Used to "flash" the control (switch it from a selected to an unselected state) a specified number of times.

Now that descriptions have been added to the LightButton control's properties, events, and methods, and the properties have been grouped into the proper categories, there's only one thing left to do until the control can be finally considered done, and that's to assign it a unique toolbox icon.

Changing the Control's Toolbox Icon

This is one of the easiest things you can do when designing controls, but it does take some graphics skills. Create a bitmap graphic 16 pixels wide by 15 pixels high and then assign that image to UserControl's ToolboxBitmap property.

You don't have to use a bitmap that is 16×15 pixels. But if you use a larger image, it will be scaled down to the correct size, and it may look odd after being scaled. Your best bet is to create an image that is exactly 16×15 pixels so that you don't get any surprises.

On the CD-ROM, you'll find a bitmap graphic for the LightButton control called LB.BMP. If you want to use that graphic to assign to the ToolboxBitmap property, feel free to do so. Or, you can create your own bitmap. You don't need a super-powerful graphics package to create the image. Windows 95's Paint program will do just fine.

Summary

In this chapter, you learned to create a control from start to finish, starting with the most important step: designing the control thoroughly.

After a solid design was created and the control's interface was mapped out, the control was built piece by piece. Several properties were added to the control to increase its functionality.

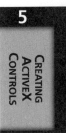

Next, the `LightButton` control's interface was completed by adding its events and methods. If you've come this far, you should know how to create your own controls from start to finish. You should also have all the code necessary for a fully functioning ActiveX control that, when compiled, can be added to your Visual Basic applications or Web pages. The next chapter will show you how to compile the control and how to deploy it.

Deploying ActiveX Controls

by Rob Thayer

IN THIS CHAPTER

- Compiling the Control   *150*
- The Package and Deployment Wizard   *155*
- Deploying .CAB Files   *156*

CHAPTER 6

Now that the LightButton control has been designed and coded, it needs to be compiled into an .OCX file. After the .OCX file has been created, the control can be used in Visual Basic applications, on World Wide Web pages, or in ActiveX documents. It can even be permanently added to VB's toolbox, if you want.

In this chapter, the LightButton control will be compiled and used first in a Visual Basic application and then on a Web page. It will be "put through its paces" and tested under many different circumstances.

Compiling the Control

When you compile an ActiveX control into an .OCX file using Visual Basic 6, you are presented with a substantial number of options. You can choose to optimize the control for speed or size, or to favor the Pentium Pro processor. You can also add documentation directly to the .OCX file, which will be displayed when the control is viewed with the Object Browser. The following section documents the options available to you when compiling controls.

Creating an .OCX File

You might think that you'll need to remove the test form from the LightButton control project group before the control can be compiled, but that won't be necessary. The control project (Project1) is completely separate from the test project (Project2), and it can be compiled separately.

Before attempting to compile the control, you have to make sure that it is not in run mode. To do so, double-click LightButton's name in the Project Explorer window. You should then see the control's Design window, indicating that the control is in design mode.

Also, unless you want the control to be named Project1, you have to change the name of Project1 to something more appropriate. Change Project1's name to LightButtonControl.

To compile the control, choose File | Make TestControl1.ocx from the menu. You should see a Make Project dialog box like the one shown in Figure 6.1.

The default name given to the .OCX file is the same as the name of the control's project (in this case, TestControl1). It would make more sense to use the name of the control instead, so change the value in the File name text box from TestControl1 to LightButton.

FIGURE 6.1.

The Make Project dialog box.

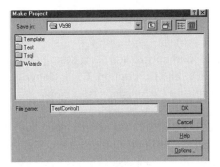

If you click OK at this point, the control will be compiled into native code and optimized for speed rather than size. Instead of compiling right now, click the Options button. You'll be given the opportunity to change the compiler options and add some documentation to the control. Figure 6.2 shows the Project Properties dialog box that appears after clicking the Options button.

FIGURE 6.2.

The Project Properties dialog box.

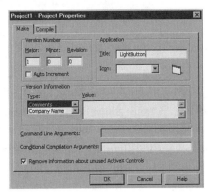

The Project Properties dialog box has two tabs, Make and Compile. The Make tab enables you to add documentation and a version number to the control. The Compile tab enables you to set the compiler's optimization options, as well as whether the control will be compiled into Native code or P-code.

On the Make tab, you can change the control's three-part version number. Because this is the first compilation of the LightButton control, it will receive the default version number of 1.0.0 (which breaks down as Major.Minor.Revision). If you check the Auto Increment box, the Revision number will be automatically incremented by one every time the control is compiled. The Revision number indicates only slight changes made to a control. If substantial changes are made, you'll need to manually change the Major or Minor version numbers and reset the Revision number to zero. I suggest changing the

Major version number any time you make changes to the control's interface such as adding new methods or properties.

The Make tab also gives you the opportunity to add short descriptions for version-related information such as Company Name, File Description, Legal Copyright, Legal Trademarks, Product Name, and general Comments. For example, you might use the Comments description to document any changes that have been made to the control since its last revision. This information will be displayed when a user views the executable file's properties in Windows (by right-clicking the program icon and selecting Properties). Because adding descriptions is not necessary, you can skip it and leave them all blank.

The Application section of the Make tab is not really used when compiling controls and applies mostly to application compilation, which enables a title and an icon to be assigned to the application.

The Command Line Arguments box also applies to application compilation, allowing you to pass command line arguments to an application when it is being run from within Visual Basic. Because controls cannot run by themselves and must be placed on a container of some sort, they obviously cannot accept command line arguments. Leave the Command Line Arguments box empty.

The Conditional Compilation Arguments box enables you to specify certain constant declarations that determine how certain parts of the control (or application) will be compiled. This is only used if there are `#If...Then` and `#End If` statements in the control or application's code. The compiler processes the `#If...Then/#End If` statements to determine what code it should include in its compilation. For example, imagine that you designed a control that consisted of several `TextBox` objects, each with a descriptive caption below it. If you wanted the captions to be available in three different languages (English, Spanish, and French), you can use conditional compilation to specify the language desired at compile time. By setting a constant in the Conditional Compilation Arguments box, a set of `#If...Then/#End If` statements could selectively assign different string values to the captions based on the value of the constant. Using the conditional compilation method in this way, you can create an English, Spanish, or French version of the control without having to change its code each time it is compiled.

Because the `LightButton` control does not require the use of conditional compilation, the Conditional Compilation Arguments box can be left empty.

The Project Properties dialog box's Compile tab gives you the capability to select either a P-code (pseudo-code) or Native code compilation. P-code is not as fast as Native code, but it doesn't take as long to compile. When compiling your controls for distribution, always select the Native code option.

When compiling a control into Native code, you are given your choice of optimization methods. You can choose to have the compiler optimize the control's code for fastest running speed or smallest .OCX size. If the control is going to be used primarily on systems that use Pentium Pro processors, you can choose to have the compiler factor these methods in when optimizing the control's code.

When compiling controls that are going to be distributed via the Internet, it makes sense to have the compiler optimize the control to be the smallest size possible. Because Internet-based controls need to be downloaded by users before they can be viewed on a Web page, the smaller the control the better. But you might want to try optimizing the control for size and then for speed and compare the size of the resulting .OCX files. Often, the size difference between the two is only a few thousand bytes, which translates to only a few extra seconds of download time. In cases in which the size of a speed-optimized .OCX file is only marginally larger than a size-optimized .OCX, I suggest optimizing for speed. As a general rule, you'll find that there is less difference in file size between speed- and size-optimized .OCX files for controls that don't have a lot of code. More sophisticated and complex controls that require a lot of code may benefit from size-optimization.

Table 6.1 shows the file sizes of three .OCX files compiled for the LightButton control. Each was compiled using a different optimization method. As you can see, there is only a 1,536-byte difference in size between the speed- and size-optimized .OCX files. The LightButton control's code is not very long or complex, so the difference is only marginal. Even when using no optimization at all, the difference is slight. For this compilation of the LightButton control, select the Optimize for Fast Code option.

TABLE 6.1. .OCX FILE SIZES FOR THE LightButton CONTROL, EACH COMPILED USING A DIFFERENT OPTIMIZATION METHOD

Optimization Method	File Size
Speed	44,544 bytes
Size	43,008 bytes
No optimization	48,128 bytes

NOTE

If you compile the LightButton control using the different optimization options listed in Table 6.1, you might get slightly larger or smaller .OCX file sizes.

No matter which optimization method you choose (speed, size, or none), you can also specify that the compiled code favor the Pentium Pro processor. Native code compiled with this option will still run on other processors, but it might be somewhat sluggish. When compiling controls for distribution on the Internet, never select the Favor Pentium Pro option. After all, you have no idea what kind of processors your Internet users will have in their systems, and it's a sure bet that many won't have a Pentium Pro.

If you have CodeView or a similar debugger, you can also choose to have the compiler generate debugging information by checking the Create Symbolic Debug Info option. In addition to the executable file normally output by the compiler, you'll also get a .PDB file that contains the debugging information. Utilities such as CodeView are used primarily for complex projects that require advanced debugging features over and above those that are offered by Visual Basic. We won't be doing any CodeView debugging, so make sure that this option is unchecked for now.

The Project Properties dialog box's Compile tab is where you set a DLL base address (the memory address at which an in-process component is loaded). Though a default value is provided, you should always change it—if another component also uses the default value, it will conflict with your component. There is no real scientific formula for coming up with new base addresses; just choose a random number between &H1000000 and &H80000000, then round it up (or down) so it is a multiple of 64K. For the LightButton control, use a DLL base address value of &H1750000. That's as good as any, and it's a multiple of 64K.

You should now have the compiler ready to compile version 1.0.0 of the LightButton control in Native code, optimized for speed. Click OK to exit the Project Properties dialog box; then click the Make Project dialog box's OK button to compile the control. The status of the compilation process will be displayed on Visual Basic's toolbar.

At this point, you should have a file called LIGHTBUTTON.OCX in the directory in which you stored the control's project files.

Using the Control in Visual Basic

To use the LightButton control in your Visual Basic programs, you need only add it to the toolbox using the Components option from VB's Project menu. Simply find the name of the control in the list, make sure that its check box is checked, and then click OK. The control will be added to the toolbox, and you can use it just like you would use any other ActiveX control.

Before you can use the control, you must make sure that it is registered on your system. Use the REGOCX32 command-line utility that comes with Visual Basic to register the .OCX file. For example, to register the TestControl.ocx file, you would change to the directory that contains the file and use REGOCX32 like this:

```
REGOCX32 TestControl.ocx
```

The control (`LightButtonControl`) would then appear the next time you displayed VB's Components dialog box.

Using the Control on a Web Page

There are two ways to include your ActiveX controls on Web pages. The first way is to use the `.OCX` file directly and add the control to the Web page using the HTML `<OBJECT>` tag (an example of how to use the `<OBJECT>` tag is shown later in this chapter). The other way is to package your control as a compressed `.CAB` file and add the `.CAB` to the Web page using the `<OBJECT>` tag. The latter method is preferred because it verifies that the system on which the control will be used already has any necessary support files, such as the Visual Basic runtime file. If any support files are missing, the `.CAB` file includes pointers to locations on the Internet where they can be found and downloaded. The whole process is transparent to the user.

Another benefit of using `.CAB` files is that they are compressed. This won't make much difference if your control is small and simple but can be beneficial when dealing with larger, more complex controls.

The good news is that `.CAB` files are easy to create using the Package and Deployment Wizard included with Visual Basic. The next section of this chapter includes detailed instructions for using the Package and Deployment Wizard to create distributable `.CAB` files for your ActiveX controls.

The Package and Deployment Wizard

The best way to package your ActiveX controls for delivery to users via the World Wide Web is by using `.CAB` files. `.CAB` (short for "CABinet") files are Microsoft's way of bundling together and compressing program and data files so that they can be installed on a user's machine. Almost all the install files on the Windows 95 CD-ROM are in `.CAB` format.

`.CAB` files can also be used to send and install ActiveX controls through the Web. Because they are compressed, download time is shorter. They can also contain any support files that the control requires. When a `.CAB` file is transferred to a user's system, it automatically uncompresses and installs itself—all of which is done seamlessly, with little or no intervention required on the part of the user.

Thankfully, Microsoft provides an easy way to create Internet-specific .CAB files by way of the Package and Deployment Wizard (formerly known as the Setup Wizard). This is the same wizard that is used to generate quick and easy setup programs for Visual Basic applications. In later versions of Visual Basic, it has been enhanced with an option for creating Internet Download Setup files.

The Package and Deployment Wizard is one of the applications in the VB6 program group. You can also use it from within Visual Basic by selecting it in the Add-In Manager.

Deploying .CAB Files

If you want to use a .CAB file on a Web page, you can use the <OBJECT> HTML tag to insert the .CAB file object. The <OBJECT> tag has the following syntax:

```
<OBJECT [ID=objectname] [CLASSID=clsid] [CODEBASE=fileinfo]>
    [<PARAM NAME=paramname VALUE=paramvalue>]
    [<PARAM NAME=paramname VALUE=paramvalue>]
</OBJECT>
```

The ID parameter is used to identify the object to scripting languages and other objects. The CLASSID is a unique 128-bit number that is assigned to each control and is used to differentiate one object from another. This number is generated by the system when the control is registered.

The CODEBASE parameter can be used to give the location of the object; that is, the URL where it can be downloaded. The object's version number can also be included so the Web browser can check to see if the object already exists on the user's system under the given CLASSID and version number.

When using the <OBJECT> tag to embed OCX controls directly onto Web pages, you can also include one or more <PARAM> tags. These tags are used to specify the control's properties (paramname) and their values (paramvalue).

A sample <OBJECT> tag for embedding the TestControl.CAB file into a Web page is shown below:

```
<OBJECT ID="LightButton"
   CLASSID="CLSID:CEB9FFE3-F500-11D1-B3B1-525400DA593D"
   CODEBASE="TestControl.CAB#version=1,0,0,0">
</OBJECT>
```

If you're anxious to see a quick sample of how the .CAB file is used on a Web page and you used the Package and Deployment Wizard to create the .CAB, you're in luck. The wizard creates a down-and-dirty Web page that includes the .CAB file. It can be found in

the same directory that you specified as the location for the new .CAB file, and its name will be the same as the .CAB file with an extension of .HTM rather than .CAB. For example, the Wizard should have created a TESTCONTROL.HTM file for you during the sample session detailed in this chapter.

Figure 6.3 shows the sample Web page in Internet Explorer. There's not much to it, but it does include a working sample of the LIGHTBUTTON.OCX control, and that's the most important part.

FIGURE 6.3.

The LightButton *control is ready to go on your Web page.*

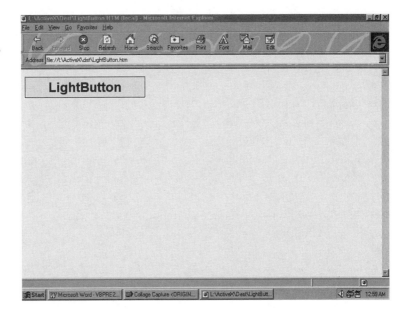

Summary

After an ActiveX control project has been compiled into an .OCX file, it can be used in Visual Basic programs or on Web pages. The best way to include ActiveX controls is by compressing them into .CAB files, which can also include any support files required by the control. The Package and Deployment Wizard that comes with Visual Basic provides an easy way to create .CAB files.

ActiveX Scripting with VBScript

by Rob Thayer

IN THIS CHAPTER

- Down-and Dirty-VBScript *160*
- More VBScript *167*

In Chapter 6, "Deploying ActiveX Controls," you learned how to add ActiveX controls to a Web page. However, controls aren't much good unless you can add code to make them interact in some way, either with the viewer of the Web page or among themselves.

Visual Basic programmers who need to write that kind of code are very fortunate. A scripting language exists—and is in wide use—that is in many ways identical to the language with which VB programmers are already familiar. Of course, I'm referring to VBScript.

VBScript, a subset of the Visual Basic programming language, is an easy way to add interactivity to a Web page. To be sure, the way VBScript works is different than the way VB works. But don't let that stop you! Experienced Visual Basic programmers should have little or no problem adapting to VBScript, though getting used to the differences may take some time.

This chapter will provide you with an introduction to VBScript. In particular, it will point out the differences, of which you need to be aware, between the scripting language and the more familiar Visual Basic development environment.

Keep in mind that this chapter is only meant to be an introduction to VBScript, not a complete reference or tutorial. Although VBScript is not nearly as complex as Visual Basic, it is still a robust language that can take some getting used to. Many excellent books have been written about VBScript, and you should strongly consider obtaining one if you plan on doing a great deal of VBScript coding.

Down-and-Dirty VBScript

As a Visual Basic programmer, you are undoubtedly used to writing code, testing it, and then compiling it into an executable file that can be distributed to others. Because VBScript is a scripting language rather than an application development language, it does not work the same way. You still write code and test it, but there is no compiler. Instead, VBScript code is embedded into a Web page and translated line by line when the Web page is viewed. In a way, it is similar to the interpreted BASIC programs of years ago.

The translation of VBScript code embedded into Web pages is a function of the Web browser. Currently, Microsoft Internet Explorer (version 3 and higher) is the most popular Web browser with built-in support for the VBScript scripting language. Unfortunately, Netscape's browser does not natively support VBScript. However, there are plug-ins available that will add this support to Netscape's product.

Although VBScript's not being pre-compiled might cause it to suffer in the way of speed, there is a very good reason for it not to be pre-compiled. By translating VBScript code on-the-fly, it can be used by any computing platform that has a VBScript virtual machine library. As Microsoft extends its reach with Internet Explorer and makes it available for more platforms, VBScript will also grow in its adaptability.

This section will teach you the basics of VBScript coding, presented from a Visual Basic programmer's point of view. It also shows you an example of an HTML document that uses VBScript code to add a certain amount of interactivity to an otherwise static Web page.

The Main Differences Between VB and VBScript

Unlike Visual Basic, VBScript is not used as a design environment; that is, you cannot lay out forms and user interfaces by dragging and dropping controls. Instead, VBScript is an after-the-fact language. The placement of ActiveX controls on a Web page, and how they got there, is not a function of VBScript. How the controls interact with the user and with each other is VBScript's true concern.

This interactivity is accomplished by setting properties of controls, performing procedures and methods, and manipulating VBScript's built-in objects and collections. Basically, it works the same way as Visual Basic after you have created an application's user interface. You then fill in the code that makes the program *dynamic*, able to interact with the actions of the user. VBScript's interface is a Web page, which might or might not contain ActiveX controls. VBScript is what makes the Web page dynamic. This is referred to as *client-side scripting*. VBScript can also be used with Active Server Pages (ASP) to provide *server-side scripting*.

Another thing you need to understand about VBScript is the fact that it has one and only one data type: the Variant. There are no strings, integers, or dates, only Variants. Of course, a Variant can hold the same kind of data as those other data types and can be of different subtypes (such as Date, String). But the point is, no matter what kind of data you are dealing with, you will have to use Variants to store it.

Because Variants are the only data type in VBScript, the use of user-defined types is excluded. Clearly, the handling of data is not one of VBScript's strong points. But that stands to reason. VBScript is a scripting language, after all, and it is not designed for extensive application development. Just try to keep that in mind when you're deciding what you want your VBScript-enabled Web page to do.

Objects in VBScript

The setting and reading of property values, calling of methods, and responding to events in VBScript is the same as it is in Visual Basic. However, the set of objects from which these properties, methods, and events originate will undoubtedly be different.

In part, the objects available for use depend on the application in which VBScript is being used. Internet Explorer has its own set of built-in objects, and your VBScript code can make use of them.

The Window object, referring to the Web browser window in which a Web page is displayed, can be utilized in several different ways by VBScript code. An OnLoad event is triggered for this object when a page is being loaded, and an OnUnload event fires just before a page is about to be unloaded. You can add code to these events to perform certain actions, just as you would use a Form's Load and Unload events in Visual Basic.

The Window object also includes a set of properties and methods that you can use in your VBScript code. One of the more popular methods is Navigate, which is used to direct the browser window to display a Web page at a given URL. For example, the following line of code will cause a browser window to display Microsoft's home page:

```
Window.Navigate("http://www.microsoft.com")
```

Other objects that originate from the Internet Explorer container application include Document, Frame, History, Link, Location, Navigator, and Script. There is also a Form object, but it's not the same as the Form object used in Visual Basic. IE's Form refers to a set of input fields, enclosed within <FORM> and </FORM> tags, that are embedded into a Web page.

VBScript has its own set of objects and collections that can be used from within script code. For the most part, VBScript's objects are used to read and write local files and perform other disk-related functions. These are the same objects as the File System Objects (FSO) that were introduced in the latest version of Visual Basic. There are two collections in the FSO model, Drives and Folders. Individual objects include Dictionary, Drive, Err, File, FileSystemObject, Folder, and TextStream. You can find a lot more about these objects and collections in the VBScript documentation that can be downloaded from Microsoft's Web site at http://www.microsoft.com/scripting/default.htm.

Though VBScript does use several built-in collection objects, it does not support the creation of user collections. You can, however, create your own arrays in VBScript.

Using Procedures in VBScript

Procedures are an important part of VBScript because all executable code must be contained within a procedure. This does not include constant and variable declarations, however, which can be either inside or outside a procedure.

Writing and using Sub and Function procedures in VBScript is basically the same as in Visual Basic. Procedures can be declared as Public or Private, but in VBScript a Public procedure can be used in any script module and Private procedures can only be used from within the same script in which they are declared.

Because VBScript only supports the `Variant` data type, you can't declare a `Function` as a certain data type using the `As Type` keyword. It's going to be a Variant, no matter what.

A Sample Script

Now that you know a little more about VBScript and how it differs from Visual Basic, let's take a look at a Web page that features VBScript code. This page also includes an embedded ActiveX `Label` control, and it uses the HTML `<IMG>` tag to display images. One of those images will be used by the VBScript code, as you'll see in just a moment.

LISTING 7.1. CH07-01.HTM—A SAMPLE HTML DOCUMENT THAT INCLUDES AN ACTIVEX CONTROL AND VBSCRIPT CODE.

```
<HTML>

<HEAD>

  <TITLE>VBScript Sample</TITLE>

  <SCRIPT LANGUAGE="VBScript">
  <!--
    Sub RevealSolution()
        Dim varSolution, varLoopCtr
        Dim varChar
        varSolution = "Vjg ocp ycu vqq ujqtv vq tgcej vjg " _
            & "dwvvqp hqt vjg hqwtvkgvj hnqqt -- dwv jg eqwnf " _
            & "tgcej vjg dwvvqp hqt vjg vygpvkgvj hnqqt!"
        lblAnswer.Caption = ""
        For varLoopCtr = 1 To Len(varSolution)
            varChar = Mid(varSolution, varLoopCtr, 1)
            If UCase(varChar) >= "A" And UCase(varChar) <= "Z" Then
                varChar = Chr(Asc(varChar) - 2)
            End If
            lblAnswer.Caption = lblAnswer.Caption + varChar
        Next
        lblAnswer.ForeColor = &H0
    End Sub
  -->
  </SCRIPT>

</HEAD>

<BODY>

<FONT FACE="Arial" SIZE=4>

<TABLE BORDER="0">
  <TR>
```

continues

LISTING 7.1.   CONTINUED

```html
<TD VALIGN="Top" WIDTH="100">
  <IMG SRC="QButton.gif" WIDTH=80 HEIGHT=100 BORDER=0
    ALT="Question Mark">
</TD>
<TD>
  <FONT SIZE=6><B><I>PUZZLE #1:</I></B></FONT>
  <BR>
  <B>A man lives on the top floor of a 40-story building.
  Every day, he rides the elevator down to the first floor
  and goes to work. However, when he comes home he takes the
  elevator up to the 20th floor, then climbs the stairs the
  rest of the way up to his home on the 40th floor. Why
  does he do that?`</B>
  <BR><BR>
  <FONT SIZE=2>
    <B>Click on <FONT COLOR="#0000FF">Solution</FONT>
    to reveal one possible answer.</B>
  </FONT>
</TD>
</TR>
<TR>
  <TD> </TD>
  <TD>
    <BR><BR>
    <IMG ID="imgSolution" SRC="ABanner.gif" WIDTH=350 HEIGHT=40
      ALT="Click here for solution" ONCLICK="RevealSolution">
    <BR><BR>
    <OBJECT ID="lblAnswer" WIDTH=467 HEIGHT=49
      CLASSID="CLSID:978C9E23-D4B0-11CE-BF2D-00AA003F40D0">
      <PARAM NAME="BackColor" VALUE="16777215">
      <PARAM NAME="ForeColor" VALUE="16777215">
      <PARAM NAME="VariousPropertyBits" VALUE="8388627">
      <PARAM NAME="Caption" VALUE="">
      <PARAM NAME="Size" VALUE="12347;1291">
      <PARAM NAME="FontName" VALUE="Arial">
      <PARAM NAME="FontEffects" VALUE="1073741825">
      <PARAM NAME="FontHeight" VALUE="240">
      <PARAM NAME="FontCharSet" VALUE="0">
      <PARAM NAME="FontPitchAndFamily" VALUE="2">
      <PARAM NAME="FontWeight" VALUE="700">
    </OBJECT>
  </TD>
</TR>
</TABLE>

</BODY>
</HTML>
```

When loaded into Internet Explorer, the Web page listed above looks like Figure 7.1. As you can see, it includes two graphic images, both of which were embedded using HTML's <IMG> tag. The ActiveX Label control is embedded onto the page using the <OBJECT> tag, and it has been assigned the ID of lblAnswer.

FIGURE 7.1.

The sample VBScript-enabled Web page. When the user clicks on the Solution button, the puzzle's solution is decoded and revealed.

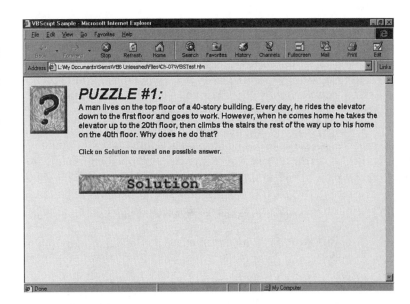

Take another look at the HTML code for the last embedded image, the Solution graphic:

```
<IMG ID="imgSolution" SRC="ABanner.gif" WIDTH=350 HEIGHT=40
 ALT="Click here for solution" ONCLICK="RevealSolution">
```

As you can see, the image has been assigned an ID name of imgSolution. An additional parameter, OnClick, is also being used. OnClick specifies the name of the procedure that will be executed when the user clicks on the image. In this case, the procedure name is RevealSolution.

It might come as a surprise to you that images that are embedded into a Web page using the <IMG> tag can generate events. Internet Explorer supports a number of events for embedded items such as images. Other parameters that can be used with the <IMG> tag include OnDblClick, OnLoad, OnMouseOver, and OnError, to name just a few. However, it should be noted that other Web browsers might not be quite so flexible.

By utilizing the OnClick parameter, an ordinary image can be turned into a makeshift button that can be used by VBScript. This frees up the overhead of having to embed an ActiveX Image control into the Web page.

So it's been established that the RevealSolution procedure will be performed when the user clicks on the Solution image. This procedure can be written in either VBScript or JScript, since Internet Explorer supports them both. Of course, we will be using VBScript. If you look at the beginning of the Web page, you'll see the following section of code:

```
<SCRIPT LANGUAGE="VBScript">
  <!--
    Sub RevealSolution()
        Dim varSolution, varLoopCtr
        Dim varChar
        varSolution = "Vjg ocp ycu vqq ujqtv vq tgcej vjg " _
            & "dwvvqp hqt vjg hqwtvkgvj hnqqt -- dwv jg eqwnf "
            & "tgcej vjg dwvvqp hqt vjg vygpvkgvj hnqqt!"
        lblAnswer.Caption = ""
        For varLoopCtr = 1 To Len(varSolution)
            varChar = Mid(varSolution, varLoopCtr, 1)
            If UCase(varChar) >= "A" And UCase(varChar) <= "Z" Then
                varChar = Chr(Asc(varChar) - 2)
            End If
            lblAnswer.Caption = lblAnswer.Caption + varChar
        Next
        lblAnswer.ForeColor = &H0
    End Sub
  -->
</SCRIPT>
```

The first thing you'll notice is that the entire procedure has been enclosed within the <SCRIPT> and </SCRIPT> tags. Appropriately enough, these tags indicate where script code begins and ends. You also notice that <!-- appears immediately after the <SCRIPT> tag, and --> appears immediately before the </SCRIPT> tag. These strange markings indicate the start and end of comments in HTML documents. Because some browsers do not support scripting, you should always enclose your VBScript code within these comment marks to avoid getting errors or other unexpected results during a page load.

The RevealSolution Sub procedure is pretty straightforward. It takes the encoded solution to the puzzle (assigned to the Variant varSolution) and decodes it character by character using a very simple decryption method. When it's done, it assigns the solution to the Caption property of the lblAnswer control, which was also embedded into the Web page. It also changes lblAnswer's ForeColor property to black so the text can be viewed against the white background of the page.

The entire section of VBScript code is contained within the HTML document's heading section, marked with the <HEAD> and </HEAD> tags. However, you can put VBScript anywhere within the document, including its body.

This simple example of a VBScript-enabled Web page is not exactly mind-blowing, that's for sure. But it does show how a Web page can become interactive with only a little effort. When the user clicks on the Solution graphic, the solution to the puzzle instantly appears. No additional data needs to be loaded, and the Web browser remains fixed on the current document instead of having to access another page. It's a neat trick, and that's just the tip of the iceberg. There are almost no limits to what can be accomplished with ActiveX components and VBScript.

More VBScript

By now, you should have a feel for how VBScript works. As a Visual Basic programmer, you are probably already able to start coding scripts or at least experimenting further with VBScript.

So you are more aware of what is available to you in VBScript, the next section details the nuts and bolts of the language: the functions, statements, and operators that are built into VBScript. Although this is not meant to be a complete reference guide to the language, it is a good start for those who want a better idea of what you can and cannot do with VBScript.

Operators

VBScript includes all of the same arithmetic operators that are found in Visual Basic, including addition (+), subtraction (-), multiplication (*), division (/), integer division (\), modulus (Mod), assignment (=), and negation (-). The concatenation operator (&) is also included. All of VB's logical operators (And, Or, Not, and Xor) and three comparison operators (Eqv, Imp, and Is) are also supported. The Like and AddressOf operators are not included in VBScript.

Functions

VBScript comes complete with a large number of built-in functions. Basically, what's available is a subset of the functions that are included in Visual Basic. Most are identical to their VB counterparts, but there are a few exceptions.

Table 7.1 lists the functions in VBScript that are the same in syntax and usage as the Visual Basic function of the same name. In case you are not familiar with a particular function, a brief description for each one has been provided. If you require more information on a function, consult your Visual Basic reference manual or obtain the full VBScript documentation from Microsoft's Web site at `http://www.microsoft.com/scripting/default.htm`.

TABLE 7.1. THE VBSCRIPT FUNCTIONS THAT ARE, FOR ALL INTENTS AND PURPOSES, IDENTICAL TO THE VISUAL BASIC FUNCTIONS OF THE SAME NAME.

Function Name	Description
Abs	Returns the absolute value of a number.
Array	Returns a variant containing an array that consists of items that were passed to the function as arguments.
Asc	Returns the ANSI character code value for the first character in the string that is passed to the function.
Atn	Returns the arctangent of a number.
Chr	Returns the ANSI character that corresponds to the numeric value that is passed to the function.
Cos	Returns a value representing the cosine of a given angle.
CreateObject	Creates a new object of a specified class and returns a reference to it.
Date	Returns the current system date.
DateAdd	Adds a specified amount of time to a given date and returns the new date value.
DateDiff	Calculates the number of specified time intervals (that is, months, days) between two dates and returns the result.
DatePart	Returns the specified part (that is, year, hour) of a given date expression.
DateSerial	Returns a date value that represents a given year, month, and day.
DateValue	Returns a date value for a given date expression.
Day	Returns a value from 1 to 31 that represents the day part of the date expression that is passed to the function.
Exp	Calculates and returns *e*, the base of natural logarithms, for a given number.
Filter	Returns an array that is a subset of another array and consists only of items that include a given search string. New in VB6.
Fix	Returns the integer portion of a number.
FormatCurrency	Returns a formatted currency when given a numeric value. New in VB6.
FormatDateTime	Returns a formatted date or time when given a valid date expression. New in VB6.
FormatNumber	Returns a formatted number when given an expression. New in VB6.
FormatPercent	Returns a formatted percentage when given an expression. New in VB6.
GetObject	Returns a reference to an existing Automation object.
Hex	Returns the hexidecimal representation of a given number.
Hour	Returns a value from 0 to 23 that represents the hour part of the time expression that is passed to the function.

Function Name	Description
InputBox	Displays a dialog box (with prompt) and waits for the user to enter text. The text that the user enters is returned by the function.
InStr	Searches for substrings within a string and returns the character position of the substring if it is found.
InStrRev	Works just like the InStr function, but starts looking for substrings from the end of the string rather than from the beginning. New in VB6.
Int	Returns the integer portion of a number.
Join	Creates a string that is composed of the elements of an array that is passed to the function, with an optional delimiter character between each element. New in VB6.
LBound	Returns the smallest possible subscript (lower bounds) for a specific dimension of an array.
LCase	Converts the alphabetic characters in a string to lowercase and returns the result.
Left	Returns a specified number of characters that are taken from the beginning (left side) of a string.
Len	Returns the number of characters in a given string or the number of bytes required for the storage of a given variable.
Log	Returns the natural logarithm of a given number.
LTrim	Removes any spaces from the beginning (left side) of a string and returns the modified string.
Mid	Returns a substring taken from another string when given the substring's starting-character position and length.
Minute	Returns a value from 0 to 59 that represents the minute part of the time expression that is passed to the function.
Month	Returns a value from 1 to 12 that represents the month part of the date expression that is passed to the function.
MonthName	Returns the long or short name of the month that corresponds to a given value. New in VB6.
MsgBox	Displays a message in a dialog box and waits for the user to click one or more buttons. The function returns a value that indicates which button was clicked.
Now	Returns a date value representing the current system time.
Oct	Returns the octal representation of a given number.
Replace	Performs a search and replace operation for a given substring within another string. New in VB6.

continues

TABLE 7.1. CONTINUED

Function Name	Description
RGB	Given values representing the red, green, and blue components of a color, returns an RGB color value.
Right	Returns a specified number of characters that are taken from the end (right side) of a string.
Rnd	Returns a randomly generated number between 0 and 1. Multiplying the result of the Rnd function by an integer number gives you a random value within a range (such as 5*RND() gives a random number from 0 to 5).
Round	Rounds a given number to a specified number of decimal places. New in VB6.
RTrim	Removes any spaces from the end (right side) of a string and returns the modified string.
Second	Returns a value from 0 to 59 that represents the second part of the time expression that is passed to the function.
Sgn	Returns a value that indicates the sign (positive, negative, or zero) of a given number.
Sin	Returns a value representing the sine of a given angle.
Space	Returns a string that contains a specified number of spaces.
Split	Separates a delimited string into individual substrings and returns those substrings as a one-dimensional array. New in VB6.
Sqr	Returns the square root of a given number.
StrComp	Compares two strings and returns the results.
String	Returns a string that consists of a character repeated a specified number of times.
StrReverse	Returns the characters of a given string in reverse order. New in VB6.
Tan	Returns a value representing the tangent of a given angle.
Time	Returns a time value representing the current system time.
TimeSerial	Returns a time value that represents a given hour, minute, and second.
TimeValue	Returns a time value for a given time expression.
Trim	Removes any spaces from the beginning and end of a string and returns the modified string.
TypeName	Returns the subtype of a given Variant variable.
UBound	Returns the largest possible subscript (upper bounds) for a specific dimension of an array.
UCase	Converts the alphabetic characters in a string to uppercase and returns the result.

Function Name	Description
VarType	Returns a numeric value that represents the subtype of a given variable.
Weekday	Returns a numeric value that indicates the day of the week for a given date expression.
WeekdayName	Returns the long or short name of the weekday that corresponds to a given value. New in VB6.
Year	Returns a value that represents the year part of the date expression that is passed to the function.

In some cases, VBScript is a few steps ahead of Visual Basic. The version of VBScript that is built into Internet Explorer 4 already included all of the functions that were just introduced in the new version of VB. These functions are listed in the table above and include Filter, FormatCurrency, FormatDateTime, FormatNumber, FormatPercent, InStrRev, Join, MonthName, Replace, Round, Split, StrReverse, and WeekdayName.

There are some functions in Visual Basic that have not been implemented in VBScript. Although they might be added to VBScript in the future, a fair number of VB functions are not included in the version of VBScript that was current as of this writing. Some, such as DoEvents, have been excluded because they don't fit in with the way scripts are processed. Others, such as the advanced financial functions DDB and FV, are probably not present due to their limited scope. Still others, which deal with disk and file operations, have been replaced with the object methods and properties discussed earlier in this chapter.

Keep in mind that the values that some VBScript functions return may be slightly different than those of the corresponding VB functions since VBScript uses only Variant data types. For example, the Atn function returns a value of type Double in Visual Basic. In VBScript, it returns a Variant value of subtype Double.

The rest of this section covers the handful of VBScript functions that differ from their Visual Basic counterparts. In most cases, the difference has to do with VBScript's use of Variants exclusively.

CBool, CByte, CCur, CDate, CDbl, CInt, CLng, CSng, and CStr

These functions, which in Visual Basic convert a value from one data type to another, are used slightly differently in VBScript. Because VBScript uses only Variants, these conversion functions convert values from one Variant subtype to another. The CSng function, for example, will convert a value to a Variant of subtype Single. Table 7.2 lists the conversion functions and provides a brief description of each.

TABLE 7.2. THE VARIABLE SUBTYPE CONVERSION FUNCTIONS IN VBSCRIPT.

Function Name	Converts a Value to a Variant of Subtype...
CBool	Boolean
CByte	Byte
CCur	Currency
CDate	Date
CDbl	Double
CInt	Integer
CLng	Long
CSng	Single
CStr	String

IsArray, IsDate, IsEmpty, IsNull, IsNumeric, and IsObject

These functions test a given variable to determine whether it is an array, a valid date expression, an un-initialized variable, a variable that contains no value at all, a numeric value, or a reference to an object. They work the same way they do in Visual Basic, but in VBScript they are applied to Variant subtypes rather than different distinct data types.

LoadPicture

VBScript's LoadPicture function works identically to the Visual Basic function of the same. It also loads a graphic image from a file. The graphic can then be assigned to the Picture property of an ActiveX control such as PictureBox or Image. The only difference is that VBScript's LoadPicture function can only be used on 32-bit platforms.

ScriptEngine, ScriptEngineBuildVersion, ScriptEngineMajorVersion, and ScriptEngineMinorVersion

These functions are intrinsic to scripting languages such as VBScript and obviously have no place in Visual Basic. They are used to determine the scripting engine that is in use and its version number.

The ScriptEngine function requires no arguments and returns a string value that indicates which scripting engine is in use. When used in VBScript, it will return a value of VBScript. Other possible values returned by this function include JScript for Microsoft's JScript (Java) scripting language and VBA for Visual Basic for Applications.

The ScriptEngineMajorVersion and ScriptEngineMinorVersion functions also require no arguments. They return numeric values indicating the version number of the DLL for the scripting language that is in use. Likewise, the ScriptEngineBuildVersion function returns the build version for the scripting language's DLL.

Statements

VBScript contains a limited subset of the statements that are available in Visual Basic. Although Visual Basic includes a total of about 75 different statements, VBScript only supports 21 of those.

Table 7.3 lists the statements that VBScript does support, along with a brief description of each. Some of these statements are slightly different in VBScript than they are in Visual Basic. These differences are discussed after the table.

7

ACTIVEX SCRIPTING WITH VBSCRIPT

TABLE 7.3. THE STATEMENTS SUPPORTED BY VBSCRIPT.

Statement	Description
Call	Executes a procedure, such as a Sub or Function
Const	Declares a constant value
Dim	Declares one or more variables
Do...Loop	Executes a block of statements while a condition is True or until the condition becomes True
Erase	Reinitializes an array and frees up the system resources it was using
Exit	Exits a procedure, For loop, or Do loop
For...Next	Executes a block of statements a specified number of times
For Each...Next	Executes a block of statements for each element in an array or collection
Function	Declares the name and arguments for a Function procedure
If...Then...Else	Executes one or more statements, depending on the evaluation results of one or more expressions
On Error	Specifies what should happen when an error condition arises
Option Explicit	Specifies that all variables must be declared before being used
Private	Declares one or more variables as being Private in scope
Public	Declares one or more variables as being Public in scope
Randomize	Initializes the random-number generator
ReDim	Redimensions array variables
Rem	Precedes program comments
Select Case	Evaluates an expression and executes the block of statements that corresponds to the value of the expression

continues

Table 7.3. CONTINUED

Statement	Description
Set	Assigns an object reference to a given property or variable
Sub	Declares the name and arguments for a Sub procedure
While...Wend	Executes a block of statements while a condition remains True

In Visual Basic, some of the statements listed above include an As Type keyword in their syntax so a data type can be specified. Because VBScript only deals in one data type (Variant), the As Type keyword has been omitted in all cases. The statements that are affected by this syntax change are Const, Dim, and Function.

VBScript procedures cannot maintain the values of their variables between calls, so the optional Static keyword has been removed from the Function and Sub statements. Also, the Friend keyword is not supported in Function and Sub statements.

Although the Call statement can execute local procedures, it cannot be used to call external routines, such as those in DLL files. VBScript does not support external procedures, and there is no Declare statement that can be used to define them.

The Dim, Private, and Public statements do not include the WithEvents keyword in their syntax. VBScript does not support class modules, so the WithEvents keyword cannot be used.

The optional As New keyword has also been omitted from the Private and Public statements' syntax. Likewise, the New keyword has been removed from the Set statement's syntax.

The On Error statement supports only one syntax, On Error Resume Next. If this statement is not used, then any runtime error is fatal and execution of the script will stop. VBScript cannot utilize error handling routines because the On Error Goto syntax is not supported.

Summary

Visual Basic programmers are lucky in that Microsoft has chosen to create a scripting language that is based on a language they already know. VBScript has been implemented in Internet Explorer to add interactivity to Web pages, and it is likely to be used in a number of other applications as well.

Although VBScript includes many of the elements that are used in Visual Basic, there are a number of differences. This chapter was meant to provide VB programmers with the information they need to start writing VBScript code.

Data Consumers and Data Sources

by Rob Thayer

IN THIS CHAPTER

- Creating a Data Source   176
- Creating a Data Consumer   192

Introduction to Data Sources and Data Consumers

VB6 enables you to create ActiveX controls that act as data consumers and data sources. A data consumer can be bound to a data source. For example, a TextBox control can be bound to a Data control by setting its DataSource and DataField properties. When you create ActiveX data consumer controls, they can act the same way.

A data source control provides an interface through which a database can be accessed. The ADO Data control, for example, acts as a data source and lets you move through the records in a recordset using the buttons that are included on the control. The database and recordset to be used are specified by the control's ConnectionString and RecordSource properties. You can bind one or more controls to the ADO Data control, and have their contents automatically updated as the record number in the ADO Data control's recordset is changed.

This chapter will show you how you can create your own data consumers and data sources. You'll build a simple data source control that you can compile and use in your own applications in lieu of the ADO Data control.

> **NOTE**
>
> In VB6, you can also build data source components as ActiveX DLLs and ActiveX EXEs using classes. This chapter will not discuss those types of data sources.

Creating a Data Source

As you'll soon see, creating an ActiveX control that acts as a data source is easy to do. However, you must have an understanding of how to create ActiveX controls in general before attempting to follow through with the example control presented here. It is strongly suggested that you read Chapter 5, "Creating ActiveX Controls," before continuing with this chapter.

The control that is built in this section looks similar to the standard ADO Data control, though it is used a little bit differently. However, instead of having a text area that shows the name of the control and two buttons that enable you to move through records one by one, a horizontal scroll bar is used. Although the scroll bar's left and right buttons can be used to move to the previous or next record in a recordset, the scroll bar can be moved to instantly change the current position of the recordset. Two command buttons (like the ones used with the ADO Data control) are also included so the user can instantly move to the first or last record. This control will be called ScrollData (and saved as "ScrData"), for "Scrolling Data Control."

The interface for the control will be, for the sake of brevity, very simple. It will consist of five properties, three methods, and no events. Table 8.1 lists the properties and methods and provides a brief description for each one.

TABLE 8.1. THE PROPERTIES AND METHODS FOR THE SCROLLDATA CONTROL.

Name	Property/Method	Description
BOFAction	Property	Specifies what to do when a BOF (Beginning of File) condition occurs
ConnectionString	Property	The connection string for connecting to a database
EOFAction	Property	Specifies what to do when an EOF (End of File) condition occurs
LargeChange	Property	The number of records to skip when the scroll bar's track is clicked
RecordSource	Property	The name of the record source (such as a table name) for the database connection
MoveFirst	Method	Moves to the first record in the recordset
MoveLast	Method	Moves to the last record in the recordset
MoveToRecord	Method	Moves to a specified record number in the recordset

The ConnectionString and RecordSource properties are strings, and the BOFAction and EOFAction properties use an enumeration; so, only certain values can be assigned to them via the control's Properties window. The LargeChange property is passed directly to the scroll bar and is an Integer value.

Under normal circumstances, you would probably want to increase the flexibility of your control by adding more properties, methods, and events to its interface. Although it is deliberately simple in its design, the sample can easily act as a starting platform for a much more complex control. However, keep in mind that simplicity can often be a virtue when creating controls, especially data conrols.

> **NOTE**
>
> Before starting on this project, you must make sure that a reference to the ADO Object Library has been established. On VB's Project menu, select the References option. On the list of available references, look to see if the box for the Microsoft ActiveX Data Objects 2.0 Library is checked. If it's not already checked, check it.

Building the Control's User Interface

Like just about any other project, the first thing to do when creating the `DataScroll` control is to build its user interface. This control will have a rather simple interface, consisting of only a horizontal scroll bar and a pair of command buttons. The positions of the elements are not very important because everything will be automatically arranged in the control's `Resize` event. The sizes of some of the elements, however, are important because they will be used to establish the default size of the control.

To build the control's user interface, use Table 8.2 and Figure 8.1 as a guide for adding the constituent controls to the `UserControl` object and for changing their properties. The `FIRST.BMP` and `LAST.BMP` files that are used with the two `CommandButton` controls can be found in VB's `SAMPLES\AXDATA` subdirectory.

TABLE 8.2. THE PROPERTIES FOR THE `UserControl` AND ITS CONSTITUENT CONTROLS, USED FOR BUILDING THE `DataScroll` CONTROL'S INTERFACE.

Control Type	Property	Value
UserControl	Name	ScrollData
	DataSourceBehavior	1 - vbDataSource
	Height	3600
	Width	4110
CommandButton	Name	cmdFirst
	AutoSize	True
	Caption	(Nothing)
	Left	240
	Picture	FIRST.BMP
	Style	1 - Graphical
	Top	1080
HScrollBar	Name	hsbRecScroll
	Height	255
	LargeChange	10

Control Type	Property	Value
	Left	600
	Min	1
	Top	1080
	Value	1
	Width	3135
CommandButton	Name	cmdLast
	AutoSize	True
	Caption	(Nothing)
	Left	3840
	Picture	LAST.BMP
	Style	1 - Graphical
	Top	1080

FIGURE 8.1.
The user interface for the ScrollData *control.*

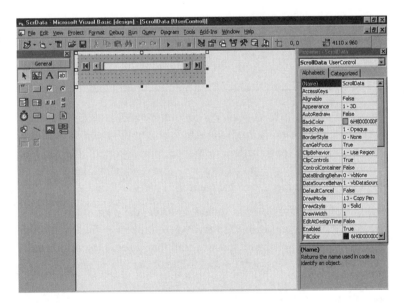

One property that needs to be discussed further is the DataSourceBehavior property of the UserControl object. DataSourceBehavior is new to VB6. Setting this property to vbDataSource is one of the keys to creating data source controls. Doing so adds a

GetDataMember event to the UserControl object, enabling the control to interact with a database. You'll see how the GetDataMember event is used later in this chapter.

As stated previously, the exact placement of the constituent controls on the UserControl object will be automatically arranged in the UserControl's Resize event. Add the code for that event procedure, as shown in Listing 8.1.

LISTING 8.1. CH08-01.TXT—THE UserControl_Resize EVENT ARRANGES THE PLACE-MENT OF THE CONSTITUENT CONTROLS WITHIN THE UserControl OBJECT.

```
Private Sub UserControl_Resize()

' Move and resize the consituent controls of the
' user control.
cmdFirst.Move 0, 15
hsbRecScroll.Move cmdFirst.Width, 0, _
    UserControl.Width - cmdFirst.Width - cmdLast.Width, _
    cmdFirst.Height + 15
cmdLast.Move cmdFirst.Width + hsbRecScroll.Width, 15

' Resize the user control.
UserControl.Height = cmdFirst.Height + 15
UserControl.Width = cmdFirst.Width _
    + hsbRecScroll.Width + cmdLast.Width

End Sub
```

The Resize event is fired when the control initializes, as well as when the user resizes the control. Although the height of the control always remains the same (primarily so the images in the command buttons do not become distorted), the width of the control is flexible. The two command buttons will always remain a fixed size, but the scroll bar's size changes with the size of the control.

Before going any further, you should now save the control to disk. But first, display the Project Properties dialog box (select Project Properties from VB's Project menu) and change the Project Name to ScrData and the Project Description to Scrolling Data Control. Then save the user control as ScrollData.ctl and the project as ScrData.vbp.

Adding Properties

The next step towards creating the ScrollData control is to add its properties. Before you can do that, however, you need to declare some variables that will hold the property values. It's also a good idea to set up some constants that will be used to store the default values for the properties. The code in Listing 8.2 should be added to the UserControl's General Declarations section.

LISTING 8.2. CH08-02.TXT—PROPERTY VARIABLE AND DEFAULT VALUE DECLARATIONS (AMONG OTHER THINGS) THAT SHOULD BE ADDED TO THE CONTROL'S GENERAL DECLARATIONS SECTION.

```
' Enumeration values for the BOFAction property.
Public Enum sdcBOFActionConstants
    sdcMoveFirst = 0
    sdcStayAtBOF
End Enum

' Enumeration values for the EOFAction property.
Public Enum sdcEOFActionConstants
    sdcMoveLast = 0
    sdcStayAtEOF
    sdcAddNewRecord
End Enum

' Declare ADO variables (recordset and connection
' objects).
Private cnMain As ADODB.Connection
Private WithEvents rsMain As ADODB.RecordSet

' Property defaults.
Const DefaultBOFAction = sdcBOFActionConstants.sdcMoveFirst
Const DefaultEOFAction = sdcEOFActionConstants.sdcMoveLast
Const DefaultConnectionString = ""
Const DefaultLargeChange = 10
Const DefaultRecordSource = ""

' Property variables.
Private msdcBOFAction As sdcBOFActionConstants
Private msdcEOFAction As sdcEOFActionConstants
Private mstrConnectionString As String
Private mstrRecordSource As String
```

8

DATA CONSUMERS
AND DATA
SOURCES

Also included in the code in Listing 8.2 are two enumerations that are used with the BOFAction and EOFAction properties. These enumerations enable the user to choose from a list of possible values for the properties, which reduces the chance that an invalid value will be assigned. The code also includes declarations for the ADO Connection and Recordset objects that will be used throughout the rest of the control project.

Each property in the control's interface uses a set of Property Let and Property Get procedures. To save some typing, you can have VB add these procedures for you by selecting the Add Procedure option from VB's Tools menu. When the dialog box appears, type the name of the property into the Name text box and make sure that Property is selected as the Type and Public is selected as the Scope. Then click on the OK button to add the procedures.

Whether you use the Add Procedure shortcut or you type in the property procedures yourself, pay close attention to the declare statements for the procedures. It's important that you use the correct names for the arguments and the correct data types.

Add the property procedures shown in Listing 8.3 to the control project.

LISTING 8.3. CH08-03.TXT—THE Property Let AND Property Get PROCEDURES ARE USED TO IMPLEMENT THE CONTROL'S PROPERTIES.

```
Public Property Get BOFAction() As sdcBOFActionConstants

' Return the value of the BOFAction property.
BOFAction = msdcBOFAction

End Property


Public Property Let BOFAction(ByVal NewValue As sdcBOFActionConstants)

' Store the new value for the BOFAction property.
msdcBOFAction = NewValue
UserControl.PropertyChanged "BOFAction"

End Property


Public Property Get EOFAction() As sdcEOFActionConstants

' Return the value of the EOFAction property.
EOFAction = msdcEOFAction

End Property


Public Property Let EOFAction(ByVal NewValue As sdcEOFActionConstants)

' Store the new value for the EOFAction property.
msdcEOFAction = NewValue
UserControl.PropertyChanged "EOFAction"

End Property


Public Property Get LargeChange() As Integer

' Return the value of the LargeChange property,
' which is the same as the hsbRecScroll control's
' LargeChange property.
LargeChange = hsbRecScroll.LargeChange
```

```
End Property


Public Property Let LargeChange(ByVal NewValue As Integer)

' Store the new value for the LargeChange property
' directly into the hsbRecScroll control's
' LargeChange property.
hsbRecScroll.LargeChange = NewValue
UserControl.PropertyChanged "LargeChange"

End Property


Public Property Get ConnectionString() As String

' Return the value of the ConnectionString property.
ConnectionString = mstrConnectionString

End Property


Public Property Let ConnectionString(ByVal NewValue As String)

' Store the new value for the ConnectionString
' property. Any extra spaces at the start or end of
' the string are trimmed.
mstrConnectionString = Trim$(NewValue)
UserControl.PropertyChanged "ConnectionString"

End Property


Public Property Get RecordSource() As String

' Return the value of the RecordSource property.
RecordSource = mstrRecordSource

End Property


Public Property Let RecordSource(ByVal NewValue As String)

' Store the new value for the RecordSource property.
' Any extra spaces at the start or end of the string
' are trimmed.
mstrRecordSource = Trim$(NewValue)
UserControl.PropertyChanged "RecordSource"

End Property
```

One other property procedure is required, but it's only a `Property Get` procedure without a corresponding `Property Let`. This is because the property is read-only. It returns the name of the `Recordset` object that is being used by the control. This object was declared in the General Declarations section and is called `rsMain`. Add the following `Property Get` procedure to the project:

LISTING 8.4. CH08-04.TXT—THE `Property Get` PROCEDURE RETURNS THE RECORDSET USED BY THE CONTROL.

```
Public Property Get RecordSet() As ADODB.RecordSet

' Return a reference to the RecordSet object that
' is used by the control.
Set RecordSet = rsMain

End Property
```

Also required for implementing properties are the `InitProperties`, `ReadProperties`, and `WriteProperties` event procedures. The `InitProperties` procedure initializes the property values using the default constants set up in the General Declarations section, and is triggered when the control is created. The `ReadProperties` and `WriteProperties` events read and write the property values from and to the property bag. Listing 8.5 contains the code for these three procedures.

LISTING 8.5. CH08-05.TXT—THE `InitProperties`, `ReadProperties`, AND `WriteProperties` EVENT PROCEDURES

```
Private Sub UserControl_InitProperties()

' Set the property values to their defaults.
msdcBOFAction = DefaultBOFAction
msdcEOFAction = DefaultEOFAction
mstrConnectionString = DefaultConnectionString
mstrRecordSource = DefaultRecordSource

' Set the hsbRecScroll.LargeChange property to
' the default value.
hsbRecScroll.LargeChange = DefaultLargeChange

End Sub


Private Sub UserControl_ReadProperties(PropBag As PropertyBag)

' Read the property values from the property bag.
msdcBOFAction = PropBag.ReadProperty("BOFAction", _
```

```
        DefaultBOFAction)
msdcEOFAction = PropBag.ReadProperty("EOFAction", _
    DefaultEOFAction)
mstrConnectionString = PropBag.ReadProperty("ConnectionString", _
    DefaultConnectionString)
mstrRecordSource = PropBag.ReadProperty("RecordSource", _
    DefaultRecordSource)
hsbRecScroll.LargeChange = PropBag.ReadProperty("LargeChange", _
    DefaultLargeChange)

End Sub


Private Sub UserControl_WriteProperties(PropBag As PropertyBag)

' Write the property values to the property bag.
Call PropBag.WriteProperty("BOFAction", _
    msdcBOFAction, DefaultBOFAction)
Call PropBag.WriteProperty("EOFAction", _
    msdcEOFAction, DefaultEOFAction)
Call PropBag.WriteProperty("ConnectionString", _
    mstrConnectionString, DefaultConnectionString)
Call PropBag.WriteProperty("RecordSource", _
    mstrRecordSource, DefaultRecordSource)
Call PropBag.WriteProperty("LargeChange", _
    hsbRecScroll.LargeChange, DefaultLargeChange)

End Sub
```

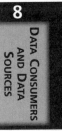

Note that in the `InitProperties` event, the default value of the `LargeChange` property is not stored in a property value. Instead, it's passed directly to the `hsbRecScroll` control.

Trying Out the Control

Now that you have the properties for the control all set up, you can give it a try to see how it looks on a form. To do this, you'll need to add a new project to your VB session. On VB's File menu, select the Add Project option. When the dialog box appears, choose the Standard EXE project and click on the OK button. This will add a standard project (`Project2`) to the project group.

In the Project Explorer window, right-click on `Project2` and select the Set as Start Up option from the pop-up menu. This will set that project as the one that executes when the Run button is clicked or the F5 key is pressed.

Save all of the projects by selecting Save Project Group from the File menu. For `Project2`, save the form as `ScrDataTest.frm`, and save the project as `ScrDataTest.vbp`. Save the project group as `ScrDataTest.vbg`.

Switch to Project2's form and add a ScrData control—its icon should be the last one in the Toolbox. Remember that before you can switch to Project2, you must close the designer window for the control project first. Otherwise, the control will be inaccessible.

If the Resize event works properly, you should see an instance of the ScrData control that looks like the one in Figure 8.2. You can try resizing the control to see how it affects the way the control is displayed.

FIGURE 8.2.

An instance of the ScrData *control. Note that the control's various components are arranged automatically, courtesy of the* Resize *event.*

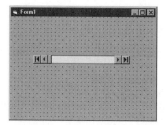

Implementing Database Functionality

After the control has been tried out and it's been established that the Resize event is working properly, it's time to go back to the control project and add some code that will let the control do what its supposed to do. For the ScrData control, that means providing database functionality. And for UserControl objects, a large part of that functionality takes place in the GetDataMember event that was mentioned at the start of the project. Listing 8.6 shows the code for the ScrData control's GetDataMember event.

LISTING 8.6. CH08-06.TXT—THE GetDataMember EVENT IS A BIG PART OF IMPLEMENTING DATABASE FUNCTIONALITY IN A CONTROL.

```
Private Sub UserControl_GetDataMember(DataMember As String, _
    Data As Object)

    On Error GoTo ErrorHandler

    If (cnMain Is Nothing) Or (rsMain Is Nothing) Then
        ' If no ConnectionString has been specified,
        ' show an error and exit this procedure.
        If mstrConnectionString = "" Then
            MsgBox "Please specify a value for the " _
                & "ConnectionString property.", _
                vbInformation, Ambient.DisplayName
            Exit Sub
        End If
        ' If no RecordSource has been specified, show
        ' an error and exit this procedure.
```

```
        If mstrRecordSource = "" Then
            MsgBox "Please specify a value for the " _
                & "RecordSource property.", _
                vbInformation, Ambient.DisplayName
            Exit Sub
        End If
        ' Set up the ADO connection using the value
        ' specified for the ConnectionString property.
        Set cnMain = New ADODB.Connection
        cnMain.ConnectionString = mstrConnectionString
        cnMain.Open
        ' Set up the ADO recordset using the value
        ' specified for the RecordSource property.
        Set rsMain = New ADODB.RecordSet
        rsMain.Open mstrRecordSource, cnMain, _
            adOpenKeyset, adLockPessimistic
        rsMain.MoveFirst
        ' Set the upper value limit of the hsbRecScroll
        ' control to the number of records in the
        ' recordset (plus one for additions).
        hsbRecScroll.Max = rsMain.RecordCount + 1
    Else
        Set cnMain = Nothing
        Set rsMain = Nothing
    End If

    ' Return the recordset in the Data argument.
    Set Data = rsMain

    Exit Sub

ErrorHandler:
    ' An error has occurred, so display the error
    ' and exit the procedure.
    MsgBox "Error: " & CStr(Err.Number) _
        & vbCrLf & Err.Description, vbOKOnly, _
        Ambient.DisplayName

End Sub
```

The first thing to note about this procedure is that a crude error handler has been added to it. You never know what kinds of errors you'll run into when trying to establish a database connection, so it's important that some type of error handler is implemented in this procedure.

Before it does anything else, the code in this procedure checks to see if the Connection and Recordset objects (cnMain and rsMain) have been assigned, and that a string value has been assigned to the ConnectionString and RecordSource properties. If any of these conditions are not met, an error message is displayed and the procedure ends.

8

DATA CONSUMERS
AND DATA
SOURCES

If everything looks okay, a connection is attempted to the database using the variable for the ConnectionString property (mstrConnectionString). If no error results, the RecordSet is opened using the variable for the RecordSource property (mstrRecordSource). If that goes through without a hitch, the hsbRecScroll constituent control's Max property is set to the total number of records in the RecordSet.

Before ending, a reference to the Recordset (rsMain) is assigned to the procedure's Data argument. You could give the control the ability to specify the DataMember that it uses by examining the DataMember argument that is also passed to this event. You should implement a DataMember property when you are designing the control to work with the Data Environment, which can contain multiple data members for the same database connection.

> **NOTE**
>
> Even though this control uses ADO as its database access method, you could just as easily use DAO or RDO as the access method.

The next section of code to be added to the control is for the hsbRecScroll_Change event. This event is triggered whenever the scrollbar's value changes. We want to act on that to change the current record in the recordset. Add the code in Listing 8.7 to the control.

LISTING 8.7.   CH08-07.TXT—THE hsbRecScroll_Change EVENT IS USED TO INSTANTLY UPDATE THE CURRENT RECORD IN THE RECORDSET.

```
Private Sub hsbRecScroll_Change()

' If rsMain has not been assigned, do nothing.
If Not (rsMain Is Nothing) Then
    ' Move to the record number indicated by the
    ' scroll bar.
    rsMain.AbsolutePosition = hsbRecScroll.Value
    ' Check for a BOF condition...
    If rsMain.BOF Then
        ' The recordset is at BOF. The action to take
        ' is specified by the BOFAction property.
        Select Case msdcBOFAction
            Case sdcBOFActionConstants.sdcMoveFirst
                rsMain.MoveFirst
            Case Else
                Exit Sub
        End Select
```

```
          Exit Sub
      End If
      ' Check for an EOF condition...
      If rsMain.EOF Then
          ' The recordset is at EOF. The action to take
          ' is specified by the EOFAction property.
          Select Case msdcEOFAction
              Case sdcEOFActionConstants.sdcMoveLast
                  rsMain.MoveLast
              Case sdcEOFActionConstants.sdcAddNewRecord
                  ' Add a new record, and update the
                  ' scroll bar's Max and Value
                  ' properties.
                  rsMain.AddNew
                  hsbRecScroll.Max = rsMain.RecordCount + 1
                  hsbRecScroll.Value = rsMain.RecordCount + 1
              Case Else
                  Exit Sub
          End Select
          Exit Sub
      End If
  End If
End If

End Sub
```

This procedure is actually quite simple. First, it checks to see if a reference has been assigned to the rsMain object. If no reference has been assigned, that essentially means that no database connection has been established, so there's no point in trying to change position in the Recordset.

If rsMain does contain a Recordset reference, the AbsolutePosition property of the rsMain object is changed to the Value of the scrollbar. AbsolutePosition changes the current record to the given logical record number. This property provides an easy way of updating the Recordset position using the scrollbar.

After a new position has been established, the BOF and EOF conditions are tested. Depending on the values specified for the control's BOFAction and EOFAction properties, certain actions are performed. For example, when an EOF condition arises and the EOFAction property has been set to sdcAddNewRecord, the AddNew method is called for rsMain and a new record is added to the end of the Recordset. The Max and Value properties for the scrollbar are updated, because the range of record numbers has been increased by one.

Now that changes in the scroll bar's value have been taken care of, the code for the First and Last buttons needs to be added. The Click events for those command buttons are short and sweet, simply calling the MoveFirst or MoveLast methods of the rsMain object after establishing that a database connection has been made. The value of the scroll bar is also updated to reflect the new record number. Listing 8.8 shows the code for the cmdFirst_Click and cmdLast_Click events.

LISTING 8.8. CH08-08.TXT—THE cmdFirst_Click AND cmdLast_Click EVENTS SIMPLY MOVE TO THE FIRST OR LAST RECORDS IN THE RECORDSET.

```
Private Sub cmdFirst_Click()

' If rsMain has been assigned, move to the first
' record in the recordset and update the scroll
' bar's position.
If Not (rsMain Is Nothing) Then
    rsMain.MoveFirst
    hsbRecScroll.Value = 1
End If

End Sub


Private Sub cmdLast_Click()

' If rsMain has been assigned, move to the last
' record in the recordset and update the scroll
' bar's position.
If Not (rsMain Is Nothing) Then
    rsMain.MoveLast
    hsbRecScroll.Value = hsbRecScroll.Max
End If

End Sub
```

The control is almost finished. The last thing to do is add the methods that have been specified for the control's interface.

Adding Methods

There are three methods in the control's interface: MoveFirst, MoveLast, and MoveToRecord. These methods are nothing more than public procedures, and the code needed to implement them is similar to the code recently added to react to the events of the scrollbar and the two command buttons. Add the code in Listing 8.9 to the control.

LISTING 8.9. CH08-09.TXT—THIS CODE IMPLEMENTS THE CONTROL'S MoveFirst, MoveLast, AND MoveToRecord METHODS.

```
Public Sub MoveFirst()

' If rsMain has been assigned, move to the first
' record in the recordset and update the scroll
' bar's position.
If Not (rsMain Is Nothing) Then
    rsMain.MoveFirst
    hsbRecScroll.Value = 1
End If

End Sub


Public Sub MoveLast()

' If rsMain has been assigned, move to the last
' record in the recordset and update the scroll
' bar's position.
If Not (rsMain Is Nothing) Then
    rsMain.MoveLast
    hsbRecScroll.Value = hsbRecScroll.Max
End If

End Sub


Public Sub MoveToRecord(RecNumber As Long)

' If rsMain has been assigned, move to the given
' record number in the recordset, but only if it
' is within the valid range.
If Not (rsMain Is Nothing) Then
    If RecNumber >= 1 And RecNumber <= rsMain.RecordCount Then
        rsMain.AbsolutePosition = RecNumber
    End If
End If

End Sub
```

8

DATA CONSUMERS
AND DATA
SOURCES

With the addition of these three procedures, the control is complete. Make sure you save it before trying it out again.

The Finished Product

To try out the control, switch back to Project2. Delete the existing instance of the control, then create a new instance. Add a text box to the form.

For the ScrData control, change the ConnectionString and RecordSource properties to something suitable. To establish a connection to the BIBLIO.MDB database, for example, you could use the ConnectionString "Provider=Microsoft.Jet.OLEDB.3.51;Data Source=C:\VStudio98\VB98\Biblio.mdb", changing the path to the BIBLIO.MDB file to whatever it happens to be on your system. You could then change the RecordSource property to Publishers or the name of any other table in the database.

For the text box, change its DataSource property to the name of the ScrData control (ScrollData1). Then change its DataField property to the name of the field to which you want to bind the text box.

Figure 8.3 shows the control in action. Here, the ScrData control is being used to quickly move through the records in the Biblio database's Publishers table.

FIGURE 8.3.

The ScrData *control in action.*

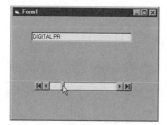

After you've verified that the ScrData control works, you can expand on it and compile it into an .OCX file. Then you can use it again and again in your own projects.

Creating a Data Consumer

Creating an ActiveX control that acts as a data consumer is as easy as creating a data source. Although this section will not present a sample data consumer control, it will tell you what you need to know to create your own data consumers.

To begin with, you must change the UserControl object's DataBindingBehavior property. This can be set to either vbNone, vbSimpleBound, or vbComplexBound. A simple bound control is bound to a single data field in the specified data source. A complex bound control, on the other hand, is bound to an entire row of data in the specified data source.

To specify a control property as bindable, use the Procedure Attributes option on VB's Tools menu (you must be in the control's code window for this option to be enabled). When the Procedure Attributes dialog box appears, click on the Advanced button. Specify the name of the property to be bound in the Name list box, and check the

Property is Data Bound box. There are then four other boxes you can check:

> Property binds to `DataField`—If selected, the property is bound to the field specified in the `DataField` property.
>
> Show in `DataBindings` collection at design time—If selected, the property appears in the control's Bindings dialog box at design time.
>
> Property will call `CanPropertyChange` before changing—If selected, the property must always call the `CanPropertyChange` method and check its return value to determine whether or not a property *can* change before its value actually is changed.
>
> Update immediate—If selected, the bound property will transmit changes immediately to the data source.

When creating a simple bound data consumer, set the `DataBindingBehavior` property to `vbSimpleBound`. You can then create a read-only property that contains the value of the bound field. On the Procedures Attribute dialog box, select that property and check the Property Binds to `DataField` box.

Creating an ActiveX control that acts as a data consumer is not difficult, but it takes some trial and error to get it right. You also need to have a solid understanding of how ActiveX controls are created.

Summary

The latest version of Visual Basic enables you to design ActiveX controls that act as data sources and data consumers. You can create and use these controls to provide unique ways of accessing and displaying information from databases in your programs.

This chapter showed you the basics of creating data sources and consumers. It also provided you with a step-by-step tutorial that illustrated how to create a data source, resulting in a simple control that can be used to access databases via the ADO access method.

Apartment Model Threading

by John D. Conley III

IN THIS CHAPTER

- **Introduction to Multithreaded Development** *196*

- **Multithreaded Development in Visual Basic 6** *198*

- **Thread Safety** *203*

- **Implementing Multithreaded Systems** *205*

- **Instantiating Externally Creatable Classes** *207*

- **Issues in Recording Apartment Events** *208*

- **Tips on Testing and Debugging Multithreaded Systems** *208*

- **Multithreading Single-Use Objects** *210*

- **The Meaning of SingleUse** *211*

Introduction to Multithreaded Development

For most Visual Basic developers, the issue of creating multiple threads and planning for concurrency and multitasking has not been even remotely material. Quite obviously, when you're working with only one processor in your computer, there is little motivation for planning for more than one application being processed by the machine. However, the rise of distributed computing over the past several years has finally caught up to the Visual Basic community because of the dominance of ActiveX/COM+ in Microsoft-based component development. Before you learn about creating multithreaded components in Visual Basic, it is important to cover the basics first. You should understand "basics," to mean the coverage of threads and concurrency.

THE BASICS OF WINDOWS ARCHITECTURE

In the Win32 architecture, a thread is the smallest unit of execution scheduled by Win32. A Win32 thread contains its own stack, each CPU register's current state, and a listing the Windows system scheduler's execution list. For each process that needs one or more threads, every one of its threads must share the resources allocated for that process.

A process is, for instance, an application you create for a user. An application (or process) can only execute in memory when the system scheduler delegates execution control to on of its threads. In essence, the system scheduler is an application execution controller in that it determines when a prioritized thread can run on behalf of a process. The higher the priority, the more often a thread will get execution control. Each thread operates independent of another, unless they share common resources, which then requires the use of semaphores for inter-thread communication.

Multithreaded development is a software development concept that enables your applications do concurrent processing (or close to concurrent) as opposed to only serial processing. Although each thread you create carries some overhead, particularly with the apartment-model threading paradigm of ActiveX/COM+, threads can help boost performance, both actual and perceived (perceived via the graphical user interface).

Defining a Thread

A thread is a set of one or more instructions given by a task (such as an application) to a central processing unit (CPU). In a sense, every time you run an application, you can think of that application instance running in memory as a thread. In single-processor machines, only one thread can be processed at one time. When more than one application needs to give instructions to the CPU for processing, the CPU must go into multitasking mode, meaning that although the client applications essentially leave several lists of instructions for the CPU to process, the CPU only accommodates one list of instructions at a time.

The necessity of implementing multiple threads in code is crucial. For instance, consider an application that needs to query every computer on which a user is currently logged. Instead of having the requesting client handle the details, it can delegate this task to some server on which a component resides that can create a thread for communicating with each client computer. Thus, the task is offloaded to a server without the client application having to take up time to contact each client serially and wait for a response from each other client. This kind of multithreading system could easily be transported to the Internet with ActiveX components.

In a distributed computing system, there are more processors that can accommodate more specialized requests, meaning the creation of multiple threads can become more specialized to handle certain requests. For instance, in a banking organization, you might have a machine that is dedicated to processing client requests for check payments, another for getting a credit report, and another for printing out reports for auditing purposes. In a telecommunications environment, you would have a machine dedicated to processing a certain telephone network service between two callers, and another to figure out the best route between the same two callers. Because of the potentially high volume of transactions in each example, each specialist machine would be required to manage multiple threads of execution.

Having multiple threads is equivalent to having more than one lane on a major highway; you expect that out of a certain population, a certain percentage of that population will travel the same road. If there were more drivers on a road than the number of lanes can handle, you'd have a traffic jam, and a lot of angry people. The same can happen with applications that don't plan for multiple requests for the same service.

9

APARTMENT
MODEL
THREADING

Understanding Concurrency

In basic terms, concurrency is the existence of more than one request for the same object at the same time. It is equivalent to having two runners reaching the finish line at the same time. In the database world, concurrency is realized when two users request write-access to the same record at the same time. In the object-oriented development world, concurrency is realized when two or more client objects attempt to invoke the same method or access the same property on another object or component at the same time with the same task priority. When object or component concurrency occurs, a locking mechanism is necessary to serialize requests. Serializing requests means that the object or component handling the request handles only one request at a time. You can also use preemptive multithreading on 32-bit systems to handle requests a lot *quicker* than serializing objects. This is because preemptive multithreading handles an additional request after starting the processing and running another thread.

The ActiveX/COM+ Approach

In the Microsoft COM world, multithreaded development has been implemented as apartment-model threading. An apartment is a term analogous for a thread. The term *apartment* is used to make the symbolic parallel between people living in an apartment and objects living in a thread of execution. Apartment-model threading provides thread safety for all COM-based transactions.

Multithreaded Development in Visual Basic 6

Apartment-model threading in Visual Basic removes conflicts that can occur when competing threads attempt to access global data. This prohibition of conflicts is put into effect by giving each apartment its own copy of global shared data. Thus, an object on one thread cannot access the global data of another thread to communicate with that object. To overcome this restriction, though, a object which is a client of, say, two apartments can pass object reference A in one apartment to object B in another, and vice versa. The client object in this scenario is a conduit, in a sense, of what is called *cross-thread marshaling*. Cross-thread marshaling provides communication synchronization between objects in an apartment.

> **NOTE**
>
> You might not want to use cross-thread marshaling by default, as it can be very time-consuming. This time consumption can affect your system's perceived (and actual) performance.

Visual Basic maintains a distinct copy of global data for each thread. Visual Basic also keeps separate copies of the data supplied by global objects. An example of such a global object is the App object. The ThreadID property of the App object will consistently return the Win32 thread ID of the apartment or thread within which the request for the ThreadID property value was handled.

Multiple threads are supported only for components that can be marked for unattended execution. Unattended execution means each apartment requires no user intervention. If your Visual Basic applications and/or components include forms, controls, ActiveX documents, or classes created with ActiveX designers, they're restricted to a single apartment.

The process for marking your component for unattended execution is pretty straightforward for simple implementations. To mark your ActiveX DLL or EXE project for unattended execution, perform the following steps:

1 Start Visual Basic, if it's not already running.

2 If it's already running, and you have an existing project open, remove all forms, controls, and UserDocuments, as well as any classes created using ActiveX Designers.

3 From the menu, choose Project *<project>* Properties, in which *<project>* is the name of your project (*Project1* for new projects). You should see the Project Properties dialog box.

4 Click on the General tab to give it the focus. Click the check box named Unattended Execution.

5 Click OK.

> **CAUTION**
>
> Keep in mind that when you configure your project for Unattended Execution, this option suppresses the display of information to the user, including message boxes and system error dialog boxes.

Understanding Apartment-Model Threading

You read earlier that an apartment is synonymous with a thread. Now let's get an even better understanding of apartment-model threading. Each component you create using Visual Basic has the apartment model at its core, whether it's single-threaded or multi-threaded. A single-threaded component has only one apartment that contains all the objects the component provides. Quite naturally, a multithreaded component has many apartments.

With the single apartment component, a single-threaded DLL created with Visual Basic, for example, is safe for use with a multithreaded client. Unfortunately, you encounter a performance trade-off for this safety. Just about all calls from client threads are marshaled as if they were out-of-process calls.

Re-Entrancy

One of the most complex concepts for anyone trying to learn about multithreaded development is *re-entrancy*. Re-entrancy is an event in which a request is made to an object in an apartment (or thread) before a previous request for that same object has been completed, prompting the yielding of processor control. In detail, re-entrancy refers to the following sequence of events:

1 A client accesses a property or method of another object or component. The object or component's code is brought into the apartment's memory.

2 While the apartment (or thread) has its focus on the property or method, another thread invokes a property or method of the same object.

3 COM automation serializes this request. By serializing the request, automation queues the request until the owning object's apartment finishes the object member that it's currently executing.

4 Right before the apartment reaches the end of the member, it executes code that yields control of the processor.

5 Automation tells the apartment to begin executing the serialized request. This action causes the thread to reenter the object's code.

The new request might be for the member the thread was already executing. In this case, the thread enters the member a second time. The request might be for another object member. If the second member doesn't yield, it will finish processing before the first member. If it changes module-level data that the first member was using, the result might be unpredictable.

By serializing property and method calls for each apartment, Automation protects you from re-entrancy. This protection is only valid as long as your code doesn't yield control of the processor. There are a few ways your code can yield control of the processor, including:

• Invoking the properties or methods of an object on another thread, or in another process.

• Calling DoEvents.

• Raising an event that's handled by an object on another thread, or in another process.

Unless you've carefully designed and written all of an object's class code so that it doesn't matter whether two members are executing at the same time, you should avoid the inclusion of code that yields control of the processor.

Serialization

As alluded to earlier, serialization is the lining up of requests in a sequential manner. Thus, given three requests, A, B, and C, request A will be handled before request B, which in turn comes before request C. Each apartment serializes requests that it encounters. Using a real-world example, given a four-lane street, with each street being equivalent to a thread, one or more cars will likely line up for each lane. When there's a traffic jam, each lane can have twenty or more cars, for instance, when there's a red light. With the lining up of these cars, only one car per lane can pass through a green light. Thus, each lane naturally goes through serialization. From time to time, apartments (or threads) experience the equivalent of a traffic jam, requiring them to serialize requests.

Thread Aggregation

Aggregation of threads, sometimes called a thread pool, can exist in out-of-process components. Aggregation of threads means a component owns a thread for the duration of that thread. An in-process component has no threads of its own. The threads that define each apartment belong to the client. On the other hand, a multithreaded out-of-process component may contain an aggregation of threads with a fixed number of threads; it can also own a separate thread for each externally created object.

As clients request objects, Visual Basic creates each object on the next thread in the pool, starting over with the first thread when it reaches the end of the pool.

For example, Figure 9.1 depicts a class diagram that shows a component, SomeComponent, with three externally creatable classes. An externally creatable class is one whose Instancing property is set to any value *except* Private or PublicNotCreatable. The classes are simply named A, B, and C. To keep track of which object was requested by which client, the square that represents each object contains the class name and the number of the client that created the instance.

FIGURE 9.1.

A class diagram showing a component, SomeComponent, with three externally creatable classes.

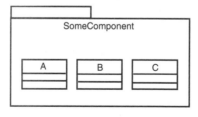

Figure 9.2 shows a simple scenario in which two clients, SomeClient1 and SomeClient2, access a member of the same class, A. Four clients have created instances of these classes. SomeClient1 requested the first object, ObjectA1, which was created on

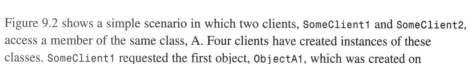

`Thread1`. `SomeClient2` then requested an object of class A, which was created on thread `Thread2`. This pattern can occur for any number of clients. Notice that both clients have multiple instances of the same class, A.

FIGURE 9.2.
A simple scenario in which two clients, `SomeClient1` *and* `SomeClient2`, *access a member of the same class, A.*

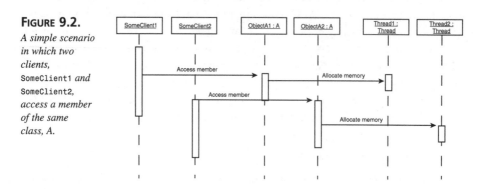

Figure 9.3 shows a situation that can occur with round-robin threading. With the round-robin threading model, you can't predict which objects will be on the same thread. Therefore you don't know who is sharing global data. Objects used by different clients may share global data, and objects used by the same client may not. For example, using Figure 9.3, the objects on thread `Thread1` are used by both `SomeClient1` and `SomeClient2`, yet they share the thread's instance of global data.

FIGURE 9.3.
The round-robin threading scenario.

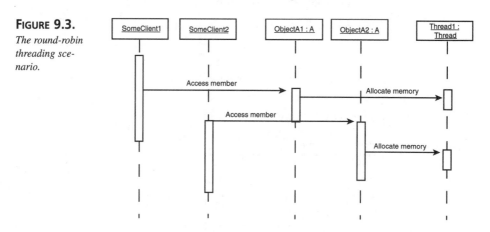

Moreover, recall that multiple accesses of the properties and methods of objects on the same thread will be serialized. Hence, these objects can block each other. That is, suppose you have a bank software system with an ActiveX component (residing on a server) that is dedicated to handling requests for loan payment histories for all client workstations across a national bank. A computer at a branch in Dallas, Texas makes a request to the component for histories on 100 customers. Another branch in Los Angeles, California makes a similar request to the same component about a minute later. They both invoke the same public method, `getPaymentHistory`. The server serializes the requests so that the Dallas request is fulfilled before the Los Angeles request.

Given the kind of this serialization described in the Dallas and Los Angeles example in the last paragraph, with its sharing of global data; you, as the architect of a client application, will not be able to (a) predict when objects will need to share global data given the dynamic nature of object interactions in apartments, and (b) you won't be able to plan when these objects will block each other's requests. Among the more academic and experienced multithreaded development practitioners, the behavior of the round-robin thread pool pattern is known as *non-deterministic*.

Benefit of the Round-Robin Threading Model

The great benefit that the round-robin threading model offers in exchange for the lack of predictability and object blocking planning mentioned earlier is that this type of model puts a limit on the total number of threads. This is a significant advantage, because multiprocessing works best if the total number of active threads roughly matches the number of processors.

As clients request objects, each object is created on a new thread. When the last client releases its last reference to objects on that thread, the thread is terminated. Retaining unused threads in this fashion will eventually degrade system performance, so avoiding dangling object references is critical when you're using a multithreaded component.

Thread Control

The big drawback to the thread-per-object model is that you have no control over the number of objects (and hence threads) that clients create. Creating too many threads will bog the operating system down in thread-maintenance overhead. Too many *active threads* (threads that are actively executing code) will be even more of a drag on the operating system. Generally speaking, you want about the same number of active threads as you have processors, to guarantee that there's never an idle processor. When you have just one processor, that's not very many active threads.

Thread Safety

Visual Basic greatly simplifies the job of authoring in-process components that can be used safely and efficiently by multithreaded clients. All in-process components created

with Visual Basic use apartment-model threading, to provide synchronous access to objects.

Using a single-threaded DLL in this way is safe, but slow. Cross-thread marshaling is almost as slow as cross-process marshaling. You can improve the performance of an in-process component when it's used with multithreaded clients by making the component multithreaded.

To make your ActiveX DLL project multithreaded, check the Unattended Execution option on the General tab of the Project Properties dialog box. This option is only enabled if the project contains no forms, controls, UserDocuments, or classes created using ActiveX designers. In-process components can only use the threads on which their clients create objects and make method calls. You cannot create additional threads within an in-process component. Thus, the other threading options in the Unattended Execution box are disabled for DLL projects. Keep in mind also that selecting the Unattended Execution option suppresses all forms of user interaction—including message boxes and system error dialog boxes.

Designating an ActiveX DLL project for unattended execution provides the following benefits:

- Each object a client creates on a given thread will be created in the same apartment (thread) of the DLL. Calls to each of these objects don't require cross-thread marshaling, which makes each object (and the apartment) more efficient.

- Because an object is only accessed on the thread in which it was created, calls are synchronized (serialized) so that a call is never interrupted by a call from another thread.

- Arguments for cross-thread calls are marshaled, and the calling thread is blocked. This synchronization of data protects the calling thread's state.

CAUTION

Note that in designing and developing the properties and methods of your classes, plan properly for reentrancy policies. Failing to do so can result in poorly performing apartment model implementations.

Implementing Multithreaded Systems

Multithreading on a single-processor machine can cause some unexpected behavior. Consider a class with two methods, getName and getAddress. These two methods are accessed at the same time.

With a single-threaded component, the requests are serialized, so that getAddress doesn't begin until getName has finished, for example. Thus, where multithreading is concerned in this scenario, the two active threads must compete for the processor's attention. Not only does the perceived average completion time increase, but also more processor time is spent switching between threads. The dilemma, then, is that two methods, getName and getAddress, take about the same amount of time.

For single-processor machines, multithreading results in a perceived performance improvement only when there exists a combination of long and short tasks. For example, if the method getAddress needs only three time slices to complete, the user of the system would perceive a significant improvement in the responsiveness of that method. Conversely, there's only a slight decrease in the time required to execute the getName method. In general, multithreading is best, at least in appearance, when most threads spend a substantial percentage of the time blocked for moderate operations. File input and output operations are examples of moderate operations. In such cases, only one or two apartments are actively executing code at any given time.

Advice for Implementing Multiple Threads of Execution

When an out-of-process code component has no user interface, you can mark it for unattended execution. Objects the component provides can run on different threads of execution.

Visual Basic provides three models for assigning objects to threads in out-of-process components. You can select one of these models using the Unattended Execution box, on the General tab of the Project Properties dialog box. See Table 9.1 for the proper settings to implement per your chosen threading model.

9

APARTMENT
MODEL
THREADING

TABLE 9.1. UNATTENDED EXECUTION SETTINGS PER MODEL.

Thread Assignment Model	Unattended Execution Settings
One thread of execution	Select the Thread Pool option with one (1) thread
Thread pool with round-robin thread assignment	Select the Thread Pool option and specify the number of threads to allow threads to allow
Every externally created object is on its own apartment	Select the Thread per Object option

Visual Basic defaults to one thread of execution after you select Unattended Execution. This option enables you to compile OLE servers created with earlier versions of Visual Basic so that you don't have to change legacy applications to take threading into account. However, the drawback with using legacy Visual Basic applications unmodified is that the code could display message boxes requiring user intervention. Re-compiling an OLE server with the Unattended Execution option minimizes the chances of showing message boxes that require operator intervention. Such messages can be logged to any source of persistence you choose, including the Windows NT event log, a database, or a text file. Keep in mind that the model you select cannot be changed at run time.

When Not to Use Multithreaded Development

Like every technique, multithreading has its limitations and drawbacks. Alex Voss, in a doctoral thesis at the Friedrich-Alexander University in Germany, listed the following as drawbacks of multithreaded development:

- Some applications do not lend themselves very well to multithreading. Synchronization and communication eat up much of the speedup achieved by parallelization.

- Parallelizing an application is a tedious job that introduces new potential programming errors. It is very difficult to test or proof the correctness of multithreaded code.

- Most operating systems today provide buffering and prefetching for I/O operations. The use of separate threads for I/O does not improve performance very much on such systems.

- Interactivity of an application can be achieved by using an event-driven programming style rather than threads. This reduces the complexity to be handled by the programmer and might even yield better performance.

Instantiating Externally Creatable Classes

Creating instances of classes that are externally creatable requires some design decisions on your part. Making these decisions before coding can be important in terms of how threads are allocated. For example, suppose you design a client that requests an instance of an externally creatable class. Visual Basic then creates the object (a) on the next thread in the thread pool, or (b) on a new thread.

Now suppose the object your client caused to be created also makes a request that causes yet another externally creatable object to be created. The outcome is dependent on the object creation implementation of the latter object. That is, Visual Basic determines if the latter object was created with the New operator or the CreateObject function.

If the latter object was created with the New operator, or with a variable declared As New, then the latter object will share the thread—and thus the global data—of the previous object that created it, which is the case with dependent objects. If created with the CreateObject function, the scenario is as if the client object, and not that previous object, requested the creation of the object. That is, although the client object, ClientObject, caused the creation of, say, FirstObject, and FirstObject then caused the creation of SecondObject. SecondObject is created as if ClientObject requested it. In any event, Visual Basic creates the object (a) on the next thread in the pool, or (b) on a new thread. The actual decision is based on the thread assignment model you specify as part of your design.

One final note on object creation. Again, the importance of making sound design decisions before actually implementing code in Visual Basic is essential. Not doing so is like gambling—you don't know if you're going to win for sure or not. Implementing object-creation code without making sound design decisions could affect apartment-model threading. If you design an object that uses the CreateObject function to create an object on another apartment/thread, every access of that latter object's members by the former object might result in cross-thread marshaling. This might enable significant performance hits that can create a noticeable perception of degraded application performance.

In coding the properties and methods of your objects, it's very important to observe the reentrancy rules you read about earlier. Multithreaded development is really of tremendous benefit when you develop scalable enterprise systems. This is particularly true where you implement components that run on remote computers, and which you require to properly scale to handle potentially thousands of clients. If you'd like to read up on

this interesting topic, you can learn more about multithreaded development for enterprise applications in the *Guide to Building Client/Server Applications with Visual Basic*, which ships with the Enterprise Edition of Visual Basic.

Issues in Recording Apartment Events

Logging apartment (or thread) events is essential to trace behavior and state changes that take place in each apartment. Visual Basic only supports multithreading in components marked for unattended execution. To permit a component to run unattended, however, the Unattended Execution option disables all user interaction, including message boxes and system error dialog boxes. This necessitates the recording of events in apartments.

There's flexibility in logging events in that you can log them to a text file, a database, or Windows NT system event log. Logging is done through the LogMode property of the App object controls. The App object's LogPath property specifies the full name, including folder, of the log file.

The items you can enter in the log file include:

- Text from message boxes that your component attempts to display to users
- System errors
- Text strings entered using the App.LogEvent method

When your component is running in the Visual Basic development environment, these entries go to the Immediate window instead of to the log file. For more information, check out Books Online reference topics or the Object Browser and look for App Object, LogEvent, LogMode, LogPath, and StartLogging. Event logging is critical for components running on remote computers, particularly as part of enterprise systems.

Tips on Testing and Debugging Multithreaded Systems

While you're in Run mode, the Visual Basic development environment only supports one thread of execution. To debug the multithreaded behavior of your component, you must run your test application against the compiled component. When you run your component in the development environment, your client test programs can create only one instance of each SingleUse class during that debugging session. After an instance of a class has been created, subsequent attempts to create an object from that class will cause Error 429, "OLE Automation server can't create object."

For debugging purposes, you can change SingleUse to MultiUse. However, to test the SingleUse behavior of your component, you must make the component executable.

Out-of-Process Components

For out-of-process components, *proper debugging* means compiling both the component and the test program, and running multiple copies of the test program. (You can also run multiple copies of the test program using multiple instances of the development environment, but you cannot trace into the compiled component.)

In-Process Components

To test the multithreaded behavior of apartment-model DLLs, split your test program into two parts—a standard executable from which you control the tests, and a multi-threaded out-of-process component. The standard executable is a client of the out-of-process component, which in turn is the test client for the DLL.

For example, the multithreaded out-of-process component might provide a TestMultiThreadDLL class, which is a hypothetical name for the class you would create to test your component. This test class can have any members you need. One such member could be a method called BeginTest. The standard executable creates any number of these TestMultiThreadDLL objects, passing each one a set of test parameters and then calling its BeginTest method.

The BeginTest method should enable a code-only timer, as demonstrated in "Creating an ActiveX EXE Component," and then return immediately, in order to avoid tying up the single-threaded Standard EXE. The TestMultiThreadDLL object's timer would control creation and testing of the objects provided by the in-process component. Each TestMultiThreadDLL object would exercise one thread (apartment) in the in-process component.

> **NOTE**
>
> To use this testing technique, you must compile both the multithreaded out-of-process component and the DLL.

Using a Native Code Debugger

If you're compiling your component to native code, and you have Microsoft Visual C++, you can compile your component with symbolic debug information for the Developer Studio debugger, which supports multithreaded debugging.

Analyzing Debug Messages

Because you can't debug multithreaded behavior in the development environment, you can't use helpful facilities such as Debug.Print and Debug.Assert to show debug message strings.

You can't use message boxes to show debug messages either because the Unattended Execution option completely suppresses user interaction.

Approaches to sending debug messages include:

- Create a single-threaded ActiveX DLL (that is, one that's *not* marked for unattended execution) with a public, creatable class that displays a modeless form with a list box. Give the class a DebugMsg method that takes a string argument and add it to the top of the list box.

  You can call this single-threaded DLL from any thread in your multithreaded ActiveX EXE project. The calls will be slow due to cross-thread marshaling (as described in "Designing Thread-Safe DLLs"), but this is not a big concern when you're debugging. You might find it helpful to include the ThreadID (an identifier for you thread) in your debug message text.

- Create a single-threaded out-of-process component that works in the fashion described above.

- Create a program that handles Windows messages, using the AddressOf operator to subclass a Visual Basic form. Use the Windows API to create and register private messages that the component you're debugging can use to send debug strings.

Multithreading Single-Use Objects

Visual Basic provides a second mechanism for using multiple threads of execution. By setting the Instancing property of a class to SingleUse, you cause each instance of the class to run in a separate instance of your component. This means that even though your component is single-threaded, each instance of the SingleUse class has its own thread of execution.

SingleUse objects require much more overhead than multiple objects in a multi-threaded component. Nonetheless, there are several reasons you might want to design and implement SingleUse objects:

- If your component must show forms, active documents, or other user interface elements, you cannot mark it for unattended execution—and thus it cannot be multi-threaded. Components that provide SingleUse objects can have forms and active documents.

- Your component can function as a standalone desktop application, and you want it to have an Application object that's not shared between clients.

- High-risk activities can be isolated in separate processes with `SingleUse` objects. If the object suffers a fatal error, other processes are not affected. By contrast, a fatal error in a multithreaded component terminates all threads.

The Meaning of `SingleUse`

After a client application creates an object from a `SingleUse` class, no client can ever create an object of that class from that instance of the component, even if the first client releases the object. That is, after the "'hole'" has been filled, it can never be empty—even if the object is destroyed.

In other words, marking a class module `SingleUse` means that during the lifetime of an instance of the component, only one instance of the class can be created externally—either by a client application, or by the component itself using the `CreateObject` function.

Out of Process Components and Multiple `SingleUse` Classes

The best way to provide exclusive use of an out-of-process component is to give it exactly one `SingleUse` class, with as many dependent objects as necessary.

If you set the `Instancing` property to `SingleUse` for more than one class module in your component, satisfying client requests for objects becomes somewhat complicated, and it becomes difficult to ensure that a client has objects from only one instance of the component. You can think of each class as a hole, which will be filled when an object of that class is created.

The lettered rectangles represent the potential to satisfy a request for an object of one of the three classes. A dotted outline indicates that the component has provided an object of that type, and so cannot provide another.

As noted previously, a better way to accomplish exclusive use of an out-of-process component is to provide one `SingleUse` object as the only externally creatable object, and as many dependent objects as you need.

Internal and External Creation of `SingleUse` Class Instances

If you design a client that creates two instances of a class marked `SingleUse`, two instances of the component executable are started. Within the component, however, it's possible to create multiple instances of such a class.

When code within the component creates an object from one of the component's own `SingleUse` classes using the `Set` statement with the `New` operator, or by declaring a variable `As New`, the object does not fill the "hole" that enables a client to create an instance of the class.

Summary

In this chapter, you learned about the basics of multithreaded development, and Microsoft's implementation of the Apartment Model Threading paradigm. You learned that an apartment is Microsoft's synonym for a thread, and that apartments can enhance the performance of ActiveX/COM+ applications and components created using Visual Basic 6.0. In understanding concurrency, you read that concurrency is the existence of more than one request for the same object at the same time. This chapter showed you the process for marking your component for unattended execution.

One of the most complex concepts for anyone trying to learn about multithreaded development is *reentrancy*. Reentrancy is an event in which a request is made to an object in an apartment (or thread) before a previous request for that same object has been completed, prompting the yielding of processor control. Serialization is the lining up of requests in a sequential manner. A thread pool is an aggregation of threads or apartments. Finally, you were given advice for implementing apartment model threading in your applications and components.

Object-Oriented Programming in Visual Basic

by John D. Conley III

IN THIS CHAPTER

- **Migrating from Legacy Programming Practices   215**
- **From OTFP to OOP   216**
- **A Primer on Classes   217**
- **Creating VB Classes   220**
- **Building Classes With the Class Builder   221**
- **Understanding the Difference Between Collections and Aggregations of Objects   227**
- **Understanding How Objects Talk to Each Other 228**
- **Understanding Subsystems   229**

Before you can get knee-deep into solid, experienced-based object oriented programming in Visual Basic, you'll need a primer on OOP. Object oriented programming (OOP) is a very complex technology. Although it's tempting to just dive right into coding objects, programmers new to object technology should view OOP as an important, new computer programming paradigm. That is, decisions about application design are made before programming (or Construction) even begins. Ad hoc assumptions about the design of an application during Construction are no longer valid. In fact, if such assumptions do occur, this indicates that the application's architecture has not been properly planned using object technology. That is, object technology requires much more organized work up front in terms of problem assessment, analysis, and design for relatively complex problems. After reading this book, you'll have a good sense of why it is important to plan your object-oriented application before you actually begin programming.

Object-oriented programming is the process of developing one to many lines of programming instructions based on well-defined design models. Such design models are graphical illustrations that represent different aspects of objects, those objects' classes from which they derive functions, and property variables and their interactions with each other.

With all the hoopla surrounding the emergence and increasing acceptance of object oriented programming, you might be saying to yourself, "Oh, boy!" Every week there seems to be some new technology pronouncing itself the guardian of true object orientation: Java/Corba, C++/Visual Basic/ActiveX/MFC, and so on. Don't worry. That's just the dynamic nature of new discoveries in the object technology community. Object technology companies are scrambling to find better and easier ways for designers and programmers of all backgrounds to migrate to the object-oriented paradigm.

Databases are becoming more object-oriented, and even the Internet is moving away from CGI (Common Gateway Interface) services and toward more robust distributed object architectures. For the seasoned object-oriented practitioner, he or she merely folds useful technologies into his or her mind with little learning curve. But, for those who are not accustomed to object technology, whose skills might still depend on more traditional development technologies, the steady rise of object-oriented programming (OOP) is a frightening, unknown menace, threatening to overturn the status quo. "What does this all mean?" you might ask.

Significant shifts in technology always seem to increase fear. But when you stop to think about this, this fear is usually derived from not knowing the technology from the ground up. Many books explain OOP (object oriented programming), but there are new groups of professionals who are not aware of some of these other books. And many OOP novices are trying to learn it through Visual Basic.

To understand how to use object-oriented programming, you will need to re-evaluate past programming habits. Nearly gone are the days when developers can try to successfully make ad hoc assumptions about business processes, intimate software design, and expected application behavior.

Migrating from Legacy Programming Practices

Without the use of a proven object-oriented methodology, the complexities of a given project tend to lead to increased risk of failure or goals that are not fully achieved. In other words, it is more difficult to measure whether or not project goals have been achieved if critical assumptions about the application's architecture are made on-the-fly. Such ad hoc designs typically add more uncontrollable complexity to the application than originally expected. One of the fundamental ideas behind object-oriented programming is to control the chaos normally associated with software development projects to promote reuse of objects. Reuse is achieved in part through well-designed classes. Well-designed classes are created from the breaking down of a complex problem into simpler abstractions. By iterating through one or more solutions to that problem, you can design classes with good attributes and methods, thus leading to a strong class interface. You will learn more about classes, as well as their methods and attributes (including public class interfaces) through the remainder of this book.

On-the-fly programming (OTFP) is the easiest, most popular, and worst programming style that ever mutated in the software development community. In OTFP, almost every function or sub is public and global, with hardly any concern for the arguments in the argument list. At least with structured analysis and structured design (SA/SD) methods, there's some thought involved in creating well-defined functions and subs (although SA/SD isn't recommended either). OTFP is a horrid mutation that evolved as a knee-jerk reaction by programmers responding to the high-pressure deadlines placed on them by sometimes unreasonable project schedules, which themselves are creatures of OTFP and chaotic project planning.

Even in small, cozy environments where everyone knows your name, OTFP tends to waste money in the long run because the resulting program depends extremely on both the original programmer and the technology it uses at a point in time. This means two things:

- If the programmer dies or quits, the often-undocumented program will have to be rewritten, and the person who rewrites it will likely use OTFP.

- If the technology becomes extinct or greatly changes (which happens very often), the programmer will have to surf through the entire code base to find every reference to members of that technology (API calls, object references, and so on).

OTFP generally leads to what's commonly referred to as *spaghetti code*. In OTFP, all code is perfect to the original programmer—but beauty is in the eyes of the beholder. Developers working in a small, informal environment can get away with OTFP because it takes far less analysis and design, and it might provide increased job security for them (but provides little benefit to their clients). But, when using OTFP, these programmers face the risk of changes in technology and user requirements now and in the future. If programmers choose to use OTFP, they have to change every line of code (which can be hundreds or thousands of lines of code) to accommodate such changes, whereas if the programmers used OOP, they would simply go to the object responsible for that technology or behavior.

What's more, OTFP doesn't lend itself at all to team development. The common response to this statement is, "Well, there are only two developers: Frank and me. We know each other well, and we just get together and hammer out our differences." This seldom (if at all) works, because this represents on-the-fly design, on which no program architecture is based. Without some organized methodology for the programming process, one person's spaghetti-code style takes precedence over that of the other programmer. This is especially damaging where that other programmer is timid and non-confrontational, which is a prevalent behavior in the programming community. More often than not, one of these programmers usually quits or in some way is removed from the project when things go wrong (and with OTFP, they very, very often do).

From OTFP to OOP

OOP—and the entire object-oriented process—provides much better and longer-lasting benefits to every project stakeholder (programmer, manager, end user, and so forth) than does OTFP. Visual Basic 6.0 offers enough features to ease the implementation of object technology and formal object-oriented analysis and design methodologies. Team development is also easier in VB6, and facilitates the creation of projects that incorporate each developer's individual talents. The VB project, in any corporate enterprise, also reflects the competence of its team members. In this context, a project represents a group of people who have as a common goal the development of an application or suite of applications to carry out some business process.

OOP lends itself well to project team development because of its capability to break down a complex system into simpler *abstractions* (understandable portions). Each abstraction, then, can be more easily assigned to team members for better definition and construction (application design and programming). Without an OOP background, VB novices tend to revert to traditional waterfall techniques (if that much) as soon as the first problem comes up in the project. This chapter will help you avoid these mistakes by helping you embrace OOP.

A Primer on Classes

A *class* is an *abstract entity* (a "thing" that carries out a subset of your user's requirements) with *behaviors* (a set of functions or methods) and *attributes* (variables or properties that identify the class).

You might say that a class is a template. Some people call classes *cookie cutters* because they can be *instantiated* (brought into your computer's memory) into real-world, *concrete* objects (with which you can interact in your application). Although this is true of *concrete classes*, this isn't completely true of *every* class. This might help you grasp the concept of classes: Classes define the behavior and identity of objects. Some classes can also define the behavior and identity of other classes. Such classes are called *base classes*. Base classes that can't be instantiated into concrete objects are called *abstract classes*. Objects implement (provide runtime code logic for) the behavior of concrete classes. Because VB isn't as object-oriented as C++ (not C) or SmallTalk, your classes will generally be concrete or *pure virtual* (its child class must implement every one of its methods).

> **NOTE**
>
> A *class* is an *abstract entity*—a "thing" that carries out a subset of your user's requirements. It represents a classification of key abstractions you discover while assessing a given problem.

The Visual Basic Class

The structure of a class is physically deployed differently in different programming languages, although the structure itself remains the same. For instance, in C++ the class is usually separated into a header file and an implementation file. The header file contains the definitions of the class itself, including its methods and properties (attributes). The implementation file shows how each member (method or property) of the class is used in a particular domain. In Visual Basic there's no such distinction. There will be more on this in a moment.

The Visual Basic class module is virtually the same as the familiar form module, which, unfortunately, has led to some confusion over the difference between the graphical user interface form object and the class module. For example, a form module and a class module can implement the interface of another class. To *implement* an interface means that the implementing class assumes the public responsibilities of the supplier class, executing method and property calls for its clients. You can add properties and methods to both form and class modules. Both have a constructor and destructor. For the form, the constructor would be `Form_Load` and the destructor would be `Form_Unload`. For the class, the constructor would be `Class_Initialize` and the destructor would be `Class_Terminate`. As a result, many VB developers place lots of business logic code into forms that make it very difficult to try to reuse such code, much less partition the application into packages that can then be assigned to individual developers on a team.

Figure 10.1 shows what a typical class module looks like.

FIGURE 10.1.

An example of a class module in Visual Basic 6.0.

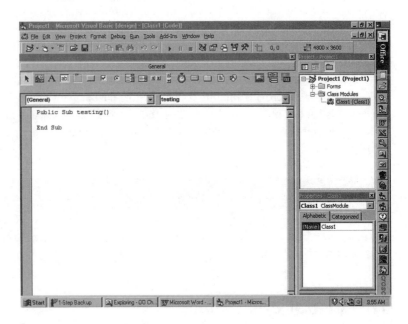

A class module consists of the definition and implementation of class members. These class members are methods (functions or subs) and properties (variables that hold information about an object whose type is defined by a class). You define the name and return type (if any) of the methods, as well as the data types of the properties. The members of a class can be defined as *public*, *private*, or *friend*.

The keyword `Public` signifies that the member is accessible to all modules within the project and in external projects. If you don't want any members to be public outside the project, you can insert the following line of code in the general declarations section of the class module:

```
Option Private
```

The keyword `Private` signifies that the member is accessible only by other members within the class module. This doesn't mean that you can't pass the value of the private property to an external module via a public property or method, however. Suppose that you have a class called `CheckingAccount` with the members in Listing 10.1.

LISTING 10.1. CLASS MEMBERS FOR THE CLASS `CheckingAccount`.

```
'General Declarations
Private mvarpAccountNumber As String

Public Property Get pAccountNumber() As String
    pAccountNumber = mvarpAccountNumber
End Property

Public Property Let pAccountNumber(ByVal sNewAccountNumber As String)
    mvarpAccountNumber = sNewAccountNumber
End Property
```

Because the property `pAccountNumber` is publicly available, the value of the private module-level variable `mvarpAccountNumber` is also publicly available, even though the variable `mvarpAccountNumber` itself isn't.

An Example of Class Identities

Now for some interesting illustrations to help you remember the object-oriented concepts previously discussed. The automotive industry provides one of the best analogies for understanding OOP. Think of Chrysler, for example, as a base class for the `Sebring` class of cars. When you go to the Chrysler dealer, you don't actually buy a `Sebring`; you buy an instance of a `Sebring`. The instance you buy is the actual `Sebring` object because you can interact with it by driving it. The `Sebring` class, then, is a concrete class, because with it, the assembly plant knows how to make real-world cars (objects) based on the `Sebring` class specification (behavior and attributes).

The `Sebring` class has methods (ways of operating), such as ignite the engine, turn the wheels, go in reverse, open doors, adjust speed, and so on. Its properties (or variables or attributes) would be color of car, current speed, maximum speed, light status (off or on), wheel base, wheel size, window tint, cabin style (sunroof, convertible, hardtop), retail price, and so on. When you instantiate a `Sebring` class into an actual Sebring car, these properties will be filled in by an *actor* (a human who interacts with a system, such as the automotive engineer or assembly person in this example). Thus, the color might be red, the window tint might be dark smoke, the wheel size might be 15 inches, the price might be $25,000, and so on. These values, taken together, represent the current *state* of the object.

Did you notice something interesting about the Sebring class? Some of its methods and properties have something in common with other cars Chrysler makes. For instance, all Chrysler cars ignite engines, turn wheels, go in reverse, open doors, adjust speed…you get the idea. They also each have color, wheel size, wheel base, and so on. So rather than re-create these methods and properties for each subclassed car (*subclass* means child class), Chrysler created abstract classes such as the H-Body cars, among others.

This is a good example of what an abstract class signifies—that is, you can't go to the Chrysler dealer and pay for an H-Body car itself. The dealer, instead, will recommend H-Body car classes, such as the Sebring. The point is that H-Body is abstract (and actually might be pure abstract because certain behavior might be implemented at a finer level for certain subclasses). The Sebring class implements the H-Body abstract class. These entities are more important to the automotive engineer and repair technician than the buyer (end user). The actual Sebring car is the object that you, the end user, buys.

Creating VB Classes

By now, you should be fairly comfortable with the idea of classes and objects and their interrelationships. Let's revisit the Visual Basic development environment, where you'll actually create a class and observe simple class behaviors at runtime.

There are four ways (also known as *development processes*) to create classes in Visual Basic:

- Add class module
- Add class from template
- Create class in Class Builder
- Create class in modeling tool

In the Learning, Professional, and Enterprise Editions of Visual Basic, you can simply add a new class module from the standard menu or the right-click pop-up menu, or by adding a new class module based on an existing class template in the \Vb\Template folder. In the Enterprise Edition, you can use the Class Builder to create a new class, or use a modeling tool such as Rational Rose/VB or Microsoft Visual Modeler.

The easiest way to add a new class to a Visual Basic project is to add a new class module from the menu. Two implementations of this process support this menu-driven approach:

- Choose Project | Add Class Module from Visual Basic's menu bar. A dialog box like the one in Figure 10.2 appears. Double-click the Class Module icon to add a new class module with the default name Class1 to your project.

FIGURE 10.2.
The Add Class Module dialog box lets you add a new class from scratch or create a new one based on one of the class templates shown.

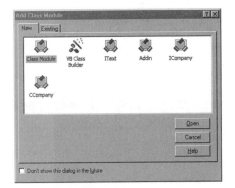

- Right-click in the Project browser on the right side of the Visual Basic IDE. From the pop-up menu, choose Add Class Module. At this point, you'll also see the Add Class Module dialog box (refer to Figure 1.2). Double-click a Class Module icon, or double-click an existing class template icon.

Building Classes With the Class Builder

If you have the Enterprise Edition of Visual Basic 6.0, you can create classes from scratch by using the helpful Class Builder. This utility is a distant cousin of Rational Rose/VB and Microsoft Visual Modeler in that it lets you build classes automatically.

If you haven't done so already, make sure that Class Builder is available in the Add-In Manager. To make it available, choose Add-Ins | Add-In Manager from the menu. You should see the Add-In Manager dialog box (see Figure 10.3). Select the VB Class Builder Utility by clicking the checkbox associated with this item. Click OK.

Now you're ready to work with Class Builder. To start this utility, choose Add-Ins | Class Builder from the menu. You should see the Class Builder utility applet, as illustrated in Figure 10.4.

10

OBJECT-ORIENTED PROGRAMMING IN VISUAL BASIC

FIGURE 10.3.
The Add-In Manager dialog box.

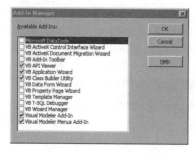

FIGURE 10.4.
Class Builder automates the process of creating classes in Visual Basic 6.0 Enterprise Edition.

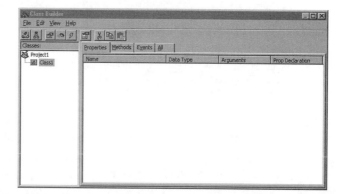

> **NOTE**
>
> If you've already added a class module to the existing project with Class Builder, you'll get an informational dialog box telling you that the hierarchy of the classes created outside Class Builder can be incorporated into Class Builder. You also can't edit or delete members of that class; if you get this dialog box, just click OK. You can always edit existing classes manually or in design tools such as Rational Rose/VB or Microsoft Visual Modeler.

Not only does Class Builder automate the process of creating classes, it also tracks the hierarchy of all your classes and collections. Class Builder also generates the skeleton code you'll need to implement the classes and collections, including the properties, methods, and events of each class.

> **NOTE**
>
> An event is similar to a method or function but is triggered by a human actor or an external system action. VB Forms have built-in events; however, you can raise

your own events as well by using the `RaiseEvent` keyword. Events are particularly useful in ActiveX controls, where you can allow programmers who use your controls to execute code for your control's event. Thus, when your control's event occurs, your programmer/user can insert code that handles further processing.

On examining the Class Builder utility environment, notice the Windows Explorer-style visual representation. The standard menu and toolbar reside at the top. Below these two is the Object Model pane on the left and the Properties, Methods, and Events pane on the right.

The Object Model pane visually displays the hierarchy of the classes and collections in your project. If you click a class in this pane, you make it available for editing in the Properties, Methods, and Events pane. In turn, if you click a method, property, or event in the Properties, Methods, and Events pane, that class member becomes available for editing.

Classes and collections that existed in previous sessions of the Class Builder can't be edited or deleted in later Class Builder sessions. Therefore, you must manually edit or delete unwanted members that survived (or persisted) beyond a previous Class Builder session.

You also can modify classes by using drag-and-drop features to, for instance, copy a property from one class to another.

The Menus

The Class Builder menus are pretty standard. The File menu offers these commands:

- If you choose New, you have the option of adding a new Class, Collection, Property, Method, or Event.
- Delete deletes the currently selected class, collection, or class member.
- Rename enables you to rename the currently selected class, collection, or class member.
- Update Project immediately updates your current Visual Basic project with the new or modified class and collection information.
- Exit closes Class Builder after saving current changes not previously updated.

The Edit menu commands are as follows:

- Cut and Copy work in the same manner as in any other Windows application. You can cut or copy the currently selected item.

10

OBJECT-ORIENTED
PROGRAMMING IN
VISUAL BASIC

- Choosing Properties displays an Edit dialog box for the currently selected class or class member.

The View menu seems insignificant at first:

- Choosing Toolbar toggles the display of the toolbar on (displayed) and off (not displayed). Simple enough.

- Choosing Options brings up the unimposing, yet far-reaching, Class Builder Options dialog box (see Figure 10.5).

FIGURE 10.5.

The Class Builder Options dialog box has far-reaching implications for your Visual Basic project.

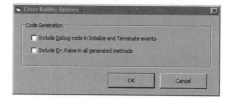

The Class Builder Options dialog box gives you two code-generation options:

- Include Debug Code in `Initialize` and `Terminate` Events
- Include `Err.Raise` in All Generated Methods

Because these two options are tightly coupled with development processes related to the design phase/iteration of the project life cycle, they are beyond the scope of this book. For now, suffice it to say that these options let you track the creation and destruction of objects at runtime, as well as trap and raise errors in each object's methods at runtime. Keep in mind that objects are runtime copies (or instances) of classes.

The Help Menu is pretty straightforward, enabling you to access information about the Class Builder utility. The Toolbar contains shortcut buttons for operations already available in the menu.

The Properties, Methods, and Events Pane

In the Properties, Methods, and Events pane on the right, you see an index tab control with four tabs: Properties, Methods, Events, and All.

The Properties page (see Figure 10.6) shows all the properties of the currently selected class. With this page, you can add, edit, and delete properties from the currently selected class. The container area is broken into four columns: Name, Data Type, Arguments, and Prop Declaration. The Name column shows the name of a given property in the class. The Data Type column shows the data type for each property. The Arguments column lists the arguments that the property method accepts (remember that properties in VB can be implemented as property methods). Finally, the Prop Declaration column indicates what type of operation the property method performs on the property.

FIGURE 10.6.

The Properties page enables you to add, edit, and delete properties from the currently selected class.

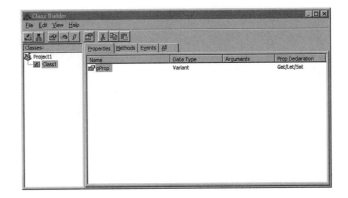

In the Prop Declaration column, the Get type enables clients (other modules needing a value or service) to access the current value or object reference of the property. The Let type enables other modules to change the value of the property. The Set type is similar to the Let type, but other modules can change only the object reference (assuming that the class property was declared as Variant or Object). If you right-click anywhere in the tab container area, a pop-up menu lets you add a new property, delete a property, perform cut and copy operations, rename the property, or display the detailed specification of each property. Figure 10.7 shows a detailed specification, which is housed in the Property Builder dialog box (double-clicking the tab container area also brings up this dialog box).

FIGURE 10.7.

The Property Builder dialog box enables you to view and modify information about each property.

By using the Property Builder, you can specify a name and data type for the property, as well as declare its scope (Public Property, Friend, or Public Variable). You also can specify that one of the properties is the default property of the class. This way, when you use the class variable in code like any other variable, the value of the default property is set or returned.

Similar to the Properties page is the Methods page, which displays the methods of the currently selected class or collection. You access the Method Builder the same way you access the Property Builder. By using the Method Builder (see Figure 10.8), you can perform the same maintenance operations as with the Property Builder. The key differences are these:

- You can specify a return value. The absence of a return value means that the method is a Sub; otherwise, it's a Function.

- You can specify that the method is a Friend, meaning that it's available to all modules in the project, but not to modules outside the project.

- You can specify whether the current method should be the default method. Therefore, if you used the class variable in code as you would a function or a sub, the VB compiler would use the default method to provide the requested service.

- There's no Prop Declaration column.

FIGURE 10.8.

The Method Builder dialog box.

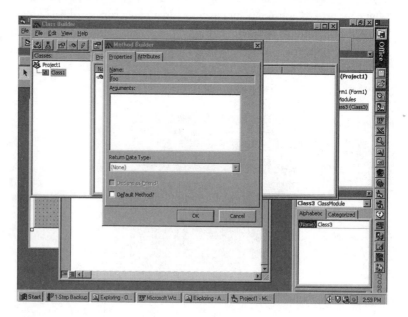

The Events page in the Class Builder shows all the events associated with the current class or collection. Because the creation and maintenance of events is the same as that of methods, double-clicking in the Events page brings up the Method Builder as well. The difference between a method and event, as far as Class Builder is concerned, is that an event doesn't require a data type.

Finally, the All page combines the specifications for every member of the current class into one convenient list.

> **TIP**
>
> To convert a class in the Object Model Pane into a collection, right-click the class and choose Set As Collection. To convert back to a class, right-click the collection and choose Set As Class.

Understanding the Difference Between Collections and Aggregations of Objects

In the earlier discussion of Class Builder, you came across the word *collection* and probably wondered what it meant. *Collection* is synonymous with the expression *object collection*, which is, well, a collection of objects. It's a list of objects, you might say. By that, you should understand that a collection is, itself, an object. This object holds references to other objects and has methods for adding, accessing, and deleting objects within it. An *aggregation* of objects is an object that contains other objects, but not in the sense of a collection. In VB, a collection is a nice object mechanism for manipulating the similarly named methods and properties of objects.

There's no sense of context (the purpose for using objects in the collection) other than for bundling them into a collection for easy access. With aggregation, though, there is a reason that the aggregate object owns other objects. That is, the subordinate object (contained object) serves the aggregate object. This means that the contained object's lifetime depends on the lifetime of the aggregate and, in particular, when the aggregate needs to use the contained object. Whew! Let's look at the Sebring example again.

On further examination, have you noticed that the Sebring is actually composed of other objects? These objects would include tires, the steering wheel, the door, the window, brakes, headlights, and so forth. You can say that the Sebring is actually an aggregate of all these objects. A collection of objects—sometimes hard to identify in the real world—might include the fuse box under the dashboard (another object) or under the hood (another object). Each fuse is an object and the fuse box is a collection of fuse objects. A key method of each fuse would be to shut down a car's electrical system to avoid major problems.

Understanding How Objects Talk to Each Other

Objects communicate with each other via their *interfaces* and the *protocols* set forth by the designer for carrying out this communication. Together, the public methods and properties of an object are the object's *interface*. This interface implements the protocol of the object. A *protocol* is the way two objects communicate with each other to properly carry out some goal. One object's interface, then, dispatches a message (a value, an object, or a pointer to a method) to another object's interface. Again, the Sebring class will help you understand the interface.

In the fuse box collection, you find that the fuses all interact with the same interface to relay electrical information to the engine (another object) and, in particular, the engine's computer (another object, which means the engine is also an aggregate). The fuse box itself has an interface to each electrical component in the Sebring. The protocol—I hope I'm not stretching this one—is based on each component expecting a particular voltage of electricity from the fuse to shut itself down when a problem is encountered. (By *problem*, I mean the state of the car. The subsequent activities related to this state would be the *scenario* for defining how these objects interact.) If the voltage isn't the one the component expects, the electrical message is ignored.

In case that wasn't straightforward enough, look at another example: think of the automatic transmission as an object. The usual methods for an automatic transmission are park, drive on normal roads, drive on slight incline, drive on steep incline, drive in reverse, and free the transmission (neutral). Together, these selections (which would be modeled as methods in your models) represent the interface to the transmission. The protocol (gulp!) would involve the nasty details of the stick interaction with the gears, among others.

Let's try another one to be safe. The air conditioner (AC) is an object whose behavior is to supply cool air when the weather is hot. Of course, you don't simply tell the AC to turn itself on and adjust itself to your favorite temperature (but that technology isn't far off). The high-level protocol calls for you to push some buttons and slide some levers. These buttons and levers are the interface to the AC. When you push the On button, this event (pushing the button) causes the button's internal methods to send an electric message to the AC to power up. Another way of explaining this power-up process is that the AC initializes itself to default (factory) settings or your previous settings. Other real-world objects have interfaces as well, such as your thermostat in your home, your microwave, and your television, among others. In turn, these objects interface with the object that supplies electricity. Because the real world operates with classes, objects, and their interfaces, why not use the same paradigm in software development?

Understanding Subsystems

Now that you've become familiar with the nature of classes and objects, it's time to introduce another concept. In the real world— at least, in theory—every object is made up of smaller objects. For instance, humans are made up of organs. In turn, these organs are made up of cells. Likewise, a well-developed object-oriented application is made up of *subsystems* (categories or packages), which are then made up of classes (or sometimes other subsystems).

Understanding Application Subsystems

A *subsystem* is a portion of the application/system that carries out a particular behavior of the entire application/system. This portion can consist of classes as well as other subsystems. For instance, you might design a portion of an application to manage all database retrieval and storage (database subsystem), another to handle the display of data in and retrieval of data from GUI objects (GUI subsystem), and yet another to handle printing and reporting (printing and reporting subsystem).

Returning to the Sebring example, the portion of the car (synonymous with application for these purposes) that handles the movement energy is the engine. The portion that handles stopping is the braking mechanism. The portion that handles air flow and temperature control is the AC. The engine *subsystem* (or portion), in turn, consists of different classes of nuts and bolts, as well as other subsystems, such as timing, cooling, starting (ignition), and so on. On another front, your house would be like an application, and it, too, has portions. Your house contains the AC subsystem (with some abstract similarities to the car's AC), the plumbing subsystem, the electrical subsystem, and so forth. Get the idea? The class, then, would be the atomic unit (assuming that it didn't contain other objects).

Understanding How Subsystems Talk to Each Other

Subsystems (categories) communicate with each other through classes that play the role of subsystem brokers or subsystem interfaces. If you think of subsystems themselves as being big classes, a class within it would act as an agent on behalf of the subsystem. You might also view this agent class as a diplomat or an ambassador. When two subsystems need to communicate, one dispatches an ambassador's envoy (a message) to the other's ambassador. The hosting ambassador validates the message (making sure that it's not a package bomb that might blow up and crash your system). If the ambassador feels the message has come to the right place, it passes the message to the proper "authorities" (some delegated class) for further processing.

Suppose that a user of your application enters some personal information such as name, address, and the like, and clicks a button to save the data to the database. At a high level this is simple: Just save it to the database straight from the form (or dialog box, for you C++ transplants). However, in OOP, the process is more method-based and organized. The form actually sends a message (packed with the data) to the GUI subsystem, which in turn separates the data from the form objects (for example, the text box, list box, and so on) and sends it to a business layer class. This business layer class places each data value to its attributes (or properties), does some business rule processing, and, if all is okay, sends this data to the database subsystem, which then saves this data to the database. (This process of saving class property values to the database is called *persistence*, because the data persists beyond the current application session.) When you finish reading this book, you should be able to think your applications through in this manner. The idea of breaking an application down into subsystems (or packages) is the core of object-oriented methods.

Summary

In this chapter, you learned about the fundamentals of object-oriented programming. At the center of this evolving technology is the class and its runtime equivalent, the object. A class is a design-time template that determines the behavior of objects based on it. Visual Basic 6.0 lets you perform OOP with the class module and the Class Builder utility.

The fundamental idea to keep in mind in OOP is that the Visual Basic project must be viewed as a round trip (or cyclical), evolving process, meaning that the artifacts of the analysis phase need to be synchronized with the design and construction phases. Without this periodic synchronization process, you lose the ability to trace the classes you create from the analysis phase down to the construction phase. This is where novice object-oriented programmers—sometimes bent on being impatient—get confused and discouraged. When requirements need to be revisited, novice Object-Oriented programmers can't tell what class corresponds to what entity in the analysis and design models. Traceability, then, is of fundamental importance to object-oriented programming.

Creating and Using Class Modules

by John D. Conley III

IN THIS CHAPTER

- Realizing the Importance of Using Analysis Methods *234*
- Building the Foundation for Object-Oriented Analysis *235*
- Implementing the Use-Case Methodology for Your Environment *239*

In basic terms, analysis is the series of acts carried out by project team members to break down complex concepts into simpler abstractions. Analysis involves looking into the problem domain in order to be able to come up with a solution.

For many years, well-intentioned programmers have gone through each project life cycle with that enduring and possibly natural enmity toward the analysis process. The standard thinking is that users don't know how to tell programmers what they want. There's some real-world precedence for this. Before business management gurus Edward Deming and Peter Drucker came on the scene, most companies tended to ignore their customers' wishes. (For that matter, monopolies have a natural tendency to ignore customers; just look at your utility monopolies' response to your billing complaints.) Deming and Drucker came along and led the corporate world toward more customer- and employee-oriented management styles.

Likewise, the three leading figures of the object-oriented software development paradigm shift—Jacobson, Booch, and Rumbaugh—have also led the software development community toward not just object-oriented styles of programming, but also toward user-oriented project-planning. The central idea behind object-oriented systems is that objects respond to stimuli (events or messages) from human users at some point in the execution of a business process. The response of the objects can incorporate issuing client requests to other external systems, which would make the client system an actor as well (more on actors in a moment).

The important thing to understand about the analysis process is that you must be able to effectively translate the initial set of user requirements into a model or foundation on which your design models can be implemented properly. Such a translation occurs within the context of a project. Planning the development of a solution to an assessed problem cannot simply occur in a vacuum. One cannot guess at the completion date for a project. Object-oriented analysis provides the best early gauge of the feasibility of successfully completing an object-oriented programming project.

Realizing the Importance of Using Analysis Methods

Now that you've gone through the object-oriented programming aspects (and there will be plenty more on OOP later), let's step back a bit and discuss analysis. Some might think that analysis is a waste of time; and some of this sentiment is justified. Most newcomers to OOP, then, bring an anti-analysis attitude with them into object oriented projects. This is the favored approach for many programmers because each programmer decides for himself how the application will work and avoids getting caught up in analysis paralysis. If there is a team of developers, each one simply splits up the user requirements document, codes in isolation, and then meets with the others to argue over who is wrong or right, what should be hacked out of the current release, and so on. As complex as user requirements are, such an approach is prone to errors, and the user typically ends up with a system he did not really ask for or want. To get along with (or out of sympathy for) the developers—who probably stayed up all night every night for a whole week—the user says something like, "Yeah, this looks okay. I guess I can do my work with this." Then a month later, the application is seldom used or is full of major bugs, and the user returns to the manual way of doing business.

The same thing applies when you try to implement OOP without doing the necessary analysis. In general, *analysis* is the process of bringing a discovered solution to a business problem from a dream in someone's head to a high-level, often user-friendly, model that can evolve into an application. Using a *methodology* (an organized, disciplined system for doing something) or carrying out some goal(s) to cultivate this evolutionary process is crucial. Perhaps the most widely used methodology for this process is the objectory method introduced by Ivar Jacobson. It's also generally known as object-oriented software engineering (OOSE). With it, you initiate a process of identifying what the current problem is, and then help users identify how they see themselves using the proposed application.

Building the Foundation for Object-Oriented Analysis

To effectively use OOA to create a solid, easily extensible system with Visual Basic, you should understand the overall approach to the project. This means that every activity you expect to undertake in creating a Visual Basic application really should be reasonably thought out beforehand. That is, you as a Visual Basic developer must concede that you usually (but not quite always) wear many hats on a typical development project, and these hats (or roles) should be identified and specified. Further, in performing these roles, you perform tasks related to each role. These tasks, too, must be identified and quantified. The roles you'll be concerned about in this chapter are *requirements gatherer*, *object-oriented analyst*, and *architect*.

The Requirements Gatherer

As a requirements gatherer, you typically interrogate end users, business managers (or domain experts), project managers, or anyone else who had the misfortune of getting in your way. Usually, there's no predefined method for gathering requirements; you simply draft an almost ad hoc list of questions centered around mouse clicks instead of business processes executed by users. A requirements model is never generated. However, as a requirements gatherer, that's exactly what you want to do. A requirements model captures all the ways users will use the Visual Basic system you're developing. Figure 11.1 shows what a typical requirements model might look like.

FIGURE 11.1.

A requirements model (the initial use-case model) visually illustrates how end users will use your system from a business processing perspective.

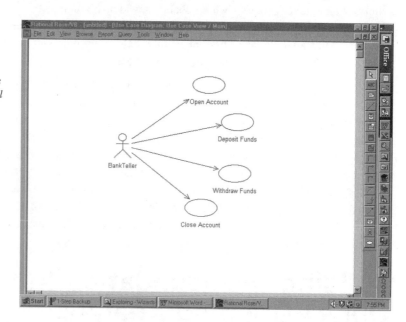

The Object-Oriented Analyst

As analysts in traditional projects, some developers are probably driven by a simplified focus of just making the gathered requirements fit into the Visual Basic project. They might have quickly come up with a list of global or form-level functions that seem to roughly provide the expected system behavior; analysis is over in a heartbeat. Analysis is actually design, if it is even that. VB developers grab some programming tips and tricks books and start forcing this analysis and design model of functions to incorporate their ideas of how the system should work. This fly-by-the-seat-of-your-pants development is also known as *programming by chaos*.

Quoting noted object-oriented methodologist Jim Rumbaugh, analysis "is the careful examination of the requirements for a system with the intent of understanding them, exploring their implications, and removing inconsistencies and omissions." Effective analysis builds on the mature (or evolved) requirements model by creating an ideal structure that endures throughout the life cycle of the proposed system under development. At this stage—which can and should be revisited throughout the project's lifetime—you don't want to try to come up with a detailed list of low-level functions that you want to rush out the door without a concern for how users use the system and how the system responds to those users. You should understand *low-level* to mean that you don't want to worry about which database you're using, which neat trick you want to incorporate to make a MAPI or Windows API call, or similar notions. This is important because changes in vendors, for instance, might necessitate changes in tools or even operating systems. Also, by avoiding the detailed design stuff early in the analysis iteration, you can better concentrate on the activities of the business process user, as the analysis model is far simpler than the design model(s).

A mature design model provides direct guidance to your programming activities, whereas an analysis model provides a solid foundation for your design model(s). Figure 11.2 gives you an example of a simple analysis model. Note how it's focused only on high-level business objects when initially created. In the User Services layer of the proposed system (on the left), a Teller Interface class encapsulates your understanding of the interaction between users and the system. Don't worry about button clicks or mouse movements. Also, there are Checking Account and Savings Account classes to encapsulate your knowledge of each account type. You could have easily had one class called Account at this stage; it just depends on your particular environment. Finally, a Persistence class is responsible for storing and retrieving information created or modified in your application, as well as getting rid of information users want destroyed. In the analysis model, it's called *persistence* rather than *database management* because you don't know whether the data repository will be a database or a flat file (regular text or binary file you store anywhere on your hard disk). That kind of detail is left to your design model.

FIGURE 11.2.

A service model.

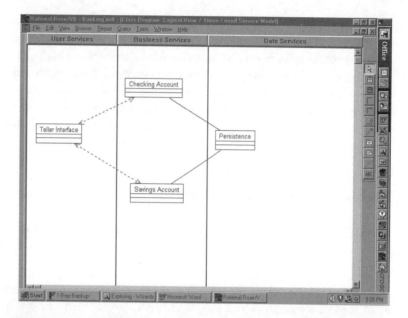

> **NOTE**
>
> Although VB6 now allows each class the ability to persist itself, you should still implement a separate persistent class to encapsulate the exact storage implementation for the class (such as flat file or database). This makes scaling your application for different implementations easier, and every class that needs persistence could reuse this one class. You won't have to go to every class whenever persistence implementation requirements change.

The Architect

The role of the architect is to formulate and facilitate the elaboration of the foundation of the system's architectural foundation. The advantage of understanding this role is that you're able to abstract the project tasks that apply only to architects. This in turn helps you focus on those tasks, should such duties be required of you. Without understanding this role, there's the risk of not concentrating on the architecture elaboration process,

Creating and Using Class Modules

CHAPTER 11

239

11

CREATING AND
USING CLASS
MODULES

which often leads to a faulty, pseudo architecture. As a pseudo-architect in a traditional shop, a developer actually does what you might call detailed analysis, but it is really ad hoc design. Such developers take the list of functions and manipulate each one to communicate with another. Often, the code for some functions is hidden behind GUI control events (for example, `Command1_Click`) for the sake of convenience (ad-hoc spaghetti architecting). Such architecting makes it extremely difficult to trace application behavior back to the requirements and analysis models.

Object-oriented architects work with analysts—and sometimes are the analysts—to ensure that project team members are able to trace the names of business objects between the requirements and analysis models. Architects also work with designers and developers, but we're mainly concerned with analysis here. In traditional analysis, end users and managers assumed that programmer-analysts had a near perfect understanding of the problem domain. This inevitably led to a decreased emphasis on analysis and more emphasis on construction activities. Because the actual gap in knowledge between the users and developers was not adequately addressed in the beginning, all of the members and beneficiaries of the project teams (also known as stakeholders) experience higher-than-necessary levels of stress as the project approaches its deadline.

> **NOTE**
>
> The *problem domain* is the business need being addressed by the proposed system under development

Implementing the Use-Case Methodology for Your Environment

When Microsoft released version 6 of Visual Basic Enterprise Edition, the Visual Basic language moved into the ballpark of object-oriented languages (though only as a "pinch hitter" perhaps, but close enough). The capability to create classes whose interfaces can be implemented by other classes and have the capability to create complex ActiveX components has really made Visual Basic a serious commercial development tool. Added to that is the automation of the design process with the help of Microsoft Visual Modeler. However, Visual Basic doesn't help with the discovery and identification of classes, actors (human and external system), and use cases. To compound this situation, the vast majority of VB programmers don't have object-oriented backgrounds, which leaves them resorting to traditional, familiar ways of developing software.

The reality is that solid system architectures and class structures seldom evolve or mature properly when programmers don't gather use cases and design classes. As a result, Visual Basic 6, which is actually a very strong development tool for implementing object technology, will continue to be maligned as you try to pour new wine into old wineskins. The rest of this chapter explains how to use object-oriented analysis techniques—specifically, use-case identification and modeling—to help you successfully initiate the analysis process and give Visual Basic a better name in the development community.

The Problem Statement

Figure 11.1 showed what a simple use-case model looks like. Of course, the elements within a use-case model don't appear out of thin air. As an analyst, you would have asked users, "In what ways do you want to use the system?" Users, who are tellers within your development context, respond that they want to be able to open an account, close an account, deposit new funds, and withdraw funds. Notice how each phrase includes important verbs, such as *open*, *close*, *deposit*, and *withdraw*. These verb phrases, as the will be called for these purposes, taken together with the actor (the teller in this case) performing these verbs, provide the context for your system. When formally written down, these phrases become the core verbiage in what's called the *problem statement*. In other words, a problem statement provides the formal boundaries (or context) for the foundation of your Visual Basic application. Figure 11.3 gives you an idea of what a problem statement might resemble.

After the problem statement matures over one or more sessions with domain experts (users knowledgeable about a particular area of concern), you'll want to peruse this document to identify key nouns and verbs. The list of nouns actually becomes a list of candidate actors or classes, whereas the list of verbs (and sometimes *gerunds*—nouns that are verbs ending with *-ing*) provides a candidate list of business processes carried out by actors (human users of your system or external systems that interact with your system) or methods that are members of a candidate class. By *candidate* I mean that these nouns and verbs require further analysis to determine whether they're truly actors, classes, business processes (or use cases), or methods.

FIGURE 11.3.

By using a word processor such as Microsoft Word, you can document a plain-English, high-level description of how users will use the system you'll be developing with Visual Basic.

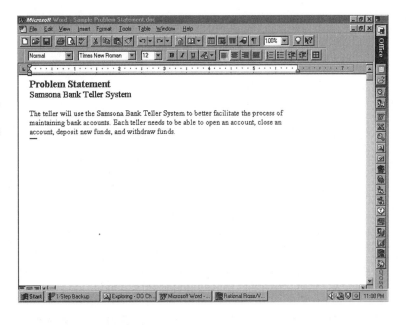

Based on your problem statement, the following list represents candidate classes and actors:

> teller
>
> Samsona Bank Teller System
>
> process
>
> bank accounts
>
> account
>
> funds

In analyzing each actor/class candidate, you or your team determines whether each item is meaningful to the context of the business processes being addressed by your system. By *meaningful*, I mean something that represents a role performed by users or external system, helps users produce a product or service that's valuable to the business, and isn't too vaguely defined within the context of your proposed system. For instance, the word *funds* is too vague for your system because the tellers don't actually create the funds or place the funds into your system. They merely accept funds from customers or give funds to them. Therefore, funds would be eliminated from your list of candidates.

If you're a beginning or intermediate object-oriented practitioner (an architect, analyst, designer, programmer, and tester), you might wonder why customers aren't mentioned in the problem statement. Answer: Customers aren't in the context of your system (your problem domain). The exchange of cash or information between tellers and customers is outside the scope of the Samsona Bank Teller System. Recall from the problem statement that your system helps tellers "better facilitate the process of maintaining bank accounts." Tellers interface with their customers in one context and then interface with your system in another. Your problem domain is concerned only with the second context. Business process engineering (designing and modeling of business tasks/responsibilities and events at the enterprise or workgroup level) would likely be concerned with the first context.

Going back to your list of candidate actors/classes, you'll notice that *teller* is obviously an important noun because this is the main actor who will use your system. Therefore, you now have your first actor. The noun *Samsona Bank Teller System* is actually the name of your system and, at this point, you assume that you don't have a compelling reason to model it as an actor or a class; therefore, it's no longer a viable candidate.

> **NOTE**
>
> In general, you wouldn't model your application as an actor or class. However, it can be modeled as a subsystem or package if it's part of a suite of applications.

The noun *process* actually describes the act of maintaining accounts and is too vague to be anything more than a description to help express the problem statement more fully for system developers. It, too, is no longer a viable candidate.

The noun *bank accounts* is a collection of accounts. Within the sentence that mentions bank accounts, you see that they're the main objects that tellers manage and, hence, as a collection, would be a strong candidate for a class (or more specifically, a collection class).

> **TIP**
>
> If you discover pluralized nouns in your problem statement that are significant to your system, make a design note to yourself that such nouns might be a collection class, which Visual Basic supports. An example of pluralized nouns is a noun with an *s* at the end that implies more than one of something.

Along similar lines, the noun *account* is also a strong candidate for a class. Again, the noun *funds* doesn't fit within your context, and is therefore not a viable candidate. Now you have a more streamlined, definitive list of actors and candidates that resembles Table 11.1.

TABLE 11.1. STRONG CANDIDATE ACTORS AND CLASSES.

Noun	Type
Teller	Actor
Bank Accounts	Class
Account	Class

You might also want to keep track of the reasons you rejected a candidate. This list is an artifact that might help future stakeholders on this project or other enterprise projects so that even the process of analyzing requirements and use cases can be reused throughout the company.

Your candidate list of verbs and verb phrases would include

> use
>
> facilitate
>
> maintaining bank accounts
>
> needs
>
> open an account
>
> close an account
>
> deposit new funds
>
> withdraw funds

Again, you want to model only meaningful verbs that provide value to the problem domain. This list of verbs and verb phrases eventually provides the context for a use-case model (which is roughly similar to the functional model of the Object Modeling Technique, or OMT), a class model, and an object model. Some verbs in your list of candidate verbs will be superfluous. Identifying such verbs might appear to be an elusive goal to beginners, but with only a few practice runs you should get a good feel for the process.

The verb *use* is too generic. It simply restates what you already know—that users will use your system. Hence, you would discard this verb from the list. The verb *facilitate* is also used merely as an expression of how users use the system; it doesn't convey any behavior that's meaningful for the actor (teller) or the system.

Maintain bank accounts sounds meaningful because, within the context of your system, tellers will do something with bank accounts, which at first glance might include some sort of management of such accounts. So let's keep it.

The verb *needs* conveys only that the following information is a requirement. Therefore, although the information that follows could very well pass from candidate to real verb, the verb *needs* by itself doesn't mean anything to the behavior of the system. So let's discard this verb.

Open an account, *close an account*, *deposit new funds*, and *withdraw funds* each sound like something tellers need to do with your system. A normal part of a teller's business processes is to open and close accounts, as well as deposit and withdraw funds. Let's keep this one.

IDENTIFYING TRUE ACTORS

Keep in mind that within the requirements context of your system, human tellers use your system, not customers. If it were customers, each teller would need to be an automated teller machine, and therefore opening and closing accounts wouldn't be meaningful to your system for logistical and legal reasons.

This is your list of verb phrases:

> maintain bank accounts
> open an account
> close an account
> deposit new funds
> withdraw funds

Now comes a gray area for most OOP novices. At this point, you could continue on to the use-case model and then on to design. However, the trained practitioner will notice that there's a potential conflict or overlapping of verbs. That is, you've just identified that your actor, the teller, can maintain accounts, as well as open and close accounts, and withdraw and deposit funds. Therefore, a question arises: Exactly what does *maintain bank accounts* mean? Is it not the operation (within your context) of opening and closing accounts and withdrawing and depositing funds? The intermediate object-oriented practitioner might say it is and proceed to eliminate the verb-like noun phrase *maintain bank accounts* from your list of system uses. However, the advanced practitioner might say that *maintain bank accounts* can be a high-level description of the grouping of operations represented as open account, close account, withdraw funds, and deposit funds.

Creating and Using Class Modules

CHAPTER 11

245

11

CREATING AND
USING CLASS
MODULES

The assessment you choose is entirely up to you; however, for the sake of simplicity, discard *maintain bank accounts*, as it's a grouping of the other verbs. Now your list looks more like this:

> open an account
>
> close an account
>
> deposit new funds
>
> withdraw funds

The Use-Case Model

The use-case model captures the verbs you discovered to be meaningful, with the actor and business domain classes that support each use case. A *use case* is an identified use by the actor of the system under development. In its simplest form, a use case is a description of one of many ways users use your system. These *ways* are also called *transactions*. Users (or human actors) perform a sequence of steps (or events) from beginning to end; that is what a use case captures. A use case can be *customized* (or instantiated) to capture how users execute the use case for a given scenario.

For instance, tellers can open accounts (a use case), but how do they open an account when a customer wants to open it with more than $10,000 cash? As you might know, in this situation the bank must file paperwork with the federal government to comply with laws that govern bank transactions involving cash amounts in excess of $10,000. This scenario, then, is a different instance (or customization) of the use case *open account*. It's certainly different from opening an account with less than $10,000 in cash. Use-case scenarios (and their corresponding sequence diagrams) describe each path (or instantiation) the use case can take.

Now re-examine the use-case model in Figure 11.1. This use-case model is the end result (or artifact) of your initial analysis process. At this point, you'd be proud to have your first use-case model complete. You're so proud, in fact, that you race off to display your stroke of genius with your domain experts (expert users or managers) who own the business process(es) behind this model.

At first, the experts are pleasantly surprised and impressed. They brag about you to an actual teller who will use the system being developed. The teller is pleased that progress is being made but notices something missing. He needs to be able to look up the customer's account information before closing it to make sure that the customer doesn't owe money to the bank and to make sure that the person is authorized to close the account. Also, he might just want to view the account information to answer a customer's questions.

In the traditional analysis process, you would have to restructure the data-flow diagrams in various places and redo the program code (because you probably already started coding the requirements). This rework usually involves patching in the new functionality, meaning new global functions were inserted in some module somewhere, or the code was tucked behind a button on a form. Some programmers may not be this motivated ; they might growl that the requested feature wasn't in the original specs and therefore can't be incorporated.

With the object-oriented analysis approach, such crucial change requests are easily incorporated, provided they naturally fit within the context of your problem domain. Clearly, the viewing of account information is a mission-critical feature (as agreed by each stakeholder in the project) and as such needs to be added to your use-case model. Because you've done no coding, the only time needed is to insert another use case into your model and update the problem statement (another often overlooked step). Figure 11.4 shows your updated problem statement; Figure 11.5 represents the updated use-case model.

FIGURE 11.4.

The updated problem statement.

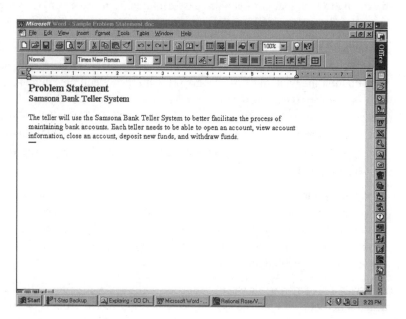

FIGURE 11.5.

The updated use-case model.

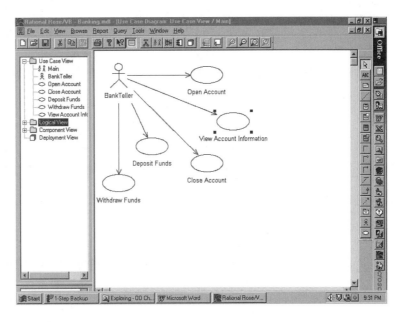

The Sequence Diagram

As alluded to earlier, a sequence diagram (also known as an *interaction diagram* or *event trace diagram*) is a diagrammatic representation of a specific instance of a use case. This specific use-case instance is called a *scenario*. There are two types of scenarios: normal and abnormal.

The *normal scenario* captures the normal interaction between the actor and the system. At the analysis level, the system is represented by the main domain object—the analysis object that interacts with the actor. You don't care about forms, buttons, or interfaces at this point; these objects are exposed during the design iteration (or phase). In diagramming a normal scenario, you're asking yourself and your project stakeholders what actions the actor will normally carry out when there are no anomalies or error conditions.

A normal scenario can take alternate paths, each of which is still normal. For instance, the use case *open account* could have at least two alternate normal scenarios: *open savings account* and *open checking account*.

Abnormal scenarios capture use-case paths that take into consideration anomalies and error conditions. For instance, an abnormal path for *close account* might be this: The account being closed doesn't exist. Also, for the *withdraw funds* use case, you'll have a scenario that deals with the situation where there aren't enough funds to withdraw.

To build a list of normal and abnormal scenarios to illustrate in your sequence diagrams, you'll need to interview domain experts and end users. Assuming that this was accomplished, the current scenarios are listed in Table 11.2.

TABLE 11.2. USE CASES AND THEIR RESPECTIVE SCENARIOS

Use Case	Scenario
Open an Account	The customer is new with no previous accounts and has the minimum required balance.
	The customer has an existing account that's active.
	The customer has an existing account that's inactive.
	The customer is new but doesn't have the minimum required balance.
	The customer is new with no previous accounts but wants to deposit more than $10,000 in cash.
Close an Account	An active account exists and the customer is authorized to close it.
	The account being closed is inactive.
	The customer isn't authorized to close the account.
	The customer is authorized to close the account, but the account is deficient or the customer owes money to the bank.
Deposit New Funds	An active account exists and the customer is authorized to deposit money in it.
	The customer isn't authorized to deposit money in the account.
	The amount being deposited exceeds $10,000 in cash.
Withdraw Funds	An active account exists and the customer is authorized to withdraw money from it.
	The customer isn't authorized to withdraw money from the account.
	The teller tries to withdraw more money at the customer's request than is available.

For simplicity's sake, you'll concentrate on the first sequence diagram for the *open an account* use case. Assume that you had a use-case meeting with the users and domain experts, who then elaborated on the steps involved.

The First Sequence Diagram

As noted in Table 11.2, the first scenario is the normal path that reads "The customer is new with no previous accounts and has the minimum required balance." Before diagramming this scenario, you should elaborate on the steps involved. A good format for proceeding would be to identify the scenario that belongs to the use case. You could assign a unique identifier to the use case as well as the scenario as follows:

Use Case 001: Open an Account

Scenario 01: The customer is new with no previous accounts and has the minimum required balance

Step 1: The Teller provides the customer information to the system

Step 2: The Teller wants to check the customer's checking history with Telecheck

Step 3: After the Teller sees that the customer has a good checking history, the Teller provides the opening deposit balance to the system

Step 4: The Teller prints out the new account information

Notice that in elaborating on the steps involved in this use case, you've actually uncovered some more significant nouns and verbs, as follows:

Nouns	Verbs
customer information	provide the customer information to the system
customer	check the customer's checking history
system	provide the opening deposit balance to the system
checking history	print out the new account information
Telecheck	
opening deposit balance	
account information	

Before creating the sequence diagram, you must again determine which nouns and verbs are significant.

The nouns *customer information* and *account information* each have a word in them that provides strong clues as to its importance in your proposed system: *information*. Words such as *customer information* or *account information* almost always imply properties (or attributes) of classes in your system. They certainly imply relational database tables. Because the words *customer* and *account* are so pivotal in your domain, the architects, analysts, and lead designers agree that these should be nominal domain classes. Let's keep them.

The noun *customer* is just another representation of *customer information*. You already decided to incorporate a nominal class named *customer*, so this is repetition. You can discard it.

The noun *system* is a more generic reference to your application name, which is Samsona Bank Teller System. If you want the analysis-view use case to remain generic enough to be reused across your enterprise, it's probably best to leave it as *system*. However, if you decide that the actual application name is more meaningful, by all means use the full system name. Because you already have identified the system as the Samsona Bank Teller System, use the full name. Thus, you've just replaced the word *system* with *Samsona Bank Teller System*.

The noun *checking history* is rather interesting. For simplicity's sake, you've left out that there's more than one kind of account in banking systems. Furthermore, in your domain (or context), the domain experts and users didn't mention any particular type of account. After a quick meeting with these stakeholders, you agreed that for this release of the system, you wouldn't consider the various kinds of accounts. Therefore, *checking history* becomes a nominal class, but not a specialization of the Account class you already identified in your earlier analysis.

> **NOTE**
>
> Many object-oriented beginners might easily miss this very important point entirely. Don't create classes and actors simply because it seems logical. Stick to the project plan. Such deviations, although thoughtful, usually slow down the object-oriented process, which then lead many people to exaggerate the length of time object-oriented projects typically take. You can speed up object-oriented projects by not adding unnecessary or uncalled-for features and objects to the project.

The noun *Telecheck* is, in the familiar English composition sense, an indirect object in that it's on the receiving end of the action initiated by the Teller. However, you don't know exactly what Telecheck means, so you ask the experts. They tell you that it's a vendor who provides research services to the bank. The Teller views the information supplied by Telecheck to determine whether the customer can establish an account. On further investigation, you discover that an electronic interface exists between the bank teller's machine and the vendor. Through this interface, the Teller sends customer information to Telecheck for verification and research. The results of the research are returned directly to the terminal screen in the current system.

Based on this behavior, you've concluded that Telecheck is an actor that you could stereotype as an *external system*. Therefore, you promote it from a noun to an actor and have to update your use-case model. Figure 11.6 shows what your new use-case model looks like.

FIGURE 11.6.

The actor Telecheck is incorporated into your use-case model.

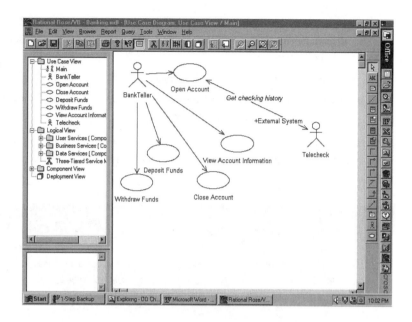

The noun *opening deposit balance* is a monetary amount. You might be tempted to model it as a class, but does it really exhibit behavior or have attributes? If it were a candidate class, it would have only one attribute (or property): Value. Identifying classes and members of classes (properties and methods) isn't always an easy process, and even the very best object technologists admit that they don't always immediately identify classes correctly the first time. So, on further analysis, you discover that *opening deposit balance* is actually a property of your Account class. How did you gather this? The adjective *opening* provides a big clue—it implies that something other than the object *balance* is going to fluctuate at some point in time. Balances fluctuate, but so do accounts. Then you remember that when you get a monthly account statement from your bank, there's a beginning balance and an ending balance. And because the account statement is merely a snapshot (or instance) of your account information, you've finally decided that Balance is an attribute of the Account class. In general, a good rule of thumb to use (loosely) is that if a candidate class has only one property (or attribute) and no methods, it might actually be a property of a larger class.

The verb phrase *provide the customer information to the system* (*system* now being *Samsona Bank Teller System*) indicates an action taken by the Teller against the system. This action is also known as an *event*. You've decided that this event is valid and, therefore, will incorporate this verb phrase into your sequence diagram.

The verb phrase *check the customer's checking history* is an action the Teller carries out by using the interface to the Telecheck system. Therefore, you should incorporate it into your sequence diagram.

The verb phrase *provide the opening deposit balance to the system* (*system* now being *Samsona Bank Teller System*) specifies information about the new account being supplied by the Teller. Thus, you should incorporate it into your sequence diagram.

The verb phrase *print out the new account information* is also an event initiated by the Teller against the system. Therefore, you should incorporate it into your sequence diagram.

> **NOTE**
>
> Because the Teller is specifying that account information be printed out, this suggests that *print* is a possible method for your Account class. This is true of each verb and verb phrase; they become possible methods for the class indicated in the indirect object part of the sentence or phrase.

Now you're ready to create your sequence diagram. Samsona Bank Teller System will be represented by some class that implements one of its behaviors. Your nominal nouns and verbs phrases list looks like this:

Nouns	Verbs
customer	provides the customer information to the Samsona Bank Teller System
Samsona Bank Teller System	checks the customer's checking history
checking history	provides the opening deposit balance to the Samsona Bank Teller System
Telecheck	prints out the new account information
account (property: Balance)	

Figure 11.7 shows what your sequence diagram looks like. The stick figures are the Jacobson symbols for actors. Although Telecheck is a machine-based system, you still model it as a stick-figure actor. The lines with the arrow at one end represent events and actions being carried out by actors and domain class instances (or objects). The rectangle preceding each line is called the *focus of control bar*. These bars indicate that each line protruding from it is part of the same event or action. For instance, the Teller-initiated event Provide Info is the only event in the Teller's focus of control (or duration of a single event or action). However, both Check lines, as well as the Supply History and Display History lines, are all part of the check history event initiated by the Teller.

FIGURE 11.7.

The sequence diagram shows the stimuli being sent from one object to another. The main actor, the Teller, initiates the events and is therefore the first object on the left.

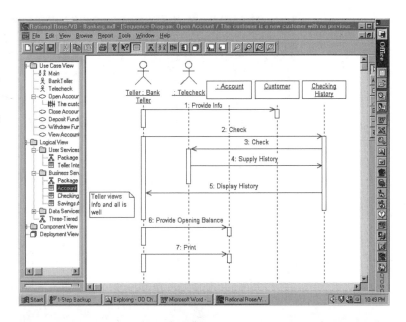

Rational Rose 98 enables you to do this type of modeling automatically. Rational Rose 98, based on the Unified Modeling Language (UML), is available for a hefty price from Rational Corporation (www.rational.com). If you don't have the resources to purchase Rational Rose, simply do the modeling by hand. Visio's latest version of its modeling tool offers limited features for the Unified Modeling Language (UML).

Visual Studio Modeler is available free to owners of Visual Studio 98 Enterprise, which includes Visual Basic 6 Enterprise Edition. It doesn't incorporate use cases, however, so you can't do sequence diagrams in it.

The Analysis Class Model

By now, you've identified a collection class (BankAccounts), and several classes (Account, Customer, CheckingHistory). The initial class model will have these three classes as model items. Figure 11.8 shows what this model looks like.

FIGURE 11.8.

The initial class model.

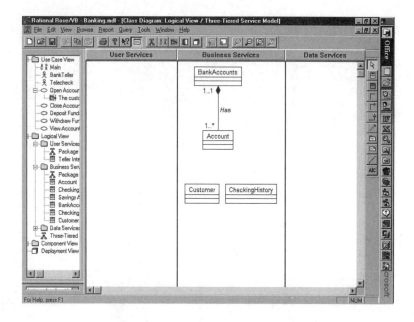

Notice that the collection class `BankAccounts` contains many `Account` class instances (or objects). The black diamond indicates this relationship, which in Visual Basic would be represented as `ByVal` (as opposed to just `ByRef`). This relationship is named *Has*, which is another way of saying that `BankAccounts` contains many `Account` objects. The notation 1..1 and 1..* together is known as the relationship's *cardinality*. Because there's only one `BankAccounts` object, its cardinality is 1..1; because you can have one to an unlimited number of Account objects in your collection, Account's cardinality in the relationship is 1..*. The asterisk (*) represents an unlimited number. The `Customer` and `CheckingHistory` classes are relationships that have meaning only with respect to the actors in your system. You can formalize these actors' events in your system through *control objects*. Control objects are responsible for controlling the flow of events between a boundary class (such as a form interface object) and the rest of the underlying application code.

Summary

In this chapter, you should have gained not only a better understanding of the role of analysis in object-oriented system development, but a lasting appreciation of it. There can be no effective object-oriented programming in Visual Basic without a thorough and iterative analysis process. Analysis should never be confused with design or programming; doing so leads to a flawed system architecture and *hacking* (or disorganized, haphazard programming). Using a *methodology* to cultivate this evolutionary process is crucial. An analysis methodology centered on how users expect to use the proposed system is absolutely necessary. Ivar Jacobson provides perhaps the best methodology for capturing these expected uses. This methodology is part of the overall objectory method and gives birth to the use-case modeling technique.

The three primary roles usually involved in the use-case identification process are the requirements gatherer, the object-oriented analyst, and the architect. The requirements gatherer typically interrogates end users, business managers (or domain experts), and project managers to draft a problem statement and, optionally, an initial requirements model. The object-oriented analyst carefully examines the requirements model to understand the requirements and elaborates on the requirements model, assesses the implications of each requirement, and removes inconsistencies and requirements discovered to no longer be valid. Object-oriented architects work with analysts and designers to ensure that project team members can trace the names of business objects between the list of requirements, analysis models, and design models. Architects sometimes perform the roles of analyst and designer; otherwise, the architect is a mediator and final decision-maker with regard to the system architecture. With the advent of the software reuse structure of the business organization, these roles will become more specialized (partitioned into smaller roles).

The problem statement is used to capture, in plain English, how users see the system helping them complete their business processes. From this problem statement, the analyst and architect identify and list meaningful nouns and verbs, which helps technicians identify potential actors, classes, class behavior, and use cases. When a list of these objects is drafted, the superfluous or vague items are discarded in favor of those with stronger meaning to the current problem domain (or business context). The main artifacts of the analysis process are the problem statement, the use-case model, and an analysis class model.

Database Programming

In This Part

- **An Overview of Database Programming in VB6** *259*

- **The ADO Data Control** *269*

- **Working in the Data Environment** *299*

- **Using the Data Report Utility** *315*

- **Database Tools and Utilites** *337*

- **Advanced Data Controls** *357*

- **SQL and the T-SQL Debugger** *391*

An Overview of Database Programming in VB6

by Rob Thayer

IN THIS CHAPTER

- Database Access Methods in VB6   *260*
- The Data View Window   *264*
- The Data Environment Designer   *264*
- Database Controls   *266*
- The Future of Data Access in VB   *266*

Database access in Visual Basic is a complicated subject. More experienced programmers are undoubtedly very familiar with the way databases work and how they are organized, but that's just the tip of the iceberg. As Visual Basic has evolved, many changes have been made concerning data access. Special data-bound controls are constantly being added to VB's toolbox to ease the creation of database applications. In fact, VB6 comes with four new data-bound controls.

The choices available for database access interfaces have also multiplied in recent years, with a considerable number of access methods on tap in VB6. In addition to the common Data Access Objects (DAO) interface, there is also RDO and the newly introduced ADO (ActiveX Data Objects).

Also new to VB6 is the Database Environment, a concept for visualizing the databases that are used in an application. The Database Environment is likely to be a big part of the future of database programming in Visual Basic, so it's important to give this new feature the attention it deserves.

Some of the biggest changes in VB6 are in the area of database access. Visual Basic is evolving into a serious tool for enterprise development, and strong database functionality is an essential means to that end. You simply cannot master Visual Basic without mastering database access.

This chapter will provide an overview of how databases are used in VB. This does not mean that it will give a detailed discussion of how databases, tables, and recordsets relate to one another. You can find that in any book for novice VB programmers. Instead of attempting to teach you the basics that you already know, the goal here is to show you what your options are when utilizing databases in your Visual Basic programs. Which database access methods are best, and why? What kind of ActiveX controls are available in the toolbox for working with databases? What is ADO all about, and what does the future hold for data access in Visual Basic? These are the types of questions that will be answered here.

Database Access Methods in VB6

The VB6 programmer has more interfaces for accessing databases available to him than ever before. When it comes to data access interfaces, there are three main choices: DAO, RDO, and ADO.

In the past, DAO (Data Access Objects) was the standard database access method for Visual Basic programmers. We've all become very familiar with DAO because it was the first database interface included with Visual Basic, introduced with VB3. RDO, which was introduced with the VB4 Enterprise Edition, has also become quite popular.

However, the heir to the throne of VB data access is a newcomer called ActiveX Data Objects or ADO. It hasn't reached its prime just yet, and it is still somewhat limited. But ADO is destined to eventually replace all of the other data access methods. Many of the enhancements to VB6 center around ADO, as you'll soon see.

With so many database access interfaces available, which one do you use? There is no clear-cut answer to this question, because the interface to use really depends on performance issues and the kind of database you'll be accessing. Is the data stored locally or remotely? Is speed or flexibility a concern? How about ease of use? These questions need to be answered before choosing a suitable access interface.

After you know the kind of database you'll be dealing with, you must also know the roles that each data access method plays. We'll start with that old stand-by, DAO.

DAO

DAO (Data Access Objects) has been around since VB3, so it has gained a strong foothold with VB programmers and is very widely used. Because it is also used in other development platforms, such as Microsoft Access, DAO is probably the most popular access method for Windows. DAO utilizes Microsoft's Jet database engine and can be used to access a wide variety of database formats, including Microsoft Access, ISAM (Indexed Sequential Access Method), and Text.

In addition to using Jet, DAO can also access ODBC (Open Database Connectivity) databases through its ODBCDirect object model. ODBC databases, such as Informix, SQL Server, or Oracle, are typically located on a separate database server.

The DAO object model consists of 17 object types, with the most basic being `Databases`, `Recordsets`, and `Fields`. Databases are accessed by opening an existing `Database` object or creating a new one. Part or all of a database table is held in a `Recordset` object. The individual fields (or columns) in a table make up a `Recordset`'s `Field` objects. With the exception of the `DBEngine` object, all of the DAO objects are members of a collection: a `Database` object belongs to the `Databases` collection, a `Recordset` belongs to the `Recordsets` collection, and so on.

When using the ODBCDirect model, the `Database` object is replaced with the `Connection` object. The two objects are similar, but the `Connection` object can include information required to access the database, such as the ODBC connect string.

To make things easier on programmers, DAO can be implemented through an ActiveX control (the `Data` control). This allows a large amount of DAO's power to be utilized without having to add a single line of code. When used in conjunction with data-aware ActiveX controls such as `TextBox` or `DBList`, the `Data` control can be very powerful.

In a nutshell, the `Data` control lets a data-aware control automatically access information from a database by binding it to a specific field in a database's table. What you can do through the `Data` control is limited, of course, and code is often needed to really tap into DAO's full functionality.

With DAO's relative ease of use and great flexibility, it seems that it would be the correct choice for a large number of database applications. But all of that flexibility comes at a price, and DAO suffers by having a large footprint and mediocre efficiency. For small-scale applications that use local databases, DAO fits the bill nicely. For enterprise development, however, there is RDO.

RDO

Similar to DAO is Remote Data Objects, or RDO. In fact, these two database interfaces sometimes work together. When DAO uses the ODBCDirect model, it does it through RDO.

RDO is essentially a wrapper around the ODBC API and the driver manager that interacts with an ODBC database. RDO is faster than DAO and uses less workstation resources. It also allows the programmer more control over connections to client/server databases and lets him fully utilize the power of ODBC. On the down side, it is somewhat harder to use than DAO. Because RDO is used primarily by professional programmers for building enterprise applications, it is only available with the Enterprise Edition of Visual Basic.

RDO has gained quite a bit of popularity over the years and is often used for accessing large relational databases from Visual Basic. Unlike DAO, RDO supports complex stored procedures.

The RDO model consists of a total of nine different object types. A connection to a database is referenced by a `rdoConnection` object. This can contain `rdoTable` objects and `rdoResultset` (recordset) objects. Other object types include `rdoQuery` and `rdoColumn`, the equivalent of DAO's `Field` object. Like DAO's objects, all of RDO's objects are also members of collections with the exception of the `rdoEngine` object.

Defining the objects that make up an RDO database system is made easier by the UserConnection designer. This utility allows you to create database connections and query objects, and to write code to respond to RDO object events.

RDO uses the Remote Data Control like DAO uses the Data control. You can use it to bind data-aware controls to fields (called columns in RDO) in a database table.

DAO works well for small-scale local databases, and RDO works well with larger relational databases in a client/server environment. For those who have become proficient in DAO and RDO, it's a great combination. But alas, DAO and RDO are being phased out. The new kid on the block is ADO, which promises to combine the benefits of both of these database access interfaces.

ADO

ADO, or ActiveX Data Objects, seems to be a one-size-fits-all approach to database access. It can connect to virtually any type of database, both relational and non-relational, local and remote. You can even use ADO to access email and file systems or custom business objects. It doesn't take up as many system resources as DAO, and it's very efficient. The current version (2.0) includes an ActiveX control somewhat similar to the Data and RemoteData controls, so data-aware components can be bound to database columns. ADO can also use the Data Environment, a graphically represented hierarchy of database connections. Sounds good, right? Well, yes and no.

Even though ADO is now in its second version, it still hasn't quite come of age yet. It does provide more functionality than RDO, but it hasn't caught up to DAO. More advanced DAO features like data definition language (DDL), users, and groups are not supported by ADO. What it boils down to is this: If you're using RDO or DAO's ODBCDirect object model, you can accomplish the same thing with ADO. On the other hand, if you're using the Jet database engine through DAO, you'll have to wait until ADO matures.

So why fix something that isn't broken? Well, because Microsoft says we should. DAO and RDO will eventually be phased out, so it makes sense to jump on the ADO bandwagon as soon as possible. It's unlikely that Microsoft will make any major improvements to ODBC, so you've probably gone just about as far as you can go with that technology. You'll also need to start using ADO if you want to exploit many of the features that are new to VB6, such as the Data Report Utility. Yet another reason is the fact that ADO is becoming the de facto standard data access method for Web applications.

ADO is also one of the key components in Microsoft's Universal Data Access Strategy. Universal Data Access defines standards for application development using a multi-tiered approach to software design. Though a detailed discussion of Universal Data Access is out of the scope of this chapter, it is important to note that ADO has been singled out as the standard for database access in the UDA strategy.

If you're using RDO in the majority of your programs, the jump to ADO will make more sense because you won't be losing any of the functionality that you already have; in fact, you'll be gaining functionality. You'll also have less of a learning curve because ADO is similar to RDO.

ADO is actually an Automation wrapper for OLE DB, a COM-based interface designed for universal data access. As you probably already know, Visual Basic is built on COM. It follows suit that this new database interface is also built on COM. Because ADO and OLE DB are COM-based, they are compatible with any development platform that supports ActiveX. This includes VBA, Active Server Pages, and scripting languages.

The ADO model consists of eight object types, many of which are similar to the objects in the RDO model and all of which are grouped into collections. The `Connection` object contains information about a data provider and its database schema. The `Recordset` object is the basic equivalent of DAO's `Recordset` object and RDO's `Resultset` object. It holds some or all of the records in a database table. Within the `Recordset` objects are `Field` objects, which are the columns in the database table.

Other objects in the ADO model include `Command`s that contain information about a command such as a query string. This is the equivalent of RDO's `rdoQuery` object. If a `Command` is parameterized, it can have one or more `Parameter` objects associated with it.

The `Error` object contains information about an error that has occurred with a data provider. It is similar to RDO's `rdoError` object; but in ADO, the `Errors` collection is on a `Connection` object instead of on the database interface engine.

ADO also provides built-in and dynamic `Property` objects for defining characteristics of an ADO object. These are similar to the `Property` objects supported by DAO.

The Data View Window

One of the new features in VB6 is the Data View window. This window lets you see the database connections for your project. It also shows the structure of the database for each connection.

Figure 12.1 shows the Data View window. Only one connection, to the Biblio database, is currently being used.

The Data Environment Designer

Visual Basic 6 introduces the Data Environment designer, a design-time tool that allows you to set up data access for your application. With it, you can add database connections, stored procedures, tables, views, synonyms, and SQL statements. All objects are organized into a hierarchy based on their relationship with one another.

FIGURE 12.1.

The Data View window shows the database connections for a project.

Figure 12.2 shows a sample Data Environment that contains a `Connection` object (`Biblio`) and three `Command` objects (`TitlesQuery`, `Authors`, and `OtherQuery`). `TitlesQuery` and `OtherQuery` are both SQL statements, and `Authors` is a table.

FIGURE 12.2.

A sample Data Environment window.

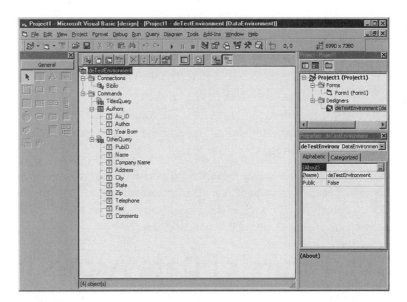

12

AN OVERVIEW OF DATABASE PROGRAMMING

You can also add code to respond to an ActiveX Data Object control's events using the Data Environment designer. You can also write code for `Connection` and `Recordset` objects.

The Data Environment designer supports drag-and-drop operations, so you can drag a field from the designer and drop it onto a Visual Basic form or the Data Report designer. The Data Report designer is discussed in Chapter 15, "Using the Data Report Utility."

Those who are familiar with RDO's UserConnection designer will see some parallels between that utility and the Data Environment designer. However, the Data Environment designer is more powerful and allows you to do things the UserConnection designer does not. For example, with the Data Environment designer, you can access multiple data sources. The UserConnection designer limits you to a single data source.

You can find more information about the Data Environment designer in Chapter 14, "Working in the Data Environment."

Database Controls

Visual Basic comes with a number of data-aware or data-bound ActiveX controls in its toolbox. Some, like the `TextBox` control, can simply be bound to a database field or column. Others, such as the new `DataGrid` control or the `DBList` control, are far more complex and can display a large amount of database information.

The introduction of the `ADO Data` control and the ADO database access method has brought some new ActiveX controls that have been optimized to work with ADO. The `DataGrid`, `DataList`, `DataCombo`, and `DataRepeater` controls all can use ADO. The new `Hierarchical FlexGrid` control works with hierarchical cursors that have been created with the Data Environment designer.

VB6's new `MonthView` and `DateTimePicker` controls can be bound to a database field to display date and time information. You can read more about these controls in Chapter 2, "New ActiveX Controls."

Standard controls that can be bound to a database field or column include: `CheckBox`, `ComboBox`, `Image`, `ImageCombo`, `Label`, `ListBox`, `MaskedEdit`, `PictureBox`, and `TextBox`. Other existing controls, such as `DBCombo`, `DBGrid`, `DBList`, `FlexGrid`, and `MSChart`, have been designed to work primarily with databases.

The Future of Data Access in VB

There's no doubt about it, ADO will eventually replace DAO and RDO. It's unlikely that Microsoft will completely remove support for DAO and RDO from Visual Basic, at least not in the next few releases. However, this support may be dropped with a subsequent release. An updated version of ADO will probably be available on the Internet before the next version of VB hits the market, and ADO will be much improved by the time VB7 is released.

ADO is still in its infancy, and it definitely has a way to go before it can completely replace DAO and RDO. But this is a hot technology, and Microsoft will undoubtedly put a lot of effort in getting it up to snuff.

You probably don't want to go through the trouble of migrating your existing RDO applications to ADO, but you should seriously consider using ADO for any new projects that you may start. If you're using the Jet database engine through DAO (as opposed to ODBCDirect), or if you're using DDL, then you'll have to wait until ADO matures.

Summary

With the addition of ADO (ActiveX Data Objects), Visual Basic programmers have more choices than ever for the method by which they access databases. This chapter discussed the three different access methods (DAO, RDO, and ADO) and the ways in which each is typically used. It also briefly discussed the new Data View window and the Data Environment designer, as well as the data-aware and data-bound ActiveX controls in VB's toolbox.

Although it focused on the present state of database access in Visual Basic, this chapter also theorized about the future of data access in VB. It showed how ADO fits into the scheme of things, and whether or not using ADO now is a good idea.

The ADO Data Control

by Loren Eidahl

IN THIS CHAPTER

- ADO: An Overview   270
- A Review of Relational Databases   270
- Examining the Use of Client/Server Design   276
- Using the ADO Control and Libraries   279
- Remoting of ADO Recordsets   295

ADO: An Overview

ActiveX Data Objects (ADO) is nearly revolutionary in its concept and scope. It is not a database connector like DAO or ODBC, rather it is an extensible set of data access objects that is a programming model. These objects are based on OLE DB, which operates at the basic API (Application Programming Interface) level. ADO wraps this functionality into an easy-to-use flexible package that will be the basis of all of Microsoft's future data access development. Even better news is that if you are familiar with DAO or RDO, you will have a very short and shallow learning curve to master ADO.

In the previous version of Visual Basic, ADO was shipped as part of the Visual InterDev product. With the release of Visual Basic 6, ADO is now the default database connection method for all versions of Visual Basic.

In the past, Visual Basic programs were created to provide access to data. The first data was simple ASCII files. This was followed by an interface known as VBSQL that was used to interface with SQL Server databases. The emphasis then shifted to ISAM databases, such as MS Access. Microsoft created the Jet Database Engine and Data Access Objects (DAO) to allow easy access to the Jet. Mixed into all of this was Open Database Connectivity (ODBC), which provided remote access to a heterogeneous group of database engines through ODBC drivers.

The latest and most significant development is OLE DB, which provides access to a heterogeneous group of types of data stores, including relational databases. The ActiveX Data Objects is a programming interface model that gives access to OLE DB.

A Review of Relational Databases

Relational databases are based on the theoretical work by E. F. Codd. Prior to Codd's concept of relational databases, attempts were made to use a number of database structures. The organizational structures were elegant and performed the task, but the inverted tree and other structures proved inflexible after their creation. Any change to the structure was a major effort and required recompilation of the database. One of the great features of relational databases is the flexibility. Adding another item of data is no problem with the relational model.

A relational database management system (RDBMS) is a software application that stores data. This data is arranged in such a way as to be available for reading, updating, adding new records, and deleting records. The RDBMS doesn't need a front-end or user interface. It is sufficient if the database accepts command-line commands (in the form of SQL statements, discussed later in this chapter), executes the command and returns a group of records, updates a record, adds a record, or deletes a record.

The user interface (UI) usually is a separate function that is in a totally separate application program called a client. The client/server design concept is explored in a later section of this chapter.

Tables

Data in a relational database is organized in tables. A table is a two-dimensional organizational structure that is composed of rows and columns. A column contains a specific category of data, such as the names or Social Security numbers of a group of people, for example. In such an example, the collection of data regarding a particular individual, such as name, Social Security number, address, and phone number, are contained within a *row*.

Table 13.1 is an example of a table that contains the contact information in a PIM (*Personal Information Manager*).

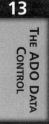

TABLE 13.1. A CONTACTS TABLE.

Last Name	First Name	Area Code	Phone No.
Jones	John	520	555-1212
Hansen	Sue	212	555-1212
Adams	Sue	602	444-3434
Adams	Phil	602	444-3434
Smith	Fred	303	222-2323

This looks very much like the information that is kept in many pocket diaries. The rows in the table are not in any particular sequence.

Primary Keys

One requirement for a table is that each row of the table be unique. This unique identifier can be a specific column that contains an item of information that is unique, such as the Social Security number of an individual or the serial number of a computer. The primary key can be composed of more than one column.

Notice in Table 13.1 that neither the last name nor the phone number will work as a primary key. Phil and Sue have the same last name and phone number. The first name will not work as the primary key because Sue Hansen and Sue Adams have the same first name. With the data contained in this table, only the combination of the first name, last name, area code and phone number can be used as the primary key to uniquely identify a record.

Experience dictates that using the first and last name as the primary key is not a good choice for a table that has many people listed in it. There are certainly many people in the world with the name John Jones. As you design the database table, think of a good choice for the primary key. One strategy is to create a unique number that is attached to each record as the primary key. This works quite well, except for the fact that you can have more than one record for the same individual and not know it.

Understanding Data Normalization

The rules of normalization are of paramount importance in the proper design of a relational database. Application of these rules keeps the database designer from falling into some traps that may cause problems. These rules are called normalization, and a database that complies is said to be in the normal form. There are three rules or normal forms that are usually applied. These are called the first, second, and third normal forms. What they lack in imaginative naming, they make up for in usefulness.

First Normal Form

A table is in the first normal form if all columns in the table contain atomic values, which means a column contains only one item of data, such as a phone number or child's name, but never two items of the same type of data, such as two or more phone numbers or the name of two or more people.

Second Normal Form

A table is in the second normal form if it is in the first normal form and every value is dependent on the primary key value. An example is if you attempt to construct a table composed of first name, last name, and phone number, where the first and last name are used as the primary key. This will work until you attempt to record the second phone number for a person, such as the work and home phone numbers. If you choose to use the phone number rather than the first and last name as the primary key, you would run into the problem of two people having the same phone number. You can begin to see the problems with different database designs and how the normalization rules can help.

> **NOTE**
>
> The language of relational databases can be somewhat arcane and obtuse. The statement that a data item must depend on the primary key is one of these cases. What this means is that without the presence of the primary key, say my Social Security number, you wouldn't have my name in the record. The two, the SSN and the name, are linked together.

Third Normal Form

A table is said to be in the third normal form if the table is in the first and the second normal forms and if every value depends on only the primary key. This is the most difficult to understand of the commonly used normal forms. An example is if you are constructing a table that includes pay rates. In your theoretical organization, all people occupying a particular job title are paid the same amount of money, regardless of their time at that job. In this case, the pay rate depends on the job title, not the person occupying the job. If you constructed a database to describe this organization, you would need to create a table of job titles and pay rates and a table of employees. You would place the key of the job title table in the employee table as a foreign or cross reference key, not the pay rate itself. In other words, the pay rate goes with the job, not the individual. The individual occupies the job and the job title has a pay rate.

> **NOTE**
>
> There are actually five normal forms. The last two are rarely used and delve into mathematical theory that is easy to forget. I have never had occasion to use the fourth and fifth normal forms.

Using Foreign Keys

Why is this important? Because a well designed relational database does not contain redundant data. An item of information, such as a name, should occur only once in a database so that if the item of data (name) needs to be changed, it needs to be changed only one time.

For example, suppose an employee of your company named Dorothy Rubyslippers marries Cal Combatboots and decides to change her name to Dorothy Combatboots. If her name appears in multiple tables in your company's database, each and every one of the tables containing her name must be located and changed. If the database is properly constructed, however, her name would need to be changed in just one place.

If a table contains multiple instances of an item of information about an individual, such as multiple phone numbers, all the phone numbers should be moved into a separate table. The two tables then need a common item of information that can be used to cross-reference the two tables. As an example, look at Tables 13.2 and 13.3.

TABLE 13.2. NAME TABLE.

SSN	Last Name	First Name	Sex
123-45-6789	Jones	John	Male
111-22-3333	Hansen	Sue	Female
012-43-8765	Adams	Sue	Female
888-22-1111	Adams	Phil	Male
666-55-4444	Smith	Fred	Male

TABLE 13.3. PHONE NUMBER TABLE.

Key	Foreign Key	Area Code	Phone No.
1	123-45-6789	520	555-1212
3	012-43-8765	212	555-1212
9	111-22-3333	602	444-3434
25	888-22-1111	312	444-3434
26	123-45-6789	520	444-3434
72	666-55-4444	215	111-2222
73	012-43-8765	212	222-3333
81	666-55-4444	215	333-4444
88	888-22-1111	312	444-5555
89	111-22-3333	602	555-6666

In Tables 13.2 and 13.3, the Social Security number (SSN) is used as the common item of information to correlate the two tables because it is the only column of information that has a unique entry for each individual. In the Names table, the SSN is the primary key. In the Phone Number table, a number is assigned as the primary key. The Phone Number table contains the SSN as a foreign key. It is the key from the Names table.

These two tables exist in a parent/child relationship; the Name table is the parent of the child Phone Number table.

The best way to decide whether data should be included in a table or moved to a separate table is to determine if the data item depends on the primary key and there is only one of them. For example, if you create a table that contains data about a group of people, each person will have only one Social Security number, only one date and place of birth, and will be either male or female. Therefore, all this data can go in one table. However, when you look at other data associated with these individuals, such as the names of their children, the makes of their cars, and their telephone numbers, you realize many of them have more than one of these items. Therefore, each of these items should be in its own separate child table.

Referential Integrity

The referential integrity of a database concerns the parent/child relationship between tables. In the preceding example regarding the Names and Phone Numbers tables, there shouldn't be a record in the Phone Number table unless there is a parent record in the Name table. If you delete the record of an individual from the Name table, all of the associated records from the Phone Number table should also be deleted. It is a violation of referential integrity if there are records in the Phone Number table that have no associated record in the Name table. In this situation, the records in the Phone Number table that have no parent records are called orphan records.

The relationships between tables are classified as one to many, one to one, many to one, and many to many. These relationships are important in the use of the database, which you will find out in the section concerning the Structured Query Language.

> **NOTE**
>
> In Microsoft Access, when the relationships between tables are set forth in a database, cascading updates and deletes can be specified. If the database engine does not provide this to be done automatically, then it needs to be done with program code. It is important that you understand the characteristics of the database engine you will be using.

Indexes

Because the rows of a table are not organized in any particular order, the RDBMS provides the capability to create one or more indexes. An index is a separate table that lists in order, either ascending or descending, the contents of a particular table with pointers to the records in the table. An index provides increased search speed when searching a database table for a specific record or set of records. Instead of reading the entire table, a search of the index is performed, and the resulting list of pointers is used to collect the records from the base table.

Views

A view is a copy of a table or tables that doesn't exist except as a results set that is created when the view is queried. For example, imagine a table in a company's personnel records database that includes the home phone number of the employee. In this company, as in many, the home phone number is considered confidential information. If the company gives employees access to the personnel table as a company directory, they will have a problem.

The solution is to create a view on the personnel table that doesn't include the column for home phone numbers and then give the employees access to the view. This will protect the security of the data. Because access to a view looks just like access to a table, no one will be able to tell the difference.

Examining the Use of Client/Server Design

Any time two computers are involved in the mutual performance of executing an application, with each performing a different function, you are undoubtedly looking at a client/server application. Many definitions of client/server are used. A definition of client/server application is an application that has a client interface and that accesses data on a remote server. The work is distributed between the client system and the remote server system, based on the capabilities of the client and server software applications. Client/server systems usually are efficient because network traffic is minimized and each portion of the application is optimized for a particular function.

Client/server applications function over any type of network, functioning at any speed. These variables are factors that affect the performance of the application, but that do not affect whether the application works.

> **NOTE**
>
> Both the client and the server must use a common communications protocol and a common data format.

The essence of a client/server application can be viewed by looking at a database application. Most relational database management systems (RDBMS), such as Microsoft SQL Server, provide a database engine that manages the data but has little or no user interface. (Exceptions are the desktop databases such as MS Access.) The interface to the RDBMS is through command-line functions. When working with this type of RDBMS, the developer needs to create the user interface application.

In this instance, the user interface application, the client, formulates a request for data that is transmitted to the system running the database, the server. This request for data is in the form of a SQL statement, such as a SQL query. The relational database engine executes the query, creates a results set, and transmits the results set back to the client.

Two-Tiered Client/Server Applications

The client/server diagram shown in Figure 13.1 is called a two-tiered client/server because the client communicates directly with the server, with no intermediary. The limitation of this model is that it is not easily scalable. If the server becomes over taxed by client traffic, the usual solution is to upgrade the server hardware to a faster processor with more memory. However, there is an upper limit to how fast the processor can be.

Multi-Tiered Client/Server Applications

It is also possible to have three or more tiers in the client/server design, which is frequently used in Internet applications. This increases the scalability of the application. An example of this multi-tiered approach can be seen with a Web page that accesses a database on the server. Frequently, the database is on a different server than the Web server. This allows the distribution of the load over multiple systems. It also creates scalability. If the database activity becomes a bottleneck for the application, the database activity can be distributed over multiple servers. If the Web server becomes the bottleneck, the Web server can be distributed over multiple servers.

There are other uses of the multi-tiered client/server model, including the following two very useful designs. The first design has a middle tier that provides an Online Analysis Processing data warehouse that is extracted from the base layer of operational databases. The second design makes use of a middle tier to enforce business rules. This separate layer for business rules makes the maintenance of the business rules much easier and less disruptive.

Understanding Thin Clients Versus Thick Clients

The terms *thin client* and *fat* or *thick clients* are being used with great frequency. The IS world is excited over the prospect of having thin clients. The advent of the thin client is not a new idea. It is a return to the model of the central computer surrounded by dumb terminals.

An understanding of the differences between thin and fat clients will provide some insight into the advantages and disadvantages of each.

Client/server implies a division of labor between the client and server systems. The usual division is that the server supplies all of the data and the client displays the data and performs manipulation of the data for the user at the user's system.

A thin client is one that provides little to the relationship except the capability to display the data transmitted by the server.

A fat client is one that provides extensive logic for the manipulation of the data transmitted by the server. This is the workstation paradigm in which a PC is the client, and the data is transmitted for the use of the client and then sent back to the server when the client has finished the task. The server is little more than a data repository.

Viewing this in light of Internet technologies and, in particular, World Wide Web technology, the Web browser is the client and the Web server is the server. In this model, the Web browser is the thin client that requires little or no maintenance for the client/server application to function. Even when client scripting is used, the browser is processing code that is transmitted each time the application is accessed. New versions of the script do not need to be installed on the client.

The primary concern in this scenario is the capability of the Web browser to support various technologies. Not all Web browsers are created equal. Web browsers vary in their support for different versions and features of HTML. Most browsers support the current 4.0 version of HTML.

In addition to the varying levels of support for HTML, there are varying levels of support for scripting languages. Netscape Navigator supports JavaScript but not VBScript. MS IE 3.0 and later supports JavaScript and VBScript. Add to this mix the complication of ActiveX support, which is present in MS IE 3.0 and later, but not Netscape Navigator without a third-party plug-in.

All of these issues, such as script language and ActiveX support, are moving the thin client of the Web browser toward a fatter client.

The most essential item to consider when analyzing Web browsers as thin clients is whether you are in an environment in which you have control over the Web browser used as a client. If you are not in such an environment, then you need to design to the lowest common denominator and use server logic to provide alternative interfaces for different browsers.

Using the ADO Data Control and Libraries

ADO 2.0 ships as two separate libraries with Visual Basic 6. The first library is called ADODB and appears in the References dialog box with the name of Microsoft ActiveX Data Objects 2.0 Library, as shown in Figure 13.1. This library contains all of the ADO objects and will most likely be suitable for the majority of your projects.

FIGURE 13.1.

The Standard version of the ADO Library supports all of the ADO objects.

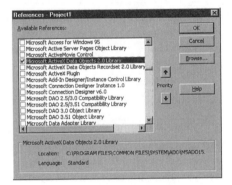

For those projects where a much less resource intensive ADO is required, the ADOR Library should be used. This Library can be found in the References dialog box under the name of Microsoft ActiveX Data Objects Recordset 2.0 Library, as shown in Figure 13.2. This library contains support for only Recordsets contributing to a decrease in resource requirements.

FIGURE 13.2.

The Light version of the ADO Library supports only the Recordset object.

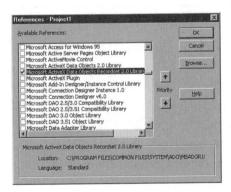

After you have selected the desired library, all of the available ADO objects, methods, and properties will then be accessible through the VBA Object Browser and the IDE Editor.

The ADO Data Control includes a number of events that are user programmable. The events listed in Table 13.4 lists the events and when they occur.

TABLE 13.4. ADO CONTROL'S PROGRAMMABLE EVENTS.

Event	Occurs
WillMove	On Recordset.Open, Recordset.MoveNext, Recordset.Move, Recordset.MoveLast, Recordset.MoveFirst, Recordset.MovePrevious, Recordset.Bookmark, Recordset.AddNew, Recordset.Delete, Recordset.Requery, Recordset.Resync
MoveComplete	After WillMove
WillChangeField	Before the Value property changes
FieldChangeComplete	After WillChangeField
WillChangeRecord	On Recordset.Update, Recordset.Delete, Recordset.CancelUpdate, Recordset.UpdateBatch, Recordset.CancelBatch
RecordChangeComplete	After WillChangeRecord
WillChangeRecordset	On Recordset.Requery, Recordset.Resync, Recordset.Close, Recordset.Open, Recordset.Filter
RecordsetChangeComplete	After WillChangeRecordset
InfoMessage	When the data provider returns a result

ADO Object Model

The ADO object model defines a collection of programmable objects that support the Component Object Model (COM) and OLE Automation to leverage the powerful partner technology called OLE DB. The ADO object model, when compared to other data access objects such as RDO or DAO, is flatter (has fewer objects) and simpler to use.

Before we begin using the ADO control, let's take a quick look at the seven objects that make up the ADO object model. These objects are shown in Figure 13.3 and briefly described in Table 13.5.

Figure 13.3.

The ADO Object Model is much less complicated than the DAO Object Model.

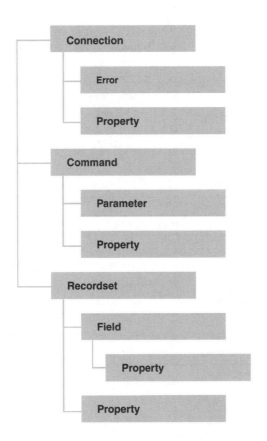

13

THE ADO DATA CONTROL

Table 13.5. ADO Object Model's Seven Objects and Four Collections.

Object	Description
Command	Maintains information about a command, such as a query string, parameter definitions, and so on
Connection	Maintains connection information with the data service provider
Error	Contains extended error information about an error condition raised by the provider
Field	Contains information about a single column of data within a Recordset
Parameter	A single parameter for a parameterized Command
Property	A provider-defined characteristic of an ADO object
Recordset	A set of records returned from a query, and a cursor into those records

For more information about the ActiveX Data Objects, check out
`http://www.microsoft.com/ado/`. This site is updated on a regular basis with information and free downloads.

Command Object

A `Command` object is the definition of a specific command, such as a SQL statement or stored procedure that you execute on a specific data source. The `Command` object contains the collections, methods, and properties as described in Tables 13.6 through 13.9, respectively.

TABLE 13.6. COLLECTIONS OF THE `Command` OBJECT.

Name	*Description*
Parameters	The collection of `Parameter` objects for the command. A `Parameter` object represents a parameter or argument associated with a `Command` object that is based on a parameterized query or stored procedure.
Properties	The set of properties for the `Command` object.

TABLE 13.7. METHODS OF THE `Command` OBJECT.

Name	*Description*
CreateParameter	Creates a new `Parameter` object.
Execute	Executes the query, SQL statement, or stored procedure specified in the `CommandText` property.

TABLE 13.8. PROPERTIES OF THE `Command` OBJECT.

Name	*Description*
ActiveConnection	Indicates the `Connection` object to which the specified `Command` object currently belongs.
CommandText	Contains the text of the SQL statement that you want to issue on a specific provider.
CommandTimeout	Determines the time to wait when attempting to establish a connection before timing out and generating an error.
CommandType	Contains the type of the command—for example, a stored procedure.
Name	Indicates the name of the object.

Name	Description
Prepared	Indicates whether or not to create a prepared or compiled statement from the command before execution.
State	Describes the current state of the object.

Connection **Object**

Connection objects can be created independently of any other previously defined object. The Connection object represents a specific unique session with a particular data source. The Connection object contains the collections, methods, and properties as described in Tables 13.9 through 13.11, respectively.

TABLE 13.9. COLLECTIONS OF THE Connection OBJECT.

Name	Description
Errors	Contains the errors generated on the connection.
Properties	The set of properties for the connection.

TABLE 13.10. METHODS OF THE Connection OBJECT.

Name	Description
BeginTrans	Starts a transaction if the database engine supports transaction processing.
Close	Closes the connection.
CommitTrans	Commits and terminates the transaction.
Execute	Executes the specified SQL statement.
Open	Opens the connection to the data source.
RollbackTrans	Reverses a transaction.
OpenSchema	Returns a Recordset object that contains schema information.

TABLE 13.11. PROPERTIES OF THE Connection OBJECT.

Name	Description
Attributes	Reads the XactAttributeEnum values for a Connection object. The value can be a sum of any one or more of the XactAttributeEnum values.
CommandTimeout	Sets the time to wait for a command to execute before timing out and generating an error.

continues

TABLE 13.11. CONTINUED

Name	Description
ConnectionString	Contains the information necessary to establish a connection, such as the DSN and password.
ConnectionTimeout	Determines the time to wait when attempting to establish a connection before timing out and generating an error.
CursorLocation	Sets or returns the location of the cursor engine.
DefaultDatabase	Indicates the default database for the Connection object.
IsolationLevel	Reads or sets the isolation level of a transaction.
Mode	Indicates the permissions that are available in a connection for modifying data.
Provider	Indicates the OLE DB Data Provider for a Connection object.
Version	Indicates the ADO version number.

Error Object and Errors Collection

An Error object is generated each time an error is encountered in an ADO operation. The Error object is part of an Errors Collection. The Error object contains the properties as described in Table 13.12

TABLE 13.12. THE Error OBJECT CONTAINS SEVEN PROPERTIES.

Property	Description
Description	Explains the error. This is the description string associated with the error.
HelpContext	Returns a context ID, as a Long integer value, for a topic in a Microsoft Windows Help file.
HelpFile	Returns a String that evaluates to a fully qualified path to a Help file.
NativeError	Indicates the provider-specific error code for a given Error object.
Number	Indicates the number that uniquely identifies an Error object.
Source	Indicates the name of the object that generated the error.
SQLState	Returns a five-character String that follows the ANSI SQL standard.

The Errors collection has one method, the Clear method, which removes all of the Error objects in the collection. The Errors collection also has two properties: Count, which indicates the total number of Error objects in the collection, and Item, which returns a specific Error object.

Field Object and Fields Collection

Field objects represent columns of data with a common data type. The Fields collection contains all stored Field objects of a Recordset object. The Field object contains one collection, the Properties collection. The Field object contains the methods and properties as described in Tables 13.13 and 13.14, respectively.

TABLE 13.13. METHODS OF THE Field OBJECT.

Name	Description
AppendChunk	Appends data to a large text or binary data Field object.
GetChunk	Returns all or a portion of the contents of a large text or binary data Field object.

TABLE 13.14. PROPERTIES OF THE Field OBJECT.

Name	Description
ActualSize	Shows the actual length of a field's value.
Attributes	Shows one or more characteristics of the Field object.
DefinedSize	Shows the defined size of a Field object.
Name	Shows the defined size of a Field object.
NumericScale	Sets or returns a Byte value, indicating the number of decimal places to which numeric values will be resolved.
OriginalValue	Shows the value of a Field that existed in the record before any changes were made.
Precision	Sets or returns a Byte value, indicating the maximum total number of digits used to represent values.
Type	Shows the data type of a Field object.
UnderlyingValue	Shows a Field object's current value in the database.
Value	Shows the value assigned to a Field object.

The Fields collection contains one method, the Refresh method, which updates the objects in the Fields collection to reflect Field objects available from, and specific to, the provider.

The Fields collection contains the Count and Item properties.

Parameter Object and Parameters Collection

A Parameter object represents a parameter or argument associated with a Command object that is based on a parameterized query or stored procedure. The Parameter object contains one method, the AppendChunk method, which is used to append a large text or binary file to a parameter. The Parameter object contains the properties and methods as described in Tables 13.15 and 13.16, respectively.

TABLE 13.15. PROPERTIES OF THE Parameter OBJECT.

Name	Description
Attributes	For the Parameter object, the value is the sum of any one or more of the ParameterAttributesEnum values.
Direction	Shows whether the Parameter represents an input parameter, an output parameter, both, or a return value from a stored procedure.
Name	The name of a parameter that can be used in references to the parameter rather than its ordinal number in the collection.
NumericScale	Sets or returns the number of decimal places to which numeric values will be resolved.
Precision	Sets or returns the maximum total number of digits used to represent values.
Size	The maximum size, in bytes or characters, of a Parameter object.
Type	The data type of a Parameter object.
Value	The value assigned to a Parameter object.

TABLE 13.16. METHODS OF THE Parameter OBJECT.

Name	Description
Append	Appends a Parameter object to the collection.
Delete	Removes a Parameter object from the collection.
Refresh	Updates the Parameter objects in the collection to show the objects available from, and specific to, the provider.

The Parameters collection also contains the two properties of Count and Item.

Count, which indicates the total number of Error objects in the collection, and Item, which returns a specific Error object.

Property Object

A `Property` object represents a dynamic characteristic of an ADO object that is defined by the provider. ADO objects contain two types of properties: dynamic and built-in. Built-in properties are available to any object. They do not appear in the object's Properties collection preventing them from being modified or deleted.

Dynamic properties appear in the object's Properties collection. They can be referenced only through the collection. A dynamic property has four built-in properties as defined in Table 13.17.

TABLE 13.17. PROPERTIES OF THE `Property` OBJECT.

Name	Description
Name	A string that identifies the property.
Type	A integer that specifies the property data type.
Value	A variant that contains the property setting.
Attributes	A long that indicates characteristics of the property specific to the provider.

13

THE ADO DATA
CONTROL

Recordset Object

You do not need to create a `Connection` object to create a `Recordset` object. This is accomplished by passing a connection string with the `Open` method. ADO creates a `Connection` object, but it isn't assigned to an object variable. If you are opening multiple `Recordset` objects over the same connection, you must create and open a `Connection` object. This assigns the `Connection` object to an object variable. If you do not use this object variable when opening your `Recordset` objects, ADO creates a new `Connection` object for each new `Recordset` object, even when you pass the same connection string.

A `Recordset` object represents the entire set of records from a base table or the results of an executed command. At any time, the `Recordset` object refers only to a single record within the set as the current record. The `Parameter` object contains the collections, properties, and methods as described in Tables 13.18 through 13.20, respectively.

TABLE 13.18. COLLECTIONS OF THE `Recordset` OBJECT.

Name	Description
Fields	Contains all stored `Field` objects of the `Recordset` object.
Properties	Contains all the `Property` objects for a specific instance of the `Recordset` object.

TABLE 13.19. METHODS OF THE Recordset OBJECT.

Name	Description
AddNew	Creates a new record for an updatable Recordset object.
CancelBatch	Cancels a pending batch update.
CancelUpdate	Cancels any changes made to the current record or to a new record prior to calling the Update method.
Clone	Creates a duplicate Recordset object from an existing Recordset object.
Close	Closes the open Recordset object and any dependent objects.
Delete	Deletes the current record or a group of records.
GetRows	Retrieves multiple records of a Recordset object into an array.
Move	Moves the position of the current record in a Recordset object.
MoveFirst	Moves to the first record in the Recordset object and makes that record the current record.
MoveLast	Moves to the last record in the Recordset object and makes that record the current record.
MoveNext	Moves to the next record in the Recordset object and makes that record the current record.
MovePrevious	Moves to the previous record in the Recordset object and makes that record the current record.
NextRecordset	Advances through a series of commands by clearing the current Recordset object and returns the next recordset.
Open	Opens a cursor.
Requery	Updates the data in a Recordset object by re-executing the query that is the basis of the object.
Resync	Refreshes the data in the current Recordset object from the underlying database.
Supports	Determines whether a specified Recordset object supports a particular type of functionality.
Update	Saves any changes you make to the current record of a Recordset object.
UpdateBatch	Writes all pending batch updates to disk.

TABLE 13.20. PROPERTIES OF THE Recordset OBJECT.

Name	Description
AbsolutePage	Sets the "page" number on which the current record is located. Uses the PageSize property to logically divide the Recordset object into a series of pages, each of which has the number of records equal to PageSize. The

Name	Description
	provider must support the appropriate functionality for this property to be available.
AbsolutePosition	Sets the ordinal position of a `Recordset` object's current record.
ActiveConnection	Shows to which `Connection` object the specified `Recordset` object currently belongs.
BOF	Shows that the current record position is before the first record in a `Recordset` object.
Bookmark	Returns a bookmark that uniquely identifies the current record in a `Recordset` object or sets the current record in a `Recordset` object to the record identified by a valid bookmark.
CacheSize	Shows the number of records from a `Recordset` object that are cached locally in memory.
CursorLocation	Sets or returns the location of the cursor engine.
CursorType	Shows the type of cursor used in a `Recordset` object—for example, Read Only or Updatable.
EditMode	Shows the editing status of the current record.
EOF	Shows that the current record position is after the last record in a `Recordset` object.
Filter	Shows a filter for data in a `Recordset`.
LockType	Shows the type of locks placed on records during editing.
MarshalOptions	Indicates which records are to be marshaled back to the server.
MaxRecords	Shows the maximum number of records to return to a `Recordset` from a query.
PageCount	Shows how many pages of data the `Recordset` object contains.
PageSize	Shows how many records constitute one "page" in the `Recordset`.
RecordCount	Shows the current number of records in a `Recordset` object.
Source	Shows the source for the data in a `Recordset` object (`Command` object, SQL statement, table name, or stored procedure) or the name of the object or application that originally generated an error.
State	Describes the current state of an object.
Status	Shows the status of the current record with respect to batch updates or other bulk operations.

Creating an OLE DB Data Source

After you have selected the appropriate ADO Object Library, the next step is to create an OLE DB data source for each database that you want to access. This necessary process only needs to be completed once and is very similar to creating an ODBC connection; however, it is specific to ADO. To create an OLE DB data source for the `Biblio.mdb` database that ships with Visual Basic 6, the following steps need to be performed:

1. Open Windows Explorer and select the folder where you want to create the OLE DB datasource. For our example, we will be opening the `\program files\Microsoft Visual Studio\VB98\` folder.

2. Right-click in the right pane of Windows Explorer. On the context menu, select the New menu option. Select the Microsoft Data Link menu option that appears in the list as shown in Figure 13.4. This creates a generic data link file in the previously specified folder.

FIGURE 13.4.

The Data Link file contains information about the location of the database.

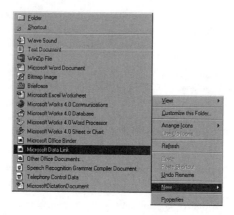

3. Rename the newly created file to `Biblio.MDL` (the file will be highlighted). The .MDL extension identifies the file as a Microsoft Data Link file.

4. Right-click on the `Biblio.MDL` file and select the Properties menu option on the context menu. This displays the Properties dialog box shown in Figure 13.5.

5. Select the Connection tab of the Properties dialog box.

6. Select Microsoft Jet 3.51 OLE DB provider from the Provider drop-down list box.

7. Enter the name of the database into the DataSource box as shown in Figure 13.6. For our example, enter the name of `Biblio.mdb`. This, of course, is assuming that the `Biblio.mdb` database has not been moved from the `\program files\Microsoft Visual Studio\VB98\` folder.

FIGURE 13.5.

The Properties dialog box.

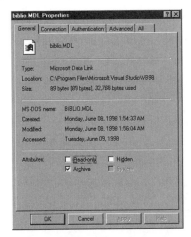

FIGURE 13.6.

Additional database information can be entered via the Properties dialog box.

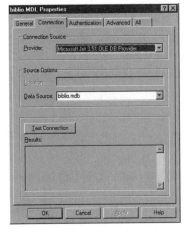

13

THE ADO DATA CONTROL

8. Click the Test Connection button to verify that a connection to the database can be made. If the connection was successful, your message should be similar to the one shown in Figure 13.7.

9. Click the OK button to close the Properties dialog box. You have now completed the process of creating an OLE DB data source link to the Biblio.mdb database.

NOTE

The Properties dialog box allows you to set a number of user authentication and database security features. Any settings that you make here will be reflected in the data link file that is generated.

FIGURE 13.7.

You need to have a successful connection before you create any applications that will be using this connection.

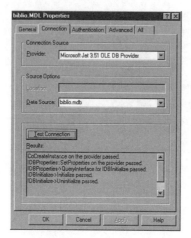

Creating an ADO Database Front End

Using the ADO Data control in your applications is no more difficult than using the standard DAO Data control. In the following example, you will create a sample front end for an ADO database. Although this application is very simplistic, it does illustrate how easy it is to create an application using ADO. To create the front end for the Biblio database, perform the following steps:

1. Confirm that you have a valid .MDL file if you will be using an OLE DB Data source.

2. Start a new project. On the form, place an ADO control. If the ADO control is not available in your toolbox, you can add it from the Components dialog box and select the Microsoft ADO Data Control option shown in Figure 13.8.

FIGURE 13.8.

The ADO Data control is added to the toolbox after the Components dialog box is closed.

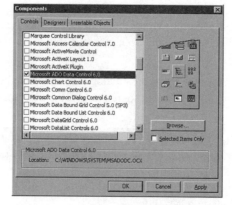

3. In the Properties window of the ADO control, click the ellipsis button on the
   `ConnectionString` property to display the ConnectionString dialog box. This is
   shown in Figure 13.9.

FIGURE 13.9.
*The property
pages allow you
to enter the
ODBC source and
connection string
information.*

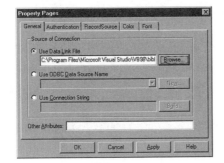

4. Select the General tab. If you have created a Data Link file (.MDL), select the Use
   Data Link File check box and click the Browse button to locate the .MDL file.

   Alternatively, you could select either the Use ODBC Data Source Name or Use
   Connection String check boxes to create a connection to your database.

5. In the Properties window of the ADO control, click the ellipsis button to display
   the Record Source dialog box. In the Command Text (SQL) text box, enter the following SQL statement:

   `SELECT * FROM Authors WHERE Au_ID = 72`

   This sets the `RecordSource` property to a SQL statement. This is shown in Figure
   13.10.

FIGURE 13.10.
*SQL statements
can also be
entered via the
RecordSource tab
on the Property
Pages dialog box.*

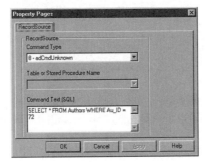

13

THE ADO DATA
CONTROL

TIP

The inclusion of a WHERE clause in the SQL statement prevents the table from locking out other users.

---

6. Place two labels and two text boxes on the form. The captions of the text boxes should be Author and Author ID.

7. Set the DataSource property for Text1 and Text2 to the name of the ADO control on the form.

8. In the properties window of Text1, set the DataField property to Author.

9. Set the DataField property of Text2 to Au_ID.

10. Press F5 to run the application. The completed form should resemble the one in Figure 13.11.

FIGURE 13.11.

The completed ADO sample.

CAUTION

The ADO Data control can be a major resource hog. The ADO control will automatically use at least two connections for the first ADO control on a form. Additional ADO controls on the same form require one connection each.

An alternative to using the ADO data control is to set the properties programmatically. The sample code segment in Listing 13.1 illustrates how this might be accomplished.

LISTING 13.1 *ADOFRM.FRM*—SAMPLE OF HOW TO SET THE PROPERTIES OF THE ADO CONTROL THROUGH CODE.

```
Private Sub Form_Load()
    With ADODC1
        .ConnectionString = "driver={SQL Server};" & _
```

```
         "server=orion;uid=sa;pwd=pwd;database=pubs"
         .RecordSource = "Select * From Authors Where Au_ID = 72"
      End With
      Set Text1.DataSource = ADODC1
      Text1.DataField = "Author"
   End Sub
```

Remoting of ADO Recordsets

Remote Data Service (RDS), an extension of ADO, is a technology based on ActiveX controls and uses ADO to retrieve data from the provider to the client. The client caches the data and can manipulate it in many ways, such as filtering and sorting. The process of *remoting* involves the passing of parameters between two different processes. This passage of data can occur over a traditional network or via the Internet. For example, on the client side of a *n*-tier client server system a call is made for data by passing a number of parameters to the middle tier. The middle tier in response accepts the call and passes it on to the data layer which in turn retrieves the specified data and passes it back to the middle tier.

The code for the server side of the application might resemble the code shown in Listing 13.2; the code for the client side might look like that in Listing 13.3.

LISTING 13.2   *SAMPLE.BAS*—SAMPLE CODE FOR THE SERVER.

```
Option Explicit

' This code segment would be placed in a .bas file

' Define a Public User Defined Type (UDT)
Public Type udtName
   ' We will define the table used in the SQL examples
   SSN As String
   Last Name As String
   First Name As String
   Sex As String
End Type

Public Function PassUDT(myrec As udtName) As udtName
   ' Code to perform some type of data modification
   ' Goes
   ' Here

   ' Return the User Defined Type
   PassUDT = myrec
End Function
```

LISTING 13.3 *SAMPLE.BAS*—SAMPLE CODE FOR THE CLIENT.

```
Option Explicit

Private myrec As udtName

Private Sub Command1_Click()
   Dim x As udtName
   x = PassUDT(myrec)
   ' Do something with the UDT data.
   ' Code to perform some type of data modification
   ' with the User Defined Type
   ' would go here
End Sub
```

An ADO recordset can be used with HTML or DHTML to access data from a Web server application via the Internet or an intranet. This is accomplished by using the Microsoft ActiveX Data Access Recordset 2.0 Library which includes only the `Recordset` object, leaving off the `Connection`, `Command`, and `Parameter` objects. Using this library allows you to create lightweight applications that can use ADO, but without a lot of the overhead that may otherwise be needed.

For more information about DHTML, see Chapter 20, "Creating DHTML Applications."

> **NOTE**
>
> The passage of User Defined Types (UDT) as parameters of public subs is now possible in Visual Basic 6.

> **TIP**
>
> Passing parameters out of process consumes more resources than if you pass them in process.

Summary

ActiveX Data Objects (ADO) represents a radical departure from the traditional methods of data access that were available to the Visual Basic programmer. With ADO your applications come closer than ever to true platform independence.

Converting existing applications that use either DAO or RDO to ADO is simply a matter of rewriting the database connection code; creating new ADO applications is no more difficult than creating a DAO based application. The short learning curve of ADO guarantees that you will be familiar with ADO after your first project. If your application is designed for a client server environment or an Intranet, ADO provides you with an excellent method of data access using the OLE DB.

Once you begin to use ADO in your applications you will most likely find new and exciting ways to use this wonderful new technology.

Working in the Data Environment

by Lowell Mauer

IN THIS CHAPTER

- Using the Data Environment   300
- Using the Data Environment to Access the Database   311

Introduction to the Data Environment

The Data Environment designer is, in effect, a very sophisticated interface that provides an interactive, design-time environment for creating programmed, runtime data access. At design time, you can set the property values for Connection and Command objects, write code to respond to the ADO events, execute commands, and create summaries and hierarchies. You can also drag Data Environment objects onto a form or report to create data-bound controls. The Data Environment designer can replace any of the three types of data access (DAO, RDO, or ADO) you might be using in your application. In addition, the Data Environment is required if you are using the Hierarchical FlexGrid control or the Data Report designer. The Data Environment designer brings together several capabilities into one complete package. Using this designer, you can perform the following:

- Define the database connection
- Create SQL commands to access the data
- Specify how separate commands are related to build complex queries
- Define aggregate functions for the query
- Specify the sort order of the data in the query

The Data Environment designer provides a means to easily access data in your Visual Basic project. In previous releases, you used the ActiveX UserConnection designer to create Remote Data Objects (RDO) at design time. Now, you can create the ADO objects at design time using the Data Environment designer.

To create the connection, the Data Environment designer displays a tabbed dialog box that helps you define the connection to the database. After the connection is defined, you can build commands by using the SQL Query designer. Together, these give you a complete point-and-click method of building the SQL connections your application needs. This section will show you how to create a Data Environment connection that will be used to display data from the database from within a Visual Basic application.

For the purposes of this chapter, you will build a query to access order information. This will be done by using both parent and child commands along with the SQL Query designer. Table 14.1 lists the tables and associated columns that will be used, as well as the command they will be added to.

TABLE 14.1. NORTHWIND DATABASE INFORMATION.

Command	Query Type	Table	Column
cmdCustomers	SQL Query	Customers	CompanyName
			Address
			City
			Region
			ContactName
			Customer ID
cmdOrders	SQL Query	Orders	Customer ID
			Order ID
			Order Date
cmdOrderDetail	Table	Order Details	<All Columns>
cmdEmployees	Table	Employees	<All Columns>

To see how to use this designer to create connections and then use them, start a new project with a single default form in it.

Defining the Connection

To access data using your Data Environment, you must first create a Connection object. This means that every Data Environment should include at least one Connection object. A Connection object represents a connection to a remote database that is used as the data source for the associated commands. A new connection called Connection1 is automatically added to the Data Environment when you add one to your Visual Basic project. At design time, the Data Environment will open the connection and obtain the metadata (database table information) from the connection, including database object names and table structures.

NOTE

If "Show Properties Immediately After Creation" is selected in the Options dialog box, the Data Link properties dialog box will be displayed when you add a Data Environment to your project.

To define the database connection, add a Data Environment object by right-clicking in the Project Explorer and choosing Add from the pop-up menu. Then choose More ActiveX Designers, Data Environment, as shown in Figure 14.1.

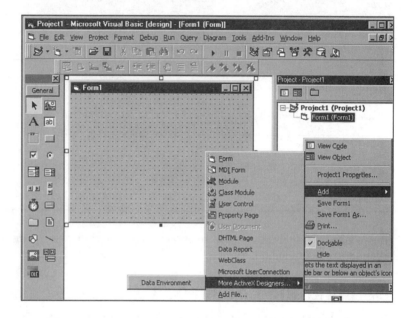

When defining the connection, you can choose from a direct connection to a Jet-supported database, a standard ODBC connection, or one of several OLE DB providers. OLE DB is the latest technique for accessing a database and will provide you access to more database-supported features. On the Provider tab of the Data Link properties dialog box (see Figure 14.2), these methods are displayed as:

- Use ODBC Data Source Name—Standard ODBC connection
- Use Connection String—OLE DB Provider connection

The NorthWind database (NWIND.MDB) will be used in this chapter. So, if you choose either the ODBC method or OLE DB method, you must define the Data Source or Data Link, respectively.

> **NOTE**
>
> I am using the OLE DB provider Data Link to allow access to the views already defined in the database.

FIGURE **14.2.**

Setting the Connection properties for the Data Environment.

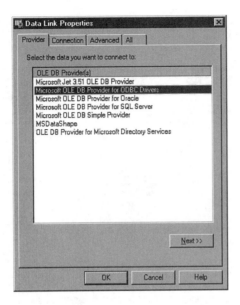

After you have defined the connection, you need to define one or more commands (SQL) to actually retrieve data from the database. Command objects define specific detailed information about which data is retrieved from the database connection. Command objects can be based on either a database object (for example, table, view, stored procedure) or a SQL query statement. To add a command, right-click on the Command folder and choose Add Command (see Figure 14.3).

If a Connection object can be identified during the add process, the ActiveConnection property of the Command object is set to that Connection object. If a Connection object is not identified, you must now select the connection the command will use to access the database. You then have a choice between using a table, view, or stored procedure directly from the database or building your own SQL query. If you choose to use a database object, select the object type and then select the object name.

Using the SQL Query Designer

You should use a table or predefined view from your database unless your application requires a more complex query. If you need a complex query, select SQL Statement on the General tab of the Command property dialog box and click the SQL Builder button, which displays the SQL Query designer, as shown in Figure 14.4.

14

WORKING IN THE DATA ENVIROMENT

FIGURE 14.3.
Adding a command to the Database connection.

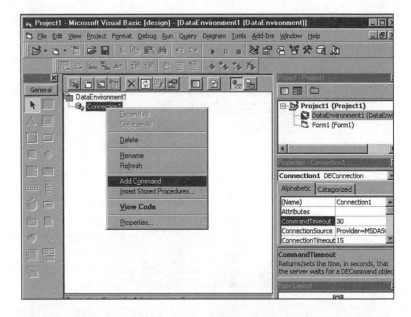

FIGURE 14.4.
Building a SQL statement is easy using the SQL Builder interface.

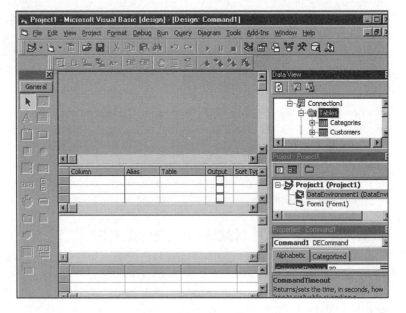

If you have ever used Microsoft Access or MSQuery, you already know how to use this SQL Query designer. Before we actually build any commands, let's take a quick look at the Query designer and its available functions. The Query designer allows you to perform the following actions:

- Create queries to retrieve data from any ODBC compliant database
- Specify the elements (tables and columns) to retrieve, the sort order, and any filters
- Preview the query results in the Results pane
- Define joins between tables to create multi-table queries
- Edit database information performing updates, inserts, and deletions
- Create action queries to modify the database

If you are familiar with SQL programming, you can also enter SQL statements directly or edit the SQL statements created by the designer. The Query designer interface consists of four panes:

- **Diagram**—Displays the input sources you are querying. Each window represents an input source and shows the available columns and the icons that indicate how each column is used in the query.
- **Grid**—This pane contains a spreadsheet-like grid where you specify the query options, such as which data columns to display, the sort order, criteria for selecting rows, and any grouping information.
- **SQL**—This displays the SQL statement for the current query. It is also where you can edit the SQL. Editing the SQL is useful if you need to create SQL statements that cannot be created using the Diagram and Grid panes.
- **Results**—Shows a grid with the results of the most recently executed Select query. You can modify the database information by editing the data directly in the cells of the grid.

You can create a query by working in and with all of the panes. You can specify a column to display by choosing it in the Diagram pane, entering it into the Grid pane, or adding it directly to the SQL statement in the SQL pane. All of these panes are synchronized, so when you make a change in one pane, the Query designer updates the other panes to reflect that change except for the Run pane which will display the results after you run the query.

In addition to the queries that you can build using the graphical panes, you can enter any SQL statement into the SQL pane. When you create queries using SQL statements that cannot be represented in the graphical panes, the Query designer dims those panes to indicate that they do not reflect the query you are creating (see Figure 14.5). However, the dimmed panes are still active and, in many cases, you can make changes to the query in those panes. If the changes you make result in a query that can be represented in the graphical panes, then those panes will no longer be dimmed.

FIGURE 14.5.

The Query designer dims the graphical panes if they cannot be used for a particular SQL statement.

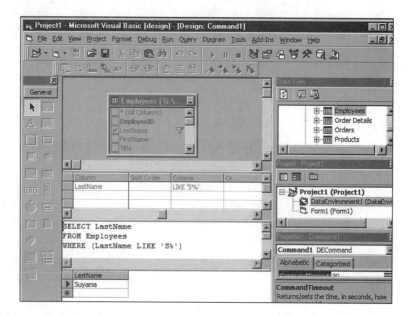

To add tables or views to the query, simply select the ones you want from the DataView window and drag them to the empty gray box. Table relationships are automatically displayed if they already exist in the database. However, if the database you are using does not have relationship information, you need to define them in the SQL Query designer. As you drag tables into the work area, you should notice that a SQL statement is being built. However, there are no columns in the statement yet.

NOTE

If the database does not have relationships specified, you can add them to the query by dragging the column(s) that define the relationship from one table to the column(s) in the other table.

Now, to add columns, you can either click the check boxes for the required columns, drag each column you want to the Column area in the middle of the dialog box, or use the drop-down list of all available columns as shown in Figure 14.6.

FIGURE 14.6.

Adding columns to the query and updating the SQL statement.

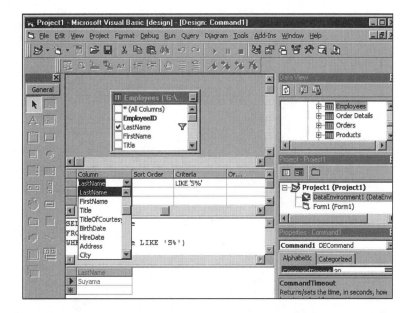

> **NOTE**
>
> Refer back to Table 14.1 for the complete list of columns to add to the primary command.

Using the Query designer, you can also add any condition or sorting required for the query. After you have finished building the query, you should test it by choosing Query, Run from the Visual Basic menu. The query is executed with the results displayed at the bottom of the SQL Builder (see Figure 14.7).

> **NOTE**
>
> This SQL Query designer lets you design any type of SQL statement that you might need (for example, Select, Update, Insert, or Delete).

After you are finished building the query and are satisfied with the results, close the designer and choose Yes to save the changes to the Command statement (see Figure 14.8).

14

WORKING IN THE
DATA
ENVIROMENT

FIGURE 14.7.

Running the completed query to test it and display the data.

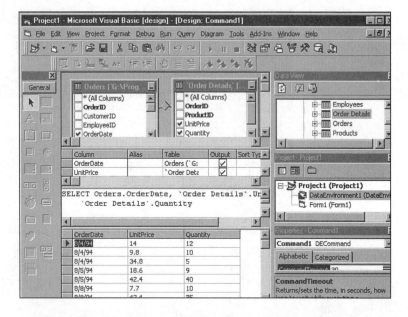

FIGURE 14.8.

The completed SQL statement is now displayed in the Connections branch of the Data Environment.

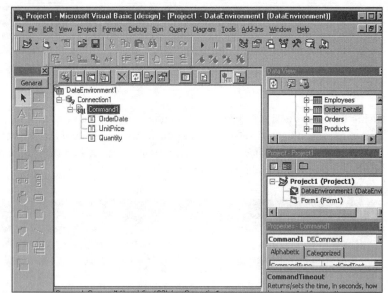

Child Commands

A child command is nothing more than a SQL query that is dependent on a previous (parent) command to create a hierarchical query, which can then be used to display data in a Data Report, Hierarchical FlexGrid control, or by using ADO coding within the application. Adding the command itself is the same as building the first query and is as simple as right-clicking the first command and then selecting ADO Child Command from the pop-up menu. However, after the command is defined, you need to define the relationship it has with its parent command. In the Child command properties dialog box, go to the Relation tab. This is where you specify the fields that relate the two commands together, creating a master/detail type relationship as shown in Figure 14.9.

FIGURE 14.9.

Defining the commands relationship with the Parent command.

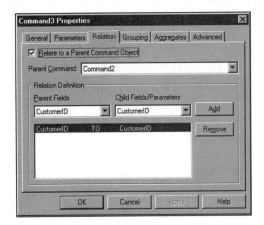

Using the information in Table 14.1, define a child command that contains the Order Detail for a customer's order. After you have done this, the Data Environment shows the child command included within the parent command, as shown in Figure 14.10.

CAUTION

A child command must contain at least one column that relates to a column in the parent command.

When the program is executed, the Data Environment constructs an ADO SHAPE command that is used by ADO to create an ADO hierarchical recordset. You can display this underlying ADO recordset and ADO SHAPE syntax by right-clicking the parent command

14

and choosing Hierarchy Info to display the generated SHAPE command as shown in Figure 14.11.

FIGURE **14.10.**

The Data Environment graphically shows which commands are children of other commands that have been defined.

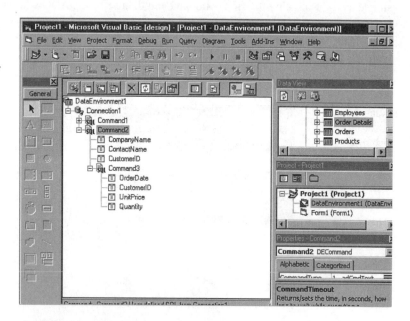

FIGURE **14.11.**

Displaying the SHAPE SQL command created by the Data Environment designer.

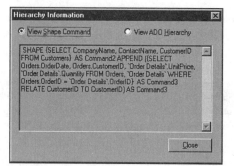

The Shape command, as shown in Figure 14.11, defines the structure of a hierarchical recordset, and the commands needed to populate it with data. A part of the Shape command is a query issued to the underlying database that returns a Recordset object. The query's syntax depends on the database you are accessing. This will usually be SQL, although ADO doesn't require the use of any particular query language. Although you can use a SQL JOIN clause to relate two tables, a hierarchical recordset will represent the information more efficiently. Each row of a recordset created by a JOIN will repeat information redundantly from the master or parent table in the relationship. A hierarchical recordset has only one parent recordset for each of the child `Recordset` objects.

To summarize the Data Environment designer's capabilities, it provides database administration allowing you to design complex queries for your application. More importantly, it provides a central repository for many commands and queries that will be used by your application. This allows you to define all of the required queries in one place to simplify the maintenance of these queries.

Using the Data Environment to Access the Database

After you have added a Data Environment to your application, you can reference the connections and commands in the program code to access data in the database. At runtime, the Data Environment creates an ADO `Command` and `Connection` object for each command and connection that you defined in the Data Environment. If the command object is marked as a recordset using the Advanced tab of the Command properties dialog box, an ADO `Recordset` object will also be created. The ADO `Command` object is added as a method of the Data Environment runtime object, and the ADO `Connection` and `Recordset` objects are added as properties.

When accessing an ADO recordset in the code, the `recordset` object names are prefixed with `rs` to distinguish them from their respective `Command` objects. For example, a `Command` object named Order creates a `recordset` object named `rsOrder`. `Recordset` objects are closed by default when the application is started and will be opened when the recordset's corresponding `Command` method is executed. In addition, you can open a `Recordset` object directly using the ADO `Open` method in the application code.

As a simple example of how to use the Data Environment to access data directly in your code, add a third command to the Data Environment as listed in Table 14.1. Then, add the controls listed in Table 14.2 to the default form as shown in Figure 14.12.

TABLE 14.2. EXAMPLE DATA ENVIRONMENT ACCESS FORM'S CONTROLS.

Control	*Property*	*Value*
Textbox	Name	txtEmployeeName
Textbox	Name	txtEmpId
Command	Name	cmdNext
	Caption	Next
Command	Name	cmdPrev

continues

Control	Property	Value
	Caption	Previous
Command	Name	cmdQuit
	Caption	Quit
Label	Name	lblID
	Caption	Employee ID
Label	Name	lblName
	Caption	Employee Name

FIGURE 14.12.

Creating an example form to access the database using the Data Environment connection.

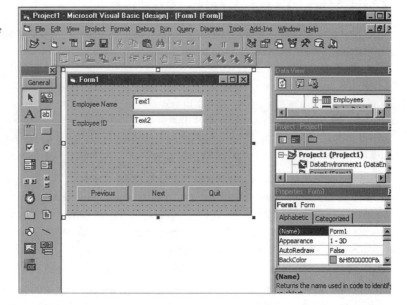

For this example, one of the text boxes will be bound to the new command, while the other one will be updated using program code. In addition, the two command buttons will allow you to move forward and backward in the query to display the data. To bind the first text box to the Customer Name, the properties need to be set as listed in Table 14.3.

TABLE 14.3. SETTING THE PROPERTIES TO BIND A TEXT BOX TO THE DATA ENVIRONMENT.

Control	Property	Value
txtEmpID	DataSource	deNorthWind
	DataMember	cmdEmployees
	DataField	EmployeeID

The first and third properties should be familiar to you; however, the second one, Data Member, is new. When you select a Data Environment as a data source, the Data Member allows you to specify which command in the Data Environment list you want to use. Finally, to add the functionality to the form, the following code sets the unbound text box, and the Move commands let you navigate the query. Add the following code to the default form:

LISTING 14.1. DBACCESS.TXT NAVIGATING THE DATABASE USING PROGRAMMED ACCESS.

```
Private Sub cmdNext_Click()
deNorthWind.rscmdEmployees.MoveNext
If deNorthWind.rscmdEmployees.Eof and deNorthWind.rscmdEmployees.Bof Then
    deNorthWind.rscmdEmployees.MoveLast
End If
txtEmployeeName.Text = deNorthWind.rscmdEmployees.Fields!firstname & _
                " " & deNorthWind.rscmdEmployees.Fields!lastname
End Sub

Private Sub cmdPrev_Click()
deNorthWind.rscmdEmployees.MovePrevious
If deNorthWind.rscmdEmployees.Eof and deNorthWind.rscmdEmployees.Bof Then
    deNorthWind.rscmdEmployees.MoveFirst
End If
txtEmployeeName.Text = deNorthWind.rscmdEmployees.Fields!firstname & _
                " " & deNorthWind.rscmdEmployees.Fields!lastname
End Sub

Private Sub cmdQuit_Click()
End
End Sub

Private Sub Form_Load()
txtEmployeeName.Text = deNorthWind.rscmdEmployees.Fields!firstname & _
                " " & deNorthWind.rscmdEmployees.Fields!lastname
End Sub
```

Now, run the application and try clicking the two command buttons to see how the Data Environment connection works the same as a Data control.

14

WORKING IN THE DATA ENVIROMENT

CAUTION

To keep this example fairly short, we have not added any programmatic update or EOF/BOF processing to this application. If you try to move past the end or beginning of the query, you will get an error message from the database.

As you can see, the Data Environment is every bit as good as the other data access methods and can be used wherever you would use a Data control or data access object.

Summary

This chapter describes Visual Basic 6's data tool that gives you the ability to create the necessary data queries you need to access the database information and use the more advanced Data controls and designers to add reporting and custom grid displays to your application. The starting point for all of these new features is the Data Environment designer, which gives you the ability to create the database connections and access commands that ADO needs to perform properly. In the next several chapters, you are going to see how to use all of these new data tools, designers, and controls in a Visual Basic application.

Using the Data Report Utility

by Rob Thayer

IN THIS CHAPTER

- Introduction to the Data Report Utility   316

- Creating a Report   316

- The Data Report Utility and Crystal Reports: How They Compare   334

Introduction to the Data Report Utility

Visual Basic 6 introduces the Data Environment, and along with it the Data Report Utility. The Data Report Utility lets you easily design and generate database reports. By using a graphic design environment, creating reports is as simple as dragging controls and database fields onto the different sections of the report. You can drag fields from the Data Environment to the Data Report Utility to add bound text fields to the report.

The Data Report Utility includes a palette of six different controls that can be added to the report in the same way that controls are added to forms. A special Function control also allows you to quickly add certain calculated values to the report, such as sums and averages.

After a report has been designed, it can be displayed on the screen simply by calling a method of the Data Report object that contains the report. You can also print the report or export it to a text or HTML file with a single method call. You can even define your own export templates.

Programmers who currently use Crystal Reports might wonder what the Data Report Utility can do for them. The two report generating tools are compared at the end of the chapter. Before proceeding with the rest of this chapter, you might want to read that section first.

Creating a Report

To show how reports can be generated with the Data Report Utility, a sample project will be created. This data report will be based on the Biblio database that comes with Visual Basic. It will show all of the publishers in the database, along with all of the book titles for each publisher. The number of titles will be calculated and printed after each publisher's titles are listed.

The report will include a page header that shows the name of the report as well as a small graphic image. Page numbers will be printed at the bottom of each page.

To create the report, the Biblio database's Publishers and Titles tables will be used. With the Data Report Utility, databases are set up in the Data Environment. So, to begin this project, the first order of business is to add and set up a Data Environment that works with the Biblio database and its Publishers and Titles tables.

Adding and Setting Up a Data Environment

To use the Data Report Utility, you first have to add a Data Environment designer to your project. Although this chapter will show you the basics of using the Data Environment with the Data Report Utility, you are urged to learn more about the Data Environment by reading Chapter 14, "Working in the Data Environment."

Start a new Standard EXE project. Add a Data Environment designer to the project by selecting Add Data Environment from VB's Project menu or More ActiveX Designers and then Data Environment from VB's Project menu. The way of adding a Data Environment is different depending on the other options that exist in the Project menu. If you don't have the Data Environment option on your menu at all, choose the Components option on the Project menu. On the Designers tab, make sure that the Data Environment and Data Report boxes are checked. You should then see the Data Environment option on the Project menu and you can add the designer to your project.

After the Data Environment designer has been added to the project, right-click on `Connection1` in the Data Environment to display the pop-up menu (see Figure 15.1). Select the Properties option and you will see the Data Link dialog box. This lets you specify which database will be used, along with the particulars of how to connect to it.

FIGURE 15.1.

Right-click on Connection1 in the Data Environment, then choose the Properties option to display the Data Link dialog box.

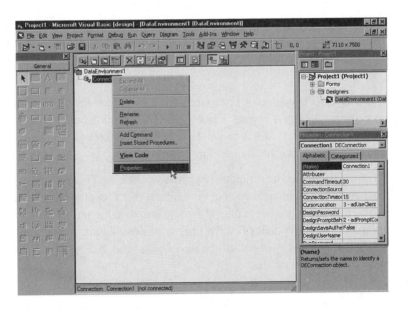

The first tab on the Data Link dialog box is used to select a data provider (see Figure 15.2). Choose the Microsoft Jet 3.51 OLE DB Provider option and click Next.

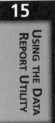

FIGURE 15.2.

The Data Link dialog box allows you to specify the database type, filename, and connection string.

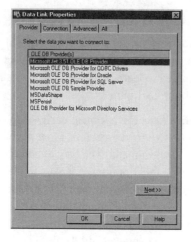

The next page on the dialog box asks for the data source for the data. Because you want to use the Biblio database, enter the path and filename of that database on your system. If you have the BIBLIO.MDB file in VB's root directory, you can simply type in BIBLIO.MDB. Otherwise, you have to provide the file's full path. Click Next when you're done.

On the next page, you are asked to enter the login name and password for the database. Because authentication is not needed to access the Biblio database, you should leave the User Name field as Admin and the Password field blank. Click Next to go to the next page.

The Data Link dialog box's final page allows you to test the database connection to make sure that everything is correct. Click the Test Connection button to see if the database is accessible. If the test fails, you will have to go back through the pages of the dialog box and make sure you entered everything correctly.

After the database connection test has passed, click the Finish button to exit the dialog box. You are then brought back to the Connection1 Properties dialog box. Note that the connection string has been filled in for you based on the information specified when using the Data Link dialog box. Of course, you could have entered the connection string yourself if you had known it off the top of your head, but the Data Link dialog box makes it a little bit easier.

To double-check that the database is accessible, click the Test Connection button on the Connection1 properties dialog box. If you get an error message, you have to click the Build button to review the connection options you've selected. If you see a message about a missing workgroup information file, then check to make sure the User Name is "Admin."

After you have established that the database can be connected properly, click the OK button. You'll then see the Data Environment hierarchy, as shown in Figure 15.3. It shows the database connection you've just established, currently called Connection1.

FIGURE 15.3.

*The Data Environment hierarchy, which includes a database connection (*Connection1*).*

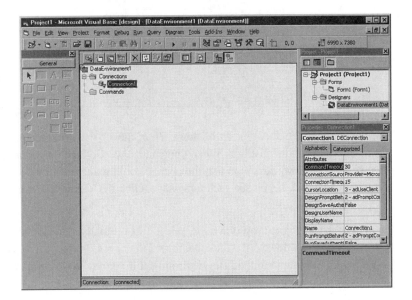

Click Connection1 in the Data Environment, then change its Name property in the Properties window. Use Biblio as the new name. Also change the Data Environment's name to deBiblio by clicking DataEnvironment1 and then modifying its Name property in the Properties window.

Because our goal is to show all of the titles for each publisher in the Biblio database, two of the database's tables (Publishers and Titles) have to be used. These two tables will be added to the Data Environment's list of Commands. As you learn in Chapter 14, a Command is some sort of database object, such as a table, stored procedure, view, or synonym.

To add a new Command, right-click on Commands in the Data Environment hierarchy. From the pop-up menu, choose the Add Command option. You will then see the Command1 Properties dialog box, as shown in Figure 15.4.

FIGURE 15.4.

*The Command1
Properties dialog
box lets you add
new Commands to
the Data
Environment.*

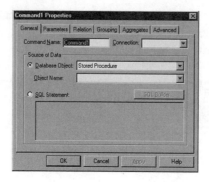

For the Command name, type **Publishers**. Then choose the Biblio connection from the
Connection drop-down list box. When you change the Connection value, you might
receive a message warning you that the change could make one or more of your
Commands invalid. If you see such a message, click the Yes button to allow the change
to the Connection value.

In the Database Object drop-down list, select Table. Finally, choose Publishers from the
Object Name drop-down list. Click OK to add the new Command. You will then see the
Publishers Command in the Data Environment hierarchy. If you expand the
Publishers Command item, you'll see a list of the columns in the Publishers table.

Next, you need to add another Command for the Biblio database's Titles table. Because
you want to relate the Titles table to the Publishers table to show all of the book titles for
each publisher, the Titles table will be a child Command of the Publishers Command.
To add the child Command, right-click on the Publishers item in the Data Environment
hierarchy. From the pop-up menu, select the Add a Child Command option. You'll then
see the Command1 Properties dialog box again.

For this Command, change the name to Titles. You don't have to specify the connection
because child Commands always use the same connection as their parent Commands.
Change the Database Object type to Table and the Object Name to Titles.

Because this is a child Command, you must specify a way of relating this Command to
its parent Command (Publishers). On the Properties dialog box's Relation tab, make
sure the Relate to a Parent Command Object box is checked. Then make sure that the
Parent Fields and Child Fields/Parameters are both set to PubID, the column that will be
used to link both of the tables together. Click the Add button to add the Pub ID-to-Pub
ID relation definition. Then click OK to add the child Command.

The Data Environment hierarchy should now show the Titles Command as a child of the
Publishers Command, indicating their relationship. Figure 15.5 shows the hierarchy completely expanded to show the columns of both the Publishers table and the Titles table.

FIGURE 15.5.

The Data Environment hierarchy, showing the Publishers Command and its child, the Titles Command.

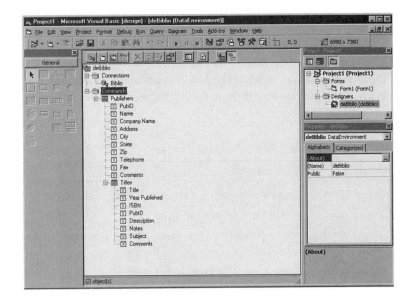

Now that the Data Environment has been set up, the next step is to actually design the report using the Data Report Utility.

Designing the Report

To begin designing the report, you must first add a Data Report to the current project. From VB's Project menu, choose the Add Data Report option. You will then see that a Data Report has been added to the Project Explorer window under the Designers folder, and the Data Report Utility will be displayed (see Figure 15.6).

FIGURE 15.6.

The newly added Data Report Utility window. Note that the Data Report has also been added to the Project Explorer.

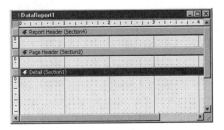

By default, the Data Report Utility consists of five different sections: Report Header, Page Header, Detail, Page Footer, and Report Footer. This is not exactly the layout that is needed for the report to be generated, however. To change the Data Report Utility to better suit the Data Environment that was previously defined, first change the Data Report's `DataSource` property to deBiblio and its `DataMember` property to Publishers. Next, right-click anywhere within the Data Report window and choose the Retrieve Structure option.

You'll be warned that all current controls will be deleted and all section and layout customizations will be cleared. Click Yes to continue.

The sections in the Data Report Utility window are now changed to reflect the Data Environment that was defined. The new sections are: Report Header, Page Header, Group Header, Detail, Group Footer, Page Footer, and Report Footer. The purpose of each section is shown in Table 15.1.

TABLE 15.1. THE SECTIONS OF A DATA REPORT.

Section	Description
Report Header	Appears only once, at the very beginning of the report.
Page Header	Appears at the top of every page.
Group Header	Appears whenever a new group starts. A group is associated with a Command in the Data Environment.
Detail	Repeated once for every record in the lowest level Command in the Data Environment.
Group Footer	Appears whenever a group ends and another is about to begin.
Page Footer	Appears at the bottom of every page.
Report Footer	Appears once only, at the very end of the report.

The structure of the Data Report is easy to understand if you relate it to the structure of the Data Environment. The Group Header and Group Footer sections correspond to the Publishers Command. Within this group are the records of the Titles Command, which make up the Detail section. For each Publisher, there may be an unlimited number of Titles. The Detail (Titles) is nested within the Group (Publishers). To make it easy to tell what is what, each header shows the name of the Data Environment Command with which it is associated in parentheses. For instance, the Group Header section shows "(Publishers_Header)" to denote that is the header section for the Publishers Command.

This is a simple example, and reports can have multiple groups nested inside one another with the Detail section being nested inside the lowest group level. Just remember that when you use the Retrieve Structure option, the sections of the Data Report correspond to the Data Environment hierarchy.

While viewing the Data Report window, you may have noticed that VB's toolbox has changed. A new tab (DataReport) has been added to the toolbox and is populated with six controls: Label, Text, Image, Line, Shape, and Function. The first five are pretty much identical to the standard VB controls of the same name. The last control, Function, is unique to the Data Report Utility and is used for generating and displaying certain kinds of information on a report. The Function control will be discussed later.

You can add any of the controls on the toolbox's DataReport tab to the sections of the Data Report. We will be using all of these controls—with the exception of the Shape control—when building the sample Biblio report.

In addition to adding controls from the toolbox to the Data Report's sections, you can also drag and drop items from the Data Environment. To do this, you must have both windows displayed on the screen at the same time. Rearrange the Data Report and Data Environment windows in a layout similar to that shown in Figure 15.7.

FIGURE 15.7.

The Data Report and Data Environment windows rearranged so both can be seen and accessed simultaneously.

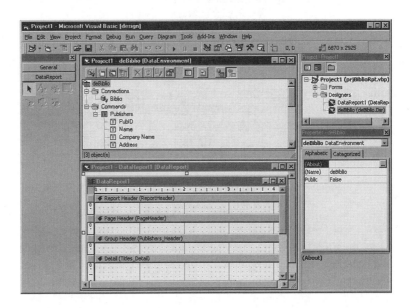

When you are able to view both the Data Report and the Data Environment windows simultaneously, drag the Company Name item from the Data Environment's Publishers Command to the Data Report's Group Header section. The Data Report Utility automatically adds two controls, a Label and a TextBox. The Label merely gives the name of the item. The TextBox is used to display the data itself, and its DataMember and DataField properties are set to reflect the database table and column to which it is bound (in this case, Publishers for the DataMember and Company Name for the DataField).

The placement of the controls within each section is important because they will have the same position on the report that is generated. Another important factor is the height of the section itself. If you have a lot of empty space in the Detail section, that same

15

USING THE DATA REPORT UTILITY

amount of empty space will be repeated for each Detail line in the report. Under some circumstances, you may want a little blank space in a section so it can be set apart from whichever section comes before it. For example, we will add a bit of space to the top of the Group Header section so the Company Name is not immediately following the last Group Footer section that is generated in the report. The resizing of sections is a trial-and-error endeavor, and you'll probably have to make several changes to a report before you get the spacing that you want.

Getting back to the Company Name field in the Group Header section, the Data Report Utility has provided us with a Label and a bound TextBox. We don't need the Label control for the sample report because there's no need to prefix each company name with "Company Name:". Make sure that only the Label control is selected, and then delete it.

Using Figure 15.8 as a guide, resize the Group Header section slightly and change the position of the Company Name field. Also, change its Font property to Arial 12-point Bold and its Width so that it spans most of the report.

FIGURE 15.8.

The Group Header section should be changed to look something like the one shown here.

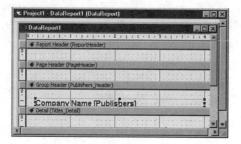

Next, drag the Titles field from the Data Environment's Titles Command and drop it on the Data Report's Detail section. Delete the accompanying Label control, leaving only the TextBox control. Then change its Font to Arial 10-point Italic and its Width to at least 6000. The position of the Titles field should be indented slightly from the Company Name field. Also, resize the Detail section so there is no empty space on the top or bottom of the Company Name field, as shown in Figure 15.9.

FIGURE 15.9.

The Titles field is added to the Data Report's Detail section and is slightly indented from the Group Header section's Company Name field.

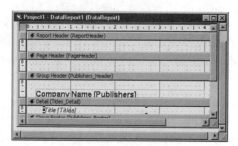

We want to add a report title at the top of each page, so that will be placed in the Page Header section. We are going to add an icon (`Image` control), a title (`Label` control), and a dividing line (`Line` control). Expand the Page Header section a little so you have some room to work in, then use Table 15.2 as a guide for adding the controls and changing their properties. When you're done, resize the Page Header section so there is just a bit of space under the `Line` control. It should look something like Figure 15.10.

TABLE 15.2. THE CONTROLS AND THEIR PROPERTIES FOR THE DATA REPORT'S PAGE HEADER SECTION.

Control Type	Property	Value
Image	Name	imgBookIcon
	Height	570
	Left	0
	Picture	BOOK02.ICO
	Top	0
	Width	720
Label	Name	lblPageTitle
	Caption	Database Book List
	Font	Arial 22-pt Bold
	Height	570
	Left	720
	Top	0
	Width	5040
Line	Name	linDivider
	Height	0
	Left	144
	Top	576
	Width	7055

NOTE

The BOOK02.ICO file, which is used by the imgBookIcon control in the preceding, can be found on the Visual Basic or Visual Studio CD-ROM. On the Visual Studio CD, it is located in the directory \COMMON\GRAPHICS\ICONS\WRITING.

FIGURE 15.10.

The changes made to the Data Report's Page Header section can be seen here.

The next thing to add to the report is a total number of titles for each publisher. This is placed in the Group Footer section, because that is the section that is displayed whenever a group (in this case, the Publishers Command) has been generated.

Add a `Label` control to the Group Footer section and change its `Caption` property to "Total Number of Titles:". Change its `Font` property to Arial 8-point Bold and its `Width` so the entire caption is displayed.

Now, you're going to need something that will calculate the number of titles in each section. Fortunately, the Data Report Utility provides just such a thing with its `Function` control. Add a `Function` control to the right of the Label control you just added and change its `Width` property to 1872.

The `Function` control can provide a total of eight different calculations, but it can only be used in the Group Footer or Report Footer sections. Table 15.3 lists `Function`'s calculation types. You can specify which type to use by setting the control's `FunctionType` property.

TABLE 15.3. THE CALCULATION TYPES PERFORMED BY THE DATA REPORT UTILITY'S FUNCTION CONTROL.

Function	Description
rptFuncSum	Sum of all items.
rptFuncAve	Average of all items.
rptFuncMin	Minimum value in a group of items.
rptFuncMax	Maximum value in a group of items.
rptFuncRCnt	Number of rows in a section.
rptFuncVCnt	Number of fields with non-null values.
rptFuncSDEV	Standard deviation.
rptFuncSERR	Standard error.

Because we need to count the number of `Title` fields in each group, we will use the `rptFuncVCnt` value. Set the `Function` control's `FunctionType` property to `rptFuncVCnt`.

Even though the `Function` control now knows that it is supposed to count the number of fields, it doesn't know which field to count. To specify that the `Title` field is to be used, you must set the control's `DataMember` property to Titles and its `DataField` property to Title.

Before finishing up with the Group Footer section, make sure that there is a little space above its `Label` and `Function` controls so the footer information won't appear immediately after the previous section on the report.

The last thing to add to the report is the page number, which will be shown at the bottom of each page. The Page Footer section contains information that is repeated on every page, so that is the section that will contain the page number.

Enlarge the Page Footer section slightly and then add a `Label` control. Change its `Caption` property to "Page:". Then right-click on blank space in the Page Footer section. From the pop-up menu, choose Insert Control and then Current Page Number. This adds a `TextBox` field that will contain the number of the current page. Move the `TextBox` control so it is right next to the `Label` control, then try to move them both so they are centered within the Page Footer section.

When you were adding the Current Page Number `TextBox`, you may have noticed that there are several other pieces of information you can add to your reports, including total number of pages, current date, current time, and report title. Each one is actually a text box that contains a code that tells the Data Report Utility what kind of value to insert. For example, the Current Page Number text box consists of the code `%p`, which indicates that the current page number should be inserted into the text box.

You are just about done designing the report. The Report Header and Report Footer sections will not be used, so you should resize those sections so there is no blank space in them. The Data Report window should look like the one shown in Figure 15.11.

Before moving on, there are just a few small changes left to be made. Click the title bar of the Data Report to display the Data Report's properties in the Property window. Change the `Caption` to `Database Book List` and the `Name` of the Data Report to `drBiblioRpt`. Finally, change the `WindowState` property to `vbMaximized`. This is a good time to save the project if you haven't done so already.

Now that the report design is finished, you can add code to display it on the screen. The next section shows you how to do just that.

FIGURE 15.11.

The Data Report window with all controls and data fields added.

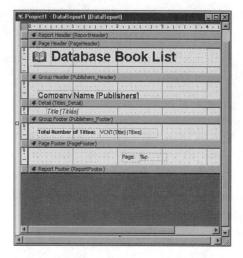

Previewing the Report

After going through all of the steps to design the Data Report, you'll be relieved to know that the code required to display the report on the screen is only one line! All you have to do is call the Show method of the Data Report object (drBiblioRpt).

Display the project's form by double-clicking Form1 in the Project Explorer. Also, switch back to the regular controls in the toolbox by selecting the toolbox's General tab.

Add the controls listed in Table 15.4 to the form and change their properties as indicated. When you're finished, the form should look like the one shown in Figure 15.12.

TABLE 15.4. THE CONTROLS AND THEIR PROPERTIES FOR THE DATA REPORT PROJECT'S FORM.

Control Type	Property	Value
Form	Name	frmBiblioRpt
	Caption	Biblio Data Report Sample
	Height	2865
	Width	4680
CommandButton	Name	cmdShow
	Caption	Show Report
	Height	495
	Left	120
	Top	240

Control Type	Property	Value
	Width	1695
CommandButton	Name	cmdPrint
	Caption	Print Report
	Height	495
	Left	120
	Top	840
	Width	1695
CommandButton	Name	cmdExport
	Caption	Export Report
	Height	495
	Left	120
	Top	1440
	Width	1695
CommandButton	Name	cmdExit
	Caption	Exit
	Height	495
	Left	120
	Top	2040
	Width	1695
Label	Name	lblWarning1
	Caption	<-- WARNING!
	Font	MS Sans Serif 10pt Bold
	Height	255
	Left	2040
	Top	960
	Width	2175
Label	Name	lblWarning2
	Caption	Don't click the Print Report button unless you want to print the entire report (several hundred pages) to your printer!
	Height	975
	Left	2040
	Top	1320
	Width	2295

FIGURE 15.12.

The form for the Data Report sample program.

The initial code to be added to the program is shown in Listing 15.1. The cmdShow_Click event calls the Data Report object's Show method, and the cmdExit_Click event ends the program.

LISTING 15.1. THE DATA REPORT SAMPLE PROGRAM'S *CMDSHOW_CLICK* AND *CMDEXIT_CLICK* EVENTS.

```
Private Sub cmdShow_Click()

    ' Use the Data Report object's Show method to
    ' display the report on the screen.
    drBiblioRpt.Show

End Sub


Private Sub cmdExit_Click()

    ' Exit the program.
    Unload Me
    End

End Sub
```

Run the program. When the Show Report button is clicked, the report is generated. This may take a short while because the Biblio database is quite large and the report will consist of several hundred pages. When the Data Report is displayed, it is enlarged to fit the screen because the WindowState property was set to vbMaximized earlier. The Data Report window should look similar to the one shown in Figure 15.13.

Note that the Data Report window includes several controls that let the user zoom in or out and page through the report. There are also buttons for printing and exporting the report. These functions can also be accomplished through code, which will be discussed next.

FIGURE 15.13.

The Data Report is generated when the Show Report button is clicked.

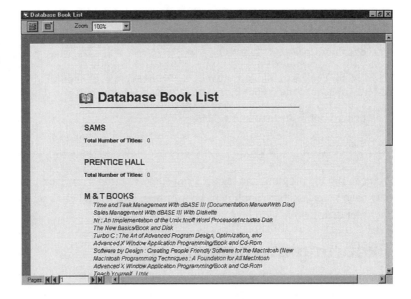

Printing the Report

Printing a data report is just as easy as showing it on the screen and is simply a matter of calling the `PrintReport` method. Although you can call `PrintReport` with no arguments to immediately start spooling the entire report to the printer, you will probably want to specify certain parameters with the method. For example, it's a good idea to display a Print dialog box before the spooling actually begins.

The syntax of the `PrintReport` method is as follows:

```
object.PrintReport(showdialog, range, pagefrom, pageto)
```

The *showdialog* argument is a Boolean value that specifies whether or not the Print dialog box is shown. Unless you want printing to start right away with no further user intervention, set this value to True.

By default, all of the report's pages will be printed. However, if you want to print a range of pages instead, set the *range* argument to the constant `rptRangeFromTo`. Then specify the starting and ending page numbers with the *pagefrom* and *pageto* arguments.

In the sample program, we want to print all of the pages in the report by default, but we also want to show the Print dialog box so a printer can be selected and a page range can be specified by the user if desired. Listing 15.2 shows the `cmdPrint_Click` event, which calls the `PrintReport` method.

15

USING THE DATA REPORT UTILITY

LISTING 15.2. THE *CMDPRINT_CLICK* EVENT, WHICH CALLS THE DATA REPORT OBJECT'S *PRINTREPORT* METHOD TO PRINT THE REPORT.

```
Private Sub cmdPrint_Click()

    ' Use the Data Report object's PrintReport method
    ' to spool the report to the printer. A Print
    ' dialog box is displayed first.
    drBiblioRpt.PrintReport True

End Sub
```

You can run the program and try the Print Report button. However, unless you want a 200-page report to start spooling to your printer, you should click the Cancel button in the Print dialog box.

Exporting the Report

One of the more interesting features of the Data Report object is its capability to export the report that it generates to an HTML or text file. The export is accomplished using the `ExportReport` method. Like the `PrintReport` method, `ExportReport` has a few parameters that allow you to control how the file is exported.

The syntax of the `ExportReport` method is as follows:

```
object.ExportReport(index, filename, overwrite,
    showdialog, range, pagefrom, pageto)
```

The `ExportReport` method uses the `ExportFormats` collection. The collection consists of templates that specify how the report is to be formatted. By default, `ExportFormats` contains four report formats: HTML (1), Unicode HTML (2), Text (3), and Unicode Text (4). You can also create your own formats and add them to the collection. For more information about how to create new export formats, see the VB6 manual or the MSDN Library.

`ExportReport`'s *index* argument specifies the index number of the `ExportFormats` collection that contains the template you want to use for the export. Although you can specify a value of 1 through 4 to use any of the default templates, it's better to use the constants that have been defined for the index argument: `rptKeyHTML`, `rptKeyUnicodeHTML_UTF8`, `rptKeyText`, and `rptKeyUnicodeText`.

The *filename* argument specifies the default filename or file filter for the exported file. If you don't specify a value for this argument and use one of the four built-in export formats, an appropriate file filter is automatically used ("`*.htm, .html`" for HTML files and "`*.txt`" for text files).

The *overwrite* argument is a Boolean value and should be set to True if you want the export file to be automatically overwritten if it already exists. Otherwise, set it to False.

The *showdialog* argument is also Boolean and specifies whether or not a Save As dialog box should be displayed. If you want to export to a file with no intervention from the user, pass this argument as False, the *overwrite* argument as True, and a valid filename in the *filename* argument.

The *range*, *pagefrom*, and *pageto* arguments are used to specify that only a certain range of report pages are to be exported. These are used the same way as they are in the PrintReport method, with *range* being set to the constant rptRangeFromTo to indicate a range is to be exported and the *pagefrom* and *pageto* arguments specifying the page range. Because the fonts used on the printer and the print preview page don't necessarily match those of the export files, the page numbers may not correspond to that of the report shown on the screen or printer using the Show or PrintReport methods.

There are a few other things you need to know about the ExportReport method. For one, it doesn't export images. Any Image controls you added to the report will not show up in the exported file, not even in HTML files.

Also, the export function is performed asynchronously. The ExportReport method returns a Long value that represents the asynchronous operation's identifier.

For the sample data report program, we want to export the entire report to an HTML file as the default. The Save To dialog box is displayed so the user can change the export range or format, if she wants. Listing 15.3 shows the final section of code for the program, the cmdExport_Click event.

LISTING 15.3. THE *CMDEXPORT_CLICK* EVENT, WHICH CALLS THE DATA REPORT OBJECT'S *EXPORTREPORT* METHOD TO EXPORT THE REPORT.

```
Private Sub cmdExport_Click()

    ' Use the Data Report object's ExportReport method
    ' to export the report to an HTML file.
    drBiblioRpt.ExportReport rptKeyHTML, , , True

End Sub
```

The sample Data Report program is now complete. Most of the work in creating it was done using the Data Report Utility. Only a few lines of code are needed to perform functions such as printing, exporting, or displaying the report on the screen.

The project created in this chapter was very simple, but the Data Report Utility can be used to create much more sophisticated reports. Multiple databases, deeply nested groups, custom calculations, and enhanced detail lines are all possible with this useful tool.

The Data Report Utility and Crystal Reports: How They Compare

Longtime users of Crystal Reports will undoubtedly want to know how the new Data Report Utility compares to that with which they are already familiar. If you are already proficient at using Crystal Reports, is the Data Report Utility worth learning about?

The answer to that question is not so simple. Crystal Reports has been around for years and has evolved into a very complex product. As a database report generating tool, it's in a class of its own. You can create significantly more robust reports with Crystal Reports than you can with the Data Report Utility.

But what the Data Report Utility lacks in flexibility, it makes up for in ease of use. After you've created one or two reports, using the Data Report Utility is a snap. It lets you build a decent-looking report in minutes with very little experience using the utility.

Another point to consider is the fact that the Data Report Utility works closely with the Data Environment. The Data Environment, though just introduced in Visual Basic 6, is bound to become a commonly-used facet of VB application development. Knowing how to use it—and the tools that are based on it—is likely to become a valuable skill.

So the answer to the question of whether or not to learn how to use the Data Report Utility is yes. It is well worth the minor investment in time to see how it works and how you can use it to develop quick and easy reports. If you want to learn more about the Data Report Utility and delve even further into its report-generating features, that's also a worthwhile endeavor.

Summary

The Data Report Utility is a simple way to create database reports. Because it works closely with the Data Environment, it is well worth learning how to use it.

The Data Report Utility uses a graphic environment for designing reports. You can drag and drop fields from the Data Environment directly onto the sections of the report. You can also use any of the six controls that are included with the utility and add them to the report, too.

The Data Report object lets you easily display the generated report on the screen or spool it to a printer. You can also export the report to an HTML or text file or create your own export templates.

Database Tools and Utilities

by Lowell Mauer

IN THIS CHAPTER

- The Data View Window   338
- The SQL Editor   339
- The Query Designer   341
- Creating Data Objects Using the Data Object Wizard   342
- Using the Data Form Wizard   349

Among the many new features that have been included with Visual Basic 6 are several database tools and utilities that help you develop more efficient applications. In addition to the Data Environment Designer and the Data Reporter, you'll see a few other data tools you can use. The first three tools discussed in this chapter are part of the Visual Data Tools that have become an integral feature of Visual Basic and the Visual Studio package. Besides these tools, there are two more wizards that will make your life much easier when designing database applications.

The Data View Window

The Data View window provides you with a way of maintaining any database connections you might need in your application. In Chapter 15, "Using the Data Report Utility," the Data Environment connections required for the Data Reporter were displayed in the Data View window (see Figure 16.1).

FIGURE 16.1

The Data View window displays all of a project's database connections.

Depending on the database type to which you are connecting, you will have one or more of the following options available to you, organized as folders:

- Database Diagrams
- Tables
- Triggers
- Views
- Stored Procedures

The Data View window gives you a way to maintain all of your database connections and information from one central location; by double-clicking, dragging and dropping, and using the right-click features, you can open, create, and edit your database objects. The next few sections show you how to use the tools accessible from the Data View window. These tools are collectively known as the Visual Data Tools and are included in both the Professional and Enterprise versions of Visual Basic 6.

The SQL Editor

The SQL Editor is a small utility that allows you to create and edit stored procedures and database triggers for both SQL Server and Oracle databases from within the Visual Basic development environment. When you are working within the editor, any SQL command will be highlighted to distinguish it from the database references or comments. If you are using one of the mentioned databases, you can use stored procedures and triggers to enhance the performance of your database access.

Stored Procedures

Stored procedures enable you to manage your server-based database and access or display information about the database or its users. As an example, you can use a stored procedure to access the order detail (from the *Order Details* table) and the Orders (from the *Orders* table) for each customer in the *customers* table. Stored procedures can contain program code, logic, and SQL queries that can be executed against the database. They can accept input values, generate parameters, return single or multiple result sets, and return values. You can use stored procedures for the same reasons that you might use SQL, with the following advantages:

- You can execute multiple SQL statements in a single stored procedure.
- Stored procedures can be referenced by other stored procedures, allowing you simply a complex series of statements.
- A stored procedure will execute faster because it is compiled and stored on the database server.

Creating a stored procedure requires a knowledge of the database's programming language. To create a new stored procedure, you would do the following:

- Display the Data View window and right-click the Stored Procedures folder; then choose New Stored Procedure from the pop-up menu. Figure 16.2 shows the SQL Editor with a default stored procedure, which contains the default SQL code generated by Visual Basic.
- Replace *Stored Procedure* in the first line of the SQL code with the name of the procedure.
- Write the remaining SQL code required for the procedure.
- Run the stored procedure to compile it and save it in the database.

16

DATABASE TOOLS
AND UTILITIES

FIGURE 16.2

Using the SQL Editor to add stored procedures to a database.

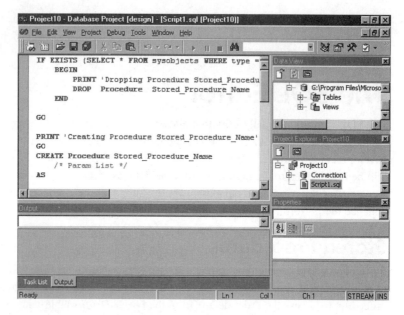

After a stored procedure is created, you can execute it by selecting the procedure in the Data View window and right-clicking on it. Then, choose the Run option from the pop-up menu. The stored procedure will then be executed like any other SQL statement. You can also copy a stored procedure and use it as a template for creating a new stored procedure. When you copy a stored procedure, it is automatically assigned a unique name in the database.

Setting Triggers

A trigger is a special kind of stored procedure that becomes active only when data is modified in a specified table using one or more data modification operations (Update, Insert, or Delete). Triggers can query other tables and can include complex SQL statements. They are very useful for enforcing complex business rules in a corporate environment. Triggers are also useful for enforcing database referential integrity, which will preserve the relationships between the tables when data is being added, updated, or deleted. However, the best way to ensure referential integrity is to define key constraints within the database. Triggers are very useful because they

- Are automatic and will be activated immediately after any modification is made to the database tables.

- Can cascade changes through any related tables in the database.

- Can be used to enforce restrictions that are more complex than those defined with check constraints. Unlike a check constraint, triggers can reference columns in other tables.

The steps required to create a trigger using the SQL Editor are the same as those for a stored procedure. In fact, the SQL Editor will work the same, except that a default trigger template is displayed in place of a stored procedure. The only difference is in the process the SQL statements will perform in the Trigger. As with stored procedures, executing the SQL for the trigger will create and save it in the database.

The Query Designer

The Query Designer (see Figure 16.3) is the third tool available to you from the Visual Data Tools set. It is an interactive database query interface that allows you to design almost any type of SQL statement required for your application processing. You can access the Query Designer either from the Visual Studio project environment or from the Data Environment Designer's SQL Builder function.

FIGURE 16.3

Making use of the Query Designer to create SQL statements for an application.

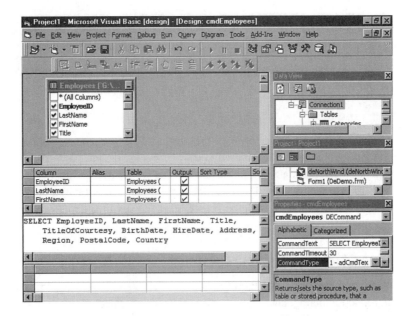

Chapter 14, "Working in the Data Environment," shows how to use the Query Designer to create SQL statements, which can be simple or very complex to be used when building Data Environment connections for ActiveX Data Objects (ADO) processing.

16

DATABASE TOOLS AND UTILITIES

Creating Data Objects Using the Data Object Wizard

Along with the numerous wizards included with Visual Basic are two database-oriented wizards that help you build data objects and forms to be used by your application. You can use the Data Object Wizard to help you create class objects and the user control objects bound to those class objects. To access this Wizard you would add it to the Add-Ins menu using the Add-Ins manager. You can use the Data Object Wizard to do the following:

- Create updateable recordsets from stored procedures
- Create user controls to display and manipulate data
- Generate Visual Basic code that defines data relationships
- Create user controls that display lookup relationships
- Provide meaningful text descriptions from reference tables using lookups
- Provide meaningful text if a field is null

> **NOTE**
>
> To use the Data Object Wizard you must first create a Data Environment that contains commands to retrieve and manipulate the data. The Data Object Wizard uses commands from the Data Environment to retrieve and update the data.

The different commands are used to define how the data is accessed from the database and how selection data will be displayed. You would first create a class object using the Wizard, and then you would create the custom data control based on the new class. Before starting to work with the Data Object Wizard, create a Data Environment containing the three commands as shown in Figure 16.4.

Creating a Class Object

When you have access to the Data Object Wizard and have started it, you will see an introduction dialog, click Next to go to the Create Object dialog (see Figure 16.5). This is where you will select either a class or control to create.

FIGURE 16.4

The Data Environment window showing the commands that will be used by the Data Object Wizard.

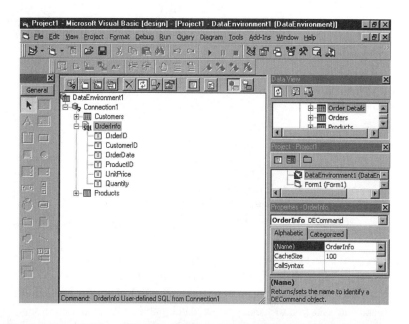

NOTE

To create a data control, you must first define a class using the Wizard.

FIGURE 16.5

Selecting the object to create.

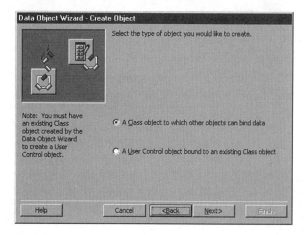

The default is a class, so click Next to continue. The dialog now displayed, as shown in Figure 16.6, lists all of the available commands defined in the Data Environment object within your project.

FIGURE 16.6

Choosing the command that will become the primary source of information for the Data Control object.

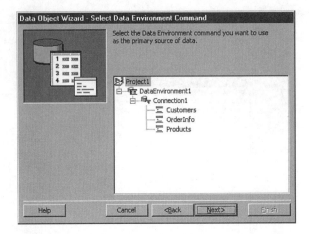

You must select the command to be used as the primary source of data for the new class you are creating. Select the OrderInfo command and click Next to continue. The Define Class Field Information dialog (see Figure 16.7) lists all the fields in the source command and asks you to specify which can be null and which are primary keys.

FIGURE 16.7

Defining the Class field information for the command.

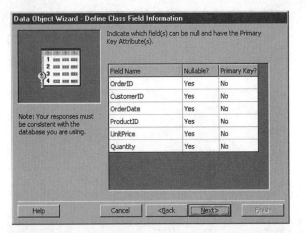

CAUTION

The values you set in this dialog must be consistent with those defined in the database definition.

When you are satisfied with these settings, click Next to define the lookup information. Lookups allow you to get description information or any other reference-type information to display along with the source data. For example, the source data might contain the product number; a lookup definition would allow you to display the product description instead of the number. In the Define Lookup Table Information dialog (see Figure 16.8), you are selecting the Data Environment commands that reference these lookup tables and will specify to which fields in the source command they are related.

> **NOTE**
>
> This is very much like a join; however, the data object is doing all the work, rather than simply accessing the extra tables in the SQL statement.

FIGURE 16.8

Defining the lookup information for the Source command data.

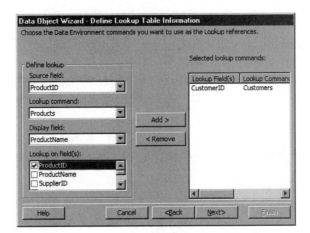

Build the Lookup command as shown in Table 16.1. As you can see, you can define as many lookup definitions as you need for your new data object class.

TABLE 16.1 DEFINING THE LOOKUP REFERENCES FOR THE SOURCE COMMAND

Source Field	Lookup Command	Lookup Field	Display Field
CustomerId	Customers	CustomerID	CompanyName

When you are finished entering lookup information, click Next to continue. The dialog shown in Figure 16.9 allows you to modify the mapping between the source and lookup fields. If you have multiple fields, they will appear separately when you click the Next button.

FIGURE 16.9

Mapping the relationships between the source command and the lookup references.

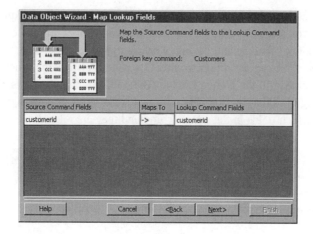

Because the default mapping is sufficient, click Next without making any changes. The next three dialogs give you the ability to define action SQL statements—such as INSERT, UPDATE, and DELETE—to be used with the source command. Figure 16.10 shows the Insert dialog, but all three have basically the same layout. The commands that could be specified in these dialogs would be the SQL commands for the associated function, as shown in the following code added to the Data Environment as a command.

```
Update [Order Details] Set UnitPrice = UnitPrice * 1.06
```

FIGURE 16.10

Defining action query commands that will be used by the custom data object.

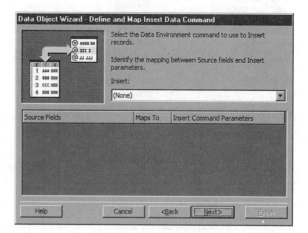

Click the Next button until you get to the final dialog, which prompts you to provide a name for the new class object. After entering a name, click Finish to actually create the class object in your project. At this point, you have a class object that can be used to create the custom data control object covered in the next section.

Creating the Custom Data Control

Now that you have the class created, you can create the data control object that will use it to display data. Restart the Data Object Wizard and select the second option, User Control Object, on the Create Object dialog and click Next. The dialog displayed (see Figure 16.11) shows each of the available commands and their associated classes in the Data Environment.

FIGURE 16.11

The Data Environment selection list showing any classes that have been defined.

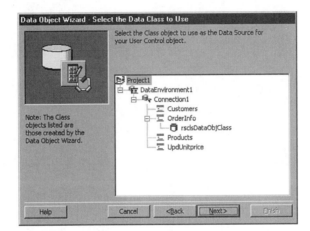

Select the class you have just created and click Next to continue the process. This will display the Select User Control Type dialog shown in Figure 16.12. When creating a data control object, you have a choice of four types of controls as shown in the figure.

FIGURE 16.12

Selecting how to display the source data in the data object.

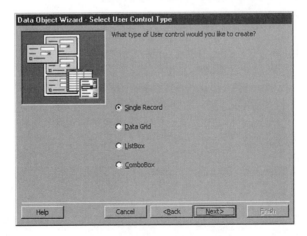

Choose the datagrid and click Next to map the class properties to control types. This dialog (see Figure 16.13) also allows you to prevent or hide any source field from being displayed by changing its associated control type to "(None)."

FIGURE 16.13

*Setting the Control
Type properties for
each of the source
command fields.*

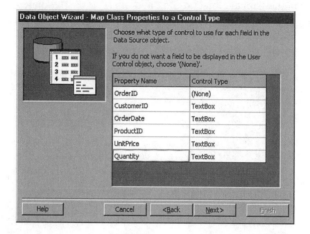

For this demo, you will leave most of the default setting for the control types. You should notice that the CustomerID and EmployeeID fields mapped to the lookup commands have control-type combo boxes. This allows you to display all of the values for the field if you want. Change these fields' settings to text box and click Next to provide a name for the new data object; then click Finish to complete the process.

Using the New Control Object

After you create the data control object, you can use it within the project like any other custom control. Figure 16.14 shows the program running with the new data control displaying the information from the orders table.

FIGURE 16.14

*Using the new data
control object in a
standard project.*

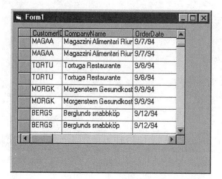

NOTE

At the time of this writing, there is very little documentation available for this Wizard and some of its features might change.

Using the Data Form Wizard

The last wizard this chapter discusses is the Data Form Wizard. By providing the Data Form Wizard, Visual Basic has made it very easy to create and include data-bound forms that give the user complete access to the data in the application's database. The Data Form Wizard is designed to automatically generate forms that contain individual bound controls and procedures used to manage the data obtained from the database. You can use the Data Form Wizard to create single-query forms to access data from a single table or query, master/detail-type forms to manage more complex one-to-many data relationships, or grid forms to manage data from a data control.

NOTE

The Data Form Wizard will work only with the new ADO Data Control.

As it takes you through several steps, the Wizard will prompt you for the information it needs to build the data forms properly. However, because the forms the Wizard builds are fairly generic, you will probably modify them to more closely resemble the remaining forms in your application. To see how this Wizard works, start a new project, and open the Data Form Wizard from the Add-Ins menu.

NOTE

If the Data Form Wizard is not on the Add-Ins menu, you must add it by using the Add-Ins Manager.

The first dialog to be displayed is the Introduction dialog, which allows you to select a data form profile you have previously saved. For this demo, click Next to choose the database type with which you are working. At this time, there are only two database types to choose from: Microsoft Access and open database connectivity (ODBC). Choose

Access and click Next to continue. After you've selected your database type, you must specify the actual database location or connection information. For Access, you are prompted for the database location as shown in Figure 16.15; however, if you are using ODBC, you will be prompted for the appropriate connection information as shown in Figure 16.16.

FIGURE 16.15

Specifying the location of the Access .mdb file.

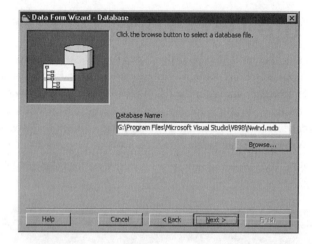

FIGURE 16.16

Setting the information required to connect to an ODBC database.

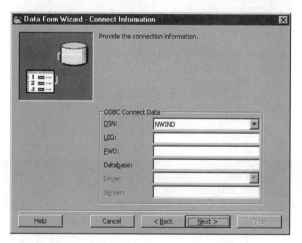

Locate and select the NorthWind database (NWIND.MDB) in the Visual Basic directory and then click Next to continue. As you move to the next dialog, the Wizard actually connects to and opens the specified database. The Form dialog (see Figure 16.17) asks you for the name of the new form, the form layout you want to create, and the type of data access connection to use.

FIGURE 16.17

Specifying the Form layout and the data access type.

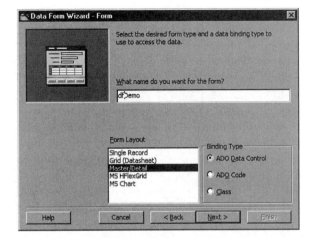

Because each of the form layouts requires slightly different information, the remaining steps will vary depending on the form layout you have chosen. For this example, choose the Master/Detail form layout and leave the default Binding type of ADO Data Control. Finally, name the new form "CH16Demo" and click the Next button. Because you selected the Master/Detail layout, you will now be prompted for the record source and fields for both the master and detail queries. The first dialog, Master Record Source (see Figure 16.18), requests the master query source.

FIGURE 16.18

Selecting the master record source for the Wizard to use.

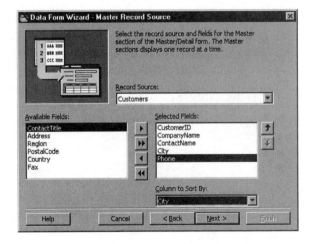

From the Record Source drop-down, select the Customers table; then select the fields shown in Figure 16.18. Finally, set the sort column to City and click the Next button to define the detail query information. As you can see from Figure 16.19, the Detail Record Source dialog looks exactly like the Master dialog.

FIGURE 16.19

Selecting the Detail information for the Master/Detail layout.

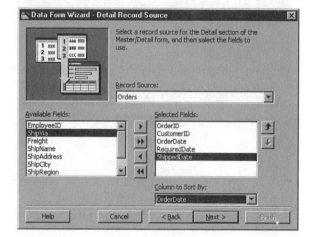

On this form, select the Orders table from the Record Source drop-down, and then select the fields shown in Figure 16.19. Again, set the sort column to OrderDate and click Next to continue. The Record Source Relation dialog (see Figure 16.20) requires you to set the relationship or "join" between the Master and Detail queries.

FIGURE 16.20

Defining the join relationship between the two queries.

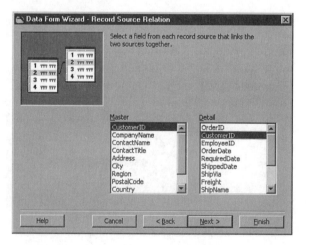

Set the CustomerID as the fields that link the two sources and click Next. The Control Selection dialog (see Figure 16.21) lets you choose the data navigation and manipulation controls you want to appear on the form and enables the Wizard to create the associated code for each selected control. The available controls to choose from are the following:

- Add—Places an Add button on the form with the associated code to add new records to the database.

- Update—Adds the Update button and its associated code to update the database from the form. This button is available only if you are using the Data Control Binding type.

- Delete—Provides the ability to delete records from the database.

- Refresh—Will add the code and command button to allow the user to request a database refresh.

- Close—Includes the code and command button to close the data form

- Show Data Control—If this checkbox is clicked, the Data Control will be displayed on the form

FIGURE 16.21

Choosing the data command buttons to place on the form.

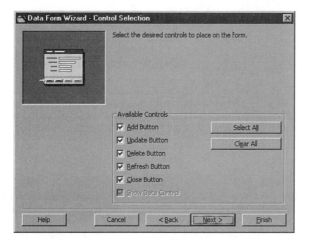

For this example, leave the defaults and click Next. You can now save all of the settings you have selected as parts of a profile. Then click the Finish button to allow the Wizard to perform its magic. The form shown in Figure 16.22 is the end result of all of the options you selected.

Try running this program to see how the Master/Detail form works. Basically, you will see one customer at a time with all of the customer's orders listed in the grid, as shown in Figure 16.23.

FIGURE 16.22

The finished data form created by the Data Form Wizard.

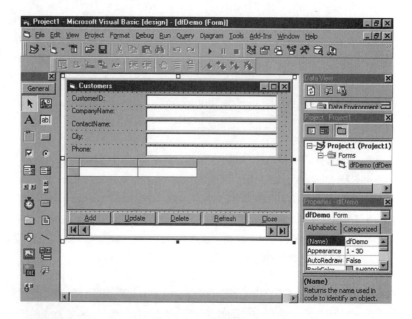

FIGURE 16.23

Using the finished form to display information from the database.

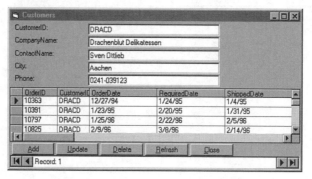

Using the Data Control, switch to a new customer and you will see the order information change as well. By using the Data Form Wizard, you can create data-aware applications with very little effort. However, after the Wizard has created the forms, you must maintain the form layout and its associated code. Finally, remember that each of the different layouts will require slightly different information to create its associated form.

Summary

This chapter explores the complete gamut of tools available to you from the Visual Basic development environment. The Data View window is really a management tool that helps you keep all the data access connections in one place, and the SQL Editor and the Query Designer help you build the SQL and other related procedures you need to create a good application. The Data Object Wizard helps you create your own data-bound custom controls without any coding. Finally, the Data Form Wizard helps you create a data access form that doesn't require you to write any code. In Chapter 17, "Avanced Data Controls," you will see the latest data-bound controls available for you to use in your application.

16

**DATABASE TOOLS
AND UTILITIES**

Advanced Data Controls

by Rob Thayer

IN THIS CHAPTER

- The DataList Control *358*
- The DataCombo Control *361*
- The DataGrid Control *363*
- The Hierarchial FlexGrid Control (MSHFlexGrid) *374*

CHAPTER 17

VB6 has introduced some considerable changes in the area of data access. The Data Environment has been added as a way of organizing data into a hierarchy format. The ADO Data control has been added to enable programmers to access databases using the new ActiveX Data Objects access method.

Because the ADO model is different than that of DAO or RDO, it stands to reason that older data-aware controls such as DBGrid will not work with this newer data access method. Therefore, Microsoft has added several new controls to VB's Toolbox. These controls have been optimized to work with ADO data sources.

Four new controls—DataList, DataCombo, DataGrid, and MSHFlexGrid—have been added to VB to take advantage of ADO. Whether you are familiar with the older data controls (DBList, DBCombo, DBGrid, and MSFlexGrid) or not, this chapter will provide you with a solid introduction to these new controls. You'll see how they are used and how you can use them in your own database applications.

The DataList Control

VB6's new DataList control bears a striking resemblance to the DBList control that has been in the Toolbox since VB4. In fact, it is completely code-compatible with the DBList control; that is, its interface includes the same properties, methods, and events that DBList does. The only difference is that DataList is designed for use with ADO data sources (such as the ADO Data control) rather than DAO or RDO data sources, which are typically provided via the Data control.

For those who are unfamiliar with the function of the DBList control, it is a list box that can be bound to a field in a Recordset. The data in the bound field of each record in the Recordset is displayed in the DBList control's list. So if you were to bind a DBList control to the Name field in the BIBLIO.MDB database's Publishers table, the control would list the name of every publisher in that table. The DataList control works exactly the same way, except that it is designed to use ADO data sources.

In addition to the properties found in the DBList control, DataList adds two of its own. Because an ADO data source can supply more than one data member, there must be a way for the DataList control to know which member to use. This is accomplished via the DataMember and RowMember properties.

For example, you might be using a Data Environment that includes a Connection with a number of Command objects. Each of the Command objects might reference a different table in the connected database. In this case, you could set the DataList control's RowSource and DataSource properties to the name of the Data Environment. Then you could set its DataMember and RowMember properties to the name of the Command object representing the table that contains the field you want to display in the DataList control (as indicated by the control's ListField property).

Of course, you don't have to use the DataList control with the Data Environment as its data source. You can use the ADO Data control as the data source instead.

For your convenience, the unique properties and methods of the DataList control are shown in Table 17.1. Again, these are, for the most part, the same properties and methods that are used with the DBList control.

TABLE 17.1. THE UNIQUE PROPERTIES AND METHODS OF THE *DataList* CONTROL

Name	Property/Method	Description
BoundColumn	Property	The source field in one Recordset object (specified by the RowSource property) that is used to supply a value to another Recordset object (specified by the DataSource property)
BoundText	Property	The value of the field specified by the BoundColumn property
DataBindings	Property	Returns the DataBindings collection object, which contains the properties of the DataList control that can be bound to a database
DataField	Property	The name of the field in the Recordset (specified by the DataSource property) to which the DataList control is bound
DataMember	Property	The data member through which the DataList control is bound, commonly used when working with data sources that can contain multiple data members (such as the Data Environment)
DataSource	Property	The ADO Data control or Command object through which the DataList control is bound
ListField	Property	The field in the Recordset (specified by the RowSource property) that is displayed in the DataList control's list
Locked	Property	Specifies whether or not the data in the DataList control can be changed by the user
MatchedWithList	Property	Returns True if the data in the BoundText property matches any of the control's list items
MatchEntry	Property	Specifies how the DataList control performs searches with user input

continues

17

ADVANCED DATA CONTROLS

TABLE 17.1. CONTINUED

Name	Property/Method	Description
RowMember	Property	The data member used to display the list items, commonly used when working with data sources that can contain multiple data members (such as the Data Environment)
RowSource	Property	The ADO Data control or Command object from which the DataList control's list is filled
SelectedItem	Property	Returns a bookmark for the record that corresponds to an item that is selected from the list
VisibleCount	Property	Returns the number of visible items in the DataList control's list portion
VisibleItems	Property	Returns an array of bookmarks for the records that correspond to the items in the DataList control's list portion
ReFill	Method	Re-creates the DataList control's list of items and repaints the control

To see how the DataList control is used, add an ADO Data control to a form and name it adoBiblioPub. Use the control's Connection String property page to establish a connection to the BIBLIO.MDB database. Choose the Use Connection String option, then click on the Build button. On the dialog box's Provider tab, choose MS Jet 3.51 OLE DB as the database provider. On the Connection tab, choose the BIBLIO.MDB file for the database name. Use the defaults for the user info, with "Admin" for the user name and no password. Then click on the Test Connection button to make sure the database connection works.

After you have a good connection, click OK to close the dialog box, then OK again to close the Connection String property page. If you are unfamiliar with how to establish database connections with the ADO Data control using the sequence of steps just listed, you may want to read Chapter 13, "The ADO Data Control." You'll have to establish a connection to the BIBLIO.MDB database if you want to try many of the samples in this chapter, so it will behoove you to become adept at doing so.

For the adoBiblioPub control's RecordSource property, click on the ellipsis button ("...") to bring up the property page. For the Command Type, choose 2 (adCmdTable). Then select the Publishers table from the Table or Stored Procedure Name drop-down list box. Then click OK to close the property page. Note that the ADO Data control's RecordSource property works differently than that of the standard Data control, which simply provides you with a list of the tables that can be accessed in the current database.

Add a `DataList` control to the form and name it `dtlPublishers`. You can now set the properties for the `DataList` control the way you would a `DBList` control. Choose `adoBiblioPub` for the `DataSource` and `RowSource` properties, and the Name field for the `ListField` property. Run the program and your `DataList` control will be populated with data from the Biblio database's Publishers table. Figure 17.1 shows how the sample program might look at runtime.

FIGURE 17.1

The `DataList` control being used with the ADO Data Control.

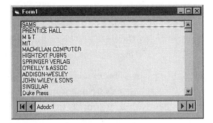

The `DataCombo` Control

Like the `DataList` control, the new `DataCombo` control is code-compatible with its predecessor, the `DBCombo` control. It has the same properties, events, and methods, adding only the `DataMember` and `RowMember` properties for working with multiple data members from a data source.

The `DBCombo` and `DataCombo` controls are combo boxes that can be bound to a field in a Recordset. The list portion of the combo box is automatically filled with the data of the bound field for each record in a Recordset. The major difference between the two controls is that the `DataCombo` control is optimized to work only with ADO data sources.

Table 17.2 lists the unique properties and methods of the `DataCombo` control. These are essentially the same as those of the `DataList` control, but have been repeated here for your convenience.

TABLE 17.2. THE UNIQUE PROPERTIES AND METHODS OF THE `DATACOMBO` CONTROL

Name	Property/Method	Description
BoundColumn	Property	The source field in one Recordset object (specified by the `RowSource` property) that is used to supply a value to another Recordset object (specified by the `DataSource` property)

continues

TABLE 17.2. CONTINUED

Name	*Property/Method*	*Description*
BoundText	Property	The value of the field specified by the BoundColumn property
DataBindings	Property	Returns the DataBindings collection object, which contains the properties of the DataCombo control that can be bound to a database
DataField	Property	The name of the field in the Recordset (specified by the DataSource property) to which the DataCombo control is bound
DataMember	Property	The data member through which the DataCombo control is bound, commonly used when working with data sources that can contain multiple data members (such as the Data Environment)
DataSource	Property	The ADO Data control or Command object through which the DataCombo control is bound
ListField	Property	The field in the Recordset (specified by the RowSource property) that is displayed in the DataCombo control's list
Locked	Property	Specifies whether or not the data in the DataCombo control can be changed by the user
MatchedWithList	Property	Returns True if the data in the BoundText property matches any of the control's list items
MatchEntry	Property	Specifies how the DataCombo control performs searches with user input
RowMember	Property	The data member used to display the list items, commonly used when working with data sources that can contain multiple data members (such as the Data Environment)
RowSource	Property	The ADO Data control or Command object from which the DataCombo control's list gets filled
SelectedItem	Property	Returns a bookmark for the record that corresponds to an item that is selected from the list
VisibleCount	Property	Returns the number of visible items in the DataCombo control's list portion

Name	Property/Method	Description
VisibleItems	Property	Returns an array of bookmarks for the records that correspond to the items in the DataCombo control's list portion
ReFill	Method	Re-creates the DataCombo control's list of items and repaints the control

You use the DataCombo control just as you would the DataList control. Its data source is specified by the RecordSource property, and the field it is bound to is specified by the DataField property. The data source and field used to fill the control's list portion are specified by the RowSource and ListField properties, respectively.

The DataGrid Control

The DataGrid control is used to display database information in a grid format. The control can be automatically filled with data from a Recordset object, and its column headers can also be obtained from a Recordset. Each cell in a DataGrid control can contain text values. Linked or embedded objects within cells are not supported by the DataGrid control at this time.

The first thing to remember about the DataGrid control is that its structure corresponds nicely to a Recordset object. The DataGrid is just what its name implies, a grid. Each row of the grid represents a record, and the columns of the grid correspond to the fields in the record. Each individual column in a row is referred to as a cell, just as you have cells in the grid of a spreadsheet.

Those who have worked with VB's DBGrid control will have no trouble adapting to the DataGrid control, which is OLEDB-aware and can be used with ADO data sources. Even if you haven't used DBGrid before, DataGrid is relatively easy to use.

DataGrid is not completely code-compatible with the DBGrid control, but it's close. The only difference between the two controls (other than the fact that DataGrid uses ADO data sources) is that the DataGrid control doesn't support the MarqueeUnique property or an unbound mode. If you need an unbound grid, use the DBGrid control.

To introduce you to the DataGrid control, you'll first learn about the control's properties, methods, and events. Then you'll try out a few examples and see how some of the control's objects work. Note that some of these items mention *columns* and *splits*. Columns and splits will be discussed in more detail later in this chapter.

DataGrid Properties

The unique properties for the DataGrid control are listed in Table 17.3. Some of them will also be discussed in more detail in this section.

TABLE 17.3. THE UNIQUE PROPERTIES OF THE DataGrid CONTROL

Property	Data Type	Description
AddNewMode	Enum	Returns a value that indicates where the current cell is in relation to the grid's AddNew row
AllowAddNew	Boolean	Specifies whether or not the user can add new records (rows) to the grid
AllowArrows	Boolean	Specifies whether or not the user can use the arrow keys to move out of the grid
AllowDelete	Boolean	Specifies whether or not the user can delete records (rows) from the grid
AllowRowSizing	Boolean	Specifies whether or not the user can resize the rows of the grid
AllowUpdate	Boolean	Specifies whether or not the user can modify data in the grid
ApproxCount	Long	Sets or returns the approximate number of rows in the grid
Bookmark	Variant	Sets or returns a bookmark for the current row of the DataGrid control
Col	Integer	The displayed column of the current cell
ColumnHeaders	Boolean	Specifies whether or not column headers are to be displayed for a grid
Columns	Collection	Returns a collection of Column objects
CurrentCellModified	Boolean	Specifies whether or not the current cell can be modified (runtime only)
CurrentCellVisible	Boolean	Specifies whether or not the current cell is visible (runtime only)
DataChanged	Boolean	Specifies whether or not the data in the grid has been changed by the user (runtime only)
DataMember	DataMember	The data member through which the DataGrid control is bound, commonly used when working with data sources that can contain multiple data members (such as the Data Environment)

Property	Data Type	Description
DataSource	DataSource	The ADO Data control or Command object to which the DataGrid control is bound
DefColWidth	Single	The default column width for the columns in the grid
EditActive	Boolean	Specifies whether or not the current cell is being edited by the user (runtime only)
ErrorText	String	Returns an error message from the DataGrid control's data source
FirstRow	Variant	Sets or returns the bookmark for the first visible row in the grid
HeadFont	IFontDisp	Sets or returns the font used in the grid's column headers
HeadLines	Single	Sets or returns the number of text lines displayed in the grid's column headers
hWndEditor	OLE_HANDLE	Returns the window handle for the DataGrid control's editing window
LeftCol	Integer	Sets or returns the leftmost visible column of the grid
MarqueeStyle	Enum	Specifies the marquee style used when cells in the grid are selected
RecordSelectors	Boolean	Specifies whether or not record selectors are displayed
Row	Integer	The displayed row of the current cell
RowDividerStyle	Enum	Specifies the border style that is drawn between rows in the grid
SelBookmarks	Collection	Returns a collection of bookmarks for all of the selected records (rows) in the grid
Split	Integer	Sets or returns the index of the current split (runtime only)
Splits	Collection	Returns a collection of Split objects (runtime only)
TabAcrossSplits	Boolean	Specifies whether or not the tab and arrow keys will move the current cell across split boundaries in the grid
TabAction	Enum	Specifies the behavior of the tab key for grid navigation

continues

TABLE 17.3. CONTINUED

Property	Data Type	Description
VisibleCols	Integer	Returns the number of visible columns in the grid (runtime only)
VisibleRows	Integer	Returns the number of visible rows in the grid (runtime only)
WrapCellPointer	Boolean	Specifies the behavior of the arrow keys for grid navigation

Data Binding

To bind a DataGrid to a data source, you need only set its DataSource property. The columns of the grid are automatically set up to accommodate the fields of the data source.

If you're using a data source that can include more than one data member, such as the Data Environment, then you will also need to set the DataGrid control's DataMember property. If you are using the DataGrid with the ADO Data control, you can leave the DataMember property blank.

Grid Navigation and User Functions

The user can use the arrow keys and the tab key to navigate through the control's grid. Exactly how these keys work is specified by the DataGrid control's TabAction, WrapCellPointer, and AllowArrows properties.

By default, the tab key is used to change the focus from control to control on a form. In this case, the TabAction property is set to 0 (dbgControlNavigation). However, you can set TabAction to 1 (dbgColumnNavigation) to cause the tab key to move from cell to cell within the grid, only changing the control focus when using the tab would cause the current row to change. You can also set TabAction to 2 (dbgGridNavigation) to cause the tab key to move from cell to cell without ever changing the focus to another control.

The cursor keys are also used to move from cell to cell within the grid when the DataGrid control has the focus. When the WrapCellPointer property is set to True, the cell pointer will move to the row's first column when the user moves to the right on the last column in the row. Or, it will move to the row's last column when the user moves to the left on the first column in the row. When the WrapCellPointer property is set to its default value of False, the pointer will not "wrap" from first to last column or vice-versa.

You can disable the use of left and right cursor key navigation within the grid by setting the `AllowArrows` property to `False`. By default, this property is set to `True`, enabling users to navigate from cell to cell within the same row.

In addition to controlling navigation, the `DataGrid` also enables you to determine what changes a user can make to the database to which it is bound. Setting the `AllowDelete` property to `False` prevents the user from deleting any records (rows) from the grid. Likewise, you can set the `AllowAddNew` property to `False` to prevent the user from adding any new records.

A setting of `False` in the `AllowUpdate` property keeps the user from making any changes to the grid's data whatsoever. Finally, the `AllowRowSizing` property can be set to `False` to prevent the user from resizing the grid's rows.

When the user selects a cell or a group of cells, the setting for the `MarqueeStyle` property determines what the selected cell will look like. Possible values for `MarqueeStyle` are: `dbgDottedCellBorder` (0), `dbgSolidCellBorder` (1), `dbgHighlightCell` (2), `dbgHighlightRow` (3), `dbgHighlightRowRaiseCell` (4), `dbgNoMarquee` (5), and `dbgFloatingEditor` (6). The default value is 6, `dbgFloatingEditor`.

Grid Display and Appearance

Several of the `DataGrid` control's properties enable you to change the way the grid and its cells appear. For example, the `ColumnHeaders`, `HeadFont`, and `HeadLines` properties are used to specify whether or not the grid displays column headers, and if so, what font they should be and how many lines of text they can have. Headers appear at the top of the grid and remain fixed in place; that is, they do not move when the grid is scrolled up or down.

The grid also includes the record number for each record along the left side of the grid. These are referred to as *record selectors*. Record selectors remain fixed and do not move when the grid is scrolled left or right. You can keep the record selectors from appearing by setting the `RecordSelectors` property to `False`.

Unless you change the width of each individual column in the grid, each column will be of equal width. You can set the default width of the cells by setting the `DefColWidth` property. You'll see how to set the size of individual columns later in this chapter.

By default, the grid's left-most column is the first column in the grid. However, you can change the left-most column to whichever column you want by setting the `LeftCol` property. Columns are numbered starting with 0, so if you want the fifth column to appear starting at the grid's left-most edge, set `LeftCol` to 4. You can change the topmost row displayed in the grid by setting the `FirstRow` property.

If you want to know how many columns and rows are being displayed by a grid, check the values of the VisibleCols and VisibleRows properties during runtime. Note that these counts include even partially visible columns and rows.

The RowDividerStyle property lets you specify how the borders between the grid's rows will look. Possible values are: No divider (0), black line (1), dark gray line (2), raised (3), inset (4), and color (5). If you set RowDividerStyle to 5, the color that is used is the one specified by the DataGrid's ForeColor property. The default value is 2 (dark gray line).

If you want to change the borders between columns, you must use the DividerStyle property for the individual Column objects. Column objects will be discussed later in this chapter.

The Current Cell

The single cell that is selected or being edited by the user is referred to as the *current cell*. You can determine which cell is current by examining the values in the Row and Col properties. These values indicate the *displayed* row and column numbers of the current cell, not the position of the cell in the grid. For example, if you have many rows in your grid and page down to the fiftieth row, it might be the third line displayed in the grid. Examining the Row property would give you a value of 2 (rows start at zero, not one) instead of 50. If you want to determine the actual row of the current cell, simply add the values of the Row and FirstRow properties. To get the actual column of the current cell, add the values of the Col and LeftCol properties.

The current cell may not be displayed on the grid at all, since the grid may have been scrolled up, down, left or right. To see if the current cell is visible on the screen, examine the CurrentCellVisible property. A value of True indicates that the current cell is visible on the screen.

You can also determine if the current cell is being edited by the user by checking the value of the EditActive property at runtime. A value of True indicates that the cell is being edited.

DataGrid Methods

The DataGrid control's interface includes several methods that can be invoked to perform some kind of operation on the control. The unique methods of the DataGrid control (that is, those that are not common to other controls as well) are listed in Table 17.4.

TABLE 17.4. THE UNIQUE METHODS OF THE DataGrid CONTROL

Method	Description
CaptureImage	Returns a snapshot image of the grid
ClearFields	Restores the default grid layout, with two blank columns
ClearSelCols	Deselects all columns in a split
ColContaining	Returns the index of a column that is located at a specified horizontal (x) coordinate
GetBookmark	Returns a bookmark for a row relative to the current row
HoldFields	Sets the grid's current column and field layout so ReBind operations will use the current layout
ReBind	Re-binds the fields in the grid to the data source and repaints the grid
RowBookmark	Returns a bookmark for a visible row in the grid
RowContaining	Returns the index of a row that is located at a specified vertical (y) coordinate
RowTop	Returns the vertical (y) coordinate of a specified row in the grid.
Scroll	Scrolls the grid horizontally and/or vertically.
SplitContaining	Returns the index of a split at the given horizontal and vertical (x, y) coordinate.

The ColContaining, RowContaining, RowTop, and SplitContaining methods are used for relating x and y coordinates to the various components of the grid. For example, the ColContaining method returns the index number of the column that is located at a given horizontal (x) coordinate within the grid. The coordinate returned by or passed to these methods is always inclusive of the grid itself and not its container; that is, the coordinate 0, 0 would indicate the upper-left corner of the grid and not the upper-left corner of the form.

The ReBind method binds all of the DataGrid's columns to the appropriate database fields and repaints the control. Whenever changes are made to the grid's layout, the ReBind method must be called.

By default, a DataGrid control conforms to its data source. For example, the columns of the grid will be set up to accommodate the fields in the data source's Recordset. However, you can manipulate the DataGrid control's columns however you like, as you'll see later. After a grid's columns have been set up, the HoldFields method can be called to set the current layout as the default for the grid. The ClearFields method restores the grid's default layout (two blank columns) and enables the grid to be automatically recreated when the ReBind method is called.

DataGrid Events

The DataGrid control's interface also includes several events. For many user actions, there are events that are fired before the action is to be performed and after the action has been performed. For example, when the user attempts to delete a row from the grid, the BeforeDelete event is fired. After the row has been deleted, the AfterDelete event is fired. Table 17.5 lists the unique events of the DataGrid control.

TABLE 17.5. THE UNIQUE EVENTS OF THE DataGrid CONTROL

Event	Fired When?
AfterColEdit	After column data has been edited.
AfterColUpdate	After data moves from a cell to the grid buffer.
AfterDelete	After a record (row) has been deleted from the grid.
AfterInsert	After a record (row) has been inserted in the grid.
AfterUpdate	After record changes have been written to the database.
BeforeColEdit	An attempt is made to edit data in a column.
BeforeColUpdate	Before data is moved from a cell to the grid buffer.
BeforeDelete	Before a record (row) is going to be deleted from the grid.
BeforeInsert	Before a record (row) is going to be inserted in the grid.
BeforeUpdate	Before record changes are written to the database.
ButtonClick	The current cell's built-in button is clicked.
ColEdit	Data in a column is edited.
ColResize	A column is resized. Note: This event is fired before the grid is repainted.
Error	An operation or action fails.
HeadClick	The user clicks on the heading for a column.
OnAddNew	An action by the user has invoked an AddNew operation.
RowResize	Rows are resized. Note: This event is fired before the grid is repainted.
Scroll	The user scrolls the grid with the scrollbars.
SelChange	The current selection changes to a different range of cells.
SplitChange	A different split becomes current.

Using the DataGrid Control

Unlike the DataList and DataCombo controls, the DataGrid control typically displays more than one database field. By default, the columns of the DataGrid conform to the columns of its data source. To see a quick example of how the DataGrid works, add an ADO Data control to a form and call it adoBiblio. Set up the ConnectionString property as discussed earlier in this chapter. For the RecordSource, choose the database's Publishers table.

Next, add a DataGrid control to the form and call it dtlPublishers. Resize the control so it is as big as possible. The only property that needs to be set for this control is its DataSource property, which should indicate the adoBiblio control as the data source. If you were using a Data Environment with the DataGrid control, you would need to set the DataMember property to specify which data member to use from the data source.

Go ahead and run the program and you should see a grid that looks something like the one shown in Figure 17.2. Even though you didn't specify any information about which fields to show in the grid's columns, the DataGrid control automatically sets up the columns for you based on the fields in the database's Publishers table.

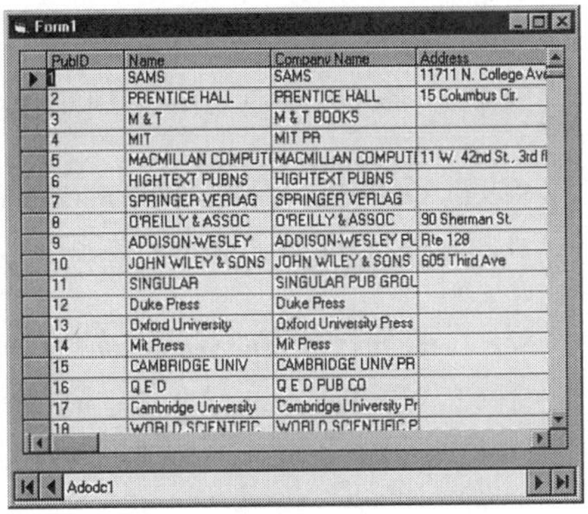

FIGURE 17.2.

The DataGrid control automatically sets up its columns to conform to the fields in the database table.

Of course, there may be times when you don't want the DataGrid control's columns to be automatically set up for you. You might want to show only certain fields from the Recordset, or you might want a column to be of a certain size. Fortunately, the DataGrid control gives you the ability to work with individual columns in the grid via a collection of objects called, appropriately enough, Columns.

Column Objects

Each grid column is actually a separate Column object, which are stored in the zero-based Columns collection. The Column objects have a number of properties (listed in Table 17.6) that can be set to specify how a column looks and what information is displayed in it.

TABLE 17.6. THE PROPERTIES OF THE COLUMN OBJECTS, WHICH CAN BE USED TO SPECIFY HOW A GRID'S COLUMNS ARE DISPLAYED

Property	Data Type	Description
Alignment	Enum	Specifies the alignment (left, right, center, or general) of the data displayed in the column
AllowSizing	Boolean	Specifies whether or not the user can resize the column
Button	Boolean	Specifies whether or not a button is displayed in the column
Caption	String	The text displayed in the column's heading area
ColIndex	Integer	A read-only value that indicates the column's position in the Columns collection and its visible position within the DataGrid control (runtime only)
DataChanged	Boolean	Specifies whether or not the column has been changed by the user (runtime only)
DataField	String	The database field to which the column is bound
DataFormat	Object	The formatting object used for the values in the column
DividerStyle	Enum	Specifies the border style drawn on the right edge of the column
Locked	Boolean	Specifies whether or not the column's data can be edited
NumberFormat	String	The string used for formatting the data displayed in the column
Text	String	Sets or returns the displayed column text for the current row
Visible	Boolean	Specifies whether or not the column is visible
WrapText	Boolean	Specifies whether or not the data in the column's cells will wrap when it hits a cell boundary

You can set most of the Column objects' properties through the DataGrid control's custom properties page. However, you will probably want to set them through code because that makes it easier to see the values that are assigned.

Try modifying the DataGrid control you added to the form earlier by inserting the following code into the Form_Load event:

```
' Remove the last 8 columns in the grid.
While (dtgPublishers.Columns.Count > 2)
    dtgPublishers.Columns.Remove _
      (dtgPublishers.Columns.Count - 1)
Wend

' Set the properties for the first column.
With dtgPublishers.Columns(0)
```

```
        .Caption = "Publisher Name"
        .DataField = "Name"
        .Width = 5000
End With

' Set the properties for the second column.
With dtgPublishers.Columns(1)
        .Caption = "State"
        .DataField = "State"
        .Width = 500
End With

dtgPublishers.HoldFields
dtgPublishers.ReBind
```

Because the Publishers table contains ten fields and the DataGrid is automatically set up to add columns for those fields, the first section of the above code removes all but the first two columns. Then it sets some of the properties for the two Column objects in the Columns collection, holding the current grid layout as the default with the HoldFields method. Finally, it calls the DataGrid control's ReBind method to re-bind the columns to the new data fields and repaint the control. The result is shown in Figure 17.3 below.

FIGURE 17.3.

The DataGrid's columns have been modified using code to show just the Publisher Name *and* State *fields.*

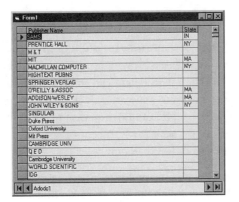

Although Figure 17.3 is a simple example, it shows you how you can modify a grid's columns to appear exactly how you want them. Just remember to call the ReBind method after you've made any changes to the grid's columns.

Split Objects

Another object type that is used with the DataGrid control is the Split object. Splits divide the grid into vertical panes so different views of the database can be provided. Each pane is a separate Split object, and all of the Split objects for a grid are contained in the Splits collection. By default, the DataGrid control uses a single Split, which is the entirety of the grid itself. This `Split` has an index of 1 because the `Splits` collection is one-based.

In many ways, `Split` objects are just smaller versions of the `DataGrid` control. The `Split` objects and the `DataGrid` control have many of the same properties, events, and methods; and they are used the same way. They even have their own `Columns` collection, and you can set up a `Split`'s columns the same way you would with the `DataGrid` control's `Column` objects.

You add a new `Split` object to a `DataGrid` just like you would add any other object to a collection, with the collection's `Add` method. Of course, you can remove a `Split` from the collection with the `Remove` method.

`Splits` can be used to keep one or more of the grid's columns from scrolling. Simply add a new `Split` to the `DataGrid` control and set it up so it contains only the columns you want to see fixed. The grid's original `Split` (index 1) can then be scrolled by the user while the second `Split` remains fixed in place.

The Hierarchical `FlexGrid` Control (`MSHFlexGrid`)

The Hierarchical `FlexGrid` Control, or `MSHFlexGrid`, is designed primarily to display data from hierarchical recordsets. The easiest way to create such recordsets is with the Data Environment designer. The Data Environment can contain database tables and procedures (called Commands) organized into a hierarchy, with parent Commands and child Commands. By assigning the name of the Data Environment to the `MSHFlexGrid`'s `DataSource` property, the format of the `MSHFlexGrid` control will automatically conform to that of the Data Environment's recordset hierarchy.

Although using the Data Environment is the preferred data source for the `MSHFlexGrid` control, you can also use `MSHFlexGrid` with the `ADO Data` control. This requires use of the `SHAPE` command in the `ADO Data` control's `RecordSource` property.

The `MSHFlexGrid` control displays data in a grid-like format. Individual cells or ranges of cells can be selected and their values determined, but the user cannot change data in the cells when the `MSHFlexGrid` is bound to a data source.

An `MSHFlexGrid` control's grid is composed of *rows*, *columns*, and *bands*. Each row represents a separate record. The columns represent fields within a record. The bands group together the fields from different recordsets. Take, for example, the grid shown in Figure 17.4. It shows an `MSHFlexGrid` control that utilizes two tables in the `BIBLIO.MDB` database, the Publishers table and the Titles table. The Titles table is set up as a child of the Publishers table. This relationship is defined in the project's Data Environment.

FIGURE 17.4.

An example of the MSHFlexGrid *control being used.*

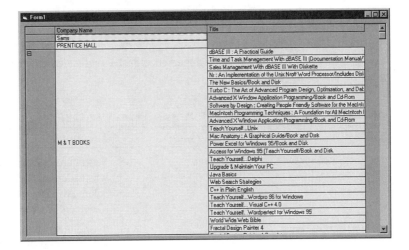

In this example, only one column exists for each band. The first band represents the Publishers table and consists of the Company Name field, which is a column in the grid. The second band represents the Titles table and consists of the Title field (column). Each row represents a different record.

Note that there is a gray area in the Title column for the publishers Sams and Prentice Hall. This is because there are no Titles records associated with these publishers. The gray area is referred to as *unpopulated space* in the parlance of the MSHFlexGrid control.

The publisher M & T Books, on the other hand, has several titles associated with it. The large area with the publisher's name is indicative that it is one record (which, you might recall, comes from the Publishers database table). Associated with this record are many different Titles records, which are displayed in the second band.

As you can see, the data in the MSHFlexGrid is displayed in a hierarchy format. You can include as many bands and levels in the hierarchy as you see fit. You can also choose which fields from each recordset will be displayed in the grid's columns.

Note the "collapse/expand" button in the gray area to the left of the first band. This button causes the levels of the hierarchy to collapse and expand, just as the levels in a TreeView control can be collapsed or expanded. When a band is collapsed, it shows up as a single row and none of the fields in its child bands are displayed.

The MSHFlexGrid control is very flexible, and you can alter just about every facet of how it displays data. To get a better feel for what you can do with the MSHFlexGrid control, first look at the properties, events, and methods that are included in its interface. Later, you'll see an example of how to use the MSHFlexGrid with the Data Environment.

MSHFlexGrid Properties

The MSHFlexGrid control has a huge list of properties, as shown in Table 17.7. Most of these properties have to do with the appearance of the grid's elements, such as the color of its headers or the font of its cells.

TABLE 17.7. THE UNIQUE PROPERTIES OF THE MSHFlexGrid CONTROL

Property	Data Type	Description
AllowBigSelection	Boolean	Sets/returns a value that specifies whether or not clicking on a row or column heading will cause the entire row or column to be selected
AllowUserResizing	Enum	Sets/returns a value that specifies whether or not the user is allowed to resize the grid's rows and columns
BackColor	OLE_COLOR	Sets/returns the background color of all non-fixed cells in the grid
BackColorBand	Array/OLE_COLOR	Sets/returns the background colors of individual bands in the grid
BackColorBkg	OLE_COLOR	Sets/returns the background color of the grid's background (except where there is a cell or a heading)
BackColorFixed	OLE_COLOR	Sets/returns the background color of all fixed cells in the grid
BackColorHeader	Array/OLE_COLOR	Sets/returns the background colors of individual headers
BackColorIndent	Array/OLE_COLOR	Sets/returns the background color of the grid's individual indented areas
BackColorSel	OLE_COLOR	Sets/returns the background color for selected cells
BackColorUnpopulated	OLE_COLOR	Sets/returns the background color of the grid's unpopulated areas
BandData	Array/Long	Sets/returns arbitrary number values to individual bands so they can be identified by those numbers in program code
BandDisplay	Enum	Specifies whether bands display horizontally or vertically in the grid

Property	Data Type	Description
BandExpandable	Array/Boolean	Sets/returns values indicating whether individual bands can be expanded and collapsed
BandIndent	Array/Long	Specifies the number of columns to indent an individual band
BandLevel	Long	Returns the band number that contains the current cell
Bands	Long	Returns the total number of bands in the grid
CellAlignment	Integer	Sets/returns a value that specifies the horizontal and vertical alignment of data in the current cell
CellBackColor	OLE_COLOR	Sets/returns the background color of individual cells or cell ranges
CellFontBold	Boolean	Specifies whether or not the current cell's text font is bolded
CellFontItalic	Boolean	Specifies whether or not the current cell's text font is italicized
CellFontName	String	Specifies the current cell's font name
CellFontSize	Single	Specifies the current cell's font size
CellFontStrikeThrough	Boolean	Specifies whether or not the current cell's text font is striked out
CellFontUnderline	Boolean	Specifies whether or not the current cell's text font is underlined
CellFontWidth	Single	Specifies the current cell's font width (in points)
CellForeColor	OLE_COLOR	Sets/returns the foreground color of individual cells or cell ranges
CellHeight	Long	Returns the height of the current cell (in twips)
CellLeft	Long	Returns the horizontal position of the current cell (in twips)
CellPicture	StdPicture	Sets/returns an image to be displayed within the current cell
CellPictureAlignment	Integer	Sets/returns the alignment of a picture displayed in the current cell or in a selected range of cells

continues

TABLE 17.7. CONTINUED

Property	Data Type	Description
CellTextStyle	Enum	Sets/returns the 3-D style of text for the current cell or in a selected range of cells
CellTop	Long	Returns the vertical position of the current cell (in twips)
CellType	Enum	Returns the type (standard, fixed, and so forth) of the current cell
CellWidth	Long	Returns the width of the current cell (in twips)
Clip	String	Sets/returns the contents of the cells in the grid's selected range
Col	Long	Sets/returns the horizontal coordinates of the active cell
ColAlignment	Array/Integer	Sets/returns the alignment of data in a column
ColAlignmentBand	Array/Integer	Sets/returns the alignment of data in a band within a column
ColAlignmentFixed	Array/Integer	Sets/returns the alignment of data in the fixed cells in a column
ColAlignmentHeader	Array/Integer	Sets/returns the alignment of data in a header within a column
ColData	Array/Long	Sets/returns arbitrary number values to individual columns so they can be identified by those numbers in program code
ColHeader	Array/Enum	Specifies whether or not headers should be displayed for individual bands
ColHeaderCaption	Array/Single	Specifies the text to display in the header for individual column bands
ColIsVisible	Array/Boolean	Sets/returns a value indicating whether or not a specific column is visible
ColPos	Array/Long	Returns the distance (in twips) between the upper-left corner of a given column and the upper-left corner of the MSHFlexGrid control

Property	Data Type	Description
ColPosition	Array/Long	Sets the position (index number) of a grid column
Cols	Array/Long	Returns the total number of columns in the grid
ColSel	Long	Sets/returns the start or end column for a range of cells
ColWidth	Array/Long	Sets/returns the width of a specific column (in twips)
ColWordWrapOption	Array/Long	Specifies whether or not word wrap is enabled for non-fixed cells in the grid
ColWordWrapOptionBand	Array/Integer	Specifies whether or not word wrap is enabled for individual bands in the grid
ColWordWrapOptionFixed	Array/Integer	Specifies whether or not word wrap is enabled for the fixed cells in a column
ColWordWrapOptionHeader	Array/Integer	Specifies whether or not word wrap is enabled for individual headers
DataField	Array/String	The database field to which an individual column is bound
FillStyle	Enum	Specifies whether changing the Text property or any other cell properties affects all selected cells or just the active cell
FixedCols	Long	Sets/returns the total number of fixed columns in a grid
FixedRows	Long	Sets/returns the total number of fixed rows in a grid
FocusRect	Enum	Specifies the kind of focus rectangle (if any) that the MSHFlexGrid control should draw around the current cell
Font	StdFont	Sets/returns the default text font or the font used in individual cells
FontBand	Array/StdFont	Sets/returns the text font used in individual bands
FontFixed	StdFont	Sets/returns the text font used in fixed cells

continues

TABLE 17.7. CONTINUED

Property	Data Type	Description
FontHeader	Array/StdFont	Sets/returns the text font used in individual headers
FontWidth	Single	Sets/returns the default font width
FontWidthBand	Array/Single	Sets/returns the font width used in individual bands
FontWidthFixed	Single	Sets/returns the font width used in fixed cells
FontWidthHeader	Array/Single	Sets/returns the font width used in individual headers
ForeColor	OLE_COLOR	Sets/returns the foreground color of all non-fixed cells in the grid
ForeColorBand	Array/OLE_COLOR	Sets/returns the foreground colors of individual bands in the grid
ForeColorFixed	OLE_COLOR	Sets/returns the foreground color of all fixed cells in the grid
ForeColorHeader	Array/OLE_COLOR	Sets/returns the foreground colors of individual headers
ForeColorSel	OLE_COLOR	Sets/returns the foreground color for selected cells
FormatString	String	Specifies a formatting string used to set the grid's column widths, alignments, fixed row text, and fixed column text
GridColor	OLE_COLOR	Sets/returns the color of the lines drawn between cells in the grid
GridColorBand	Array/OLE_COLOR	Sets/returns the color of the lines drawn between individual bands in the grid
GridColorFixed	OLE_COLOR	Sets/returns the color of the lines drawn between fixed cells in the grid
GridColorHeader	Array/OLE_COLOR	Sets/returns the color of the lines drawn between individual headers in the grid
GridColorIndent	Array/OLE_COLOR	Sets/returns the color of the lines drawn between indented cells in the grid

Property	Data Type	Description
GridColorUnpopulated	OLE_COLOR	Sets/returns the color of the lines drawn between unpopulated areas of the grid
GridLines	Enum	Specifies the type of lines (if any) drawn between cells in the grid
GridLinesBand	Array/Enum	Specifies the types of lines (if any) drawn between individual bands in the grid
GridLinesFixed	Enum	Specifies the types of lines (if any) drawn between fixed cells in the grid
GridLinesHeader	Array/Enum	Specifies the types of lines (if any) drawn between individual headers in the grid
GridLinesIndent	Array/Enum	Specifies the types of lines (if any) drawn between indented cells in the grid
GridLinesUnpopulated	Enum	Specifies the types of lines (if any) drawn between unpopulated areas of the grid
GridLineWidth	Integer	Sets/returns the width (in pixels) of lines drawn between cells in the grid
GridLineWidthBand	Array/Integer	Sets/returns the width (in pixels) of lines drawn between individual bands in the grid
GridLineWidthFixed	Integer	Sets/returns the width (in pixels) of lines drawn between fixed cells in the grid
GridLineWidthHeader	Array/Integer	Sets/returns the width (in pixels) of lines drawn between individual headers in the grid
GridLineWidthIndent	Array/Integer	Sets/returns the width (in pixels) of lines drawn between indented cells in the grid
GridLineWidthUnpopulated	Integer	Sets/returns the width (in pixels) of lines drawn between unpopulated areas of the grid

continues

17

ADVANCED DATA CONTROLS

TABLE 17.7. CONTINUED

Property	Data Type	Description
HighLight	Enum	Specifies how and when selected cells in the grid appear highlighted
LeftCol	Long	The left-most visible column in the grid
MergeCells	Enum	Sets/returns a value that indicates when and how cells with the same contents should be grouped (merged) together
MergeCol	Array/Boolean	Sets/returns a value that indicates which columns can have their contents merged (see the MergeCells property)
MergeRow	Array/Boolean	Sets/returns a value that indicates which rows can have their contents merged (see the MergeCells property)
MouseCol	Long	Returns the column coordinate of the mouse cursor
MouseRow	Long	Returns the row coordinate of the mouse cursor
Picture	StdPicture	Returns a snapshot of the MSHFlexGrid control
PictureType	Enum	Sets/returns the type of picture that will be used with the Picture property
Redraw	Boolean	Sets/returns a value that indicates whether or not the MSHFlexGrid control should be redrawn after every change
Row	Long	Sets/returns the vertical coordinates of the active cell
RowData	Array/Long	Sets/returns arbitrary number values to individual rows so that each can be identified by the numbers in program code
RowExpandable	Boolean	Specifies whether or not the current row can be expanded
RowExpanded	Boolean	Returns a value that indicates whether or not the current row is expanded

Property	Data Type	Description
RowHeight	Array/Long	Sets/returns the height of individual rows (in twips)
RowHeightMin	Long	Sets/returns the minimum height (in twips) for all the rows in the grid
RowIsVisible	Array/Boolean	Sets/returns a value indicating whether or not a specific row is visible
RowPos	Array/Long	Returns the distance (in twips) between the upper-left corner of a given row and the upper-left corner of the MSHFlexGrid control
RowPosition	Array/Long	Sets the position (index number) of a grid row
Rows	Long	Returns the total number of rows in the grid, or the total number of rows in an individual band
RowSel	Long	Sets/returns the start or end row for a range of cells
RowSizingMode	Enum	Sets/returns a value that indicates whether resizing a row affects all rows in the grid or just the row that is being resized
ScrollBars	Enum	Sets/returns a value that indicates the types of scrollbars the MSHFlexGrid control has, if any
ScrollTrack	Boolean	Sets/returns a value that indicates whether the grid should scroll as the user moves the scroll box along the scroll track, or whether the grid position should update only after the scrolling is finished
SelectionMode	Enum	Sets/returns a value that indicates the kind of selection that is allowed in the MSHFlexGrid control, such as selection by row, selection by column, or free cell selection
Sort	Enum	Sets a value for sorting selected rows by some criteria

continues

TABLE 17.7. CONTINUED

Property	Data Type	Description
Text	String	Sets/returns the text content of a cell or a range of cells
TextArray	Array/String	Sets/returns the text contents of an arbitrary cell without changing the Row and Col properties
TextMatrix	Array/String	Sets/returns the text contents of a cell at a specified row and column
TextStyle	Enum	Sets/returns the 3D text style for regular cells in the grid
TextStyleBand	Array/Enum	Sets/returns the 3D text style for individual bands in the grid
TextStyleFixed	Enum	Sets/returns the 3D text style for fixed cells in the grid
TextStyleHeader	Array/Enum	Sets/returns the 3D text style for individual headers in the grid
TopRow	Long	Sets/returns the uppermost visible row in the grid
Version	Integer	Returns the version of the MSHFlexGrid control that is being used
WordWrap	Boolean	Specifies whether or not the contents of the cells in the grid word wrap when the cells' boundaries are reached

MSHFlexGrid Methods

The MSHFlexGrid control only has six unique methods in its interface. They are listed in Table 17.8.

TABLE 17.8. THE UNIQUE METHODS OF THE MSHFlexGrid CONTROL

Method	Description
AddItem	Adds a new row to the grid
Clear	Clears the contents (including text, pictures, and cell formatting) of the grid. The number of rows and columns in the grid is not affected by this method
ClearStructure	Clears the structure (mapping information) of the grid

Method	Description
CollapseAll	Collapses all rows of a specified band in the grid
ExpandAll	Expands all rows of a specified band in the grid
RemoveItem	Removes a row from the grid

The AddItem and RemoveItem methods can be used to add or remove rows (bands) from the grid. To collapse or expand all of the rows for a specified band in the grid, the CollapseAll and ExpandAll methods can be used.

The Clear method clears the contents of the grid, but leaves the number of rows and columns intact. To clear the structure of the grid, including the order and name of the grid's columns, use the ClearStructure method.

MSHFlexGrid Events

The MSHFlexGrid control is capable of triggering only a few unique events. These events are listed in Table 17.9.

TABLE 17.9. THE UNIQUE EVENTS OF THE MSHFlexGrid CONTROL

Event	Fired When?
Collapse	The user collapses a row in the grid
Compare	The Sort property is set to CustomSort, enabling the user to customize the sort process
EnterCell	A new cell becomes the currently active cell
Expand	The user expands a row in the grid
LeaveCell	Before a new cell becomes the currently active cell
RowColChange	A new cell becomes the currently active cell
Scroll	The contents of the grid are scrolled using the keyboard, scroll bars, or when the contents are scrolled programmatically
SelChangeEvent	A new range of cells is selected

The EnterCell, LeaveCell, and RowColChange events are all related because they are all fired whenever a new cell becomes the currently active cell. The actual order of events is: LeaveCell, EnterCell, and then RowColChange.

The Collapse and Expand events are triggered when a row (band) is collapsed or expanded by the user. The Col and Row properties can be used to determine the cell used to collapse or expand the band.

17

ADVANCED DATA
CONTROLS

The `Compare` event occurs once for each pair of rows in the grid when the `Sort` property is set to 9 (Custom Sort). The custom sort enables you to sort a row by any column or cell property you choose. Note that doing a sort this way can be significantly slower than using a built-in sort.

The `Scroll` event is triggered when the grid is scrolled, no matter how the scroll is accomplished (by keyboard, by the scroll bars, or by program code). This event is also fired while the user drags or scrolls with the mouse, but only if the `ScrollTrack` property is set to `True`. If `ScrollTrack` is set to `False`, the `Scroll` event is only triggered once after the drag action is complete.

The `SelChange` event fires when the selected range of cells changes. The selected range can be changed by the user (by pressing and holding the Shift key while using the arrow keys) or by program code (using the `Row`, `Col`, `RowSel`, and `ColSel` properties).

Using the `MSHFlexGrid` Control

The `MSHFlexGrid` control is typically used with the Data Environment because it conforms nicely to the Environment's hierarchical structure. In fact, after you set up the Data Environment, you can just assign its name to the `MSHFlexGrid` control's `DataSource` property and you're ready to go—the `MSHFlexGrid`'s structure will be created to match that of the Data Environment.

To see how this works, create a new project. Add a Data Environment to the project by selecting the Add Data Environment option from VB's Project menu. Rename the Data Environment to `deBiblio` and the Connection to `conBiblio`.

Next, right-click on `conBiblio` to display its pop-up menu. Choose the Properties option to bring up the Data Link Properties dialog box. Choose Microsoft Jet 3.51 OLE DB Provider as the data provider, then click Next. On the Connection tab, choose the `BIBLIO.MDB` file as the database name. Leave the user information as it is. Press the Test Connection button to ensure that the connection to the database can be made. After you have checked the connection, click on the OK button. You should now be back at the Data Environment window.

Again, right-click on `conBiblio` to display its pop-up menu. This time, choose the Add Command option to add a new Command object to the connection. Right-click on the new Command object (`Command1`) to display its pop-up menu, then select the Properties option. In the properties dialog box that appears, change the Command Name to Publishers and choose Table for the Database Object. For the Object Name, choose Publishers. This will set up the `conBiblio` Command object to access the Publishers table of the Biblio database. Click OK to close the dialog box and return to the Data Environment window.

You should now see the `Publishers` Command nested underneath the `conBiblio` Connection in the Data Environment. Right-click on the `Publishers` Command to display its pop-up menu. Choose the Add Child Command option and you will then see another Command object (`Command1`) nested underneath the `Publishers` Command. The `Command1` object is a *child Command* to the `Publishers` Command, its *parent Command*.

Right-click on the `Command1` Command object and choose Properties from the pop-up menu. Change the Command Name to Titles, the Database Object to Table, and the Object Name to Titles. This will set up the child Command (now called `Titles`) to access the Titles table of the Biblio database.

Because the `Titles` Command is a child of the `Publishers` Command, there has to be some sort of a relationship between them. To establish this relationship, display the Relation tab of the Properties dialog box. The Relate to a Parent Command Object box should be checked, and the Parent Command should already be selected as the `Publishers` Command. To define the relationship between the two Command objects, make sure the PubID field is selected in both the Parent Fields and Child Fields/Parameters list boxes. This is the field that links the two database tables (Publishers and Titles). Click the Add button to add the PubID-to-PubID relationship. Then click OK to close the Properties dialog box.

The Data Environment has now been set up with a `Publishers` Command and the `Titles` Command as a child Command. Your Data Environment window should look like the one shown in Figure 17.5.

FIGURE 17.5.

The Data Environment window should include a Publishers Command with a Titles Command as its child.

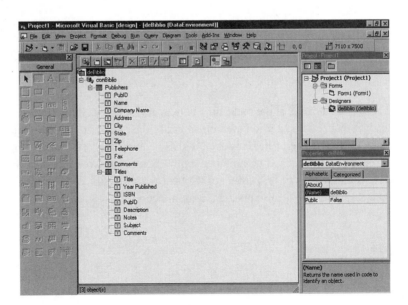

Now that the Data Environment is finished, all that's left to do is add an MSHFlexGrid control to the project's form. Resize the form so it is as wide as possible, but still fits on the screen, then add an MSHFlexGrid control. Resize the control so it uses most of the form's space. Finally, change its DataSource property to deBiblio. Then go ahead and run the program.

You'll see that the MSHFlexGrid control utilizes the Data Environment's hierarchy to display a data grid that shows information from both the Publishers table and the Titles table (see Figure 17.6). The columns for the Publishers table are first, followed by those of the Titles table. If a Publishers record does not have any Titles records associated with it (that is, no records in the Titles table have a PubID field that match the PubID field of the Publishers record), the space for the Titles columns is gray. If a Publishers record has associated Titles records, the Titles columns are filled in.

FIGURE 17.6.

The MSHFlexGrid is being used to display data in the Publishers and Titles table of the Biblio database. Note that the data is organized into a hierarchy.

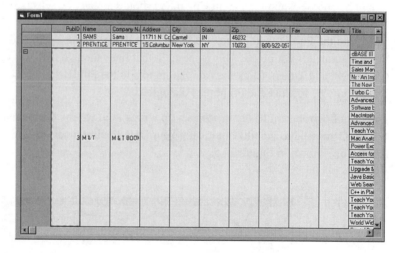

The MSHFlexGrid is at the same time both a simple and a complex control. It's simple in the fact that creating a grid based on an established Data Environment hierarchy is easy to do, as you've seen here. However, it's also complex in that there are many different ways in which you can fine-tune it and modify it to suit your particular needs. The dozens and dozens of properties for the MSHFlexGrid enable you to change just about every aspect of the grid's appearance and function.

Summary

With the addition of the Data Environment and the ADO Data control, VB6 also includes several new controls that are designed to work with these data sources. The DataList, DataCombo, DataGrid, and MSHFlexGrid controls have all been optimized for ADO.

Those who are familiar with DBList, DBCombo, and DBGrid will have no trouble adapting to the new controls because they are code-compatible with these previous controls. The MSHFlexGrid is different than the older MSFlexGrid control, however, because it is designed to work with hierarchical data sources such as the Data Environment.

This chapter provided an introduction to these new controls. It should give you enough information so you can start using them right away, even if you're not familiar with the older data-aware controls.

17

ADVANCED DATA
CONTROLS

SQL and the T-SQL Debugger

by Loren Eidahl

IN THIS CHAPTER

- Working with Standard SQL   *392*
- Using the T-SQL Debugger   *412*

This chapter serves two distinct purposes. It begins with an overview of Structured Query Language (SQL), describing what it is and how it works from an ANSI perspective. The first section provides many tables and examples to illustrate the syntax used for communicating with a database engine, as well as a general discussion of the different ways you can handle the data you retrieve. The second half of the chapter deals with Microsoft's T-SQL Debugger (short for "Transact-SQL Debugger"), a tool for debugging stored procedures on an SQL Server. You will walk-through working with the debugger, and examples and options are pointed out to give you a thorough understanding of how it simplifies further communication with the server.

Working with Standard SQL

Structured Query Language (SQL) has quickly become the standard relational database language. SQL gives you a way to impose standards when you use a relational database. Some relational databases still don't support SQL, but the vast majority of them do. Here are some of the relational databases that support SQL:

- SQL Server
- Access
- Sybase
- Oracle
- Informix

> **NOTE**
>
> This chapter covers some of the basics of SQL language—that is, the American National Standards Institute (ANSI 92) SQL. It's not database-specific, which means that certain database engines can have a slightly different syntax. This also means that some of the code presented in this chapter might not work correctly for a given database engine. Consult the documentation for your specific database engine to be sure.

You can use this SQL standard in a client/server environment or in a standalone environment. Either way, SQL is the language used to query the database engine. A *database engine* is the heart of the database; it's the way the database vendor decides how the database operates and functions, how data is stored, how syntax is used, and how processing occurs.

You can actually use SQL to do more than construct queries. Using SQL implies that you're querying the database to get data returned from it. In fact, there's much more to it than this. You use SQL to insert new data, update existing data, and even control the parameters of the database engine.

You can send SQL to a database engine by many means. The database engine comes with some sort of interactive tool for sending SQL statements to get some result. This can be *Interactive Structured Query Language (ISQL)* for MS-SQL or *SQL Datasheet* in Oracle.

This chapter deals with SQL as a whole. SQL can be, and has been, the subject of entire books. This chapter can't cover every aspect of SQL, but it covers the basics. The chapter also doesn't discuss specific database engines. Certain things are common in all SQL databases. These basic commonalties are the subject of the rest of this chapter. However, for the examples, the following sample data is used. The data is broken up into four tables, shown in Tables 18.1 through 18.4.

TABLE 18.1. THE INVENTORY TABLE.

Product ID	Description	Supplier ID	Quantity
MS001	Visual Basic 6	M001	2
MS002	Word for Windows	M001	1
MS003	Excel	M001	1
SO001	Norton Utilities	S002	1

TABLE 18.2. THE SALE STABLE.

Product ID	Staff ID	Date Sold	Quantity Sold
MS001	E1234	7/01/98	5
SO001	E1235	7/01/98	5

TABLE 18.3. THE STAFF TABLE.

Staff ID	Last Name	First Name
E1234	Jefferson	Tom
E1235	Lincoln	Abe
E1236	Newton	Ike

TABLE 18.4. THE SUPPLIER TABLE

Supplier ID	Supplier
B001	Borland
I001	Intuit
M001	Microsoft
S001	Sams Publishing
S002	Symantec

The tables give you an idea of the structure of a database and how the fields relate to each other. Designing databases isn't the topic of this chapter; however, it's important to understand how the data relates so that the examples presented later make sense.

By looking at Tables 18.1 through 18.4, you can see that the INVENTORY table contains a list of all items a company can stock. The table also contains a field for the quantity in stock and the product ID used to identify when a sale is made in the SALES table. Listing the description of the product every time a sale occurs is inefficient. Also, a supplier ID field identifies the company that supplies the product from the SUPPLIER table.

The SALES table relates to the tables discussed in the preceding paragraph, but also has a field for the staff ID (the person selling the item). The name of the person selling the item is looked up in the STAFF table, based on the staff ID.

That's how the four tables relate to each other. Each table contains simple data. However, if the database is designed correctly, it makes no difference how much data is in the tables.

Retrieving Data

By far the most common SQL statement is the SELECT statement. This statement is used to retrieve rows of data from a table as well as for many other purposes (which are presented in the rest of this chapter). To use this statement, you must know the names of the columns in the table you're trying to receive, or you can use an asterisk to specify all columns. The SELECT statement for Microsoft Jet SQL has the following general syntax:

```
SELECT [ALL¦DISTINCT] [TOP xx [PERCENT]] select_list
FROM table_names
[WHERE {search_criteria¦join_criteria}
[{AND¦OR search_criteria}]]
[GROUP BY [ALL]aggregate_free_expression [,aggregate_free_expression...]]
[HAVING search_conditions]
[ORDER BY {field_list} [ASC¦DESC]]
```

in which:

- ALL specifies that every row is returned, including duplicates. (This is the default and doesn't need to be used.)

- DISTINCT specifies that only non-duplicate rows are to be returned.

- TOP specifies that you want only the top *xx* number of records returned. You can also specify the PERCENT keyword after the number *xx* to return only the top *xx* percentage of the total records to be returned. (See the later section "Limiting the Selection" for more information.)

- *select_list* is the list of column names in the tables to return, separated by commas.

- *table_names* is the list of tables that return data.

- *search_criteria* is the list of column names in the tables to return.

- *join_criteria* is the list of column names in one table that joins to other column names in a different table.

- *aggregate_free_expression* is an expression that doesn't include an aggregate. Refer to Table 18.6 later in this chapter for a list of aggregate functions that can't be included in this expression.

- *field_list* is a list of the columns the data is sorted on.

- ASC specifies that the sort order is ascending. (This is the default and doesn't need to be used.)

- DESC specifies that the sort order is descending.

If you're not intimately familiar with SQL, the preceding information can seem pretty confusing. Let me simplify it by providing examples from Tables 18.1 through 18.4.

18

SQL AND THE
T-SQL DEBUGGER

> **NOTE**
>
> The keywords throughout this chapter, such as SELECT, FROM, and so on, aren't case-sensitive. They're listed here in uppercase to set them apart from the regular text, but you can type them in lowercase.

Selecting Records

To use the SELECT statement, you must know what you want to select and from what you want to select it. In other words, you need to know the column names and the table names you're trying to select. If you don't know the column names, you must use an asterisk to select all columns in the tables. For example, if you want to select all values from the Supplier column in the SUPPLIER table, you use this statement:

```
SELECT *
FROM SUPPLIER
```

> **NOTE**
>
> Even though the keywords aren't case sensitive, some databases have case-sensitive column names and table names. For this example, the table names have been designated in uppercase, whereas the column names have been designated in lowercase. Columns are sometimes referred to as *fields* and column names as *field names*. They're synonymous.

> **NOTE**
>
> Even though an SQL statement can consist of many lines of text, it's actually one statement. To help you understand this concept, as a general rule, a statement consists of all lines of SQL text between two SELECT keywords.
>
> Even though these SQL text lines are shown on separate lines, they actually can be put on one line. They're generally constructed on multiple lines because that way they're easier to read. The SQL standard calls for the database engine (whichever one is used) to ignore the carriage return between SQL keywords in the statement.

The preceding SQL statement produces a complete list of the suppliers in the SUPPLIER table, but the order returned is the order in which they're entered into the table. If you want to sort the list alphabetically, you can use this statement:

```
SELECT Supplier
FROM SUPPLIER
ORDER BY Supplier
```

The ORDER BY keyword (sometimes referred to as the ORDER BY *clause*) needs a column name to know on which column to sort. This ensures that the data is ordered by the Supplier column. By default, the data is ordered in ascending order. To sort in descending order, use this statement:

```
SELECT Supplier
FROM SUPPLIER
ORDER BY Supplier DESC
```

If you want to select multiple columns, use the following statement:

```
SELECT Supplier,Supplier_ID
FROM SUPPLIER
ORDER BY Supplier
```

This statement selects the Supplier column first, followed by the Supplier_ID column. All values in the table are returned because you didn't limit the search. Two columns are selected in the preceding statement (which, coincidentally, is the total number of columns in the SUPPLIER table). However, if you have a table with 100 columns and you want to select all the columns, you don't have to type the names of all 100 columns. You can select all columns in a table with a statement like this:

```
SELECT *
FROM SUPPLIER
ORDER BY Supplier
```

The asterisk indicates that all columns are selected from the SUPPLIER table. The table is still sorted by the Supplier column in ascending order. Although this method is quick, it is not generally recommended because the SQL statement has to scan every single record of the table.

Limiting the Selection

You don't have to return all data from a table; you can limit the number of rows returned by using the WHERE keyword. Suppose you want to find out what the supplier ID is for Symantec. You want to limit the number of rows in the SUPPLIER table to all rows where the supplier is equal to "Symantec". You can do this with the following code:

```
SELECT *
FROM SUPPLIER
WHERE Supplier = "Symantec"
ORDER BY Supplier
```

The data returned is only the data that matches the WHERE keyword (also referred to as the WHERE clause). If no supplier is named Symantec, no rows are returned.

18
SQL AND THE
T-SQL DEBUGGER

> **NOTE**
>
> The string literal in the WHERE clause is case sensitive. Therefore, "Symantec" isn't the same as "SYMANTEC".
>
> Also, some implementations of SQL require the use of single quotation marks (apostrophes) rather than double quotation marks.

The ORDER BY clause isn't necessary in the preceding statement, but it doesn't hurt it either. By design, each supplier appears in the SUPPLIER table only once. Because you're looking for only one supplier, the order is irrelevant. However, if you're looking for more than one supplier, it becomes relevant. Suppose that you're looking for "Symantec" or "Microsoft". Use this SQL statement:

```
SELECT *
FROM SUPPLIER
WHERE Supplier = "Symantec" OR Supplier = "Microsoft"
ORDER BY Supplier
```

In this case, two rows are returned: first the "Microsoft" row and then the "Symantec" row, thanks to the ORDER BY clause.

Another way to write the preceding statement is to use the IN keyword, which lets you list a range of values to test for. The values are separated by a comma. The preceding statement is rewritten as the following:

```
SELECT *
FROM SUPPLIER
WHERE Supplier IN ("Symantec","Microsoft")
ORDER BY Supplier
```

Using the IN keyword can generally save a lot of typing because the column name doesn't have to be repeated. Table 18.5 lists additional keywords that you can use in the WHERE clause.

CAUTION

There is a direct correlation between database performance when using the IN clause and the number of records contained therein. To limit performance nightmares, create a temporary database that contains the items of the IN clause and create a join to the table used in the Select statement.

TABLE 18.5. KEYWORDS THAT YOU CAN USE IN A WHERE CLAUSE.

Keyword	Purpose
IN	Tests for values in a specified range
NOT IN	Tests for values not in a specified range
LIKE	Tests for values that are like a specified value
NOT LIKE	Tests for values that aren't like a specified value
IS NULL	Tests for null values
IS NOT NULL	Tests for non-null values

Keyword	Purpose
AND	Tests for multiple conditions
OR	Tests for either specified condition
BETWEEN	Tests for values between a set of specified values
NOT BETWEEN	Tests for values not between a set of specified values
EXISTS	Tests for existing values
NOT EXISTS	Tests for non-existing values
ANY	Tests for any values
ALL	Tests for all values

A common necessity is to return values that, for example, start with a certain letter, such as *S*. You can do this by using the LIKE keyword. If you want to return all rows from the SUPPLIER table for a supplier starting with an *S*, use this statement:

```
SELECT *
FROM SUPPLIER
WHERE Supplier LIKE "S%"
ORDER BY Supplier
```

This statement returns rows containing the suppliers "SAMS Publishing" and "Symantec". The following is the syntax for using the LIKE keyword, where you might have a percent sign before the *constant*, after the *constant*, or both:

```
LIKE "[%]constant[%]"
```

The *constant* is the value for which you're testing. The percent signs are wildcard symbols, just like asterisks in DOS. If you're looking for any supplier with an *S* in its name, use this statement:

```
SELECT *
FROM SUPPLIER
WHERE Supplier LIKE "%S%"
ORDER BY Supplier
```

NOTE

Microsoft Access uses an asterisk (*) wildcard symbol in place of the percent sign (%) when accessed through DAO. The percent sign applies to SQL Server and other client/server databases, as well as Access via ODBC. The rest of the syntax is the same. Also, the expression placed between wildcard symbols is case sensitive.

18

SQL AND THE
T-SQL DEBUGGER

> **NOTE**
>
> You must use at least one percent sign in a LIKE clause. If you don't, no rows are returned.

Because the SELECT keyword is used to return values, you can even go so far as to return a value that's not part of the database. This is referred to as a *calculated column*. For example, you can return a percentage of the quantity in the INVENTORY table. Instead of the following SQL statement, which returns the quantity that's actually in the database,

```
SELECT Quantity
FROM INVENTORY
```

you can use this SQL statement to return 10 percent of the quantities:

```
SELECT Quantity * .10
FROM INVENTORY
```

This works only for a numeric data type. You certainly can't do this if Quantity is a string.

Another way to limit the number of records returned is to use the TOP keyword. Suppose that you want to test a SQL statement to determine whether you've used the correct syntax. However, you don't want to return potentially millions of rows of data for a test. You can use the optional TOP keyword to limit the number of rows.

The TOP keyword without a following PERCENT keyword returns only the first *xx* number of records of the total recordset. For example, the following will return only the first 10 records from the SUPPLIER table:

```
SELECT TOP 10 *
FROM SUPPLIER
ORDER BY Supplier
```

If 250 records were in the table, only the first 10 would be returned. Likewise, this example will return the first 10 percent of the total records from the SUPPLIER table:

```
SELECT TOP 10 PERCENT *
FROM SUPPLIER
ORDER BY Supplier
```

Again, if 250 records were in the table, only the first 25 would be returned.

Setting Up Joins

A *join* is a way to return data from two tables. The key to doing this is that you must join or link the columns of data between the two tables so that the database engine knows how to look up the join. You create the join in the WHERE clause. If you want to select all items in the INVENTORY table but also with the company that supplied the item, you have to do a join between the INVENTORY and SUPPLIER tables. This is because a column (Supplier_ID) is common to both tables, and this column is what the join is based on. This is also called a *common key*, which is a "key" field used as a join. For the SUPPLIER table, it's the primary key, which means that this column is used to access a row in the table. It's not the primary key in the INVENTORY table because it isn't used to access a row in this table; the Product_ID column is the primary key in that table. How to determine primary keys and database design isn't the purpose of this chapter.

To perform the join mentioned here, use this code:

```
SELECT Supplier, Description, Quantity
FROM SUPPLIER s, INVENTORY i
WHERE i.Supplier_ID = s.Supplier_ID
ORDER BY Supplier
```

This statement selects the Supplier, Description, and Quantity columns from the SUPPLIER and INVENTORY tables. For every occurrence of a supplier ID in the INVENTORY table, the supplier is looked up by using the same Supplier_ID column, and the values are assigned to be equal.

The individual letters s and i that you see in the preceding code are *aliases*. You use these to identify a column in a table that has the same name in another table you're trying to access. If you don't specify this alias, you receive an error telling you that the column name is ambiguous. This alias gives the database engine a way to decipher to which column you're referring. The alias name goes after the table names in the FROM clause. The name can be any unique value (treated as a string without quotes) as long as it isn't the name of a table you're trying to access.

After the alias is established in the FROM clause, you can reference it by using this format, where *alias* is the name of the alias defined and *column* is the name of the column in the aliased table:

```
alias.column
```

For example, consider the WHERE clause in the previous statement:

```
WHERE i.Supplier_ID = s.Supplier_ID
```

It follows the syntax of `alias.column` on each side of the = sign. After the alias is established, you can use it in any of the SQL clauses that are part of that same statement.

If you're trying to select (return) columns in different tables, you must also reference the alias to avoid any ambiguity. Even if you aren't selecting columns with the same name, you might still use the alias. For example, the following isn't incorrect:

```
SELECT s.Supplier, i.Description, i.Quantity
FROM SUPPLIER s, INVENTORY i
WHERE i.Supplier_ID = s.Supplier_ID
ORDER BY s.Supplier
```

It performs the same function. However, it does introduce a possible element of error. At least one field in the ORDER BY clause needs to be in the SELECT clause. If you change the last line to the following, you receive an error because the Supplier column doesn't exist in the INVENTORY table:

```
ORDER BY i.Supplier
```

You can create even more complex joins. Suppose that you want to select the supplier, product description, and quantity, but return only the rows in the INVENTORY table where the supplier is "Microsoft". You have to do a join again to the SUPPLIER table because the only reference to SUPPLIER in the INVENTORY table is an ID, Supplier_ID, which is used as a lookup key in the SUPPLIER table. You can do the join with this statement:

```
SELECT s.Supplier, i.Description, i.Quantity
FROM SUPPLIER s, INVENTORY i
WHERE i.Supplier_ID = s.Supplier_ID
AND s.Supplier = "Microsoft"
ORDER BY s.Supplier
```

Again, the ORDER BY clause isn't absolutely necessary because only one row can be in the SUPPLIER table with the name "Microsoft".

You can use the techniques and topics discussed here to join multiple tables in your application. However, remember that the more joins you do, the longer it takes the database engine to come back with the results.

Working with Aggregates

An *aggregate* is a mathematical SQL function. Table 18.6 lists the types of SQL aggregates available.

TABLE 18.6. SQL AGGREGATES.

Aggregate	Purpose
COUNT()	Counts the number of rows returned
SUM()	Sums the number of rows returned
AVG()	Averages the number of rows returned
MAX()	Finds the maximum value in the rows returned
MIN()	Finds the minimum value in the rows returned

In each aggregate listed in Table 18.6, an expression (typically a column name) is expected in the parentheses. However, the expression can be any valid SQL expression.

If you want to find out how many rows are returned from this statement,

```
SELECT s.Supplier, i.Description, i.Quantity
FROM SUPPLIER s, INVENTORY i
WHERE i.Supplier_ID = s.Supplier_ID
ORDER BY s.Supplier
```

you can use this statement instead:

```
SELECT COUNT(*), s.Supplier, i.Description, i.Quantity
FROM SUPPLIER s, INVENTORY i
WHERE i.Supplier_ID = s.Supplier_ID
ORDER BY s.Supplier
```

This statement returns four columns: the count of the number of rows returned, the supplier, the description, and the quantity. The joins in the statement were discussed earlier in the "Setting Up Joins" section.

When using an aggregate function, you can use a GROUP BY clause to tell the database engine how to do the calculation. For example, if you want to sum the number of items stocked for each supplier, you must use a GROUP BY clause. If you don't, how would the database engine know how to return the sum? Refer to Table 18.1 to follow this example. Would the database engine sum the quantities for each Product_ID, Description, Supplier_ID, or a combination of the three? That's where the GROUP BY clause comes in. In this scenario, you can perform the necessary function by using this statement:

```
SELECT SUM(Quantity)
FROM SUPPLIER s, INVENTORY i
WHERE i.Supplier_ID = s.Supplier_ID
GROUP BY s.Supplier
ORDER BY s.Supplier
```

This means that for every new supplier, the Quantity is summed. If the GROUP BY clause is omitted, only one row is returned, and it's the sum of all quantities.

Inserting Data

Without inserting data, there would never be the need to perform any UPDATE, DELETE, or SELECT statements. Inserting rows (or records) into a table requires an INSERT statement. The syntax of the INSERT statement is

```
INSERT INTO table[(column_list)]
VALUES{(insert_values)}|sql_select_statement
```

where

- *table* is the name of the table to insert into.
- *column_list* is a listing of columns that have data inserted, separated by commas.
- *insert_values* is the list of values to be inserted into the columns in *column_list*. The same number of values must be in the *insert_values* list as is in the *column_list* list.
- *sql_select_statement* is an alternative way to insert values into a table. You can select values of another table to be inserted. In this case, you don't use the VALUES keyword. You must make sure that the number of columns you're returning in your SQL statement is the same number as in the *column_list* list.

NOTE

Microsoft Access requires the INTO keyword; SQL Server doesn't.

To use the INSERT statement to insert a new supplier into the SUPPLIER table, you can use this statement:

```
INSERT SUPPLIER(Supplier_ID,Supplier)
VALUES ("C001","Crystal Services")
```

The row is simply inserted into the table. Here are some considerations, however:

- Does the primary key field already exist?
- Are you concerned about case sensitivity?
- Are you inserting values with the correct data type?

These questions are important. Except for the case sensitivity question, the questions presented here can result in errors if they aren't addressed properly. For example, the following will result in error:

```
INSERT INTO SUPPLIER(Supplier_ID,Supplier)
VALUES (1,"Crystal Services")
```

The Supplier_ID column doesn't expect a numeric data type; it expects a string data type. If you aren't going to include any characters, you must construct the SQL statement this way:

```
INSERT SUPPLIER(Supplier_ID,Supplier)
VALUES ("1","Crystal Services")
```

Rather than insert into a table by hard-coding the values, you can insert by selecting the values from another table. Suppose that you have a table, MASTER, which also has

Supplier_ID and Supplier columns from which you'll select values. You can insert all items from the MASTER table like this:

```
INSERT SUPPLIER(Supplier_ID,Supplier)
SELECT Supplier_ID,Supplier
FROM MASTER
```

On the other hand, if you wanted to insert based only on a certain value from the MASTER table, you could construct your SQL SELECT statement based on any valid SQL rule. You could do this:

```
INSERT SUPPLIER(Supplier_ID,Supplier)
SELECT Supplier_ID,Supplier
FROM MASTER
WHERE Supplier="Crystal Services"
```

As presented in the "Retrieving Data" section earlier in the chapter, the WHERE clause limits the number of rows returned.

Deleting Data

Deleting rows (or records) from a table requires a DELETE statement. The syntax of the DELETE statement is

```
DELETE FROM table
[WHERE search_conditions]
```

in which *table* is the name of the table to delete from, and *search_conditions* are any valid SQL expressions to limit the number of rows deleted.

The DELETE statement deletes an entire row or rows in the database. You can't delete only one column.

You can use the DELETE statement to delete all rows in the SUPPLIER table by using this statement:

```
DELETE FROM SUPPLIER
```

> **CAUTION**
>
> You don't receive a confirmation when you use the DELETE statement. If the statement is executed, the rows are deleted. It's that simple. Be very careful when you use the DELETE statement.

18

**SQL AND THE
T-SQL DEBUGGER**

If you want to delete the rows only where the supplier is a certain value, you do it like this:

```
DELETE FROM SUPPLIER
WHERE Supplier = "Borland"
```

This statement deletes all values in the SUPPLIER table where the Supplier is "Borland".

> **NOTE**
>
> Be careful when you delete (or update) a row in a table in case a value relates to a value in a different table. If it does, you might possibly orphan a row of data in the other table. Creating an *orphan* means that the value related to data in the table from which you deleted now has no way of being referenced and that the row in the second table is just taking up space.
>
> There are ways around this that aren't within the scope of this chapter, as stated earlier. When you design the database, you can place a trigger on the column so that orphaning doesn't happen inadvertently.

Updating Data

Updating rows (or records) in a table requires an UPDATE statement. The syntax of the UPDATE statement is

```
UPDATE table
SET assignment_list
[WHERE search_conditions]
```

in which:

- *table* is the name of the table to insert into.

- *assignment_list* is a listing of all updates that will take place.

- *search_conditions* are any valid SQL expressions to limit the number of rows updated.

If you want to update the Supplier_ID column of the SUPPLIER table, you can use the UPDATE statement:

```
UPDATE SUPPLIER
SET Supplier_ID="XXX"
```

All rows in the Supplier_ID column are updated to "XXX". To prevent the rows from being updated, you need to limit the search by using a WHERE clause with any valid SQL expression. You can limit the updating, as described earlier, to only where the Supplier is equal to "Borland". You do this as follows:

```
UPDATE SUPPLIER
SET Supplier_ID="XXX"
WHERE Supplier = "Borland"
```

> **CAUTION**
>
> You don't receive a confirmation when you use the UPDATE statement. If the statement is executed, the rows are updated. It's that simple. Be very careful when you use the UPDATE statement.

On the other hand, if you want to update based only on a certain value from another table, you can use any valid SQL SELECT statement in place of *assignment_list* in the syntax presented earlier. Suppose that you have a table, MASTER, that also has Supplier_ID and Supplier columns out of which you'll select values. You can insert an item from the MASTER table to update a record in the SUPPLIER table like this:

```
UPDATE SUPPLIER
SET Supplier_ID = (SELECT Supplier_ID
FROM MASTER
WHERE Supplier = "Symantec")
WHERE Supplier = "Symantec"
```

The last two lines of the preceding statement look as though they're repeated, but they really aren't. The parentheses around the statement between the second and fourth lines indicate a query within a query. The inner query selects from the MASTER table the supplier ID where the supplier is "Symantec". The outer query, the UPDATE statement, updates the Supplier_ID column to the value returned from the inner query but limits the rows for which this applies to where the supplier is equal to "Symantec". If the last line isn't present, all rows in the Supplier_ID column are updated.

The query-within-a-query concept (called *nested queries*) opens up more possibilities for you when you use SQL. As you develop more advanced applications that retrieve data, you'll find that understanding SQL is vital.

Grouping SQL Statements into Transactions

A transaction is an important part of proper database design. A *transaction* provides a way to group a series of critical SQL statements. That way, if something fails, the database can be reverted to the state it was in before the statements were issued. The following three statements handle transactions:

- BEGINTRANS marks the beginning of a transaction.
- COMMITTRANS marks the end of a transaction.

- ROLLBACK rolls the transaction back to the state the database was in before BEGINTRANS was issued.

You indicate the beginning of the group of statements with the BEGINTRANS keyword. If there are no errors, the transaction ends with the COMMITTRANS keyword, which commits all statements executed since BEGINTRANS was issued. However, any errors must be handled in an error handler, which must tell the database not to issue any of the statements executed since the BEGINTRANS was issued. This is done with the ROLLBACK keyword.

The database can do this because it stores the data in a transaction log. The transaction log stores the data in the state that it was at the time the BEGINTRANS was issued. Therefore, the data can be rolled back by using the transaction log.

A good example of when you might use transactions is in an order entry/accounting application. In one transaction, with one order, you want to do the following things:

- Let the shipping department know about the items to be shipped
- Update the customer's record
- Decrease inventory

All these items need to be handled at once. If any of them fails, they all need to fail. For example, if the SQL statement to decrease the inventory fails and you don't force the customer's record and the shipping department transactions to fail, there's no integrity between the sets of data. The customer's record would say that an item was ordered, the shipping department would ship the item, but the inventory wouldn't be decreased. As this situation continues, the inventory database would show a large number of items, but these items wouldn't actually exist because the shipping department keeps receiving orders to ship them out. The code fragment in Listing 18.1 illustrates how to use transactions with your SQL statements.

LISTING 18.1. MULTIPLE SQL STATEMENTS WRAPPED IN A TRANSACTION.

```
'Handle Error
On Error Goto SaveError
'Begin the transaction
BeginTrans
'Instruct the shipping department to ship the item
sCmd = "INSERT INTO Shipping(Cust_ID, Stock_Num, Qty) "
sCmd = sCmd + "VALUES (101, '119945A', 2) "
'issue statement
dbMain.Workspaces(0).Execute sCmd

'Update the customer's record
sCmd = "INSERT INTO Order(Cust_ID, Stock_Num, Qty, Price, Date) "
sCmd = sCmd + "VALUES (101, '19945A', 2, 19.95, '12/15/96') "
```

```
'issue statement
dbMain.Workspaces(0).Execute sCmd

'Update inventory
sCmd = "UPDATE Inventory "
sCmd = sCmd + "SET On_Hand = On_Hand - 2 "
sCmd = sCmd + "WHERE Stock_Num = '19945A' "
'issue statement
dbMain.Workspaces(0).Execute sCmd

'there were no errors, commit
CommitTrans
Exit Sub

'error handler
SaveError:
    MsgBox Error$
    Rollback
    Exit Sub
```

Altering the Database Structure with Data Definition Statements

You can use data definition statements to create or alter the database structure itself. You can use them to do the following:

- Create tables
- Add columns to tables
- Add indexes on tables
- Delete tables and indexes

These statements are issued from Visual Basic just as any other statement would be issued—by using the EXECUTE method of the database object.

Creating Tables

To create a table, you use the CREATE TABLE keywords, which use the syntax

```
CREATE TABLE table (field1 type [(size)] [index1] [, field2 type [(size)]
➡[index2] [, ...]][, multifieldindex [, ...]])
```

in which:

- *table* is the name of the table to be created.
- *field1*, *field2...* are the names of fields to be created in the new table. (At least one field must be created at this time.)

- *type* is the data type of the new field.

- *size* is the field size in characters for a text field.

- *index1, index2...* specifies a CONSTRAINT clause defining a single-field index.

- *multifieldindex* specifies a CONSTRAINT clause defining a multiple-field index.

Suppose that you wanted to create a table named Orders. This table would have five columns: Cust_ID, Stock_Num, Qty, Price, and OrderDate. Also, there would be a primary key index on the Cust_ID column:

```
CREATE TABLE Orders (Cust_ID Double CONSTRAINT PKey PRIMARY KEY, Stock_Num
➡TEXT(10), Qty Integer, Price CURRENCY, OrderDate DATE)
```

If you want to make the Cust_ID, Stock_Num, and OrderDate the primary key, you would do so like this:

```
CREATE TABLE Orders (Cust_ID Double, Stock_Num TEXT(10), Qty Integer,
➡Price CURRENCY, OrderDate DATE, CONSTRAINT PKey PRIMARY KEY(Cust_ID,
➡Stock_Num, OrderDate))
```

Adding or Deleting Columns and Indexes

To alter a table, use the ALTER TABLE keywords with the following syntax:

```
ALTER TABLE table {ADD {[COLUMN] field type[(size)] [CONSTRAINT index] I
CONSTRAINT multifieldindex} ¦
DROP {[COLUMN] field I CONSTRAINT indexname} }
```

in which:

- *table* is the name of the table to be altered.

- *field* is the name of the field to be added to or deleted from the table.

- *type* is the data type of the field.

- *size* is the field size in characters for text fields.

- *index* is the index for the field.

- *multifieldindex* is the definition of a multiple-field index to be added to table.

- *indexname* is the name of the multiple-field index to be removed.

Suppose that you wanted to add a Ship_Date column to the previous example. You could do that like this:

```
ALTER TABLE Orders
ADD COLUMN Ship_Date DATE
```

If you then wanted to delete a column, you could do that like this:

```
ALTER TABLE Orders
DROP COLUMN Ship_Date
```

You can use this same general syntax to add or delete indexes. The only difference is that you must follow the rules for the CONSTRAINT clause, which follows one of two basic syntaxes. The first is for a single field index, which follows this basic syntax:

```
CONSTRAINT name {PRIMARY KEY ¦ UNIQUE ¦
REFERENCES foreigntable [(foreignfield)]}
```

in which:

- *name* is the name of the index to be created.

- *foreigntable* is the name of the foreign table containing the field or fields specified by *foreignfield1*, *foreignfield2*, and so on.

- *foreignfield1*, *foreignfield2...* are the names of the fields in *foreigntable* specified by *ref1* and *ref2*. You can omit this field if the referenced field is the primary key of *foreigntable*.

The second is for a multiple field index, which follows this basic syntax:

```
CONSTRAINT name
{PRIMARY KEY (primary1[, primary2 [, ...]]) ¦
UNIQUE (unique1[, unique2 [, ...]]) ¦
FOREIGN KEY (ref1[, ref2 [, ...]]) REFERENCES foreigntable
➡[, [(foreignfield1 foreignfield2 [, ...]])]}
```

in which:

- *name* is the name of the index to be created.

- *primary1*, *primary2...* are the names of the fields to be designated as the primary key.

- *unique1*, *unique2...* are the names of the fields to be designated as unique keys.

- *ref1*, *ref2...* are the names of foreign key fields that refer to fields in another table.

- *foreigntable* is the name of the foreign table containing the field or fields specified by *foreignfield1*, *foreignfield2*, and so on.

- *foreignfield1*, *foreignfield2...* are the names of the fields in *foreigntable* specified by *ref1* and *ref2*. You can omit this field if the referenced field is the primary key of *foreigntable*.

Deleting Tables and Indexes

Deleting tables or indexes requires a simple SQL statement that uses the DROP keyword. Of course, you know the name of the table to delete, but it can be difficult to know the name of an index. If you created it, you would know the naming conventions you've used. For example, a primary key index could be called Pkey. However, if you've used

18

**SQL AND THE
T-SQL DEBUGGER**

some other tool to create the tables and indexes, you might not know the name. One thing you could do is cycle through the Indexes collection to determine all index names.

The DROP keyword is used with this general syntax:

```
DROP {TABLE table ¦ INDEX index ON table}
```

in which *table* is the name of the table to delete or the name of the index to delete that resides in a table, and *index* is the name of the index to delete.

If you wanted to delete the table Orders, you would do so like this:

```
DROP TABLE Orders
```

You'll receive no confirmation prompt before the table or index is deleted. Issuing the statement will perform the action.

> **NOTE**
>
> Client/server databases, such as SQL Server, also enable you to DROP databases, provided that you have the appropriate permissions to do so.

Using the T-SQL Debugger

The Transact-SQL Debugger (T-SQL Debugger) included in Visual Basic 6 Enterprise Edition, first made its appearance in Visual Basic 5 Enterprise Edition. Before the T-SQL Debugger existed, debugging stored procedures on SQL Server required a large amount of time. You had to raise errors under certain circumstances to know what was going on within the stored procedure. In other words, you had to devise a custom method of debugging stored procedures. The T-SQL Debugger changes all that by providing a way to debug stored procedures from within Visual Basic.

Installing the T-SQL Debugger

To install the T-SQL Debugger, you need to know a few things. First, there is a client-side setup and there is a server-side setup. The client-side setup is installed automatically when you choose the Typical installation option. If you choose the Custom installation option, you must select the SQL Debugging option under Enterprise Features.

NOTE

The process of installing the T-SQL Debugger is documented in the README.TXT file located in VB6.0\TOOLS\TSQL\SRVSETUP on the VB6 Enterprise Edition CD-ROM. The location of the file on your CD might be slightly different if you are using a different implementation of Visual Basic.

The server-side setup is a little more complicated:

1. Confirm that your version of NT 4.0 is running service pack 3 or greater. If you have not already upgraded your NT 4.0 system, you can use the upgrade provided on the Visual Basic 6.0 CD-ROM. Make sure that you reboot your system after the Service Pack has been installed.

2. Make sure that SQL Server 6.5 or greater is installed, as well as SQL Server Service Pack 4 (SP4). On the Visual Basic 6.0 CD-ROM, the SP4 is located in the \SQL\SERVPACK4\I386 subdirectory. If your copy of VB resides on a different CD (such as Visual Studio), the location of the Service Pack might be different. In any case, install the Service Pack and reboot when prompted.

NOTE

Make sure that no errors occur when you install SQL Server 6.5 Service Pack 4 because installing the service pack alters the database by issuing scripts that are necessary for you to continue. If any errors occur, your database won't be updated. Also, make sure that you reboot each time you're prompted. If you don't, this could affect the overall installation process.

3. Set up the actual T-SQL Debugger by running the SDI_NT4.EXE program on Visual Basic 6.0's CD-ROM in the \TOOLS\TSQL\SRVSETUP subdirectory.

Even though you're set up to debug your stored procedures, you should consider a few points before continuing:

- Make sure that the MSSQLServer service is *not* set up to log on as a system account. Make sure that it's set to log on as a local account (see Figure 18.1).

- If you're using TCP/IP as a protocol, make sure that the machines communicate with each other by typing **PING** at the server's command prompt, followed by the name of the computer you're trying to connect with.

18

SQL AND THE T-SQL DEBUGGER

FIGURE 18.1

MSSQLServer service startup parameters.

- Make sure that you have Remote Data Objects 2.0 or later installed on the client computer.

- Make sure that the RPC Services (Remote Procedure Call and Remote Procedure Locator) are running on the Windows NT server.

If you have problems, the system will tell you to look in the client and server logs but won't tell you where the logs are located. The server log is actually the Windows NT Application event log. The client log, AUTMGR32.LOG, is on the client machine in the \WINDOWS\SYSTEM subdirectory. This is a cumulative log, with the most recent entries at the bottom.

> **NOTE**
>
> If everything looks fine, but you can't figure out why stored procedures aren't debugging, it's best to first reboot the client machine. If that doesn't work, try rebooting the server.

Using the T-SQL Debugger

As an add-in, the T-SQL Debugger must be selected for use. Choose Add-Ins | Add-In Manager from the Visual Basic menu. Make sure that a check mark is next to the VB T-SQL Debugger option (see Figure 18.2).

After you select it, notice that the Automation Manager is running. The Automation Manager runs because it's necessary to coordinate Remote Procedure Calls (RPC) with the server. Next, choose Add-Ins T-SQL Debugger from the menu to start the debugger.

FIGURE 18.2

Selecting the T-SQL Debugger for use.

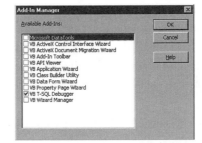

> **NOTE**
>
> You might notice that the T-SQL Debugger is actually offscreen. Apparently, Microsoft didn't take into account the resolution of the add-in. Simply move it to the center of the screen for use.

Creating Queries

When you invoke the T-SQL Debugger, you should notice a dialog box with three tabbed pages. You must fill in the first page, Settings, to establish an ODBC connection with SQL Server before you can continue. The following fields are required:

- DSN
- SQL Server
- UID
- Password (if any)

To begin, select a Data Source Name (DSN), a 32-bit data source registered with ODBC. If you don't have one on your machine, you can create one by clicking the Register DSN button and configuring a 32-bit DSN in the dialog box that appears.

Next, select or enter the name of the server where SQL Server is installed. For example, you might name your server SERVER-A. After you successfully log on, this server will be conveniently added to the drop-down list for future use.

Enter the database. If you leave the Database field blank, the default database (usually Master) is used. For example, type **pubs**.

UID is the user ID registered with SQL Server. Type a valid user ID, such as **sa** (the default administrator logon). Also type the password, if one exists.

Although they aren't necessary to change for you to continue, the following RDO (Remote Data Objects) options are available:

18

SQL AND THE T-SQL DEBUGGER

- Lock Type specifies the type of RDO locking that will occur. The possible values are `rdConcurReadOnly`, `rdConcurValues`, `rdConcurLock`, `rdConcurRowver`, and `rdConcurBatch`.

- Result Set specifies the type of RDO resultset that will be returned. The possible values are `rdOpenKeyset`, `rdOpenForwardOnly`, `rdOpenStatic`, and `rdOpenDynamic`.

- Options specifies miscellaneous options for how queries are executed. The possible values are `rdNone` and `rdExecDirect`.

Figure 18.3 shows how the Settings page looks when configured properly.

FIGURE 18.3.

The Settings page of the T-SQL Debugger.

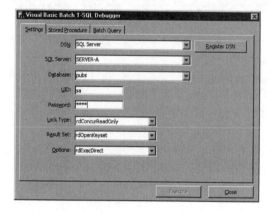

After the required fields are filled in, notice that the Stored Procedure and Batch Query tabs are enabled. Click the Stored Procedure tab to establish an RDO connection with the server. You'll see a list of stored procedures contained within the database (`pubs`) you selected in the earlier example. You'll see these possible stored procedures:

- `byroyalty`
- `reptq1`
- `reptq2`
- `reptq3`

Select a stored procedure to run (for example, the `byroyalty` stored procedure). Figure 18.4 shows how the Stored Procedure page now looks.

Notice at the bottom of the dialog box that the Execute button becomes enabled. This is because the T-SQL Debugger is ready to debug the stored procedure.

Alternatively, you can traverse the list of parameters shown on the left and set values for them in the Value text box. That way, you can try different values to debug the stored procedures. However, as you'll see shortly, you can actually change the value in the debugger, just as you would in the Visual Basic debugger. As you change the values, notice that the Query text box changes to reflect the new values. This is the actual query that will be sent to the server.

FIGURE 18.4.

The Stored Procedure page of the T-SQL Debugger.

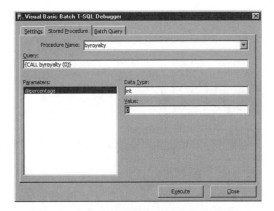

> **NOTE**
>
> Although you can actually change the value in the Query text box, it's not recommended because the Value text box doesn't reflect a change in this case.

If you want to execute the query at this time, see the next section, "Executing Queries."

You use the Batch Query page to place text that will be used in a batch query. A *batch query* is a series of SQL statements transmitted to the server, one after another, in a group. Figure 18.5 shows a sample batch query. Each item in the batch must be separated by the keyword GO.

Executing Queries

To execute the query, simply click the Execute button. Doing so establishes another connection with the server and places the query in the debugger window (see Figure 18.6, showing the byroyalty stored procedure).

The debugger window has four panes:

- The top unlabeled pane contains the actual stored procedure text.
- The Local Variables pane lists the local variables in the stored procedure.
- The Global Variables pane lists global variables within SQL Server 6.5.
- The bottom unlabeled pane is the results window.

Figure 18.5.

The Batch Query page of the T-SQL Debugger.

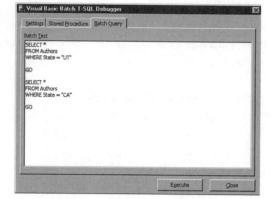

Figure 18.6.

The T-SQL Debugger with a stored procedure to execute.

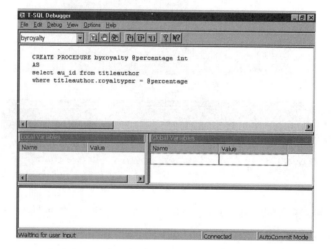

To execute the query, click the Go toolbar button, press the F5 key, or choose Debug | Go from the menu.

If you receive the error message shown in Figure 18.7, refer to the steps listed earlier in the "Installing the T-SQL Debugger" section or refer to the online help. If you don't receive an error, the stored procedure is executed (see Figure 18.8).

Figure 18.7.

A T-SQL Debugger server error.

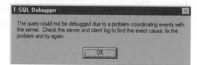

FIGURE 18.8.

The T-SQL Debugger after a stored procedure is executed.

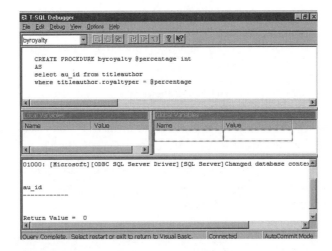

After you execute a query, notice that the Go toolbar button becomes disabled. To enable it, choose Debug | Restart from the menu or press Shift+F5. Now you can execute the query as before.

Debugging Queries

Debugging a query with the T-SQL Debugger is similar to debugging a query in Visual Basic. A *breakpoint* tells the debugger to pause execution when it reaches the code line containing the breakpoint. That way, you can check the values of variables at a specific point. You can set breakpoints by clicking a line of text in the query and then clicking the Set/Remove Breakpoint toolbar button, pressing the F9 key, or choosing Edit | Set Breakpoint from the menu. A red dot appears in the margin of the line containing the breakpoint.

After you set a breakpoint, you can step through the code as you would in Visual Basic. You have the following options:

- Step Into
- Step Over
- Run To Cursor

To activate the Step Into option, click the Step Into toolbar button, press the F8 key, or choose Debug | Step from the menu. Step Into executes every line of code. If the code calls a label or another procedure, Step Into steps through each line in that code as well. As each line is executed, the system pauses after each line of code. It's useful to set a breakpoint at a specific point in the code where you suspect a problem to be located, allowing the program to pause execution. Then, stepping through the code to watch program execution helps find errors in code.

Activate the Step Over option by clicking the Step Over toolbar button (Step Over has no hotkey or menu option). The Step Over option executes each line in the current procedure but not every line of code of a called procedure. The code is executed, but not every line is shown.

The Run To Cursor option lets you determine which line of code is executed next. To use it, place the cursor on the line you want to execute. Then click the Run To Cursor toolbar button or choose Debug | Run To Cursor from the menu (no hotkey is available). All lines of code between where the cursor was and where the cursor currently is will be skipped.

While you're debugging code (by setting breakpoints), you can query or set the values of variables to test different scenarios without having to rerun your query externally. Figure 18.9 shows the code stopped at a breakpoint, with the values of all local variables.

FIGURE 18.9.

The T-SQL Debugger stopped at a breakpoint.

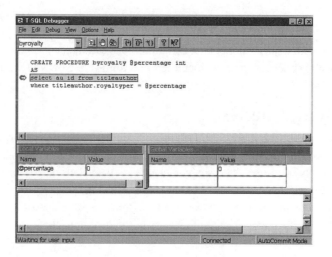

Notice in the Local Variables pane that the value of the @percentage variable is 0. Another way to tell the value of your variables is to place the mouse pointer over the variable to see the value in a ToolTip.

To change the value, simply click the Value field in the Local Variables pane and manually change the value. After you change it, press Enter. Notice that placing the cursor over the variable changes it immediately. You then can step through the rest of the procedure and view the results. Change the percentage to 25 to view the results as shown in Figure 18.10. Two author IDs are returned at 25 percent.

You use the Global Variables pane to query or set the values of global variables. These global variables, stored within SQL Server, are available to all stored procedures and queries. Again, only while debugging can you query or set the value of these options. For example, stop a query at a breakpoint and type the global variable @@OPTIONS, which stores different options within SQL Server. (All global variables begin with @@.) Press Enter to see the value of the global variable. This value might not be included in the stored procedure. Figure 18.11 shows what this pane looks like.

FIGURE 18.10.

The T-SQL Debugger after a variable value is changed.

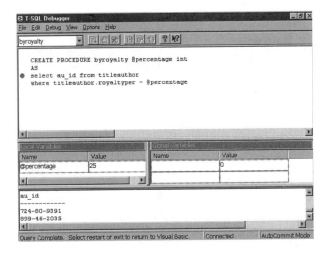

FIGURE 18.11.

The T-SQL Debugger after a global variable is entered.

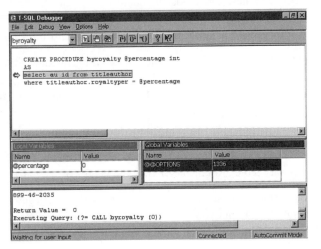

T-SQL Debugger Options

You can set two options while using the debugger. One is to view the call stack. If one stored procedure calls another, you'll have more than one query in the call stack. To view this stack, choose View | Call Stack from the menu. Figure 18.12 shows this window.

FIGURE 18.12.

*The T-SQL
Debugger call
stack.*

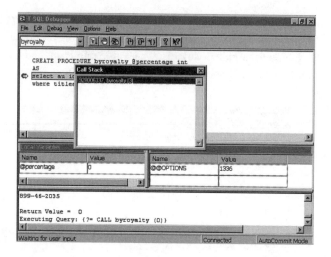

The other option is the mode that the debugger is in. You can choose between Auto Commit and Auto Rollback. With Auto Rollback, a query is automatically rolled back if it's not committed in code. With Auto Commit, every complete transaction is automatically committed when it's executed.

You can toggle between these two modes by choosing Options | Safe (Auto Rollback) Mode from the menu. If a check mark is next to this item, the debugger is in Auto Rollback mode; if there isn't a check mark, the debugger is in Auto Commit mode.

You can also add a watch to a global variable, just as you can add a watch in Visual Basic. A *watch* shows the value of specified variables. To add a watch, select Edit | Add Watch from the menu to place the watch in the Global Variables pane. To remove the watch, simply click it and press Delete.

Another nice feature is the ability to view the contents of a temporary table. To view the contents, simply choose View | Temp Table Dump from the menu. At the prompt, type the name of the temporary table. You then can view the results of the table.

You can view the results of your stored procedures or any messages in the Output window. You can toggle the Output window on and off by choosing View | Output Window. If a check mark is next to the option, the Output window will be shown.

In addition to these stated options, you can choose your own colors for items in the debug window by choosing Options | Colors. The following items can have colors assigned:

Comment	Keyword
Constant	Number
Datatype	Operator

Function	String
Identifier	Execution Indicator

You can also choose the font for the text in the debugger by choosing Options | Font from the menu.

> **NOTE**
>
> You can also debug a stored procedure from within Visual Basic in break mode via the UserConnection object. You can right-click the object to see an option labeled Debug Stored Procedure. This will begin the debugging session listed throughout this chapter.

Summary

SQL is important because it has become the standard language of most databases. SQL varies slightly among different databases, but the core components discussed in this chapter are common to most databases, except where noted. This chapter gives a good insight into SQL and how it's used.

Microsoft's introduction of the T-SQL Debugger into the Enterprise Edition of Visual Basic 6.0 is a tremendous improvement. Until now, debugging stored procedures was difficult, if not impossible: You had to devise your own schemes for returning values and error codes from stored procedures, a cumbersome task because the stored procedures had to be recompiled after these schemes were put in place.

The T-SQL Debugger makes it easy to debug stored procedures. It allows you to step through your stored procedures, as well as query and set the value of variables. Using the T-SQL Debugger saves countless hours of tedious work.

Internet Programming

PART
IV

IN THIS PART

- Creating ActiveX Documents   *427*
- Creating DHTML Applications   *453*
- Mail-Enabling Your Applications With MAPI   *483*
- Using the Internet Transfer Control   *519*
- Client/Server Programming With Winsock *535*

Creating ActiveX Documents

by Loren Eidahl

IN ·THIS CHAPTER

- Understanding ActiveX Documents **428**

- Exploring the `UserDocument` Object **430**

- ActiveX Document DLLs Versus ActiveX Document EXEs **436**

- Creating Your First ActiveX Document *437*

- Menu Design for ActiveX Documents *442*

- Adding Forms and Documents to ActiveX Documents **445**

- Deploying an ActiveX Document in Internet Explorer *447*

- Using the ActiveX Document Migration Wizard *448*

Whether you are creating a Web page or designing a multiuser application, your choice of development tools can make a big impact on the level of functionality your product can possess and the speed with which it can be completed. Visual Basic 6 provides a number of tools that can help you create better and faster applications. One of these tools, ActiveX documents, actually comes in a couple of different flavors depending on your application's needs. In this chapter you will learn how ActiveX documents can be used to make Internet programming available to even the most casual of developers.

Understanding ActiveX Documents

ActiveX documents can in some cases be thought of as the embodiment of the code reuse paradigm. They allow you to create applications that can run as stand-alone applications or as part of a much larger Internet or Intranet application. ActiveX documents are similar to Hypertext Markup Language (HTML) documents in that they both require that a container be used to view them, such as a Web browser. However, this is where the similarity ends.

What Is an ActiveX Document?

In its most basic form, an ActiveX document is an application that runs inside a container, such as Internet Explorer, instead of running as a stand-alone program. Figure 19.1 shows an example of an ActiveX document.

FIGURE 19.1.

An ActiveX document can run in a container such the Office binder or a browser.

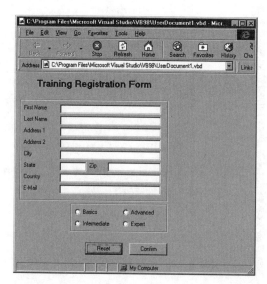

ActiveX documents get their name from their similarity to word processing documents (.DOC) or spreadsheet documents (.XLS). These files must be viewed using a container program such as Microsoft Word or Microsoft Excel. Files that need containers to be viewed cannot be launched independently of the required viewer. For example, you can view a spreadsheet created in Excel only on machines that have Excel installed on them.

Fortunately, there are many containers that support ActiveX documents, including Internet Explorer, Microsoft Office binders, and the Visual Basic Integrated Development Environment (IDE). Users will run your program inside one of these container applications.

The key item to note about ActiveX documents is that they are entire applications. Unlike ActiveX controls that are placed on a form to create an application, ActiveX documents are form objects that have controls placed on them to create the user interface. This method of creating applications allows the developer to create ActiveX documents that can be treated as objects to create applications that are component based.

Understanding the Advantages of ActiveX Documents

The primary reason to use ActiveX documents in Visual Basic is to create component-based applications that can be used either on the desktop or the Internet without a separate interface for each. The Active desktop of Internet Explorer 4.0 is an excellent example of how ActiveX documents can be used to create interfaces that are component based.

ActiveX documents provide you with a number of distinct advantages when creating applications. Some of these advantages include the following:

- Creating ActiveX documents does not require you to learn another programming language. In fact, it does not require you to learn any arcane functions or Application Programming Interface (API) calls with Visual Basic (VB). It just requires you to look at your application in a new way.
- If you are creating Internet-specific applications, the Visual Basic IDE can save you countless hours of development time compared to languages that offer no such tool.
- Debugging your ActiveX document application is no different than debugging a traditional Visual Basic application.
- The Hyperlink object allows you to navigate to any page from the browser. These pages can be ActiveX documents or Web pages.

One advantage that has special importance to developers of intranets or Internet applications is the capability of ActiveX documents to be downloaded from the Web server. This means that users accessing an ActiveX document page will always have access to the latest version. ActiveX documents use script commands in the HTML file to alert the server if a new version of the document cabinet (.CAB) should be downloaded from the server. The approach simplifies the process of maintaining code and version control.

Exploring the UserDocument Object

The UserDocument provides many of the same features and the functionality that a form object provides. Following is a list of some of the key similarities between a UserDocument and a form object:

- They both hold key roles in the creation of applications.
- Controls can be placed on either one.
- They can display graphics and information.

As you can see, a UserDocument shares many of the key features of a form. This provides great flexibility in the design of your documents and the manner in which you present information to the user.

Key Events and Properties

The UserDocument and the form object are very similar; however, there are key properties, methods, and events that make the UserDocument unique. Conversely, there are properties, methods, and events that the UserDocument does not support.

The key events the UserDocument object does not support are the Activate, Deactivate, Load, and Unload events. To make up for the loss of these key events, the UserDocument object offers developers the following events not supported by the form object:

- AsyncReadComplete—Occurs when the container holding the document has finished an asynchronous read request.
- EnterFocus—Occurs when the ActiveX document receives focus.
- ExitFocus—Occurs when the ActiveX document loses focus.
- Hide—Occurs when the user navigates from the current ActiveX document to another document.
- InitProperties—Occurs when the document is first loaded. However, if any

properties have been saved using the `PropertyBag` object, the `ReadProperties` event will occur instead.

- `ReadProperties`—occurs in place of the `InitProperties` event if items are stored in a `PropertyBag` object. This event also occurs as the document is first loaded.

- `Scroll`—Occurs when the user uses the scrollbar of the container in which the ActiveX document is running.

- `Show`—Occurs when the user navigates from another document to the ActiveX document.

- `WriteProperties`—Occurs as the program is about to be terminated. This event happens right before the `Terminate` event, but only occurs if the `PropertyChanged` statement has been used to indicate that a change has occurred in a property's value.

Creating and Storing Properties for a UserDocument

If you have used the form object, the `UserControl` object, or the `UserDocument` object, you most likely have noticed some similarities between the three. These objects all have one common thread: They are extensible. All three objects have the capability to create properties, methods, and events. However, only two of these objects, `UserControl` and `UserDocument`, allow you to use the `PropertyBag` object. The `PropertyBag` object, you might recall, stores data contained in public properties for use between sessions. Despite the similarities between the `UserDocument` and a form, there are some ways in which the `UserDocument` is much more similar to a `UserControl` than to a form. All three objects— the form, the `UserControl`, and the `UserDocument`—enable you to create properties and methods to extend their capabilities. However, only `UserControl` and `UserDocument` have the capability to use the `PropertyBag` object.

This chapter won't go into great detail on the process of creating properties. However, if you would like a refresher on this topic, you might want to check out Chapter 5, "Creating ActiveX Controls." For the sake of the current discussion, the following list briefly describes the steps involved. To create and store properties for the `UserDocument`, you will need to follow these steps:

1. Create a property by using the `Property Let` and `Property Get` procedures. You can create the shell of the property by using the Add Procedure dialog box, accessible from the Tools menu of Visual Basic.

2. To indicate that the value of a property has changed, place the `PropertyChanged` statement in the `Property Let` procedure of each property whose value you want to store.

3. To store the values of the property, use the WriteProperty method of the PropertyBag object to output the values of the changed properties. The code for this is placed in the WriteProperties event of the UserDocument.

4. To retrieve the values of the property, use the ReadProperty method of the PropertyBag object to output the values of the changed properties. The code for this is placed in the ReadProperties event of the UserDocument.

Asynchronous Downloading of Controls

One of the primary concerns for Internet developers is the speed at which the end user can download or retrieve the desired application. The User Interface is usually the first component of an application that gets judged. If the interface is slow or boring, the application is off to a very rough start in terms of user acceptance. Although the Web developer cannot do much about the speed at which the users are connected, a few programming ideas can help increase the speed at which the application downloads data to end users' machines.

Downloading ActiveX documents can sometimes slow down or stall other actions on a Web page. To overcome this problem, the ActiveX specification includes a provision to asynchronously download data. This means that while a control is being downloaded to a site, the other elements on that site are free to function as planned, without a noticeable delay in processing. ActiveX documents created in Visual Basic 6 can use the following methods and event or the UserControl object to control the download process:

- AsyncRead method
- CancelAsyncRead method
- AsyncReadComplete event

> **NOTE**
>
> The AsyncRead method first appeared in Visual Basic 5. Since then, several changes have been made to this method that allow for greater flexibility in implementation.

The AsyncRead Method

The AsyncRead method begins the download process. The declaration for this method is

object.**AsyncRead** Target, AsyncType [, PropertyName], [AsyncReadOptions]

In actual practice, the call for the AsyncRead method would look like the following:

```
AsyncRead "http://www.mysite.com/file.dat" vbAsyncTypeFile, "Data"
```

The `Target` argument denotes the actual location of the data to be requested. This can be a path or a uniform resource locator (URL). The `AsyncType` argument indicates the type of data being requested. The data can be one of the three following types:

Constant	Description
VbAsyncTypePicture	The data is a picture.
VbAsyncTypeFile	The data is a file.
VbAsyncTypeByteArray	The data is a byte array.

The `Property` argument is a string identifying the name of the download operation. This is useful if multiple download processes are occurring simultaneously. You can also use this value in the `CancelAsyncRead` method.

The `AsyncRead` method will raise some errors on its own; however, it is a good idea to have sufficient error handling in place. If no data is available for download, then the `AsyncRead` method will return to the calling procedure.

The `CancelAsyncRead` Method

The `CancelAsyncRead` method cancels the specified download process. The declaration for this method is

```
object.CancelAsyncRead [PropertyName]
```

If `PropertyName` is provided, only the download process specified in `PropertyName` will be canceled. If it is not provided, the last call to the `AsyncRead` method that did not provide a `PropertyName` will be canceled.

The `AsyncReadComplete` Event

The `AsyncReadComplete` event signals the application that the download process has been completed. The declaration for this method is

```
Sub AsyncReadComplete(AsyncProp As AsyncProperty)
```

After the completion of each download, the `AsyncReadComplete` event is fired. The argument of the `AsyncReadComplete` event is a reference to an `AsyncProperty` object, which can be used to identify the downloaded property and retrieve the downloaded data.

The `AsyncProperty` object has three properties, as shown in the following table. These properties allow the control to determine what download has completed and the type of data returned.

19

CREATING
ACTIVEX
DOCUMENTS

Constant	Description
AsyncProperty.PropertyName	This property contains the name of the property being downloaded.
AsyncProperty.AsyncType	This property contains the same value as the AsyncType argument of the AsyncRead method that initiated the download process.
AsyncProperty.Value	This property contains the downloaded data.

The following code illustrates how you might use the AsyncReadComplete event to signal the completed download of a graphic.

```
Private Sub UserControl_AsyncReadComplete( AsyncProp As AsyncProperty)
On Error Resume Next
  If AsyncProp.PropertyName = "DownloadedGraphic" then
     Set picture1 = AsyncProp.Value
     Debug.Print "Download Complete"
  End If
End Sub
```

> **NOTE**
>
> The AsyncReadComplete event needs to have some type of error handling. Any error that isn't handled has the potential for stopping the download process (such as a lost Internet connection). If an error occurs during the transfer, the vbAsyncStatusCodeError status code is returned.

In the example, the Value property will contain the data from the download—in this case a picture. However the Value property could just as easily contain a file or a byte array, as defined in the AsyncRead call. In all cases it is assumed that the control will know how to handle the incoming data. If a file was downloaded, the Value property will contain a path on the local machine. Typically, all files are downloaded to the c:\windows\temp folder, where they are assigned a temporary filename. At this point a Visual Basic application can open the file using standard file handling methods.

Using the Hyperlink Object

The UserControl.HyperLink property provides a reference to the Hyperlink object. The Hyperlink object gives your control access to ActiveX hyperlinking functionality. This allows your ActiveX documents to navigate to a specific URL or navigate through the history file. The main requirement for this object is that the ActiveX control must be placed in a Hyperlink-aware container such as Internet Explorer (IE) 3.0 or 4.0.

The following code segment assumes that the control's URLText property contains a URL string. Clicking on the control causes it to request that its container navigate to that URL. If a valid URL is not provided as a target, an error will occur.

```
Private Sub UserControl_Click()
    HyperLink.NavigateTo Target:=URLText
End Sub
```

The following table describes the methods associated with the Hyperlink object.

Method	Description
NavigateTo	Accepts an optional Location argument, which specifies a location within the target URL. If a location is not specified, the server will jump to the top of the URL or document. This method also accepts an optional FrameName argument, which specifies a frame within the target URL.
GoForward	Navigates forward in the History list.
GoBack	Navigates backward in the History list.

> **NOTE**
>
> If your control is placed on a non-Hyperlink-aware container, an application in your system that supports Hyperlink will be launched to handle the request.

The following code segment illustrates how the GoForward and the GoBack methods might be called:

```
Hyperlink.GoForward
```

Attempting to call either the GoForward or the GoBack methods when the History list is empty will cause an error condition. The following code segment illustrates how to handle such an error.

```
Private Sub Mback_Click()
    On Error Goto ErrHandler
    UserDocument.Hyperlink.GoBack
```

```
'****************************************
' Additional operational code goes here
'****************************************
    Exit Sub
ErrHandler:
    MsgBox "You have reached the end of the History list"
End Sub
```

> **NOTE**
>
> A container such as Internet Explorer, which supports hyperlinking, will execute on its own the jump specified in a `NavigateTo` method. A container such as Office 97 Binder, which does not support hyperlinking, will start a hyperlink-capable program to process the jump.

ActiveX Document DLLs Versus ActiveX Document EXEs

ActiveX components, whether they be ActiveX documents or ActiveX controls, provide the Visual Basic developer with the ability to create reusable code components. These code components typically will contain properties and methods that the client application can call. This type of code reuse enables Visual Basic developers to create a standard set of objects that can be used in other applications without having to recode them each time. Properly designed, you can use these code components in multiple projects with only a few slight changes to the passed parameters.

One of the key points to understanding ActiveX components is their relationship to the client that calls them. All ActiveX components—whether they be ActiveX controls, ActiveX document executables (EXEs), or ActiveX document dynamic link libraries (DLLs)—can be categorized in one of the following ways:

- In-process component
- Out-of-process component

ActiveX document DLLs and ActiveX controls are in-process components. This means they run in the same memory space as any client applications that call them. A client application might also be another ActiveX document DLL. ActiveX document EXEs are out-of–process components. This means they run in their own address space, whereas the client application typically runs in its own process or thread of execution.

> **NOTE**
>
> The choice of whether to create ActiveX document DLLs or EXEs is somewhat dependent on what type of document you wish to display. ActiveX document DLLs can display only modal forms. If your application uses modeless forms, you must create an ActiveX document EXE file. Another factor that will determine whether to create a ActiveX document as a DLL or EXE is performance. ActiveX DLLs use the same memory space as their host and as a result are much faster than ActiveX EXEs.

Creating Your First ActiveX Document

The steps required to create an ActiveX document are similar to those needed to create standard applications using VB 6. In this section you will create an ActiveX document that can be used as a template for creating additional ActiveX documents.

The steps that you will use to create a new ActiveX document are as follows:

1. Determine functionality of ActiveX document.
2. Design the interface for the document. This includes the properties, methods, and events that the document will expose.
3. Create a project that contains the ActiveX document and any supporting forms.
4. Add necessary controls or code to the UserDocument object.
5. Add necessary controls or code to complete the interface and supporting forms.
6. Compile document to a .vbd file and test it with potential target applications.
7. Use the Package and Deployment Wizard to create an Internet download setup.

These steps serve only as a rough outline for your development efforts. Obviously, there are a number of details involved in each of these steps, but you can see that the process is similar to creating non-ActiveX document applications.

> **NOTE**
>
> The preceding steps refer to creating an application. Because an ActiveX document is an interactive application, containing any number of forms and controls, throughout this chapter *application* will often refer to an ActiveX document.

Starting an ActiveX Document Project

The first step toward creating an ActiveX document is to start your project. You do this by selecting the New Project item from the File menu. From the New Project dialog box, select the option to create an ActiveX Document EXE by double-clicking the icon. This starts the new project and displays a blank UserDocument form on the screen.

> **NOTE**
>
> If the UserDocument is not displayed automatically, double-click the UserDocument object in the Project window to display it.

After you have created the project, change the properties of the project and the UserDocument to descriptive names, like those listed in Table 19.1. To access the properties of the project, choose ProjectName Properties from the Project menu. The properties of the UserDocument are accessible from the Properties window (View | Properties Window). After setting the properties, save the files of the project by clicking the Save button on the toolbar. You must then specify names for each of the new files.

TABLE 19.1. PROJECT PROPERTIES FOR ACTIVEX DOCUMENT EXE PROJECT

Property	Setting
ProjectType	ActiveX EXE
ProjectName	Register
ProjectDescription	ActiveX Document—Registration
UserDocument Name	RegisDoc

> **DOCUMENT FILENAMES**
>
> The source code of ActiveX documents is saved in a text file, much the same way a form is saved. The description of the UserDocument object and any controls is stored along with the code of the document in a file with the extension .dob. This is similar to the .frm file of a form. If there are any graphic components of the interface, these are stored in a .dox file, similar to the .frx file for forms. When you compile your ActiveX document, you create either an .exe or a .dll file, along with a .vbd file. The .vbd file is the one accessed by Internet Explorer. This .vbd file is the "document" part of the file, similar to a .doc file from Microsoft Word.

Creating the Interface for the Document

Drawing controls on the UserDocument object creates the interface of your ActiveX document, just like drawing them on the form of a standard program. You can use almost any Visual Basic control to create your document. The only exception is that you cannot use the object linking and embedding (OLE) container control as part of an ActiveX document. Another restriction is that an ActiveX document cannot contain embedded objects such as Word or Excel documents.

CAUTION

If you use third-party or custom controls in your project, you need to check the licensing requirements before you plan on distributing your ActiveX documents.

To create the interface for the sample application, add the controls to the UserDocument object as listed in Table 19.2. When you have finished adding the controls and setting their properties, your form should look like that shown in Figure 19.2.

TABLE 19.2. MAJOR PROPERTY SETTINGS FOR THE CONTROLS THAT MAKE UP THE REGISTRATION APPLICATION'S USER INTERFACE

Control Type	Property	Value
TextBox	Name	txtFirstName
	Name	txtLastName
	Name	txtAddress1
	Name	txtAddress2
	Name	txtCity
	Name	txtState
	Name	txtZip
	Name	txtCountry
	Name	txtEmail
Label	Name	lblHeader
	Caption	Registration Form
	Name	lblFirstName
	Name	lblLastName
	Name	lblAddress1

continues

TABLE 19.2. CONTINUED

Control Type	Property	Value
	Name	lblAddress2
	Name	lblCity
	Name	lblState
	Name	lblZip
	Name	lblCountry
	Name	lblEmail
CommandButton	Name	cmdReset
	Caption	Reset
	Name	cmdConfirm
	Caption	Confirm
Frame	Name	fraUser

FIGURE 19.2.

You can use the registration form as the basis for a number of Internet applications.

Adding Code to the Document

After you have created the interface, you are ready to write the code that makes the document perform a task. As with the forms in a non-ActiveX document program, any code you write will need to be placed in the various events of the controls that make up the document. For the sample application you must enter the code from Listing 19.1 in the Click event of the cmdReset button.

LISTING 19.1. REGISTER.DOB—CODE REQUIRED TO RESET THE CONTROLS

```
Private Sub cmdReset_Click()
    txtFirstName = ""
    txtLastName = ""
    txtAddress1 = ""
    txtAddress2 = ""
    txtCity = ""
    txtState = ""
    txtZip = ""
    txtCountry = ""
    txtEmail = ""
End Sub
```

Testing Your ActiveX Document

After you have created the interface and entered all of the necessary code, you are ready to begin the testing process of the document. To test your code, follow these steps:

1. Run your document by pressing F5 or clicking the Start button on the toolbar.

2. Click the OK button on the Debugging form. Internet Explorer should now launch your document, as shown in Figure 19.1.

3. Enter values into the text boxes. When you click the reset button, the text boxes should be reset.

> **CAUTION**
>
> Terminating your program without closing Internet Explorer can cause errors in IE. Therefore, you should close and restart IE each time you run your document.

Compiling Your Document

After you have finished testing and debugging your document, you are ready to compile the document for distribution. To start the compilation process, select the Make Register.exe menu option from the File menu of Visual Basic. This will then open the Make project dialog box, prompting you to supply a name and location for the EXE or DLL file. The name of the .vbd file is based on the Name property of the UserDocument object. This file is placed in the same folder that you specified for the EXE file.

After you have compiled the ActiveX document, you can view it in any container program that handles ActiveX documents. Internet Explorer and Office Binder are two such programs. At the time this book is being written, Netscape Navigator 4.0 does not support ActiveX documents.

19

CREATING
ACTIVEX
DOCUMENTS

If you would like to use your ActiveX documents in Microsoft Office 97 Binder, start the Binder and then select the Add from File item in the Section menu. This opens a dialog box that enables you to specify the file to be loaded. You specify the name and location of your .vbd file and then click the OK button to load the document. Figure 19.3 shows the Register document running inside the Office 97 binder.

FIGURE 19.3.

The Office 97 Binder provides another means with which to run your ActiveX documents.

If your desire is to place your ActiveX documents on the Internet, you first need to run the Package and Deployment Wizard. The Wizard will create a CAB file that contains the required components, as well as sample HTML that shows you how to include your document on a Web page.

Menu Design for ActiveX Documents

How to create a menu system is one topic that deserves special attention in any discussion of how to create ActiveX documents. This is because of the special relationship that exists between an ActiveX document and its container. An ActiveX document is dependent on the host to display its menu; however, most containers have their own dedicated menus that are displayed. This can cause a situation where the document and the container are competing with each other to display the menus that each need. Ultimately the container makes the final decision on what menu to display, and unless there is no existing menu the ActiveX document will lose the battle.

When designing menu systems for ActiveX documents, you can provide guidelines for the container to follow should there ever be any question about what menu system to display. The process of adding menus to your ActiveX document is very similar to adding menus to traditional Visual Basic applications. You can use the menu editor to add menus to your ActiveX documents just as in a normal application. The one special item about ActiveX document menus is the `NegotiatePosition` property. This box allows you to select the position the menu will have in the container. `NegotiatePosition` must be set to reflect the relative position of the document menu to the container menu. The valid choices for the `NegotiatePosition` property are as follows:

- Left—The menu will appear leftmost on the menu bar of the ActiveX documents container.

- Right—The menu will merge the document menu with the container's rightmost menu. As a result of this merging, any Help menu options for the document will be displayed as a submenu option of the container's Help menu.

- Middle—The menu will be to the right of any menus set to display in the leftmost position.

- None—The menu is not displayed in the container.

> **TIP**
>
> It is generally a good idea not to include a File menu in an ActiveX document. The container will usually supply this menu.

To get a better understanding of how menus work with ActiveX documents, create a sample project. For your sample project you will use the registration form you created earlier. Follow these steps to create the sample project:

1. Open the Register project.

2. Choose the Menu Editor menu option from the Tools menu.

3. Create a new menu option with the caption of &Help and the name of `mnuHelp`.

4. In the NegotiatePosition box, select the 3-Right option.

5. Add the menu and submenu options as shown in Table 19.3 and Figure 19.4.

19

CREATING ACTIVEX DOCUMENTS

TABLE 19.3. MENU AND SUBMENU OPTIONS FOR THE SAMPLE PROJECT

Caption	Name	Level	NegotiatePostion
About Register	mnuAbout	Sub	0-None
&Left Option	mnuLeft	Main	1-Left
&Middle Option	mnuMiddle	Main	2-Middle

FIGURE 19.4.

The Menu Editor allows you to customize how menus are viewed in a container.

6. Run the application by pressing F5 or the Start menu option. Internet Explorer should now display the sample project as shown in Figure 19.5.

FIGURE 19.5.

Internet Explorer now has two additional menus and a new submenu option.

Adding Forms and Documents to ActiveX Documents

As in most applications, the space available on any one form is limited. In most applications there will be secondary forms to collect and display additional information. In the sample application you created only one UserDocument. However, you are not limited to only one document. You can create any number of documents and navigate between them. You also have the ability to include standard forms in your ActiveX document applications. This section will quickly examine what it takes to add additional documents and forms to your ActiveX document application.

Adding Additional Documents

The process of adding additional documents is straightforward; however, the methods used for communication between these documents deserves some discussion. In addition, the UserDocument object does not support some standard methods available to forms such as Load, Unload, Show, and Hide.

To add an additional document to your project, choose the Add User Document item from the Project menu. This places a new document in your project, under the UserDocuments folder. After you have added this new document, it is a good idea to save it with a descriptive name as part of your project. After you have added the document, you are free to create whatever interface you desire.

As mentioned earlier, UserDocument does not support certain methods. One of these, the Show method, is typically used to display a form in a standard application. To address this problem the UserDocument object supports the use of the NavigateTo method of the Hyperlink object. This method allows you to specify a file path or URL where the target ActiveX document page is located. This method provides for a convenient way to create applications that are just as at home on the Internet as they are on the desktop. A typical use of the NavigateTo method is shown in the following few lines of code:

```
Private Sub cmdConfirm_Click()
    Hyperlink.NavigateTo App.Path & "\confdoc.vbd"
End Sub
```

In the sample code, the NavigateTo method is passed in the relative path of the ActiveX document (confdoc.vbd). The use of the App.Path property allows the document to be accessed from the current directory. In cases where files are located over a network the Universal Naming Convention (UNC) is supported. Figures 19.6 and 19.7 show two pages of an ActiveX document application that are displayed in the browser. You can access the second document by clicking on the Confirm button located on the first

19

CREATING
ACTIVEX
DOCUMENTS

document. The code to do this is placed in the click event of the command button. Listing 19.2 shows the code used to navigate from the first document to the second and back again.

LISTING 19.2.   REGISTER.DOB—CODE REQUIRED TO NAVIGATE BETWEEN FORMS

```
Private Sub cmdConfirm_Click()
    Hyperlink.NavigateTo App.Path & "\confdoc.vbd"

End


Sub Private Sub cmdGoBack_Click()
    Hyperlink.NavigateTo App.Path & "\regisdoc.vbd"

End Sub
```

FIGURE 19.6.

The Registration document is the first document of a multiple document application.

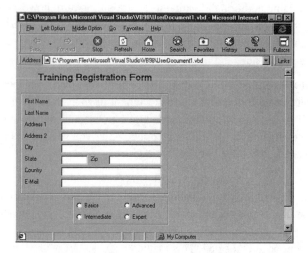

When you launched the Confirmation document in the application, Internet Explorer enabled its Back button. This is another way ActiveX documents can be navigated. However, it is not good design to depend on the browser to provide a method of navigating your documents. For this reason you should always use the NavigateTo method to provide navigational ability. Another reason for not using the browser's Back button is that the first document might not always be the previous document in the history list. Also, if the first document has scrolled out of the history list, the NavigateTo method is the only way to get to the document again.

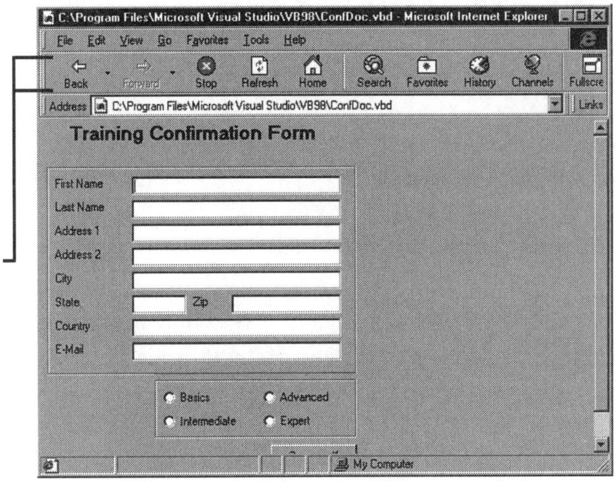

FIGURE 19.7.

The Confirmation document is the second document of a multiple document application.

Training Confirmation Form

First Name

Last Name

Address 1

Address 2

City

State   Zip

Country

E-Mail

○ Basics   ○ Advanced

○ Intermediate ○ Expert

Back button is enabled

In addition to working with more than one document, you can work with standard forms in your ActiveX document applications. To use a form in a project, you create it the same way you would create a form for a standard project—draw the interface of the form and write the code to perform tasks. To display the form from your document, use the Show method. Then, to remove the form, use the Unload statement.

Although forms can be part of your application, they are not handled the same way as documents. Forms are not contained within the application that contains the ActiveX document. They are independent of the container. Figure 19.8 shows an ActiveX document with an About form dialog box displayed.

Deploying an ActiveX Document in Internet Explorer

The process of linking an ActiveX document with an HTML page involves a little bit of coding in VBScript and HTML. The following steps show how this is accomplished:

1. The OBJECT tag is placed on a separate HTML page because the ActiveX document will replace the HTML page in IE. When clicked, this page will disappear when the ActiveX document is loaded. The code in Listing 19.3 will create a hyperlink from the calling page to the ActiveX document.

2. Listing 19.4 shows the code necessary to download and register the ActiveX document in the registry.

FIGURE 19.8.

Forms are outside the boundaries of the document container.

3. The code in Listing 19.5 provides a way for IE to navigate to the requested .vbd file. This example assumes that the .vbd file will reside in the same folder as the .htm file.

LISTING 19.3. Register.HTM—CODE REQUIRED TO CREATE A HYPERLINK TO THE ACTIVEX DOCUMENT

```
<a href="RegisDoc.htm">Register for a Class</a>
```

LISTING 19.4. Register.HTM—CODE REQUIRED TO DOWNLOAD AND REGISTER AN ACTIVEX DOCUMENT

```
<OBJECT
    classid="clsid:2F330484-1C7D-11D0-1233-00A0C70385C4"
    codebase="RegisDoc.cab#version=1,0,0,0">
</OBJECT>
```

LISTING 19.5. Register.HTM—CODE REQUIRED TO NAVIGATE TO THE REQUESTED .VBD FILE

```
<SCRIPT LANGUAGE="VBScript">
Sub Window_OnLoad
    Document.Open
    Document.Write "<FRAMESET>"
    Document.Write "<FRAME SRC=""RegisDoc.vbd"">"
    Document.Write "</FRAMESET>"
    Document.Close
End Sub
</SCRIPT>
```

Using the ActiveX Document Migration Wizard

Creating an ActiveX document from scratch can be a rewarding experience. Before you go out and create a new suite of ActiveX documents from scratch, you should look at the ActiveX Document Migration Wizard.

The ActiveX Document Migration Wizard helps convert the forms and make up existing applications in ActiveX documents. For developers who have a large library of code and applications, this can result in a great deal of time savings. Before you convert all your existing Visual Basic applications, you should know that the Wizard is designed to provide the rough framework only; it is not designed to create entire robust applications. The following steps outline the operations the ActiveX Document Migration Wizard performs when converting an application.

- The Wizard copies the properties of the form object to a new `UserDocument` object.
- The Wizard copies any menu items from the source form to the new `UserDocument`.
- All controls from the source form are copied to their matching position on the `UserDocument` object. The only exceptions to this are any OLE and embedded OLE controls, which are not copied.
- All code from the source form event procedures is copied to corresponding procedures in the `UserDocument`.
- Any unsupported code is commented out. This includes code that includes the `Load`, `Unload`, and `End` statements.

The ActiveX Document Migration Wizard is an excellent tool to do the grunt work required to migrate to a `UserDocument` object. However, there is some detail work that needs to be done by you—the developer—before distribution can take place.

The first thing you need to do is to convert the code in the unsupported events to those events supported by the `UserDocument` object. If you have code in the `Load` and `Unload` events, you will want to move it to the `Initialize` and `Terminate` events.

Next, you should make sure that you are not referencing any objects that no longer exist. You should make sure that your code does not reference any forms by name (for instance, "frmSales").

Running the ActiveX Document Migration Wizard

The ActiveX Document Migration Wizard must be available to the Visual Basic IDE. If you have not already done so, you can make the Wizard available by selecting it from the Add-In Manager dialog box, which is accessible by choosing the Add-In Manager item from the Add-Ins menu. After you have added the Wizard to your desktop, you can run it by choosing the ActiveX Document Migration Wizard item from the Add-Ins menu.

To begin the conversion process, the project whose forms you want to convert must be open. After you have opened the project, launch the ActiveX Document Migration Wizard. At this point you will be presented with a series of screens that will guide you through the conversion process. The first of these screens is introductory only, so click the Next button to continue.

The second screen of the Wizard, shown in Figure 19.9, includes a list box from which you can select the forms that you would like to convert. Any forms that have been defined for this project will be displayed in this list box. To select forms, simply click in the check box next to the name of the form. When you have made all your selections, click the Next button to continue.

The Options page of the ActiveX Document Migration Wizard, shown in Figure 19.10, lets you control how the Wizard will process the forms you have selected. The three

FIGURE 19.9.

You can select multiple forms in the list box.

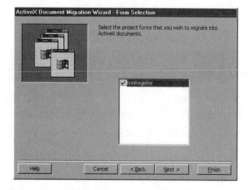

options enable you to do the following:

- Choose to comment out invalid code. This option will comment out statements such as Load, Unload, or End that are not supported by ActiveX documents.

- Remove original forms after conversion. This option will remove the forms from the current project after the conversion is made. Typically, you will *not* want to check this option because you will want your original project intact.

- Choose whether to convert your project to an ActiveX EXE or ActiveX DLL project. The option defaults to ActiveX EXE. (ActiveX DLLs are used for creating shared components rather than applications.)

After making your choices, click the Next button to continue. The last page of the Wizard allows you to view a summary report that describes the Wizard's actions. After making your selection, click the Finish button to begin the conversion. The summary report is a valuable development tool because it provides you with information regarding the steps you need to complete. Figure 19.11 shows the summary report.

FIGURE 19.10.

Select the options that are appropriate to your needs.

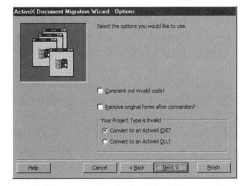

FIGURE 19.11.

The ActiveX Document Migration Wizard uses a summary report to guide you through the rest of the conversion process.

Viewing the Wizard's Work

When the ActiveX Document Migration Wizard has finished its work, it places the newly created `UserDocument` objects in the same project as the original forms. The document source files are stored in the same folder as the original form files and are given similar names, with the appropriate extension. For example, a form stored in the file `frmTest1.frm` creates a `UserDocument` stored in the file `docTest1.dob`. As previously stated, the controls of the form are copied to the `UserDocument` and their relative positions are preserved.

Also, as stated previously, most of the code from your original form is copied over to the UserDocument. Invalid code is commented out and identified by the ActiveX Document Migration Wizard. (This assumes that you chose to comment out invalid code on the Options page of the Wizard.) Figure 19.12 shows an example of this process.

19

CREATING
ACTIVEX
DOCUMENTS

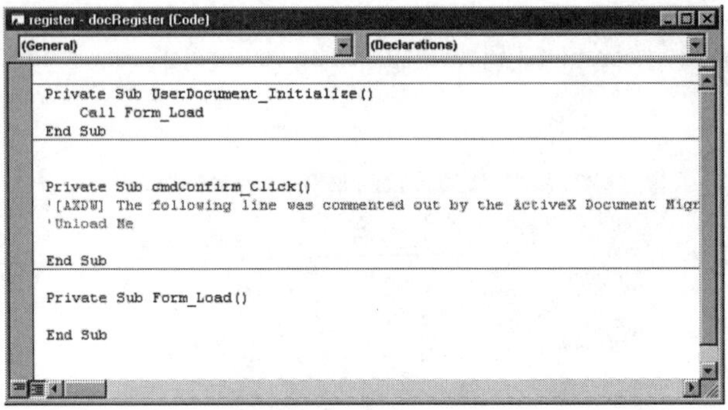

FIGURE 19.12.

Invalid code is identified by the [AXDW] mark in a comment statement.

```
register - docRegister [Code]
(General)                              (Declarations)

Private Sub UserDocument_Initialize()
    Call Form_Load
End Sub


Private Sub cmdConfirm_Click()
'[AXDW] The following line was commented out by the ActiveX Document Migr
'Unload Me

End Sub

Private Sub Form_Load()

End Sub
```

Summary

Understanding how ActiveX documents can be used is the first step in creating Internet applications quickly. The UserDocument object provides you with the ability to create any number of document objects that can be linked via classes in your applications. This method of code reuse guarantees that your Internet development efforts are rewarded with applications that are robust and that meet the needs of your users.

Creating DHTML Applications

by Loren Eidahl

IN THIS CHAPTER

- An Overview of Dynamic HTML *454*
- Applications: What Are They? *455*
- Understanding the DTHML Object Model *457*
- Understanding the DHTML Project Type *463*
- Implementing DHTML Applications *473*

The Internet is growing at exponential rates every year. To support this meteoric growth the language of the Web, HTML has evolved far beyond it humble beginnings. Over the past 18 months, a number of new features have been added to HTML. Collectively, these new features are called Dynamic HTML. Some of these new features support the Netscape browser and some support Microsoft's browser. Whatever browser you choose to implement Dynamic HTML, one thing is certain. Web development will never be the same.

An Overview of Dynamic HTML

Excerpt from the Book of Browsers, circa 1997 AD.

The Holy Browser Wars:

In the beginning, there was HTML and it was named 1.0. And the people said it was good. The people loved HTML 1.0 and used it to fill their lives and Web pages with blinking text and colors. Life was good.

Then the lord of the browser decreed, "I will give the people more." The duke of windows also decreed, "I will give the people more." Thus began the Holy Browser Wars. Each side battled mightily for the right to have their browser used by the people. Once, twice, thrice they battled over land and sea. At the end of the third battle, the lord and the duke both declared victories; they had each given the people what they wanted.

The people chose sides and proclaimed, "We want more!"

The love of power and wealth caused greed to color the hearts of the lord and duke. So began the fourth battle of the browser wars...

When HTML was first introduced, the combination of hypertext linked documents with images was intoxicating. This new form of communication created a wave of technological advancements that revolutionized communication as we know it. This also had the added affect of guaranteeing the success of the Internet, which at that time was nothing more than a way for people in academic institutions to exchange information. HTML effectively gave everyone the ability to express themselves in ways they never imagined, as well as provided everyone with the ability to reach people all over the globe.

Over the years, as our experience with HTML and the Internet progressed, we pushed the limits of HTML. One hurdle that we could not quite get over was the fact that HTML pages were static documents. To add any kind of movement or animation to an HTML document, it was necessary to incorporate some embedded components, such as Java applets or ActiveX controls. This provided some quick relief from static pages, but still did not address the fundamental need. In response, Netscape and Microsoft both developed extensions to HTML that were designed to solve this problem. These various extensions have been collectively referred to as Dynamic HTML.

Unfortunately, Dynamic HTML (DHTML) is still not quite a standard; both Netscape and Microsoft have released versions that are incompatible with each other. The World Wide Web consortium (W3) has also released what it defines to be Dynamic HTML. Expectedly, their definition combines elements from both Microsoft and Netscape's implementations. The W3 view of Dynamic HTML can be found at the Web site `http://www.w3.org/DOM/`.

Unfortunately, the W3 is still a ways away from codifying what Dynamic HTML is. Until such time, Microsoft and Netscape will continue on two separate paths. The only thing that will determine the outcome of this battle is the camp in which the Web developers and members of the Internet community feel the most comfortable.

DHTML Applications: What Are They?

In its most basic form, a Dynamic HTML application is a combination of Dynamic HTML pages and compiled Visual Basic code designed to process user-initiated events. This application is usually an interactive application that is designed to perform a specific task or process, such as inventory control or creating a purchase order. The application uses the browser on the client machine to respond to actions such as clicking the mouse, dragging and dropping items, and general text entry.

A Dynamic HTML application can be as simple as a single HTML form, or as complicated as an entire corporate intranet. Ideally, a Dynamic HTML application is an application that enables users to interact and control the application through a browser. A Dynamic HTML application can connect to a database and retrieve data specific to each user based on user actions, such as clicking the mouse or selecting controls in a particular order.

In the past, this type of interaction with the user required some level of CGI scripting or other types of server-side support. A DHTML application uses Visual Basic code and Internet Explorer 4.01 or greater to perform those tasks on the client side, although some applications might make calls to the server. This shift can have profound effects on the types of applications that can be created. No longer does the server have to be bogged down in the process of validating requests from every client. Performing the bulk of the work on the client (browser) frees up the server making the applications run quicker.

In an intranet, implementation DHTML applications provide a number of key benefits, the most important of which are the speed at which the application runs and the security of sensitive information. Because Visual Basic code is used to create the underlying processes, you have complete control over what information is passed to another client or to the server.

The following lists a few of the advantages of creating DHTML applications.

- Server Load Reduction—In traditional applications that rely upon CGI to perform form and data validation, each request must be routed to the Web server where it can be processed. Applications created in DHTML do not need to use the server for form validation. Each request made by the client skips being routed to the Web server, therefore, speeding up the server and saving resources.

- Faster Response Time—In a DTHML page, layout changes and code processing can be accomplished without refreshing the page from the server. In a standard Web page, changes to the page require that the page be refreshed from the server

- Dynamic Interaction—HTML elements can be directly controlled by Visual Basic code that create new versions of Web pages on-the-fly.

- State Management—DHTML can pass state information between pages. This eliminates the need for cookies, which have been the traditional answer to HTML lack-of-state support.

- Offline capability—DHTML applications enable users to make updates and changes while they are online. When users are offline, the application can be still be used through the user's cache.

- Code Security—In a traditional HTML page, any embedded JavaScript or VBScript can be easily downloaded or changed. This can lead to a potential security risk and a lot of development effort given away for free. In a DHTML application, the underlying Visual Basic code is complied and is totally separate from the HTML page. This level of separation provides a high level of security and guarantees that your code will not find its way into someone else's Web page.

> **NOTE**
>
> To create Dynamic HTML applications with Visual Basic, the client machines need to have Internet Explorer 4.01 installed. DHTML applications impose no specific server-side requirements, however.

Understanding the DHTML Object Model

Before DHTML, accessing specific element information in a traditional HTML page was difficult at best. The object model exposed only a limited number of properties and any HTML elements exposed were mainly form elements.

With the introduction of the Dynamic HTML object model, all that changed. The object model exposes every tag, as well as the contents of HTML container tags. In addition, each element is now available as an object that possesses its own attributes, properties, events, and methods. This means that you can write applications that change the characteristics of the `<td>` tag or the `<P>` tag, as well as the contents with just a few lines of code. This capability enables you to create applications that dynamically change the layout, position, and attributes of every element and container on your HTML page through Visual Basic code.

The document object model shown in Figure 20.1 exposes user actions, such as mouse clicks and keyboard activity as events, enabling you to create event handlers in Visual Basic. These event handlers can simply collect the data or they can intercept the data and replace it with a different value. For example, you could create an event handler on the mouse that trapped for the double-click event and displayed a specialized menu. This menu could be coded to enable the user to custom configure various elements on the Web page.

Dynamic HTML Objects

The DHTML object model contains a number of objects that that can be accessed through Visual Basic code as shown in Tables 20.1 and 20.2.

Table 20.1.   PRIMARY DHTML OBJECTS.

Object	Description
BaseWindow	Represents an instance of the browser. This object is also used to display the Document object
Document	Represents the HTML page currently viewed in the browser

FIGURE 20.1

The BaseWindow object corresponds to the topmost window object in the IE 4 DHTML object model.

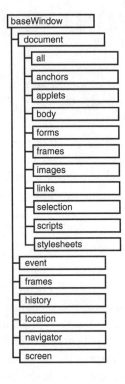

TABLE 20.2. SECONDARY DHTML OBJECTS.

Object	Description
All	Provides access to the HTML tags that are part of the document.
Applets	Contains information about any Java applets.
Forms	This object can actually be a compilation of a number of objects relating to the HTML form. There is only one form object for each HTML page.
Frames	A collection of window objects, one for each separate frame in the current window.
Images	A collection that contains one element for each image in the document.
Links	A collection of links referenced in the current document.
Selection	Represents the current active selection.
Scripts	A collection of all of the script elements within the document.
Stylesheets	A collection of the style sheets attached to the current document.
Event	Maintains the state of events occurring within the browser.

TABLE 20.2. CONTINUED

Object	Description
History	Maintains a list of the most recently visited URLs.
Location	Maintains information on the current URL.
Navigator	Maintains information specific to the browser.

Dynamic HTML Events

The majority of the events in DHTML are similar to the events in Visual Basic; therefore, the learning curve needed to use the events in DHTML should be reasonably small. The reason is that most of the events in the DHTML object model mimic those in Visual Basic.

> **TIP**
>
> All event names in Dynamic HTML have the word "on" as a prefix, as in onkeydown and onhelp. This prefix makes them easy to locate when looking them up in source code or help files.

Keyboard Events

One of the new features brought about by Internet Explorer 4.x support of DHTML is keyboard events. The keyboard events supported by DTHML and Visual Basic are very closely matched as described in the following list:

- onkeydown—This event is triggered when a key is pressed. This event will return the number of the keycode for the key pressed. An event handler can be coded to watch for this event and return a different value to override the original keystroke.

  Visual Basic equivalent: keydown

- onkeyup—This event is triggered when a user releases a pressed key. An event handler can be assigned to this key to intercept, override, and/or nullify the actual key pressed.

  Visual Basic equivalent: keyup

- onkeypress—This event is triggered for a valid key press. An event handler can be assigned to this key to intercept, override, and/or nullify the actual key pressed.

  Visual Basic equivalent: keypress

- onhelp—This event is triggered when the user presses the F1 key or clicks the help button on Internet Explorer.

   Visual Basic equivalent: n/a

The keycode property of DHTML event object contains the unicode keycode for any keyboard event that occurs. This value can be used to change the key associated to the event by changing the value of the keycode property or by returning an integer value. The event can be canceled by returning a zero or false.

Mouse Events

Mouse events in DHTML and Visual Basic are very similar. In both cases, they are triggered by some type of action from the mouse. The following list describes the DHTML events and their Visual Basic counterparts:

- onclick—This event is triggered when the user presses and releases the left mouse button on an element. It can also occur when the user presses Enter on a button or any element that can receive focus.

   Visual Basic equivalent: click

- ondbclick—This event is triggered when the user clicks twice on an object.

   Visual Basic equivalent: doubleclick

- onmouseout—This event is triggered when a user moves the mouse out of a given element.

   Visual Basic Equivalent: n/a

- onmousedown—This event is triggered when a user presses the mouse button.

   Visual Basic Equivalent: mousedown

- onmouseup—This event is triggered when a user releases a pressed mouse button.

   Visual Basic Equivalent: mouseup

- onmousemove—This event is triggered when the mouse is moved.

   Visual Basic equivalent: mousemove

- onmouseover—This event is triggered when the mouse is moved into an object. It occurs only when the mouse is first moved into the object.

   Visual Basic equivalent: n/a

When the mouse moves the pointer into an object, the following events occur in order:

1. onmousemove

2. onmouseover

3. onmouseout

Focus and Selection Events

These events are used to track the cursor as it moves around the HTML document. They can be used with either form or non-form elements. The following list describes the events and their Visual Basic counterparts:

> **NOTE**
>
> Although the `focus` and `selection` events have similar counterparts in non-DHTML Visual Basic, they are handled differently.

- `onfocus`—This event is triggered when the mouse moves into an element capable of receiving input. An example might be a button, frame, form element, or another application on the desktop.

  Visual Basic equivalent: `gotfocus`

- `onblur`—This event is triggered when the user moves the mouse off of an element that is capable of receiving input. An example might be a button, frame, form element, or another application on the desktop.

  Visual Basic equivalent: `lostfocus`

- `onselectstart`—This event is triggered when a selection if first initiated, such as when a user clicks a character in a document.

  Visual Basic equivalent: `selchange`

- `onselect`—This event is triggered when the user changes the selection, such as moving the mouse over characters in a document while holding the mouse button down.

  Visual Basic equivalent: `selchange`

- `ondragstart`—This event is triggered when the user begins a drag selection.

  Visual Basic equivalents: `dragdrop, dragover`

- `onchange`—This event is triggered when a user uses the Tab key or Enter key to move off the element. In Visual Basic, the `change` event is triggered whenever an action takes place in the control.

  Visual Basic equivalent: `change`

Page Events

The following list describes those Dynamic HTML events that can be used to control the loading and unloading of documents in a Web browser. Their Visual Basic equivalents are provided:

- onload—This event is triggered after the document is loaded and all associated page elements are downloaded. It is typically used to monitor the status of the HTML page; however, it can be used with images, RealAudio, or any other Web-supported object loaded with the HTML document.

  Visual Basic equivalent: load

- onunload—This event is triggered immediately before the current page is unloaded.

  Visual Basic equivalent: unload

- onready—This event is triggered as soon as the page can be interacted with by the user, such as by scrolling or clicking elements.

  Visual Basic equivalent: initialize

- onbeforeunload—This event is triggered before an HTML document is unloaded when navigating to another document. An event handler can be used to intercept this event so that a user has the ability to change his or her mind and remain on the current page.

  Visual Basic equivalent: n/a

Other Events

The following list describes those Dynamic HTML events that don't lend themselves to a specific category. Their Visual Basic counterparts are also listed:

- onerror—This event is triggered if an error occurs while loading a document, image, form element, or script. Error messages can be suppressed by setting the onerror attribute of the element to "null."

  Visual Basic equivalent: error

- onresize—This event is triggered when an object it is attached to is resized. Code does not need to be written to handle the resizing of the elements on a page, as you would do in Visual Basic.

  Visual Basic equivalent: resize

- onscroll—This event is triggered when the scroll box for the page or element is repositioned, such as in a resize.

  Visual Basic equivalent: scroll

DHTML Form Events

The following list includes those Dynamic HTML events for which there is no equivalent Visual Basic event:

- `onabort`—This event is triggered when the user aborts the download process by pressing the Stop button on the browser.

- `onreset`—This event is triggered when the Refresh button on the browser is pressed.

- `onsubmit`—This event is triggered when the user selects the Submit button on a form. An event handler can be attached to this event on the client side to validate data before it is processed by the server.

- `onfilterchange`—This event is triggered when a filter changes state or completes a transition from one state to another.

- `onbeforeunload`—This event is triggered before an HTML document is unloaded when navigating to another document. An event handler can be used to intercept this event so that a user has the ability to change his mind and remain on the current page.

- `onhelp`—This event is triggered when the user presses the F1 key or clicks the Help button on Internet Explorer.

- `onmouseout`—This event is triggered when a user moves the mouse out of a given element.

- `onmouseover`—This event is triggered when the mouse is moved into an object. It occurs only when the mouse is first moved into the object.

Understanding the DHTML Project Type

Now that we have covered what Dynamic HTML and Dynamic HTML applications are, let's take a look at what it takes to actually create a DHTML application. Visual Basic 6 supplies a template project type that makes the creation of DHTML projects easy. This template (shown in Figure 20.2) creates a project that includes a module and a designer.

FIGURE 20.2.
The DHTML Project Template.

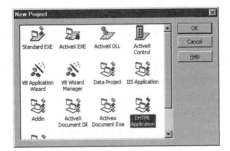

The module contains the code to use Internet Explorer's property bag object to maintain state from one DHTML page to another DHTML page. The Page Designer enables you to create the pages that will comprise the interface to your application.

Using the Page Designer

The page designer's primary purpose is to act as an interface for your DHTML application development efforts. The page designer provides you with a highly specialized IDE from which DHTML applications are launched and saved. The page designer provides you with the ability to create your own HTML pages or to import pre-existing pages into the designer. If you use the designer to create your HTML pages, any required code will be automatically generated by the designer. The page designer is shown in Figure 20.3.

FIGURE 20.3.
The Page Designer.

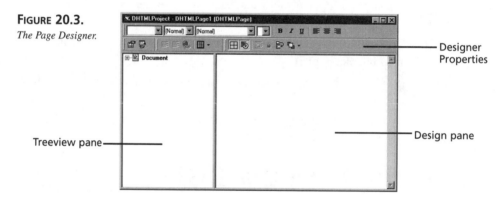

The module contains the code to use Internet Explorer's property bag object to maintain

Designing Pages for DHTML

Creating pages for DHTML applications in Visual Basic 6 can be accomplished in one of the following ways:

- Pages can be created from scratch by adding the HTML elements from the toolbox in VB6 to the page designer.

- Pages can be created in an external HTML editor.

- Pages can be created by using a combination of these methods.

Using the designer in Visual Basic to create pages is simply a matter of adding the various elements from the toolbox and positioning them to create the desired page. This method is useful if your goal is to create a page relatively quickly for prototyping purposes or really simple applications. Using Visual Basic to create your pages isolates you from having to concern yourself with knowing any of the underlying HTML tags and attributes of the various elements.

If your goal is to have maximum control over the code, then creating your HTML files in an external editor and importing them into Visual Basic is the desired alternative. This approach provides you with many benefits. Some of these benefits include the following:

- Ability to use HTML editor of your choice.
- Graphics can be created externally by you or a graphics designer.
- Version Control programs such as Microsoft's Visual Source Safe (VSS) can be used more effectively.
- Ability to use portions of the HTML file in similar non DHTML projects.
- Complete control of layout and content.

Using External Pages with the Page Designer

The page designer enables you to import pre-existing HTML pages into your DHTML application, which enables you to have greater control over the complexity of the page. External HTML files that are imported into designer enable you to access and modify the HTML code whereas pages created in the designer do not.

To import an external HTML page into the designer, carry out the following steps:

1. Select the desired HTML file to import. For this example, the HTML page shown in Figure 20.4 will be used.

FIGURE 20.4.

The HTML page to be imported.

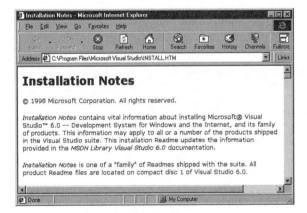

2. If necessary, add a new designer to your project. This is done by selecting the Add DHTML Page menu option from the Project menu.
3. Open up the DHTML Properties dialog box and select the Save HTML in an External File option.
4. Click the Open button and select the name and location of the desired HTML file you want to import and click OK. This is shown in Figure 20.5.

FIGURE 20.5.

The dialog box enables you to create a new HTML file or use an existing one.

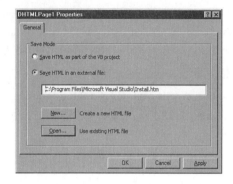

5. The file loads when you close the dialog box, and is displayed in the designer window as shown in Figure 20.6.

FIGURE 20.6.

The imported HTML page in the designer.

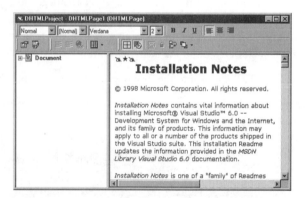

> **NOTE**
>
> There is a one-to-one match between DHTML pages and designers. For every new DHTML page that you want to add to your project, you must add a corresponding designer.

When the designer loads the page, it checks to see what elements are on the page. It then compiles a list of these elements and displays them in the left (treeview) pane of the designer.

After you have successfully imported the HTML page, you can make any modifications that you like. Modification might include the addition of elements from the toolbox or adjusting the properties of the existing elements within the page.

Creating New Pages in the Page Designer

The DHTML Page Designer also enables you to create HTML pages in Visual Basic. The designer utilizes an interface that enables you to draw the controls on a page without the need to create HTML code. The Page Designer enables you to arrange the controls on the form and set their properties. The code that Visual Basic generates for each can be stored in an external HTML file or within the designer.

Creating pages using the designer is quick; however, this speed comes at the price of flexibility. The Page Designer is ideal for those quick user interfaces or as a method of prototyping an interface. The designer cannot handle the more advanced HTML layout options that are required for production-level applications. Even with this apparent drawback, the designer is an excellent tool for creating simple interfaces very quickly.

The designer supports a number of traditional HTML elements to aid you in the designing of your forms. Any controls that are intrinsic to Visual Basic cannot be used—only those controls that appear in the HTML tab in the Toolbox, as shown in Figure 20.7. In addition to the HTML controls contained in the Toolbox, the designer also enables you to add ActiveX controls to your pages.

The following is a list of the HTML controls that are supported by the designer:

- Button
- SubmitButton
- ResetButton
- TextField
- TextArea
- PasswordField
- Option
- CheckBox
- Select
- Image
- Hyperlink
- HorizontalRule
- FileUpload
- HiddenField
- InputImage
- List

FIGURE 20.7.

HTML controls in the toolbox.

The HTML tab

To create a new page using the Page Designer, perform the following steps:

1. Start a new DHTML project in VB6.
2. Open the Page Designer by clicking the Designers folder in the project window and select the DTHMLPage1 item. This is shown in Figure 20.8.

FIGURE 20.8.

The Designers folder contains one designer for each HTML page in the application.

3. Click the desired control in the Toolbox. Draw the desired control in the right pane of the designer.
4. Set properties for the control by clicking the control and changing the appropriate property in the properties window. The properties window can be made visible by selecting View, Properties Window. This is shown in Figure 20.9.
5. Repeat steps 3 and 4 for each element to be placed on the form.
6. Press F5 to run the application. The completed form is displayed in the browser as shown in Figure 20.10.

FIGURE 20.9.
Each control needs to have an ID.

FIGURE 20.10.
A completed form in the browser.

20

CREATING
DHTML
APPLICATIONS

TIP

To manipulate controls that appear as invisible in the designer, select the control in the Treeview pane.

NOTE

There is a one-to-one match between DHTML pages and designers. For every new DHTML page that you want to add to your project, you must add a corresponding designer.

Using DHTML to Maintain State

Whether you are creating a small Internet application or a large multisite, multilingual intranet, sooner or later you are going to have to pass data from one page to another page. In a normal application, this does not present any kind of mental dilemma for the developer; however, the Internet is vastly different. The reason is that the Internet is stateless. This simply means that the protocol that passes the requests from the client (Web browser) to the server is not able to store that information for later processing. This dilemma presents itself again in DHTML applications, in that the protocol is not capable of carrying any data between pages.

In order to pass information between pages another method had to be developed. In a DHTML application, the GetProperty and PutProperty functions are used to store data. These functions are also used to retrieve data, provided that the client (Web browser) is active. In Listing 20.1 you see the code that gets added to each DHTML application that is created from the DHTML application template.

> **NOTE**
>
> The GetProperty and the PutProperty are both methods of the IE4.x property bag. They can be used in either DHTML applications or Active Server Pages (ASP).

LISTING 20.1. modDHTML.bas—GENERATED CODE TO MAINTAIN STATE USING THE GetProperty AND PutProperty.

```
'The following code allows you to use the Web browser's property bag
'    to persist information across different DHTML pages.
Public objWebBrowser As WebBrowser

'PutProperty: Store information in the Property bag by calling this
'             function.  The required inputs are the named Property
'             and the value of the property you would like to store.
'
Public Sub PutProperty(strName As String, vntValue As Variant)

    'Check whether we have an instance of the browser.
    If objWebBrowser Is Nothing Then Set objWebBrowser = New WebBrowser

    'Call the browser's PutProperty method to store the value.
    objWebBrowser.PutProperty strName, vntValue

End Sub
```

```
'GetProperty: Retrieve information from the Property bag by calling this
'            function.  The required input is the named Property,
'            and the return value of the function is the current value
'            of the property.
'
Public Function GetProperty(strName As String) As Variant

    'Check whether we have an instance of the browser.
    If objWebBrowser Is Nothing Then Set objWebBrowser = New WebBrowser

    'Call the browser's GetProperty method to retrieve the value.
    GetProperty = objWebBrowser.GetProperty(strName)

End Function
```

To store information, the `PutProperty` is used; to retrieve information, the `GetProperty` is used.

To create the DHTML state example, perform the following steps.

1. Begin a new DHTML project.

2. Add a second designer to the project.

3. In the first designer, create the form as shown in Figure 20.11. The form should contain a button and a text field.

FIGURE 20.11.

A cookie is created that stores the value using the `PutProperty`.

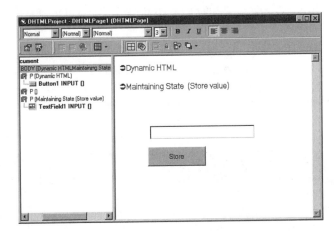

4. Add the code in Listing 20.2 to the `onclick` event of the Store button.

5. Create the page shown in Figure 20.12 in the second designer. The form should contain a button and a text field.

FIGURE 20.12.

The form returns the value from the cookie using the GetProperty.

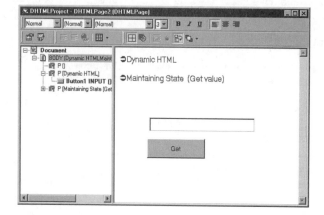

6. Add the code in Listing 20.3 to the `onclick` event of the Get button.

7. Press F5 to run the application.

After the application is running, enter a value in the text box on the Store form and press the button. Although it might have appeared as though nothing happened, the value that you entered was actually stored in the `PutProperty` function as shown in Listing 20.2. The use of the `PutProperty` is roughly analogous to the action that takes place in a more traditional "cookie." Now to retrieve the value, change the URL so that it now refers to `\DHTML_Project\DHTML_Page2.html`

This change is needed so as to load the second page of the sample. The use of the `GetProperty` to load the data is shown in Listing 20.3. After the Get page is loaded, press the button. The text box should now contain the value that originated in the Store page.

TIP

If you need to create a number of forms that are very similar, you can select all of the elements on one form, copy them to the Clipboard, and paste them on a new form. This method retains all of the property settings and saves you time.

LISTING 20.2. modDHTML.bas—CODE REQUIRED TO LOAD THE COOKIE USING THE PutProperty FUNCTION.

```
Private Function Store_onclick() As Boolean
PutProperty BaseWindow.Document, "Property1", TextField1.Value
End Function
```

LISTING 20.3. modDHTML.bas—CODE REQUIRED TO EXTRACT THE VALUE FROM THE COOKIE USING THE GetProperty FUNCTION.

```
Private Function Get_onclick() As Boolean
TextField1.Value = "The value of the property is " & _
    GetProperty(BaseWindow.Document, "Property1")
End Function
```

In the previous example, there was no easy way to navigate from the Store page to the Get page, other than manually changing the URL. This problem is easily solved with a line of code that calls the navigate method of the BaseWindow object. The following line of code is an example;

```
BaseWindow.navigate "Project1.DHTMLPage2.html"
```

This code segment assumes that there is a compiled page called Project1.DHTMLPage2.html. This line of code could be called from a click event from an element on the page or after specific user-supplied criteria have been met.

Implementing DHTML Applications

The time has come for you to prepare your DHTML application for release to the masses. One nagging question remains: Is your application ready?

This question can sometime cause the most experienced developer to lose sleep and gain a few gray hairs. Visual Basic takes the worry out of deploying your application in a number of different ways. First, Visual Basic includes a rich tool set designed to aid in everything from the debugging process up to the point at which the application is installed on the client. Second, this tool set operates the same for both ActiveX controls and for DHTML applications, making for a smooth transition and a very small learning curve. The following list describes at a high level the processes involved in taking an application from the Visual Basic IDE to the Client's machine:

- Debug application using Visual Basic's Debugger
- Compile application using the Make utility

- Use the Package and Deployment Wizard to create .cab files containing all necessary files
- Digitally sign your application
- Use the Package and Deployment Wizard to deploy your application to the desired Web server
- Copy any supporting files to the necessary folder on the Web server

> **NOTE**
>
> Visual Basic does not have any built-in facility to digitally sign files. The ActiveX SDK available from Microsoft's Web site provides all of the necessary tools except for the private key. The private key needs to be applied for from a certificate authority such as VeriSign. VeriSign can be reached at http://www.verisign.com/.

In this section, you look at what it takes to deploy a DHTML application.

Debugging DHTML Applications

The process required to debug an DHTML application is similar to that involving a standard Visual Basic application. In both cases, Visual Basic's built-in Debugger is pressed into service.

An additional tool to aid in the debugging process is the Debugging tab in the project's properties window. The debugging tab on the Project Properties dialog box, shown in Figure 20.13, enables you to control how the system will respond to you during the debugging process. On this tab you can set values that enable you to start a new instance of Internet Explorer or use an existing instance.

Compiling Your Application

Compiling a DHTML application and a standard application are both handled the same way—by choosing the Make menu option from the File menu. A DHTML application is in reality just a Visual Basic application with a DHTML designer.

When a DHTML application is compiled, Visual Basic creates a DLL that contains all of the designers and modules that comprise your application. Any secondary files such as HTML files, images, or AVI files are not compiled into the DLL and must be shipped as separate files.

FIGURE 20.13.

The Debugging tab enables you to select how the application will be started.

The file types listed in Table 20.3 are created when Visual Basic compiles a DHTML application.

TABLE 20.3. FILES TYPES CREATED WHEN COMPILING A DHTML APPLICATION.

File Type	Description
.mod	Visual Basic module. This contains all of the specific event code.
.dsr	Text file that contains the designer source code and references to the HTML pages contained therein.
.dsx	A binary file containing information about the designer.
.vbw	Contains layout information.
.vbp	Visual Basic project file.

> **NOTE**
>
> A DHTML application must be built as an inprocess component (DLL file).

When Visual Basic runs the completed application, a number of things happen behind the scenes. First, an <OBJECT> tag is inserted into the body of each HTML page. This provides a method to download the HTML page when the application is deployed. Second, a classID, a reference ID, and a <CODEBASE> are inserted in the <OBJECT> tag. These IDS are used to determine where the page resides in the registry, to determine where it resides in the DLL, and client's to instruct the browser where to find the page on the client's computer.

Deploying DHTML Applications

One of the exciting new features of Visual Basic 6 is the Package and Deployment Wizard. To say that this wizard is a replacement for the Setup Wizard found in Visual Basic 5 is comparable to saying that Visual Basic 6 is a replacement for Visual Basic 3 or GW-Basic.

The Package and Deployment Wizard enhances and extends the functionality found in the original Setup Wizard by adding special features for Web-based installations. Microsoft didn't forget about the desktop either, and now includes enhanced support for CAB files. The following are just a few of the new features that are part of the packaging portion of the Package and Deployment Wizard:

- You have the ability to create a group folders and choose an icon for the installation.
- You now have the ability to specify the file destination of each file that is part of the final project. For example, you can now create install scripts that install all of the databases into their own folders.
- You can choose what files are to be shared with other applications.
- You have the ability to create an install script that saves your preferences for a later use. This should save a lot of time on those multiple install jobs.
- Specific to the Internet additions, you now have the ability to select what components IE can download from a Web site. This enables you to write an install script that checks a specific URL or UNC for individual downloadable components. This alone could be worth the admission price for those intranet applications.
- The wizard enables you to create a detailed dependency file that can be used to check for upgraded files and resources.

The wizard also enables you to deploy your application or component to a specific Web server of a UNC folder. Some of the highlights of the deployment portion of the wizard are as follows:

- You can deploy applications to either a Web server using the WEBPOST method, or to a traditional UNC.
- You can select specific files to deploy.
- You have the ability to add additional files to the deployment group.
- The Deployment Wizard portion enables you to specify a specific Web server and the method of deployment. On my test machine, my options were FTP, HTTP, Microsoft Content Replication System, and FrontPage Extended Web.

- You have the ability to choose a specific folder on the server to post the files to. This works in conjunction with the ability to create a base folder on the development machine and have the application deployed to the same folder structure on the server.

The Package and Deployment Wizard makes extensive use of the CAB technology as well as Diamond Directive Files (DDF) files, Microsoft's compression technology. As you probably already know, cabinet files (CAB) are specially formatted files that contain ActiveX controls along with all of the necessary support files. These files contain information about the control and the necessary support files that tell the Web browser what files need to be downloaded. The Web browser takes the information from the cabinet file and compares it to the files already on the computer to determine whether any of the files need to be downloaded. This enables the Web browser to avoid downloading any unnecessary files.

Installing the Package and Deployment Wizard

To use the Package and Deployment Wizard, you will need to install it by using the Add-In Manager. To do this, select Add-Ins; then click the Add-In Manager. You will see a dialog box showing a list of the available add-ins. Highlight the Package and Deployment Wizard option and select the Load on Startup and the Loaded/Unloaded options, as shown in Figure 20.14. Close down the Add-In Manager window and the new wizard will be added to your list of available Add-Ins.

FIGURE 20.14.
The Visual Basic Add-In Manager enables you to add a number of different Add-Ins to your development environment.

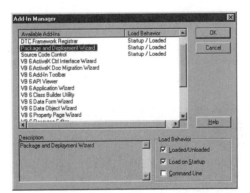

Using the Package and Deployment Wizard

The first thing that needs to be done is to open up the project file for the application. After you have loaded the project, select the Package and Deployment Wizard from the Add-Ins menu. The Package and Deployment Wizard's main screen will present three options from which you can choose, as shown in Figure 20.15.

FIGURE 20.15.

The Package and Deployment Wizard's main screen enables you to select the project you want to create a package for.

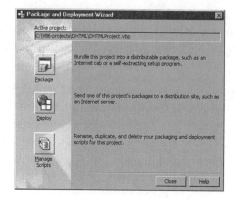

These three options—Package, Deploy, and Manage Scripts—enable you to create an install package, deploy a project to a server, and manage your package and deployment scripts. For the following example, you will need to select the first menu option Package. The next few sections describe the individual screens that you will use to enter the parameters to create the install package.

Package Type Dialog Box

Here is where you choose the type of package that you want to create. Your choices are as follows:

- Standard Setup Package
- Internet Package
- Dependency File

For this example, choose the Internet Package option. Your screen should now look like Figure 20.16. Choose Next to go to the next dialog box.

FIGURE 20.16.

The Dependency File option creates a file that contains information about all of the .dlls, .ocxs, and other resource files that your project needs.

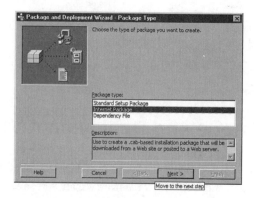

Package Folder Dialog Box

This dialog box enables you to enter the location of where you would like the final package to be assembled, as shown in Figure 20.17. Choose Next to go to the next dialog box.

FIGURE 20.17.
The Package Folder dialog box creates a default folder for the package in the folder that contains your project files.

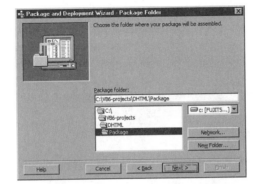

Included Files Dialog Box

The Include Files dialog box enables you to select what additional files are to be included in the package. For this example you can use the default file list provided, as shown in Figure 20.18.

The Package and Deployment Wizard analyzes your project and looks for any ActiveX controls that you might be using as server-side controls. If your control uses any server-side components, either as local or remote components, add them with this dialog box.

If your control is to be distributed to other developers for use in building Web pages, you need to include the Property Page DLL with your file distribution. This provides developers with the ability to specify property settings for the control in other, non–Visual Basic development environments. Choose Next to go to the next dialog box.

FIGURE 20.18.
You can add or remove files from the list by clicking the checkbox located next to the filename.

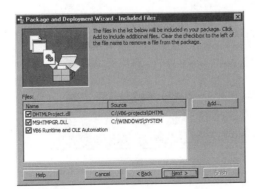

File Source Dialog Box

The File Source dialog box asks you to decide where you want to locate the runtime components of your applications, as seen in Figure 20.19. You can either select your own location on one of your own servers, or download runtime components from the Microsoft Web site. Specifying a location on an internal server might be better if you don't have a fast connection to the Internet. On the other hand, by specifying the Microsoft Web site at `http://www.microsoft.com/vbasic/icompdown`, you guarantee that your users always get the latest copies of the runtime components. Choose Next to go to the next dialog box.

FIGURE 20.19.

You can specify your own Web site to download the latest version of the files needed by the package.

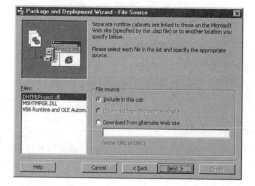

Safety Settings Dialog Box

The Safety Settings dialog box enables you to set the safety levels for each ActiveX control in your project. If your control is safe for initialization, check Safe for Initialization. If your control is safe for scripting, check Safe for Scripting, as shown in Figure 20.20. Click both of the safety selection boxes; then click Next to go to the next dialog box.

FIGURE 20.20.

By marking your control as safe for initialization and scripting, you are placing your guarantee in your control that it cannot harm the user's computer, even if being used in HTML documents that you did not build.

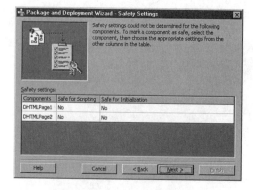

CHAPTER 20

481

The Finished! Dialog Box

If you would like to save the information that was collected by the wizard, you can do so now (see Figure 20.21). You will need to provide a script name only—the wizard places the script in the package folder in your project. At this point, you are prompted to enter the name of the script. Choose Finish to build the package and go to the next dialog box.

FIGURE 20.21.

If you need to make any changes to the wizard options, now is the time to do it.

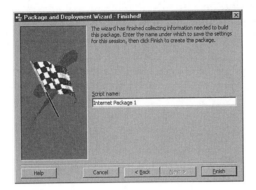

Packaging Report

The Packaging Report provides any last-minute information that you might need to know about the package just created. This is shown in Figure 20.22. Choose Close to go to the main menu of the Package and Deployment Wizard.

FIGURE 20.22.

The Packaging Report provides valuable information.

At this point, you would normally sign your files and use the Package and Deployment Wizard to deploy your application to the Web server.

Summary

Dynamic HTML is an excellent tool to create applications designed to run on intranets and even on the Internet. One of the best things about learning DHTML is that is opens up more doors for creative expression. Now, your favorite Visual Basic applications can have a Web front end with very little effort. Or, your favorite HTML applications can have the security that Visual Basic provides. Either way you look at it, one thing is for sure; DHTML has added an exciting and bold dimension to traditional application development.

Mail-Enabling Your Applications with MAPI

by Rob Thayer

IN THIS CHAPTER

- **Understanding the MAPI Specification** *484*

- **Using the MAPI Controls: MAPISession and MAPIMessages** *488*

- **Creating MAPI Programs with Visual Basic** *493*

As the use of intranets and the Internet becomes more common, application program-mers must learn to tap into the power of this new technology. In the past, standalone programs were the norm, but the next generation of applications will require the capabil-ity to communicate on a global scale. For example, a few years ago it was sufficient to design a program to monitor machines in a factory and produce reports concerning their efficiency. Today, that same program might be expected to send those reports automati-cally to the factory foreman or to other management personnel thousands of miles away. The easiest way to do that is through electronic mail (e-mail). And that's where MAPI comes in.

In a nutshell, MAPI (Mail Application Programming Interface) is a specification that defines a complete messaging subsystem. Primarily, it defines common interfaces by which mail-related components can interact. These components include service providers such as *message store providers* that can create, submit, and store mail mes-sages; *address book providers* that can maintain a database of message recipients; and *transport providers* that handle the actual transmission of messages. It may sound com-plicated, but it's not. This chapter provides you with a better understanding of what MAPI is and how it works. This chapter also shows how you can use MAPI to add elec-tronic messaging functionality to your Visual Basic programs.

Understanding the MAPI Specification

Microsoft created MAPI to establish a common interface for various mail-related com-ponents, including those developed by other vendors. Primarily, it allows client applica-tions (such as ones written in Visual Basic) to interact with service providers. In this context, *service providers* are programs that perform mail-related tasks. Three principal types of service providers are defined under MAPI: address book providers, message store providers, and transport providers. These provider types are discussed in more detail later, along with another important part of the MAPI system—the MAPI Spooler.

The MAPI specification uses a layered model (see Figure 21.1). At the top of the model are the client applications, which sometimes provide an interface that simplifies the use of e-mail messaging for end users. In other types of client applications, the messaging might be transparent to users.

The bottom layer of the model is the various service providers that furnish MAPI-compliant message services. It doesn't matter which programming language these com-ponents are written in as long as they "speak MAPI." Microsoft Exchange is a good example of a MAPI-compliant component because it acts as an address book provider and as a message store provider.

FIGURE 21.1.

The MAPI specification uses a layered model, with MAPI providing an interface between client applications and various service providers.

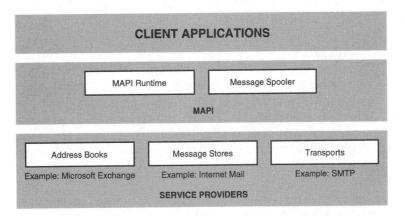

The MAPI Layered Model

> **NOTE**
>
> It's the job of the transport provider to translate messages into the different messaging system formats such as SMTP. These messaging systems are actually the lowest level in the MAPI model. But because this translation process is transparent to the MAPI programmer, it isn't discussed in this chapter.

Tying together the top and bottom layers of the model is MAPI itself, which consists of the MAPI runtime system (DLLs) and the Message Spooler. MAPI provides interfaces to the client applications and the service providers, acting as a middleman or interpreter so that the two can "talk together."

At a basic level, MAPI functions resemble the print spooler built into Windows 95 or Windows NT. When you're writing an application that prints a report, you don't have to worry about who manufactured the printer that will receive the report. That task is left to the Windows print spooler, which translates the report so that it will look fundamentally the same no matter what printer is being used. MAPI works the same way: It enables your application to send and receive e-mail messages no matter what transport provider your system uses (as long as the transport provider is MAPI-compliant). It also enables you to use the services of MAPI-compliant address book and message store providers.

> **NOTE**
>
> As an experienced Visual Basic programmer, you might be a little confused that MAPI stands for *Mail Application Programming Interface* because it doesn't function like the APIs you're used to. Under normal circumstances, an API consists of a related set of functions that can be called from within a VB program. Microsoft's first implementation of MAPI worked that way (that implementation is now referred to as *Simple MAPI*). Extended MAPI, which is used in VB6, doesn't work that way; instead, all MAPI services are accessed with two ActiveX controls (or COM objects). Like other ActiveX controls, they have events, methods, and properties. By responding to events, calling methods, and setting properties, much of MAPI's functionality is available to VB programmers.

MAPI Service Providers

MAPI service providers do the bulk of the work in the MAPI system. They also shield client application programmers from a great deal of additional coding, as you'll see later.

Although most programmers choose to use existing MAPI service providers such as Microsoft Exchange, it's possible to create your own custom service providers—doing so, though, can be difficult and requires a lower-level language such as C++. If you're interested in learning more about service provider creation, I recommend *Inside MAPI* by Microsoft Press.

Address Book Providers

Address book providers contain databases of addressing information for message recipients. These databases are organized into hierarchies, using *containers* that hold information for various recipients.

When a new message is created, it might be given an e-mail address such as jdoe@xyzco.com as its recipient. In that case, the address book provider is sidestepped, and the message is sent to its destination. If a literal name such as John Doe is given as the message's recipient, however, that name must be translated into a valid e-mail address. In that case, you use the address book provider to look up the literal name. If the name is found, the message is assigned an e-mail address, and it can continue on to the message store provider for delivery. If the name isn't found, a dialog box might appear that allows users to add the name (and a corresponding e-mail address) to their personal address book for later use.

Among other functions that improve the efficiency of e-mail messaging for end users, address books are also useful for creating distribution lists. A *distribution list* consists of one or more related e-mail addresses lumped together under a single name. When a message is addressed to that name, a copy is sent to each person in the distribution list. For example, business owners might want to send copies of their promotional newsletters to a hundred different subscribers each month. Rather than send 100 messages individually (a time-consuming chore), they can send the newsletter to a single address created as a distribution list. The address book provider does all the work and sends a copy of the message to each person on the list. By providing this kind of functionality, address book providers can be an important part of the MAPI system.

Note that on any given computer, more than one address book provider might be in use. MAPI merges all of them together, however, so that they appear as a single provider to the client application.

Message Store Providers

Message store providers maintain e-mail messages in some sort of database system, typically organized as a hierarchy that uses folders to group messages pertaining to a particular user or subject. Although the message store provider's code (in most cases, a DLL or OCX) is actually executed on the same machine as the client application that's using it, the message database itself can reside locally or on a network.

Message store providers also have another important function. They handle the transmission and receipt of e-mail messages, working closely with the system's transport provider. The following section discusses this in more detail, but keep in mind that it's through the message store provider that your client application will send outgoing messages and receive incoming messages.

Examples of message store providers include Microsoft Exchange, Lotus's cc:Mail, and Hewlett-Packard's OpenMAIL, although many more are available. Some message store providers, such as Exchange, can function as address book providers as well.

Transport Providers

Several underlying messaging protocols have become de facto standards, such as SMTP and X.400. Other protocols might be proprietary in nature. Regardless of which protocol is being used to send messages to and from the Internet or an intranet, it's the transport provider's job to translate those messages to work with the given protocol. Here's how it works:

1. Outbound messages (sent *from* the client application) are sent to the message store provider.

2. The message store provider hands the message over to the MAPI Spooler, which sends it to the transport provider.

3. The transport provider converts the message into a stream of bytes compatible with the messaging protocol being used.

Inbound messages work the same way, only in reverse:

1. The transport protocol receives a byte stream and converts it into a MAPI message.

2. The message is sent to the Spooler, which places it into a receive folder furnished by the message store provider.

3. The client application now has access to the new message and can retrieve it from the message store provider.

Because the message store providers and the MAPI Spooler handle transmission and receipt of messages, your client applications probably won't deal with transport providers at all. It helps, though, to know the role that these components play within the MAPI system.

The MAPI Spooler

Like transport providers, your client applications can't deal directly with the MAPI Spooler. But you should be aware of how the Spooler works.

The MAPI Spooler runs in a completely separate process from the client application, just as the Windows print spooler runs in its own process. Even if more than one client application is running, a single instance of the MAPI Spooler is used. When inbound messages are received, the Spooler must determine to which message store provider they should be delivered. Outgoing messages from different message store providers are sorted by submission order, placed into a common queue, and then sent to the appropriate transport providers one by one.

Using the MAPI Controls: MAPISession and MAPIMessages

All the MAPI functionality in Visual Basic 6 is provided by two powerful ActiveX controls: MAPISession and MAPIMessages. The MAPISession control is the simplest of the two and is used only to begin and end MAPI sessions. The MAPIMessages control, on the other hand, provides all the message-related services available under MAPI. Both are invisible controls—they aren't displayed on the form when the program is in run mode.

The sequence of events for a typical MAPI application is as follows:

- Set properties for the MAPISession control that will affect the way in which a MAPI session will be started.

- Call the MAPISession control's `SignOn` method, which begins a new MAPI session.
- Use one or more MAPI services by setting properties or calling methods provided by the MAPIMessages control.
- Call the MAPISession control's `SignOff` method to terminate the MAPI session.

The MAPIMessages control allows you to retrieve messages from the mail server's inbox, perform operations on retrieved messages, and create new messages. It works closely with the mail server, which provides several dialog boxes related to many of the MAPI services. For example, when you create a new message with the MAPIMessages control's `Compose` and `Send` methods, a dialog box appears that facilitates the composition of a new message, saving you from an incredible amount of programming.

The way in which you use the MAPIMessages control might seem a little strange at first; I admit that it was a bit hard for me to get used to. But when you understand how the various properties and methods of the MAPIMessages control work together, you'll master MAPI programming very quickly. The two sample applications created later in this chapter give you a good introduction to how MAPI works in Visual Basic, so relax if you don't yet fully understand how the MAPI controls function. When you see them in action, they'll be much easier to comprehend.

Tables 21.1 and 21.2 list the unique methods and properties available for each control. Note that neither control has events and that standard properties, such as `Name` and `Index`, are excluded.

TABLE 21.1. METHODS AND PROPERTIES FOR THE MAPISESSION CONTROL.

Name	Description
Methods	
`SignOff`	Ends a MAPI session.
`SignOn`	Starts a MAPI session.
Properties	
`Action`	Starts or ends a MAPI session. This property should no longer be used but is included to provide backward compatibility with a previous version of MAPI.
`DownloadMail`	Specifies whether new mail should be downloaded from the mail server after beginning a MAPI session.
`LogonUI`	Specifies whether a dialog box should appear when a MAPI session is started.
`NewSession`	Specifies whether a new MAPI session should be started if a valid MAPI session already exists.

continues

TABLE 21.1. CONTINUED

Name	Description
	Properties
Password	Specifies the password for the account associated with the UserName property.
SessionID	Returns the handle for the current MAPI session. This value is set when the SignOn method is called.
UserName	Specifies the user or profile name to be used when starting a MAPI session.

TABLE 21.2. METHODS AND PROPERTIES FOR THE MAPIMESSAGES CONTROL.

Name	Description
	Methods
Compose	Clears all components of the compose buffer.
Copy	Copies the currently indexed message to the compose buffer so that it can be edited.
Delete	Deletes a message, a recipient, or an attachment.
Fetch	Creates a message set from messages in the inbox. You can specify the type of messages included in the set by using the FetchMsgType and FetchUnreadOnly properties. The message set can also be sorted by first setting the FetchSorted property.
Forward	Copies the currently indexed message into the compose buffer so that it can be sent (forwarded) to another e-mail address.
Reply	Copies the currently indexed message into the compose buffer so that a reply can be sent to the originator of the message.
ReplyAll	Sends copies of the reply to all recipients of the currently indexed message; it's similar to the Reply method.
ResolveName	Searches the address book for the currently indexed recipient of a message and returns an error if it's not found. If the AddressResolveUI property is True, a dialog box for address resolution is displayed rather than an error.
Save	Saves the message in the compose buffer.
Send	Sends the message in the compose buffer to the mail server for delivery.
Show	Displays the Address Book dialog box.

Mail-Enabling Your Applications With MAPI

CHAPTER 21

491

21

MAIL-ENABLING
YOUR
APPLICATIONS

Name	Description
	Properties
Action	Performs a number of message-related functions. This property is no longer used but is included to provide backward compatibility with a previous version of MAPI.
AddressCaption	Specifies the caption that appears at the top of the Address Book dialog box.
AddressEditFieldCount	Specifies which editing controls are displayed in the Address Book dialog box.
AddressLabel	Specifies the caption on the To: button in the Address Book dialog box.
AddressModifiable	Specifies whether users can modify the address book.
AddressResolveUI	Specifies whether a dialog box should be displayed when the ResolveName method is called.
AttachmentCount	Returns the number of attachments for the currently indexed message.
AttachmentIndex	Sets or returns the pointer to the currently indexed attachment of a message.
AttachmentName	Specifies the filename of the currently indexed attachment.
AttachmentPathName	Specifies the full path to the currently indexed attachment.
AttachmentPosition	Specifies the position of the currently indexed attachment within the body of the message (in characters).
AttachmentType	Specifies the type of the currently indexed attachment (data file, embedded OLE object, or static OLE object).
FetchMsgType	Specifies the type of messages to be included in the message set when the Fetch method is called.
FetchSorted	Specifies the order in which the messages in the message set are sorted when the Fetch method is called.
FetchUnreadOnly	Specifies that only unread messages should be retrieved from the inbox when the Fetch method is called.
MsgConversationID	Identifies that the currently indexed message is part of a message thread.
MsgCount	Returns the total number of messages included in the current message set.
MsgDateReceived	Returns the date on which the currently indexed message was received.

continues

TABLE 21.2. CONTINUED

Name	Description
	Properties
MsgID	Returns the ID number of the currently indexed message. This number is generated internally by the MAPI subsystem and should be unique for each message in the message set.
MsgIndex	Sets or returns the pointer to the currently indexed message.
MsgNoteText	Specifies the body of the currently indexed message.
MsgOrigAddress	Returns the address of the originator (sender) of the currently indexed message.
MsgOrigDisplayName	Returns the name of the originator (sender) of the currently indexed message.
MsgRead	Returns a value indicating whether the currently indexed message has been read.
MsgReceiptRequested	Specifies whether a return receipt has been requested for the currently indexed message.
MsgSent	Specifies a value indicating whether the currently indexed message has been sent to the mail server for delivery.
MsgSubject	Specifies the short subject description of the currently indexed message.
MsgType	Specifies the type of the currently indexed message.
RecipAddress	Specifies the e-mail address for the recipient of the currently indexed message.
RecipCount	Returns the total number of recipients for the currently indexed message.
RecipDisplayName	Specifies the name of the currently indexed message recipient.
RecipIndex	Sets or returns the pointer to the currently indexed message recipient.
RecipType	Specifies the type of the currently indexed message recipient.
SessionID	Returns the handle to the current MAPI session.

As you can see, there is quite a bit to these two controls, especially MAPIMessages. Don't worry; I'll go through just about all of it in this chapter.

Creating MAPI Programs with Visual Basic

You're almost ready to start creating some sample MAPI programs with Visual Basic. Before you do, I'd like to briefly explain the three different types of MAPI applications: mail-enabled, electronic mail (e-mail), and mail-aware. Each provides a different level of e-mail functionality:

- *Mail-enabled applications* are applications whose main function isn't specifically e-mail-related but contain some e-mail messaging services, often transparently to users. The example given earlier in this chapter of a program that monitors machines in a factory and e-mails information regarding their efficiency is a mail-enabled application. The first sample program that follows this section is also an example of a mail-enabled application.

- *Electronic mail, or e-mail applications*, provide electronic messaging services as their main function. These programs typically have a user interface that simplifies the creation and handling of e-mail messages by end users. Microsoft's Internet Mail is just one example of an e-mail application.

- *Mail-aware applications* are similar to e-mail applications, but their main function might not be messaging-related. A word processor, for example, might allow you to compose a document and e-mail it to another person. In that way, it functions like an e-mail application. However, the capability to send the document is more a bonus than the main function of the program. Microsoft Word 97 allows you to e-mail its documents, so it's an example of a mail-aware application.

As time goes on, more and more programs will feature some degree of electronic messaging functionality. Most of these applications will be mail-enabled or mail-aware, incorporating e-mail services into their basic design as just another basic feature demanded by end users.

CAUTION

Before you begin creating MAPI client applications in Visual Basic, you must have a properly configured MAPI-compliant mail server on your system. A standalone or network computer running Windows 95 or Windows NT might use Microsoft Exchange, which is included with those operating systems. Not having the necessary components installed can result in unpredictable errors and the inability of the following sample applications to work properly. If

continues

you're unsure of whether your system has a mail server installed, consult the online help system or your network administrator.

Creating Mail-Enabled Applications

You first will create a mail-enabled program because such an application provides a good introduction to how MAPI works with Visual Basic without going into too much too soon. Later, you'll create a more robust program that covers many more of the services provided by MAPI.

This program is a simple login/logout interface that might be used to track employee activity of some kind. Perhaps it could be a front end to another application. When employees begin to use the application, they log in with their username and password. When finished, they log out, and someone else can use the application.

When three employees have logged in and out, an activity report with all six transactions (three logins and three logouts) is automatically generated and sent to a manager or supervisor for review. To make testing of the program easier, a button has been added so that the activity report can be sent immediately instead of waiting until all six transactions take place.

The program interface will look like the one shown in Figure 21.2. Notice that there are places for employees to enter their username and password. There are also Log In and Log Out buttons, as well as a button to immediately generate and send the activity report.

FIGURE 21.2.

The interface for the employee login/logout program.

To create the program interface, add the various controls to the form; then refer to Table 21.3 to change the properties of the controls.

TABLE 21.3. CONTROL PROPERTIES FOR THE EMPLOYEE LOGIN/LOGOUT PROGRAM.

Control	Property	Setting
Form	Name	frmMAPIApp1
	Caption	MAPIApp1

Mail-Enabling Your Applications With MAPI

CHAPTER 21

495

21

MAIL-ENABLING
YOUR
APPLICATIONS

Control	Property	Setting
	Height	3315
	Left	60
	Top	345
	Width	3120
Label	Name	lblTitle
	Alignment	2 ignmentp
	Caption	Security Check
	Height	255
	Left	120
	Top	120
	Width	2775
Label	Name	lblName
	Alignment	1 ignmentCheckty
	Caption	Name
	Height	255
	Left	120
	Top	510
	Width	855
Label	Name	lblPassword
	Alignment	1 ignmentrdeckty
	Caption	Password
	Height	255
	Left	120
	Top	870
	Width	855
TextBox	Name	txtName
	Height	285
	Left	1080
	Text	" "
	Top	480
	Width	1815
TextBox	Name	txtPassword
	Height	285
	Left	1080
	PasswordChar	*
	Text	(Nothing)
	Top	840
	Width	1815

continues

TABLE 21.3. CONTINUED

Control	Property	Setting
CommandButton	Name	cmdLogIn
	Caption	Log In
	Height	375
	Left	120
	Top	1320
	Width	1335
CommandButton	Name	cmdLogOut
	Caption	Log Out
	Height	375
	Left	1560
	Top	1320
	Width	1335
CommandButton	Name	cmdSendLog
	Caption	Send Log Report
	Height	375
	Left	120
	Top	1800
	Width	2775
MAPISession	Name	mpsSession
	Left	120
	Top	2280
MAPIMessages	Name	mpmSendLog
	Left	2280
	Top	2280

NOTE

If the two MAPI ActiveX controls (MAPISession and MAPIMessages) aren't already in your toolbox, press Ctrl+T or choose Project | Components. In the Components dialog box, double-click Microsoft MAPI Controls 6.0 so that its box is checked; then click OK to add the two controls to your toolbox.

After you create the form, it's time to do some coding. This program uses only four sub-routines, and only one actually uses the MAPI controls. I'll save that subroutine for last so that I can discuss it in more detail.

Mail-Enabling Your Applications With MAPI

CHAPTER 21

497

21

MAIL-ENABLING
YOUR
APPLICATIONS

Before you start coding these four subroutines, you need to add two module-level variables to the General Declarations section. These two variables will be used throughout the rest of the program:

```
Dim mintLogCount As Integer
Dim mstrLogActivity(6) As String
```

> **NOTE**
>
> When naming objects and variables in Visual Basic, I prefer using Microsoft's coding conventions. Notice that a three-character pneumonic precedes every object and variable name to indicate its type (frm for Forms, cmd for Command Buttons, int for integers, and so on). You also can precede variable names with a one-character scope indicator (g for global or m for module-level). I have found these coding conventions useful, and I advise you to consider adopting their use.

The first subroutine is for the Log In button's Click event (see Listing 21.1). When the event is triggered, the program verifies that users have typed something in the Name and Password text boxes. (Of course, the verification process would be much more involved if this were more than just a simple test program, with all names and passwords being looked up in an employee database. In the interest of keeping it simple, I'll ease up on the security a bit.)

LISTING 21.1. CODE FOR cmdLogIn's Click EVENT.

```
Private Sub cmdLogIn_Click()

    ' Make sure that both a name and a password have been
    ' entered.
    If txtName.Text = "" Or txtPassword.Text = "" Then
        MsgBox "Please enter your name and password."
        Exit Sub
    End If

    ' If this was a real application, code for checking the
    ' user's login information would go here.

    cmdLogIn.Enabled = False    ' Disable LogIn button and...
    cmdLogOut.Enabled = True    ' ...enable LogOut button.

    txtName.Enabled = False
    txtPassword.Text = ""
    txtPassword.Enabled = False
```

continues

LISTING **21.1.** CONTINUED

```
    ' Add this login to the activity log.
    mintLogCount = mintLogCount + 1
    mstrLogActivity(mintLogCount) = "User " _
        & UCase$(txtName.Text) & " logged IN at " _
        & Time$ & " on " & Date$

End Sub
```

When an employee logs in, a transaction line with the username and the login date and time is added to the mstrLogActivity array. Later, this array is used to generate the activity report e-mailed to a supervisor.

The next section of code is for the Log Out button's Click event (see Listing 21.2). Like the routine in Listing 21.1, it adds a transaction line to the mstrLogActivity array. If the array has six transactions, the SendActivityLog subroutine is called. That's the subroutine that actually uses the two MAPI controls, which I'll discuss in just a moment.

LISTING **21.2.** CODE FOR cmdLogOut's Click EVENT.

```
Private Sub cmdLogOut_Click()

    ' Add this logout to the activity log.
    mintLogCount = mintLogCount + 1
    mstrLogActivity(mintLogCount) = "User " _
        & UCase$(txtName.Text) & " logged OUT at " _
        & Time$ & " on " & Date$

    ' If the activity log is "full", then send it out via
    ' e-mail.
    If mintLogCount = 6 Then
        SendActivityLog
    End If

    txtName.Text = ""
    txtName.Enabled = True
    txtPassword.Enabled = True

    cmdLogIn.Enabled = True
    cmdLogOut.Enabled = False

End Sub
```

Next, you have yet another Click event, this time for the Send Log Now button (see Listing 21.3). It also calls the SendActivityLog subroutine to e-mail the login/logout report.

Mail-Enabling Your Applications With MAPI

CHAPTER 21

499

21

MAIL-ENABLING
YOUR
APPLICATIONS

LISTING 21.3. CODE FOR cmdSendLogNow's Click EVENT.

```
Private Sub cmdSendLog_Click()

' Check to see if there's actually anything in the activity
' log before sending it.
If mintLogCount = 0 Then
    MsgBox "Activity log empty - nothing to send!"
    Exit Sub
End If

SendActivityLog

End Sub
```

Now that you've taken care of the overhead, it's time to get down to business. Listing 21.4 shows the SendActivityLog subroutine.

LISTING 21.4. THE SendActivityLog SUBROUTINE, WHICH HANDLES ALL THE MAPI SERVICES USED BY THE LOGIN/LOGOUT PROGRAM.

```
Public Sub SendActivityLog()

    Dim intMsgLoop As Integer
    Dim strMsgBuffer As String

    On Error GoTo SendActivityLogError

    ' Establish a MAPI session.
    mpsSession.UserName = "security"
    mpsSession.Password = "test"
    mpsSession.DownLoadMail = False
    mpsSession.LogonUI = False
    mpsSession.SignOn
    mpmSendLog.SessionID = mpsSession.SessionID

    ' Create the body of the message in a temporary buffer.
    strMsgBuffer = ""
    For intMsgLoop = 0 To mintLogCount
        strMsgBuffer = strMsgBuffer _
            & mstrLogActivity(intMsgLoop) & Chr$(13) & Chr$(10)
    Next intMsgLoop

    ' Compose and send the message.
    mpmSendLog.Compose
    mpmSendLog.RecipAddress = "schief@mapiland.com"
    mpmSendLog.RecipDisplayName = "Security Chief"

    mpmSendLog.MsgSubject = "Activity Log - " & Date$ _
```

continues

LISTING 21.4. CONTINUED

```
            & "/" & Time$
    mpmSendLog.MsgNoteText = strMsgBuffer
    mpmSendLog.Send

    ' Set the activity log's index to zero, effectively
    ' "clearing out" the log.
    mintLogCount = 0

    mpsSession.SignOff

    Exit Sub

SendActivityLogError:
    MsgBox Error$, vbCritical, "Critical Error: " & Str(Err)
    End

End Sub
```

Because this routine does most of the work in the program and contains all the MAPI-related code, let's look at it in more detail.

To begin with, notice that an error handler has been implemented. Whenever you're working with the MAPI controls, it's always a good idea to set up some kind of error handling. Many things can go wrong if you're not careful in your coding. In fact, the MAPI specification defines 36 different error conditions that can arise when using the MAPI controls. Under normal circumstances, you'll probably want to implement a much more robust error-handling routine that traps for specific errors or offers the users options when an error occurs. But in the interest of simplicity, you'll display only the error description and its value and then end the program. If you have the necessary 32-bit MAPI DLLs installed properly on your system, you won't run into any problems.

Because the subroutine in Listing 21.4 contains all the MAPI-related action in the program, I'll go through it section by section and discuss each part in more detail.

Establishing the MAPI Session

The following code segment establishes a MAPI session by using the MAPISession control (mpsSession):

```
' Establish a MAPI session.
mpsSession.UserName = "security"
mpsSession.Password = "test"
mpsSession.DownLoadMail = False
mpsSession.LogonUI = False
mpsSession.SignOn
mpmSendLog.SessionID = mpsSession.SessionID
```

The `UserName` and `Password` properties are changed to reflect the login information you want to use (in this case, a username of `security` and a password of `test`). If you want to run this program on your system, you'll have to change these two properties to something that works with your mail server—your own name and password, for example.

> **NOTE**
>
> You don't need to specify a password at all if you use a profile name rather than a username. Most MAPI-compliant mail servers (including Microsoft Exchange) allow you to set up different profiles. A discussion of profiles and how Windows Messaging works is beyond the scope of this chapter. However, you can use the Windows help system to learn more on those topics.

The `DownLoadMail` property is set to `False`, specifying that any new messages shouldn't be retrieved when the user has signed on. Because this program's only function is to send an employee activity report to the appropriate party, it's not set up to receive mail.

The `LogonUI` property is also set to `False`. If it's set to `True`, a dialog box will appear that prompts for the username and password to log on to the service provider. Because you don't want the dialog box to appear, you set this property to `False`, and no user intervention is required. If you use invalid values for the `UserName` and `Password` properties, the dialog box appears whether the `LogonUI` property is `True` or `False`. On the other hand, if you assign valid `UserName` and `Password` property values, the dialog box still won't appear, even if the `LogonUI` property is set to `True`.

After all the necessary properties are set, the MAPISession control's `SignOn` method is called. When a MAPI session is started, it's assigned a Session ID number. In the preceding code segment, that number is placed into `mpsSession`'s `SessionID` property. You must copy that value so that the MAPIMessages control knows which MAPI session to use when its own methods are called. Note that when a MAPI session has been initiated, the MAPISession control isn't used again until the MAPI session is to be terminated (using the `SignOff` method).

Adding Elements to a Temporary String Used to Hold the Message Body

The following code segment loops through the `mstrLogActivity` array and adds its elements to a temporary string (`strMsgBuffer`) used to hold the body of the e-mail message:

```
' Create the body of the message in a temporary buffer.
strMsgBuffer = ""
```

```
For intMsgLoop = 0 To mintLogCount
    strMsgBuffer = strMsgBuffer _
        & mstrLogActivity(intMsgLoop) & Chr$(13) & Chr$(10)
Next intMsgLoop
```

A carriage return and linefeed are added to the end of each element so that the information doesn't get lumped into one long line of text.

Addressing and Sending the Message

Now, you need to address and send the message. First, you call the MAPIMessages control's Compose method to clear all the components in the compose buffer, which is used to create new messages (or to edit and resend existing messages, as you'll see later):

```
' Compose and send the message.
mpmSendLog.Compose
mpmSendLog.RecipAddress = "manager@mapiland.com"
mpmSendLog.RecipDisplayName = "Mr. Manager"
mpmSendLog.MsgSubject = "Activity Log - " & Date$ _
    & "/" & Time$
mpmSendLog.MsgNoteText = strMsgBuffer
mpmSendLog.Send
```

The RecipAddress property is assigned the e-mail address of the person receiving the message, and the RecipDisplayName property gets the name of the recipient. In the example, I've used a fabricated e-mail address and name; you might want to change these two properties to a valid e-mail address that you can use to test the program.

Next, you give the message a subject, using the MsgSubject property, and assign the temporary string you created earlier to the message body (the MsgNoteText property). Now you're ready to send it. To do so, the MAPIMessages control's Send method is called. This sends the message to the mail server, which in turn relays it to the recipient specified by the RecipAddress property.

Resetting the Activity Log

After the activity log is sent, it should be reset, or cleared out, so that it can be used again. By setting the log's counter back to zero, you can record more employee activity in the log:

```
' Set the activity log's index to zero, effectively
' "clearing out" the log.
mintLogCount = 0

mpsSession.SignOff
```

Finally, you close your MAPI session by calling the MAPISession control's SignOff method. You don't have to tell the MAPIMessages control that the session is over, but you can no longer use that control's methods until a new session is started. Calling any of its methods without having a MAPI session in progress results in an error.

Saving the Project

Save the project as CH2101.VBP and the form as CH2101.FRM; then compile and run the program. If you aren't on a network with an e-mail gateway or have to use dial-up networking to connect to the Internet, make sure that you've established a connection to the Internet first.

When the program runs, type a username and password—anything will do because you don't perform any validation on what's entered. Click the Log In button. The password will disappear, and text boxes are disabled until you click the Log Out button, so do that now. Then enter another name and password, if you want, and log in and out. Now, click the Send Log Report button to send the activity log. All this work is transparent to the user, so it might not seem like anything has happened. But if you check the mailbox for the recipient assigned to the message, you'll see some new mail.

Before moving on to the next MAPI application, try a few things. Exit the program and change the line in the SendActivityLog subroutine from

```
mpmSendLog.Send
```

to

```
mpmSendLog.Send True
```

and run the program again. When you click the button to send the activity log, you'll see a window similar to the one shown in Figure 21.3.

FIGURE 21.3.

The window displayed when the Send *method is called with a* True *argument.*

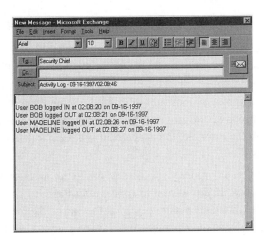

The mail server displays this window, so it might look different on your system if you're not using Microsoft Exchange. You'll see more of this window when you create the next application. For now, exit the program and remove the True argument from the line of code you just changed.

Now, try adding an attachment to the message sent by the login/logout application. Suppose that, along with the employee activity log, you want to include another log file created by the application that the employees are using. This file is a simple ASCII text file named USE.LOG and is located in the C:\APP directory (for testing purposes; feel free to change the filename and path to indicate a file that exists on your system). To add the attachment to the message, modify the section of code in the SendActivityLog subroutine so that it looks like Listing 21.5.

LISTING 21.5. THE MODIFIED CODE SEGMENT IN THE SendActivityLog SUBROUTINE SO THAT AN ATTACHMENT IS ADDED TO THE MESSAGE BEING SENT OUT.

```
' Compose and send the message.
mpmSendLog.Compose
mpmSendLog.RecipAddress = "manager@mapiland.com"
mpmSendLog.RecipDisplayName = "Mr. Manager"
mpmSendLog.MsgSubject = "Activity Log - " & Date$ _
    & "/" & Time$
mpmSendLog.MsgNoteText = strMsgBuffer
mpmSendLog.AttachmentType = mapData
mpmSendLog.AttachmentName = "Program Use Log"
mpmSendLog.AttachmentPathName = "C:\App\Use.log"
mpmSendLog.AttachmentPosition = Len(mpmSendLog.MsgNoteText)
mpmSendLog.Send
```

As you can see, four new lines have been added to SendActivityLog. All of them set properties of the mpmSendLog control:

- The AttachmentName property specifies a descriptive name for the attachment.

- The AttachmentPathName property specifies its full path and filename. To test the use of attachments, you have to change the AttachmentPathName property to reflect a file that exists somewhere on your system.

- The AttachmentType property indicates what kind of object the attachment is. It can be a data file (mapData), an embedded OLE object (mapEOLE), or a static OLE object (mapSOLE). In the example, the attachment is a regular data file, so the mapData constant is used.

- The AttachmentPosition property specifies where in the message body the attachment will be positioned. If you want it to appear after the third character, this property is set to 3. Often, attachments are placed at the end of the message. This is the case in the sample code, so the AttachmentPosition property is set to the length of the entire message body.

That just about wraps it up for the login/logout application. In the next section, you create a simple e-mail program that demonstrates how to use many more of the MAPI services in Visual Basic.

Creating E-Mail Applications

In the preceding section, you created an application that sends e-mail transparently—users weren't involved in the process of sending the messages. Now, you'll create an application that relies totally on users: a simple e-mail program displaying messages read in from the mail server and allowing users to create and send new messages as well as perform various services on existing messages. Although it's a primitive and simple program, it provides an example of an e-mail application.

The program consists of three main sections. At the top is a ListBox containing the subjects of all messages read in from the mail server. In the middle is a Label displaying header information for the currently selected message. The last section is a TextBox displaying the body of the currently selected message.

When users click one of the message subjects in the ListBox, the name of the sender, the subject, and the date the message was received appear in the Label. The body of the message appears in the TextBox.

When a message is selected, users can click any of the following command buttons that perform message services: Reply, Reply All, Forward, Copy, and Delete. If users click the New button, they can compose and send a new message. Last but not least, users can view the address book by clicking the appropriately named Address Book button.

You might think that even a simple program like this would take quite a bit of coding. If so, you'll be pleasantly surprised. Because MAPI does most of the work for you, the amount of program code is minimal.

Begin by assembling the program's interface. By using Table 21.4 as a guide, add the various components and change their properties so that your form looks like the one shown in Figure 21.4.

TABLE 21.4. CONTROL PROPERTIES FOR THE SIMPLE E-MAIL APPLICATION.

Control	Property	Setting
Form	Name	frmMAPIApp2
	Caption	MAPIApp2
	Height	6465
	Left	60
	Top	345
	Width	6615
Label	Name	lblTitle
	Alignment	2 - Center
	Caption	Simple E-Mail Application

continues

TABLE 21.4. CONTINUED

Control	Property	Setting
	Font	MS Sans Serif 12pt
	Height	375
	Left	1320
	Top	120
	Width	3975
CommandButton	Name	cmdMsgNew
	Caption	New
	Height	255
	Left	120
	Top	600
	Width	975
CommandButton	Name	cmdMsgReply
	Caption	Reply
	Height	255
	Left	1200
	Top	600
	Width	975
CommandButton	Name	cmdMsgReplyAll
	Caption	ReplyAll
	Height	255
	Left	2280
	Top	600
	Width	975
CommandButton	Name	cmdMsgForward
	Caption	Forward
	Height	255
	Left	3360
	Top	600
	Width	975
CommandButton	Name	cmdMsgCopy
	Caption	Copy
	Height	255
	Left	5520
	Top	600
	Width	975
CommandButton	Name	cmdMsgDelete
	Caption	Delete
	Height	255

Control	Property	Setting
	Left	5520
	Top	600
	Width	975
ListBox	Name	lstMessages
	Height	1035
	Left	120
	Top	1080
	Width	6375
Label	Name	lblMsgInfo
	BorderStyle	1 rderStyleen am
	Font	MS LineDraw 8pt
	Height	735
	Left	120
	Top	2280
	Width	6375
TextBox	Name	txtMsgBody
	Height	2775
	Left	120
	MultiLine	True
	ScrollBars	2 rollBarsw
	Top	3000
	Width	6375
CommandButton	Name	cmdAddrBook
	Caption	Address Book
	Height	255
	Left	3120
	Top	6120
	Width	1575
CommandButton	Name	cmdExit
	Caption	Exit Program
	Height	255
	Left	4800
	Top	6120
	Width	1695
MAPISession	Name	mpsSession
	Left	120
	Top	5880
MAPIMessages	Name	mpmMessages
	Left	720
	Top	5880

FIGURE 21.4.

The interface for the simple email application.

When your form design is complete, you can begin adding the program's code. I'll take the sections one by one so that I can explain each part in more detail.

Listing 21.6 shows the code for the form's Load event. There's really nothing new here. When the program starts, it first displays itself and then establishes a MAPI session. When a session is started, the FetchMessages subroutine is called. As you'll see in just a moment, that routine reads in the messages from the mail server and displays their subjects onscreen.

LISTING 21.6. CODE FOR THE FORM'S Load EVENT.

```
Private Sub Form_Load()

    On Error GoTo ErrHandler

    ' Show the form so it shows up behind the login
    ' dialog box.
    Me.Show

    ' Start a new MAPI session.
    mpsSession.DownLoadMail = True
    mpsSession.LogonUI = True
    mpsSession.SignOn
    mpmMessages.SessionID = mpsSession.SessionID

    ' Read messages from the message server's InBox.
    FetchMessages

    ' If there are messages, display the first one.
    If lstMessages.ListCount > 0 Then
        lstMessages.ListIndex = 0
```

```
            lstMessages_Click
        End If

    Exit Sub

ErrHandler:
    CriticalError

End Sub
```

Note that I've added error handling to this code. In fact, I've done so in all the routines and events that perform some sort of MAPI function. Any error that arises will be handled by the `CriticalError` routine (see Listing 21.7). If an error does occur—and let's hope it doesn't—this routine displays a message box with the error number and description. It also terminates the MAPI session if it has already been started.

LISTING 21.7. THE `CriticalError` ROUTINE, WHICH HANDLES ANY ERRORS THAT MAY OCCUR THROUGHOUT THE PROGRAM'S VARIOUS SUBROUTINES AND EVENTS.

```
Public Sub CriticalError()

    ' An error has occurred. Inform the user and exit
    ' the program.
    MsgBox Error$, vbCritical, "Critical Error: " & Str(Err)
    If mpsSession.SessionID Then
        mpsSession.SignOff
    End If
    End

End Sub
```

The next code section (see Listing 21.8) is for the `FetchMessages` routine mentioned earlier. Its job is to retrieve all the messages in the mail server's inbox.

LISTING 21.8. THE `FetchMessages` ROUTINE, WHICH RETRIEVES MESSAGES FROM THE MAIL SERVER.

```
Public Sub FetchMessages()

    Dim intMsgIndex As Integer

    On Error GoTo ErrHandler

    ' Read all messages (read and unread) from the server,
    ' and sort as specified by the user's InBox.
    mpmMessages.FetchSorted = True
```

continues

LISTING 21.8. CONTINUED

```
    mpmMessages.FetchUnreadOnly = False
    mpmMessages.Fetch

    ' Clear the List Box and add to it all of the
    ' messages just read.
    lstMessages.Clear
    intMsgIndex = 0
    If mpmMessages.MsgCount > 0 Then
        Do
            mpmMessages.MsgIndex = intMsgIndex
            lstMessages.AddItem mpmMessages.MsgSubject
            intMsgIndex = intMsgIndex + 1
        Loop Until (intMsgIndex = mpmMessages.MsgCount)
    End If
    Exit Sub

ErrHandler:
    CriticalError

End Sub
```

The first thing the routine in Listing 21.8 does is set some of the properties for the
MAPIMessages control's `Fetch` method. The `FetchSorted` property is set to `True`,
specifying that the messages should be retrieved in whichever order they are in the mail
server's inbox. If the default value (`False`) was used, the messages would be retrieved in
the same order in which they were received.

The `FetchUnreadOnly` property is also set here. By assigning it to `False`, it specifies that
all messages should be retrieved, not just the unread ones. The default value for this
property is `True` (retrieve unread messages only).

Next, the `Fetch` method is called. It sends all the messages in the mail server's inbox to
your application and stores them in a message set. You can think of the *message set* as a
kind of array because you can access messages in the set individually, just as you can
access elements of an array individually. To index a message, you simply change the
MAPIMessages control's `MsgIndex` property to point to the message you want to access.
You can then read other properties that apply to the message, such as `MsgSubject`,
`MsgNoteText`, or `MsgDateReceived`. You also can call methods that perform some sort of
function on the currently indexed message. For example, if you want to forward the current message, you would call the `Forward` method. It might sound a little strange, and it
does take a little getting used to, but using the MAPI controls is really a snap.

Okay, back to the `FetchMessages` routine. Now that you have all the messages in the
mail server's inbox stored in the message set, you need to list them onscreen.

Mail-Enabling Your Applications With MAPI

CHAPTER 21

511

21

MAIL-ENABLING
YOUR
APPLICATIONS

This is where the ListBox control (lstMessages) comes in. The next piece of code adds all the message subjects in the message set to lstMessages (after clearing whatever was in there before).

First, you need to tell just how many messages had been read in when the Fetch method was called. This data is stored in the MAPIMessages control's MsgCount property. If it's more than zero, you know that at least one message has been retrieved and is stored in the message set. In that case, you use a Do...Loop Until structure to loop through the message set and add each message subject to the ListBox. Note that you have to set msmMessages's MsgIndex property to point to a different message each time the loop is performed.

Listing 21.9 shows the Click event for the New button, which allows users to create a new mail message and send it to the mail server for delivery. Only two lines of this code actually perform that function, and they both call methods of mpmMessages, the MAPIMessages control. The Compose method is called first. It clears all components of the compose buffer. Next, the Send method is called. Use the True argument to indicate that a dialog box should be displayed so that users can add the various elements of the message (subject, body, and so on). The dialog box appears when the Send method is provided by the mail server, so it might be different from machine to machine.

LISTING 21.9. CODE FOR THE NEW BUTTON'S Click EVENT.

```
Private Sub cmdMsgNew_Click()

    On Error GoTo ErrHandler

    ' Create a new message.
    mpmMessages.Compose
    mpmMessages.Send True

    lstMessages.SetFocus
    Exit Sub

ErrHandler:
    CriticalError

End Sub
```

If you're delighted to find out that it takes only two lines of code to create and send a new message with the MAPI controls, you'll be glad to know that all the other message services are just as easy.

> **NOTE**
>
> After the Send method is complete, the program focus is set to the lstMessages control. I added this line so that the focus would be taken off the New button—more of a cosmetic touch than anything else. I've also done the same in all the other CommandButton Click events, as you'll see.

Now, start adding the code for the other buttons' Click events. They're all similar. Listing 21.10 shows the first, cmdMsgReply_Click.

LISTING 21.10. CODE FOR THE REPLY BUTTON'S Click EVENT.

```
Private Sub cmdMsgReply_Click()

    On Error GoTo ErrHandler

    ' Reply to currently indexed message.
    mpmMessages.MsgIndex = lstMessages.ListIndex
    mpmMessages.Reply
    mpmMessages.Send True

    lstMessages.SetFocus
    Exit Sub

ErrHandler:
    CriticalError

End Sub
```

As promised, the code is short and simple. The MAPIMessages control's MsgIndex property is set to reflect the message number selected in the ListBox (lstMessages). This makes that message the currently indexed message. Next, mpmMessages's Reply method is called, which copies the current message to the compose buffer and adds RE: at the beginning of its Subject line. Finally, the Send method is called, and the message dialog box is displayed.

As you can see, the code for the Reply All button's Click event (see Listing 21.11) is almost identical to Reply's Click event. The only difference is that rather than the Reply method be called, the ReplyAll method is used.

LISTING 21.11. CODE FOR THE REPLYALL BUTTON'S Click EVENT.

```
Private Sub cmdMsgReplyAll_Click()

    On Error GoTo ErrHandler
```

```
    ' Reply to all recipients of the currently indexed
    ' message.
    mpmMessages.MsgIndex = lstMessages.ListIndex
    mpmMessages.ReplyAll
    mpmMessages.Send True

    lstMessages.SetFocus
    Exit Sub

ErrHandler:
    CriticalError

End Sub
```

These two buttons do have slightly different functions. The Reply button sends a reply message only to the originator (sender) of the message. The Reply All button, however, sends a copy of the reply message to all the recipients of the original message.

Moving on, you have the Forward button's `Click` event (see Listing 21.12). Again, it's similar to the last two code listings. The `Forward` method copies the currently indexed message to the compose buffer. The message is then edited in the dialog box displayed when the `Send` method is called. The Subject line in the dialog box is prefixed with `FW:` when the `Forward` method is used.

LISTING 21.12. CODE FOR THE FORWARD BUTTON'S `Click` EVENT.

```
Private Sub cmdMsgForward_Click()

    On Error GoTo ErrHandler

    ' Forward the currently indexed message.
    mpmMessages.MsgIndex = lstMessages.ListIndex
    mpmMessages.Forward
    mpmMessages.Send True

    lstMessages.SetFocus
    Exit Sub

ErrHandler:
    CriticalError

End Sub
```

Listing 21.13 shows the code for the Copy button's `Click` event. The `Copy` method simply copies the currently indexed message into the compose buffer. It doesn't alter the Subject line like some of the previously discussed methods.

LISTING 21.13. CODE FOR THE COPY BUTTON'S Click EVENT.

```
Private Sub cmdMsgCopy_Click()

    On Error GoTo ErrHandler

    ' Copy the currently indexed message.
    mpmMessages.MsgIndex = lstMessages.ListIndex
    mpmMessages.Copy
    mpmMessages.Send True

    lstMessages.SetFocus
    Exit Sub

ErrHandler:
    CriticalError

End Sub
```

The last of the message services' code is for the Delete button (see Listing 21.14). It's different from the rest of the listings thus far because it doesn't call the Send method. After pointing to the current message, the Delete method is called, and the message's subject is removed from the ListBox control.

LISTING 21.14. CODE FOR THE DELETE BUTTON'S Click EVENT.

```
Private Sub cmdMsgDelete_Click()

    On Error GoTo ErrHandler

    ' Delete the currently indexed message and remove its
    ' subject from the ListBox.
    mpmMessages.MsgIndex = lstMessages.ListIndex
    mpmMessages.Delete
    lstMessages.RemoveItem lstMessages.ListIndex

    ' Some odds and ends to take care of.
    If lstMessages.ListCount > 0 Then
        lstMessages.ListIndex = 0
    Else
        lblMsgInfo = ""
        txtMsgBody = ""
    End If

    lstMessages.SetFocus
    Exit Sub

ErrHandler:
    CriticalError

End Sub
```

Mail-Enabling Your Applications With MAPI

CHAPTER 21

515

21

MAIL-ENABLING
YOUR
APPLICATIONS

This routine also does a bit of housekeeping when a message is deleted. If no message subjects are left in the ListBox control, it blanks out any message currently onscreen. If some message subjects still remain in the ListBox control, it changes the ListBox pointer to highlight the first message in the list.

When users click one of the message subjects in the ListBox control, you want the corresponding message to be displayed. The code in Listing 21.15 displays the message's originator (sender), subject, and date received in the lblMsgInfo Label control and the body of the message in the txtMsgBody TextBox control.

LISTING 21.15. lstMessages's Click EVENT, DISPLAYING A MESSAGE WHEN USERS CLICK A MESSAGE SUBJECT.

```
Private Sub lstMessages_Click()

    ' When the user clicks on a message's subject, display
    ' the info (From, Subject, and Date) in the lblMsgInfo
    ' box and the message body in txtMsgBody.
    mpmMessages.MsgIndex = lstMessages.ListIndex
    lblMsgInfo = "From: " + mpmMessages.MsgOrigDisplayName + Chr$(13) _
        + "Subj: " + mpmMessages.MsgSubject + Chr$(13) _
        + "Date: " + mpmMessages.MsgDateReceived
    txtMsgBody = mpmMessages.MsgNoteText

End Sub
```

A single MAPIMessages method, Show, allows you to display an Address Book dialog box provided by the mail server. Listing 21.16 shows the code that displays the dialog box when the Address Book button is clicked.

LISTING 21.16. CODE FOR THE ADDRESS BOOK BUTTON'S Click EVENT.

```
Private Sub cmdAddrBook_Click()

    On Error GoTo ErrHandler

    ' Show the Address Book dialog box.
    mpmMessages.Show

    lstMessages.SetFocus
    Exit Sub

ErrHandler:
    CriticalError

End Sub
```

You're almost finished—only a few more subroutines to go! The Click event for the Exit button (see Listing 21.17) verifies that the users want to exit the program. It then terminates the current MAPI session and ends the program if users decide to proceed with the exit.

LISTING 21.17. CODE FOR THE EXIT BUTTON'S Click EVENT.

```
Private Sub cmdExit_Click()

    Dim intExit As Integer

    ' Make sure the user really wants to exit the
    ' program.
    intExit = MsgBox("Exit the program?", vbYesNo, _
        "Exit Program")
    If intExit = vbYes Then
        mpsSession.SignOff
        End
    End If

    lstMessages.SetFocus

End Sub
```

The last thing to add to the program is the bit of code shown in Listing 21.18. It prevents users from typing anything into the TextBox control (txtMsgBody), which contains the body of the currently selected message.

LISTING 21.18. CODE FOR txtMsgBody'S KeyPress EVENTS, PREVENTING USERS FROM TYPING ANYTHING INTO THE TEXT BOX USED TO DISPLAY THE MESSAGE BODY.

```
Private Sub txtMsgBody_KeyPress(KeyAscii As Integer)

    ' Prevent users from typing into the text box that
    ' contains the message body.
    KeyAscii = 0

End Sub
```

Finally, you're ready to try out the program. Save the project as CH2102.VBP and the form as CH2102.FRM; compile and run the program. The first thing you'll see is a dialog box similar to the one shown in Figure 21.5 (again, yours might look different if you're using a mail server other than Microsoft Exchange).

After establishing a MAPI connection, the program receives messages from the mail server's inbox. It might take a few moments after the MAPI session is established, but

Mail-Enabling Your Applications With MAPI

CHAPTER 21

517

21

MAIL-ENABLING
YOUR
APPLICATIONS

you'll then see a dialog box telling you that the program is checking for messages (see Figure 21.6).

FIGURE 21.5.

When the program is run, the mail server requests a profile name.

FIGURE 21.6.

The program retrieves messages from the mail server's inbox.

When mail retrieval is completed, you'll see a list of the messages (if any) that were in the mail server's inbox. Try sending a new message by clicking the New button. When you do, a window pops up like the one shown in Figure 21.7. (Again, yours might be different, based on the kind of mail server you're using.)

FIGURE 21.7.

When sending a new message, the mail server provides a window where you can compose and send the message.

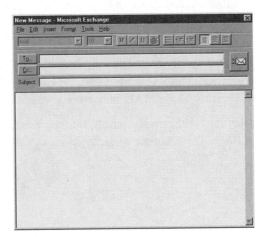

Don't forget to click the Send button when you're finished composing your message. For the dialog box provided by Microsoft Exchange, the button to send the message is located to the right of the Subject line.

Try using some of the other message services in the program. Then click the Address Book button to display the Address Book dialog box (see Figure 21.8). In the Address Book dialog box, you can add new entries to your personal address book. You can also delete entries, create distribution lists, and perform several other operations.

FIGURE 21.8.

The Address Book dialog box lets you change your personal address book.

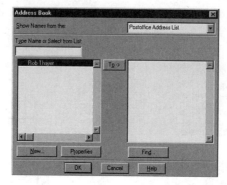

That's it for the tour of the simple e-mail application. True to its name, the application is simple and does lack in some areas. For instance, the application doesn't support message attachments, but it does show almost all the services supported under MAPI.

Summary

This chapter introduces the creation of MAPI applications with Visual Basic. The chapter first discusses the MAPI specification and its various components. You learned that MAPI acts as a standard interface between electronic messaging client applications and service providers.

You also learned about the two powerful MAPI ActiveX controls, MAPISession and MAPIMessages. The MAPISession control is used to start and end MAPI sessions, and the MAPIMessages control provides all the MAPI message services.

The sample applications using the two ActiveX controls illustrate how easily you can implement MAPI in Visual Basic. These sample applications provide an introduction to MAPI programming.

Using the Internet Transfer Control

by Rob Thayer

IN THIS CHAPTER

- Properties, Methods, and Events *521*
- Using the Internet Transfer Control with a Proxy Server *529*
- Accessing Files and Documents with the OpenURL Method *530*
- Accessing FTP Servers with the Execute Method *531*

The popularity of the Internet has created a new challenge for Windows programmers. In addition to being able to use files and documents stored on a local server, today's applications are expected to extend their reach globally. A program should provide the flexibility of being able to retrieve a document from the local hard drive, other accessible systems on a network, or any computer connected to the Internet.

Luckily for Visual Basic programmers, Microsoft has created an ActiveX control that makes accessing files on the Internet very easy. This control, called the Internet Transfer Control or Inet for short, allows you to send or retrieve files and documents using File Transfer Protocol (FTP) and Hypertext Transfer Protocol (HTTP). It also lets you send specific commands to perform operations for either protocol. For example, you can delete and rename files with the DELETE and RENAME commands when you are connected to an FTP host system.

Using the Internet Transfer Control is simple. First, you set the properties that pertain to the connection to be made to the host system: protocol, username, password, remote server name, and so on. You can then use the control's methods to retrieve files or send commands. In some cases, issuing a command will result in data being placed into the Internet Transfer Control's buffer. You can read the information from the buffer using another of the control's methods.

The Internet Transfer Control is invisible on a form—like the Timer Control. All of its functionality is implemented through its methods, and it requires no user interface.

The Internet Transfer Control supports both synchronous and asynchronous file transfers. This means that depending on the control methods you use to retrieve files and documents, you can have the program wait until the data is transferred, or you can issue the command and then simply monitor the progress of the transfer while your application does other things.

To be sure, the Internet Transfer Control is a component that every Visual Basic programmer should know how to use. If you want to extend the reach of your applications to access other servers around the world via the Internet, it's the tool to use.

> **NOTE**
>
> If the Internet Transfer Control is not included on a project's Toolbox, it probably has to be loaded. Right-click the Toolbox and select the Components option. When the Components dialog box appears, make sure there is a check mark in the box for Microsoft Internet Transfer Control 6.0. Then click OK and the control will be added to the Toolbox.

Properties, Methods, and Events

In order to fully understand how the Internet Transfer Control works, you must first understand how to use its properties, methods, and events. There aren't very many of each, but there are enough to connect to and interact with any FTP or HTTP server. The lean interface of the Internet Transfer Control is a testament to its exceptional design.

The following sections discuss the control's unique properties, methods, and events in detail. Later in this chapter, you'll see examples of how some of these interface elements are used.

Properties

The Internet Transfer Control has only 14 unique properties included in its interface. Table 22.1 lists these properties.

TABLE 22.1. THE UNIQUE PROPERTIES OF THE INTERNET TRANSFER CONTROL

Property Name	Data Type	Description
AccessType	Enum	Sets/returns a value that determines whether the control will access the Internet directly or via a proxy server
Document	String	Sets/returns the file or document to be used with the Execute method
hInternet	Long	Returns the Internet handle from the Application Programming Interface (API), used to make direct calls to the API; not used in Visual Basic
Password	String	Sets/returns the password for logon requests to remote computers
Protocol	Enum	Sets/returns the protocol (that is, FTP, HTTP, Secure HTTP) to be used with the Execute method
Proxy	String	Sets/returns the name of a proxy server used to access the Internet
RemoteHost	String	Sets/returns the address of the remote system to which the control sends and/or receives data
RemotePort	Integer	Sets/returns the port number of the remote system to which the control connects
RequestTimeout	Long	Sets/returns the length (in seconds) to wait before a request times out

continues

TABLE 22.1. CONTINUED

Property Name	Data Type	Description
ResponseCode	Long	Returns an error code from a remote connection
ResponseInfo	String	Returns an error message from a remote connection
StillExecuting	Boolean	Returns a value that indicates whether or not the control is busy executing an operation
URL	String	Sets/returns a uniform resource locator (URL) to be used with the Execute or OpenURL methods
UserName	String	Sets/returns the username for logon requests to remote computers

In addition to those listed in Table 22.1, the Internet Transfer Control also has the following properties: Index, Name, Object, Parent, and Tag. These are standard properties and are used just as they would be with any other ActiveX control. The following sections discuss the unique properties of Table 22.1 in more detail.

AccessType Property

The AccessType property sets or returns a value that determines how you are accessing the Internet. If you are accessing the Internet via a proxy server, you should set this property to icNamedProxy (2). If you are accessing the Internet directly, you should set AccessType to icDirect (1). You can also use the default settings for the system by setting AccessType to icUseDefault (0).

For more information about using the Internet Transfer Control with a proxy server, see the section "Using the Internet Transfer Control with a Proxy Server" later in this chapter.

Document Property

When performing host operations with the Execute method (discussed later in this chapter), you sometimes must specify a file or document. In these cases, you should set the Document property with the name of the file or document.

hInternet Property

The hInternet property is used to obtain an Internet handle from the WININET.DLL API so direct calls can be made to the API. This property is not used in Visual Basic.

Protocol Property

Before establishing a connection with a server using the Internet Transfer Control, you should set the Protocol property to specify the transfer protocol you'll be using.

Possible values for this property include icUnknown (0), icDefault (1) for the default protocol, icFTP (2) for FTP, icHTTP (4) for HTTP, and icHTTPS (5) for Secure HTTP. The value 3 (icReserved) is reserved for future use and you should not use it at this time. The default value for this property is icDefault (1).

Proxy Property

The Proxy property is only used when accessing the Internet via a proxy server, and you should assign it with the name of the proxy server. For more information, see the section "Using the Internet Transfer Control with a Proxy Server" later in this chapter.

RemoteHost and RemotePort Properties

The RemoteHost and RemotePort properties are used to specify the host name (or Internet Protocol [IP] address) and port number for the remote server to which the Internet Transfer Control will be connecting. The RemoteHost property can contain either a host name (such as ftp://ftp.microsoft.com) or an IP address (such as 123.45.6.78). The RemotePort property specifies the connection port for the remote host. For FTP connections, the port number is typically 21. For World Wide Web connections, it's usually 80. If you set the Protocol property, the RemotePort property is set automatically for you.

RequestTimeout Property

When the Internet Transfer Control makes a request to a remote host, the request will timeout within a certain amount of time if there is no response. Setting the RequestTimeout property changes the number of seconds until a timeout occurs. The default value is 60, for 60 seconds. Setting RequestTimeout to 0 will cause the control to wait indefinitely for a response.

ResponseCode and ResponseInfo Properties

When an error occurs with the host connection, the error number is placed in the ResponseCode property and the error message is placed in the ResponseInfo property. The StateChanged event also is triggered, and the State becomes 11 (icError). For more information on the StateChanged event, see the section "Events" later in this chapter.

StillExecuting Property

You can check the status of the Internet Transfer Control by examining the StillExecuting property. A value of True indicates that the control is busy executing some kind of operation, such as a file transfer.

URL Property

Before using the Internet Transfer Control's `Execute` and `OpenURL` methods, you must first assign a valid URL to this property. The URL should contain the protocol and the remote host name (for example, `http://www.microsoft.com`).

UserName and Password Properties

When establishing an FTP connection with a remote server, you must send a username and password. Some servers allow anonymous users to log on, but others require a valid username and password. In the case of the latter, you must make sure to set the `UserName` and `Password` properties accordingly before you can establish a connection.

If you are accessing an anonymous FTP server, you can leave the `UserName` and `Password` properties empty. The Internet Transfer Control will automatically assign values for them. The `UserName` property will be set to "anonymous" and the `Password` property will be set to the current user's e-mail name.

> **NOTE**
>
> Setting the `Password` property and leaving the `UserName` property empty will result in an error when the Internet Transfer Control attempts to connect with the host server.

Methods

Although the Internet Transfer Control includes only a few methods in its interface, each method plays a significant role in how the control is used. Table 22.2 lists the control's five methods and provides a brief description of each.

TABLE 22.2. THE METHODS OF THE INTERNET TRANSFER CONTROL

Method	Description
Cancel	Cancels the current request or operation and closes any established connections
Execute	Executes a request or operation to a remote server
GetChunk	Retrieves data from a remote server
GetHeader	Retrieves header text from an HTTP file
OpenURL	Opens and retrieves a document at a specified URL

The syntax for the Internet Transfer Control's methods plus more detailed descriptions are provided in the following sections.

Cancel **Method**

The Cancel method cancels the current request (if any) and closes any connections that have been established. The syntax for the Cancel method is as follows:

```
object.Cancel
```

Execute **Method**

The Execute method allows you to pass commands to an HTTP or FTP server, causing some operation to be performed. For example, you could tell an FTP server to retrieve a certain directory by sending it a DIR command via the Execute method. This will then place the directory information in the Internet Transfer Control's buffer, and it can be read using the GetChunk method.

The syntax for the Execute method is as follows:

```
object.Execute url, operation, data, requestheaders
```

Each of the Execute method's four arguments are optional. The url argument specifies the URL to be applied to the operation being performed. For example, if you're issuing a DELETE command, the URL should contain the name of the FTP server and the pathname to the filename to be deleted (such as ftp://ftp.mycompany.com/dave/test.dat). Instead of specifying the URL in this argument, you can specify it in the control's URL property.

The operation argument is the operation or command to be executed. Table 22.3 lists valid operations. Some operations work only with the FTP protocol and some work only with the HTTP protocol. Note that some operations require arguments of their own. Both the command and any necessary arguments should be included in the Execute method's operation argument.

TABLE 22.3. VALID OPERATIONS FOR THE INTERNET TRANSFER CONTROL'S EXECUTE METHOD

Protocol	Operation/Syntax	Description
HTTP	GET	Retrieves data from the URL specified by the URL property.
HTTP	HEAD	Sends the requestheaders argument.
HTTP	POST	Posts data from the *data* argument to the server.
HTTP	PUT	Sends (puts) a page, located in the data argument, overwriting any existing page.

continues

22

THE INTERNET TRANSFER CONTROL

TABLE 22.3. CONTINUED

Protocol	Operation/Syntax	Description
FTP	CD *dir*	Changes the directory specified by *dir*.
FTP	CDUP	Changes the current directory's parent directory.
FTP	CLOSE	Closes the current connection.
FTP	DELETE *file*	Deletes the file specified by *file*.
FTP	DIR *dir*	Searches the directory specified by *dir*. The GetChunk method must be used to retrieve the directory data.
FTP	GET *file1 file2*	Retrieves the file specified by *file1* and saves it locally in the pathname and filename specified by *file2*.
FTP	LS *dir*	Searches the directory specified by *dir*. The GetChunk method must be used to retrieve the directory data.
FTP	MKDIR *dir*	Creates the directory specified by *dir*.
FTP	PUT *file1 file2*	Sends the local file specified by *file1* and writes it to the remote system using the pathname and filename specified by *file2*.
FTP	PWD	Returns the current directory name. The GetChunk method must be used to retrieve the data.
FTP	QUIT	Terminates the current user.
FTP	RECV *file1 file2*	Retrieves the file specified by *file1* and saves it locally in the pathname and filename specified by *file2*. Same as the GET operation.
FTP	RENAME *file1 file2*	Renames the file specified by *file1* to the name specified by *file2*.
FTP	RMDIR *dir*	Removes the directory specified by *dir*.
FTP	SEND *file1 file2*	Sends the local file specified by *file1* and writes it to the remote system using the pathname and filename specified by *file2*. Same as the PUT operation.
FTP	SIZE *dir*	Returns the size of the directory specified by *dir*.

NOTE

Some of the operations listed in Table 22.3 might not be permitted by the remote server. For example, the MKDIR operation might not be allowed if the user privileges for creating new directories are not in effect for the current FTP connection.

Certain operations also require that data be available to them. For example, the HTTP POST and PUT operations require data to be sent to the remote server. In these cases, the necessary data should be passed to the Execute method's data argument.

When issuing the HTTP HEAD operation, header information must be sent to the remote server. The appropriate header data should be passed to the Execute method's requestheaders argument. You can include more than one header line in this argument, but each line must terminate with a carriage return and line feed (vbCrLf). The format for header lines is as follows:

```
headername: headervalue vbCrLf
```

Typical header names include "Date," "Content-type," and "Last-modified."

GetChunk Method

Certain operations use the Execute method, and they retrieve data from the host and place it into the Internet Transfer Control's buffer. To read the data in the buffer, use the GetChunk method.

The syntax for the GetChunk method is as follows:

```
object.GetChunk(size,[, datatype])
```

The size parameter specifies the number of bytes to retrieve from the buffer. You can use the optional datatype parameter to specify whether the data is retrieved as a string or as a byte array. For strings, pass the constant icString for the datatype parameter or simply omit the datatype parameter (icString is the default). To retrieve the data into a byte array, pass the constant icByteArray for the datatype parameter. Byte arrays are typically used when binary data has been placed in the Internet Transfer Control's buffer.

You'll see an example of how to use the GetChunk method later in this chapter in the section titled "Accessing FTP Servers with the Execute Method."

GetHeader Method

HTTP files typically include header information in addition to the actual text of the file. You can retrieve a file's header information using the GetHeader method.

The syntax for the GetHeader method is as follows:

```
object.GetHeader([headername])
```

Headers consist of several different pieces of information. You can specify the kind of information you want to retrieve by passing a header name in the optional headername parameter. Typical header names include "Content-length," for the number of bytes in the file; "Content-type," for the multipurpose Internet mail extensions (MIME) content type of the data; "Date," for the time and date of the document's transmission; "Last-modified," for the time and date of the document's last modification; and "Server," for the name of the server. If you want to retrieve all of the header information, omit the `headername` parameter.

OpenURL

One of the more useful methods of the Internet Transfer Control is `OpenURL`. This method allows a file or document (HTTP or FTP) to be retrieved from the host.

The syntax for the `OpenURL` method is as follows:

```
Object.OpenURL url [, datatype]
```

All you have to do to retrieve a file or document with the `OpenURL` method is pass it a valid URL, such as `http://www.microsoft.com/index.htm`. The `OpenURL` function returns the contents of the file or document and can place them into a string variable, a text box, or any other object that can hold a string.

By default, the `OpenURL` method reads files as strings. However, you can specify that it read a file as a byte array by passing the constant `icByteArray` for the optional `datatype` parameter. Byte arrays are typically used when retrieving binary files.

For some examples of how to use the `OpenURL` method, see the section "Accessing Files and Documents with the `OpenURL` Method" later in this chapter.

Events

The Internet Transfer Control has only one event, but it is a significant one. The `StateChanged` event is fired whenever there is a change in the connection to the remote system. The syntax for the `StateChanged` event is as follows:

```
object_StateChanged(ByVal State As Integer)
```

The `StateChanged` event provides an integer value (`State`) that indicates the current state of the connection. Table 22.4 lists the possible values for `State`.

TABLE 22.4. THE POSSIBLE VALUES FOR THE *StateChanged* EVENT'S *State* PARAMETER

VB Constant	*Value*	*Control State*
icNone	0	No state to report
icHostResolvingHost	1	Looking up the IP address of the host computer
icHostResolved	2	Successfully found the IP address of the host computer

VB Constant	Value	Control State
`icConnecting`	3	Establishing a connection to the host computer
`icConnected`	4	Successfully connected to the host computer
`icRequesting`	5	Sending a request to the host computer
`icRequestSent`	6	Successfully sent request to the host computer
`icReceivingResponse`	7	Receiving a response from the host computer
`icResponseReceived`	8	Successfully received a response from the host computer
`icDisconnecting`	9	Disconnecting from the host computer
`icDisconnected`	10	Successfully disconnected from the host computer
`icError`	11	Error has occurred in communicating with the host computer
`icResponseCompleted`	12	Request successfully completed and all data has been received from the host computer

22

THE INTERNET TRANSFER CONTROL

When a command or operation is issued to the remote server using the `Execute` method, the `StateChanged` event might fire a number of times as the steps for sending the request are completed. For example, it is not uncommon for the `StateChanged` event to trigger eight times in a row with the `State` value changing each time the event is fired: first when the host's IP address is being looked up (`State` = 1), then when the IP address is found (`State` = 2), then when the connection to the host is being established (`State` = 3), and so on until a response is successfully received from the host (`State` = 8). Of course, a problem (such as an IP address never being resolved) could interfere with sending the request.

Using the Internet Transfer Control with a Proxy Server

If you're accessing the Internet via a proxy server, there are some special considerations you need to be aware of before using the Internet Transfer Control. You must set the control's `Proxy` and `AccessType` properties when using a proxy server.

First, set the `Proxy` property to the name of the proxy server. If you're unsure of the name of the proxy server for your system (or if your system uses a proxy server), open the Windows 9x/NT Control Panel and double-click the Internet icon. Then select the Connection tab on the Internet Properties dialog box. If the Connect Through a Proxy Server box is checked, you are accessing the Internet through a proxy server. To determine the name of the proxy server, click the Settings button. You will then see a list of the proxy servers used for different protocols such as HTTP and FTP.

After you have established the proxy server name and have set the `Proxy` property, change the `AccessType` property to `icNamedProxy`. That's all there is to it. You can now access the Internet via the Internet Transfer Control and the proxy server.

Accessing Files and Documents with the `OpenURL` Method

You can retrieve Web pages and files easily using the Internet Transfer Control's `OpenURL` method. In fact, it takes only one line of code to retrieve a document with `OpenURL`. Consider the following example:

```
rtbHTMLDoc = icWebServer.OpenURL("http://www.microsoft.com")
```

This code would read in the default page at `www.microsoft.com` into a RichTextBox control called `rtbHTMLDoc` using an Internet Transfer Control called `icWebServer`. Note that a RichTextBox control is used so the spacing and formatting of the page remain intact.

You can also use `OpenURL` with FTP files, as in this example:

```
txtFTPFile = icFTPIn.OpenURL("ftp://ftp.fakeco.com/test.txt")
```

This code would retrieve a file called `test.txt` and place it into the `txtFTPFile` text box control. In this example, the Internet Transfer Control used to perform this operation is called `icFTPIn`.

If you want to retrieve a file or document and save it to a file, one way to do it is to assign the file to a string variable; then write the string to a file using Visual Basic's `Open`, `Write`, and `Close` statements. This works fine for text files, but you might run into a problem when transferring binary files. To retrieve and save a binary file, use a procedure like the following one:

```
Private Sub GetBinaryFile(strURL As String, _
    strFileName As String, icITControl As Inet)

Dim bytDataIn() As Byte
Dim intFileNum As Integer

bytDataIn() = icITControl.OpenURL(strURL, icByteArray)

intFileNum = FreeFile()
Open strFileName For Binary As #intFileNum
Put #intFileNum, bytDataIn()
Close #intFileNum

End Sub
```

This simple procedure uses the `OpenURL` method to read in a file (specified by the `strURL` argument) as a byte array. The byte array is then written to the file specified by the `strFileName` argument. The name of the Internet Transfer Control is also passed to the procedure in the `icITControl` argument.

Accessing FTP Servers with the Execute Method

22

The Internet Transfer Control can transmit data both *synchronously* and *asynchronously*. When using the `OpenURL` method, the data is transmitted synchronously. That is, no other operations can be performed until the transfer is complete. Using the `Execute` method, data can be transmitted asynchronously.

To illustrate how to use the `Execute` method, consider the following section of code used to retrieve the root directory from an FTP server. This code assumes that the program contains a list box called `lstDirItems` and an Internet Transfer Control called `icRemote`. It also assumes that the `ConnectToFTP` procedure is being called from somewhere else in the program:

```
Public strBuffer As String
Public strExecuteCmd As String


Private Sub ConnectToFTP()

With icRemote
    .AccessType = icDirect
    .RequestTimeout = 10
    .Protocol = icFTP
    .URL = "ftp://ftp.microsoft.com"
End With

strExecuteCmd = "DIR"
icRemote.Execute , "DIR /"

End Sub


Private Sub icRemote_StateChanged(ByVal State As Integer)

If State = icResponseCompleted Then
    ' Retrieve the data from the host.
    strBuffer = GetFTPData(icRemote)
    If strExecuteCmd = "DIR" Then
        ' Fill in the lstDirItems list box with
```

```
                ' the directory names just retrieved.
            FillDirList lstDirItems
        End If
    End If

    End Sub


    Private Function GetFTPData(icServer As Inet) As String

    Dim strDataChunk As String
    Dim strDataInput As String

    ' Get a 1024-byte chunk of data for the host.
    strDataChunk = icServer.GetChunk(1024, icString)

    Do While (Len(strDataChunk) > 0)
        ' Build a buffer of received data in the
        ' strDataInput variable.
        strDataInput = strDataInput & strDataChunk
        ' Get another chunk of data from the host.
        strDataChunk = icServer.GetChunk(1024, icString)
    Loop

    GetFTPData = strDataInput

    End Function


    Private Sub FillDirList(lstDirList As ListBox)

    Dim lonBufferPos As Long
    Dim lonLastPos As Long
    Dim strDirItem As String

    lstDirList.Clear

    lonBufferPos = InStr(strBuffer, vbCrLf)
    While (lonBufferPos <> 0)
        strDirItem = Mid$(strBuffer, lonLastPos + 1, _
            lonBufferPos - lonLastPos - 1)
        lstDirList.AddItem strDirItem
        lonLastPos = lonBufferPos + 1
        lonBufferPos = InStr(lonLastPos + 1, strBuffer, vbCrLf)
    Wend

    End Sub
```

The ConnectToFTP procedure sets up the properties for the Internet Transfer Control and executes a DIR operation with the Execute method. The module-level variable strExecuteCmd is set to DIR so the code in the StateChanged event knows how it should act when a directory is retrieved from the host.

The StateChanged event procedure checks to see whether the State is icResponseCompleted. If so, that could mean that the DIR command has been executed and the directory information has been retrieved into the Internet Transfer Control's buffer. First, the buffer is read using the GetFTPData function. This function uses the GetChunk method to read in 1KB chunks of data from the buffer. The contents of the buffer are returned by the GetFTPData function as a string. Returning back to the StateChanged event procedure, the FillDirList procedure is called if the operation that was executed was DIR. FillDirList parses the string returned by the GetFTPData function (strBuffer) and adds each line to the list box that is passed as an argument to the function (in this case, lstDirItems).

Figure 22.1 shows a simple user interface you might use with the previously listed code. The Connect command button calls the ConnectToFTP procedure, and the Cancel command button invokes the Cancel method to terminate the connection. You can alter the URL via a text box at the top of the form. You can also monitor the StatusChanged event with a Select...Case statement being used to display the current status in a label at the bottom of the form.

FIGURE 22.1.

A simple program that uses the Internet Transfer Control to retrieve a directory from a host FTP server.

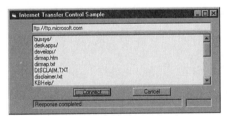

This is not a complete program, and it doesn't do anything other than read in the root directory of an FTP host server. But you can expand the code relatively easily so the items in the list box (lstDirItems) can be retrieved when they are clicked. Or, if the item you click is a directory name, you can change the directory of the host FTP server to the new directory name and read a new directory list.

Summary

The Internet Transfer Control provides an easy way for Visual Basic programs to access files and documents on Internet servers around the world using the FTP and HTTP protocols. It allows you to send specific operations or commands to these servers or to retrieve a file with a single method call.

This chapter provides an introduction to the Internet Transfer Control, including detailed information on the properties, methods, and events that make up its interface. With what you've learned here, you should have no trouble extending your applications so they can interact on a global level with other servers.

Client/Server Programming with Winsock

by Loren Eidahl

IN THIS CHAPTER

- TCP/IP Fundamentals   536
- Using the Microsoft Winsock Control 539
- Creating the Price Lookup Example 547

In Chapter 22, "Using the Internet Transfer Control," you were introduced to one of Visual Basic's exciting new Internet-specific controls, the Internet Transfer control. This control enables you to create applications that use Hypertext Transfer Protocol (HTTP) and File Transfer Protocol (FTP) for communication to the outside world with an external application.

In addition to the Internet Transfer control, Visual Basic includes in its suite of Internet-specific controls the Winsock control. The Winsock control enables you to create applications that access the low-level functions of the Transmission Control Protocol/Internet Protocol (TCP/IP), thereby providing an alternative to HTTP or FTP for communication purposes.

TCP/IP Fundamentals

Exchanging information from computer to computer requires that they be able to speak in a common language. One of the most common languages in use today is the Transmission Control Protocol/Internet Protocol. TCP/IP is a specification that defines a series of protocols used to standardize how computers exchange information with each other.

The protocols in TCP/IP are arranged in a series of layers known as a *protocol stack* (see Figure 23.1). What happens within a layer is isolated from the layer above it or below it. There is a physical layer, not shown in the figure, that deals with the actual communications hardware (modems, Ethernet cards, and so on). Above this is the IP layer that handles moving data from one node in the network to the next. Above the IP layer is a layer called the TCP layer, which deals with how to move data from the source to the destination, ignoring any nodes in between. At the top of the stack is the application layer, which deals with more familiar functions, such as FTP and HTTP, as shown in Figure 23.1. If security is required, it is handled in the stack above the TCP layer.

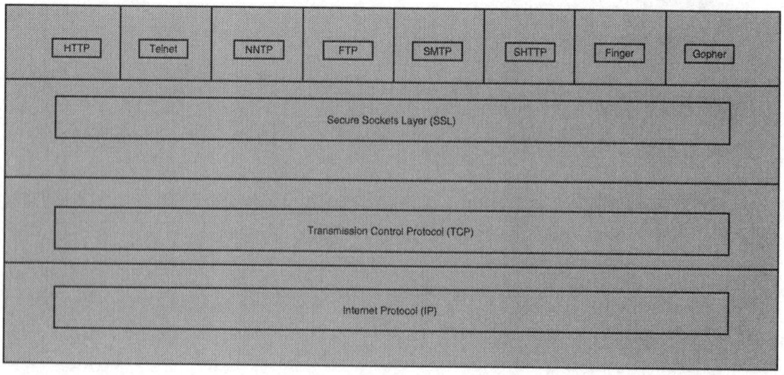

FIGURE 23.1

The TCP/IP stack diagram.

| HTTP | Telnet | NNTP | FTP | SMTP | SHTTP | Finger | Gopher |

Secure Sockets Layer (SSL)

Transmission Control Protocol (TCP)

Internet Protocol (IP)

The creation of the TCP/IP answered several concerns about how computers would talk to each other over the Internet. An even bigger question was still to be answered: How would applications talk to other applications over the Internet? To put it another way, how would they talk to the TCP/IP stack. This problem was particularly vexing for developers on the Windows platform. The development of Winsock solved this problem early in the history of the Internet.

Winsock is short for Windows Sockets. It was created in the fall of 1991 and is used in the interface between TCP/IP and Windows TCP/IP. Today's most popular Internet applications for Microsoft Windows and Microsoft NT are developed according to the Winsock standard.

Refer to the MSDN Library: Windows Socket Specification or to the TechNet Library for information about TCP/IP.

How Does It Work?

Winsock is a standard that is maintained by Microsoft. This standard is basically a set of routines that describe communications to and from the TCP/IP stack. These routines reside in a dynamic link library (DLL) that runs under Windows 3.1, Windows NT, and Windows 9x. The Winsock DLL is interfaced with TCP/IP and from there through the Internet.

The easiest way to show how Winsock works is with the diagram in Figure 23.2.

FIGURE 23.2
The Winsock layer.

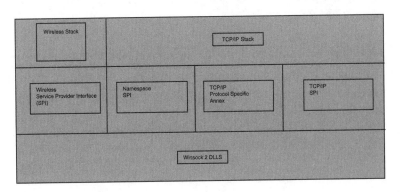

The Winsock DLL is a layer between an application and the TCP/IP stack. The application tells the Winsock DLL what to do. These instructions then go to the TCP/IP stack, and the TCP/IP stack passes them along to the Internet.

The Winsock Application Programming Interface (API) in the Win32API includes Microsoft's own INetAPI Internet extensions. The extensions found in the INetAPI extend the functionality of the HTTP and FTP. These same extensions are encapsulated in the Winsock and Internet Transfer controls that ship with Visual Basic 6.

> **NOTE**
>
> For more reading on TCP/IP, you might want to check out the MDSN Library or Microsoft's TechNet CD-ROM. Many Web sites and books can supply you with a wide range of information on TCP/IP.

A Word About Clients and Servers

Before beginning to create your own client or server program, it would be wise to consider just what you are attempting to create.

In a typical networking environment, the client application requests information from the server application; as soon as the server application receives the client request, the server application responds with the appropriate information. The important thing to note about client/server programming using the Winsock control is that the client always makes the request for a connection.

In a typical Winsock application, the server is constantly listening for a client request. On receipt of a client request, the server first responds to the initial request. When they are connected, a peer relationship exists in which either the client or the server can request information of each other.

Domain Names and IP Addresses

As computers became more closely networked, a system became necessary to give remote computers the capability to recognize other remote computers; thus was born the method of IP addressing. An *IP address* uniquely identifies any computer connected to a network. This address is a four-byte number with each byte separated from the next by a period. This number is uniquely assigned to your computer, whether you are connected to another computer via your company network, to the Internet, or to a wide area network that spans the entire globe.

As networks increased in popularity, network administrators found it increasingly difficult to remember all the IP addresses for each computer to which they needed to connect. The domain name service (DNS) was designed to enable the administrators of these networks to quickly access a specific computer by its own unique name.

Understanding Ports

You have already seen how TCP/IP forms the backbone of all Internet communication between computers, but do you know how the various applications on different computers talk to each other?

The answer is ports. A *port* is a special location in the computer's memory that exists when two computers are in communication via TCP/IP. Applications use a port number as an identifier to other computers; both the sending and receiving computers use this port to exchange data.

To make the job of communication easier, some port numbers have been standardized. These standard port numbers have no inherent value other than that users have agreed to use them with certain applications. Table 23.1 lists a number of popular and publicly accepted port numbers and their corresponding applications.

TABLE 23.1 PUBLICLY ACCEPTED PORTS AND THEIR POINTS OF CALL

Service	Port
HTTP (WWW)	80
FTP	20,21
Gopher	70
SMTP	25
POP3	110
Telnet	23
Finger	79
Local loops/callbacks	0

Using the Microsoft Winsock Control

The Microsoft Winsock control makes using the TCP/IP a breeze. Microsoft has wrapped up the Winsock and INetAPI API calls into a nice neat package that you can easily incorporate into your Visual Basic applications.

To illustrate the use of the Winsock control, this chapter's example demonstrates most of the control's methods and events. You will build a client/server application that consists of both a client application and a server application. You can use this application as the basis for a wide range of client/server applications using the Winsock control.

The client application will have the capability to connect to the Winsock control and exchange data. The server portion will have the capability to accept multiple server connections and report on the status of each connection as it is created.

Winsock Operating Modes

Before you begin developing with the Winsock control, you must decide which of the two available protocols you are going to use. The Winsock control supports the following two operating modes:

- `sckTCPProtocol`   The Winsock control will be operating in TCP mode.
- `sckUDPProtocol`   The Winsock control will be operating in User Datagram Protocol (UDP) mode.

TCP Basics

The TCP enables you to create and maintain a connection to a remote computer. By using the connection, both computers can stream data between each other.

If you are creating a client application, you must find out the server computer's name or IP address (`RemoteHost` property), as well as the port (`RemotePort` property) on which it will be listening. Then invoke the `Connect` method.

If you are creating a server application, set a port (`LocalPort` property) on which to listen, and invoke the `Listen` method. When the client computer requests a connection, the `ConnectionRequest` event will occur. To complete the connection, invoke the `Accept` method within the `ConnectionRequest` event.

When a connection has been made, both computers can send and receive data. To send data, invoke the `SendData` method. Whenever data is received, the `DataArrival` event occurs. Invoke the `GetData` method within the `DataArrival` event to retrieve the data.

UDP Basics

UDP is a connectionless protocol. Unlike TCP operations, computers do not establish a connection. Also, a UDP application can be either a client or a server.

To transmit data, first set the client computer's `LocalPort` property. The server computer then needs only to set the Remote Host to the Internet address of the client computer, set the `RemotePort` property to the same port as the client computer's `LocalPort` property, and invoke the `SendData` method to begin sending messages. The client computer then uses the `GetData` method within the `DataArrival` event to retrieve the sent messages.

Properties of the Winsock Control

Winsock enables you to create clients and servers using the same control. This dual functionality enables you to specify through property setting the type of application you will be building. The Winsock control uses a number of the same properties, whether you are creating a client or a server, thereby all but eliminating the learning curve needed to create applications. The next couple of sections describe the properties available to the Winsock control and how they can be called in an application.

BytesReceived Property

The BytesReceived property tells you the number of bytes currently in the receive buffer. BytesReceived is read-only and is unavailable at design time. The value returned is a long integer. The following is an example of the syntax; the code here, and in the next sections, applies to a Winsock control with the default name of Winsock1:

```
RetVar = Winsock1.BytesReceived
```

You might use the BytesReceived property to determine the size of a display area for the data or to see whether there is any data in the buffer.

LocalHostName Property

The LocalHostName property returns the name of the local host system. LocalHostName is read-only and is unavailable at design time. The value returned is a string. The following is an example of the syntax:

```
RetVar = Winsock1.LocalHostName
```

LocalIP Property

The LocalIP property returns the local host system IP address in the form of a string, such as 204.246.66.6. This property is read-only and is unavailable at design time. The value returned is a string. An example of the syntax is

```
RetVar = Winsock1.LocalIP
```

LocalPort Property

The LocalPort property returns or sets the local port number. LocalPort can be both read from and written to and is available both at design time and runtime. The value returned is a long integer. The following is an example of the syntax to read the property:

```
RetVar = Winsock1.LocalPort
```

To set the property, you use the following:

```
Winsock1.LocalPort = 1007
```

23

CLIENT/SERVER
PROGRAMMING
WITH WINSOCK

An example of using this property is setting the port prior to using the `Listen` method to set the port number for the application. This allows selection of the port at runtime.

Protocol Property

The `Protocol` property returns or sets the protocol of either UDP or TCP. This property can be both read from and written to and is available both at design time and runtime. (Note that at runtime the control must be closed—see the section "`State` Property" later in this chapter.) The value returned is `0` (or the constant `sckTCPProtocol`) or `1` (or `sckUDPProtocol`). The following is an example of the syntax to read this property:

```
RetVar = Winsock1.Protocol
```

To set the property, you use

```
Winsock1.LocalPort = sckTCPProtocol
```

RemoteHost Property

The `RemoteHost` property returns or sets the remote host. `RemoteHost` can be both read from and written to and is available both at design time and runtime. The value returned is a string and can be specified either as an IP address (such as `204.246.66.6`) or as a DNS name (such as `www.microsoft.com`). The following is an example of the syntax to read the property:

```
RetVar = Winsock1.RemoteHost
```

To set the property, you use

```
Winsock1.RemoteHost = "127.0.0.1"
sClientMsg = "Sending data to " & Winsock1.RemoteHostIP
```

Setting this property at runtime enables the user to select the remote host when the application starts or base the selection on some criteria.

RemotePort Property

The `RemotePort` property returns or sets the remote port number. This property can be both read from and written to and is available both at design time and runtime. The value returned is a long integer. An example of the syntax to read the property is

```
RetVar = Winsock1.RemotePort
```

To set the property, use the following:

```
Winsock1.RemotePort = 1007
```

This property can be used to select the application that is to be contacted at the remote host.

State Property

The State property returns the state of the control as expressed by an enumerated list. This property is read-only and is unavailable at design time. The State property is set by using various methods and events. The syntax to read the property is

RetVar = *Winsock1*.State

Table 23.2 shows the settings for the State property.

TABLE 23.2   SETTINGS FOR THE STATE PROPERTY CAN PROVIDE SOME LEVEL OF EXCEPTION HANDLING

Constant	*Value*	*Description*
sckClosed	0	Default closed
sckOpen	1	Open
sckListening	2	Listening
sckConnectionPending	3	Connection pending
sckResolvingHost	4	Resolving host
sckHostResolved	5	Host resolved
sckConnecting	6	Connecting
sckConnected	7	Connected
sckClosing	8	Peer is closing the connection
sckError	9	Error

23

CLIENT/SERVER PROGRAMMING WITH WINSOCK

TIP

The State property needs to be checked via some built-in code routines before state-changing methods are used. For example, attempting to open a closed Winsock control will result in an error.

Methods of the Winsock Control

Methods are predefined functions used to perform various tasks on the control. There are methods that open and close a connection and methods that accept a request for the connection. The following sections discuss some of the important methods used with the Winsock control.

Accept Method

The Accept method is used for the TCP server applications only. It accepts the request for connection from a client system. For the Accept method to be used, the control must be in a *listening state*. This method is used in conjunction with the ConnectionRequest event, which is discussed later in this chapter.

The syntax for the Accept method appears as follows:

```
Private Sub Winsock1 ConnectionRequest (ByVal requestID as Long)
    Winsock1(NumSockets).Accept requestID
End Sub
```

Close Method

The Close method terminates a TCP connection from either the client or server applications. The syntax is

```
Winsock1.Close
```

GetData Method

GetData is the method that retrieves the current block of data from the buffer and then stores it in a variable of the variant type. The syntax is

```
Winsock1.GetData DataVar
```

PeekData Method

The PeekData method operates in a fashion similar to the GetData method. However, it does not remove data from the input queue. This method is available only for TCP connections. The following is the syntax:

```
Winsock1.PeekData DataVar
```

Listen Method

The Listen method is invoked on the server application to have the server application wait for a TCP request for connection from a client system. The syntax is

```
Winsock1.Listen
```

SendData Method

The SendData method dispatches data to the remote computer. It is used for both the client and server systems. The syntax is

```
Winsock1.SendData OutVar
```

The following is a code segment that illustrates its usage:

```
Private Sub cmdSend_Click()
    If Winsock1.State = sckConnected Then
        Winsock1.SendData txtClientData.Text
        sClMessage = "Sending data to " & Winsock1.RemoteHostIP
        List1.AddItem (sClMessage)
    Else
        MsgBox "Not currently connected"
    End If
End Sub
```

Connect Method

The Connect method requests a connection to a remote computer. The syntax is

```
object.connect remotehost, remoteport
```

The Remotehost argument is required and contains the name of the remote computer to connect to. The RemotePort argument contains the name of the port on the desired remote computer.

Events

Events are the triggers that invoke the methods. An example of an event is a mouse click. The events from other objects, such as a command button, trigger some of the methods in the preceding section. The Winsock control generates events that also can be used. Some of these events, such as the ConnectionRequest event, happen at the server as a result of an action taken by the client. The events generated by the Winsock control make it possible for an unattended system to participate in a network communications session.

Close Event

The Close event occurs when the remote computer closes the connection. The event can do cleanup work at the end of a session. The syntax is

```
Private Sub Winsock1_Close(Index As Integer)
    sServerMsg = "Connection closed: " & Socket(Index).RemoteHostIP
    List1.AddItem (sServerMsg)
    Socket(Index).Close
    Unload Socket(Index)
    NumSockets = NumSockets - 1
End Sub
```

Connect Event

The Connect event occurs after the connection with the remote computer has been made. The syntax is

```
Private Sub Winsock1_Connect()
    If Winsock1.State = sckConnected Then
        sClientMsg = "Connection Successful!"
        List1.AddItem (sClientMsg)
    End If
End Sub
```

ConnectionRequest Event

The ConnectionRequest event occurs when the server receives a request for connection from a client system. The syntax is

```
Private Sub Winsock1_ConnectionRequest(requestID As Long)
```

This example shows the code necessary to connect a Winsock control using the TCP. The code runs on the machine that is accepting the connection request. The RequestID parameter identifies the request. This is passed to the Accept method, which accepts the particular request. The following code segment illustrates how this event might be used:

```
Private Sub WinsockTCP_ConnectionRequest _
(requestID As Long)
    If Winsock1.State <> sckClosed Then Winsock1.Close
    Winsock.Accept requestID
End Sub
```

DataArrival Event

The DataArrival event occurs when new data arrives. The syntax is

```
Private Sub Winsock1_DataArrival(ByVal bytesTotal As Long)
    Dim sData As String
    Winsock1.GetData sData, vbString
    sClMessage = "Received data " & sData & " from " &
     ③Winsock1.RemoteHostIP
    List1.AddItem (sClMessage)
End Sub
```

SendComplete Event

The SendComplete event occurs when a send operation is completed. The syntax is

```
Winsock1_SendComplete
```

SendProgress Event

The SendProgess event occurs while data is being sent. The syntax is

```
Winsock1_SendProgress(bytesSent As Long, bytesRemaining As Long)
```

BytesSent indicates the number of bytes sent since the last time this event was fired.

BytesRemaining indicates the number of bytes in the send buffer waiting to be sent.

Error Event

The `Error` event occurs whenever a background process such as connecting, sending, or receiving fails to complete or generates an error. The syntax is

```
Winsock1_Error(number As Integer, Description As String, Scode As Long,
  ➥Source As String, HelpFile As String, HelpContext As Long,
  ➥CancelDisplay As Boolean)
```

Creating the Price Lookup Example

One of the current trends in software development today is the issue of thick clients versus thin clients. A *thick client* is basically an application that performs the bulk of the processing on the individual client PC, whereas a *thin client* performs the processing on the server. The next example explores how the Winsock can help with the creation of thin clients.

Traditional client/server systems rely on a closed system to exchange data between two sites or between a client and a server. The Internet has created new possibilities for creating networks and ways for applications to exchange data. The Winsock control gives you the ability to easily create clients that are thin—with just a few lines of code.

The project that you will create enables a client application to request price information from a server connected to a database. To use this example, the products database that comes on the CD-ROM needs to be on your system.

You can find the complete source code for the Price Lookup project in the \Ch31\PLU folder on the CD-ROM included with this book.

Creating the Client

The client portion of our project is designed to enable a user to enter a product item number and then click the Lookup button to view the current price of the item. Sounds simple, doesn't it? Actually, it is. The client takes the value entered into the `txtItem` field and sends it to the server applications that use it to look up the price in a database. The server then sends the data back to the client, where it is displayed in the `lblPrice` field. To create the client application, perform the following steps:

1. Start a new Standard EXE in Visual Basic with the name of Client2.vbp.

2. Confirm that you have the Winsock control in your ToolBox.

3. Place the Winsock control and the other controls on the form, as shown in Figure 23.3.

4. Set their properties as follows:

Control	Value	Name
Command1	Close	cmdClose
Command2	Connect	cmdConnect
Command3	Send	cmdSend
text1	txtItem	
text2	txtPrice	
shape1	circle	shpGO
shape2	circle	shpWait
shape3	circle	shpError
Winsock	sckTCP	Winsock1

5. Your screen should now resemble the one in Figure 23.3.

6. Write the code for the command buttons and the Winsock control.

7. Save your work and build your executable file, client2.exe, using the file menu|make exe.

FIGURE 23.3

The client portion of the Price Lookup example enables users to retrieve price information from a remote database.

The complete source code for the client can be found on the CD-ROM included with this book.

Listing 23.1 shows the complete source code for the client.

LISTING 23.1   CLIENT2.EXE—THE CLIENT USES THE WINSOCK CONTROL TO SEND THE ITEM NUMBER TO THE SERVER

```
Option Explicit
Private Sub cmdClose_Click()
    Winsock1.Close
    shpGo.Visible = False
```

```
        shpWait.Visible = False
        shpError.Visible = True
End Sub

Private Sub cmdConnect_Click()
    Winsock1.RemoteHost = "127.0.0.1"
    Winsock1.RemotePort = 1007
    Winsock1.Connect
    shpGo.Visible = True
    txtItem.SetFocus

End Sub

Private Sub cmdSend_Click()
 If Winsock1.State = sckConnected Then
        Winsock1.SendData txtItem.Text
        shpGo.Visible = True
        lblMessage.Caption = "Sending Data"
    Else
        shpGo.Visible = False
        shpWait.Visible = False
        shpError.Visible = True
        lblMessage.Caption = "Not currently connected to host"
    End If
End Sub

Private Sub Winsock1_DataArrival(ByVal bytesTotal As Long)
    Dim sData As String

    Winsock1.GetData sData, vbString
    lblPrice.Caption = sData

    lblMessage.Caption = "Received data"
    shpGo.Visible = True
    shpWait.Visible = False
    shpError.Visible = False

End Sub

Private Sub Winsock1_SendComplete()
    lblMessage.Caption = "Completed Data Transmission"
End Sub
```

Creating the Server

The server portion of the Price Lookup example is designed to accept the item number sent from the client and look up the associated price in a database. The server then sends the price information back to the client.

The connection to the database is made in the `DataArrival` event of the Winsock control. The following code segment opens the database and finds the first occurrence of the value in `sItemData`. When the record is found, the value contained in the price field is sent back to the client.

```
        ' Get clients request from database
    strData = "ItemNumber = '" & sItemData & "'"
    Data1.Recordset.MoveLast
    Data1.Recordset.FindFirst strData
    strOutData = Data1.Recordset.Fields("Price")
```

To create the server portion of the example, perform the following steps:

1. Start a new Standard EXE in Visual Basic with the name Server2.vbp.

2. Confirm that you have the Winsock control in your ToolBox.

3. Place the Winsock control and the other controls on the form, as shown in Figure 23.4.

4. Set their properties as follows:

Control	Name	Value
List11	list1	
Label1	lblHostName	Host
Label2	lblIP	IP Address
Label3	blUsers	Connections
Label4	lblHostId	
Label5	lblAddress	
Label6	lblConnections	
Winsock	Socket(0)	

5. Your screen should now resemble the one in Figure 23.4.

6. Write the code for the command buttons, labels, and Winsock control. Listing 23.2 shows the complete source code. The server is going to respond to the initial client request about a price lookup and will act as a client to a database server to retrieve the value from the database.

7. Save your work and build your executable file server2.exe, using the file menu|make exe.

FIGURE 23.4

The server portion of the Price Lookup example connects to a database to find the price, based on the item number sent from the client.

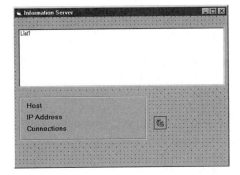

LISTING 23.2 SERVER2.EXE—THE SERVER PORTION OF THE PRICE LOOKUP EXAMPLE ENABLES USERS TO RETRIEVE PRICE INFORMATION FROM A REMOTE DATABASE

```
Option Explicit
Dim iSockets As Integer
Dim sServerMsg As String
Dim sRequestID As String


Private Sub cmdStop_Click()

End Sub
Private Sub Form_Load()
    '------------------------------------------------------------
    ' Program :    Server2.exe
    ' Author:      Loren D.Eidahl
    ' Noticce:
    '
    '------------------------------------------------------------
    frmServer.Show
    lblHostID.Caption = Socket(0).LocalHostName
    lblAddress.Caption = Socket(0).LocalIP
    Socket(0).LocalPort = 1007
    sServerMsg = "Listening to port: " & Socket(0).LocalPort
    List1.AddItem (sServerMsg)
    Socket(0).Listen
End Sub

Private Sub socket_Close(Index As Integer)
    sServerMsg = "Connection closed: " & Socket(Index).RemoteHostIP
    List1.AddItem (sServerMsg)
    Socket(Index).Close
    Unload Socket(Index)
    iSockets = iSockets - 1
    lblConnections.Caption = iSockets

End Sub
```

continues

23

CLIENT/SERVER
PROGRAMMING
WITH WINSOCK

LISTING 23.2 CONTINUED

```
Private Sub socket_ConnectionRequest(Index As Integer,
➡ ByVal requestID As Long)
    sServerMsg = "Connection request id " _
& requestID & " from " & Socket(Index).RemoteHostIP
  If Index = 0 Then
    List1.AddItem (sServerMsg)
    sRequestID = requestID
    iSockets = iSockets + 1
    lblConnections.Caption = iSockets
    Load Socket(iSockets)
    Socket(iSockets).LocalPort = 1007
    Socket(iSockets).Accept requestID
  End If

End Sub

Private Sub socket_DataArrival(Index As Integer, ByVal bytesTotal As Long)
    Dim sItemData As String
    Dim strData As String
    Dim strOutData As String

    ' get data from client
    Socket(Index).GetData vtData, vbString
    sServerMsg = "Received: " & vtData & " from " & _
Socket(Index).RemoteHostIP & "(" & sRequestID & ")"
    List1.AddItem (sServerMsg)

    ' Get clients request from database
    strData = "ItemNumber = '" & sItemData & "'"
    Data1.Recordset.MoveLast
    Data1.Recordset.FindFirst strData
    strOutData = Data1.Recordset.Fields("Price")

    'send data to client
    sServerMsg = "Sending: " & strOutData & " to " &
    ➡ Socket(Index).RemoteHostIP
    List1.AddItem (sServerMsg)
    Socket(Index).SendData strOutData

End Sub
```

A NOTE FROM THE AUTHOR

I realize that some readers might question the use of a `DataControl` to connect to the database on the server side.

Please understand that this chapter focuses on how to use the Winsock control, not on how to connect to a database. The point of this application is to show how the Winsock control can be used with just a few lines of code. Placing the necessary Active Data Objects (ADO) code into the application would easily have obscured the small amount of code required for the Winsock control.

In any real-world application, you would use whatever data connection mechanism is dictated by the application and the required data source.

Running the Example

After you have entered the code for both the client and the server, you will need to compile them into two separate executables.

The client and server applications you just created can run quite well on local or networked machines. To test the client and the server, perform the following steps:

1. Create executables for both the client and the server.

2. Confirm that you have TCP/IP installed on your machine. Windows 95 users might need to manually install the TCP/IP through Network Settings in the Control Panel, as shown in Figure 23.5. Windows NT users most likely will already have TCP/IP installed.

FIGURE 23.5

Install the TCP/IP protocol by selecting Add on the Configuration tab to the Network menu.

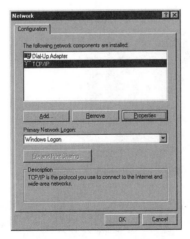

3. Launch the server component. The server should respond with a message indicating that it is listening to a particular port.

4. Launch an instance of the client application. Press the Connect button to establish a connection to the server. The green light on the client form should come on, indicating that the connection was successful. The server should also indicate that a client request was made, as shown in Figure 23.6.

FIGURE 23.6

The server will show the client ID number and the number of active connections.

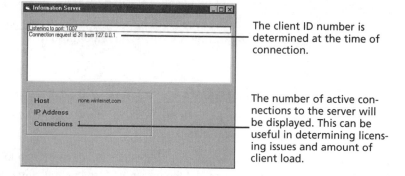

The client ID number is determined at the time of connection.

The number of active connections to the server will be displayed. This can be useful in determining licensing issues and amount of client load.

5. Launch a second instance of the client application and connect to the server.

6. From the first client application, enter the value 500 into the item number field and press the Lookup button. The value 8.9 should be displayed in the price field.

7. From the second instance of the application, enter the value 400 into the item number field and press the Lookup button. The value 23.46 should be displayed in the price field, as illustrated in Figure 23.7.

FIGURE 23.7

The server uses the DataControl to connect to a database

NOTE

Because of the lack of error handling in the client and server applications, it is quite possible that an error could occur that resets the client or server, or both, during the testing process.

Enhancements to the Price Lookup Example

As you worked your way through the Price Lookup example, undoubtedly a number of improvements and an application idea or two came to mind. As I mentioned earlier, this example is meant to be built on and enhanced.

The following ideas would improve the stability and performance of both the client and server applications:

- **Improvement of error handling**

  Currently there is no error handling in place for invalid client requests, problems with creating a connection, client losses of connection, and so forth. The error-handling portion of the server will most likely be the single largest area for improvement.

- **Implementation of a remote data connection**

  The example assumes that the database is located in the same path as the server. In real-life applications, the database could reside on a database server. There must be code to account for a distributed network of servers. One possible solution is to use the Remote Data Connection control (RDC) in VB 6.

- **Creation of log files for the server and client**

  In the first example, you printed various messages to a list box for public viewing. In a real-world application, printed log files would need to be generated indicating what level of activity is occurring on the server.

- **Use of classes to handle database connectivity**

  The server currently connects to the database in the `DataArrival` event of the Winsock control; this type of setup is far from ideal. A better solution would have the Winsock control reference a class object that made the database connection and returned the data to the server via an ActiveX EXE.

- **Implementation of cross-platform support**

  This chapter doesn't discuss this in detail; however, note that different platforms might respond differently or produce unexpected results. One possible solution to cross-platform woes is to use Windows API calls on those areas that could cause problems—such as interface and database connectivity.

- **Use of ActiveX Components**

  The server is an ideal candidate to be implemented as ActiveX EXE or ActiveX DLL with a separate interface connection—possibly through an ActiveX document.

All the preceding ideas for improvement can easily be implemented using the techniques mentioned in this book.

Summary

At this point you should have a clear idea of how to use the Winsock control in your applications. As you have seen from the example, you don't need to code for hours on end to create sophisticated client/server applications. The Winsock control provides you with the ability to access one of the most popular communication protocols available, guaranteeing that your applications can run on the Internet and your corporate intranet.

Advanced Programming Topics

PART

V

IN THIS PART

- **Using Office 97 Components With Visual Basic** *559*
- **Using Windows API Functions** *579*
- **Useful API Functions** *597*
- **Creating Telephony Applications With TAPI** *617*
- **Adding Speech Recognition With SAPI** *627*
- **Creating Your Own Add-Ins** *643*
- **Accessing the System Registry** *689*
- **Creating Online Help Systems** *737*
- **Debugging and Testing Techniques** *781*
- **Dynamic Control Creation and Indexing** *793*
- **Implementing OLE Drag and Drop Capabilities** *809*
- **Tuning and Optimizing Your Application** *831*
- **Algorithms for VB Programmers** *857*
- **Differences Between VBA and VB6** *875*
- **Programming for Microsoft Transaction Server** *889*
- **Visual SourceSafe: A Necessity for Serious Developers** *915*

Using Office 97 Components With Visual Basic

by Rob Thayer

IN THIS CHAPTER

- OLE *560*
- The OLE Control *561*
- OLE Automation *569*

CHAPTER 24

Although Visual Basic is a powerful language, there are times when the components that you need already exist in another application. Instead of recoding such components, it is sometimes possible to "borrow" them from another application.

All the applications in the Microsoft Office suite are based on object libraries that contain many external components. For example, Microsoft Excel makes available object types such as Worksheets and Charts. You can use these object types in your Visual Basic programs using the OLE container control or OLE automation.

The OLE container control can be used to link or embed objects directly into your programs. For instance, you can have a Microsoft Word document displayed in a window on a form. The document can be edited by double-clicking on the window. This enables you to implement the full functionality of the complex Word application with little or no coding.

OLE automation gives you access to the hundreds of object classes that were used to build the Microsoft Office applications. You can use these classes just as you would the classes that you create yourself.

This chapter will introduce you to the OLE control and OLE automation. With even a basic understanding of how OLE objects can be used, you will be able to utilize an extraordinary number of new program components and object classes.

OLE

OLE is a cornerstone of both the Windows operating system and Visual Basic. It provides a way for applications to communicate with one another and to share each other's components. For example, you can add the functionality of the various Office 97 applications (such as Word and Excel) right into your own Visual Basic programs. This is easily accomplished by using OLE technology.

OLE used to be short for Object Linking and Embedding, and that is a large part of what OLE does—it enables objects (documents) to be linked to or embedded into applications. It also does much more than that (which is why OLE no longer stands for the restrictive Object Linking and Embedding description), and these are the functions that will be discussed in this chapter. From a programmer's point of view, linking and embedding enables you to add an object, such as a Word document or an Excel spreadsheet, into your application without having to do a lot of extra coding to support it. In fact, an OLE object can be completely self-sufficient and not require a single line of code, as you'll see by following some of the examples given in this chapter.

Although linking and embedding both allow the functionality of one application (the *server*) to be added to another application (the *container*), they each go about it differently. When an object is linked, the container application is given a *reference* to the object rather than the object itself. This way, the data can be shared simultaneously among more than one application. If a change is made to the data in one application, any other applications that share the same data will also show the change. On the other side of the coin, embedded objects (and their data) actually exist within the container application. If the data is changed, any other applications that contain copies of the same data will not show the change. You'll see examples of both linked and embedded objects later in this chapter.

This might sound like cutting edge technology, but OLE is nothing new. In fact, it's beginnings go all the way back to 1991. Over the years, OLE has been refined and enhanced, resulting in the current version (2.0). In addition to linking and embedding documents within applications, OLE now deals with many more issues, such as object storage and reuse. The ActiveX controls in VB's Toolbox are based on OLE technology. In fact, the .OCX (OLE Custom Control) extension was given to ActiveX components because they communicate via 32-bit OLE interfaces. Controls in previous versions of Visual Basic (VBXes) were not based on OLE and used the Windows messaging services for communication.

Although it is not discussed in this chapter, there is another way for objects to communicate with each other. DDE, which stands for Dynamic Data Exchange, also provides a way for data and functions to be shared between applications. However, DDE, an older technology, is far more limited than OLE and should not be used unless OLE is for some reason not supported.

In Visual Basic, OLE objects can be used in two different ways. The first is through the OLE control, which enables an object to be embedded (or linked) into a Visual Basic program. The other way is through OLE automation, which accesses objects directly and enables you to manipulate them from within your VB programs. Both the OLE control and OLE automation will be covered in this chapter.

The OLE Control

Visual Basic supports OLE linking and embedding via its OLE control. Using this control, you can add the functionality of complex programs, such as Word and Excel, directly into your programs with a minimum of effort. The best way to understand how the OLE control works is to see it in action, so the first thing you'll do is create a program that contains linked and embedded objects.

This example will embed a Microsoft Word document into a Visual Basic program. For the program to work, you must have Microsoft Word installed on your system. Although OLE enables you to "borrow" the functionality of other applications (servers) and use

24

them in your own programs (containers), the server application must be present on whichever system you are running the container program.

> **NOTE**
>
> If you don't have Microsoft Word, you can substitute any other kind of linkable object available on your system. A list of available linkable objects is displayed in the Insert Object dialog box, which appears when an OLE control is added to a form.

To create the sample program, start a new project (Standard EXE). Use Table 24.1 as a guide for placing the controls on the form and building the program:

TABLE 24.1. THE CONTROLS (AND THEIR PROPERTY VALUES) THAT MAKE UP THE OLE TEST PROJECT

Control Type	Property	Value
Form	Name	frmOLETest
	Caption	OLE Test
	Height	6030
	StartUpPosition	2 - Center Screen
	Width	6735
CommandButton	Name	cmdSave
	Caption	Save
	Height	495
	Left	2880
	Top	4680
	Width	1215
OLE	Name	oleObject
	Height	4185
	Left	390
	Top	240
	Width	5895

Note that when you place the OLE control on the form, you will see the Insert Object dialog box shown in Figure 24.1.

FIGURE 24.1.

The Insert Object dialog box appears automatically whenever an OLE control is added to a form.

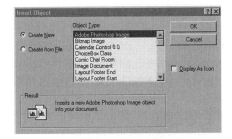

The Insert Object dialog box provides a list of all object types available on your system (your list will most likely be different from the one shown in Figure 24.1). You are also given two options for how you want to insert the object: `Create New` or `Create from File`. If you select the `Create New` option, an object with no data (a new object) will be embedded into your application. If you select the `Create from File` option, a specific object will be inserted. For this example, select `Create from File`.

When you select the `Create from File` option, the list of embeddable objects disappears, and you are asked to specify a filename. You can use any file you want, but for this example, the Microsoft Word document OLETEST.DOC, which can be found on the CD that accompanies this book, will be used.

After you specify the file to be used, click the `Open` button. You will be returned to the Insert Object dialog box. For now, leave the `Link` and `Display as Icon` options unchecked. You'll learn more about them in just a moment. Click `OK` to insert the object.

You should then see a copy of the object (OLETEST.DOC or whatever file you specified) inside the OLE control (see Figure 24.2). You can now finish changing the OLE control's properties as shown in Table 24.1.

FIGURE 24.2.

An embedded object (Microsoft Word file OLETEST.DOC) inside an OLE control.

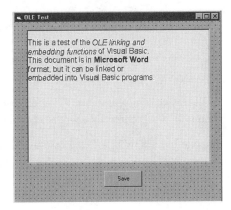

24

USING OFFICE 97 COMPONENTS WITH VB

Go ahead and run the program. The object still appears in the OLE control, no surprise there. But double-click on the OLE control and see what happens. You are allowed to edit the object (in this case, a Word document) right from within your application. Essentially, you've embedded a copy of the object, along with the server application that it belongs to, in your own application (see Figure 24.3).

FIGURE 24.3.

Editing the embedded object from within the running VB application.

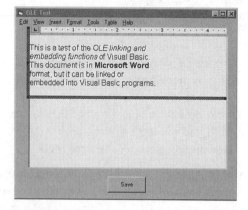

Notice also that after the document has been activated (by double-clicking on it), your application is provided with a menu bar that it did not have before. These menu options are taken directly from Word and can be used to make changes to the document, just like they would if you had loaded the document into Word and edited that way.

> **NOTE**
>
> If your application already has a menu bar and an embedded object is activated, it will merge its menu options with those of your application.

You can make as many changes as you want to the embedded document, but you'll find that there is no way to save them because Word's File menu is missing. Why is that?

When you embed an object in Visual Basic, you have to use VB code to save changes to the object. This is accomplished using the OLE control's SaveToFile method.

Exit the program and then add the code in Listing 24.1 to the cmdSave CommandButton's Click event.

LISTING 24.1. CH24-01.TXT—THE cmdSave_Click EVENT, WHICH SAVES THE DATA OF THE oleObject OLE CONTAINER CONTROL.

```
Private Sub cmdSave_Click()

Dim intFileNum As Integer

' Get the next available file number.
intFileNum = FreeFile

' Open a binary file with the name of the embedded
' object (oleObject.SourceDoc) and write out the
' object's data to that file using the OLE control's
' SaveToFile method.
If oleObject.OLEType = vbOLEEmbedded Then
    Open oleObject.SourceDoc For Binary As #intFileNum
    oleObject.SaveToFile intFileNum
    Close #intFileNum
End If

End Sub
```

In the preceding code, the SaveToFile method is only used if the object is embedded rather than linked (oleObject.OLEType = vbOLEEmbedded). SaveToFile works with linked objects too (oleObject.OLEtype = vbOLELinked), but it doesn't save the object's data. Instead, it saves the link information and an image of the data to the file.

To save the object's data to a file, you need to open a binary file, call the SaveToFile method, and then close the file. The filename used in the preceding procedure comes from the OLE control's SourceDoc property, which contains the name of the file specified in the Insert Object dialog box.

NOTE

If you want to save the object in OLE version 1.0 format, use the SaveToOle1File method in place of SaveOleFile.

If you run the program again, make some changes to the embedded object, and then click the Save button, the object's data will be saved. You can verify this by stopping the program and running it again. When the object data is loaded in, it should include the changes that you made.

To try some other variations of embedded objects, stop the program and then right-click the oleObject OLE control. You will see a pop-up menu of options. Choose Insert Object and the Insert Object dialog box opens.

Once again, choose the `Create from File` option and specify the OLETEST.DOC file (or any other object). Then make sure that the Link option is checked. Click `OK`, and you should see a message that asks you whether you want to delete the current embedded object (see Figure 24.4). Choose `Yes`.

You now have a linked object contained in your application. It might look the same as an embedded object, but as you'll soon see, it acts differently.

Run the program; then double-click the object. Instead of being able to edit the object within your application, the object's server application (in this case, Microsoft Word) is invoked. The object can then be edited and saved within the server application. When the file is saved, it is automatically updated in your application.

Stop the program; then go back to the Insert Object dialog box by right-clicking the `oleObject` control and choosing `Insert Object` from the pop-up menu. Choose the `Create from File` option; then specify the same file you've been working with. This time, leave the `Link` option unchecked, but check the `Display As Icon` option. Click `OK` to accept your choices.

You'll get another prompt, but this time it asks whether you want to delete the current link. Remember, a linked object is only a reference to an object and not the object itself. The last object that was inserted into the application was linked, not embedded. So you are asked whether you want to delete the link rather than the embedded object. Choose `Yes`.

Because you selected the `Display As Icon` option, you'll see an icon rather than the object's data (see Figure 24.5). If you run the program and double-click the icon, the object's server application will again be invoked, and the object can be edited (and saved). The `Display As Icon` option is useful if you don't want to actually display an object's data but still want the user to be able to edit it indirectly through your program.

If you don't want to embed an existing object, you can use the `Create New` option on the Insert Object dialog box. This will embed a blank object in the OLE container control. It's basically the same as using the `Create from File` option, but because it's a new file, there isn't any data associated with it. Figure 24.6 shows an embedded Microsoft Excel Chart object.

FIGURE 24.5.

An embedded Word document with the Display As Icon *option selected.*

FIGURE 24.6.

An embedded Microsoft Excel Chart object.

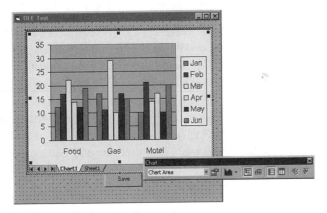

Along with the chart is a toolbar that enables you to specify how the chart will look. For example, you can choose the type of chart displayed by using the Chart Type pull-down icon. When the program is run, the toolbar will disappear. It reappears when the user double-clicks the embedded object to make it active.

There are probably dozens of different embeddable object types available on your system. You can use any of them in your programs, but keep in mind that the object's server application must be present on each user's system if you plan to distribute your programs. So if you choose to use Microsoft Excel charts in your application, you must be sure that anyone who uses the application also has Microsoft Excel installed on her system.

OLE Control Properties and Methods

Like any other ActiveX control, the OLE container control has properties that can be used to specify how it looks and acts. It also has a few methods that can be called to accomplish certain tasks. This section gives brief descriptions of some of the more important properties and methods of the OLE container control.

Objects often have many operations that can be performed on them. These are called *verbs*. If you right-click an embedded object at runtime, the pop-up menu that appears will show all the valid verbs for the object. For example, if you run the program with the embedded Microsoft Excel Chart object and right-click the object, the pop-up menu contains two options (verbs): Open and Edit. The Open verb opens the object's server application (in this case, Microsoft Excel) and displays the object's data. The Edit verb allows the chart to be edited within the OLE container control, just as if you had double-clicked the object. You can disable the pop-up verb menu by setting the AutoVerbMenu property to False. A setting of True enables the pop-up menu (the default).

You can obtain a list of all of an object's valid verbs using the ObjectVerbs and ObjectVerbsCount properties. ObjectVerbs is a zero-based string array that contains all the supported verbs for the object, and ObjectVerbsCount specifies the number of elements in the ObjectVerbs array. The default verb for the object is always contained in ObjectVerbs(0). The ObjectVerbFlags property can be used to determine the menu state of a verb when passed the verb's element number in the ObjectVerbs array. Possible values are vbOLEFlagChecked (&H0008), vbOLEFlagDisabled (&H0002), vbOLEFlagEnabled (&H0000), vbOLEFlagGrayed (&H0001), and vbOLEFlagSeparator (&H0800). To update the list of verbs that an object supports, call the FetchVerbs method.

If you want to cause an object to perform the operation associated with one of its supported verbs, you can use the DoVerb method. The DoVerb method takes only one argument, and that is a numeric value that indicates the verb to be performed. Possible values for the argument are: vbOLEShow (-1), vbOLEOpen (-2), vbOLEHide (-3), vbOLEUIActivate (-4), vbOLEInPlaceActivate (-5), and vbOLEDiscardUndoState (-6). If you want to perform the operation for the object's default verb, either call the DoVerb method without an argument or use the value vbOLEPrimary (0).

The AutoActivate property specifies how an object can become activated. The default value is vbOLEActivateDoubleclick (2), which means that the user needs to double-click the object to activate it. However, you can change this property to vbOLEActivateManual (0), which means that you must call the DoVerb method to activate the object; vbOLEActivateGetFocus (1), which activates an object when it receives the focus (by single-clicking it); or vbOLEActiveAuto (3), which activates an object when it gets the focus or when it is double-clicked.

If you want to check to see whether an object's server application is running, then examine the value of the AppIsRunning property. A value of True indicates that the server application is running. The AppIsRunning property is only available at runtime.

To specify how the object appears within the OLE container control, use the SizeMode property. The default value (vbOLESizeClip, 0) indicates that the object is displayed at its actual size. If the OLE control is too small to display all the data, the data is clipped. You can change this property to vbOLESizeStretch (1), which resizes the object so that it will fit within the OLE control; vbOLESizeAutoSize (2), which resizes the OLE control automatically to fit all of the object; and vbOLESizeZoom (3), which resizes the object to fit the container control the best it can while still maintaining the object's original proportions.

As you saw earlier in this chapter, a linked object is updated whenever it is changed by its server application. The UpdateOptions property can be used to change when and how linked data gets updated. The default is vbOLEAutomatic (0), which means that the object is updated whenever its data changes. Other possible values are vbOLEFrozen (1), which indicates that the data should only be updated when its linked data is saved by the server application; or vbOLEManual (2), which indicates that the data should only be updated when the OLE control's Update method is called. Keep in mind that the UpdateOptions property only works for linked objects, not embedded objects.

If you want to display only a specific section of an object's data rather than all the data, you can use the SourceItem property. For example, if you only wanted the OLE control to contain a range of cells for an Excel spreadsheet, you might set the SourceItem property to "R1C1:R5C5." This would display only the cells in rows 1 through 5, and columns 1 through 5. Of course, the type of information that you use with the SourceItem property depends on the type of object with which you are dealing.

Finally, if you want to display the Insert Object dialog box, call the OLE control's InsertObjDlg method. This will enable the user to specify the type of object that should be contained by the OLE control.

OLE Automation

Another way to integrate Microsoft Office and other applications' components into your own programs is by using OLE automation. OLE automation does not require that you use the OLE control. Instead, you define objects of different classes in your code.

Before you can use OLE automation, you need to know the class of the object that you want to use. The easiest way to list available classes on your system is to use the References dialog box (see Figure 24.7). Choose Project | References from VB's menu.

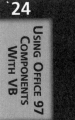

24

USING OFFICE 97 COMPONENTS WITH VB

You will be shown a list of object libraries available on your system. Simply check the ones you want to use; then click OK.

FIGURE 24.7.

The References dialog box lists available OLE object libraries on your system.

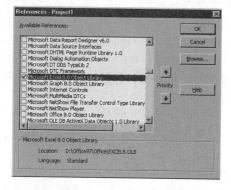

In this example, the Microsoft Excel 8.0 Object Library is used. This object library contains a number of Excel-specific objects that can be used by the VB programmer.

To see the objects now available to you, use VB's Object Browser (see Figure 24.8). Press F2 to display the Object Browser.

FIGURE 24.8.

The Object Browser, which can be used to display the objects available in all referenced object libraries.

By default, the Object Browser shows all the objects in all the object libraries referenced by your project. This can be a little confusing because you only want to see the objects available from the Excel 8.0 object library. Use the Object Browser's top list box to select Excel so that only the Excel objects will be shown.

You should now have a list of objects in the Excel 8.0 Object Library (see Figure 24.9). As you can see, quite a few objects are still available to you just from this one library. These are the object classes that the Excel application uses. The classes are defined as public, so they are exposed to outside applications, such as your Visual Basic programs.

FIGURE 24.9.

The Object Browser, showing only the objects exposed by the Excel 8.0 Object Library.

If you select one of the object classes, such as Worksheet, you will see the list of properties, methods, and events for that class. After you look at some of the object classes in an object library, it becomes obvious that OLE automation can provide your programs with an incredible amount of complex prewritten software components. However, keep in mind that you cannot use these classes in your programs if your users do not also have the object library installed on their system (that is, if they do not have Microsoft Excel on their system).

So how do you use these object classes in your programs? Simple: Declare an object variable of a particular class just as you would any other object. For example, the following sections of code:

```
Dim objSpread As New Excel.Worksheet
```

or

```
Dim objSpread As Object
Set objSpread = New Excel.Worksheet
```

declare the variable objSpread to be of class type Worksheet, which was one of the object classes exposed in the Excel 8.0 Object Library. The second object declaration method shown above is used as a work-around for a problem in VB that sometimes causes multiple object references to be created when using the New keyword. You must have established a reference to the object library you will be using before using any classes

from that library. A reference to the Excel library was previously established using the References dialog box.

Declaring an object this way is known as *early binding* because the compiler knows the type of object that the variable will hold when the program is compiled. Objects can also be declared using *late binding*, where the variable is declared as type `Object`, but the actual class is not specified. For example, the Excel `Worksheet` object (`objSpread`) declared previously could also be declared by using the following code:

```
Dim objSpread As Object
Set objSpread = CreateObject("Excel.Worksheet")
```

The variable is declared to be of type `Object` and then is assigned an actual object type using the `CreateObject` statement. Late binding is appropriate if you don't know an object's class when the variable that holds it is declared. However, you should try to use early binding whenever possible because it is more efficient.

After an object has been declared using either early or late binding, you might want to load some existing data into the object. This is accomplished using the `GetObject` statement. For example, to declare an object to be of Microsoft Word's `Document` class and to load in the `OLETEST.DOC` document used in earlier examples, the following code might be used:

```
Dim objDocument As New Word.Document
Set objDocument = GetObject("OLETest.doc")
```

The `GetObject` statement can also be used to define the class of the object while also specifying its data, such as:

```
Dim objDocument As Object
Set objDocument = GetObject("OLETest.doc", Word.Document)
```

After you've defined an object, you can use its properties, methods, and events to specify how it should look and what it should do. Because of the complexity of the Microsoft Office object libraries and their many object classes, a discussion of how to use individual components is beyond the scope of this chapter. Because the Office components are used the same way through OLE automation as they are in VBA, it is recommended that you use a comprehensive book on VBA for more information.

When you are finished using an object, you should close it (using a `Quit` or `Close` method works for some objects) and set the object to `Nothing`. This will free up any system resources that the object might have been using.

Using OLE Automation

To illustrate how OLE automation works, the following sample program can be constructed. It uses two objects, one of the `Word.Application` class and one of the

`Word.Document` class. Together, they are used to display an instance of the Word application and a new document. The application will be displayed on the screen, and the document will be given some text. Command buttons in the sample program will enable the document's data to be saved and the application to be closed.

Start a new project (Standard EXE). Using the References dialog box, make sure that the Microsoft Word 8.0 Object Library is checked. Note that you must have Microsoft Word installed on your system to follow along with this example.

Add a new module to the project. In the module's General Declarations section, add the following lines of code:

```
Public objWordApp As New Word.Application
Public objWordDoc As Object
```

This will declare the two objects that will be used in the program. One (`objWordApp`) will be early-bound, and one (`objWordDoc`) will be late-bound.

To build the program's user interface, go back to the project's form and use Table 24.2 and Figure 24.10 as a guide for adding the various components and changing their properties:

TABLE 24.2. THE COMPONENTS THAT MAKE UP THE OLE AUTOMATION SAMPLE PROGRAM

Control Type	*Property*	*Value*
Form	Name	frmOLEAuto
	Caption	OLE Automation
	ControlBox	False
	Height	3105
	StartUpPosition	2 - CenterScreen
	Width	1665
CommandButton	Name	cmdLaunch
	Caption	Launch App
	Height	495
	Left	180
	Top	165
	Width	1215
CommandButton	Name	cmdSaveDoc
	Caption	Save Doc
	Height	495
	Left	180

24

continues

TABLE 24.2. CONTINUED

Control Type	Property	Value
	Top	795
	Width	1215
CommandButton	Name	cmdCloseApp
	Caption	Close App
	Height	495
	Left	180
	Top	1425
	Width	1215
CommandButton	Name	cmdExit
	Caption	Exit
	Height	495
	Left	180
	Top	2070
	Width	1215

FIGURE 24.10.
The OLE Automation sample program's user interface.

After the program's user interface has been created, some code needs to be added. The first section of code (see Listing 24.2) is for the first command button, which launches the Word application.

LISTING 24.2. CH24-02.TXT—THE CODE FOR THE cmdLaunch_Click EVENT, WHICH LAUNCHES THE WORD APPLICATION USING OLE AUTOMATION.

```
Private Sub cmdLaunch_Click()

' Check to see if application has already been
' launched.
If Not (objWordDoc Is Nothing) Then
    MsgBox "Application already launched!"
    Exit Sub
End If
```

```
' Set up the size of the Word application window and
' make the app visible.
objWordApp.Width = 300
objWordApp.Height = 200
objWordApp.Left = 0
objWordApp.Top = 0
objWordApp.Visible = True

' Add a document to the Word application.
Set objWordDoc = objWordApp.Documents.Add()

' Give the document some text.
objWordDoc.Content = "This is a test"

End Sub
```

This event procedure first checks to see whether the application has already been launched. It does this by evaluating the `objWordDoc` object to see whether it is `Nothing`. If it is `Nothing`, that means it hasn't yet been assigned an object class and, consequently, that the application hasn't been launched. Note that the `objWordApp` object cannot be compared to `Nothing` because it was assigned an object type (`Word.Application`) when it was declared.

Next, the size of the Word application window and its position (upper-left corner of the screen) are specified using the `objWordApp` object's `Top`, `Left`, `Height`, and `Width` properties. Then the application is revealed by setting its `Visible` property to `True`.

A document is added to the newly launched Word application by using the `Add` method for the application's `Documents` collection (`objWordApp.Documents.Add`). This new document is represented by the `objWordDoc` object. Some content is added to the document using the `Content` property.

The rest of the command buttons' `Click` events are shown in Listing 24.3.

LISTING 24.3.   CH24-03.TXT—THE `Click` EVENTS FOR THE REST OF THE COMMAND BUTTONS IN THE OLE AUTOMATION SAMPLE PROGRAM.

```
Private Sub cmdSaveDoc_Click()

' Check to see if objWordDoc is Nothing. If it is,
' then the app hasn't been launched, so nothing can be
' saved. Otherwise, use objWordDoc's Save method to
' save the document.
If objWordDoc Is Nothing Then
    MsgBox "Application not launched!"
Else
    objWordDoc.Save
```

continues

24

USING OFFICE 97
COMPONENTS
WITH VB

LISTING 24.3. CONTINUED

```
End If

End Sub


Private Sub cmdCloseApp_Click()

' Check to see if objWordDoc is nothing. If it is,
' then the app cannot be closed because it hasn't yet
' been launched. Otherwise, quit the app and assign
' objWordApp and objWordDoc to Nothing to free up
' resources.
If objWordDoc Is Nothing Then
    MsgBox "Application not launched!"
Else
    objWordApp.Quit
    Set objWordDoc = Nothing
    Set objWordApp = Nothing
End If

End Sub


Private Sub cmdExit_Click()

' Check to see if objWordDoc is Nothing. If it is,
' then exit the program. Otherwise, notify the user
' that the app must be closed first.
If objWordDoc Is Nothing Then
    Unload Me
    End
Else
    MsgBox "Close application first!"
End If

End Sub
```

In all the Click events, the objWordDoc object is checked to see whether it is Nothing before the rest of the procedure is executed. In the cmdSaveDoc_Click event, the document cannot be saved if the application has not been launched. In the cmdCloseApp_Click event, the application cannot be closed if it hasn't been launched. And in the cmdExit_Click event, the program can only be exited if the objWordDoc is equal to Nothing (indicating that the application either hasn't been launched or has been closed).

The cmdSaveDoc_Click event is triggered when the Save Doc command button is clicked. It uses the objWordDoc object's Save method to save the document.

The `cmdCloseApp_Click` event closes the application and is triggered when the Close App button is clicked. To close the application, the `objWordApp` object's `Quit` method is called. Then the `objWordApp` and `objWordDoc` objects are both set to `Nothing` to free up any system resources they were using.

Finally, the `cmdExit_Click` event ends the program. By the time the program ends, the application must have already been closed (if it was launched in the first place).

When you run this sample program, you should see a small form with four buttons on it. Clicking the `Launch App` button will launch the Word application, create a new document, and add some text to it (see Figure 24.11).

FIGURE 24.11.

The OLE automation sample program can launch the Microsoft Word application.

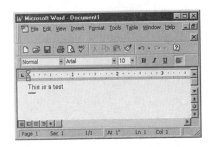

If you click the `Save Doc` button, you'll be asked to provide the filename of the document. If you click `Cancel`, the program will give you an error. That's because the program returns an error that you can trap for if the user chooses not to save the document. Otherwise, you wouldn't be able to tell whether the document was actually saved. The sample program doesn't trap for the error, so an error condition results.

The `Close App` button will quit the application. If the document hasn't been saved since it was last changed, you will be prompted if you want to save the document before exiting. Choose No to close the application. Click the `Exit` button to exit the program.

Admittedly, the sample program doesn't do much. But it does show how OLE automation can be used with Microsoft Office components (or any components, for that matter) to add extra functionality to your programs.

24

USING OFFICE 97
COMPONENTS
WITH VB

Summary

The Windows operating system has a built-in way of enabling components from one application to be used in another application. OLE enables an application's objects to be linked or embedded into other programs. In Visual Basic, the OLE control is used to implement linking and embedding of objects.

Another way of using an application's exposed classes (object types) is through OLE automation. OLE automation lets you use component types from applications such as Microsoft Word and Excel right in your VB programs.

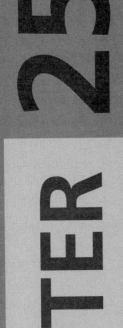

Using Windows API Functions

by Rob Thayer

IN THIS CHAPTER

- The Windows API Library Files *580*
- Declaring a Windows API Function *583*
- Passing Arguments by Value and by Reference *585*
- `Declare` Statement Argument Data Types *586*
- The API Text Viewer *589*
- Using Windows API Functions in Your Applications *592*
- How to Use Windows API Callbacks *594*

The Visual Basic programming environment is a very powerful platform for creating Windows applications. Sometimes, however, you will want to extend the features of Visual Basic to do things that are possible in the Windows environment but are not directly supported by Visual Basic.

An example of extending Visual Basic is printing angled, or slanted, text. In the Visual Basic environment, all text is displayed horizontally, usually within the confines of a text box or some other control. If you want to display text at any angle other than 45 degrees—and you don't have an ActiveX control that will do it for you—you have to call a Windows function that is located in the Windows Application Programming Interface (API).

The Windows API can also be used to create windows in shapes other than rectangular. Your application would really be unique if it used a circular or triangular window! The API opens up a world of possibilities for the serious developer.

The Windows API is a set of several hundred functions and subroutines that are located in a set of files called dynamic link libraries (DLLs). You can make a function from the Windows API available to your Visual Basic program by "declaring" the function to be callable from your program. You can then use the Windows API function as you would any built-in Visual Basic function or a function you have written yourself. After you master the use of the Windows API, you'll have a powerful new tool that will enable you to break out of the confines of Visual Basic and extend your programs in ways you might not have thought were possible.

This chapter covers the following topics concerning using the Windows API:

- The set of dynamic link libraries and how they are used
- How to include Windows API functions in your programs—the `Declare` statement
- The syntax and data types of the `Declare` statement
- How to use the API Text Viewer program
- Examples of using Windows API functions in your applications
- How to use Windows API callbacks

The Windows API Library Files

The Dynamic Link Library (DLL) files that make up the Windows API are commonly located in the Windows SYSTEM subdirectory. These files are found on every PC that is running Windows, so you don't have to worry about including them if you create a set of setup disks for distribution.

The three Windows DLLs are USER32.DLL, KERNEL32.DLL, and GDI32.DLL. Several smaller DLLs are known as extension DLLs and provide functions in addition to those found in the three major DLLs. Some useful extension DLLs include the following:

```
COMDLG.DLL

DLLLZ32.DLL

VERSION.DLL

APIGID.DLL

COMCTL32.DLL

MAPI32.DLL

NETAPI32.DLL

ODBC32.DLL

WINMM.DLL
```

Figure 25.1 details the relationship between the three major DLLs and the Windows operating system.

FIGURE 25.1.
The relationship of the major DLLs to the Windows operating system.

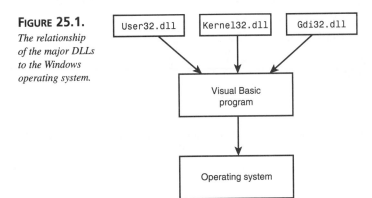

The following sections discuss in some detail the primary purposes of each DLL as well as some examples of the functions they provide.

USER32.DLL

The USER32.DLL library file contains functions that relate to managing the Windows environment, such as

- Handling messages between windows
- Managing cursors
- Managing menus
- Handling other non-display functions

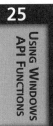

The following list outlines some of the functions of the USER32 library:

GetCursorPos& returns the cursor's screen position in X and Y coordinates.

SetWindowPos& sets a window's position, size, state, and Z-order.

GetParent& returns the handle of a parent window.

GetActiveWindow& returns the handle of the active window, or zero if no window is active.

SendMessage& sends a message to a window, triggering an event for that window or telling it to perform some action.

GDI32.DLL

The GDI32.DLL library file (the Graphics Device Interface library) contains functions that help manage output to different devices, especially the screen. Following are some of the functions in GDI32:

BitBlt& copies a bitmap image from one device context to another.

DeleteObject& deletes a GDI object (that is, fonts or bitmaps) from memory.

RoundRect& draws a rectangle with rounded corners.

SelectObject& selects a graphics object into a device context.

StretchBlt& stretches and manipulates a bitmap image as it copies it from one device context to another.

KERNEL32.DLL

The KERNEL32.DLL library contains functions that manage the low-level operating system functions. These functions include

- Memory management
- Task management
- Resource handling
- File and directory management
- Module management

Here are some of the functions in the KERNEL32 library:

GetSystemDirectory& returns the full path of the Windows system directory.

GetTempFileName& returns the path and name of a temporary file that can be used by an application.

GetModuleFileName& returns the full path name for a module (that is, DLL or application) that is loaded into memory.

GetVersionEx& returns the versions of DOS and Windows currently running on the system.

The Extension DLL Libraries

The extension DLLs are libraries added to Windows when the functionality of Windows has changed in some way, usually with the addition of new features to the operating system. Instead of completely rewriting the operating system whenever a new feature is added, a new DLL is added to the system that includes the functions that add the new feature to the operating system. For example, when Microsoft added multimedia capabilities to Windows, it created a new DLL that includes the multimedia functions, WINMM.DLL.

The major extension libraries that are a part of Windows are

- COMCTL32.DLL adds the new Windows common controls that are part of Windows 9*x* and Windows NT 4.0. Examples of these include the ToolBar and TreeView controls.

- MAPI32.DLL implements the functions that let any application work with electronic mail.

- NETAPI32.DLL adds a set of functions that enable applications to access and control networks.

- ODBC32.DLL implements a set of functions that let applications work with databases that are ODBC-compliant. ODBC stands for Open Database Connectivity.

- WINMM.DLL implements a set of functions that access the operating system's multimedia capabilities, such as playback of sound and video.

- TAPI32.DLL adds a set of functions that provide telephony functionality in Windows. Telephony is the merging of telephones and computers and is commonly used in voice mail and automated attendant phone systems.

These are the library files and extensions to the Windows operating system you will call when you write programs that access the Windows API. After you learn how to call these libraries from your Visual Basic applications (the subject of the next section), you can tap the full power of the Windows environment.

Declaring a Windows API Function

To include a Windows API function in your Visual Basic programs, use the Declare statement to "declare" the function to be a part of your program. The Declare statement is added to the General Declarations section of either a standard module or a form. If the Declare statement is added to a standard module, the function is considered Public and can be called from anywhere in your application. If the Declare statement is added to the General Declarations section of a form, the function is local to that form and can only be called from within that form. In the latter case, you must precede the declaration with the Private keyword.

The syntax of the Declare statement depends on whether or not the procedure you call returns a value. If the procedure does return a value, you use the Function form of the Declare statement:

```
[Public ¦ Private] Declare Function publicname Lib "libname"
➥[Alias "alias"] _
 [([[ByVal ¦ ByRef] argument [As Type] [,[ByVal ¦ ByRef] argument
➥[As Type]]...])] [As Type]
```

If the procedure does not return a value, you use the Sub form of the Declare statement:

```
[Public ¦ Private] Declare Sub publicname Lib "libname" [Alias "alias"] _
 [([[ByVal ¦ ByRef] argument [As Type] _
 [,[ByVal ¦ ByRef] argument [As Type]] ...])]
```

This might look pretty complicated, but it isn't when you break it down into its separate parts. The Public and Private options define the scope of the function and determine whether or not it can be used outside of the module in which it is declared. The name of the function is defined by the publicname parameter, and the DLL library in which it is located is specified by the libname parameter.

> **NOTE**
>
> Although API routines that return a value are defined as Functions, and those that do not are defined as Subs, the word "function" is typically used to indicate either case. So whenever you see the word "function" used in the text of this chapter, take it to mean "a Windows API routine."

Some functions have aliases, or alternate names by which they can be called. For example, the SetFocus function has an alias of SetFocusAPI. Without the alias, the function would not be usable from within Visual Basic because its name conflicts with the SetFocus method. The use of aliases will be discussed in more detail later in this chapter.

The next part of the Declare statement is an optional list of arguments. Arguments can be passed to the function by reference (the default), or by value using the ByVal keyword. You'll learn more about this in the next section.

Finally, in the case of a Function (and not a Sub) you might need to define the type of value that is returned by the function using the optional As Type construct. The only difference between subs and functions is that functions return a value and subs do not. The majority of the Windows API is made up of functions, and they typically return a long integer value that indicates the success or failure of the function. You can either define the type of return value using the `As Type` construct, or you can simply append an identifier to the function name itself. For example, `BitBlt&` indicates that the `BitBlt` function returns a long integer.

Here is an example of calling a Windows API function using the `Function` form of the `Declare` statement from a standard module. This function returns the handle of the currently active window on a desktop:

```
Declare Function GetActiveWindow Lib "User32" () As Long
```

Here is an example of calling a Windows API function using the sub form of the `Declare` statement from the General Declarations section of a form. This Windows API function moves the referenced window and changes its size:

```
Private Declare FunctionSub MoveWindow& Lib "User32" (ByVal hWnd As _
    Long, ByVal X As Long, ByVal Y As Long, ByVal _
    nWidth As Long, ByVal nHeight As Long, ByVal _
    bRepaint As Long)
```

The two sample Windows API function calls only had long integer argument types. However, many more data types are used in calling Windows API functions. Some of these data types are standard Visual Basic data types, but some are based on C++ data types and can be tricky to use for a programmer who doesn't have experience in C++. The following sections cover in more detail the structure of the `Declare` statement's arguments, including how the arguments are passed to the Windows API and the legal data types for `Declare` statement arguments.

Passing Arguments by Value and by Reference

You can pass arguments to a function by value or by reference. Passing an argument by value means that a copy of the argument is sent to the function. Passing arguments by value means that the function cannot change the value of the actual argument because it is only working with a copy of the argument.

Passing an argument by reference means that the function is actually passing a 32-bit pointer to the memory address where the value of the argument is stored. When an argument is passed to a function by reference, it is possible for the function to actually change the value of the argument because the function is working with the actual memory address where the argument's value is stored and not just a copy of the argument's value.

With Windows API functions, the passing of arguments by value or by reference is not simply a matter of programmer choice. The functions that make up the Windows API expect its arguments to be passed either by value or by reference. It is up to you, the programmer, to know the proper way to pass arguments to a particular function. If you pass an argument by value when the function expects the argument to be passed by reference, or vice versa, the function will receive the wrong type of data and will probably not work correctly. And when you're dealing with system-level functions, the results can be very unpredictable indeed.

Visual Basic, by default, passes arguments to functions by reference. It is not necessary then, when writing a `Declare` statement, to explicitly pass an argument to the function using the `ByRef` keyword. When passing arguments by value, however, you must explicitly use the `ByVal` keyword.

Some Windows API functions that require more than one argument might have some arguments that must be passed by value and some arguments that are passed by reference. In this case, you have to use `ByVal` for the arguments passed by value, but you can use the `ByRef` keyword or leave it out for arguments passed by reference.

The following code shows an example of a `Declare` statement that declares a function that requires some arguments to be passed by value and some to be passed by reference:

```
Declare Function CreateIcon& Lib "user32" (ByVal hInstance As Long, _
    ByVal nWidth As Long, ByVal nPlanes As Byte, ByVal nBitsPixel As Byte, _
    lpANDbits As Byte, lpXORbits As Byte)
```

Two of the arguments to this function, `lpANDbits` and `lpXORbits`, are passed by reference (the default), whereas the other arguments are passed by value.

Declare Statement Argument Data Types

The functions that make up the Windows API are written in C. The data types that C accepts are often similar to the data types of Visual Basic, but in some cases, there are significant differences between the data types of the two languages. Not having a clear understanding of these differences can lead to Windows API function calls that don't work properly or don't work at all in some cases. The following sections discuss the most common data types the different Windows API functions expect and how they are declared in Visual Basic.

INTEGER

The `INTEGER` data type is used for 16-bit numeric arguments that correspond to the C data types `short`, `unsigned short`, and `WORD`. Arguments of the `INTEGER` data type are passed by value, and are typically written as `(ByVal argument As Integer)` or `(ByVal argument%)`.

LONG

The LONG data type is used for 32-bit numeric arguments that correspond to the C data types int, unsigned int, unsigned long, BOOL, DWORD, and LONG. LONG data type arguments are passed by value, and are typically written as (ByVal *argument* As Long) or (ByVal *argument*&). This is the most common data type used with Windows API functions.

STRING

The Windows API functions expect the LPSTR C data type, which is a memory pointer to characters (in C, a string is an array of characters). STRING data type arguments are passed by value and are typically written as (ByVal *argument* As String) or (ByVal *argument*$). When a string parameter is passed to a Windows API function, the string is supposed to be passed as a pointer to a null terminated string, which is a string with a last character with the ASCII value 0. Visual Basic automatically converts a string passed by value to this type of string by adding a null termination character.

STRUCTURE

Some Windows API functions expect their arguments to be of a STRUCTURE type. A STRUCTURE in C++ is the equivalent to a user-defined type (UDT) in Visual Basic. UDT data type arguments are passed by reference, and are typically written as (*argument* As UDT). For example, an argument shown as (myRect As RECT), where RECT is a UDT that defines a rectangle structure which is very common in controlling windows with the Windows API. Before declaring and calling API functions that use STRUCTURE argument types, you must be sure to define the structure first in your program using a Type...End Type construct.

> **NOTE**
>
> The file WIN32API.TXT that comes with Visual Basic contains Type...End Type constructs for all of the STRUCTUREs used by the Windows API functions. You can cut and paste what you need from that file, or you can use the API Text Viewer tool that also comes with Visual Basic. That program is discussed in more detail in the next section.

ANY

Some Windows API functions accept more than one data type for the same argument. If you want to be able to pass more than one data type with the argument, use the ANY data type. The ANY data type is passed by reference and is typically written as (*argument* As Any).

These are the major data types you will encounter when calling Windows API functions. But before you look at some examples of actually using the Windows API in a program, some other aspects of the Declare statement need to be discussed.

Using Aliases

Some Windows API functions are named using characters that are illegal in Visual Basic. A very common example is the underscore, as in _lopen. Trying to reference this name in Visual Basic generates an error because of the underscore character. The way around this is to "alias" the name in the Declare statement. For example, to use the _lopen function, the following Declare statement will work:

```
Declare Function lopen Lib "kernel32" Alias "_lopen" _
(ByVal lpPathname As String, ByVal ireadWrite As Long) As Long
```

The Windows API function _lopen is renamed lopen so that it is recognized as a legal name in Visual Basic. The Alias keyword lets Visual Basic know that the function it is really working with is _lopen.

Another use of the Alias keyword is to change the name of a function, usually for readability reasons. For example, the GetRgnBox& function might be renamed GetRegionBox& through the use of the Alias keyword so its purpose is more apparent.

You have to be careful when using aliases because they sometimes change from version to version of an API. For example, a function's alias in the 16-bit Windows API may not be the same in the Win32 API.

Using Ordinal Numbers as Function Names

Sometimes a Windows API function can be named with its ordinal number rather than a more descriptive text name. Using an ordinal number requires less system resources, so it is slightly more efficient than using a text name.

If you want to refer to a function by its ordinal number, use the Alias keyword to refer to the number, as in

```
Declare Function GetWindowsDirectory Lib "kernel32" Alias "#432" _
 (ByVal lpBuffer As String, ByVal nSize As Long) As Long
```

> **NOTE**
>
> To find the ordinal number of a Windows API function, you must use a utility program such as Dumpbin.exe, which is included with Microsoft Visual C++.

The API Text Viewer

As you have probably surmised by now, creating a `Declare` statement that gets the right Windows API function and declares it using the proper syntax and data types can be a little tricky. Starting with Visual Basic 4, Microsoft included with the Visual Basic distribution a utility program to help with finding the right API function and declaring it legally and properly within an application—the API Text Viewer. The API Text Viewer, or just the API Viewer, separates three different aspects of calling API functions—constants, declares, and types—into groups that can be viewed together. You can then select an item from the group, and the proper syntactical form is displayed in the API Viewer. You can then take the form and cut and paste it directly into your application. This helps ensure that you do not have a mistake in a `Declare` statement or a `Constant` declaration.

The API Viewer is usually found in the same program group as Visual Basic. Figure 25.2 shows the API Viewer in all its glory.

FIGURE 25.2.

The API Viewer form.

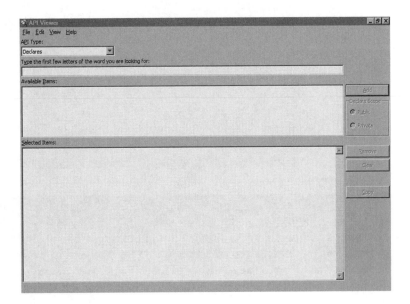

The API Type ComboBox enables you to select the type of API information you want to view. There are three types available:

- Declares
- Constants
- Types

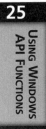

These three API types are stored in a text file called `Win32api.txt`. When you select one of the types from the API Type listbox, that section of the `Win32api` text file is displayed.

To load the text file, select File | Load Text File from the API Viewer menu. Then select the `Win32api` file from the dialog box that appears. This is a pretty big file, so it may take a few moments to load in. Figure 25.3 shows the API Viewer form after the `Win32api` text file is loaded.

FIGURE 25.3.

The API Viewer form displaying Declare API types from the `Win32api` *text file.*

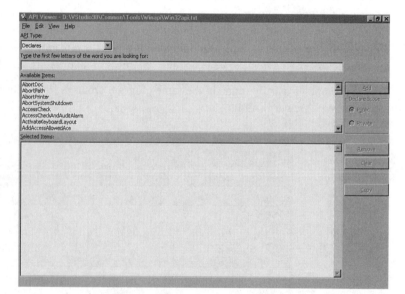

> **NOTE**
>
> After the `Win32api` text file loads, a dialog box might pop up asking if you want to convert the text file to a database (`.MDB`) file. Converting the text file to a database file enables the API types to load faster. After you do this, you select `Load Database File` instead of `Load Text File` from the File menu.

All of the API functions are displayed in the Available Items ListBox in alphabetical order. To select a function to view, double-click the item or click on the Add button. The function declaration statement is then added to the Selected Items text box. Figure 25.4 shows the `GetWindowTextLength` function declaration displayed in the Selected Items text box.

FIGURE 25.4.

The Get Window-
Text Length
*function displayed
in the API Viewer.*

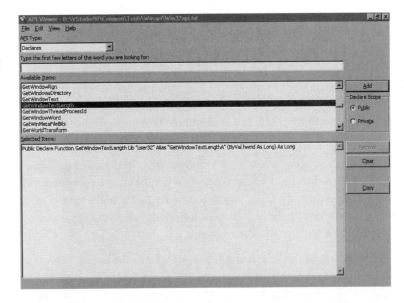

Note that there are two radio buttons with which you can choose a Public or Private
scope declaration of the function you will be using. You need to select one or the other
before adding the function to the Selected Items text box. The default scope is Public.

After you select a Declare statement to view, you can copy it to the Clipboard by clicking the Copy button located to the right of the Selected Items text box. After the text is on
the Clipboard, you can easily paste it into your Visual Basic application.

You can also copy Type structures and constants that are used by the Win32 API functions by selecting either Types or Constants in the API Type list box, then repeating the
same steps that you did for copying Declare statements. Of course, you will need to
know which constants and Type structures your API functions use. You can find this
information in an API reference, such as Dan Appleman's *Visual Basic Programmer's
Guide to the Win32 API.*

Using Windows API Functions in Your Applications

There are many ways to use the Windows API functions in your applications. One set of API functions you will use often when you start writing advanced Windows applications is the set of API functions that deal with getting information about a window or set of windows.

Every window in the Windows operating system is identified by a handle. The desktop window has a handle, a Visual Basic form displayed in an application has a handle, and even the controls on a form, which are themselves actually windows, have handles. You can gather a lot of information about the windows in your application after you get the handle of the window that interests you.

To get the handle of the active window on your desktop, you need to use the function GetActiveWindow. This function returns the handle of the active window. To use this function in your application, add the following line to a standard module:

```
Declare Function GetActiveWindow Lib "user32" () As Long
```

With this function declared, you can now add code to your application to call the function. For example, to use this function in a simple application, create a form with one command button on it. Add the following code to the Command button's Click event:

```
Dim lonHwnd As Long
lonHwnd = GetActiveWindow&
MsgBox "Active Window Handle: " & Str$(lonHwnd)
```

When you run this application and click the Command button, you see the message box shown in Figure 25.5.

FIGURE 25.5.

Getting the handle of the active window.

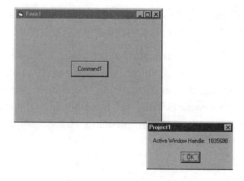

After you get the handle of a window, you can use that information to do other things with the windows on your desktop using the Windows API. For example, to make a window the active window, you can pass its handle to the SetActiveWindow& function, which makes active the window associated with whichever handle it is passed.

The Declare statement for SetActiveWindow& is

```
Declare Function SetActiveWindow Lib "user32" (ByVal hWnd As Long) As Long
```

You can add this function to your code to make a window the active window:

```
Dim lonStatus as Long
lonStatus = SetActiveWindow(lonHwnd)
```

The argument lonHwnd is the handle of a window, which was acquired through another Windows API function such as GetActiveWindow&. The variable lonStatus is used because the SetActiveWindow& function returns a long integer that represents the handle of the previously active window.

> **NOTE**
>
> Most of the ActiveX controls in Visual Basic have an hWnd property that you can use to obtain its handle.

The preceding examples give only a hint of the power of the Windows API functions. Every aspect of the Windows environment, from the Windows environment itself to handling hardware such as printers and disk drives, can be controlled to a greater or lesser extent by using Windows API functions. Taking the time to learn these functions can help you gain greater control over your applications' environment, and you can often achieve significant efficiency gains using the API functions in your applications. Chapter 26, "Useful API Functions," details many more handy API functions and provides examples of how to use them.

> **CAUTION**
>
> When writing Windows API functions, be sure to save your work often because it is easy to crash your system and lose your work if one of your API functions goes awry. In fact, many programmers set up their Visual Basic environment to prompt them to save the project every time they run it. The setting for a project to automatically save the program when it is run can be found on the Environment tab of the Options dialog box (select the Options menu item from VB's Tools menu).

25

USING WINDOWS API FUNCTIONS

How to Use Windows API Callbacks

The Windows API includes several functions called enumeration functions. An example of a Windows API enumeration function is EnumWindows. EnumWindows provides a list of the handles of all parent windows in the Windows environment. It does this by sending the list to a user-defined function that handles the list in some way, say by adding the handles to a ListBox control. For this to work, Visual Basic must be able to call the user-defined function *from within* the Windows API function—in this case, EnumWindows. The technique for doing so is called a callback.

To perform a callback, a function pointer that points to the memory address where the function is stored must be in the argument list of the Windows API function. Visual Basic 5.0 introduced the AddressOf operator. AddressOf can provide an API function with the memory address of the function it is associated with. The AddressOf operator is used this way:

```
AddressOf functionname
```

functionname is the name of the function to which AddressOf points. To see a callback in action, try out the following program. It uses the EnumWindows function to compile a list of all current parent windows and displays them in a ListBox control.

Create a project with one form and one module. Add a ListBox control to the form, and call it lstWinHandles. Then add the following code to the Form_Load event:

```
Private Sub Form_Load()

    Module1.GetWinHandles

End Sub
```

Type the following code into the module you added earlier:

```
Declare Function EnumWindows& Lib "user32" (ByVal lpEnumFunc As Long, _
    ByVal lParam As Long)

Public Sub GetWinHandles()

    Dim lonStatus As Long
    Dim lonDummy As Long

    lonStatus = EnumWindows&(AddressOf EnumWindowsProc, lonDummy)

End Sub
```

```
Function EnumWindowsProc (ByVal AddhWnd As Long, ByVal OptParam As Long)
➥As Long

    Form1.lstWinHandles.AddItem Str$(AddhWnd&)
    EnumWindowsProc = True

End Function
```

The first thing that happens when you run this program is that the `ListWinHandles` sub-routine in Module1 is called. This subroutine in turn calls the Windows API function `EnumWindows`, passing to it the memory address of your own `EnumWindowsProc` function and a dummy parameter value.

The `EnumWindowsProc` function is very simple. It takes the information that was passed from the `EnumWindows` API function (`AddhWnd`) and adds it to the `lstWinHandles` list box. The second parameter passed to `EnumWindowsProc` (`OptParam`) is not used. Note that `EnumWindowsProc` might be called several times, once for each parent window that is found by the `EnumWindows` API function.

The `AddressOf` operator is used to determine the memory address of the `EnumWindowsProc` function, which will act as the callback function in this example. Therefore, when the `EnumWindows` API function executes, it will send information to the `EnumWindowsProc` function (more about this in just a moment). Although it's not used in this example, the `lonDummy` argument is also passed to the `EnumWindowsProc`. This optional parameter gives the programmer some additional control as to how the callback function will work. For example, the argument could be changed from a long integer to a ListBox so the name of the ListBox that is used to hold the windows handles obtained by the `EnumWindows` API function could be specified at runtime. As it is now, the ListBox `lstWinHandles` is hard-coded into the `EnumWindowsProc` function, so that ListBox is used every time the function is called.

In the example, the API function (`EnumWindows`) passes two arguments to the callback function (`EnumWindowsProc`). The first is a window handle (remember, the whole purpose of the `EnumWindows` API function is to get the handles of all current parent windows). The last argument is of our own design, and it can be any type we define it to be.

Other API functions pass different arguments to the callback function. If you want to try implementing callbacks with other API functions, you'll have to do some research to find out which arguments they will pass to your callback function.

Summary

The Windows API function library provides the Visual Basic programmer with all the power available from the Windows platform. Every aspect of Windows, from the desktop environment to the hardware environment, can be controlled with one or more API functions. However, using the API functions can be tricky for a number of reasons, most of which revolve around the fact that the functions themselves are written in C and are not always compatible with Visual Basic. Many Visual Basic programmers are afraid to use the API functions because of this difficulty. However, by learning the syntax of the API functions you want to call, you can avoid the unexpected results and system crashes that have given the Windows API a bad name in Visual Basic circles. Using the API Text Viewer program can also help you get a handle on the complexity of the API functions.

Useful API
Functions

by Rob Thayer

In This Chapter

- Graphics and Display Functions   599
- System Functions   607

Visual Basic is a powerful language. It has literally hundreds of built-in functions and statements that can be used to accomplish many small miracles, such as determining how many days have elapsed between two dates or reading information from a disk file. Add to that functionality a full palette of ActiveX controls that can be used as building blocks for creating some extraordinary applications, and you have one incredible development environment that is capable of doing just about anything. Well, almost anything.

Even with the power of VB's built-in library of functions and statements and its unlimited toolbox of external controls, there are still things that VB either cannot do or cannot do efficiently. For example, copying one section of memory—including video memory—to another is not directly supported in Visual Basic. You could probably write a routine that would accomplish this seemingly simple feat, but it would be painfully slow. Unfortunately, VB is not equipped to handle things like that.

If you wanted to add some animation to your Visual Basic program, you might find that there is no efficient way to do so and surmise that VB simply is not the kind of development environment that supports animation. And, in a way, you would be right. But VB can tap into a huge library of functions that extend it in ways you might not have imagined. The best part is that the users of your VB program already have this library of functions built into their operating system, so you don't have to distribute any extra files or libraries for your program to make use of them.

So what is this library called? It's the Win32 API (Application Programmer's Interface), and it's built into every copy of Windows 95. Consisting of several DLLs (Dynamic Link Libraries), it contains thousands of functions that can be easily accessed from within Visual Basic or any other high-level language.

This chapter details some of the more important and useful functions accessible through the Win32 API. Of course, what is shown here is only a smattering of what is actually available. If you want to find out more about the API functions, I suggest you look at Dan Appleman's *Visual Basic Programmer's Guide to the Win32 API*. It's the definitive guide to all the API functions, and it was written with the VB programmer in mind.

If you want to learn more about how to actually call API functions from within Visual Basic, see Chapter 25, "Using Windows API Functions." This chapter assumes that you have some knowledge of how to call API functions, so you will want to read Chapter 25 first if you are not already familiar with how to do so. You should also be aware of the

WIN32API.TXT file, which contains all the declarations for the Win32 API functions as well as various constants and type structures used by the API functions. The WIN32API.TXT file is also covered in Chapter 25.

Graphics and Display Functions

One of the most useful aspects of the Win32 API is improving the performance of graphics. Even relatively simple graphics operations can require a great deal of calculation and memory manipulation. As a high-level language, Visual Basic is inadequate for performing such operations. For smooth animation and efficient graphic displays, Win32 API functions are often necessary.

Two of the most important API functions for graphics are BitBlt and StretchBlt, both of which copy bitmap images from one location to another. Among other uses, they can help create fast and smooth animation by quickly copying graphics images from one area of the screen to another.

Other graphics-related API functions include RoundRect, which can be used to draw rectangles with rounded corners; CreateFontIndirect and SelectObject, which can display text at any angle; and FlashWindow, which flashes a window's caption, perhaps in an attempt to get the user's attention. All these functions are detailed in this section.

Many more graphics functions are included in the Win32 API. Some provide services already covered by VB's built-in functions and statements, but others offer unique services that can only be accomplished through the API.

Copying Images: BitBlt& and StretchBlt&

Although you can copy one PictureBox image to another using a single line of code, there are times when you require more control over how the copy operation is performed. For example, you might want to copy only a portion of the source image to the destination image. For that, you'll need to use the Win32 API's BitBlt& function, which is declared as follows:

```
Declare Function BitBlt& Lib "gdi32" (ByVal hDescDC As Long, _
    ByVal x As Long, ByVal y As Long, ByVal nWidth As Long, _
    ByVal nHeight As Long, ByVal hSrcDC As Long, _
    ByVal xSrc As Long, ByVal ySrc As Long, ByVal dwRop As Long)
```

The arguments for the BitBlt& function are described in Table 26.1.

TABLE 26.1. THE ARGUMENTS OF THE BitBlt& API FUNCTION.

Argument	Description
hDescDC	The device context of the destination image
x	The logical x (horizontal) coordinate of the destination image's upper-left corner
y	The logical y (vertical) coordinate of the destination image's upper-left corner
nWidth	The width of the destination image
nHeight	The height of the destination image
hSrcDC	The device context of the source image
xSrc	The logical x (horizontal) coordinate of the source image
ySrc	The logical y (vertical) coordinate of the source image
dwRop	The raster operation to be used during the memory transfer

Typically, the BitBlt& function is used to copy all or part of the contents of a PictureBox control to another PictureBox control. Because the arguments of the function deal in pixels, the ScaleMode property of each PictureBox control should always be set to 3 (Pixel). The x and y arguments specify the logical coordinates *within the destination device context*, which means that an x, y coordinate of 0, 0 would indicate the upper-left corner of the source image, not the upper-left corner of the video screen. The same is true of the xSrc and ySrc arguments, though they refer to the logical coordinates of the source device context. The nWidth and nHeight arguments specify how much of the source image to transfer to the destination image.

The dwRop argument specifies the type of raster operation that should be performed during the image transfer. In most cases, this argument will be set to &HCC0020, which indicates a straight copy should be performed. However, other dwRop values are shown in the following table. The mnemonic (that is—SRCCOPY) is the constant for the value as defined in the WIN32API.TXT file.

SRCCOPY	&HCC0020	Destination = Source
SRCPAINT	&HEE0086	Destination = Source OR Destination
SRCAND	&H8800C6	Destination = Source AND Destination
SRCINVERT	&H660046	Destination = Source XOR Destination
SRCERASE	&H440328	Destination = Source AND (NOT Destination)
NOTSRCCOPY	&H330008	Destination = NOT Source
NOTSRCERASE	&H1100A6	Destination = (NOT Source) AND (NOT Destination)
MERGECOPY	&HC000CA	Destination = Source AND Pattern
MERGEPAINT	&HBB0226	Destination = (NOT Source) OR Destination

PATCOPY	&HF00021	Destination = Pattern
PATINVERT	&H5A0049	Destination = Pattern XOR Destination
PATPAINT	&HFB0A09	Destination = (NOT Source) OR Pattern OR Destination
DSTINVERT	&H550009	Destination = NOT Destination
BLACKNESS	&H42	Destination = 0
WHITENESS	&HFF0062	Destination = All bits set to 1

NOTE

The preceding raster operation codes suggest that certain types of bit manipulation be performed on the destination image. This can result in some strange effects. You might want to try experimenting with them to see what results you come up with.

All this might sound a bit confusing, but it's actually pretty simple. Basically, you define a source image and a destination image (hDescDC and hSrcDC) by providing a device context for each, which can be easily obtained using the PictureBox's hDC property. You also define the coordinates for the point within the source image (xSrc, ySrc) where the copying should begin as well as the number of pixels across (nWidth) and down (nHeight). You also specify the coordinates within the destination image (x, y) where the copied image should be placed. Finally, the dwRop argument determines which raster operations should be performed during the image transfer.

Take the following example. Suppose that a form has two PictureBox controls, picSource and picDest. The picSource control is the larger of the two, about 100×100 pixels square in size. picDest is only about 25×25 pixels square. If you wanted to copy a portion of the picSource image into picDest, the best way to do it would be to use the BitBlt& function, as shown in the following code:

```
Dim lonSrcX As Long
Dim lonSrcY As Long
Dim lonStatus As Long
Dim lonRasterOp As Long

' The ScaleMode property for the PictureBox controls
' must be set to 3 (Pixel).
picSource.ScaleMode = 3     ' Pixel
picDest.ScaleMode = 3       ' Pixel

' The lonSrcX and lonSrcY variables are used to specify
' the upper-left corner within the source image of where
```

```
' to start copying.
lonSrcX = 10
lonSrcY = 10

' Specify the raster operation to use during the image
' transfer. A straight copy is &HCC0020.
lonRasterOp = &HCC0020

lonStatus = BitBlt&(picDest.hDC, 0, 0, 25, 25, _
    picSource.hDC, lonSrcX, lonSrcY, lonRasterOp)
```

The preceding code will copy the source image (picSource), starting at 10 pixels left and 10 pixels down from its upper-left corner, to the destination image (picDest). The copy will be placed starting in the upper-left corner of picDest because 0,0 has been specified for the BitBlt& function's x and y arguments. The nHeight and nWidth arguments are both set to 25, so a portion of the picSource image 25 pixels high and 25 pixels wide will be placed into picDest (which, coincidentally, is the same size as the picDest control). The dwRop argument is set at &HCC0020, which specifies that a straight copy with no image manipulation or raster operation should be performed.

If you try out the sample code, make sure that you declare the BitBlt& function in a code module and that an image is assigned to the picSource control. Otherwise, you might get unexpected results.

You might have already picked up on BitBlt&'s major limitation: it can only be used to copy images (or portions of images) directly with no resizing or scaling. If, for example, you wanted to copy a source image 200 pixels wide × 200 pixels high into a destination image that is 50 pixels wide × 40 pixels high, you can't do it with BitBlt& because the source image would have to be scaled to fit the destination image. However, there is a slightly different version of BitBlt& that will accomplish this task: StretchBlt&. The declaration for the StretchBlt& function is shown below.

```
Declare Function StretchBlt& Lib "gdi32" (ByVal hDC As Long, _
    ByVal x As Long, ByVal y As Long, ByVal nWidth As Long, _
    ByVal nHeight As Long, ByVal hSrcDC As Long, _
    ByVal xSrc As Long, ByVal ySrc As Long, ByVal nSrcWidth As Long, _
    ByVal nSrcHeight As Long, ByVal dwRop As Long)
```

The StretchBlt& function has the same arguments as BitBlt&, with the addition of nSrcWidth and nSrcHeight. The function works in exactly the same way as BitBlt&, but you can now specify the height and width of the destination image, which BitBlt& assumed from the source image's height and width. If the source's height and width are different from the destination's height and width, the source image will be automatically reduced or enlarged to fit the parameters of the destination image.

Draw a Rectangle with Rounded Corners

Perhaps this isn't the most useful API function, but it can be used to create a more interesting program interface. With RoundRect&, you can draw rectangles with rounded corners. You can do the same thing with VB's Shape control, but RoundRec& can be used to draw rectangles inside other objects, such as PictureBox controls. The function is declared as follows:

```
Declare Function RoundRec& Lib "gdi32" (ByVal hDC As Long, _
    ByVal X1 As Long, ByVal Y1 As Long, ByVal X2 As Long, _
    ByVal Y2 As Long, ByVal X3 As Long, ByVal Y3 As Long)
```

The arguments of the RoundRect& function are detailed in Table 26.2.

TABLE 26.2. THE ARGUMENTS OF THE RoundRect& API FUNCTION.

Argument	Description
hDC	The device context for the object on which the rectangle will be drawn.
X1, Y1	The logical coordinates for the upper-left corner of the rectangle.
X2, Y2	The logical coordinates for the lower-right corner of the rectangle.
X3	The width (in pixels) of the ellipse used to round the corners of the rectangle. Use zero for no rounding.
Y3	The height (in pixels) of the ellipse used to round the corners of the rectangle. Use zero for no rounding.

Using the RoundRect& function is straightforward. You need only specify the device context of the object on which the rectangle will be drawn (hDC), the upper-left coordinates of the rectangle within the device context (X1, Y1), the lower-left coordinates of the rectangle (X2, Y2), and the height and width of the ellipse used for the rounding effect (X3 for the height, Y3 for the width). If you don't want any rounding at all, use zero for both X3 and Y3.

The RoundRect& function uses pixels for all its arguments, so you should always set the ScaleMode property of the object that is being used to 3 (Pixel). An example of how the RoundRect& function might be used follows. It draws a rectangle with rounded corners onto a PictureBox control called picCommand.

```
Dim lonDC As Long
Dim lonStatus As Long

picButton.ScaleMode = 3
lonDC = picButton.hDc
```

```
Status& = RoundRect&(lonDC, 5, 5, picButton.ScaleWidth - 5, _
    picButton.ScaleHeight - 5, 20, 20)
```

The rectangle starts 5 pixels left and 5 pixels down from `picButton`'s upper-left corner. The rectangle's lower-right corner will be 5 pixels right and 5 pixels up from `picButton`'s lower-right corner. An ellipse 20 pixels wide and 20 pixels high is used to round the corners.

Rotating Text

If you want to display text sideways or at any other degree of rotation, you'll need to use three Win32 API functions: `CreateFontIndirect&`, `SelectObject&`, and `DeleteObject&`.

The first function in this trio, `CreateFontIndirect&`, does the bulk of the work. It actually creates a new font, based on an existing TrueType font. The new font will be rotated at the correct degree of rotation, and you can display it on the screen just as you would any other font.

The `Declare` statement for the `CreateFontIndirect&` function should look like this:

```
Declare Function CreateFontIndirect& Lib "gdi32" _
    Alias "CreateFontIndirectA" (lpLogFont As LOGFONT)
```

It looks simple, and it is. Its single argument, `lpLogFont`, is a user-defined type called `LOGFONT` that contains specific information about the font to be created. The `LOGFONT` type (and the `LF_FACESIZE` constant that it uses) should be defined as follows:

```
Public Const LF_FACESIZE = 20

Public Type LOGFONT
    lfHeight          As Long
    lfWidth           As Long
    lfEscapement      As Long
    lfOrientation     As Long
    lfWeight          As Long
    lfItalic          As Byte
    lfUnderline       As Byte
    lfStrikeOut       As Byte
    lfCharSet         As Byte
    lfOutPrecision    As Byte
    lfClipPrecision   As Byte
    lfQuality         As Byte
    lfPitchAndFamily  As Byte
    lfFaceName        As String * LF_FACESIZE

End Type
```

To create a new font, you need only assign values to the various items of the `LOGFONT` type and then call the function. For example, to create a new font that is based on the

Arial TrueType font and rotated at 45 degrees, you would assign the string "Arial" (terminated with a null character, ASCII 0, at the end) to the lfFaceName item, and the degree of rotation multiplied by ten (450) to the lfEscapement item.

Setting the height of the font is a little trickier. You must multiply the desired point size by -20 and then divide it by the Screen object's TwipsPerPixelY property. You'll see an example of this later in this section.

The CreateFontIndirect& function returns a zero if it is not successful. If that is the case, you can use GetLastError& to determine the nature of the error. If the function is successful, however, it will return the handle for the new font which, as you'll soon see, will be used with the SelectObject& function.

After the new font has been created, you have to select the new font to the device context in which it will be used with the SelectObject& function. For example, if you will be displaying the new font inside a PictureBox control, then you must use SelectObject& to specify that the new font's handle should be associated with the PictureBox control.

The SelectObject& function's Declare statement is as follows:

```
Declare Function SelectObject& Lib "gdi32" (ByVal hDC As Long, _
    ByVal hObject As Long)
```

The hDC argument specifies the device context of the object that will be using the new font. In the case of a PictureBox control, you can use its hDC property.

The hObject argument refers to the handle of the newly created font. This is the same value that was returned by the CreateFontIndirect& function.

If the SelectObject& function is successful, it will return a handle to the object previously assigned to the device context. So if you're assigning a font to an object with SelectObject&, it will return the handle of the font previously assigned to the object. If the function is unsuccessful, it will return zero.

After the font is created and assigned to an object, you can use the object's CurrentX and CurrentY properties to change the position at which the text will be displayed. You can then use the object's Print property to display the text.

When you're finished using the new font, it's a good idea to delete it to free up system resources. This is done using the DeleteObject& function. It is declared as shown in the following line:

```
Declare Function DeleteObject& Lib "gdi32" (ByVal hObject As Long)
```

The only argument for this function is hObject, which should be the handle of the font.

If the DeleteObject& function is not successful, it returns zero. Otherwise, it will return a nonzero value.

The following code segment shows how the CreateFontIndirect&, SelectObject&, and DeleteObject& functions might be used to display text upside down inside a PictureBox named picShowText.

```
Dim udtLOGFONT As LOGFONT
Dim lonFontSize As Long
Dim lonFontHandle As Long
Dim lonLastFont As Long
Dim lonStatus As Long

lonFontSize = 20

' Set up the items in the udtLOGFONT type, which will
' determine what the new font will look like.
udtLOGFONT.lfEscapement = 1800              ' Degree of rotation * 10.
udtLOGFONT.lfFaceName = "Arial" & Chr$(0)       ' Font name.
udtLOGFONT.lfHeight = (lonFontSize * -20) / Screen.TwipsPerPixelY

' Create the new font and get its handle.
lonFontHandle = CreateFontIndirect&(udtLOGFONT)

' Assign the new font to the picShowText object, and
' get the handle of the previous font assigned to that object.
lonLastFont = SelectObject&(picShowText.hDC, lonFontHandle)

' Print some upside-down text.
picShowText.CurrentX = picShowText.Width - 300
picShowText.CurrentY = picShowText.Height - 300
picShowText.Print "This is upside-down!"

' Assign the last font used back to the picShowText object.
lonStatus = SelectObject&(picShowText.hDC, lonLastFont)

' Destroy the new font.
lonStatus = DeleteObject&(lonFontHandle)
```

Flash a Window's Caption

If you want to get your user's attention, one good way is to flash the caption of your form. To do that, you'll use the FlashWindow& API function.

The Declare statement for the FlashWindow& function is as follows:

```
Declare Function FlashWindow& Lib "user32" (ByVal hWnd As Long, _
    ByVal bInvert As Long)
```

The hWnd arguments specify the handle of the window that will have its caption flashed. If you want to flash the caption of a form, you can pass the form's hWnd property as the argument, as you'll see later.

The bInvert argument is either True or False and specifies the state of the window's caption. True makes the caption inverse, and False returns it back to its original state.

The FlashWindow& function returns a True value if the window was active before the function was called, or a False value if it was not active.

The best way to establish a steady flashing rhythm for the caption is to use a Timer control. The following example shows the Timer event for a Timer control called timFlashTimer. Every time the event is triggered, it calls the FlashWindow& function to flash Form1's caption. The static booState variable is used to determine whether the caption should be inverse or normal. The value of booState flip-flops every time the Timer event is executed. You can set the Timer's Interval property to whatever value you think is appropriate, such as 1000 for one second.

```
Private Sub timFlashTimer_Timer()

Static booState As Boolean
Dim lonStatus As Long
Dim lonFormHandle As Long

' Get Form1's handle.
lonFormHandle = Form1.hWnd

' Call the FlashWindow& function.
lonStatus = FlashWindow&(lonFormHandle, booState)

' Flip-flop booState's value.
booState = Not booState

End Sub
```

If you were to use this event in a program, you would have to add some way of controlling timFlashTimer. By disabling and enabling the Timer, you can control when the form's caption is flashed. You can also change the Timer's Interval property to specify how quickly or how slowly the caption is flashed.

System Functions

Many functions provided by the Win32 API deal with core features of the Windows operating system. This section shows you how you can use some of the API's system functions to do things that Visual Basic doesn't let you do.

By dealing directly with the operating system through the API, you can gain more control over how child processes are handled within your programs. The API functions CreateProcess&, WaitForSingleObject&, and CloseHandle& can be used together to spawn child processes and wait until they are finished executing before continuing on with the processing of the application that started the new process.

Other API functions such as SystemParametersInfo& enable you to keep users from rebooting the system using Ctrl+Alt+Del or switching applications with Ctrl+Tab. When you do want the system rebooted, the ExitWindowsEx& function lets you do it right from within your program.

You can also obtain information about the system by using API functions. For example, you can determine the locations of the Windows and Windows System directories using the API functions GetWindowsDirectory& and GetSystemDirectory&.

The system functions detailed here are just the tip of the iceberg, of course. Hundreds more are available in the Win32 API.

Wait for a Child Process

When you want to run another program from inside your Visual Basic program, you use VB's Shell command. But unfortunately, using Shell doesn't give you much control over the new process. If you want to wait until the process is finished before your program has control again, the Shell command leaves you in the lurch.

Fortunately, three API functions can be used together to give you more control over the child processes that your programs start. The CreateProcess& function starts the process, the WaitForSingleObject& function is used to wait until the process is finished, and the CloseHandle& function destroys the process.

The CreateProcess& function is declared as follows:

```
Declare Function CreateProcess& Lib "kernel32" _
    Alias "CreateProcessA" (ByVal lpApplicationName As String, _
    ByVal lpCommandLine As String, _
    lpProcessAttributes As SECURITY_ATTRIBUTES, _
    lpThreadAttributes As SECURITY_ATTRIBUTES, _
    ByVal bInheritHandles As Long, ByVal dwCreationFlags As Long, _
    lpEnvironment As Any, ByVal lpCurrentDirectory As String, _
    lpStartupInfo As STARTUPINFO, _
    lpProcessInformation As PROCESS_INFORMATION)
```

That's a long Declare statement, but it's primarily because the CreateProcess& function gives you such control over the process that is created. The arguments for the function are detailed in Table 26.3:

TABLE 26.3. THE ARGUMENTS FOR THE CreateProcess& API FUNCTION.

Argument	Description
lpApplicationName	The name of the application that will be executed.
lpCommandLine	The command line to be executed.
lpProcessAttributes	Defines the security for the process. This argument can also be declared as ByVal As Long and passed as zero if the process does not allow inheritance.
lpThreadAttributes	Defines the security for the primary thread of the process. This argument can also be declared as ByVal As Long and passed as zero if the process does not allow inheritance.
bInheritHandles	Specifies whether the handles in the current process can be inherited by the child process. A value of True enables the handles to be inherited.
dwCreationFlags	Specifies how the process is run and what priority it is given.
lpEnvironment	A pointer to an environment block.
lpCurrentDirectory	The path of the directory to use for the new process, or null to specify the directory that is in use when the function is called.
lpStartupInfo	Various information about how to create the process.
lpProcessInformation	The process and thread identifiers of the new process and a new process and thread handle for the new process.

Several type structures are required for passing information to the CreateProcess& function. We'll take a look at them one by one.

The SECURITY_ATTRIBUTES structure is used by both the lpProcessAttributes and the lpThreadAttributes arguments. In both cases, you don't have to use the SECURITY_ATTRIBUTES structure if the process does not allow inheritance. Instead, declare the lpProcessAttributes and lpThreadAttributes as ByVal As Long and pass zero values for both arguments when the function is called.

When it is used, the SECURITY_ATTRIBUTES structure is declared as follows:

```
Type SECURITY_ATTRIBUTES
    nLength As Long
    lpSecurityDescriptor As Long
    bInheritHandle As Long
End Type
```

Because a discussion of inheritance and process security is beyond the scope of this brief explanation of the API functions, the SECURITY_ATTRIBUTES structure will not be used in the sample code at the end of this section.

Another type of structure used by the CreateProcess& function is STARTUPINFO, which contains information about how the process should be started. It is declared as follows:

```
Type STARTUPINFO
    cb As Long
    lpReserved As String
    lpDesktop As String
    lpTitle As String
    dwX As Long
    dwY As Long
    dwXSize As Long
    dwYSize As Long
    dwXCountChars As Long
    dwYCountChars As Long
    dwFillAttribute As Long
    dwFlags As Long
    wShowWindow As Integer
    cbReserved2 As Integer
    lpReserved2 As Byte
    hStdInput As Long
    hStdOutput As Long
    hStdError As Long
End Type
```

In many cases, the only item in the STARTUPINFO structure that you need to set is cb. The cb item specifies the length of the STARTUPINFO structure, and it should be set using a line of code such as:

```
udtStartupInfo.cb = Len(udtStartupInfo)
```

The rest of the items in the STARTUPINFO structure can be left alone. Of course, you can set them to obtain greater control over your child process. A detailed description of each item is beyond of the scope of this discussion, however.

The final type structure used by the CreateProcess& function is PROCESS_INFORMATION, which is defined as follows:

```
Type PROCESS_INFORMATION
    hProcess As Long
    hThread As Long
    dwProcessId As Long
    dwThreadId As Long
End Type
```

The PROCESS_INFORMATION structure is used to return the process and thread identifiers for the new process as well as its process and thread handle. The process handle will be used to specify which process to wait for when the WaitForSingleObject& function is called.

One argument of the `CreateProcess&` function requires a closer look. The `dwCreationFlags` argument is used to specify how the process will run and what priority it is given. This is done using constants that can be found in the `WIN32API.TXT` file. These constants are also shown in the following list along with their values.

Constant Name	Hex Value	Description
CREATE_SUSPENDED	&H4	Suspends the new process immediately. The process will not start again until the `ResumeThread&` function is called.
IDLE_PRIORITY_CLASS	&H40	The process is given a very low priority.
HIGH_PRIORITY_CLASS	&H80	The process is given a very high priority.
NORMAL_PRIORITY_CLASS	&H20	The process is given a normal priority.

The `CreateProcess&` function returns a nonzero value if it is successful, and a zero value if it fails. In the case of an error, you can use `GetLastError&` to determine the problem.

After the process has been created, a second API function should be called to wait until the process has finished executing. The `WaitForSingleObject&` function does just that, and it is declared as follows:

```
Declare Function WaitForSingleObject& Lib "kernel32" _
    (ByVal hHandle As Long, ByVal dwMilliseconds As Long)
```

The `hHandle` argument specifies the handle of the process that should be waited on. The process handle is returned by the `CreateProcess&` function in the `PROCESS_INFORMATION` structure.

The `dwMilliseconds` argument specifies how long the function should wait for the process to finish, in milliseconds. If its value is zero, then the function will return immediately. If it is set to the constant `INFINITE` (`-1`), then it will wait as long as it takes for the process to complete.

After the process is finished, it should be closed using the `CloseHandle&` function. The declaration for that function is as follows:

```
Declare Function CloseHandle& Lib "kernel32" (ByVal hObject As Long)
```

The only argument that needs to be passed to the `CloseHandle&` function is the handle of the process that will be closed. Again, the handle process is returned by the `CreateProcess&` function in the `PROCESS_INFORMATION` structure.

The following sample code begins printing the numbers from 1 to 100 to VB's Immediate window. When it gets to 50, it stops and creates a new process that runs Windows' Calculator application. As soon as the Calculator program is closed, the printing of numbers continues until 100 is reached. Note that because the SECURITY_

ATTRIBUTES structures are not needed, the `CreateProcess&` function should be declared with the `lpProcessAttributes` and `lpThreadAttributes` arguments defined as `ByVal As Long`.

```
Dim intCount As Integer
Dim lonStatus As Long
Dim lonProcHandle As Long
Dim strCmdLine As String
Dim udtProcessInfo As PROCESS_INFORMATION
Dim udtStartupInfo As STARTUPINFO

strCmdLine = "c:\Win95\calc.exe"
udtStartupInfo.cb = Len(udtStartupInfo)

For intCount = 1 To 100
    Debug.Print intCount
    If intCount = 50 Then
        ' Create the process.
        lonStatus = CreateProcess&(vbNullString, strCmdLine, _
            0, 0, 1, &H40, 0&, vbNullString, udtStartupInfo, _
            udtProcessInfo)
        ' Determine the new process' handle.
        lonProcHandle = udtProcessInfo.hProcess
        ' Wait until the process is finished.
        lonStatus = WaitForSingleObject&(lonProcHandle, -1)
        ' Close the process.
        lonStatus = CloseHandle&(lonProcHandle)
    End If
Next intCount
```

Exit Windows

The `ExitWindowsEx&` function is simple in its implementation, but its effects are profound. It causes a shutdown of the Windows operating system.

The `Declare` statement for the `ExitWindowsEx&` function is as follows:

```
Declare Function ExitWindowsEx& Lib "user32" (ByVal uFlags As Long, _
    ByVal dwReserved As Long)
```

The only argument you have to worry about when calling `ExitWindowsEx&` is uFlags. The dwReserved argument is reserved by the operating system and should always be set to zero.

The uFlags argument specifies how the system should be shut down. Its possible values are shown in the following table. The mnemonic refers to the constant defined in the `WIN32API.TXT` file, and the number indicates the value assigned to the constant.

EWX_LOGOFF	0	Terminates all processes; then logs off.
EWX_FORCE	4	Terminates processes, including those that do not respond, and then logs off.

| EWX_REBOOT | 2 | Reboots the system. |
| EWX_SHUTDOWN | 1 | Shuts down the system (ready for power off). |

ExitWindowsEx& returns a nonzero value if it is successful and zero if an error occurs. Use GetLastError to determine the error.

The following sample code shows how the ExitWindowsEx& function can be used to reboot a system.

```
Dim lonStatus As Long
Dim lonShutdownFlags As Long

lonShutdownFlags = 2 ' Value of EWX_REBOOT.

' Reboot the system.
lonStatus = ExitWindowsEx&(lonShutdownFlags, 0)
```

Stop Ctrl+Alt+Del and Ctrl+Tab

When your VB application is running, you might want to disable the user's ability to reboot the system using Ctrl+Alt+Del or to switch applications using Ctrl+Tab. If that is the case, then you'll need to use the SystemParametersInfo& API function.

SystemParametersInfo& actually enables you to retrieve and set a wide variety of Windows system parameters. However, the only service of the function that will be discussed here is the disabling of the Ctrl+Alt+Del and Ctrl+Tab keys.

The Declare statement for the SystemParametersInfo& function should be as follows:

```
Declare Function SystemParametersInfo& Lib "user32" _
    Alias "SystemParametersInfoA" (ByVal uAction As Long, _
    ByVal uParam As Long, lpvParam As Any, ByVal fuWinIni As Long)
```

The uAction argument specifies which system parameter should be set. There is a long list of possible parameters for this argument, but the one we're interested in is SPI_SCREENSAVERRUNNING, a constant defined in the WIN32API.TXT file. Its value is 97.

The second argument for the function is uParam. The possible values for the uParam argument depend on the system parameter specified by the uAction argument. For the SPI_SCREENSAVERRUNNING parameter, the possible values are True and False. A value of True will disable the Ctrl+Alt+Del and Ctrl+Tab keys, whereas a value of False will enable them.

The lpvParam argument can have several uses depending on which system parameter is being used with the function. In some cases, it returns the value of the system parameter before it is changed. The lpvParam argument can be any kind of variable type, but it should match the variable type used by the uParam argument. Because the values of uParam are of type Boolean for the SPI_SCREENSAVERRUNNING system parameter, a Boolean variable should be declared and passed to the function as the lpvParam argument.

If the lpvParam argument is of type Integer or Long or is a data structure, it should be passed to the function by reference (ByRef). In all other cases, it should be passed by value (ByVal).

The final argument, fuWinIni, determines whether the system parameters being changed by the SystemParametersInfo& function should be stored in the WIN.INI file, the System Registry, or both. A value of zero prevents any updates.

An example of using the SystemParametersInfo& function to disable the Ctrl+Alt+Del and Ctrl+Tab keys follows:

```
Dim booOldValue As Boolean
Dim lonStatus As Long
Dim lonSysParam As Long

lonSysParam = 97 ' Value for SPI_SCREENSAVERRUNNING

' Disable Ctrl+Alt+Del and Ctrl+Tab.
lonStatus = SystemParametersInfo&(lonSysParam, True, _
    booOldValue, 0)

' Enable Ctrl+Alt+Del and Ctrl+Tab.
lonStatus = SystemParametersInfo&(lonSysParam, False, _
    booOldValue, 0)
```

Find the Windows and System Directories

If you need to obtain the full path for a system's Windows directory or the WINDOWS\ SYSTEM directory, you can use the API functions GetWindowsDirectory& and GetSystemDirectory&.

The GetWindowsDirectory& function should be declared using the following Declare statement:

```
Declare Function GetWindowsDirectory& Lib "kernel32" _
    Alias "GetWindowsDirectoryA" (ByVal lpBuffer As String, _
    ByVal nSize As Long)
```

The Declare statement for the GetSystemDirectory& function is:

```
Declare Function GetSystemDirectory& Lib "kernel32" _
    Alias "GetSystemDirectoryA" (ByVal lpBuffer As String, _
    ByVal nSize As Long)
```

Both the `GetWindowsDirectory&` and the `GetSystemDirectory&` functions have two arguments, `lpBuffer` and `nSize`. The `lpBuffer` argument is a fixed-length string that will hold the directory path returned by either function. `nSize` indicates the size of the `lpBuffer` string. The functions always return the size of the path, regardless of whether the `lpBuffer` string is large enough to hold it. If the string is not large enough, then the return value should be used to resize the string to the proper size, and the function should be called again. If you define the string used for the `lpBuffer` argument as at least 255 characters, it is unlikely you will encounter a directory path that won't fit into the string.

The following section of code shows how the `GetWindowsDirectory&` and `GetSystemDirectory&` functions might be used in a program:

```
Dim strDirPath As String * 255
Dim lonStatus As Long

strDirPath = Space$(255)

lonStatus = GetWindowsDirectory&(strDirPath, 255)
Debug.Print strDirPath

lonStatus = GetSystemDirectory&(strDirPath, 255)
Debug.Print strDirPath
```

Summary

Visual Basic can let you do many things, but it won't let you do everything. Sometimes, you have to bypass VB and interact directly with the Windows operating system. This is accomplished through a huge library of functions called the Win32 API.

The Win32 API has hundreds of built-in functions. This chapter shows you how to use a few of them to accomplish tasks that would be impossible or inefficient in Visual Basic.

Creating Telephony Applications with TAPI

by Rob Thayer

IN THIS CHAPTER

- How It Works   *619*
- Creating a TAPI Application   *620*
- Other TAPI Functions   *625*

TAPI, (Telephony Applications Programmer Interface), is a library of functions that can be used to provide programs with telephony support. So what is telephony? In a nutshell, *telephony* is a term that refers to the merging of computers and the telephone system. Under Windows 9x and Windows NT, telephony is facilitated through a group of functions and procedures in a dynamic link library (DLL) file. These functions and procedures comprise a programmable interface that allows developers to write programs that utilize telephone technology.

"The telephone system" is a broad category and can include many different communication media. The most common is POTS, which stands for Plain Old Telephone System. POTS is the phone system that has existed for years, and we use it every day. More recent communication protocols include ISDN (Integrated Services Digital Network) and T1, which were designed to be faster and handle a greater volume of data than POTS.

The protocol used for data and voice communication is inconsequential with TAPI. It enables your programs to work with different phone systems through a standard interface.

As stated previously, telephony (and therefore TAPI) is a merging of computers and telephones. This goes far beyond voice communications. You can use TAPI to perform operations directly with the phone system, such as obtaining Caller ID information, recording and playing back audio through voice phone lines, or monitoring for digits pressed by a caller. With TAPI, you can create a complete voice mail system as well as many other telephone-based applications.

TAPI is extremely versatile. Unfortunately, there is a price to be paid. TAPI is somewhat difficult to work with because it is implemented as a library of functions rather than as an ActiveX control (like MAPI, the Messaging API). The number of TAPI functions is high—well over 100 in TAPI version 2.1. What's worse, little information is currently available for Visual Basic programmers who want to utilize the TAPI library. In-depth use of the TAPI functions in VB requires an investment of time and a great deal of patience as well as a certain amount of skill in using C functions.

The good news is that many third-party components now on the market make TAPI development much easier. Artisoft's Visual Voice Pro and Pronexus' VBVoice are but two such products, though there are many others available from other vendors. It's recommended that you at least consider purchasing third-party software if you plan to do any serious TAPI development.

Another piece of good news is that TAPI 3.0 is on the horizon and promises to be easier to use than TAPI 2.1; it might even include ActiveX controls to help facilitate TAPI development. As of this writing, TAPI 3.0 was only available as a part of the Windows NT 5.0 Beta CD.

This chapter introduces you to the basics of using the TAPI library directly. A sample application that initiates a TAPI-based phone call will be created so that you can see exactly how a TAPI session can be constructed in Visual Basic.

How It Works

The TAPI library acts as a layer between an application and the physical telephone line, be it POTS, ISDN, T1, or PBX, analog or digital. In fact, TAPI can communicate with multiple telephone lines (called *line devices*) simultaneously and can merge two. For example, a voice line can be merged with a fax line to create fax-on-demand services through a voice mail system.

TAPI can also communicate with *phone devices*, which are telephones emulated by PCs. The Windows Phone Dialer is an example of a simple phone device because it emulates a telephone and can be used with physical phone lines attached to the system.

At times, other components are also used by TAPI. For example, call managers are programs that actually establish a connection with a line device and also communicate with TAPI to provide that service to other applications. In addition to being a phone device, the Windows Phone Dialer can also be used as a call manager.

TAPI has various levels of service, depending on the type of telephony operations required and the type of communication medium being used. *Basic Telephony* provides only a minimum of functions that can be used on POTS lines. *Supplementary Telephony* includes more advanced services, such as call holding, transferring, and conferencing. Finally, *Extended Telephony* is an extension to the TAPI library and is particular to a specific TAPI service provider.

There are many different levels to TAPI, and many different aspects of how it communicates with devices and applications. A more detailed description is beyond the scope of this chapter. However, you can find several resources on the Internet and on Microsoft's Web site that discuss how the TAPI system works.

> **NOTE**
>
> As of this writing, the current working version of TAPI was 2.1. However, TAPI 3.0 will be included with Windows NT 5. For more information about the new version, see Microsoft's Web site at http://www.microsoft.com/communications/tapilearn30.htm.

Types of TAPI Applications

There are basically two types of TAPI applications: Full Telephony and Assisted Telephony. Full Telephony applications do not require additional components (other than the TAPI library) to utilize TAPI services. This is because Full Telephony applications operate at a lower level and have to call more basic TAPI functions to establish and manage TAPI sessions.

Assisted Telephony applications require components or programs, such as call managers, to use TAPI services. These applications work at a higher level and are easier to program because there isn't as much overhead required when managing TAPI sessions.

To illustrate the difference between a Full Telephony and an Assisted Telephony application, consider the steps needed to take to establish a TAPI session and make a phone call. A Full Telephony application would have to do the following:

- Call the `lineInitialize` function to start the TAPI session.
- Call the `lineNegotiateAPIVersion` function to establish that the correct TAPI services are installed and are being used.
- Call the `lineOpen` to connect to the appropriate line device.
- Set up the necessary calling parameters in the `LINECALLPARAMS` structure.
- Call the `lineMakeCall` function to dial a phone number.

In addition to the preceding steps, you would also have to write a callback function to be used with the `lineInitialize` function.

In an Assisted Telephony application, you need only pass four arguments to the `tapiRequestMakeCall` function. The call manager (a separate program) does everything else for you. The sample program shows how to create an Assisted Telephony application using `tapiRequestMakeCall`.

Creating a TAPI Application

In this section, you'll build an Assisted Telephony application in Visual Basic that will start a TAPI session by dialing a given phone number. The dialing will actually be done by another program, the Windows Phone Dialer utility. The VB program will also end the session. You can then "fill in the blanks" and use other TAPI functions during the session.

Before you can begin building the program, you'll need to make sure that you have the necessary components. Read the following section to see whether you have everything you need or you need to download something that is missing.

27

CREATING
TELEPHONY
APPLICATIONS

What You Need

In Windows 95 and certain versions of Windows NT, the TAPI library is not included. However, it can be downloaded from Microsoft's Web site for free. The file, TAPI21.EXE, can be found at http://www.microsoft.com/communications/telephony.htm.

TAPI21.EXE is a self-extracting archive. When you run it, it will ask you the name of the directory to which its files should be extracted. When the file extraction is finished, the directory contains additional executable programs that install the TAPI library on different operating system platforms. For example, the file TAPI2195.EXE is the TAPI implementation for Windows 95, and TAPI21NT.EXE is TAPI for Windows NT. Install the one that is appropriate for your system, but first consult the README.TXT file in the same directory. It will give you specific information on how to install TAPI.

If you'll be using TAPI through an ordinary modem, you might also need to download Unimodem, a driver that converts TAPI functions to standard AT modem commands. It also functions as a TAPI service provider. You can find it at http://www.microsoft.com/hwdev/devdes/modemddk.htm.

For the example included in this chapter, you'll also need the Windows Phone Dialer utility. This is included with Windows 95 and should be found in the Accessories group.

A Sample Program

Now that you're sure that you have all the necessary components, you can start building the sample program. Invoke Visual Basic and start a new project (Standard EXE).

The first thing you need to do to build the sample TAPI session is to design a user interface. Use Figure 27.1 and Table 27.1 as a guide for adding the controls to the form and changing their properties.

FIGURE 27.1.

The user interface for the sample TAPI application.

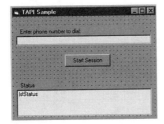

TABLE 27.1. THE CONTROLS AND THEIR PROPERTIES FOR THE SAMPLE TAPI APPLICATION'S USER INTERFACE.

Control Type	Property	Value
Form	Name	frmTAPITest
	Caption	TAPI Sample
	Height	3210
	StartUpPosition	2 - Center Screen
	Width	4605
Label	Name	lblEnterPhone
	Caption	Enter phone number to dial:
	Height	255
	Left	240
	Top	360
	Width	3855
TextBox	Name	txtPhoneNum
	Height	285
	Left	120
	Top	600
	Width	4335
CommandButton	Name	cmdStartSession
	Caption	Start Session
	Height	375
	Left	1680
	Top	1200
	Width	1455
Label	Name	lblStatus
	Height	255
	Left	240
	Top	2040
	Width	1095
ListBox	Name	lstStatus
	Height	840
	Left	120
	Top	2280
	Width	4335

After the user interface has been designed, a module needs to be added to the project so that the TAPI functions can be declared. Add a module to the project; then add the code in Listing 27.1 to the module.

LISTING 27.1. THE FUNCTION DECLARATION FOR `tapiRequestMakeCall`, PLUS SOME GLOBAL ERROR CONSTANTS—TO BE PLACED INTO A MODULE.

```
Declare Function tapiRequestMakeCall Lib "tapi32" _
    (ByVal lpszDestAddress As String, _
     ByVal lpszAppName As String, _
     ByVal lpszCalledParty As String, _
     ByVal lpszComment As String) As Long

Global Const TAPIERR_CONNECTED = 0&
Global Const TAPIERR_DROPPED = -1&
Global Const TAPIERR_NOREQUESTRECIPIENT = -2&
Global Const TAPIERR_REQUESTQUEUEFULL = -3&
Global Const TAPIERR_INVALDESTADDRESS = -4&
Global Const TAPIERR_INVALWINDOWHANDLE = -5&
Global Const TAPIERR_INVALDEVICECLASS = -6&
Global Const TAPIERR_INVALDEVICEID = -7&
Global Const TAPIERR_DEVICECLASSUNAVAIL = -8&
Global Const TAPIERR_DEVICEIDUNAVAIL = -9&
Global Const TAPIERR_DEVICEINUSE = -10&
Global Const TAPIERR_DESTBUSY = -11&
Global Const TAPIERR_DESTNOANSWER = -12&
Global Const TAPIERR_DESTUNAVAIL = -13&
Global Const TAPIERR_UNKNOWNWINHANDLE = -14&
Global Const TAPIERR_UNKNOWNREQUESTID = -15&
Global Const TAPIERR_REQUESTFAILED = -16&
Global Const TAPIERR_REQUESTCANCELLED = -17&
Global Const TAPIERR_INVALPOINTER = -18&
```

27

**CREATING
TELEPHONY
APPLICATIONS**

The code in the module also includes several global constants for the TAPI error conditions. Many of these won't be used in the sample program, but you'll want to add them anyway. If you start experimenting with other TAPI functions, it will help to know exactly the error that is being returned. A `Sub` procedure that will be added later will use these constants to display the TAPI error that occurred.

The next section of code to add is for the `cmdStartSession` CommandButton's `Click` event (see Listing 27.2). This is where the TAPI session will be started, and where the `tapiRequestMakeCall` function will be called.

LISTING 27.2. THE CODE FOR THE TAPI SAMPLE PROGRAM. WHEN THE START SESSION BUT-
TON IS CLICKED, THE tapiRequestMakeCall FUNCTION IS CALLED.

```
Private Sub cmdStartSession_Click()

Dim lonTAPIStatus As Long

' Check to see if a phone number was entered.
If RTrim(txtPhoneNum.Text) = "" Then
    lstStatus.AddItem "Err: No Phone Number Entered"
    Exit Sub
Else
    strPhoneNum = RTrim(txtPhoneNum.Text)
End If

' Initiate the TAPI session with the
' tapiRequestMakeCall function.
lonTAPIStatus = tapiRequestMakeCall(strPhoneNum, _
    "TAPI Sample", strPhoneNum, "")

' Report the status.
Call TAPIStatus(lonTAPIStatus)

End Sub
```

Note that after the tapiRequestMakeCall function is called, another routine named
TAPIStatus (see Listing 27.3) is also called. This is used to sort out the different TAPI
error codes and report back (in the lblStatus ListBox) a readable error message. This
routine will be handy if you go farther with TAPI and start using the other TAPI
functions.

LISTING 27.3. THE TAPIStatus Sub PROCEDURE, WHICH IS USED TO REPORT THE STATUS OF
A TAPI FUNCTION CALL.

```
Private Sub TAPIStatus(lonStatCode As Long)

' Based on the TAPI status code (passed to this
' procedure in lonStatCode), add an appropriate message
' to the lstStatus ListBox.
Select Case lonStatCode
    Case TAPIERR_CONNECTED
        lstStatus.AddItem "Ok"
    Case TAPIERR_DROPPED
        lstStatus.AddItem "Dropped"
    Case TAPIERR_NOREQUESTRECIPIENT
        lstStatus.AddItem "Err: No Request Recipient"
    Case TAPIERR_REQUESTQUEUEFULL
        lstStatus.AddItem "Err: Request Queue Full"
    Case TAPIERR_INVALDESTADDRESS
        lstStatus.AddItem "Err: Destination Address Invalid"
```

```
        Case TAPIERR_INVALWINDOWHANDLE
            lstStatus.AddItem "Err: Window Handle Invalid"
        Case TAPIERR_INVALDEVICECLASS
            lstStatus.AddItem "Err: Device Class Invalid"
        Case TAPIERR_INVALDEVICEID
            lstStatus.AddItem "Err: Device Class ID"
        Case TAPIERR_DEVICECLASSUNAVAIL
            lstStatus.AddItem "Err: Device Class Unavailable"
        Case TAPIERR_DEVICEIDUNAVAIL
            lstStatus.AddItem "Err: Device ID Unavailable"
        Case TAPIERR_DESTBUSY
            lstStatus.AddItem "Destination Busy"
        Case TAPIERR_DESTUNAVAIL
            lstStatus.AddItem "Destination Unavailable"
        Case TAPIERR_UNKNOWNWINHANDLE
            lstStatus.AddItem "Err: Unknown Windows Handle"
        Case TAPIERR_UNKNOWNREQUESTID
            lstStatus.AddItem "Err: Unknown Request ID"
        Case TAPIERR_REQUESTFAILED
            lstStatus.AddItem "Err: Request Failed"
        Case TAPIERR_REQUESTCANCELLED
            lstStatus.AddItem "Err: Request Cancelled"
        Case TAPIERR_INVALPOINTER
            lstStatus.AddItem "Err: Invalid Pointer"
End Select

End Sub
```

Before you run the program, make sure that you load the Windows Phone Dialer utility (look for it in Windows' Accessories group). That program will act as the call manager and will handle the dialing of the phone number that is passed to the `tapiRequestMakeCall` function.

Running the program will invoke the call manager, and the call manager then dials the number entered in the `txtPhoneNum` TextBox. Figure 27.2 shows the TAPI sample program and the Windows Phone Dialer.

The sample program gets you started with using the TAPI library. You can now use the other TAPI functions to start building more complex telephony applications.

Other TAPI Functions

The `tapiRequestMakeCall` function used in the sample program is just one of the more than 100 functions in the TAPI library. Although it does establish a TAPI connection, it cannot be used to access media streams. Instead, the `tapiRequestMediaCall` function should be used. The function definition for `tapiRequestMediaCall` is as follows:

```
Declare Function tapiRequestMediaCall Lib "tapi" _
```

FIGURE 27.2.

*The TAPI sample
program in action,
using the Windows
Phone Dialer as a
call manager.*

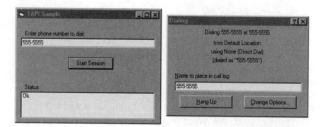

```
(ByVal hWnd As Long, ByVal wRequestID As Long, _
ByVal lpszDeviceClass As String, _
ByVal lpDeviceID As String, ByVal dwSize As String, _
ByVal dwSecure As Long, ByVal lpszDestAddress As String, _
ByVal lpszAppName As String, _
ByVal lpszCalledParty As String, _
ByVal lpszComment As String) As Long
```

There are many more functions in the TAPI library. If you want to learn more about how TAPI works, access Microsoft's Web site and search for "TAPI." Another good reference source is the *MAPI, SAPI, & TAPI Developer's Guide*, also published by Sams Publishing.

Summary

Telephony has become a buzzword in the last few years. As communication media improve and newer and faster protocols are devised, the marriage between the computer and the telephone will become commonplace.

Microsoft's TAPI library enables PC developers to take advantage of some impressive telephony operations. However, in its current implementation, TAPI is not very easy to use for Visual Basic programmers. Third-party vendors offer controls that ease the TAPI development process and should be strongly considered.

This chapter introduced TAPI and showed how to create an Assisted Telephony application that uses a call manager to dial a phone number. This simple application can act as a starting point for anyone who wants to further explore the TAPI library.

Adding Speech Recognition with SAPI

by Loren Eidahl

IN THIS CHAPTER

- Overview of SAPI 4.0   *628*
- Creating a Speech Recognition Application   *629*
- Creating a Text-to-Speech Application   *635*

Microsoft has recently released version 4 of its Speech Application Programming Interface (SAPI). The SAPI is a set of functions that enable you to incorporate text-to-speech and speech recognition into your applications. The next few sections provide you with a brief look at some of the features of the Speech API and how you can use them to add speech and voice recognition to your applications.

Overview of SAPI 4.0

The SAPI is designed to provide an API layer between applications that use speech technology and the speech engines. In this way, programs that utilize SAPI can use an upgraded version of the speech engine without having to be recompiled. An additional benefit is the ability to share the various speech resources between applications.

The SAPI Suite is a collection of tools, source code, documentation, and speech engines designed for developing text-to-speech and speech recognition applications.

The SAPI SDK includes source code and binary files for the following development tools:

- Visual Basic
- Java
- C++
- COM

You can download the SAPI SDK Suite from Microsoft's research site at the following address: http://www.research.microsoft.com/research/sdk/

Text-to-Speech is a technology that enables a written text to be spoken through a sound card in your computer. Voice recognition is a complementing technology that enables voice commands to direct the flow of a program or the actions of your computer. These voice commands are issued through a microphone attached to the sound card in your computer.

The Software Developer's Kit (SDK) provides you with everything that you need to begin using the Speech API (except the microphone and soundcard). The SDK contains a large number of samples written in Visual Basic, C++, and Java. The SDK includes six ActiveX controls that enable you to create applications ranging from simple speech recognition to a voice-operated word processor.

The ActiveX controls that are included in the Speech API SDK cover the following areas:

- Direct Speech recognition
- `Voice` commands
- Dictation
- Direct Speech synthesis
- `Voice Text` control
- Speech Telephony

Those controls that are prefixed with "Direct" give access to the complete Speech API. These controls load all of the speech engines as in-process controls. Developers seeking the maximum amount of control and flexibility will want to use these controls.

The `Voice` command and `Voice Text` control do not provide nearly the level of access to the API that their Direct counterparts do. However, what you lose in flexibility is made up for in the ability to develop applications that use these controls with just a few lines of code. If you are planning on using these controls in a real-world application, you will most likely want to use the Direct versions, as they are quicker. These controls are out-of-process controls that provide for resource and memory sharing between voice applications.

If you were planning to create a new word processor that responds to voice commands, the `Dictation` control would be an excellent place to start. This control enables you to add such features as inverse text and word correction.

The Telephone control is designed to aid you in the creation of Telephony applications. This control combines voice synthesis, voice recognition, and DTMF into a single ActiveX control.

28

ADDING SPEECH
RECOGNITION
WITH SAPI

Creating a Speech Recognition Application

The creation of a speech recognition application is just as easy as creating any other application in Visual Basic. This ease is primarily because all of the necessary API calls are encapsulated into a set of six ActiveX controls.

One popular use of speech recognition is the ability for a user to speak a word or phrase and have the computer perform a specific task based on what it heard. This method of speech recognition is commonly referred to as "Command and Control." Some popular uses for this type of speech recognition include the following:

- Automatic e-mail handling
- Computer activated security systems
- Computer controlled devices
- Games
- Remote data entry
- Learning systems

Command and Control can be used in most every case where a directive must be issued to a computer to perform a specific task. Until now, these directives have been limited to responses via a mouse or a keyboard only; however, with the advent of enhanced speech engines, speech can also be added as a form of input to a computer.

In this section you will get the opportunity to create your own version of an application that can be used to respond to voice commands. This application (although limited) can be used as the core of a much more sophisticated application. As you use the Speech SDK to build your application you will find that the underlying code for each one is nearly identical; the major changes come in the design of the interface.

Setting up the Microphone

Before you can begin building any application that depends upon speech recognition, the speech engine needs to be trained to the type of microphone that is to be used as well as your individual speech pattern.

The opening page of the Speech SDK Web page includes a link to enable you to adjust the microphone to the speech engine (see Figure 28.1). The Microphone Setup Wizard is accessed from the link, as shown in Figure 28.2.

After it is installed on your computer, the Microphone Setup Wizard prompts you to enter the type of microphone that you have and the type of speakers. After you have answered these questions, you need to adjust the microphone levels. This task is accomplished simply by speaking into the microphone and reciting a specific paragraph, shown in Figure 28.3. After you have done this, click the Finish button to complete the setup process.

> **TIP**
>
> The Microphone Setup Wizard can be re-run as often as you like. It is also a good idea to run the Microphone Setup Wizard if you have recently changed the type of microphone that you're using.

FIGURE 28.1.

The Welcome page of the Speech SDK Web page provides links to sample applications.

FIGURE 28.2.

The Microphone setup page of the Speech SDK includes links to utilities and source code.

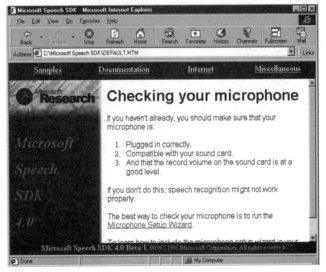

Using the Direct Speech Control

To create the Direct Speech application, start a new Visual Basic 6 project and perform the following steps:

1. Add the Microsoft Direct Speech control to your toolbox, as shown in Figure 28.4.

2. Add the controls to the form and set their properties as shown in Table 28.1. When it is complete, your form should resemble the one shown in Figure 28.5.

FIGURE 28.3.

A good quality microphone will reproduce your speech more accurately than one of a lesser quality.

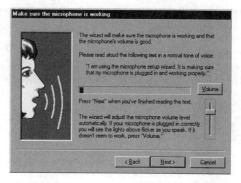

3. Add the code in Table 28.1.

4. Save your project and run the application.

FIGURE 28.4.

The Direct Speech Control is one of six ActiveX controls in the SAPI.

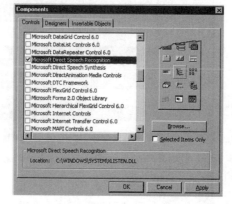

TABLE 28.1. THE MAJOR CONTROLS FOR THE SPEECH RECOGNITION PROGRAM

Control	Property	Setting
TextBox	Name	txtCommand
Direct Speech Recognition	Name	DirectSR

FIGURE 28.5.

The completed Command and Control application.

The Form_Load() event in Listing 28.1 loads the Direct Speech control with the specified grammar in the text string. This text string contains the words or phrases that the speech engine is expecting to hear. The DirectSR_PhraseFinish() property is called when the user is done speaking. This property is then used to compare what was heard with the phrases in the grammar file. If a match is found, the appropriate application is launched.

LISTING 28.1. COMMAND.FRM—THE CODE REQUIRED TO LAUNCH APPLICATIONS WITH THE SPOKEN WORD.

```
Private Sub Form_Load()
Dim retval As Integer

DirectSR.GrammarFromString "[Grammar]" + vbNewLine + _
                           "type=cfg" + vbNewLine + _
                           "[<start>]" + vbNewLine + _
                           "<start>=Launch Notepad" + vbNewLine + _
                           "<start>=Launch Browser" + vbNewLine + _
                           "<start>=Launch Calculator" + vbNewLine


DirectSR.Activate
End Sub

Private Sub DirectSR_PhraseFinish(ByVal flags As Long,
➥ByVal beginhi As Long, ByVal beginlo As Long,
➥ByVal endhi As Long, ByVal endlo As Long,
➥ByVal Phrase As String, ByVal parsed As String,
➥ByVal results As Long)
txtCommand.Text = Phrase

Select Case Phrase
    Case Is = "Launch Notepad"
      retval = Shell("C:\windows\Notepad.exe", 1)
    Case Is = "Launch Browser"
      retval = Shell("C:\windows\Iexplore.exe", 1)
    Case Is = "Launch Calculator"
      retval = Shell("C:\windows\Calc.exe", 1)

End Select

End Sub
```

28

ADDING SPEECH RECOGNITION WITH SAPI

TIP

The Phrase keyword is case sensitive. Make sure that the phrase in your grammar matches the case in your Select statements.

After the application has started, speak one of the phrases in the grammar string. If the speech engine was able to properly discern what was said, the desired application should be launched.

Properties and Methods of the Direct Speech Control

The `Direct Speech` ActiveX control has a rich collection of properties and methods that enable you to configure the control to your needs. Due to space limitations, not all of the properties are discussed here; only those used in the sample project are covered.

Activate

The `Activate` method tells the speech recognizer to start listening. The recognizer must be initialized and a grammar must be loaded before calling `Activate`.

GrammarFromString

The `GrammarFromString` method loads a grammar from a string. When creating a grammar string pay special attention to the explicit use of the `vbNewLine` character. It automatically initializes the speech engine if it has not already been done. The declaration for this property is:

```
GrammarFromString(grammar As String)
```

This method is similar in nature to the `GrammarFromFile`, and `GrammarFromResource` methods.

PhraseFinish

The property is called when the user has finished speaking a phrase and the speech-recognition engine is certain about the words that were spoken. The declaration for this property is:

```
PhraseFinish(flags As Long, beginhi As Long, beginlo As Long, endhi As
➥Long, endlo As Long, Phrase As String, parsed As String, results As Long)
```

DO YOU HAVE THE POWER?

Developing applications using any of the ActiveX controls included with the Speech SDK takes a lot of computer power. Due to the type of processes that are happening in your computer, what would seem like a "normal" amount of RAM can be woefully inadequate.

Microsoft indicates that the speech engines require that your computer be a Pentium with at least 16MB of RAM. I tested the Speech API on a number of machines ranging from a Pentium 75 to a Pentium 233 with anywhere from 16 to 64MB of RAM.

The final results showed that if your machine has upwards of 32MB of RAM and a processor greater than 150 MHz, the speech engines produce excellent results. Any systems that have less than 32MB of RAM suffer from missed words and the inability to process both speech recognition and text-to-speech in the same application.

Creating a Text-to-Speech Application

Text-to-Speech applications have recently gotten easier to develop with the introduction of the ActiveX `Text-to-Speech` and Direct Speech Synthesis controls found in the SAPI SDK. These controls provide you with a wide range of flexibility in creating applications that can convert written text to speech.

In this project you will create a sample application that uses the Voice Text ActiveX control. This control is somewhat easier to use in test applications than the Direct Speech Synthesis control, however it does not have the same amount of flexibility.

NOTE

The Voice Text control shares its resources with other applications. If you are creating an application that cannot share resources on a global level you might want to use the Direct Speech `Synthesis` control. This replacement control has the added benefit of a more sophisticated interface.

Creating the Text-to-Speech Project

To create the Text-to-Speech application, start a new Visual Basic 6 project and perform the following steps:

1. Add the `Microsoft Voice Text` control to your toolbox, as shown in Figure 28.6
2. Add the controls to the form and set their properties, as shown in Table 28.2. When complete, your form should resemble that shown in Figure 28.7. I have placed some additional graphic controls on the form for aesthetic purposes only.

28

ADDING SPEECH
RECOGNITION
WITH SAPI

3. Add the code in Listings 28.2 and 28.3.

4. Save your project and run the application.

FIGURE 28.6.

Adding the Microsoft Voice Text *control to your toolbox.*

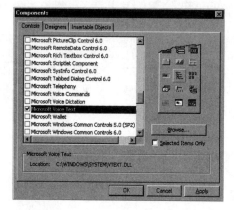

TABLE 28.2. KEY CONTROLS FOR TEXT-TO-VOICE

Control	Property	Setting
Label	Name	lblHeader
	Caption	Visual Text to Speech
Label	Name	lblText
	Caption	Text to Speak
Label	Name	lblStyle
	Caption	Voice Style
TextBox	Name	txtText
	Caption	[None]
	Multiline	True
	ScrollBars	2- Vertical
ComboBox	Name	cmbVoiceType
	Style	2- Dropdown List
CommandButton	Name	cmdSpeak
	Caption	Speak
TextToSpeech	Name	TextToSpeech1

The code in the Form_Load() event is used to initialize the speech engine and load the voice type combo box with all of the available voices. The code for the Form_Load() event is shown in Listing 28.2.

FIGURE 28.7.

The Voice Text
*ActiveX control
has a mouth as its
interface.*

LISTING 28.2. VOICE.FRM—THE CODE REQUIRED TO INITIALIZE THE SPEECH ENGINE.

```
Private Sub Form_Load()
Dim strVoiceType As String
Dim intEngine As Integer
Dim i As Integer

intEngine = TextToSpeech1.Find("Mfg=Microsoft;Gender=1")
TextToSpeech1.Select intEngine

For i = 1 To TextToSpeech1.CountEngines
    strVoiceType = TextToSpeech1.ModeName(i)
    cmbVoiceType.AddItem strVoiceType
Next i
cmbVoiceType.ListIndex = TextToSpeech1.CurrentMode - 1

End Sub
```

The click events of the Voice Type combo box and the Speak button are used to set the
speech engine to the desired voice and to speak the text respectively. The code for the
click events of the Voice Type combo box and the Speak button is shown in listing 28.3.

LISTING 28.3. COMMAND.FRM—THE CODE REQUIRED TO SELECT A SPECIFIC VOICE TYPE.

```
Private Sub cmbVoiceType_Click()
    TextToSpeech1.CurrentMode = cmbVoiceType.ListIndex + 1
    If (TextToSpeech1.Gender(TextToSpeech1.CurrentMode) = 1) Then
        TextToSpeech1.LipType = 0
    Else
        TextToSpeech1.LipType = 1
    End If
End Sub
```

continues

28

ADDING SPEECH
RECOGNITION
WITH SAPI

LISTING 28.3. CONTINUED

```
Private Sub cmdSpeak_Click()
    TextToSpeech1.Speak txtText.Text
End Sub
```

After the application has started, type some text into the first combo box and press the speak button. If your speakers are connected you should hear the female voice speak your words. The second box can be used to adjust the voice type.

Properties and Methods of the Text-to-Speech Control

The Text-to-Speech ActiveX control has a rich collection of properties and methods that enable you to configure the control to your needs. Should you find that the standard Text-to-Speech control does not address all of your needs, you might want to consider using the Direct Speech Synthesis control in your applications. Due to space limitations, all of the properties and methods are not discussed; only those that are used in the sample project are covered.

CurrentMode

This is the index for the currently selected voice engine, as passed into the various engine information calls and properties. The declaration for this property is:

```
CurrentMode As Long
```

In actual practice the call to the CurrentMode property would resemble the following:

```
cmbVoiceType.ListIndex = TextToSpeech1.CurrentMode - 1
```

CountEngines

This is the number of Speech Synthesis Engines installed on the local computer. This property is read-only and represents the largest number that can be used as an index to indexed properties and methods. The declaration for this property is:

```
CountEngines As Long
```

The following code segment illustrates how the call to the CountEngines property would be used:

```
For i = 1 To TextToSpeech1.CountEngines
    strVoiceType = TextToSpeech1.ModeName(i)
    cmbVoiceType.AddItem strVoiceType
Next i
```

Find

The Find property is read-only and returns the index of an engine that most closely matches the input parameter list, ranked in order. The declaration for this property is:

```
Find(RankList As String) As Long
```

The syntax for RankList is:

```
<field>=<value>;<field>=<value>...
```

The following values can be used in the field/value pairs of the previous syntax.

- EngineID
- MfgName
- ProductName
- ModeID
- ModeName
- LanguageID
- Dialect
- Speaker
- Style
- Gender
- Age
- Features
- Interfaces
- EngineFeatures

The following code fragment illustrates how the Find property can be used to indicate the type of engine.

```
intEngine = TextToSpeech1.Find("Mfg=Microsoft;Gender=1")
```

In this example the manufacturer of the speech engine is Microsoft and the gender of the voice is female.

Gender

Gender is a read-only property that returns the gender of the voice. The Gender property can be either a 1 for Female or a 2 for Male. The declaration for this property is:

```
Gender(index As Long) As Long
```

The following code segment illustrates how the call to the `Gender` property would be used:

```
intEngine = TextToSpeech1.Find("Mfg=Microsoft;Gender=1")
```

LipType

The lips on the Mouth of the ActiveX control can vary in appearance based on the engine selected. To create lips that are female, this property should be set to 0, creating red lips. For Male lips this property should be set to 1. The declaration for this property is:

```
LipType As Short
```

The following code segment illustrates how the call to the `LipType` property would be used:

```
TextToSpeech1.LipType = 0
```

> **NOTE**
>
> There are numerous properties, methods, and events that give you complete control over the mouth and how it relates to the spoken text. Using them in your application enables you to control everything from the placement of the teeth and tongue to complete replacement of the mouth with one of your own design.

ModeName

This property sets the text-to-speech mode; for example, "Female Voice" or "Male Robot Voice." The declaration for this property is:

```
ModeName(index As Long) As String
```

The following code segment illustrates how the call to the `ModeName` property would be used:

```
strVoiceType = TextToSpeech1.ModeName(i)
```

Select

This method selects a text-to-speech engine for `Speak` to use. The declaration for this method is:

```
Select(index As Long)
```

The following code segment illustrates how the `Select` method would be used:

```
TextToSpeech1.Select intEngine
```

Speak

This method causes the text to speech control to speak the text. The declaration for this method is:

```
Speak(text As String)
```

The following code segment illustrates how the Speak method would be used:

```
TextToSpeech1.Speak txtText.Text
```

Summary

The examples in this chapter only touched on the power and flexibility in the SAPI and the SAPI SDK. Even with this light treatment you should see how speech recognition and text-to-speech are tools that can be used to effectively communicate to and control computer applications. As speech recognition technology improves, we will see many more applications that use speech to communicate. Although the level of computer generated speech in popular science fiction shows might be years away, we can enjoy the benefits that the current technology affords us now.

28

ADDING SPEECH
RECOGNITION
WITH SAPI

Creating Your Own Add-Ins

by Loren Eidahl

IN THIS CHAPTER

- Understanding the Extensibility Model   644
- Assessing the Extensibility Object Model   644
- Understanding the Core Objects Package   645
- Understanding the Form Manipulation Package   651
- Understanding the Event Response Package   652
- Understanding the Add-In Management Package   652
- Implementing the Extensibility Model in a Practical Way   654
- Understanding What Makes a Wizard   661
- Planing the Computer Wizard   662
- Using the Wizard Manager   665
- Modifying the Code   675
- Using the Wizard Resource File   683

Whether you have been using Visual Basic for two months or two years, it seems like there is always a feature or two that you just can't seem to live without and Microsoft hasn't yet implemented. On some projects you might find that a built-in word processor for your code would save you hours of work, perhaps on other projects you might find that a built in utility to extract your comments to a text files would be a handy tool.

Microsoft has done an admirable job of adding new features to each release of Visual Basic, and VB6 is no exception. However, as the popularity of VB6 increases, so do those "must have" utilities that developers can't live without. Microsoft, anticipating that it could not answer the desires of every programmer, made Visual Basic an extensible product, thereby providing the way for VB developers to create their own features in VB6.

Understanding the Extensibility Model

The key principle behind extensibility is that it enables you to extend some object beyond its core base of behavior. You might say that one attribute of a good system is that its users can effectively extend it without jeopardizing the primary engine that drives it.

Visual Basic 6 is such a system. The core VB development environment is a robust beast. But even this great system needs to be tweaked from time to time, especially where repetitious development chore patterns emerge. For instance, when you're building a huge SQL string, you must break up the string into repetitious lines of code, such as the following:

```
Dim strSQL As String
strSQL = strSQL & "SELECT SomeColumn FROM SomeTable "
strSQL = strSQL & "WHERE SomeIndex = '"  & strAnotherString
...
```

By implementing some clever extensible behavior to Visual Basic, you can automate the process of building large SQL strings so that all you need to do is add the column name(s), values, and WHERE clause constraints.

Assessing the Extensibility Object Model

To implement extensibility features, Visual Basic offers the powerful Extensibility Object Model (EOM). Through EOM, many core objects in Visual Basic itself are available to you at no extra charge. Of course, just because the EOM is a powerful interface into the rich world of the VB engine doesn't mean that it's easy to learn, much less to implement. If it were that simple, you could probably just as easily develop your own Visual Basic compiler.

The EOM consists of six loosely coupled packages of objects with methods that implement key services of the Visual Basic development environment. (*Package* is an object-oriented term that refers to a group of related but distinct objects that carry out a common subsystem behavior.) These six object packages in the EOM are

- Core Objects
- Form Manipulation
- Event Response
- Add-in Management
- Project and Component Manipulation
- Code Manipulation

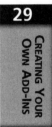

Understanding the Core Objects Package

The Core Objects package contains the bread and butter of Visual Basic extensibility. In a loose sense, it has the same importance as the MFC (Microsoft Foundation Classes) has in Visual C++. Its objects include the following:

- The root object
- The IDTExtensibility Interface object
- The Visual Basic instance variable

The Root Object

Just as CObject is the base class of the MFC in Visual C++, so is the VBE (Visual Basic Environment) object to the extensibility services of Visual Basic. The VBE object is also known as the root object of the extensibility model. It's the base object for every extensibility object and collection in Visual Basic. Each object and collection owns a reference to the VBE object via a VBE property. The collections owned by the VBE object include the following:

- VBProjects
- Windows

- CodePanes
- CommandBars

The VBProjects Collection

The VBProjects collection enables you to access a set of Visual Basic properties. This feature can be helpful if your development environment has an established process for developing software—that is, you could easily audit projects quickly to make sure that they're on track. You also could use this facility to rapidly and automatically add enterprise-wide classes or frameworks, or to complete subsystems into a set of projects before a developer adds the first line of new code.

Table 29.1 shows some of the more important properties and methods for the VBProjects collection. It also provides brief descriptions of each.

TABLE 29.1. A FEW KEY PROPERTIES AND METHODS OF THE VBPROJECTS COLLECTION.

Name	Type	Description
Filename	Property	Returns the full pathname of the group project file.
StartProject	Property	Returns or sets the project that will start when users choose Start from the Run menu, click the Run button, or press the F5 key.
AddFromFile	Method	Enables you to add or open a project or group project. Its only required argument is the string representing the path of the file you want to add. Also, an optional Boolean argument, if set to True when the file being added isn't a group project file, closes the existing group project; subsequently, the new project is created as the only open project. If it's set to True when the file being added is a group project file, the current group project is replaced by the one you're adding. If it's set to False when the file being added is a group project file, each project in the corresponding group project is inserted into the current group project. The AddFromFile method returns a reference to the VBNewProjects collection.
AddFromTemplate	Method	Enables you to add project templates into the VBProjects collection. Its only required argument is the string representing the path of the file you want to use as a template. This method is similar to AddFromFile, except that you're dealing with project templates rather than project files.

The `Windows` Collection

With the `Windows` collection, you can access windows such as the Project and Properties windows. Also, this collection enables you to access a group of all currently open code windows and designer windows. VB adds a window to this collection each time you open a code or designer window. Similarly, each window you close is removed from this collection. With each window in the collection, for instance, you can show, hide, or position windows.

Invoking the `Close` method has different implementations for different types of windows. For instance, if you invoke `Close` on a code or designer window in the collection, that window is simply closed and removed from the collection. However, if you invoke it on a window that's a linked window frame, the window isn't closed, but rather unlinked from the other windows. If you invoke the `Close` method on a Project or Properties window, the object's `Visible` property is set to `False`, but it remains in the collection.

Table 29.2 shows some of the properties and methods for `Window` objects in the `Windows` collection as well as brief descriptions of each:

TABLE 29.2. SOME OF THE PROPERTIES AND METHODS OF WINDOW OBJECTS (IN THE WINDOWS COLLECTION).

Name	Type	Description
`LinkedWindowFrame`	Property	A read-only property that returns the `Window` object representing the frame that contains the window. With this property, you can access the object representing the *linked window frame*. A linked window frame is a window frame (a listview style area) containing links to more than one window. The Project and Properties windows in VB6 are examples of window frames. The linked window frame has properties distinct from the window(s) it contains. If the window has no links with other windows in the frame, the `LinkedWindowFrame` property returns `Nothing`. An example of such a linked window frame would be the Project and Properties windows that are linked by default when you run Visual Basic 6.
`CreateToolWindow`	Method	This method creates a new tool window containing a reference to the *DocObj* object you pass in as the fifth argument. See more about the `CreateToolWindow` method in the following paragraph.

29

CREATING YOUR
OWN ADD-INS

The `CreateToolWindow` method mentioned in Table 29.1 has the following syntax:

```
object.CreateToolWindow(AddInInst, ProgId, Caption, GuidPosition, DocObj) _
    As Window
```

The first argument, *AddInInst*, is an object instance of an add-in from the development environment you pass in. The *ProgId* argument is of the `String` data type and represents the program identifier of the ActiveX `Document` object. The *Caption* argument is also a `String` that contains text you want displayed as the caption for the window. The *GuidPosition* argument is a `String` that holds a unique identifier for the window.

The *DocObj* argument in the preceding code is an object that represents an ActiveX `Document` object. When you call this method, the *DocObj* argument you pass in will be set to an actual ActiveX `Document` object.

Collections of the `Windows` Collection

The `Windows` collection uses the `CodePanes` and `CommandBars` collections.

The `CodePanes` collection enables you to access the collection of code panes now open in your Visual Basic project.

The `CommandBars` collection enables you to access the collection of command bars. Each command bar object is a menu-style toolbar, combining the best of the menus and toolbars that users have come to expect. Each command bar object in the collection can itself contain other command bar objects, given the type of command bar you implement. The different types of command bars are

- Pop-up
- ComboBox
- Button

The `VBE` object has a `CommandBarEvents` property that, when accessed, returns the current `CommandBarEvents` object. Also, the user of your command bar can actually move to another area inside a menu or toolbar. Programmatically speaking, you shouldn't hard-code its actual position.

Referencing an object within the `CommandBars` collection can be straightforward. To reference the Add-Ins menu object, you would declare a command bar object variable and instantiate it as follows:

```
Set objCmdBar = VBInstance.CommandBars("Add-Ins")
```

With this approach, you don't have to memorize the object's ordinal position.

> **TIP**
>
> Because some built-in attributes of the `CommandBars` collection and each command bar object might change with subsequent versions of Visual Basic, you might consider creating your own classes to encapsulate its methods and properties. That way, the other classes and modules in your system will refer to your class, which in turn delegates its methods and property assignments to the `CommandBars` collection, the command bar object, or both.
>
> This is useful, especially in those cases where the software manufacturer changes the name of a method or property in a new version of its software, yet you had already implemented the previous version in numerous systems across your enterprise. Then you can carefully implement the new version of that software with later versions of your own.
>
> Suppose that you have a third-party component with a class `BankAccount` in it, and that class has an attribute (property) called `AccountNum`. That's the current version, and you use that component in ten systems within your company (and each system, in turn, uses the component in 20 subsystems). When the new version comes out, the software company changed the attribute name to `AccountNumber`. You can see how much work that would be if you didn't encapsulate that component into a class (interface class). With an interface class, all enterprise systems would refer to it, and in turn this class would delegate its members to the component. When the component changes, only the interface class is affected; all other classes can stay in production.

You use the `Events` object to access properties that enable add-ins to connect to all events in Visual Basic for Applications. The properties of the `Events` object return objects of the same type as the property name. For example, the `CommandBarEvents` property returns the `CommandBarEvents` object.

You can use the `SelectedVBComponent` property to return the active component. (The *active component* is the component being tracked in the Project window.) If the selected item in the Project window isn't a component, `SelectedVBComponent` returns `Nothing`.

The `IDTExtensibility` Interface Object

The `IDTExtensibility` Interface object exposes the public methods and properties of the extensibility model. By *exposes*, I mean that because you don't directly use the services (methods) and properties of the underlying extensibility model, you need to invoke the methods of the model's agent, so to speak. You can think of interfaces as public agents for the private implementation of an extensibility model object you instantiate.

To use the IDTExtensibility object, you must add a reference to it in your project. To do this, choose Project|References from VB's menu. When the References dialog box appears, find the Microsoft Visual Basic 6.0 Extensibility object and put a check mark next to it. Then click OK.

Before you use the IDTExtensibility Interface object, you also need to designate a class to implement it. To implement this interface, insert the following line in the General Declarations section of your class module:

```
Implements IDTExtensibility
```

This line causes a new entry to appear under the Class item in the left-hand drop-down box (object list) of your class module. You'll insert your implementation code in the methods and properties associated with IDTExtensibility.

The four methods for Add-In servicing (for managing your Add-Ins) are shown in Table 29.3. These methods define the Add-Ins interface with Visual Basic and are called by the VB IDE at specific times. For example, the IDTExtensibility_OnConnection method is called when VB starts (and the Add-In is part of the current project), when the Add-In is selected via the Add-In Manager, or when the Add-In is selected by the user from VB's Add-In menu.

TABLE 29.3. THE FOUR METHODS THAT DEFINE AN ADD-INS INTERFACE WITH VISUAL BASIC.

Method Name	Function
IDTExtensibility_OnConnection	Called when the Add-In is being connected to the VB IDE
IDTExtensibility_OnDisconnection	Called when the Add-In is no longer being used by the VB IDE
IDTExtensibility_OnStartupComplete	Called when the Add-In has been connected to the VB IDE, though it is only used when the Add-In has been connected when Visual Basic starts
IDTExtensibility_OnAddInsUpdate	Called whenever the VBADDIN.INI file has been modified

If you noticed, the methods listed in Table 29.3 have names similar to those of events. When an actual event occurs, these methods (known as *Add-In event handlers*) are fired. The class in your code that implements IDTExtensibility must implement these four event-handling methods, even if that means you put a REM comment command or a comment character (') in the interface method.

The Visual Basic Instance Variable

The Visual Basic instance variable (also known as a *dynamic identification variable*) identifies a particular instance of your Visual Basic session. This instance identifier enables you to have separately identifiable running instances of Visual Basic in memory.

The instance variable is of the type VBIDE.VBE. To use this variable, declare it in a class module or general module (also known as a *class utility* in MS Visual Modeler, a software design tool now available for Visual Basic 6). Therefore, if you declared it in a class module as private, the declaration would look like the following:

```
Private mVBInst As VBIDE.VBE
```

The prefix m identifies the variable as a module-level variable.

> **NOTE**
>
> The VBIDE.VBE object will not be accessible by your programs unless you have a reference to the IDTExtensibility object. See "The IDTExtensibility Interface Object" section earlier in the chapter.

Understanding the Form Manipulation Package

The objects and object collections within the Form Manipulation package offer methods (or services) that enable you to automate common development tasks particular to forms in your Visual Basic projects. That is, you can iterate through all the forms (each of type VBForm) in a project, much the way you're probably accustomed to doing by using the Forms collection. Along the same lines, you can manipulate all the controls on a VBForm object by using the VBForm's public collection, VBControls.

Within the Form Manipulation package are several objects, including CommandBar and CodePane.

The CommandBar Object

The CommandBar object enables you to work with menus and toolbars. Using Visual Basic you can create and delete command bars as well as modify their attributes, such as size, location on the form, and their icons. You also can handle the events associated with command bars by using the Events.CommandBarEvents collection of the current instance of VB (VBInst).

The `CodePane` Object

The `CodePane` object enables you to display the lines of code you may have in a given object. This object is a public member of the `CodeModule` object. You refer to a `CodePane` object by using syntax similar to this:

```
Set MyCodePane = MyVBComponent.CodeModule.CodePane
```

Understanding the Event Response Package

Obviously, when you extend Visual Basic with the EOM, you require some mechanism for processing every action VB users carry out. The EOM provides the capability to respond to such events. The source of events can be an object or a collection of objects. Now, you can process events for the VBA object, as well as collections such as `VBProjects`, `VBComponents`, `VBControls`, and `References`. Typical events you might want to process could include

- Starting a new project
- Ending an existing project
- Adding a member to or deleting a member from a project (that is, forms, components, classes, and so on)
- Adding an object to or removing an object from a collection (that is, forms, components, classes, projects, and so on)
- Adding a reference to or deleting a reference from a project

You can probably find many more uses for Event Response objects. The idea is that you can better manage the methodology and process of developing Visual Basic software systems by using the capability to respond to events in the Visual Basic development environment.

Understanding the Add-In Management Package

Managing add-ins is essential to using the EOM. Visual Basic provides you with the `AddIns` collection and the `AddIn` object for working with add-ins. By using each `AddIn` object, you can connect and disconnect add-ins, as well as use objects exposed within them.

Understanding the Project and Component Manipulation Package

Visual Basic's Extensibility Object Model enables you to manipulate one or more projects and components within a corresponding project or component collections. Remember that a project is the development environment entity that contains all the components that make up your current software-development effort. A component, in turn, is a member of that project and can be a form, code module, control, or whatever member is necessary to implement your project.

The object types for project objects are VBProject (a single object) and VBProjects (a collection of VBProject objects). The object types for component objects are VBComponent (a single object) and VBComponents (a collection of VBComponent objects). When you add a new VBProject to the VBProjects collection, the VBProjects collection returns a reference to the newly added VBProject object after it's finished adding the object to the collection. The same pattern applies to VBComponent and VBComponents as well.

Understanding the Code Manipulation Package

At the center of the Code Manipulation package is the CodeModule object. Unlike the CodePane object, which allows only read-only access to code, the CodeModule object enables you to alter code. In turn, unlike the CodePane object, the CodeModule object doesn't let you view the code. Therefore, if you want to view and alter code, you need the services of the CodePane object in the Form Manipulation package. This combined use of services would loosely couple the Code Manipulation and Form Manipulation packages.

In saying that you can alter the code, I mean that you can add, delete, or replace blocks of code. So if you decided to create your own version of Visual Modeler (Microsoft's object-oriented modeling tool for VB6), you could use the CodeModule object to automatically create the code from your models.

The CodeModule object is useful, particularly for software development managers, system architects, and the like. You can use the CodeModule object, for instance, to count the number of lines of code in a component's module. The CodeModule property for the line count is CountOfLines. CodeModule would be a public object within a VBComponent object.

With the CountOfLines property, you could use the CodeModule's Line property to refer to a particular line of code (represented as a string). Therefore, by using the

CountOfLines and Lines properties, you could grab all the text in a module by using syntax similar to the following:

```
For lonCurrentLineNumber = 1 To MyVBComponent.CodeModule.CountOfLines
    strAllCodeText = strAllCodeText & _
    MyVBComponent.CodeModule.Lines(lonCurrentLineNumber, 1) & vbCrLf
Next lonCurrentLineNumber
```

There is a property that applies to the code pane. That is: "CountOfVisibleLines". This property returns the number of visible code lines in a code panein which lonCurrentLineNumber is the number representing the current line of code, MyVBComponent is an arbitrary project component you specify (that is, form, class, and so on), lonCurrentLineNumber in the Lines(lonCurrentLineNumber,1) represents the starting line number of the block of lines to be returned, and the 1 represents the number of lines to be returned in the Lines property, and strAllCodeText is the string value that represents all the lines of code you just accumulated.

Implementing the Extensibility Model in a Practical Way

Now that you know a little more about the Extensibility Model, it would be a good idea to exercise that knowledge by creating a simple Add-In. In this section, you'll build a sample Visual Basic Add-In that will count the number of lines of code for a given program component.

To begin creating the sample Add-In, start a new project. Choose the AddIn project type (see Figure 29.1).

FIGURE 29.1.

To create the sample Add-In, first start a new project of the AddIn type.

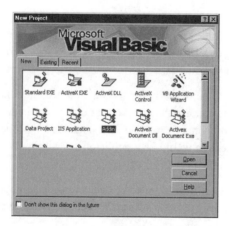

The `AddIn` project type includes many components necessary for creating Visual Basic Add-Ins. There is a form (`frmAddIn`) that you can modify to provide a user interface for your Add-In. There's also a Designer module (`Connect`) that contains the four methods (`AddToAddInCommandBar`, `Hide`, `Show`, and `IDTExtensibility_OnStartupComplete`) that are needed for the Add-In's interface to Visual Basic.

In this sample, you won't have to worry about any of the project's components except the form and the `Connect` module. You'll change it so that the user can enter the name of a component (and the project to which it belongs) that will have its number of code lines counted.

Display the form onscreen. It should look like the one shown in Figure 29.2.

FIGURE 29.2.

The form for the AddIn project before it is modified to fit the purposes of the sample Add-In.

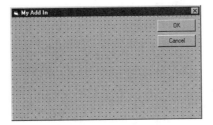

Notice that two `CommandButton` controls are included on the form for you. We won't be using them, so go ahead and remove them from the form.

To build the Add-In's user interface, use Figure 29.3 and Table 29.4 as a guide for adding the different controls and changing their properties.

TABLE 29.4. THE CONTROLS AND THEIR PROPERTIES THAT MAKE UP THE SAMPLE ADD-IN'S USER INTERFACE.

Control Type	Property	Value
Form	Name	frmAddIn
	Caption	Code Line Counter
	Height	3480
	StartUpPosition	2 - Center Screen
	Width	3825
Label	Name	lblProject
	Caption	Project
	Height	255

continues

TABLE 29.4. CONTINUED

Control Type	Property	Value
Value	Left	360
	Top	240
	Width	1695
TextBox	Name	txtProject
	Height	315
	Left	240
	Text	" "
	Top	480
	Width	3135
Label	Name	lblComponent
	Caption	Component
	Height	255
	Left	360
	Top	1080
	Width	1695
TextBox	Name	txtComponent
	Height	315
	Left	240
	Text	" "
	Top	1320
	Width	3135
CommandButton	Name	cmdCountCodeLines
	Caption	Count Code Lines
	Height	375
	Left	240
	Top	2040
	Width	1695
CommandButton	Name	cmdDone
	Caption	Done
	Height	375
	Left	240
	Top	2520
	Width	1695

Control Type	Property	Value
Label	Name	lblCodeLines
	Alignment	2 - Center
	Caption	Code Lines
	Height	255
	Left	2400
	Top	2280
	Width	855
TextBox	Name	txtCodeLines
	Alignment	2 - Center
	Enabled	False
	Height	315
	Left	2400
	Text	" "
	Top	2520
	Width	855

Next, you need to add a few short event procedures to frmAddIn. Listing 29.1 shows these procedures.

FIGURE 29.3.

The user interface (frmAddIn) for the sample Add-In.

LISTING 29.1. FRMADDIN.FRM—THE CODE PROCEDURES FOR THE SAMPLE ADD-IN, WHICH SHOULD BE ADDED TO THE frmAddIn FORM.

```
Private Sub cmdCountCodeLines_Click()

Dim strVBProject As String
Dim strVBComponent As String
Dim objVBComponent As VBComponent
```

continues

LISTING 29.1. CONTINUED

```
' form's two TextBox controls.
strVBProject = txtProject.Text
strVBComponent = txtComponent.Text

' Set objVBComponent to the program component suggested
' by strVBProject and strVBComponent.
Set objVBComponent =
VBInstance.VBProjects.Item(strVBProject).VBComponents.Item(strVBComponent)

' Assign the number of lines of code (CountOfLines) of the
' component objVBComponent to the txtCodeLines TextBox.
txtCodeLines.Text = Str(objVBComponent.CodeModule.CountOfLines)

End Sub


Private Sub cmdDone_Click()

' Hide the Add-In window.
Connect.Hide

End Sub
```

Before going any further, let's take a closer look at the two event procedures you just added. The first, cmdCountCodeLines_Click, is triggered when the user clicks on the Count Code Lines button. It uses the project and component names that were typed into the form's TextBox controls (txtProject and txtComponent) to assign that component to the objVBComponent object. Note the hierarchy used to obtain a component item in the following line of code:

```
Set objVBComponent = _
VBInstance.VBProjects.Item(strVBProject).VBComponents.Item(strVBComponent)
```

First, the VBInstance object is referenced and then its VBProjects collection. The string value strVBProject included in the first set of parentheses indicates the project name, which is used as the key argument for the VBProjects collection's Item method.

After the project has been referenced from the VBProjects collection, that project's VBComponents collection is accessed by using the strVBComponent string as a key argument for the collection's Item method. This long sequence of referencing ultimately assigns the specified component (strVBComponent) that is part of the specified project (strVBProject) to the objVBComponent object.

The following line of code

```
txtCodeLines.Text = Str(objVBComponent.CodeModule.CountOfLines)
```

is used to access the `CodeModule` of the newly assigned `objVBComponent` object. The `CountOfLines` property of the `CodeModule` object contains the number of lines of code in that particular component. This number is assigned to the `txtCodeLines` TextBox so that the user can see the results.

The second event procedure that was added is the `cmdDone_Click` event. This contains only a single line of code that calls the `Connect` object's `Hide` method, hiding the Add-In's user interface. The `Connect` object is an instance of the `Connect` class, which, as you might remember, is a part of the `AddIn` project. It is defined in the form's General Declarations section.

You can remove the `Click` events for the `CancelButton` and `OKButton` objects because they were deleted earlier. These event procedures are no longer valid because they will never be triggered.

The last change that you need to make is a small one, and project will be finished. Bring up the code in the `Connect` Designer. In the `AddInInstance_OnConnection` procedure, there is a line of code that looks like this:

```
Set mcbMenuCommandBar = AddToAddInCommandBar("My AddIn")
```

Change the `"My AddIn"` to `"Code Line Counter"`. If you don't, then the Add-In will appear on VB's Add-In menu as "My AddIn," which isn't very descriptive.

That's all there is to the sample Add-In. However, you need to do something before you save the project. Choose Project MyAddIn Properties from the menu. Change the project name from `"MyAddIn"` to something more appropriate, such as `"CodeLineCounter"`. The final item is to change the project type to that of an ActiveX DLL. After doing this you can click the OK button. Now you can save the project. Save the form as `CLCFORM.FRM`, the designer as `CLCCONNECT.DSR`, and the project as `CODELINECOUNTER.VBP`.

Compile the Add-In by choosing File | Make CodeLineCounter.dll from the menu. When the Make Project dialog box appears, be sure to specify that the executable file be placed in the same directory as Visual Basic. You want VB to have access to the Add-In later.

Before you can use the Add-In, you have to make a change to the `VBADDIN.INI` file so that Visual Basic will know that the Add-In is available. You'll find that file in your

29

CREATING YOUR
OWN ADD-INS

Windows directory, and you can edit it with a text editor. Add the following line to the end of the file:

```
CodeLineCounter.Connect=0
```

Save the file; then get back into Visual Basic. Open any project that you might happen to have handy. Then choose Add-In | Add-In Manager from the menu. You should see a list similar to the one shown in Figure 29.4, though the items on your screen might be different.

FIGURE 29.4.

Visual Basic's Add-In Manager.

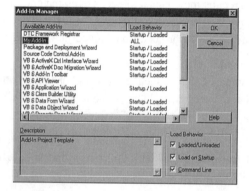

Notice that you now have an option for My AddIn. Select the Load on Startup and the Loaded/Unloaded check boxes; then click OK.

As soon as the Add-In loads, it is added to VB's AddIn menu. Invoke it by choosing it from that menu, and its user interface shows onscreen. Enter the name of a project currently loaded into Visual Basic and then the name of one of its components. For example, if you have a project named Project1, which contains a form named Form1, then enter those names in the appropriate text boxes. Then click on the Count Code Lines button. You should then see the number of lines of code in the Code Lines text box. Try it with other components if you want. When you're finished, click the Done button.

> **NOTE**
>
> If you go back to make changes to the sample Add-In, make sure that you remove it from the AddIns menu using the Add-In Manager. Otherwise, you won't be able to recompile the project.

Admittedly, this is a simple Add-In. It could use some work. For example, instead of having the user enter the project and component names into text boxes, you might want to use combo boxes that contain the names of all available projects and components so that the user need only select the ones he wants. But it does serve as an example of how to use the Extensibility Model in Visual Basic and should provide a starting point for further explorations into this area of programming.

Understanding What Makes a Wizard

If you take a look at any of the popular programs on the market toady, you will find that they generally do one of two things in a repetitive manner. When you create a program in Visual Basic, most of your programs will require some type of main form and menu system. Visual Basic includes the Application Wizard to automate the task of creating the basics for your application. Most likely, any application that requires the user to perform a series of steps to arrive at a predetermined result can benefit from a wizard.

The Setup Wizard that comes with Visual Basic is a good example of how a wizard can be used in an application or as an application. The Setup Wizard prompts the user for specific information about the type of application, how many disks to use, any additional support files. The Setup wizard then takes all of the information entered and retrieves all of the necessary .dlls , ocxs, and support files to create the .cab and .dep files. After this process, the Setup Wizard creates the actual setup program in the desired distribution format. What is created is a professional looking installation program that will install your application to the Internet or to a local system.

Determining When a Wizard is Needed

To determine if a wizard could be useful in an application, you first need to know what processes are involved when a wizard is launched. One of the first things that occur when the setup wizard launches, is a series of questions that determine what type of setup program the user desires. After answering these high level questions the wizard will ask questions at the next lower level of detail; for example, how would you like to distribute your application. This process continues until all questions have been asked. One of the key things to note about a wizard is that the user is always presented with a limited number of questions on any one page. This limitation helps direct and create the logic flow that the wizard follows. Upon completing all of the questions the user is presented with a confirmation that the desired choices were implemented successfully. At no time was the user aware that there was code being created in the background, all they were aware of was the questions posed by the wizard.

There is a wide range of applications that can easily benefit from a wizard, some of the more popular types of application are as follows:

- Application submissions
- Build-to-Order systems
- Reservation Systems
- Credit applications
- Computer-based training

Effective Wizard Design

The process of designing a wizard starts out the way any other application design should start—it starts with a clear set of goals and objectives. After the goal of the wizard is determined, the next step involves organizing the logical steps into the order that they occur. For example the setup wizard would not be overly useful if it created a list of dependency files before it asked about the application to be installed. Likewise a wizard designed to process reservations would not ask a user to select the room they desired to stay in without first determining if the room was available during the dates desired. One of the final elements of information is the confirmation and future-step area of the wizard. Wizards generally are designed to automate mundane tasks, even so the user needs to know that the process has completed successfully and what steps remain that require user attention.

Planning the Computer Wizard

The key to creating a successful wizard is careful attention to the steps that comprise the task your are attempting to automate. The creation of wizards requires that you pay close attention to the small details that make up your process. It is not so uncommon for developers to sit down in front of our computers without much more than a few notes on a napkin and code an application. This off-hand approach to application development might promote creativity in some developers, but it is destined to create a wizard that is both hard to use and fails to collect important information from the user. This obviously necessitates that proper planning and design have taken place well before the actual development process is begun. Overall, this type of attention to detail means that you will not have to go back and redesign a major section of the wizard after an error was discovered.

Most wizards today are actually subsets of much larger applications. This is not to say that a wizard can not be a stand-alone application, the example that you'll be building in this chapter is meant to be the basis for a stand-alone application.

The wizard that you'll design is a front end for the ordering of customized personal computers. The system will ask the users a series of questions based upon their desires and preferences for a computer system. After the user has answered all of the necessary questions, the wizard will prompt the user for confirmation of the order to begin processing. If the user accepts the order, the wizard will then generate the order for processing by the computer manufacturer. This quick example should show you how you can create powerful Intranet applications with very little effort.

Now that we have discussed the importance of planning , lets begin the process of planning what information you need to obtain from the user. The first thing you need to do is collect some basic information about the user such as his name, phone number, and so forth. If this wizard were tied directly to a database, you could ask the use to supply some identifying criteria , such a customer id or possibly a phone number.

> **NOTE**
>
> A nice feature for the computer wizard would be a customer database that would automatically retrieve specific customer information.

After you have collected the basic user information, you'll need to determine what kind of computer you need to build. To do this, you need to ask the user a series of questions that are designed to guide the user to select the proper components. These choices will include the type and speed of the computer, its the amount of RAM, the size of its hard drive, and the size of the monitor. After you have compiled the information, you need to present the user with the ability to order accessory items such as tape backup units, modems, surge protectors, and so on.

So far you have just defined in one paragraph what our wizard is going to do and some of the screens required to make it happen. In addition to the screens that will present the computer options, you also need to create the splash or welcome screen and some type of completion screen at the end of the questions. These last two screens won't ask the user any specific information about their system; rather, they serve as general information screens. At this point, it might be a good idea to review how many screens we will be creating and their intended purpose.

- Introduction Screen—This screen is an introduction to your wizard.

- User Profile Screen—This screen enables the user to enter his name, address, and phone number.

- Computer Type—This screen asks the user about what type of computer he would like—a workstation or a network server—and the type of CPU he is using.

- Processor—The user should be able to select the processor he would like in his system.

- Type of OS—This screen will ask the user what type of operating system he would like; such as Windows 95/98, NT 4/5.

- Amount of RAM—This screen prompts the user to enter the amount of RAM that is to be in his computer system.

- Size of Hard Drive—The user also has the opportunity to enter the size of the hard drive he would like in their system.

- Video—This screen presents a number of video card and monitor choices to the user for selection.

- Accessories—This screen lists a number of optional items that the user can choose from, such as modems, tape drives, and so on.

- Conclusion—The is the last screen in the wizard. This will enable the user to complete his order and send it to be processed.

A NOTE FROM THE AUTHOR

The Computer Wizard originally had a number of additional screens. These screens however were determined to be unneeded to attain the goal of the chapter. During the process of paring down the number of screens used, the processor screen was inadvertently removed. It was not until after most of the screen controls had been defined for the remaining screens that the omission was noticed, much to my chagrin. The insertion of the screen was simple; redoing all of the controls to be consecutively numbered took a great deal more time.

Even that best planning can sometimes be subject to a small but time consuming oversight.

Now that the screens have been defined, you can actually begin design phase of the individual screens that are to comprise the wizard.

Using the Wizard Manager

The Wizard Manger is a tool designed to simplify the process of building a wizard add-ins in Visual Basic 6.0. The Wizard Manager, first introduced in Visual Basic 5, is not designed to respond to or evaluate every possible scenario that you can think of; rather, it was designed to create a template upon which you can build. As your skills and requirements for wizards increase, you might find that the Wizard gets in your way of the development process.

To install the Wizard Manger, select Add-Ins; then click the Add-In Manager. You will see a dialog box showing a list of the available add-ins. Highlight the VB 6 Wizard Manager option and select the Load on Startup and the Loaded/Unloaded option, as show in Figure 29.5.

FIGURE 29.5.

The Visual Basic Add-In Manager enables you to add a number of different Add-Ins to your development environment.

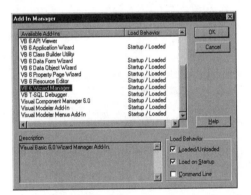

Next, select the Add-Ins menu option and select the Wizard Manager option. The Wizard Manager form will be displayed as shown in Figure 29.6.

FIGURE 29.6.

You can create a template wizard by following the prompts from the Wizard Manager Add-In.

You are almost ready to begin building your wizard.

Creating the Template

To begin, start a new project and name it "Computer Wizard." Now select Add-Ins from the menu bar and select the Wizard Manager. Immediately, you see the template forms for a generic wizard in the Wizard menu frame. If you don't see the pre-built steps— Introduction, Steps 1, 2, 3, 4, and Finished!—right-click the Wizard Manager and select New Wizard. The Wizard Manger creates two forms automatically (Wizard.frm and Confirm.frm) and opens the Wizard template screens, as shown in Figure 29.7.

> **NOTE**
>
> You must name the main form in your wizard application `frmWizard`!

> **NOTE**
>
> The complete Computer Wizard project is on the CD-ROM that accompanies this book.

FIGURE 29.7.

The Wizard Manager pre-builds the wizard template forms, which you can modify for your own wizard application.

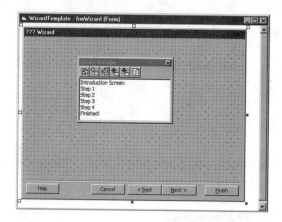

In addition to the four steps previously mentioned, the wizard created the supporting code for the project. The following are the various files created by the Wizard Manager:

- Confirm.frm
- Wizard.frm
- Wizard.bas

- Wizard.CLS
- Wizard.Res

Building the Wizard from the Template

The default number of screens that the wizard created is not enough for our application, so you will need to create a few additional screens. To create the additional screens that are needed, click the Add A Step button and add three more. You'll be asked to supply a name for each of the additional screens, but for now, just name them Step 5, Step 6, Step 7, and Step 8.

Next, double-click each of the Step *x* captions and change them, as shown in Table 29.5 and shown in Figure 29.8.

29

CREATING YOUR
OWN ADD-INS

FIGURE 29.8.

After you have set all the captions, you will have ten screens in the Computer Wizard.

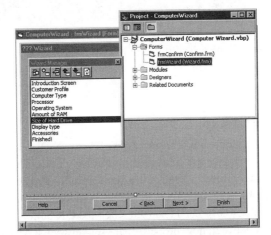

> **TIP**
>
> You can change the name of the screen by right-clicking on the screen and selecting the Edit Name menu option.

TABLE 29.5. THE COMPUTER WIZARD STEPS

Original Caption	New Caption
Introduction	Introduction
Step 1	Step 1: Customer Profile
Step 2	Step 2: Computer Type

continues

TABLE 29.5. CONTINUED

Original Caption	New Caption
Step 3	Step 3: Processor
Step 4	Step 4: Operating System
Step 5	Step 5: Amount of RAM
Step 6	Step 6: Hard Drive
Step 7	Step 7: Display type
Step 8	Step 8: Accessories
Finished!	Finished!

> **TIP**
>
> You don't have to rename the items in the Wizard Manager, but you'll find it easier to maintain your wizards if you give the frames meaningful names instead of something overly generic, such as in Step 7.

Using the Template

By default, the Wizard Manger creates a project type of ActiveX DLL and the startup object is set to (none), allowing for the creation of an ActiveX DLL. The Computer Wizard will be a stand-alone project, so select the Standard EXE project type and frmWizard as the startup object in the project properties window. If you get a message indicating that property values have been changed, click the OK button. This is normal because of the differences between how properties are set between a ActiveX DLL and a Standard EXE.

> **NOTE**
>
> You can easily turn the Computer Wizard into an ActiveX EXE by adding a Sub Main() module to your application. When you are ready to compile select a project type of ActiveX EXE and a startup object of Sub Main in the project properties window.

You'll notice that the Wizard Manager has inserted the appropriate navigation buttons into the form for you. All that's remaining for you to do is add the graphics and appropriate text to create the visual portion of the interface.

Now close the application and return to Visual Basic. Examine the Wizard form and note how you can navigate among the various frames by clicking the appropriate screen title in the Wizard Manager, as explained earlier.

The various Wizard screens are saved on frame controls. Start by selecting the first frame in the array, the introduction screen. This frame contains three controls: a picture box, a label, and a check box. Usually, the check box should be left as it is, which enables users to select the Skip this screen in the future option. The Wizard Manager creates the code to activate this check box option, too. The Step frames, however, have only two controls each: the picture box and a single label. These controls are all control arrays; thus, it is simple to correlate them with the frame names as you work.

> **TIP**
>
> On new step screens, the image control sets the Stretch property to False. To prevent the image control from resizing when a bitmap is inserted that is smaller, set the Stretch property to True. This causes the Bitmap to stretch to the size of the image control.

If you would like to create your own version of the Computer Wizard, Figures 29.9–29.16 and Tables 29.6–29.13 can be used as a guide for control placement.

TABLE 29.6. THE CONTROLS FOR THE CUSTOMER PROFILE SCREEN ARE PLACED INSIDE THE FRAME CONTROL.

Control	Name	Caption
Frame	Frame(0)	Customer Profile
TextBox	Text(0)	
TextBox	Text(1)	
TextBox	Text(2)	
TextBox	Text(3)	
TextBox	Text(4)	
Label	Label(0)	First Name
Label	Label(1)	Last Name
Label	Label(2)	Phone Number
Label	Label(3)	Credit Card Number
Label	Label(4)	Exp Date

FIGURE 29.9.

The text box and label controls for the Customer Profile Screen are placed on a frame control.

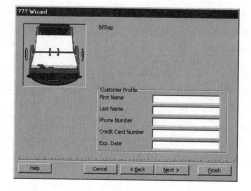

TABLE 29.7. THE COMPUTER TYPE SCREEN USES TWO FRAMES TO DIFFERENTIATE BETWEEN THE COMPUTER TYPE AND CASE DESIGN.

Control	Name	Caption
Frame	Frame(1)	Computer Type
OptionBox	Opt(0)	Desktop
OptionBox	Opt(1)	LAN Server
OptionBox	Opt(2)	Web Server
Frame	Frame(2)	Case Design
OptionBox	Opt(3)	Desktop
OptionBox	Opt(4)	Mini-Tower
OptionBox	Opt(5)	Full-Size Tower
OptionBox	Opt(6)	Rack

FIGURE 29.10.

The Computer Type screen uses two frames to differentiate between the computer type and case design.

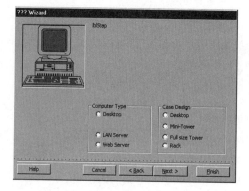

TABLE 29.8. THE PROCESSOR SCREEN USES TWO FRAMES TO PROVIDE A LOGICAL GROUPING FOR THE DATA.

Control	Name	Caption
Frame	Frame(3)	Processor
OptionBox	Opt(7)	200 Pentium
OptionBox	Opt(8)	233 Pentium II
OptionBox	Opt(9)	266 Pentium II
OptionBox	Opt(10)	333 Pentium II
Frame	Frame(4)	Number of Processors
OptionBox	Opt(11)	1
OptionBox	Opt(12)	2
OptionBox	Opt(13)	4
OptionBox	Opt(14)	8

29

CREATING YOUR
OWN ADD-INS

FIGURE 29.11.

The Processor screen uses two frames to provide a logical grouping for processors and the numbers of processors.

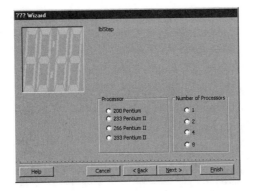

TABLE 29.9. THE OPERATING SYSTEM

Control	Name	Caption
Frame	Frame(5)	Operating System
OptionBox	Opt(15)	Windows 95
OptionBox	Opt(16)	Windows 98
OptionBox	Opt(17)	NT 4.0
OptionBox	Opt(18)	NT 5.0
OptionBox	Opt(19)	Unix/Linux

FIGURE 29.12.

The Operating System screen enables users to select their favorite OS.

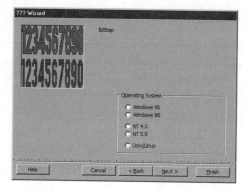

TABLE 29.10. AMOUNT OF RAM

Control	Name	Caption
Frame	Frame(6)	RAM
OptionBox	Opt(20)	16 MB
OptionBox	Opt(21)	24 MB
OptionBox	Opt(22)	32 MB
OptionBox	Opt(23)	64 MB
OptionBox	Opt(24)	96 MB
OptionBox	Opt(25)	128 MB
OptionBox	Opt(26)	250 MB
OptionBox	Opt(27)	512 MB
OptionBox	Opt(28)	784 MB
OptionBox	Opt(29)	1 GB

FIGURE 29.13.

Users can select the appropriate amount of RAM.

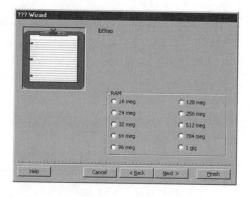

TABLE 29.11. THE HARD DRIVE

Control	Name	Caption
Frame	Frame(7)	Hard Drive Size
OptionBox	Opt(30)	2.1 GB
OptionBox	Opt(31)	3.2 GB
OptionBox	Opt(32)	4.3 GB
OptionBox	Opt(33)	6.4 GB
OptionBox	Opt(34)	8.4 GB
OptionBox	Opt(35)	2.1 GB SCSI
OptionBox	Opt(36)	4.3 GB SCSI
OptionBox	Opt(37)	8.4 GB SCSI
OptionBox	Opt(38)	9.1 GB SCSI
Frame	Frame(8)	QTY
OptionBox	Opt(39)	1
OptionBox	Opt(40)	2
OptionBox	Opt(41)	4
OptionBox	Opt(42)	6
OptionBox	Opt(43)	8
OptionBox	Opt(44)	10

FIGURE 29.14.

The Hard Drive screen has option boxes in two frames.

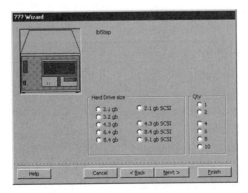

TABLE 29.12. THE DISPLAY TYPE SCREEN

Control	Name	Caption
Frame	Frame(9)	Video Adapters
OptionBox	Opt(45)	2 MB Video RAM

continues

TABLE 29.12. CONTINUED

Control	Name	Caption
OptionBox	Opt(46)	4 MB Video RAM
OptionBox	Opt(47)	8 MB Video RAM
OptionBox	Opt(48)	16 MB Video RAM
Frame	Frame(10)	Monitors
OptionBox	Opt(49)	15" .28 13.9" Display
OptionBox	Opt(50)	17" .26 15.8" Display
OptionBox	Opt(51)	19" .26 18" Display
OptionBox	Opt(52)	21" .26 19.9" Display

FIGURE 29.15.

The Display Type screen uses two frames to provide user options.

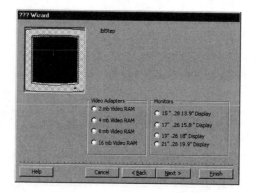

TABLE 29.13. THE ACCESSORIES SCREEN USES CHECKBOXES TO ENABLE THE USER TO SELECT MULTIPLE ADD-ON ITEMS.

Control	Name	Caption
Frame	Frame(11)	Accessories
CheckBox	Chk(0)	Network Card
CheckBox	Chk(1)	8 GB Tape Backup
CheckBox	Chk(2)	Zip Drive
CheckBox	Chk(3)	Backup Power Supply
CheckBox	Chk(4)	Surge Protector
CheckBox	Chk(5)	Sound Card w/Speakers
CheckBox	Chk(6)	DVD ROM Drive
CheckBox	Chk(7)	CD-R ROM Drive

In a typical wizard application, the Finish button is active only on the final frame or next to final frame. The Wizard Manager creates the "Finished!" frame for you; in most cases, there is no need to make extensive modifications to this frame. One possible change could be changing the text on the "Finished" button to "Order." That decision is left for you to make. The chkSaveSettings control can be used to enable the customer to make the same order next time. These settings are typically written to the registry of the local machine, however they could just as easily be written to a database for later use. In this example, the ability to save order information could be helpful for those individuals who are buying computers for a large office.

FIGURE 29.16.

The Accessories Screen uses check-boxes to enable the user to select multiple add-on items.

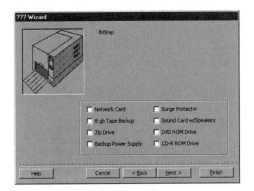

The Confirm dialog box, illustrated in Figure 29.17, appears last. It is a separate form that serves to confirm that the order has been sent. This is the point at which the Computer Wizard would create the order and either send via email or save it to a database for processing.

FIGURE 29.17.

The Confirm dialog box signals the end of the wizard's operations.

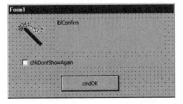

Modifying the Code

Now that you have built the interface, you can run the wizard, and even compile it, but it is still just a series of screens. Some of the required code changes include modifying the code that calls the Finish button, and changing the captions to reflect the proper forms. A few changes also need to be made to the code that the wizard created. In Listing 29.2 the code that was generated for the declarations section is shown.

LISTING 29.2 WIZARD.FRM—DECLARATIONS CREATED BY THE WIZARD MANAGER

```
Option Explicit

Const NUM_STEPS = 6

Const RES_ERROR_MSG = 30000

'BASE VALUE FOR HELP FILE FOR THIS WIZARD:
Const HELP_BASE = 1000
Const HELP_FILE = "MYWIZARD.HLP"

Const BTN_HELP = 0
Const BTN_CANCEL = 1
Const BTN_BACK = 2
Const BTN_NEXT = 3
Const BTN_FINISH = 4

Const STEP_INTRO = 0
Const STEP_1 = 1
Const STEP_2 = 2
Const STEP_3 = 3
Const STEP_4 = 4
Const STEP_FINISH = 5

Const DIR_NONE = 0
Const DIR_BACK = 1
Const DIR_NEXT = 2

Const FRM_TITLE = "Blank Wizard"
Const INTRO_KEY = "IntroductionScreen"
Const SHOW_INTRO = "ShowIntro"
Const TOPIC_TEXT = "<TOPIC_TEXT>"

'module level vars
Dim mnCurStep       As Integer
Dim mbHelpStarted   As Boolean

Public VBInst       As VBIDE.VBE
Dim mbFinishOK      As Boolean
```

In Listing 29.3 you can see what the declarations section should look like after the necessary code changes.

LISTING 29.3 WIZARD.FRM—THE MODIFIED DECLARATIONS FOR frmWizard INCLUDES CODE TO HANDLE FORMS.

```
Option Explicit

Const NUM_STEPS = 10
```

```
Const RES_ERROR_MSG = 30000

'BASE VALUE FOR HELP FILE FOR THIS WIZARD:
Const HELP_BASE = 1000
Const HELP_FILE = "MYWIZARD.HLP"

Const BTN_HELP = 0
Const BTN_CANCEL = 1
Const BTN_BACK = 2
Const BTN_NEXT = 3
Const BTN_FINISH = 4

Const STEP_INTRO = 0
Const STEP_1 = 1
Const STEP_2 = 2
Const STEP_3 = 3
Const STEP_4 = 4
Const STEP_5 = 5
Const STEP_6 = 6
Const STEP_7 = 7
Const STEP_8 = 8
Const STEP_FINISH = 9

Const DIR_NONE = 0
Const DIR_BACK = 1
Const DIR_NEXT = 2

Const FRM_TITLE = "Blank Wizard"
Const INTRO_KEY = "IntroductionScreen"
Const SHOW_INTRO = "ShowIntro"
Const TOPIC_TEXT = "<TOPIC_TEXT>"

'module level vars
Dim mnCurStep        As Integer
Dim mbHelpStarted    As Boolean

Public VBInst        As VBIDE.VBE
Dim mbFinishOK       As Boolean
```

Notice that changes were made to the number of individual step forms that are to be initialized. The next batch of changes involves changing the number of step forms in the frmWizard's SetStep() subroutine as shown in the code segment in Listing 29.4.

LISTING 29.4 WIZARD.FRM—CORRESPONDING CHANGES IN THE *SETSTEP* SUBROUTINE

```
Select Case nStep
      Case STEP_INTRO
```

continues

LISTING 29.4 CONTINUED

```
        Case STEP_1

        Case STEP_2

        Case STEP_3

        Case STEP_4

        Case STEP_5

        Case STEP_6

        Case STEP_7

        Case STEP_8
            mbFinishOK = False
        Case STEP_FINISH
            mbFinishOK = True

    End Select
```

Notice that the number of steps was increased to reflect the addition of the new forms. The other major change was to place the code that enabled the Finish button on the last screen. This prevents the Finish button from being clicked on before all the forms have been seen.

The SetStep() procedure enables you to insert code that enables other wizard forms or options. One example might to be create a form that only gets called under pre-set conditions.

Providing Exception Handling

An important part of any program is proper error or exception handing. A properly designed wizard is no exception. In this example only the most rudimentary of error handling is provided. This was done primarily to show how error handling can be implemented—not what to error handle. From this basic example you will be able to construct your own specific error handling routines.

The Wizard Manager generates an error handling subroutine called IncompleteData designed to display error messages based on information passed from another routine. The IncompleteData routine is very basic but it does serve as a starting point for a more sophisticated routine. Before you can use the built-in routine, you need to create your own routine that will be able to detect if an error or exception occurred. In this example the `ValidateUserInput` routine passes the error information to the `IncompleteData` routine and a message is displayed. The `ValidateUserInput` routine is shown in Listing 29.5.

LISTING 29.5. WIZARD.FRM—THE VALIDATEUSERINPUT ROUTINE NEEDS TO BE ADDED TO THE EXISTING CODE IN FRMWIZARD.

```
Private Sub ValidateUserInput(nStep As Integer)
    Select Case nStep
        Case STEP_INTRO

        Case STEP_1
            If Text(0) = "" Then
                IncompleteData (mnCurStep)
            End If
        Case STEP_2

        Case STEP_3

        Case STEP_4

        Case STEP_5

        Case STEP_6

        Case STEP_7

        Case STEP_8

        Case STEP_FINISH

    End Select
End Sub
```

The next step is to create the code that calls the newly created subroutine. The code in Listing 29.6 shows where to place the call to the `ValidateUserInput` routine.

To call the subroutine from the next button, simply call the function with a simple `If...Then` statement, as in Listing 3.6.

LISTING 29.6. WIZARD.FRM—CALLING THE VALIDATEUSERINPUT SUBROUTINE FROM THE *CMDNAV_CLICK* PROCEDURE

```
Private Sub cmdNav_Click(Index As Integer)
    Dim nAltStep As Integer
```

continues

29

CREATING YOUR
OWN ADD-INS

LISTING 29.6. CONTINUED

```
    Dim lHelpTopic As Long
    Dim rc As Long
    ValidateUserInput (mnCurStep)
    Select Case Index
        Case BTN_HELP
            mbHelpStarted = True
            lHelpTopic = HELP_BASE + 10 * (1 + mnCurStep)
            rc = WinHelp(Me.hwnd, HELP_FILE, HELP_CONTEXT, lHelpTopic)

        Case BTN_CANCEL
            Unload Me

        Case BTN_BACK
            'place special cases here to jump
            'to alternate steps
            nAltStep = mnCurStep - 1
            SetStep nAltStep, DIR_BACK

        Case BTN_NEXT
            'place special cases here to jump
            'to alternate steps
            nAltStep = mnCurStep + 1
            SetStep nAltStep, DIR_NEXT

Case BTN_FINISH
            'wizard creation code goes here

            Unload Me

            If GetSetting(APP_CATEGORY, WIZARD_NAME, CONFIRM_KEY,
vbNullString) = vbNullString Then
                frmConfirm.Show vbModal
            End If

    End Select
End Sub
```

The cmdNavClick() subroutine is an excellent place to place additional type of exception handling or conditional branching routines.

Controlling the Flow

The previous sections mentioned how code could be inserted that could branch to other forms based on users input. This is all good, but the question remains—how do you determine what selections have been made? In the Computer wizard example you might want to limit the user to choices on a form based on a choice previously made. The following provides an example of the criteria or business rules that some of our wizard forms should follow:

- If a user selects a Desktop computer, they cannot have a case design of a Rack mount. This criterion needs to be applied as soon as the Desktop button is clicked.

- If a user selects a Desktop computer their choices for hard drives, RAM and accessories will be limited.

- If a user selects a 2 MB video card they cannot purchase monitors over 17 inches.

The code in Listing 29.7 checks to see if the Opt(0) (Desktop) was clicked. If it was, it disables the "Rack" case design menu option and disables the number of memory choices and accessory choices. The code also moves the Hard Drive frame after it hides the frame that enables users to enter the number of hard drives desired. Additional functions of the code include the disabling of the 19" and 21" monitor choices if a 2MB video card is desired.

LISTING 29.7. WIZARD.FRM—THE `Opt_click()` SUBROUTINE IS CALLED WHENEVER AN OPTION BUTTON IS CLICKED.

```
Private Sub Opt_Click(Index As Integer)
Select Case Index
    Case 0                          ' desktop computer
        Opt(6).Enabled = False
        Opt(12).Enabled = False
        Opt(13).Enabled = False
        Opt(14).Enabled = False
        Opt(17).Enabled = False
        Opt(18).Enabled = False
        Opt(19).Enabled = False
        Opt(26).Enabled = False
        Opt(27).Enabled = False
        Opt(28).Enabled = False
        Opt(29).Enabled = False
        Frame(7).Top = 2280
        Frame(7).Left = 3720
        Frame(8).Visible = False
        Chk(1).Enabled = False
    Case 1                          ' LAN Server
        Opt(6).Enabled = True       ' Rack mount case
        Opt(12).Enabled = True
        Opt(13).Enabled = True
        Opt(14).Enabled = True
        Opt(17).Enabled = True
        Opt(18).Enabled = True
        Opt(19).Enabled = True
        Opt(26).Enabled = True
```

continues

LISTING 29.7. CONTINUED

```
        Opt(28).Enabled = True
        Opt(29).Enabled = True
        Frame(7).Top = 2280
        Frame(7).Left = 2400
        Frame(8).Visible = True
        Chk(1).Enabled = True
    Case 2                          ' Web Server
        Opt(6).Enabled = True
        Opt(12).Enabled = True
        Opt(13).Enabled = True
        Opt(14).Enabled = True
        Opt(17).Enabled = True
        Opt(18).Enabled = True
        Opt(19).Enabled = True
        Opt(26).Enabled = True
        Opt(27).Enabled = True
        Opt(28).Enabled = True
        Opt(29).Enabled = True
        Frame(7).Top = 2280
        Frame(7).Left = 2400
        Frame(8).Visible = True
        Chk(1).Enabled = True
    Case 45                         ' 2 meg graphic board
        Opt(51).Enabled = False     ' 19" monitor
        Opt(52).Enabled = False     ' 21" monitor
    Case 46                         ' 4 meg graphic board
        Opt(51).Enabled = True      ' 19" monitor
        Opt(52).Enabled = True      ' 21" monitor
    Case 47                         ' 8 meg graphic board
        Opt(51).Enabled = True      ' 19" monitor
        Opt(52).Enabled = True      ' 21" monitor
    Case 48                         ' 16meg graphic board
        Opt(51).Enabled = True      ' 19" monitor
        Opt(52).Enabled = True      ' 21" monitor

End Select

End Sub
```

The opt_Click() event occurs whenever one of the OptionBoxes is clicked. Because all of the OptionBoxes are part of an array, you can trap for any one of the OptionBoxes in the same procedure. This method can also be used on the TextBoxes, Frames, Labels and CheckBoxes that make up the individual forms in the ComputerWizard. The use of a control array enables you to create only one reference to the OptionBox object. The computer considers this array to be a single resource, thereby saving on program overhead.

To test out this new function, run the example and click on the desktop option and see what options are still available. When you get to the Monitor Type screen select a 2MB video card and watch what menu options become available.

The use of control arrays might provide for somewhat cryptic variable names, but the benefits of increased flexibility, reduction in code, and decreased overhead might be worth it. Of course if the code is properly commented it isn't a big problem.

Using the Wizard Resource File

The Wizard Manager creates an easily maintainable program skeleton, which requires the minimal code manipulation listed in the previous sections. Much of what the user sees in the interface, however, is customized and controlled from a resource file.

A resource file can be added and removed from the Visual Basic project just as any other object, except that you can't work with the file directly from Visual Basic. First, you need to create the source file, then compile it into a resource .res file.

The Wizard Manager creates a template resource file that holds strings for the captions of the various buttons and labels in the wizard application. The source code created by the Wizard Manager for the template resource file is contained in Listing 29.8.

LISTING 29.8. WIZARD.RC—THE RESOURCE FILE SOURCE CODE AS GENERATED BY THE WIZARD MANAGER.

```
STRINGTABLE DISCARDABLE
BEGIN
        //Wizard Caption
        10          "Wizard Template"
        15          "Wizard Template..."

        //Button Captions for Navigation Control:
        100         "Help"
        101         "Cancel"
        102         "< &Back"
        103         "&Next >"
        104         "&Finish"

        //Intro Info:
        1000        "Introduction"
        1001        "The ??? Wizard will help you ..."
        1002        "&Skip this screen in the future."

        //Other Step Control Captions:
        2000        "Step 1"
        2001        "Instructions for this step."
```

continues

LISTING 29.8. CONTINUED

```
2002        "Step 2"
2003        "Instructions for this step."
2004        "Step 3"
2005        "Instructions for this step."
2006        "Step 4"
2007        "Instructions for this step."

//Finish Step:
3000        "Finished!"
3001        "The ??? Wizard is finished collecting
3002        "information.\r\n\r\n_"
3003        "To build your ???, press Finish!"
3004        "Save current settings as default"

//Confirmation dialog
10000       "??? Created"
10001       "The ??? has been created."
10002       "Don't show this dialog in the future."
10003       "OK"

//Misc strings:
20000       "(None)"

//Error messages:
30000       "Incomplete Data."
30001       "You must ... before you can continue."

END


5000    BITMAP      wizmenu.bmp
```

You can modify each of the strings in the preceding source code to match what you want your wizard to say to the user. The numbers to the left of each string refer to the Tag property of the controls on the wizard. Note that the /r/n characters in the resource file signals the compiler to insert a carriage return and new line into your text.

> **NOTE**
>
> If you are interested in seeing how the code refers to the Tag property, examine the code in the Wizard.bas module on the companion CD.

To modify your own resource file, use a text editor and open the file wizard.rc in your working directory. Make the changes listed in Listing 29.9 to the source code.

LISTING 29.9. WIZARD.RC—MODIFY THE SOURCE CODE FOR THE RESOURCE FILE TO YOUR WIZARD'S REQUIREMENTS

```
STRINGTABLE DISCARDABLE
BEGIN
        //Wizard Caption
        10          "Computer Wizard"
        15          "Computer Wizard..."

        //Button Captions for Navigation Control:
        100         "Help"
        101         "Cancel"
        102         "< &Back"
        103         "&Next >"
        104         "&Finish"

        //Intro Info:
        1000        "Introduction"
        1001        "The Computer Wizard will take you step-by-step
        1002        "through the order process. The Wizard will ask
        1003        "a series of questions about the options you
        1004        "would like in your computer.
        1005        "When complete your request will be processed!"
        1006        "&Skip this screen in the future."

        //Other Step Control Captions:
        2000        "Step 1"
        2001        "Enter  your Name and Phone Number:"
        2002        "Step 2"
        2003        "What type of  Computer?"
        2004        "Step 3"
        2005        "What type of Processor ?."
        2006        "Step 4"
        2007        "Select your desired Operating System."
        2008        "Step 5"
        2009        "How much RAM do you need?."
        2010        "Step 6"
        2011        "What Size of Hard Drive?"
        2012        "Step 7"
        2013        "What Type of Display?"
        2014        "Step 8"
        2015        "Do you need anything else?"

        //Finish Step:
        3000        "Finished!"
        3001        "The Computer Wizard is finished collecting
        3002        "the information that it needs to create your
        3003        "order. To confirm your order, press Finish!"
        3004        "Save current settings as default"
```

continues

LISTING 29.9. CONTINUED

```
10000       "Order Created"
10001       "Your computer order has been created."
10002       "Don't show this dialog in the future."
10003       "OK"

//Misc strings:
20000       "(None)"

//Error messages:
30000       "Incomplete Data."
30001       "You must enter required information
30002       "before you can continue."

END
```

Note that most of the modifications in the code in Listing 29.9 are simply changes to the text strings. But as you add screens, you need to go back to the interface and check the Tag properties on the controls for the screens that you add. If you neglect this step, your controls will not display the label text you entered in Listing 29.9.

If the Resource Compiler is not already installed on your system, you need to copy it from the Visual Basic CD. You'll find it in the \Microsoft Visual Studio\VB98\ Wizards\ folder. There is no install process; simply copy the rc.exe and rcdll.dll files to your hard drive. You will find it helpful to copy the Resource Compiler directly into the directory where you are working with your wizard.

> **NOTE**
>
> The modified code does not include any bitmaps. In the example on the CD-ROM, the bitmaps are imbedded directly into the controls. However, you might want to refer to your own wizards in the resource file. If you do, make sure that they are in the application directory, where the wizard is installed.

The Resource Compiler is discussed extensively in the VB Books Online on your Visual Basic CD and in the readme file in the Resource Compiler tool directory, but you only need to know the basics to compile your resource file. To compile the file, run the following in the working directory:

```
RC /v /r wizard.rc
```

The RC runs the Resource Compiler, the /v parameter turns on messages (so that you can see what the compiler is doing), the /r parameter tells the compiler to create the .res file, and the wizard.rc specifies the file name.

If you run the Resource Compiler and receive an error message, the /v parameter tells you which line(s) you need to correct. When you have successfully compiled the resource .res file, return to Visual Basic, open the Computer Wizard project, and run it. You will now see your changes in the resource file reflected in the program, as illustrated in Figure 29.18.

After you have created the Wizard.res file you can use the Resource Editor to make changes to the text strings.

FIGURE 29.18.

The control tags are associated with the appropriate strings in the compiled resource file.

Summary

In this chapter, you learned about the Extensibility Object Model and its various members. After reading this chapter you might have thought of a number of new features that your would like to add to Visual Basic. The EOM enables you to transform Visual Basic into the application development environment that meets your particular needs.

The use of Add-ins, whether they are ActiveX components or Wizards, enables you to have greater flexibility and control over an already feature rich development environment. This ability enables you to create applications that transcend any of the apparent shortcomings of the current release.

Accessing the System Registry

by Rob Thayer

IN THIS CHAPTER

- INI Files   691
- The System Registry   715

When developing more complex applications, it is often desirable to implement a feature that will store information such as user settings to disk so they can be reinstated the next time the program runs. This saves the user the hassle of having to modify these settings every time he starts the program.

In the past, persistent program information was usually saved in INI (initialization) files, sometimes called profile files. These were simple text files, and they typically contained a list of parameter names (called *keys*) and their values. INI files did work, but they lacked an efficient organization method. Related keys could be grouped together into sections, but because INI files were text files, there was no way of quickly obtaining a particular key's value. Instead, the file would have to be read sequentially until the desired section and key were located.

Although Visual Basic does not include built-in functions specifically for reading or writing to INI files, there are some functions available via the Windows API that can be used to retrieve or update key values. Although these functions do make dealing with INI files easier, the use of sequential text files is still not very efficient.

With the introduction of Windows 95, a new way of storing program information came into vogue. Instead of using many individual INI files, program settings and information could be stored in a central repository called the System Registry. The Registry is organized into a hierarchy format, enabling searches for specific keys to be much more efficient. We'll talk more about the Registry's organization scheme later.

Visual Basic includes built-in functions for accessing keys in the System Registry, but they are somewhat limited. These functions only enable you to add, change, or delete keys and their values in a specific section of the Registry that is reserved for applications. Under most circumstances, this is exactly where you would want the information about your program to be stored. However, there are times when you need access to other parts of the Registry. Again, the Windows API fills the gap. There are several API functions for reading and manipulating keys in the Registry.

Though accessing the System Registry is typically more efficient than using INI files, the latter still has its place in the storage of program settings and other persistent information. Rather than make INI files obsolete, the Registry sometimes complements them.

This chapter discusses the System Registry and how it can be accessed using both inherent Visual Basic functions and external Windows API functions. INI files will also be discussed, along with the API functions that are used to read and write to them.

INI Files

INI (Initialization) files are text files that contain information specific to a Windows application. Although they can be easily displayed and modified using any text editor (such as Notepad), they are not so easily manipulated from within a Visual Basic program. No built-in VB functions exist specifically to deal with these kinds of files. Instead, Windows API functions need to be used.

Before we go into how you can use these API functions in your programs, it's necessary that you see how a typical INI file is organized. The easiest way to do that is to view one or two of them with a text editor. Most of them are found in the Windows directory or in the subdirectory of the application to which they belong, and they usually have the standard filename extension .INI.

Take, for example, the VBADDIN.INI file. This file is used specifically to store the list of Add-Ins that are available to Visual Basic. Though it might appear differently on your system, based on the Add-Ins you have installed, the contents of a typical VBADDIN.INI file might look like this:

```
[Add-Ins32]
VBSDIAddIn.Connect=0
DataToolsAddIn.Connect=1
AppWizard.Wizard=1
WizMan.Connect=0
ClassBuilder.Wizard=0
AddInToolbar.Connect=0
ControlWiz.Wizard=0
DataFormWizard.Wizard=0
ActiveXDocumentWizard.Wizard=1
PropertyPageWizard.Wizard=0
APIDeclarationLoader.Connect=0
CodeLineCounter.Connect=0
vbscc=1
```

Let's start from the top. The first line, [Add-Ins32], is a section name. Although this file only has one section, other INI files might be organized into multiple sections, each with a unique name.

The rest of the file is composed of keys and their values. Keys are used to store individual program settings and other vital pieces of information. The values can be either integers or strings.

Visual Basic, the application that will use this INI file, will read in these settings when it starts up. Based on the individual key values, VB can determine which Add-Ins it should and should not load.

A small INI file such as this one makes sense because it can be read in sequentially and the key values can be obtained as a group. Under most circumstances, individual key values do not have to be accessed singularly.

Depending on how you look at it, the fact that an INI file like this can be easily modified by the program's user can be either good or bad. An INI file like the one shown above is pretty straightforward, making modifications easy. If, however, an INI file is more complex, you might not want your users poking around in it and potentially damaging the existing settings.

INI files really weren't designed to be edited manually. Instead, they should be modified using the application to which they belong. Although you could easily change the VBADDIN.INI file yourself with a text editor, it's a much better idea to use VB's Add-In Manager utility. That way, you are prevented from assigning invalid key values or corrupting the file.

Accessing INI Files With the Windows API

There are two basic types of INI files, system and private. A System INI refers exclusively to the WIN.INI file that is used by Windows. Private INIs refer to everything else, including the INI files that you use for your own applications. There is really no difference between a system INI and a private INI, though the distinction is important, as you'll soon see.

In order to add, delete, or change keys and their values in INI files, you need to use functions from the Windows API. A separate set of functions exists for accessing the system INI as opposed to private INIs, but the corresponding functions are used the same way. Table 30.1 lists the API functions for accessing the system INI and Table 30.1 lists the functions for accessing private INIs:

TABLE 30.1. THE WINDOWS API FUNCTIONS FOR ACCESSING THE SYSTEM INI (WIN.INI).

Function Name	Description
GetProfileInt	Retrieves the integer value of an individual key.
GetProfileSection	Retrieves all key values in a given section.
GetProfileString	Retrieves the string value of an individual key.
WriteProfileSection	Updates all keys in a given section, or creates a new section.
WriteProfileString	Updates or creates an individual key value. Can also be used to delete a key or a section.

TABLE 30.2. THE WINDOWS API FUNCTIONS FOR ACCESSING PRIVATE INI FILES.

Function Name	*Description*
GetPrivateProfileInt	Retrieves the integer value of an individual key.
GetPrivateProfileSection	Retrieves all key values in a given section.
GetPrivateProfileString	Retrieves the string value of an individual key.
WritePrivateProfileSection	Updates all keys in a given section, or creates a new section.
WritePrivateProfileString	Updates or creates an individual key value. Can also be used to delete a key or a section.

The matching functions in Tables 30.1 and 30.2 are almost identical. The only difference is that you do not have to specify an INI file name for the functions that deal with the system INI because it is assumed that it's called WIN.INI, and that it's located in the Windows directory.

> **NOTE**
>
> On Windows NT, some of the sections in the WIN.INI file are mapped to the System Registry. This means that when you think you are changing data in the WIN.INI file with the Windows API function, the changes are actually being made to parts of the System Registry. Be careful!

You might have noticed that although there are separate functions for retrieving integer and string values for individual keys, there is only one function for updating or creating key values. That's because all key values are actually stored as strings. When retrieving integer values, the string is converted to a numeric value. For example, a key value of "8732ab" would cause the GetPrivateProfileInt function to translate that as an integer value of 8732. Of course, if the key value was simply "8732", the function would also translate it as an integer value of 8732.

Each of the ten API functions has a different syntax. The functions will be discussed in sets of two, one for accessing private INI files and the corresponding function for accessing the system INI file.

30

ACCESSING THE SYSTEM REGISTRY

> **NOTE**
>
> When specifying section and key names with these functions, the names are not case sensitive. Also, when specifying the name of the INI file for the private INI functions, the functions will automatically look for the file in the Windows directory if no path is given.

GetPrivateProfileSection and GetProfileSection

```
Declare Function GetPrivateProfileSection Lib "kernel32"
    Alias "GetPrivateProfileSectionA"
    (ByVal lpApplicationName As String,
     ByVal lpReturnedString As String,
     ByVal nSize As Long,
     ByVal lpFileName As String) As Long

Declare Function GetProfileSection Lib "kernel32"
    Alias "GetProfileSectionA"
    (ByVal lpApplicationName As String,
     ByVal lpReturnedString As String,
     ByVal nSize As Long) As Long
```

The GetPrivateProfileSection and GetProfileSection API functions retrieve the entire list of key names and values for a given section (specified by the lpApplicationName argument) in an INI file. The list is placed in a fixed-length string specified by the lpReturnedString argument, with the byte size of the string given in the nSize argument. Items in the list are delimited by Null characters, with one item equaling a key and its value. The GetPrivateProfileSection function has an additional argument, lpFileName, for specifying the path and name of the INI file.

Both functions return a value that indicates how many bytes were placed in the lpReturnedString argument. If the lpReturnedString buffer was too small to accommodate the entire list of keys and their values, then the function returns a value that is two less than the size of the buffer, which was specified by the nSize argument.

GetPrivateProfileInt and GetProfileInt

```
Declare Function GetPrivateProfileInt Lib "kernel32"
    Alias "GetPrivateProfileIntA"
    (ByVal lpApplicationName As String,
     ByVal lpKeyName As String,
     ByVal nDefault As Long,
     ByVal lpFileName As String) As Long

Declare Function GetProfileInt Lib "kernel32"
```

```
    Alias "GetProfileIntA"
    (ByVal lpApplicationName As String,
     ByVal lpKeyName As String,
     ByVal nDefault As Long) As Long
```

With the `GetPrivateProfileInt` and `GetProfileInt` API functions, you specify a section name (`lpApplicationName`) and a key name (`lpKeyName`) to retrieve a key value. When using the `GetPrivateProfileInt` function, you must also specify the path and name of the INI file with the `lpFileName` argument.

As mentioned earlier, all key values are stored as strings. `GetPrivateProfileInt` and `GetProfileInt` convert a key value string to a long integer and return the result. If the key is not found, then the value specified by the `nDefault` argument is returned by the function.

GetPrivateProfileString and GetProfileString

```
Declare Function GetPrivateProfileString Lib "kernel32"
    Alias "GetPrivateProfileStringA"
    (ByVal lpApplicationName As String,
     ByVal lpKeyName As String,
     ByVal lpDefault As String,
     ByVal lpReturnedString As String,
     ByVal nSize As Long,
     ByVal lpFileName As String) As Long

Declare Function GetProfileString Lib "kernel32"
    Alias "GetProfileStringA"
    (ByVal lpApplicationName As String,
     ByVal lpKeyName As String,
     ByVal lpDefault As String,
     ByVal lpReturnedString As String,
     ByVal nSize As Long) As Long
```

Like the `GetPrivateProfileInt` and `GetProfileInt` functions, `GetPrivateProfileString` and `GetProfileString` are also used to retrieve key values. However, these functions retrieve string values rather than integer values.

The arguments `lpApplicationName` and `lpKeyName` are used to specify the section and key names, respectively. For the `GetPrivateProfileString` function, the `lpFileName` argument indicates the path and name of the INI file. The key value is placed into the buffer string specified by the `lpReturnedString` argument, which is a fixed-length string `nSize` bytes long. If the key is not found, then the string value given as the `lpDefault` argument is placed in the `lpReturnedString` buffer.

30

ACCESSING THE
SYSTEM REGISTRY

If the function is successful, it will return the number of bytes that were placed into the lpReturnedString buffer. If the buffer is too small, the function will return a value that is one or two less than the size of the buffer as specified by the nSize argument.

The GetPrivateProfileInt and GetProfileInt functions can also be used to list all of the keys contained in a given section, or all of the sections in the INI file. To retrieve a list of keys in a section, set the lpKeyName argument to a Null string value (vbNullString). To retrieve a list of sections, set the lpApplicationName argument to vbNullString. In either case, the list that is returned has each item delimited with a Null character.

WritePrivateProfileSection and WriteProfileSection

```
Declare Function WritePrivateProfileSection Lib "kernel32"
    Alias "WritePrivateProfileSectionA"
    (ByVal lpApplicationName As String,
     ByVal lpString As String,
     ByVal lpFileName As String) As Long

Declare Function WriteProfileSection Lib "kernel32"
    Alias "WriteProfileSectionA"
    (ByVal lpApplicationName As String,
     ByVal lpString As String) As Long
```

The WritePrivateProfileSection and WriteProfileSection API functions are used to add or update a section and the keys that are contained within it. They can also be used to create new sections.

The section name is always specified by the lpApplicationName argument. The lpFileName argument is used with the WritePrivateProfileSection function to specify the path and name of the INI file.

If you want to provide a list of keys and their values, pass the list to the function as the lpString argument with each item in the list delimited with a Null character. The key names and values currently existing in the section will be replaced by those in the list, so be careful when updating keys this way.

If you want to create a new section with no keys in it, pass an empty string ("") for the lpString argument.

These functions return a non-zero value when successful, or zero when unsuccessful. In the case of the latter, you can use the GetLastError API function for more information on the error that was generated.

WritePrivateProfileString and WriteProfileString

```
Declare Function WritePrivateProfileString Lib "kernel32"
    Alias "WritePrivateProfileStringA"
```

```
    (ByVal lpApplicationName As String,
     ByVal lpKeyName As Any,
     ByVal lpString As String,
     ByVal lpFileName As String) As Long

Declare Function WriteProfileString Lib "kernel32"
    Alias "WriteProfileStringA"
    (ByVal lpApplicationName As String,
     ByVal lpKeyName As Any,
     ByVal lpString As String) As Long
```

The `WritePrivateProfileString` and `WriteProfileString` API functions are used primarily to add or update keys and their values. However, you can also use these functions to delete keys.

The `lpApplicationName` argument specifies the section name in which a key is located, and the `lpKeyName` argument specifies the name of the key. Use the `lpString` argument to give the value of the key. If you want to delete a key, set the `lpString` argument to `vbNullString`. If you want to delete all of the keys in a section, set the `lpKeyName` argument to `vbNullString`.

For the `WritePrivateProfileString`, the `lpFileName` argument specifies the path and name of the INI file. If the file is not found, a new file will be created.

These functions return a non-zero value on success or a zero value when they fail. If the function is unsuccessful, you can use the `GetLastError` API function for more specific information on the error that occurred.

Creating an INI File Editor

Now that you are familiar with the set of API functions that are used to access INI files, a sample program that better illustrates how the functions are used is in order. The program only uses the functions for accessing private INI files because it's not a good idea to casually fool around with the system INI file (WIN.INI).

The program that is created here will be built on later in this chapter in order to show how the API functions for accessing the System Registry are used. For now, however, we'll only concentrate on the INI functions.

To create the sample program, first build its user interface using Table 30.3, Table 30.4, and Figure 30.1 as guides. Table 30.3 lists the various controls that make up the interface, along with their properties. Table 30.4 lists the menu items that need to be added to the program's menu using VB's Menu Editor (accessed from VB's Tools menu):

30

ACCESSING THE SYSTEM REGISTRY

TABLE 30.3. THE CONTROLS AND THEIR PROPERTIES FOR THE INI FILE/SYSTEM REGISTRY
EDITOR PROGRAM.

Control Type	Property	Value
Form	Name	frmINIEdit
	Height	6570
	StartUpPosition	2 - Center Screen
	Width	6555
Label	Name	lblSectionName
	Caption	Section Name
	Height	255
	Left	240
	Top	120
	Width	1815
TextBox	Name	txtSectionName
	Enabled	False
	Height	285
	Left	240
	Top	360
	Width	4575
Label	Name	lblKeyName
	Caption	Key Name
	Height	255
	Left	240
	Top	720
	Width	1575
TextBox	Name	txtKeyName
	Enabled	False
	Height	285
	Left	240
	Top	960
	Width	4575
Label	Name	lblValue
	Caption	Value
	Height	255

Control Type	Property	Value
	Left	240
	Top	1320
	Width	1575
TextBox	Name	txtValue
	Enabled	False
	Height	285
	Left	240
	Top	1560
	Width	4575
CommandButton	Name	cmdRetrieve
	Caption	Retrieve
	Enabled	False
	Height	375
	Left	240
	Top	2040
	Width	1095
CommandButton	Name	cmdUpdate
	Caption	Update
	Enabled	False
	Height	375
	Left	1440
	Top	2040
	Width	1095
CommandButton	Name	cmdAdd
	Caption	False
	Height	375
	Left	2640
	Top	2040
	Width	1095
CommandButton	Name	cmdDelete
	Caption	False

continues

30

ACCESSING THE
SYSTEM REGISTRY

TABLE 30.3. CONTINUED

Control Type	Property	Value
	Height	375
	Left	3840
	Top	2040
	Width	1095
CommandButton	Name	cmdRefresh
	Caption	False
	Height	375
	Left	5040
	Top	2040
	Width	1095
Label	Name	lblFileContents
	Caption	INI File Contents
	Height	255
	Left	240
	Top	2640
	Width	1575
ListBox	Name	lstFileContents
	Height	2205
	Left	240
	Top	2880
	Width	5895
Label	Name	lblLastOpStatus
	Caption	Last Operation Status
	Height	240
	Left	240
	Top	5280
	Width	1575
Label	Name	lblStatus
	Alignment	2 - Center
	BorderStyle	1 - Fixed Single
	Height	255

Control Type	Property	Value
	Left	240
	Top	5520
	Width	5895
CommonDialog	Name	dlgGetFilename
	Left	5160
	Top	480
	FileName	*.ini
	Filter	*.ini
OptionButton	Name	optType
	Caption	Registry
	Enabled	False
	Height	255
	Index	1
	Left	5160
	Top	1440
	Value	True
	Width	1215
OptionButton	Name	optType
	Caption	INI File
	Enabled	True
	Height	195
	Index	0
	Left	5160
	Top	1200
	Value	False
	Width	1095

TABLE 30.4. THE MENU ITEMS FOR THE SAMPLE PROGRAM, TO BE ADDED WITH VB'S MENU EDITOR.

Menu Item Name	Caption
mnuFile	File
mnuFileOpenINIFile	Open INI File...
mnuExit	Exit

FIGURE 30.1.

The INI File/System Registry Editor program's user interface (in design mode).

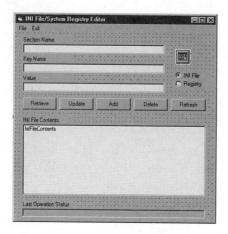

After the user interface has been designed, the program code can be added. But first, add a new module to the project so the API functions can be declared. Call the module INIEdit; then add the code in Listing 30.1.

LISTING 30.1.   CH30-01.TXT—THE CODE FOR THE INIEdit MODULE.

```
Public Declare Function GetPrivateProfileSection Lib "kernel32" _
    Alias "GetPrivateProfileSectionA" (ByVal lpAppName As String, _
    ByVal lpReturnedString As String, ByVal nSize As Long, _
    ByVal lpFileName As String) As Long
Public Declare Function GetPrivateProfileString Lib "kernel32" _
    Alias "GetPrivateProfileStringA" (ByVal lpApplicationName _
    As String,ByVal lpKeyName As Any, ByVal lpDefault As String, _
    ByVal lpReturnedString As String, ByVal nSize As Long, _
    ByVal lpFileName As String) As Long
Public Declare Function WritePrivateProfileSection Lib "kernel32" _
    Alias "WritePrivateProfileSectionA" (ByVal lpAppName As String, _
    ByVal lpString As String, ByVal lpFileName As String) As Long
Public Declare Function WritePrivateProfileString Lib "kernel32" _
    Alias "WritePrivateProfileStringA" (ByVal lpApplicationName _
    As String, ByVal lpKeyName As Any, ByVal lpString As Any, _
    ByVal lpFileName As String) As Long

Public gstrKeyValue As String * 256
```

Note that in the previous code, a global fixed-length string (gstrKeyValue) is also declared. This string will be used as the buffer for retrieving or setting key values using the API functions.

The next section of code to be added (see Listing 30.2) is for the cmdAdd CommandButton control's Click event and INIAdd, the function that it calls to add a section or key to an INI file.

LISTING 30.2. CH30-02.TXT—THE cmdAdd_Click EVENT AND THE INIAdd FUNCTION, WHICH ADDS A SECTION OR KEY TO THE INI FILE.

```
Private Sub cmdAdd_Click()

' Make sure the user entered a section name.
If txtSectionName.Text = "" Then
    MsgBox "Please enter a section name first."
    Exit Sub
End If

' For INI files, call the INIAdd function. For
' the Registry, call the RegAdd function.
If optType(0).Value = True Then
    lblStatus = INIAdd()
Else
    lblStatus = RegAdd()
End If

End Sub


Private Function INIAdd() As String

Dim lonStatus As Long
Dim strSectionName As String

' Remove brackets from section name, if necessary.
strSectionName = FixSectionName(txtSectionName.Text)

If txtKeyName.Text = "" Then
    ' No key name was specified, so add a new (empty)
    ' section with the WritePrivateProfileSection
    ' API function.
    lonStatus = WritePrivateProfileSection(strSectionName, _
        "", dlgGetFilename.FileName)
    ' Determine the status of the operation.
    If lonStatus = 0 Then
        INIAdd = "Error - Section could not be added"
    Else
        INIAdd = "Section added succesfully"
        ReadFile
    End If
Else
    ' Use the WritePrivateProfileString API function
    ' to add the key and, if necessary, the section.
    lonStatus = WritePrivateProfileString(strSectionName, _
```

continues

LISTING 30.2. CONTINUED.

```
        txtKeyName.Text, txtValue.Text, dlgGetFilename.FileName)
    ' Determine the status of the operation.
    If lonStatus = 0 Then
        INIAdd = "Error - Key could not be added"
    Else
        INIAdd = "Key added successfully"
        ReadFile
    End If
End If

End Function
```

The cmdAdd_Click event first ensures that a section name has been entered in the txtSectionName text box. It then calls one of two functions, INIAdd or RegAdd, based on the state of the INI File/Registry option buttons. Each function returns a string value that indicates the status of the operation. This status string is displayed in the lblStatus Label control. This format—checking the text boxes, calling separate routines for INI file or Registry operations, and then displaying the status—is used for all of the command buttons except the Refresh button, which is disabled when the Registry option button is selected.

The RegAdd function will be added later in this chapter when the Registry functions are discussed. No error can occur because the Registry option button is currently disabled.

The INIAdd function first calls the FixSectionName function, which removes brackets that enclose the section name. This function will be added later.

If no key name has been provided by the user in the txtKeyName text box, it is assumed that a section is to be added. Because it has already been verified that a section name has been entered, the procedure can then use the WritePrivateProfileSection API function to create the new section. Note that the lpString argument for the API function is passed as an empty string (""), indicating that there is no list of keys to be updated.

If a key name has been provided, then the procedure uses the WritePrivateProfileString API function to add or update the key and its value. The key value is taken from the txtValue text box.

The name and path of the INI file, which is obtained using the CommonDialog control dlgGetFilename, is passed to the API functions as the lpFileName argument. It is the same way in the rest of the INI functions that compose the sample program.

After the `WritePrivateProfileSection` or `WritePrivateProfileString` functions are called, the status of the operation is returned by the `INIAdd` function. If the functions are successful, the contents of the INI file are re-displayed using the `ReadFile` procedure, which will also be added later.

The next section of program code (see Listing 30.3) is for the Retrieve button. Again, two procedures are used: the `cmdRetrieve_Click` event and the `INIRetrieve` function.

LISTING 30.3.   CH30-03.TXT—THE `cmdRetrieve_Click` EVENT AND THE `INIRetrieve`
FUNCTION, WHICH RETRIEVES A GIVEN KEY'S VALUE FROM THE INI FILE.

```
Private Sub cmdRetrieve_Click()

Dim lonOpStatus As Long

' Make sure both a key name and a section name
' have been specified by the user.
If txtSectionName.Text = "" Then
    MsgBox "Please enter a section name first."
    Exit Sub
End If
If txtKeyName.Text = "" Then
    MsgBox "Please enter a key name first."
    Exit Sub
End If

' For INI files, call the INIRetrieve function. For
' the Registry, call the RegRetrieve function.
If optType(0).Value = True Then
    lblStatus = INIRetrieve()
Else
    lblStatus = RegRetrieve()
End If

End Sub


Private Function INIRetrieve() As String

Dim lonValueSize As Long
Dim strSectionName As String

' Remove brackets from section name, if necessary.
strSectionName = FixSectionName(txtSectionName.Text)

' Use the GetPrivateProfileString API function to
' retrieve the key's value from the file. A default
' value of "?!?" is used to see if the key has been
```

30

ACCESSING THE SYSTEM REGISTRY

continues

LISTING 30.3.   CONTINUED

```
' retrieved successfully.
lonValueSize = GetPrivateProfileString(strSectionName, _
    txtKeyName.Text, "?!?", gstrKeyValue, 256, _
    dlgGetFilename.FileName)

' Determine the status of the operation. If the
' value of the key is the same as the default value
' ("?!?"), then the key was probably not found.
If Left$(gstrKeyValue, 3) = "?!?" Then
    INIRetrieve = "Error - Key could not be located"
Else
    INIRetrieve = "Key retrieved successfully"
    txtValue.Text = Left$(gstrKeyValue, lonValueSize)
End If

End Function
```

You already know how the cmdRetrieve_Click event works, since it is very similar to the cmdAdd_Click event that was added earlier. Therefore, we'll press on to the discussion of the INIRetrieve function.

The first thing the INIRetrieve function does is strip the brackets from the section name using the FixSectionName function. This is pretty much standard in all of the program's INI functions.

The GetPrivateProfileString API function is used to retrieve the key's value. A default value of "?!?" is given so the success of the operation can be determined later. If the function places a value of "?!?" in the buffer (gstrKeyValue), it's a pretty safe bet that the key was not found.

The gstrKeyValue, which is used as the buffer in which the key value is to be placed by the function, was declared globally in the module that was added earlier. It is a fixed-length string of 256 characters, so a value of 256 is passed as the API function's nSize argument.

If the key is found (that is, a value of anything other than "?!?" is placed in gstrKeyValue), then the key value is displayed in the txtValue text box. Again, the status of the operation is returned by the function.

Next, add the code for the Update button (see Listing 30.4). The cmdUpdate_Click event and the INIUpdate function are the procedures that are used.

LISTING 30.4. CH30-04.TXT—THE cmdUpdate_Click EVENT AND THE INIUpdate FUNC-
TION, WHICH UPDATES A GIVEN KEY'S VALUE IN THE INI FILE.

```
Private Sub cmdUpdate_Click()

' Make sure both a key name and a section name
' have been specified by the user.
If txtSectionName.Text = "" Then
    MsgBox "Please enter a section name first."
    Exit Sub
End If
If txtKeyName.Text = "" Then
    MsgBox "Please enter a key name first."
    Exit Sub
End If

' For INI files, call the INIUpdate function. For
' the Registry, call the RegUpdate function.
If optType(0).Value = True Then
    lblStatus = INIUpdate
Else
    lblStatus = RegUpdate
End If

End Sub


Private Function INIUpdate() As String

Dim lonStatus As Long
Dim strSectionName As String

' Remove brackets from section name, if necessary
strSectionName = FixSectionName(txtSectionName.Text)

' Use the WritePrivateProfileString API function to
' update the key.
lonStatus = WritePrivateProfileString(strSectionName, _
    txtKeyName.Text, txtValue.Text, dlgGetFilename.FileName)

' Display the status of the operation and update
' the file contents list box if successful.
If lonStatus = 0 Then
    INIUpdate = "Error - Key could not be updated"
Else
    INIUpdate = "Key updated successfully"
    ReadFile
End If

End Function
```

If you've been following along, the INIUpdate function will be pretty easy to figure out. First, the FixSectionName function strips the brackets from around the section name, if necessary. The WritePrivateProfileString function is then called and is passed the section name, key name, and value. The status of the operation is returned by the INIUpdate function and the contents of the INI file are re-read and displayed using the ReadFile function if the operation is successful.

The next command button to be coded is the Delete button. Add the code for the cmdDelete_Click event and the INIDelete function as shown in Listing 30.5.

LISTING 30.5. CH30-05.TXT—THE cmdDelete_Click EVENT AND THE INIDelete FUNC-
TION, WHICH ARE USED TOGETHER TO DELETE A KEY OR SECTION FROM THE INI FILE.

```
Private Sub cmdDelete_Click()

' Make sure the user entered a section name.
If txtSectionName.Text = "" Then
    MsgBox "Please enter a section name first."
    Exit Sub
End If
' Check for a key name only when accessing the
' Registry.
If optType(1).Value = True Then
    If txtKeyName.Text = "" Then
        MsgBox "Please enter a key name first."
        Exit Sub
    End If
End If

' For INI files, call the INIDelete procedure. For
' the Registry, call the RegDelete procedure.
If optType(0).Value = True Then
    lblStatus = INIDelete()
Else
    lblStatus = RegDelete()
End If

End Sub


Private Function INIDelete() As String

Dim lonStatus As Long
Dim lonYesNo As Long
Dim strKeyName As String
Dim strSectionName As String

' Remove brackets from section name, if necessary.
```

```
strSectionName = FixSectionName(txtSectionName.Text)

If txtKeyName.Text = "" Then
    ' No specific key name was specified, so the
    ' entire section will be deleted. Ask the user
    ' if this is okay as a safety measure.
    lonYesNo = MsgBox("Delete all keys in section?", vbYesNo)
    If lonYesNo = vbNo Then
        INIDelete = "Delete operation aborted"
        Exit Function
    End If
    ' When deleting a section, the key name passed
    ' to the API function should be vbNullString.
    strKeyName = vbNullString
Else
    ' When deleting a specific key, the key name
    ' is passed to the API function.
    strKeyName = txtKeyName.Text
End If

' Use the WritePrivateProfileString API function to
' delete specific keys or entire sections.
lonStatus = WritePrivateProfileString(strSectionName, _
    strKeyName, vbNullString, dlgGetFilename.FileName)

' Display the status of the operation and update
' the file contents list box if successful.
If lonStatus = 0 Then
    INIDelete = "Error - Key could not be deleted"
Else
    INIDelete = "Key deleted successfully"
    txtKeyName.Text = ""
    txtValue.Text = ""
    ReadFile
End If

End Function
```

The cmdDelete_Click event is slightly different than the rest of the Click events so far. For INI files, it only checks to see if the section name has been entered. This is because it is possible to delete an entire section from the INI file, so a key name is not necessary. When dealing with the Registry, however, both the txtSectionName and txtKeyName text boxes need to be used.

The INIDelete event is perhaps a little more complicated than the other procedures, but it's still pretty straightforward. As always, the FixSectionName function is called. Then the txtKeyName text box is examined to see if a key name was entered. If not, it is assumed that the section is to be deleted. The user is prompted to ensure that this is really what was intended. If the user okays the section deletion, the strKeyName variable is set to vbNullString. Later, this variable will be passed to the WritePrivateProfileString API function. The vbNullString value tells the function that the entire section is to be deleted rather than an individual key.

If the txtKeyName text box does contain a key name, the name is assigned to the strKeyName variable. When that value is passed to the API function, the function knows that it is supposed to delete a single key.

After the strKeyName variable has been assigned, the WritePrivateProfileString API function is called. The status is returned by the INIDelete function. If the operation is successful, the txtKeyName and txtValue text boxes are cleared because the key no longer exists, and the contents of the INI file are re-displayed with the ReadFile function.

The last button event code to add is for the cmdRefresh_Click event (see Listing 30.6).

LISTING 30.6. CH30-06.TXT—THE cmdRefresh BUTTON'S Click EVENT, WHICH SIMPLY USES THE ReadFile FUNCTION TO RE-DISPLAY THE INI FILE'S CONTENTS.

```
Private Sub cmdRefresh_Click()

' Update the contents of the list box with the
' ReadFile procedure.
ReadFile

End Sub
```

The cmdRefresh_Click event simply calls the ReadFile procedure, which re-displays (refreshes) the contents of the INI file in the lstFileContents ListBox control.

The ReadFile procedure is to be added next (see Listing 30.7).

LISTING 30.7. CH30-07.TXT—THE ReadFile PROCEDURE, USED FOR READING THE CONTENTS OF THE INI FILE AND DISPLAYING THEM IN A LIST BOX.

```
Private Sub ReadFile()

Dim intFileNum As Integer
Dim strLineIn As String

' Re-read the current INI file and display it
' in the list box lstFileContents.
lstFileContents.Clear
If Dir$(dlgGetFilename.FileName) <> "" Then
    intFileNum = FreeFile
```

```
    Open dlgGetFilename.FileName For Input As #intFileNum
    While Not EOF(1)
        Line Input #intFileNum, strLineIn
        lstFileContents.AddItem strLineIn
    Wend
    Close #intFileNum
End If

End Sub
```

This is another simple piece of code. The file name specified by the `CommonDialog` control's `FileName` property (`dlgGetFilename.FileName`) is read sequentially, with each line being added to the `lstFileContents` list box.

Another procedure that has been used often in the functions added earlier is the `FixSectionName` procedure (see Listing 30.8):

LISTING 30.8.   CH30-08.TXT—THE `FixSectionName` FUNCTION, USED TO REMOVE THE BRACKETS FROM AROUND A SECTION NAME.

```
Private Function FixSectionName(sOldName As String) As String

Dim strNewName As String

' Remove the [brackets] around the section name
' field. The Windows API functions add the brackets
' for you.
If Left$(sOldName, 1) = "[" Then
    strNewName = Mid$(sOldName, 2)
Else
    strNewName = sOldName
End If
If Right$(sOldName, 1) = "]" Then
    strNewName = Left$(strNewName, Len(strNewName) - 1)
End If
FixSectionName = strNewName

End Function
```

Again, this procedure is pretty simple. The left and right brackets are removed from the section name that is passed to the function, and the new section name is returned by the function.

This function is necessary because the API functions that write sections add the brackets automatically. If you already have the brackets around the section name, the result will be a section name with double brackets added to the INI file.

Because the contents of the INI file are displayed in a ListBox control, it would be nice to make use of the situation and have a key or section name appear in the program's text box fields when it is clicked on. In order to facilitate such a feature, code needs to be added to the lstFileContents_Click event (see Listing 30.9).

LISTING 30.9.   CH30-09.TXT— THE lstFileContents_Click EVENT, WHICH TRANSFERS A KEY OR SECTION NAME TO THE PROGRAM'S TEXT BOXES WHEN IT IS CLICKED IN THE LIST BOX.

```
Private Sub lstFileContents_Click()

Dim intEqualPos As Integer
Dim lonListPtr As Long
Dim strListItem As String

txtKeyName.Text = ""
txtValue.Text = ""

' Get the item that was chosen from the list box.
strListItem = lstFileContents.List(lstFileContents.ListIndex)

' Did the user click on a section name (enclosed in
' brackets) or a key name?
If Left$(LTrim$(strListItem), 1) = "[" Then
    txtSectionName.Text = strListItem
Else
    txtSectionName.Text = ""
    ' Separate the key info into the key name and
    ' its value.
    intEqualPos = InStr(strListItem, "=")
    If intEqualPos > 1 Then
        txtKeyName.Text = Left$(strListItem, intEqualPos - 1)
        txtValue.Text = Mid$(strListItem, intEqualPos + 1)
    End If
    ' Loop backwards through the list and try to
    ' find the section name to which the key belongs.
    For lonListPtr = lstFileContents.ListIndex To 0 Step -1
        strListItem = LTrim$(lstFileContents.List(lonListPtr))
        If Left$(strListItem, 1) = "[" Then
            txtSectionName.Text = strListItem
            Exit For
        End If
    Next lonListPtr
End If

End Sub
```

The first thing this procedure needs to determine is if the user clicked on a section name or a key name. This is easy to figure out because section names are always enclosed in brackets.

If a section name is clicked, the name of the section is placed in the `txtSectionName` control and the procedure ends. However, if a key name is clicked, things are a little more complicated. The key name and it's value have to be separated, because they are listed in the INI file using the format *key=value*. Also, it is a good idea to determine the section in which the key is contained. This requires looping back through the INI file contents to find the first section name, which is placed in `txtSectionName`.

The next procedures that need to be added to the program are for the two menu items (see Listing 30.10):

LISTING 30.10. CH30-10.TXT—THE CODE FOR THE PROGRAM'S MENU ITEMS.

```
Private Sub mnuExit_Click()

' Exit the program.
Unload Me
End

End Sub

Private Sub mnuFileOpenINIFile_Click()

Dim intFileNum As Integer
Dim strFileName As String

' Show the Open File dialog box.
dlgGetFilename.FileName = "*.ini"
dlgGetFilename.Filter = "*.ini"
dlgGetFilename.ShowOpen

' If a file was selected, then enable some of the
' components of the user interface. Then read in
' and display the contents of the file.
strFileName = dlgGetFilename.FileName
If strFileName <> "" And strFileName <> "*.ini" Then
    txtSectionName.Enabled = True
    txtKeyName.Enabled = True
    txtValue.Enabled = True
    cmdRefresh.Enabled = True
    ' If no file for the selected name exists,
    ' make one.
    If Dir$(strFileName) = "" Then
        intFileNum = FreeFile
```

continues

30

ACCESSING THE SYSTEM REGISTRY

LISTING 30.10. CONTINUED

```
        Open strFileName For Output As #intFileNum
        Close #1
    End If
    ' Show the file name in the status area.
    lblStatus = "File " & strFileName & " opened."
    ReadFile

End If

End Sub
```

The `mnuExit_Click` routine simply ends the program. The `mnuFileOpenINIFile_Click` routine uses the `dlgGetFilename CommonDialog` control to determine the name and path of the INI file that is to be edited. If the file is found, its contents are displayed using the `ReadFile` procedure added earlier.

Because none of the API functions are valid until at least the name of a section has been entered, code needs to be added to keep the user from clicking on any of the command buttons until they have entered a section or key name. The last three procedures for the sample program (see Listing 30.11) implement this safety measure:

LISTING 30.11. CH30-11.TXT—PROCEDURES NEEDED TO ENSURE THAT NO COMMAND BUTTONS ARE USED UNTIL AN INI FILE HAS BEEN SELECTED.

```
Private Sub txtKeyName_Change()

' Check the status of the txtKeyName and
' txtSectionName fields to see if some command
' buttons can be enabled.
ToggleCmdButtons

End Sub

Private Sub txtSectionName_Change()

' Check the status of the txtKeyName and
' txtSectionName fields to see if some command
' buttons can be enabled.
ToggleCmdButtons

End Sub

Private Sub ToggleCmdButtons()

' Disable/enable certain command buttons based on
```

```
' whether or not the txtSectionName and txtKeyName
' fields are blank.
If txtSectionName.Text = "" And txtKeyName.Text = "" Then
    cmdRetrieve.Enabled = False
    cmdAdd.Enabled = False
    cmdDelete.Enabled = False
    cmdUpdate.Enabled = False
Else
    cmdRetrieve.Enabled = True
    cmdAdd.Enabled = True
    cmdDelete.Enabled = True
    cmdUpdate.Enabled = True
End If

End Sub
```

That's all there is to the sample program. When you try it out, it's probably a good idea to create a new INI file just for fooling around with. Select the Open INI File option from the File menu and type in the name of an INI file that doesn't already exist, such as *VBU-CH30.INI*.

Try experimenting with the Add, Update, Retrieve, and Delete buttons. Just remember that you have to enter at least a section name before choosing any of the options.

If you haven't already, make sure you save the program because it will be used in the next section for performing System Registry editing functions.

The System Registry

The System Registry first made its appearance with Windows 3.1, but it played only a minimal part in the storage of parameters and settings under that operating system. Windows 95 and Windows NT, on the other hand, use the Registry extensively. It's not uncommon to find a Registry that is several megabytes in size, filled with all manners of settings and other information.

The System Registry is organized into a hierarchy format that makes it easy to locate a desired key, provided you know the "path" in which the key is contained. If the concept of a hierarchy is unfamiliar to you, don't worry. It will all be apparent in just a moment.

One of the best ways to learn about the Registry is by using a utility called RegEdit. RegEdit comes with Windows, and it enables you to navigate through the many keys and subkeys that make up the Registry. Figure 30.2 shows RegEdit in action.

RegEdit is divided into two window panes, with the Registry's hierarchy of subkeys shown in the left pane. The right pane is used to display keys and values, as you'll soon see.

FIGURE 30.2.

The RegEdit utility, which is used to view and change Registry keys.

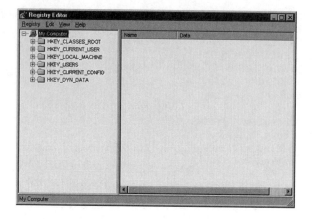

Figure 30.2 shows the Registry's six *root keys*: HKEY_CLASSES_ROOT, HKEY_CURRENT_USER, HKEY_LOCAL_MACHINE, HKEY_USERS, HKEY_CURRENT_CONFIG, and HKEY_DYN_DATA. Each of these root keys can contain hundreds or even thousands of *subkeys*, which in turn contain one or more keys and their values.

For example, Figure 30.3 shows the subkeys of the HKEY_CURRENT_USER root key. Many of these subkeys can themselves contain subkeys, and so on. The small plus sign next to a subkey or root key is used to open it up, and the small minus sign is used to close it.

FIGURE 30.3.

The HKEY_CURRENT_USER *root key is opened to display the subkeys it contains. Many of these subkeys have subkeys of their own.*

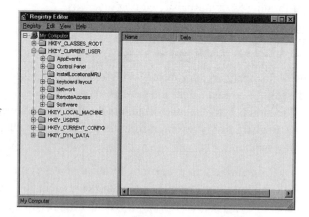

The hierarchy organization of the System Registry can be seen in this "nesting" of subkeys. The path for a key is shown at the bottom of the RegEdit window. For example, Figure 30.4 shows the subkey path My Computer\HKEY_CURRENT_USER\Software\Microsoft\Internet Explorer\Settings. However, when specifying key paths, you

typically discard the My Computer root designation, leaving
HKEY_CURRENT_USER\Software\Microsoft\Internet Explorer\
Settings. HKEY_CURRENT_USER is the root key, Software is a subkey of
HKEY_CURRENT_USER, Microsoft is a subkey of Software, and so on.

FIGURE 30.4.

RegEdit shows the path of the currently selected subkey at the bottom of its window.

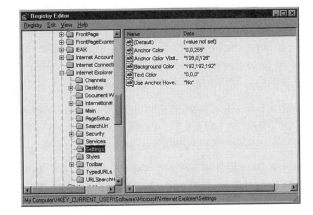

Note that in Figure 30.4, the keys for the subkey Settings are shown in RegEdit's rightmost pane. Each subkey can have multiple key values.

Registry keys can have string values or binary values. Take a look at the keys shown in Figure 30.5. The string keys are denoted with an "ab" icon to their left. Their values are also enclosed in quotes. Binary keys, on the other hand, are denoted with "001 110" icons. Their values are shown as hexadecimal numbers.

FIGURE 30.5.

Some keys have string values, and some have binary values. You can tell which are which by the icon to the left of the key name.

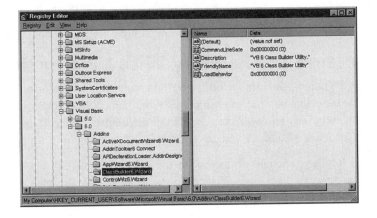

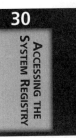

30

ACCESSING THE
SYSTEM REGISTRY

To change a key value, double-click on the name of the key. You will then be prompted to enter the key's value. To add a key, right-click on the empty space in RegEdit's right pane. Then use the pop-up menu to add a new key and specify its value type.

You can also right-click on the subkeys shown in RegEdit's left pane in order to add new subkeys. To delete a subkey, right-click on its name and choose Delete from the pop-up menu.

As you can see, the organization of the Registry is far more complex than that of INI files. INI files have sections that contain individual keys, and the Registry contains subkeys of subkeys of subkeys. The keys can be found contained within the subkeys.

Even though the Registry's organization is complex (at least in terms of size), it is still easily navigated. You need only know a key's path to access it, and the key can be read in almost no time regardless of how large the Registry might become.

You should now have a good idea of how the Registry works, and how individual keys can be specified. The next step is learning how to manipulate the Registry from within your Visual Basic programs. Depending on which area of the Registry you want to change, this can be accomplished using a few built-in VB functions or a set of Windows API functions.

CAUTION

Before experimenting with the System Registry, make sure that you back it up first. You can do this using Export function of the RegEdit program, but it's better to use a backup program. The Registry is fragile, and sometimes even minor changes to it can have a devastating effect on your system.

Accessing the Registry With VB Functions

Although Visual Basic does include some built-in functions for manipulating the System Registry, the extent of what you can do with these functions is somewhat limited. Basically, they only let you access one part of the Registry. In addition, they restrict the number of levels of subkeys you can create.

The VB Registry functions always access the path `HKEY_CURRENT_USER\Software\VB and VBA Program Settings\`. You can create subkeys from this path, but the VB functions limit you to this specific part of the Registry. If you want access to other areas, you'll have to use Windows API functions, which are discussed in the next section of this chapter.

There are a total of four VB functions and statements for accessing the Registry. They are listed in Table 30.5. Note that in Visual Basic, a key is sometimes referred to as a *setting*.

TABLE 30.5. THE VISUAL BASIC FUNCTIONS FOR ACCESSING THE SYSTEM REGISTRY.

Function/Statement	Description
SaveSetting	Adds or updates keys and their values
GetSetting	Retrieves a key value
GetAllSettings	Retrieves a list of keys and their values
DeleteSetting	Deletes a subkey or key

These functions and statements are discussed in more detail in the sections that follow.

The `SaveSetting` Statement

The SaveSetting statement updates a key value. It can also create new keys. Its syntax is:

```
SaveSetting appname, section, key, setting
```

The appname argument specifies the name of the application to which the key belongs. The section argument specifies the subkey, key specifies the name of the key, and setting gives the value of the key.

If you were to use the SaveSetting statement in a program called MyCompany Demo and you wanted to save screen settings such as background color, the code might look like this:

```
SaveSetting "MyCompany Demo", "Screen", "BGColor", "&HFFFFFF"
```

This would result in a key with the following path being created in the Registry:

```
HKEY_CURRENT_USER\Software\VB and VBA Program Settings\MyCompany
Demo\Screen\BGColor
```

Of course, if the key already existed, the new value ("&HFFFFFF") would be assigned to the key.

The `GetSetting` Function

The GetSetting function does the opposite of the SaveSetting statement. It retrieves a key value from the Registry. Its syntax is:

```
GetSetting(appname, section, key[, default])
```

Again, the *appname*, *section*, and *key* arguments specify the application name, subkey name, and key name. The optional *default* argument is used to specify a value that will be returned by the function if the key cannot be located. If no `default` is given, the default return value is assumed to be an empty string (`""`).

If you had used the example code given for the `GetSetting` statement above, the following line of code

```
strValue = GetSetting("MyCompany Demo", "Screen", _
    "BGColor", "&H000000")
```

would result in the value "&HFFFFFF" being assigned to `strValue`. If the key did not exist, `strValue` would be assigned "&H000000".

The `GetAllSettings` Function

If you want to retrieve all of the keys and their values in a particular subkey, you can use the `GetAllSettings` function. Its syntax is:

```
GetAllSettings(appname, section)
```

As before, the `appname` argument specifies the application name and the section argument specifies the name of the subkey. The value returned by the function is a Variant that is a two-dimensional array of strings containing all of the keys and their values in the subkey.

The `DeleteSetting` Statement

To delete a key or subkey from the Registry, use the `DeleteSetting` statement. Its syntax is:

```
DeleteSetting appname, section[, key]
```

Once again, the `appname` argument specifies the application name and the `section` argument specifies the name of the subkey. If you leave out the optional `key` argument, the subkey will be deleted. If you do specify a `key`, only that key will be deleted.

Accessing the Registry With the Windows API

When the VB functions and statements for accessing the Registry don't give you the flexibility you desire, you'll probably have to turn to the Windows API. The API actually has quite a few functions that deal directly with the Registry. They are all listed here, but only the more useful ones are covered in any detail.

TABLE 30.6. THE WINDOWS API SYSTEM REGISTRY FUNCTIONS.

Function Name	Description
RegCloseKey	Closes an open key.
RegConnectRegistry	Opens a key on a remote system.
RegCreateKey	Creates a new key.
RegCreateKeyEx	Creates a new key or opens an existing key.
RegDeleteKey	Deletes a key.
RegDeleteValue	Deletes a key's value.
RegEnumKey	Returns a list of the subkeys of a given key.
RegEnumKeyEx	Returns a list of the subkeys of a given key. Gives you more control than RegEnumKey.
RegEnumValue	Returns a list of the values for a given key.
RegFlushKey	Makes sure that changes to keys have been written to disk.
RegGetKeySecurity	Returns the security information for a key.
RegLoadKey	Loads Registry information from a disk file.
RegNotifyChangeKeyValue	Notifies a program when a key's value changes.
RegOpenKey	Opens a key.
RegOpenKeyEx	Opens a key. Gives you more control than RegOpenKey.
RegQueryInfoKey	Retrieves information about a key.
RegQueryValue	Retrieves a key value.
RegQueryValueEx	Retrieves a key value. Gives you more control than RegQueryValue.
RegReplaceKey	Replaces Registry information with Registry data from a disk file.
RegRestoreKey	Restores Registry information from a disk file.
RegSaveKey	Saves Registry information to a disk file.
RegSetKeySecurity	Sets security information for a key.
RegSetValue	Sets a key value.
RegSetValueEx	Sets a key value. Gives you more control than RegSetValue.
RegUnloadKey	Closes an open key on a remote system.

As you can see in Table 30.6, the Windows API gives you a far greater control of System Registry manipulation than the VB functions. With the API, you can access security information for keys, manage keys on remote systems, or transfer Registry information to and from disk files.

30

ACCESSING THE SYSTEM REGISTRY

The API functions that will be covered in this section include `RegCloseKey`, `RegCreateKey`, `RegDeleteValue`, `RegOpenKeyEx`, `RegQueryValueEx`, and `RegSetValueEx`. If you want more information on any of the other functions, *Dan Appleman's Visual Basic Programmer's Guide to the Win32 API* is strongly recommended.

RegOpenKeyEx

```
Declare Function RegOpenKeyEx Lib "advapi32"
    Alias "RegOpenKeyExA"
    (ByVal hKey As Long,
     ByVal lpSubKey As String,
     ByVal ulOptions As Long,
     ByVal samDesired As Long,
     phkResult As Long) As Long
```

Before a Registry subkey can be accessed, it must first be opened. The `RegOpenKeyEx` API function opens a subkey and returns its handle, a unique number that is used to reference the subkey. If the function is successful, the handle is placed in the variable specified as the `phkResult` argument.

The first argument to the function, `hKey`, refers to the handle of the subkey that precedes the subkey to be opened. For example, if you were using a subkey path such as `HKEY_CURRENT_USER\Software\MyApplication`, the handle for the `Software` subkey would have to be given before the `MyApplication` subkey could be opened.

The `lpSubKey` argument specifies the name of the subkey to open. Continuing with the example given above, this would be `"MyApplication"`.

The `ulOptions` argument is not used and should be set to zero. The `samDesired` argument specifies the types of operations that can be performed on the subkey. Table 30.7 lists some of the constants that can be used for the `samDesired` argument and their values.

TABLE 30.7. CONSTANTS THAT CAN BE USED WITH THE SAMDESIRED ARGUMENT.

Constant	Value
KEY_EVENT	&H1
KEY_QUERY_VALUE	&H1
KEY_SET_VALUE	&H2
KEY_CREATE_SUB_KEY	&H4
KEY_ENUMERATE_SUB_KEYS	&H8
KEY_NOTIFY	&H10

Constant	Value
KEY_CREATE_LINK	&H20
KEY_ALL_ACCESS	&H3F

The RegOpenKeyEx function returns a zero value if the subkey can be opened and non-zero if there is a problem.

RegCloseKey

```
Declare Function RegCloseKey Lib "advapi32"
    (ByVal hKey As Long) As Long
```

The RegCloseKey API function is used to close a currently open subkey. Its only argument is hKey, which specifies the handle of the open subkey. RegCloseKey returns zero if successful and non-zero on failure.

RegCreateKey

```
Declare Function RegCreateKey Lib "advapi32"
    Alias "RegCreateKeyA"
    (ByVal hKey As Long,
     ByVal lpSubKey As String,
     phkResult As Long) As Long
```

To create a new subkey, first make sure the subkey that will contain it has been opened with the RegOpenKeyEx function. You'll need the handle of that subkey to pass to the RegCreateKey function in the hKey argument. The lpSubKey argument is the name of the key value, and phkResult is the assigned the handle of the new subkey (provided the function is successful). The function will return a zero value on success or non-zero on failure.

RegDeleteKey

```
Declare Function RegDeleteKey Lib "advapi32"
    Alias "RegDeleteKeyA"
    (ByVal hKey As Long,
     ByVal lpSubKey As String) As Long
```

To delete a subkey, use the RegDeleteKey API function. Simply pass it the handle of the open subkey that contains the subkey to be deleted in the hKey argument, and the name of the subkey to be deleted in the lpSubKey argument. The functions returns zero if successful and non-zero on failure.

RegDeleteValue

```
Declare Function RegDeleteValue Lib "advapi32"
    Alias "RegDeleteValueA"
    (ByVal hKey As Long,
     ByVal lpValueName As String) As Long
```

To delete a key value, use `RegDeleteValue`. Simply pass it the handle of the subkey that contains the value in `hKey`, and the name of the key value in `lpValueName`. The function returns zero if successful and non-zero if it fails.

RegQueryValueEx

```
Declare Function RegQueryValueEx Lib "advapi32"
    Alias "RegQueryValueExA"
    (ByVal hKey As Long,
     ByVal lpValueName As String,
     ByVal lpReserved As Long,
     lpType As Long,
     lpData As Any,
     lpcbData As Long) As Long
```

To retrieve the value of a key, use the `RegQueryValueEx` function. You must first open the subkey that contains the key value so you can pass its handle to this function as the `hKey` argument. The `lpValueName` argument specifies the name of the text value. `lpReserved` is not used and should be set to 0. The type of data to be retrieved is specified by the `lpType` argument (see Table 30.8), and the `lpData` argument specifies a buffer into which the value will be placed. The `lpcbData` argument should indicate the size of the buffer. Zero is returned by the function if successful and non-zero is returned on failure.

TABLE 30.8. THE CONSTANTS FOR SPECIFYING KEY VALUE TYPES.

Constant	Value	Description
REG_NONE	0	Undefined
REG_SZ	1	String (Null terminated)
REG_EXPAND_SZ	2	Non-expanded environment string
REG_BINARY	3	Binary data
REG_DWORD	4	32-bit
REG_DWORD_LITTLE_ENDIAN	4	32-bit with high-order byte first
REG_DWORD_BIG_ENDIAN	5	32-bit with low-order byte first
REG_LINK	6	Symbolic link
REG_MULTI_SZ	7	Multiple strings
REG_RESOURCE_LIST	8	Resource list for device driver

RegSetValueEx

```
Declare Function RegSetValueEx Lib "advapi32"
    Alias "RegSetValueExA"
    (ByVal hKey As Long,
     ByVal lpValueName As String,
     ByVal Reserved As Long,
     ByVal dwType As Long,
     lpData As Any,
     ByVal cbData As Long) As Long
```

The `RegSetValueEx` API function sets a key value. `hKey` is the handle of the subkey that contains the key value, and `lpValueName` is the name of the value itself. `Reserved` is not used and should be set to 0. The type of value is specified by `dwType` (refer to Table 30.8), and `lpData` is the buffer that contains the value. The size of the buffer is specified by `cbData`. The function returns zero on success and non-zero if unsuccessful.

Creating a System Registry Editor

To illustrate how the Windows API Registry functions can be used to add, retrieve, update, and delete key values, the program that was started earlier in this chapter will be built upon so it can be used to edit INI files and the Registry. To keep things simple, only individual key values will be accessible.

To begin modifying the sample program, first add the following declarations and constants to the `INIEdit` module (see Listing 30.12):

LISTING 30.12. CH30-12.TXT—FUNCTION DECLARATIONS AND CONSTANTS TO BE ADDED TO THE INIEdit MODULE.

```
Public Declare Function RegCloseKey Lib "advapi32" _
    (ByVal hKey As Long) As Long
Public Declare Function RegCreateKey Lib "advapi32" _
    Alias "RegCreateKeyA" (ByVal hKey As Long, _
    ByVal lpSubKey As String, phkResult As Long) As Long
Public Declare Function RegDeleteValue Lib "advapi32" _
    Alias "RegDeleteValueA" (ByVal hKey As Long, _
    ByVal lpValueName As String) As Long
Public Declare Function RegOpenKeyEx Lib "advapi32" _
    ByVal lpSubKey As String, ByVal ulOptions As Long, _
    ByVal samDesired As Long, phkResult As Long) As Long
Public Declare Function RegQueryValueEx Lib "advapi32" _
    Alias "RegQueryValueExA" (ByVal hKey As Long, _
    ByVal lpValueName As String, ByVal lpReserved As Long, _
    lpType As Long, lpData As Any, lpcbData As Long) As Long
Public Declare Function RegSetValueEx Lib "advapi32" _
```

continues

30

ACCESSING THE
SYSTEM REGISTRY

LISTING 30.12. CONTINUED

```
     Alias "RegSetValueExA" (ByVal hKey As Long, _
     ByVal lpValueName As String, ByVal Reserved As Long, _
     ByVal dwType As Long, lpData As Any, _
     ByVal cbData As Long) As Long

Public Const REG_NONE = 0
Public Const REG_SZ = 1
Public Const REG_EXPAND_SZ = 2
Public Const REG_BINARY = 3
Public Const REG_DWORD = 4
Public Const REG_DWORD_LITTLE_ENDIAN = 4
Public Const REG_DWORD_BIG_ENDIAN = 5
Public Const REG_LINK = 6
Public Const REG_MULTI_SZ = 7
Public Const REG_RESOURCE_LIST = 8
```

The first procedure that needs to be added to the program is a function called
GetKeyHandle (see Listing 30.13). This function uses the RegOpenKeyEx API function
to open a subkey and get its handle, a unique number that can be used to reference the
subkey.

LISTING 30.13. CH30-13.TXT—THE GetKeyHandle FUNCTION, WHICH OPENS A SUBKEY
AND RETURNS ITS UNIQUE HANDLE.

```
Private Function GetSubkeyHandle(sSubkey As String) As Long

Dim intSubkeyCount As Integer
Dim intSubkeyLoop As Integer
Dim intSubkeyPtr As Integer
Dim lonHandle(1 To 32) As Long
Dim lonLastHandle As Long
Dim lonStatus As Long
Dim strKeyPath As String
Dim strSubkeys(1 To 32) As String
Dim strTempKeys() As String

' Trim any spaces from left and right sides of the
' subkey path.
strKeyPath = Trim$(sSubkey)

' Use VB's Split function to break the key's path
' into subkeys.
```

continues

```
strTempKeys = Split(strKeyPath, "\")

' Transfer the elements of the strTempKeys()
' array to strSubkeys(), but leave out any blank
' elements.
For intSubkeyLoop = 0 To UBound(strTempKeys)
    If strTempKeys(intSubkeyLoop) <> "" Then
        intSubkeyCount = intSubkeyCount + 1
        If intSubkeyCount <= 32 Then
            strSubkeys(intSubkeyCount) = strTempKeys(intSubkeyLoop)
        Else
            ' Error - too many subkeys in path.
            GetSubkeyHandle = -1
            Exit Function
        End If
    End If
Next intSubkeyLoop

For intSubkeyPtr = 1 To intSubkeyCount - 1
    ' For the first subkey, use the defined
    ' constants - this is the root key.
    If intSubkeyPtr = 1 Then
        Select Case UCase$(strSubkeys(1))
            Case "HKEY_CLASSES_ROOT":
                lonLastHandle = &H80000000
            Case "HKEY_CURRENT_USER":
                lonLastHandle = &H80000001
            Case "HKEY_LOCAL_MACHINE"
                lonLastHandle = &H80000002
            Case "HKEY_USERS":
                lonLastHandle = &H80000003
            Case "HKEY_PERFORMANCE_DATA":
                lonLastHandle = &H80000004
            Case "HKEY_CURRENT_CONFIG":
                lonLastHandle = &H80000005
            Case Else:
                GetSubkeyHandle = -1
                Exit Function
        End Select
    End If
    ' Open the next subkey.
    lonStatus = RegOpenKeyEx(lonLastHandle, _
        strSubkeys(intSubkeyPtr + 1), 0, &H3F, _
        lonHandle(intSubkeyPtr))
    ' A non-zero value returned by the
    ' RegOpenKey function indicates an error.
    If lonStatus Then
```

continues

30

ACCESSING THE
SYSTEM REGISTRY

LISTING 30.13. CONTINUED

```
        ' opened subkeys.
        For intSubkeyLoop = 2 To (intSubkeyPtr - 1)
            lonStatus = RegCloseKey(lonHandle(intSubkeyLoop))
        Next intSubkeyLoop
        GetSubkeyHandle = -1
        Exit Function
    End If
    lonLastHandle = lonHandle(intSubkeyPtr)
Next intSubkeyPtr

' Return the value of the last subkey handle.
GetSubkeyHandle = lonLastHandle

' Close all subkeys but the last one.
For intSubkeyLoop = 1 To (intSubkeyCount - 2)
    lonStatus = RegCloseKey(lonHandle(intSubkeyLoop))
Next intSubkeyLoop

End Function
```

The object of this function is to return the handle of the last subkey in the path, which is provided by the user via the txtSectionName text box. Keep in mind that a path can be a long series of subkeys, such as HKEY_CURRENT_USER\Software\Test App or something even longer. It is within the last subkey that the individual keys and their values are contained. So it is that last subkey that has to be opened.

Unfortunately, that's not an easy task. To access the last subkey in the path, all of the preceding subkeys have to be opened, one at a time. So first you would open the HKEY_CURRENT_USER root key, then the Software subkey, then finally the Test App subkey.

The first thing that needs to be done is to make sure there are no spaces surrounding the subkey path. Then the path is broken down into its various subkeys using VB's Split function, which was just introduced in VB6. This handy function saves a bit of coding! It uses the backslash ("\") delimiter of the path to break down the txtSectionName string into individual items, which are stored in the strTempKeys array.

Because empty subkey names would be invalid, the strTempKeys array is transferred to the strSubkeys array and any empty items are weeded out. The strSubkeys array is only dimensioned for 32 elements, so a path with more subkeys than that will cause the function to fail.

Now that the subkey path has been broken down, the function loops through the subkeys and opens each one. To see how that is done, take a look at the call to the RegOpenKeyEx API function:

```
lonStatus = RegOpenKeyEx(lonLastHandle, _
        strSubkeys(intSubkeyPtr + 1), 0, &H3F, _
    _    lonHandle(intSubkeyPtr))
```

The first argument to the function is the handle of the last subkey that was opened (`lonLastHandle`). Because this is not available for the first subkey in the path, a `Select...Case` statement is used to assign a value to `lonLastHandle` based on the first subkey, which must be one of the Registry's six root keys. If it's not, the path is invalid and the `GetSubkeyHandle` function fails.

The second argument to the `RegOpenKeyEx` function is the name of the subkey to be opened. That's easy; it's the next subkey in the `strSubkeys` array. The third argument is unused and is set to zero. The next argument is a Long value that specifies the operations that can be performed on the subkey. In this case, a value of `&H3F` is used to provide full access to the subkey. The final argument is assigned the handle of the subkey that is opened, which will be stored in the `lonHandle` array.

If for some reason the `RegOpenKeyEx` function is not successful, then the `GetSubkeyHandle` function fails. But first, any currently open subkeys need to be closed with the `RegCloseKey` API function. You always want to make sure that you close any subkeys that you open.

If all of the calls to the `RegOpenKeyEx` function are successful, then the `GetSubkeyHandle` function returns the handle of the last subkey that was opened. All of the handles that preceded it are closed before the function ends, leaving only the last subkey open.

This is a pretty complicated routine, but if you break it down into its parts it may be easier to understand. Navigating along a subkey path is one of the more difficult aspects of Registry API programming.

The next procedure to add (see Listing 30.14) is a far more simple one. It closes a subkey when given its handle.

LISTING 30.14. CH30-14.TXT—THE CloseSubkey FUNCTION, WHICH CLOSES AN OPEN SUBKEY.

```
Private Function CloseSubkey(lHandle As Long) As Long

Dim lonStatus As Long

' Close the key with the handle specified by the
' lHandle argument.
lonStatus = RegCloseKey(lHandle)
```

continues

LISTING 30.14. CONTINUED

```
CloseSubkey = 0
If lonStatus Then CloseSubkey = -1

End Function
```

Once again, the `RegCloseKey` API function is used to close a subkey. The `CloseSubkey` function will be used in the next procedure to be added, the `RegRetrieve` function (see Listing 30.15).

LISTING 30.15. CH30-15.TXT—THE `RegRetrieve` FUNCTION, WHICH IS USED TO RETRIEVE A KEY VALUE FROM THE REGISTRY.

```
Private Function RegRetrieve() As String

Dim lonSubkeyHandle As Long
Dim lonStatus As Long
Dim lonValueType As Long
Dim lonValueSize As Long

' Use the GetSubkeyHandle function to determine the
' handle of the subkey given in txtSectionName.
lonSubkeyHandle = GetSubkeyHandle(txtSectionName.Text)
If lonSubkeyHandle = -1 Then
    ' Subkey could not be located.
    RegRetrieve = "Error - Subkey could not be located"
    Exit Function
End If

' Use the RegQueryValueEx API function to retrieve
' the value of the key given in txtKeyName.
lonValueType = REG_SZ
lonValueSize = 256
lonStatus = RegQueryValueEx(lonSubkeyHandle, _
    Trim$(txtKeyName.Text), 0, lonValueType, _
    ByVal gstrKeyValue, lonValueSize)
If lonStatus <> 0 Then
    ' Key could not be located.
    RegRetrieve = "Error - Key could not be located"
Else
    RegRetrieve = "Key retrieved successfully"
    txtValue.Text = Left$(gstrKeyValue, lonValueSize)
End If

' Close the open subkey with the CloseSubKey
```

```
' function.
lonStatus = CloseSubkey(lonSubkeyHandle)

End Function
```

If you remember back to the cmdRetrieve_Click event that was added earlier in this chapter, the RegRetrieve function is called when the Retrieve button is clicked and the Registry option button is selected. This function does basically the same thing that the INIRetrieve function does, except instead of retrieving a key from an INI file, it retrieves it from the Registry.

This function assumes that the txtSectionName text box contains the name of the subkey path and the txtKeyName text box contains the name of the key value to be retrieved. To get to the key, the subkey path has to be followed and the last subkey has to be opened. This is accomplished with the GetSubkeyHandle function discussed earlier.

After the subkey handle has been provided, the RegQueryValueEx API function is used to obtain the key value. If successful, the function places the value in the specified buffer, which in this case is gstrKeyValue.

The lonValueType variable is set to REG_SZ, a constant that has a value of 1. This variable is passed to the RegQueryValueEx function to specify the type of value to be retrieved. The sample program will only deal with string values for simplicity's sake, but there are actually a number of different value types you can retrieve from a key, including binary data and long integers. The possible values are shown in Table 30.8.

After the RegQueryValueEx function has been called, the status of the operation is determined and will be returned by the RegRetrieve function. If successful, the value in gstrKeyValue is displayed in the txtValue text box. Before the function ends, the subkey that was opened is closed because it is no longer needed.

The next procedure to be added is the RegDelete function (see Listing 30.16). It's used to delete a key and its value.

LISTING 30.16. CH30-16.TXT—THE RegDelete FUNCTION, WHICH DELETES KEY VALUES.

```
Private Function RegDelete() As String

Dim lonSubkeyHandle As Long
Dim lonStatus As Long

' Use the GetSubkeyHandle function to determine the
' handle of the subkey given in txtSectionName.
lonSubkeyHandle = GetSubkeyHandle(txtSectionName.Text)
```

continues

30

ACCESSING THE SYSTEM REGISTRY

LISTING 30.16. CONTINUED

```
If lonSubkeyHandle = -1 Then
    ' Subkey could not be located.
    RegDelete = "Error - Subkey could not be located"
    Exit Function
End If

' Use the RegDeleteKey API function to delete the
' key.
lonStatus = RegDeleteValue(lonSubkeyHandle, _
    txtKeyName.Text)
' Check status of the operation.
If lonStatus <> 0 Then
    RegDelete = "Error - Key could not be deleted"
Else
    RegDelete = "Key deleted sucessfully"
End If

' Close the open subkey with the CloseSubKey
' function.
lonStatus = CloseSubkey(lonSubkeyHandle)

End Function
```

Once again, the GetSubkeyHandle function is used to open the last subkey in the path given in the txtSectionName text box. Then the RegDeleteValue API function is used to delete the key value. The subkey is then closed because it is no longer needed.

The next two procedures, RegUpdate and RegAdd, are almost identical (see Listing 30.17). That's because the same API function (RegSetValueEx) is used to add or update a key value.

LISTING 30.17. CH30-17.TXT—THE RegUpdate AND RegAdd FUNCTIONS, WHICH BOTH USE THE RegSetValueEx API FUNCTION TO ADD OR UPDATE A KEY VALUE.

```
Private Function RegUpdate() As String

Dim lonSubkeyHandle As Long
Dim lonStatus As Long

' Use the GetSubkeyHandle function to determine the
' handle of the subkey given in txtSectionName.
lonSubkeyHandle = GetSubkeyHandle(txtSectionName.Text)
If lonSubkeyHandle = -1 Then
    ' Subkey could not be located.
    RegUpdate = "Error - Subkey could not be located"
    Exit Function
```

```
End If

' Use the RegSetValueEx API function to update the
' key's value.
lonStatus = RegSetValueEx(lonSubkeyHandle, _
    txtKeyName.Text, 0, REG_SZ, ByVal txtValue.Text, _
    Len(txtValue.Text))

' Check status of the operation.
If lonStatus <> 0 Then
    RegUpdate = "Error - Key could not be updated"
Else
    RegUpdate = "Key updated sucessfully"
End If

' Close the open subkey with the CloseSubKey
' function.
lonStatus = CloseSubkey(lonSubkeyHandle)

End Function


Private Function RegAdd() As String

Dim lonSubkeyHandle As Long
Dim lonStatus As Long

' Use the GetSubkeyHandle function to determine the
' handle of the subkey given in txtSectionName.
lonSubkeyHandle = GetSubkeyHandle(txtSectionName.Text)
If lonSubkeyHandle = -1 Then
    ' Subkey could not be located.
    RegAdd = "Error - Subkey could not be located"
    Exit Function
End If

' Use the RegSetValueEx API function to create a
' new key and set its value.
lonStatus = RegSetValueEx(lonSubkeyHandle, _
    txtKeyName.Text, 0, REG_SZ, ByVal txtValue.Text, _
    Len(txtValue.Text))

' Check status of the operation.
If lonStatus <> 0 Then
    RegAdd = "Error - Key could not be added"
Else
    RegAdd = "Key added sucessfully"
End If
```

continues

LISTING 30.17.   CONTINUED

```
' Close the open subkey with the CloseSubKey
' function.
lonStatus = CloseSubkey(lonSubkeyHandle)

End Function
```

In both procedures, the GetSubkeyHandle function is used to get the handle of the last subkey in the path. Then the RegSetValueEx API function is called. The REG_SZ constant is used again here to indicate that the value to be added or updated is of type string.

The final bit of code to be added is for the optType option buttons, which are used to select whether an INI file or the System Registry is to be accessed. The optType_Click event (see Listing 30.18) enables and disables command buttons and text boxes depending on which option is selected.

LISTING 30.18.   CH30-18.TXT—THE optType_Click EVENT, WHICH IS TRIGGERED WHEN THE USER SELECTS EITHER THE INI FILE OR REGISTRY OPTION BUTTONS.

```
Private Sub optType_Click(Index As Integer)

' Enable/disable options depending on the state
' of the option buttons for INI files/Registry.
If Index = 1 Then
    txtSectionName.Enabled = True
    txtKeyName.Enabled = True
    txtValue.Enabled = True
    cmdRefresh.Enabled = False
    mnuFile.Enabled = False
    lstFileContents.Enabled = False
Else
    cmdRefresh.Enabled = True
    If dlgGetFilename.FileName = "*.ini" Then
        txtSectionName.Enabled = False
        txtKeyName.Enabled = False
        txtValue.Enabled = False
        cmdAdd.Enabled = False
        cmdRetrieve.Enabled = False
        cmdUpdate.Enabled = False
        cmdDelete.Enabled = False
        cmdRefresh.Enabled = False
    End If
    cmdRefresh.Enabled = True
    mnuFile.Enabled = True
    lstFileContents.Enabled = True
End If

End Sub
```

The only thing left to do is make a few changes to the user interface. Change the caption of `lblSectionName` to `Section Name/Subkey Path` because the text box it labels now serves a dual purpose. Also, change the `optType(1)` option button's `Enabled` property to True so the Registry option can now be selected.

Make sure you save the program before running it because an errant API function can cause Visual Basic to crash. Also, heed this warning: Back up your System Registry before fooling around with modifying and deleting keys! One wrong move can have serious repercussions!

To use the Registry editing functions of the program, first select the `Registry` option button. Then enter the path of a valid subkey in the Subkey Path text box, remembering that it must begin with one of the six root keys (see Figure 30.6). Enter a key name and a value in the appropriate text boxes. Then use the `Add`, `Retrieve`, `Update`, or `Delete` buttons to perform operations on the Registry. You can use the RegEdit program to build subkeys that you can experiment with. You can also use that program to visualize any changes that you make.

FIGURE 30.6

The INI File/System Registry Editor dialog box. To manipulate keys, put the subkey path in the top text box and the key name in the middle text box.

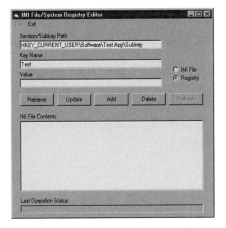

Summary

When designing complex software applications, it is sometimes necessary to save information about the program so they can be retrieved when the program is next run. For example, you might want to enable the user to save certain settings or preferences so she doesn't have to change them every time she uses the program.

The best way to do this used to be by using INI files. Although they still serve some purposes today, most programmers prefer to save their program information in the System

Registry. The Registry is a central database that holds data on just about every facet of the Windows operating system, including data specific to individual programs.

In order to access INI files and the System Registry from within Visual Basic, it is necessary to utilize Windows API functions. VB does contain a few built-in functions and statements for accessing the Registry, but they are limited.

This chapter discussed how INI files and the System Registry work. It also showed you how you can use the Windows API to store and retrieve information in both.

Creating Online Help Systems

by Lowell Mauer

IN THIS CHAPTER

- Building a Help System   *738*
- Creating a Standard Help Project   *747*
- Moving to HTML Help *762*
- Accessing Help from a Visual Basic Application *775*

Every Windows application must provide to users a way of getting help when faced with questions about the application. These days, Help systems are more than just having the manual available as a file on the PC. Help systems now consist of text, sound, video, and more. This chapter can't answer the question of what the content of your Help system should be, but it will show you what's available for you to use and how to create the Help system.

If you think that adding a complete Help system to your application is as difficult as creating your application, you're very wrong. Most applications make use of the built-in Windows Help application providing only the Help system files (.hlp) that WinHelp uses to display the Help information. Deciding what the content of the Help system should be is the hardest part of the process.

As you advance into the next generation of programming tools, such as Visual Basic 6, you are given a choice as to how your Help System can be implemented. Besides the standard WinHelp style Help systems, you can now create HTML-based Help systems using the new HTML Help workshop which is also included with Visual Basic 6. This chapter will show you how to build, compile, and test a standard Help system that you can add to your Visual Basic application. Then, you will create a second version of the same Help system using the new HTML format and also attach it to your Visual Basic application. You'll also see some of the different features you can add to you Help system.

Building a Help System

A Help system is made up of one or more document files that you create. Some of these files will contain the text or graphics that appear in your finished Help topics. Other files will contain the information that controls how your Help windows will look and act. In the final compile process, all of these files are turned into a finished Help system. The best part of this process is that if you don't like any part of the finished product, you can quickly change it and recompile.

By using the Help Contents page, users can select an item to view and then navigate from one topic to another, based on what they need to find out. In addition to topic jumping, application Help systems usually provide pop-up windows that give detailed information about a particular word, phrase, or picture without actually going to another Help page. Follow these steps to create your own custom Help system:

1. Create the Help topics files in an Rich Text Format (RTF) with any word processor that supports the RTF format, such as Microsoft Word.

2. Create the Project file for the application.

3. Create the contents file to display the Table of Contents.

4. Compile and test the Help files by using the Help Workshop.

5. Attach your finished Help system to your Visual Basic application when and where needed.

When finished, you need to distribute only two file types with your application: the actual Help files (`.hlp`) and the contents file (`.cnt`). Help files can be as simple or as complex as you want them to be. To create the topics files, you need to know how to perform the following tasks in a word processor:

- Saving files in Rich Text Format (`.rtf`)
- Inserting and displaying footnotes
- Formatting text as hidden, underlined, and double-underlined
- Changing line spacing
- Inserting page breaks
- Inserting graphics into a text document

31

CREATING ONLINE HELP SYSTEMS

> **NOTE**
>
> All examples in this chapter were created with Microsoft Word as the word processor. If you're using WordPerfect, refer to its help documentation on how to perform these tasks.

The Help text or topics files contain topics linked together via hypertext "jump words" or special hypergraphics. Without linking, the topics in a Help file would be isolated islands of information; users couldn't move from one topic to another. They would have to return to the Table of Contents to go to another topic in the Help system. The easiest way to link topics is to create hypertext that allows users to jump between topics or display a pop-up window. These jumps serve the same purpose as cross-references in a book and consist of coded text or graphics that tell WinHelp to display another topic in the main Help window.

Building a Topics File

Topics files are nothing more than fancy word processing files, each file containing one or more topics. A completed Help file is a combination of these topics files that provides users with information they need. When designing and creating topics files, you want to decide what the flow will be from one topic to another. Each page in the document file that is separated from the next by a hard coded page break creates one topic in the Help system.

NOTE

If you intend to create an HTML Help system, each Topic should be placed in its own document files.

Because Help is an online facility, each topic can be as long as needed. To create a Help text file, you'll work with the following formatting commands:

- Underline
- Double-underline
- Hidden text

TIP

It's helpful to reveal all formatting codes while you create your topics files.

A topics file contains the words, pictures, sounds, and videos that make up your Help system. To create most topics files, all you need to do is the following:

1. Enter the text for each topic.
2. Separate each topic with a page break.
3. Add footnotes to activate Help features.
4. Add any graphics or multimedia files.

Double-underlining the jump phrases in the text creates hypertext jumps; any pop-up phrases are formatted with single-underlining. Both have a context string or "tag" formatted as hidden text that's used as the location for the jump or pop-up to go to.

CAUTION

When creating a jump to another topic, be careful not to have spaces between the double-underlined text and the hidden text. This will prevent the jump from occurring.

Entering the Text

Open your favorite word processing program to start the text-entry process. For the examples in this chapter, small text files are used to demonstrate hyperlinks, pop-ups, and other Help system features. Figure 31.1 shows the Contents topics page for a completed Help file.

FIGURE 31.1.

A completed Contents topics page shown in Microsoft Word.

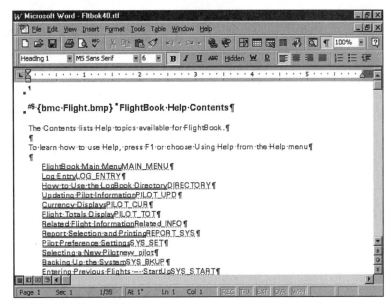

First notice the use of double-underlining in Figure 31.1. Double-underlined words or phrases will appear as green in the document and as single-underlined hypertext in your Help system. When users click these words or phrases, WinHelp automatically jumps to the page referenced by the jump tag, which is the hidden text immediately following the jump phrase.

NOTE

For HTML Help topics, the jumps will be added as HTML hyperlinks, as described later in this chapter.

Your demo Help file will contain three topics pages taken from this chapter, the Table of Contents page, and three secondary topics page (see Figure 31.2). As the first page of your topics file, enter the text from Listing 31.1. Don't forget to save your work after entering each page.

FIGURE 31.2.

The completed topics file using Listings 31.1 through 31.4 as input.

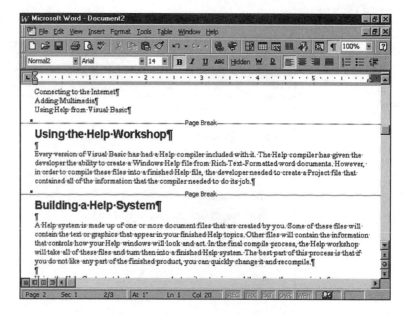

LISTING 31.1   CH31TOC.TXT—TABLE OF CONTENTS TEXT FOR THE DEMO HELP FILE

```
Every Windows application must provide to the user a way of
getting Help when faced with questions about the application.
These days Help systems are more than just having the manual
available as a file on the PC. Help systems now consist of
text, sound, video and more. While this chapter cannot answer
the question of what the content of your Help system should be,
it will show you what is available for you to use and how to
create the Help system.

Using the Help Workshop
Building a Help System
Connecting to the Internet
```

Now, press Ctrl+Enter to insert a page break and then enter the text shown in Listing 31.2. This will become the second page of your topics file.

LISTING 31.2   CH31TOPIC1—USING THE HELP WORKSHOP

```
Every version of Visual Basic has had a Help compiler included
with it. The Help compiler has given the developer the ability
to create a Windows Help file from Rich-Text-Formatted Word
documents. However, in order to compile these files into a
finished Help file, the developer needed to create a Project
file that contained all of the information that the compiler
needed to do its job.
```

Insert another page break into the file and then enter the text shown in Listing 31.3. Repeat this process for the Listing 31.4.

LISTING 31.3   CH31TOPIC2—BUILDING A HELP SYSTEM

```
A Help system is made up of one or more document files that are
created by you. Some of these files will contain the text or
graphics that appear in your finished Help topics. Other files
will contain the information that controls how your Help windows
will look and act. In the final compile process, the Help Workshop
will take all of these files and turn then into a finished Help
system. The best part of this process is that if you do not like
any part of the finished product, you can quickly change it and
recompile.
Using the Help Contents tab, the user can select an item to view
and then from there, navigate from one topic to another, based on
what the user needs to find out. In addition to 'topic jumping',
application Help systems usually provide pop-up windows that give
detailed information about a particular word, phrase or picture
without actually going to another Help page.
```

LISTING 31.4   CH31TOPIC3—CONNECTING TO THE INTERNET

```
Many of the newer applications like Microsoft Office 97 use
jumps in their Help system to take the user to specific pages
on the World Wide Web. When creating your Help system, you can
also provide the user with a way to locate your web site or any
other web site on the Internet. To make this happen, the macro
ExecFile will be used. This macro will run programs that will
connect to the Internet using Internet Explorer.
```

Finally, for each topic that you have, you can add a title in a bold, larger font size at the top of the page.

Labeling the Topics

Now that you have some topics, you need to identify them by assigning a unique *topic ID* to each one. This way, WinHelp knows the location of each topic in the Help system. Footnotes are used to create these topic IDs. You'll use three symbols in the footnote area to set up the important features of the Help system (see Table 31.1).

TABLE 31.1 CUSTOM FOOTNOTE SYMBOLS USED IN DEFINING THE HELP TEXT FILE

Footnote Symbol	Description
#	Defines a topic ID for each topics page in the file
$	Sets the page title, which will appear in the Help system's Search list box
K	Defines one or more keywords that users can then search for on the Index page

In the footnote section, the # symbol is used to connect a topics page with its topic ID or jump tag. This identifies each topic in the Help system. Each tag must be unique within the Help system. Although the compiler can successfully compile topics that don't have jump tags, users of the Help system won't be able to view these topics unless they contain keywords that can be searched for.

> **NOTE**
>
> If a topic has no topic ID or keywords defined, users can't view the topic.

The $ symbol is used to define the title for each Help topic in the file. Titles usually appear at the beginning of the topic and in the Bookmark menu and Search list box, if the topic contains keywords.

The final symbol, K, is used to specify the topic keywords that may be used to search for related topics. The WinHelp system lists matching topics by their titles in the Search dialog box. This symbol is the only one of the three that enables multiple words or phrases to be listed. The following footnote example shows a keyword list for the topic titled `aligning` found in the Microsoft Word Help system:

```
K drawing object;graphics;tables;text
```

The custom footnote symbols must be the first items that appear on the jump page, followed by the Help topic title, if any, and then by any text that you want in the topic. To insert a footnote in Word, position the cursor at the beginning of the page and then choose Insert | Footnote from the menu to display the Footnote and Endnote dialog box (see Figure 31.3).

FIGURE 31.3.

Using the Footnote and Endnote dialog box makes inserting footnotes easy.

31

CREATING ONLINE
HELP SYSTEMS

Click the Custom Mark option button and then enter one of the three symbols described in Table 31.2. When you click OK, the screen splits into two windows, one with the topics page and the other showing the footnotes (see Figure 31.4).

FIGURE 31.4.

Footnotes added to a topic are displayed at the bottom of the Word window.

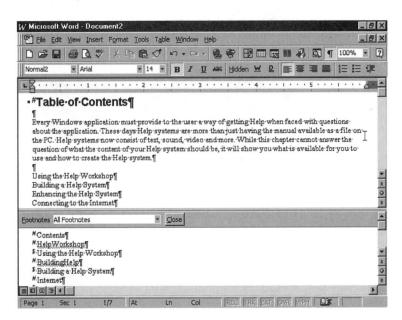

Set the topic IDs by adding the footnotes in Table 31.2 to each page of the topics file. The custom footnote symbol that you should use for now is #.

TABLE 31.2 TOPIC ID TEXT FOR EACH PAGE IN THE DEMO HELP FILE

Page	Footnote Text
1	Contents
2	HelpWorkshop
3	BuildingHelp
4	Internet

By setting these footnotes, you can now set the jump hyperlinks within each topic to enable users to jump between topics. To set a link for a topic, you need to format the word or phrases that you want as the links. On the first page of the Help topics file, place the cursor at the end of the sentence Using the Help Workshop and enter the topic ID **HelpWorkshop**. Now select the sentence Using the Help Workshop and double-underline it. Next, select the word HelpWorkshop and format it as hidden text. This will take the user to the topic defined by the jump topic **Help Workshop**. You should notice that the hidden text that you entered matches the topic ID for the page to which the user will jump.

Now, perform the same tasks for the remaining topic jumps listed on page 1, as shown in Figure 31.5. All three of these jumps should be double-underlined.

FIGURE 31.5.

The topics file showing the hyperlinks and footnotes for each topic in the file.

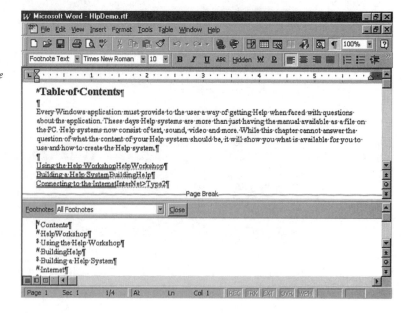

Save your Help topics file in Rich Text Format and close your word processor. Congratulations, you've created your first Help topics file. You must now create the project file that will be used to compile the topics into a working Help system.

Creating a Standard Help Project

The Help project file contains the instructions for compiling your Help topics files into a working Help system. When you use the standard Help Workshop to create the project file, the minimum information you need to have is specified for you when you choose File|New from the menu. The remaining information that you can specify depends on the size and complexity of the Help file that you're creating, as well as your own creativity.

Follow these steps to build the project file:

1. Start the Help Workshop by choosing Microsoft Help Workshop and then Help Workshop from the Start Menu.
2. Choose File|New from Help Workshop's menu.
3. In the New dialog box, select Help Project and click OK.
4. The Project File Name selection dialog box appears. Enter **VBDemo** as the project name and click Save. (Don't worry about the Save as Type box; you can leave it blank.) The workshop screen is now displayed with the default options for your project.
5. Specify where your topics files are located and their names. Click the Files button on the right to display the Topic Files dialog box, where you can add or remove file references from your Help project (see Figure 31.6).

FIGURE 31.6.

Adding the topics files to your project by using the Workshop dialog boxes.

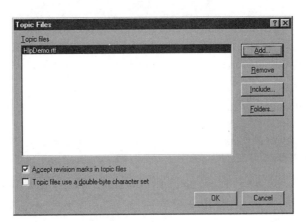

6. Click the Add button to display the Open dialog box, locate the topics file you've already created, and select it. Click the Open button and then OK to add this file to the project.

7. To tell the project where to find the bitmap you added to the topics file, click the Bitmaps button that appears on the main Help Workshop screen. In the Bitmaps dialog box, locate the folder the bitmap is in and then click OK.

The project file now has enough information to compile your topics file into a working Help file (see Figure 31.7).

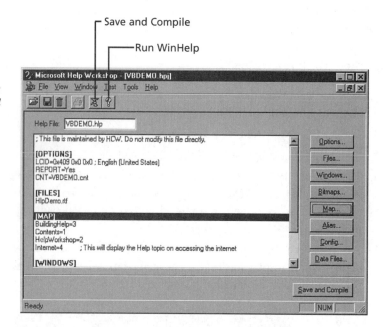

FIGURE 31.7.

The finished project file contains several parameter sections that were added.

To compile your Help project, click the Compile button (refer to Figure 31.7); the Compile to a Help File dialog box appears (see Figure 31.8), which lets you set the Help project filename to compile.

Click the Compile button in the Compile a Help File dialog box to complete the process of compiling the topics files into a Help file. If you didn't select the option to have WinHelp automatically display the Help file when completed, you need to click the Run WinHelp button. This will display the View Help File dialog box (see Figure 31.9).

This dialog box will display the current help project file that is open, the defined Help file path, and name and a list of any mapped topic IDs. Using this dialog box, you can view your new Help file as though it were opened by a program, as though users double-clicked its file icon in Windows Explorer, or as a pop-up using a mapped topic ID to select a given topic. Select the A Double-Clicked File Icon option and click View Help to display the Table of Contents topic from the new Help file (see Figure 31.10).

FIGURE 31.8.

Compiling the Help project with the Compile a Help File dialog box.

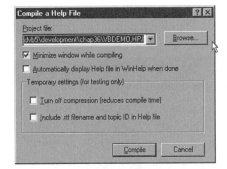

FIGURE 31.9.

Using the View Help File dialog enables you to test the Help file in the way it would be used.

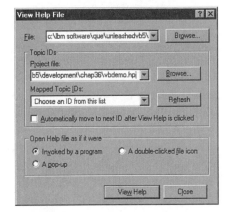

FIGURE 31.10.

The compiled Table of Contents as users will see it.

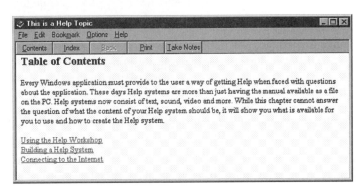

31

CREATING ONLINE HELP SYSTEMS

You might have noticed that the workshop fills in the names of the Help project and finished Help files for you in the appropriate boxes. When testing your new Help file, you'll find that there are no mapped topic IDs, because you haven't added any to the project yet. To add topic ID mapping, you should first close the Help file if it's still open, and then click the Map button in the workshop window to display the Map dialog box (see Figure 31.11). This dialog box lists the topic IDs that have been mapped and their related values. To add a new one to this list, click Add to display the Add dialog box.

FIGURE 31.11.

Mapped topic IDs are defined and listed in the Map dialog box.

Using numeric values to reference Help topics makes it easier to use the Help file when adding it to your Visual Basic application. The mapped numbers are used in the program calls to the WinHelp application. In the Add dialog box, you can enter only three values: the topic ID defined in the topics file, a numeric value, and an optional comment. To see how mapped topic IDs works, enter the topic ID HelpWorkshop and the numeric value 2; if you want, you then can enter a comment describing this topic. When you're finished, click OK to add this topic to the mapped list. Then click OK again to return to the main workshop window. Your project file should now have a new section in it called MAP.

Recompile the Help file and then click the Run WinHelp button. You should now have the new mapped topic ID listed in the Mapped Topic IDs drop-down box as shown in Figure 31.10. Select the mapped value, select A Pop-Up as the way to display the Help file, and click View Help. The topic that you selected displays as a pop-up immediately (see Figure 31.12).

When adding mapped topic IDs, you should decide on an organized numbering scheme that will enable you to keep track of the topics you are using. You now have a completed Help system. It doesn't look any different than the old non-Windows Help design, however, because you haven't created the new Help Topics dialog box yet. The next section shows you how and why the Help Topics dialog box is used.

FIGURE 31.12.

Displaying Help information as a pop-up.

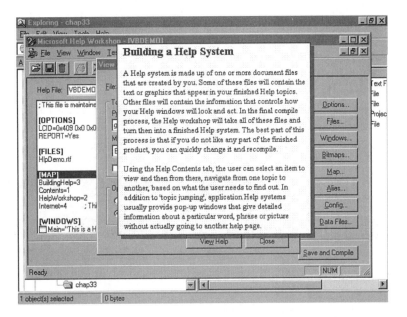

Using the Help Topics Dialog Box

The easier it is for your users to find Help, the less frustrated they will be when looking for solutions and answers in your application. Users will access the Help system from several locations within your application as well as display it by double-clicking its icon in Windows Explorer. In the Help system that you've created, you can see that the Index button at the top of the Help dialog box is grayed out, because no keywords are defined in any of the topics files you created.

When the Help Topics dialog box appears, you can determine which of three default pages appear. You can also determine the information that appears on two of those pages. If you want a Contents page to appear, you must provide a contents file along with the Help file. If you want the Index page to appear, you must define keywords in your topics. Finally, the Find page always appears, unless you specify that you don't want it to be displayed.

The items listed on the Contents page are defined in the contents file created with the Help Workshop. Because the Contents page information is kept in a separate file, whatever appears on the Contents page is dynamic, meaning that you can add or remove items from the list independent of the Help system content. As your application is enhanced, you don't have to change the original Help file; you just add a second Help file to your application and include the topics in the contents file.

Creating a contents file is really easy when using the Help Workshop. As you create the contents file, the Help Workshop displays each item with a book or page icon, depending on the position of the item. This way, you can see the finished list as you create it.

Building the Contents File

In the Help Workshop, choose File | New from the menu; then select Help Contents from the new list and click OK. An empty Contents window appears in the Help Workshop (see Figure 31.13). This is where you'll create the contents file.

FIGURE 31.13.

The contents file creation window will display the Contents list as you work.

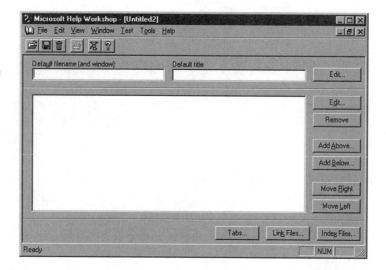

When the contents file is first created, you need to specify default information that WinHelp will use to locate the entries in the contents file, display the correct title at the top of the Help Topics dialog box, and display the Help information in the correct window type. To set this default information, click the Edit button located at the top-right of the window to display the Default Help Information dialog box (see Figure 31.14). In the Default Help Filename text box, enter the name of your Help file. Then, in the Default Window text box, enter the window type you want to use to display the topics in your Help file. Finally, in the Default Title text box, you can optionally enter the title you want displayed in the Help Topics dialog box. You can change any of these default settings when entering the actual items in the contents list.

FIGURE 31.14.

The Default Help Information for the Help Topics dialog box.

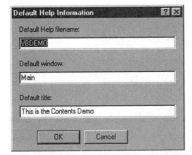

> **NOTE**
>
> Help window types are defined in the project file. The window type of Main is the default type generated in the project file for you.

Before going any further, save the contents file. The name that you give it doesn't have to be the same name as the Help file, as long as you set the contents file name parameter in the project file. You can add four types of entries to the contents file, each entry giving users the capability of performing a particular function (see Table 31.3).

TABLE 31.3 CONTENTS FILE ENTRY OPTIONS

Option	Description
Heading	Used to define a category level shown as a Book icon
Topic	Defines each main page of the Help system
Macro	Enables users to launch a macro directly from the Topics dialog box
Include	Includes other contents files in the main contents file

> **NOTE**
>
> If a heading has no topic titles beneath it, it won't appear in the Topic dialog box.

When adding items, remember that headings are identified by book icons that can be double-clicked to display the subheadings or topics that they contain. To add the first entry to the list, you can click the Add Above or Add Below button, it doesn't matter. The Edit Contents Tab Entry dialog box appears (see Figure 31.15).

FIGURE 31.15.

Adding entries to the Contents page is done with the Edit Contents Tab Entry dialog box.

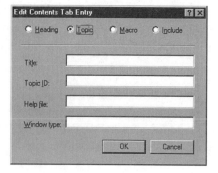

This is where you can override the default settings for the contents file. For the first item, select the Heading option at the top of the form. Then enter `Giving Your Users Help` as the Title and click OK. You should see a book icon appear with the title you entered next to it. Next, add the remaining topics and headings, as listed in Table 31.4.

TABLE 31.4 TOPICS ITEMS ADDED TO THE CONTENTS FILE

Entry Type	Title	Topic ID
Topic	Table of Contents	Contents
Heading	Giving Your Users Help	
Topic	Using the Help Workshop	HelpWorkshop
Topic	Building the Help System	BuildingHelp
Heading	Enhancing the Help System	
Topic	Connecting to the Internet	Internet

After you add these entries, the Contents dialog box should look like the one shown in Figure 31.16.

FIGURE 31.16.

The finished Contents page displayed in the Help Workshop.

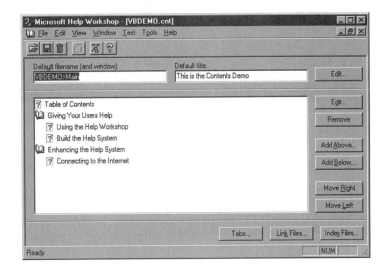

After saving the changes to the contents file, you can test it. The Contents file name should be set on the File page of the Options dialog box in the Help Workshop for your project. To test the contents file, click the Run WinHelp button, select the Invoked by a Program option, and click View Help. The Help Topics dialog box appears, as shown in Figure 31.17. Try clicking the book icons and then the item icons to see what happens.

FIGURE 31.17.

The finished Help Topics dialog box is displayed to users.

31

CREATING ONLINE
HELP SYSTEMS

Adding Keywords to the Index Page

If you recall, the Index page appears only if you have keywords defined in your topics files. Then, by double-clicking a keyword displayed on the Index page, users can display the related topic. To add keywords to your Help topics, you add a K footnote to the topics to which you want to add keywords. For each K footnote, you can define as many keywords as you need for the topic page, each one separated by a semicolon (;). If you assign the same keyword to more than one topic, the keyword appears only once in the index. However, when users double-click that keyword, the Topics Found dialog box appears (see Figure 31.18).

FIGURE 31.18.

The Topics Found dialog box displays multiple topics for a keyword.

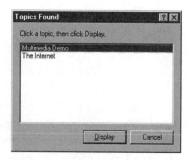

Add some keywords to the demo Help file, using the techniques and syntax described earlier in this chapter. Remember that the K footnote symbol must be uppercase, and each keyword is separated by a semicolon (;). Unlike the Contents page, you must recompile the Help file for the keywords to be included on the Help Topics dialog box. After recompiling, test your Help file again to see how the Index page works.

Because indexes can sometimes contain several levels of entries, just as the Contents page does, second-level entries are indented under their related first-level entry, listing the specific topics within that category. You can create the same effect in your Help Index by defining first- and second-level keywords. The Windows Help Index is a good example of this technique (see Figure 31.19).

Creating first- and second-level keywords requires only a slight change in the way you define the keywords. To add a first-level keyword to your Help file, add a K footnote and type the keyword followed by a comma (,) and a semicolon (;), as follows:

```
K Workshop,;
```

Neither the comma nor the semicolon appears in the Index text. Next, immediately following the semicolon, type the first-level keyword again, followed by a comma, a space, the second-level keyword, and another semicolon, as follows:

```
K Workshop,; Workshop, Using the Help Workshop;
```

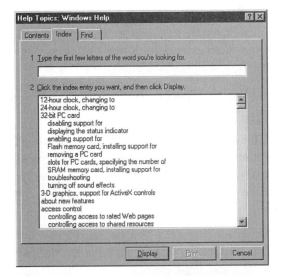

FIGURE 31.19.

The Windows Help Index, with second-level indexes listing related keywords.

> **NOTE**
>
> To use the same first-level keyword in multiple topics, you need to specify it the same way in each topic.

Add a few first- and second-level keywords to your Help file, recompile it, and see what it looks like.

Setting Up the Find Page

The Find page enables users to perform a full text search through every word in a Help file. For example, if users enter the word *open* on the Find page in the Windows Help Topics dialog box, every topic that contains the word *open* is listed. When users click the Find tab for the first time, the Find Setup Wizard appears to help users set up the full-text search index. Users have to do this only once, unless they deleted the index file (.fts) that contains this information.

> **NOTE**
>
> The only topics included in the Find page search are the ones with Titles defined as $ footnotes.

If you want a full text search index to be available to your users immediately, you can have it created when you create the Help file by specifying it on the FTS tab of the Options dialog box. You then need to include this new file (.fts) with the contents file (.cnt) and the Help file (.hlp) when you distribute your application.

Understanding the Difference Between the Index Page and the Find Page

The Index page contains the keywords that you've defined in the Help file. They can be terms for beginners or for advanced users. The keywords can be synonyms for terms used in the topic, or can be words that describe the topic. The index provides users with many ways of getting to the information. The more ways you give users, the easier it will be for them to find what they want.

The Find page lists only words that appear within the Help topics. To find a topic, users must use a word exactly as it appears in the text. By using the Find page, users can easily list every topic that contains a specific word.

> **TIP**
>
> If the name of a program element changes, you can use the Find tab to locate each occurrence of it in your Help file.

You now have a Windows Help system that contains the new Help Topics dialog box and uses the full text search capabilities of WinHelp. Next, you will see how to add a few of the more advanced features to your Help system.

Enhancing the Standard Help File

Although you can add many more features to the Help file, this section will discuss only a few of the following features:

Video and sound files	Training card Help
WinHelp macros	A customized Help display
Internet access	Secondary Help windows
Context-sensitive Help	Complex graphics with hotspots

Using Secondary Window Formats

You can use two types of windows in your Help files: main and secondary. The main window has a menu bar and a button bar, and can't be sized automatically. A Help file has only one of this type of window. The menu bar in the main window provides the Display History option, which enables users to display a list of topics that have been accessed during this session. The other option is the Bookmark menu, which enables users to mark a topic to return to later.

Although a secondary window doesn't have a menu bar, it can have a button bar and can be sized automatically. You can define up to 255 secondary windows in a Help file, with a maximum of nine displayed at any one time.

To see how all this works, define a main and a secondary window to your Help project by using the Windows button in the Help Workshop. In the Windows Properties dialog box (see Figure 31.20), define new windows for your project. You also can customize the position, color, buttons, and macros that will appear in each window, as well as set the default title for the top of each window.

FIGURE 31.20.

Defining new window styles in the Window Properties dialog box.

To create a secondary window, all you need to do is name it. You can then use this name in your project, contents, and topics files to specify in which window you want the topic displayed.

In the Window Properties dialog box, click the Add button to display the Add a New Window Type dialog box. To create a main window, use Main as the new window name; otherwise, enter the name that you want to use, up to eight characters. As a starting point, select one of the three standard window types listed in the drop-down box:

- *Procedure*. This window type is normally used for displaying procedures. It's autosizing, contains three buttons on the button bar, and is positioned in the upper-right corner of the screen.

- *Reference*. This window type is normally used for displaying reference material. It's autosizing, contains three buttons on the button bar, is positioned on the left side of the screen, and takes up approximately two-thirds of the screen's width.

- *Error message*. This window type is normally used for displaying error messages. It's autosizing, contains no buttons, and lets WinHelp determine the position (upper-right corner of the screen, unless users change the position).

These are the types used in Windows Help. Think of them as templates to get you started; you can modify them as you see fit.

Select one of these types and click OK. Next, change a reference in a topic to use this new window. In the topic with the ID of Internet, change the hyperlink jump tag to

```
Internet>window2
```

in which *window2* is the name of the secondary window that you just defined. Recompile the Help project and open the Help file. Navigate to the Contents Page and click Internet Jump. You'll see that, rather than change the content of the main window, the Help system displays a new, secondary window (see Figure 31.21).

FIGURE 31.21.

Secondary windows enable you to give users information in separate windows.

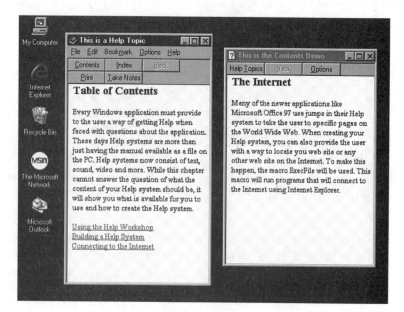

Linking to the Internet

Many of the newer applications, such as Microsoft Office 97, use jumps in their Help systems to take users to specific pages on the World Wide Web. When creating your Help system, you can also provide users with a way to locate your Web site or any other Internet Web site. To make this happen, the macro `ExecFile` will be used to connect to the Internet, using Internet Explorer.

The `ExecFile` macro works as though you were running a program from the command prompt. You specify the file or program and the arguments for the program you're running. As an example, if you wanted to use Internet Explorer to jump to the Sams Publishing home page, the jump text in the topics file would look like the following code:

```
Sams Publishing! ExecFile(start,http://www.mcp.com)
```

in which everything from the exclamation point on is set as hidden text.

The program used in this example is `start`, which connects to the Internet and passes the Web address specified in the macro. (This program is included with Windows, so don't worry about whether you have it.)

Adding Multimedia

Another way to enhance your Help system is by adding video and sound clips to it. Video can be useful and fun to include in your Help system. Windows uses video in its *Online User's Guide*. Several topics include animation to explain how to perform a particular function. You can include video in any topic window, including pop-ups. An embedded window is created for the multimedia file and is automatically resized to accommodate the image or controller (see Figure 31.22).

FIGURE 31.22.

Running a video in the Help system.

To add a video clip to your Help file, you use the following syntax:

```
{mci [_left, _right] [[options,] filename.ext}
```

If you want to have the video clip aligned, you use the _left or _right parameters. The options parameter can be one of the several values listed in Table 31.5.

TABLE 31.5 VIDEO DISPLAY OPTIONS

Option	Description
External	Doesn't include the video file in the Help file itself
Noplaybar	Hides the playbar (use only for autoplay and repeat)
Nomenu	Hides the menu button on the playbar
Repeat	Repeats the file automatically
Play	Plays the file automatically when the MCI window is displayed

If you wanted to add a video clip to your Help system that will display the drill bit video included in the Visual Basic installation, add the following line to your topics file:

```
{mci repeat, Drillrle.avi}
```

Moving to HTML Help

HTML Help is the next generation of online help authoring systems that have been created by Microsoft. It uses the underlying components of Microsoft's Internet Explorer to display the Help information, supporting HTML, ActiveX, Java, scripting (both JavaScript and VBScript), and HTML image formats such as jpeg and gif. If you've ever used WinHelp or the standard Help Workshop before, you will be very familiar with many of the features of HTML Help and its associated workshop.

Like WinHelp, HTML Help uses a project file to combine help topic, contents, index, image, and other source files into one compressed help file. HTML Help also provides you with a workshop that helps you in creating the Help file. Unlike WinHelp, HTML Help has no limits to the size of the Help file you can create or to the size of any of the other features in the Help file. The only limitations that you have are those of the computer and any the Hypertext Markup Language (HTML) might have.

As you have seen, navigation within a standard Help system is done by using embedded commands that defines which topic should be displayed next. When using the new HTML Help system, these commands have been replaced with HTML tag codes that instruct the Help browser to locate and display another Help topic file. The new interface provides greater ease of movement and a 'cleaner' interface to the user, as shown in Figure 31.23.

FIGURE 31.23.

The new HTML Help system Interface makes it easier for the user to find the information they need

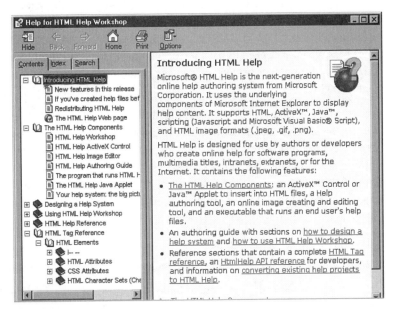

When using the new HTML Help system, the documents you design are created using Hypertext Markup Language or HTML. Each topic you create has a corresponding HTML file. Although each Help topic you create appears to be a document with text, graphics, or images on it, the html files are actually text documents that contain the HTML formatting codes. The codes, or tags, tell the Help browser how to display each page and supply the locations of any files that are referenced on that page.

> **NOTE**
>
> You don't have to limit yourself to using a word processor; you can use any HTML authoring tool such as Microsoft FrontPage to create your HTML files.

Your first task when creating an HTML Help system is to design the overall look of your topic pages. Only then can you continue on and actually create the topic files. By using the Table of Contents tab, users can select an item to view and then navigate from one topic to another, based on what they need to find out. The steps to create an HTML Help system are basically the same as a Standard Help system, except that you are now creating HTML pages instead of RTF documents.

When you have finished creating the HTML Help system, you only need to distribute the actual Help file (.chm) with your application. Because HTML Help is a relatively new technology, you cannot assume that every user will have the files needed to view the HTML Help. The Package and Deployment Wizard will add a dependency to your application installation for the HTML Help files referenced in your application. To create the topics files, you either need to have a working knowledge of HTML programming to design fancy Help topics or you can use any of the word processors that can save a document in HTML format.

The Help text or topics files are linked together by adding the HTML anchor tags <A>...</A> which include the reference to the next topic file, or you can use a special ActiveX control that comes with the HTML Help workshop to enable the user to click a button and jump to another topic. The process of building topic files has not changed except for one very important item—each topic should now be a separate document that is then converted into HTML format. To create most topics files, all you need to do is the following:

1. Enter the text for each topic.
2. Add the HTML tags to support the included features (Links, Images, and so on).

Because you have already seen how to build topic files, take the existing document from the Standard Help system you created earlier and break it into four separate documents. Then, if your word processor supports it, convert the documents into HTML format. If your word processor does not support this function, you will need to create each HTML file manually and add the text to each.

> **NOTE**
>
> When saving these files as HTML, you should use the listing names as they will be referenced later in this chapter when adding HTML tag codes.

Unlike the old Windows Help system, to set a link for a topic, you need to know the name of the HTML file to which you want to jump. This requires that you create most of the topic files before you start adding links and pop-ups to the topic files themselves. This changes the process into a two-step process, one to create the topic files, and the second one to add any required links. To see how to add a link to a topic, open the table of contents file (CH31TOC.HTM) in notepad, then find the sentence, "Using the Help Workshop" and replace it with the following statement.

```
<A HREF="CH33TOC.HTM">Table of Contents</A>
```

As you can see, the file that you want to jump to is inserted into the <A> tag code. Now, perform the same process for the remaining topic links listed on the table of contents, as shown in Figure 31.24. All three of these links should use the <A> tag.

31

CREATING ONLINE
HELP SYSTEMS

FIGURE 31.24.

The Table of Contents topic page showing the links inserted for each main topic listed.

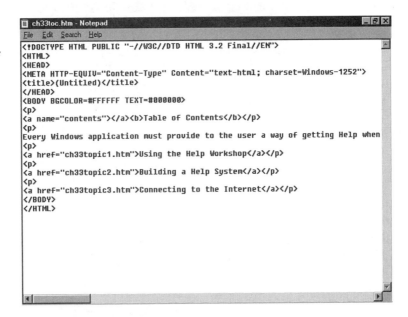

```
ch33toc.htm - Notepad
File  Edit  Search  Help
<!DOCTYPE HTML PUBLIC "-//W3C//DTD HTML 3.2 Final//EN">
<HTML>
<HEAD>
<META HTTP-EQUIV="Content-Type" Content="text-html; charset=Windows-1252">
<title>(Untitled)</title>
</HEAD>
<BODY BGCOLOR=#FFFFFF TEXT=#000000>
<p>
<a name="contents"></a><b>Table of Contents</b></p>
<p>
Every Windows application must provide to the user a way of getting Help when
<p>
<a href="ch33topic1.htm">Using the Help Workshop</a></p>
<p>
<a href="ch33topic2.htm">Building a Help System</a></p>
<p>
<a href="ch33topic3.htm">Connecting to the Internet</a></p>
</BODY>
</HTML>
```

At this point, you have created several HTML files for your help system, but there is nothing that actually makes it into a Help system yet. The best you can do with it is to display the files in a Web browser. In the next section, you will see how to use the new HTML Help workshop to take these files and create the actual help file for you to use.

Using the HTML Help Workshop

The HTML Help workshop gives you the tools to create an easy to use Help system that performs much like an Internet Web site. As with the Standard Help system, you need to build a project file that is used by the compiler to create the final HTML Help file. The best way of producing the project file is by using the new HTML Help workshop.

- Start the HTML Help Workshop from the Start menu
- Choose File | New from the Workshop's menu
- In the New dialog box, select Project and click OK

A New Project wizard is displayed asking if you want to convert an older WinHelp project. Leave the option unchecked and click Next. Enter **VBDemoHTML** as the project name and click Next to continue. The next dialog box (see Figure 31.25) lets you specify any files you have already created and want to add to the project.

FIGURE 31.25.

Adding existing files to the new HTML Help project.

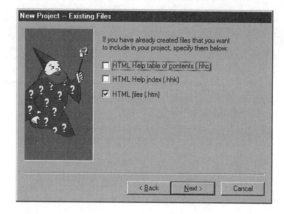

If you check any of these, you are asked to enter the location and name of the file(s). Because you have already created the HTML topic files, click the third selection and click Next. In this dialog box (see Figure 31.26) add the topic files you previously created.

FIGURE 31.26.

Adding the Topic files you have already created.

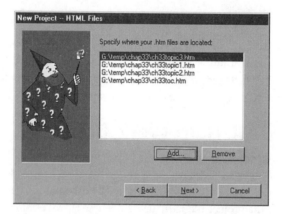

Select all of your HTML topic files and click Next, then Finish to complete the project's creation. The last step that you need to do is to set the default topic for the Help file. The easiest way to change a project setting is by double-clicking on the setting you want to change in the Options list.

Then, set the default topic file to CH31TOC.HTM. The project file now has enough information to compile your topic files into a working Help file (see Figure 31.27).

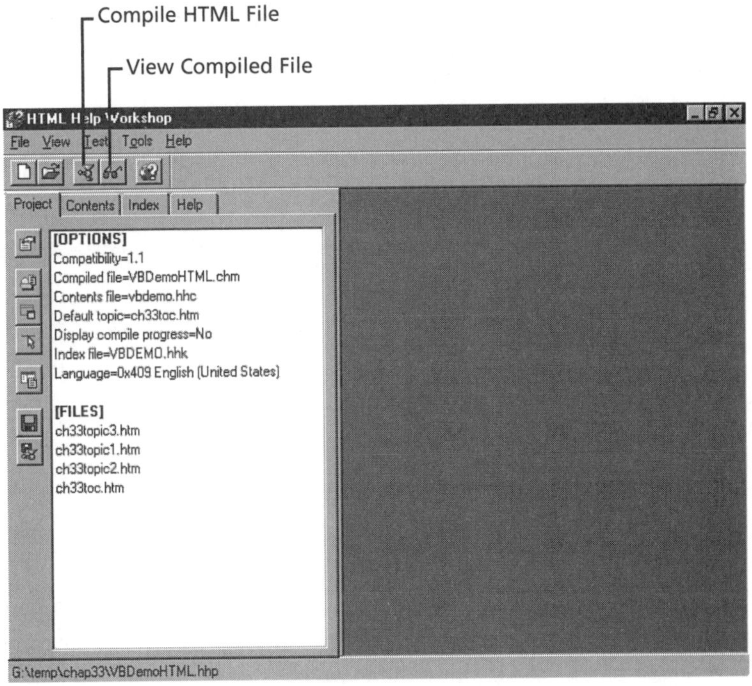

Compile HTML File

View Compiled File

FIGURE 31.27.

The finished project file contains several parameter sections that were added.

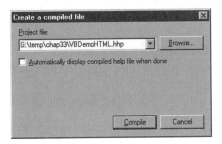

The workshop toolbar in Figure 31.27 contains two buttons that you'll be using to compile and then test your Help file. To compile your Help project, click the Compile HTML File button, the Create a Compiled File dialog box appears (see Figure 31.28). This dialog box lets you set the Help project filename to compile.

FIGURE 31.28.

Compiling the Help project with the Create a completed file dialog box.

Click the Compile button in the Compile a Help File dialog box to complete the process of compiling the topics files into a Help file. After the compile is completed, click the View Compiled File button to display the Table of Contents topic from the new Help file (see Figure 31.29).

31

CREATING ONLINE
HELP SYSTEMS

FIGURE 31.29.

The compiled Table of Contents as the users will see it.

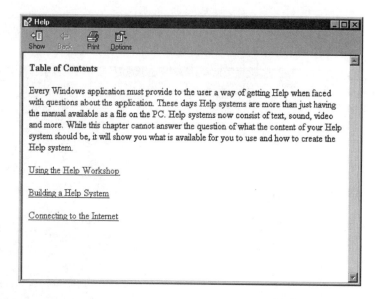

You now have a completed Help system; however, you can see that there is no Tab frame to the left of the Help information window. This is because you have not created the Contents or Index files. If you want a Contents tab to appear, you must define a contents file within the Help project. If you want the Index tab to appear, you must define an Index file that contains keywords for your topics. Finally, the Search tab will appear only if you specify that you want it.

Building the Contents Tab

In the HTML Help Workshop, click on the Contents tab to display the Contents window. When you do this for the first time, a dialog box will appear, asking if you are creating a new Contents file or using an existing one. Leave the default to create a new one and click OK. The Windows Save As dialog box is displayed for you to enter the new file name. Once again, leave the default name and click Save. An empty Contents window appears in the Help Workshop (see Figure 31.30). This is where you'll create the contents file.

You can add two types of entries to the contents file, each entry giving users the capability of performing a particular function (see Table 31.6).

TABLE 31.6 CONTENTS FILE ENTRY OPTIONS

Option	Description
Heading	Used to define a category level shown as a Book or Folder icon
Topic	Defines each main page of the Help system

FIGURE 31.30.

The Contents tab displays the Contents list as you work.

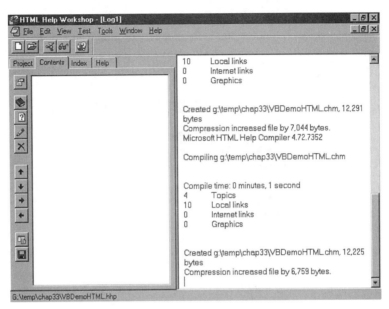

When adding items, remember that headings are identified by book or folder icons that can be double-clicked to display the topics that they contain. To add the first entry to the list, you can click the Insert a Heading button or Insert a Page button, it doesn't matter. The Contents Entry dialog box appears (see Figure 31.31).

FIGURE 31.31.

Adding entries to the Contents tab is done with the Table of Contents Entry dialog box.

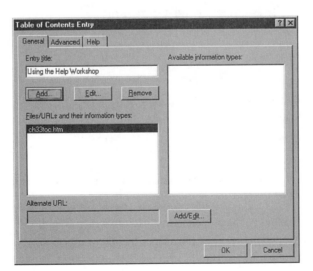

The Content Enter dialog box is where you specify the title of the entry and the associated page or Web link for that item. In fact, a heading can now have a topic page associated with it. When you hit the Add button, the path or URL dialog appears (see Figure
31.32) listing the available HTML file titles (not the filenames) from which to select.

FIGURE 31.32.

*Selecting the HTML
topic files for the
Contents file.*

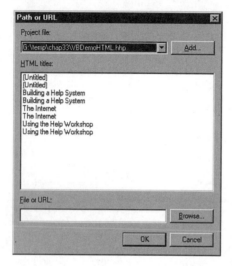

Add the items listed in Table 31.7 to the contents file.

TABLE 31.7 TOPIC ITEMS ADDED TO THE CONTENT FILE

Entry Type	Title	Topic File
Heading	Giving your Users Help	CH31TOC
Page	Using the Help Workshop	CH31TOPIC1
Page	Building the Help System	CH31TOPIC2
Heading	Enhancing the Help System	
Page	Connecting to the Internet	CH31TOPIC3

After you add these entries, the Contents tab should look like the one shown in Figure
31.33.

After saving the changes to the contents file, test it by compiling the Help file and viewing it. To test the Contents file, click the View Compiled File button to see the new Help
system, shown in Figure 31.34. Try clicking the book icons and then the item icons to
see what happens.

FIGURE 31.33.

The finished Contents tab displayed in the Help Workshop.

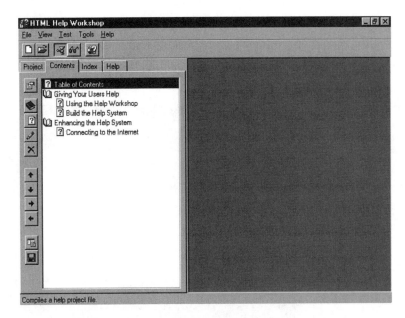

FIGURE 31.34.

The finished Help file, including a Contents Tab.

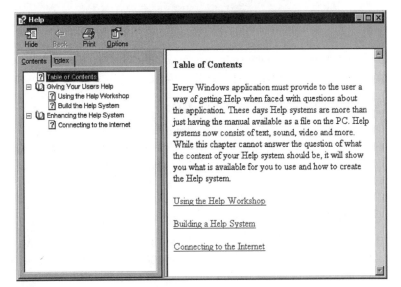

Adding Keywords to Index Tab

If you recall, the Index tab appears only if you have keywords defined for your topic pages. Then, by double-clicking a keyword displayed on the Index tab, users can display the related topic. You would add keywords to the Index the same way as you added items to the Contents tab. By clicking the Index tab in the HTML Help workshop, you are prompted for the name of the new Index file to create. Also you can add multiple topic pages to a keyword definition as shown in Figure 31.35.

FIGURE 31.35.

Adding multiple topic pages to an Index keyword.

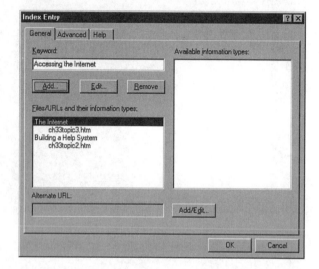

Then, when you are in the Help system and click on that topic, a selection list is displayed as shown in Figure 31.36.

Setting up the Search Tab

The Search tab enables users to perform a full text search for every word in a Help file. For example, if users enter the OPEN on the Search tab in the Windows Help browser, every topic that contains the word OPEN is listed. If you choose to have the project compile a full-text search file (.chg), you must distribute it with the Help file.

Converting from Older Help Projects

If you are a Visual Basic developer that has already created help systems for your applications, don't panic; the HTML Help workshop has a conversion feature that enables you to easily create an HTML Help project from an existing WinHelp project. The New Project Wizard will convert the WinHelp project file (.hpj) to an HTML Help project file (.hhp), the topic files (.rtf) to HTML topic files (.htm), the contents file (.cnt) to the HTML Help contents file (.hhc), and any index files to the new format (.hhk). Any bitmap images you might have in the files will be converted to gif, jpeg, or png, depending on your target browser. If you want, see how this works by converting the Standard Help project that you created at the beginning of this chapter.

FIGURE 31.36.
Getting a Related Topics Selection list on the Index Tab.

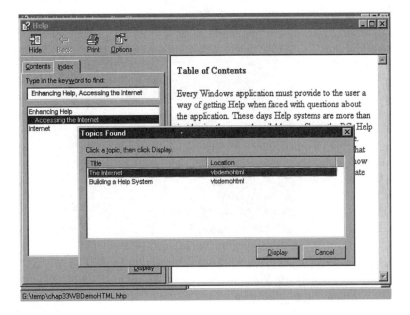

Using Advanced HTML Help Features

There are many different components that you can add to your Help system by making use of the different HTML code tags. HTML tags support everything from adding images to an HTML page to having animations or movie clips displayed on the HTML page. In addition, by using the HTML Help workshop, you can define different window formats so that you can have certain topics displayed differently than others. The types of windows that you can create or customize are:

- Default window: This is the window in which topics will automatically appear. You never have to create the default Help window, but you can customize them.

- Secondary window: This is a custom window in which you can assign topics to display.

- Embedded window: This is also a secondary window, but rather than staying on top of the Help display, embedded windows are nested into the software program.

To define a new window, go to the Project tab and click the Add/Modify Windows Definition button. Now, enter the name for the new window and click OK to go to the Window Type dialog box as shown in Figure 31.37.

FIGURE 31.37.

Defining a new window to be used by the Help system.

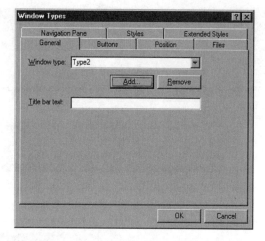

This dialog box enables you to customize almost every aspect of a window frame. Then to use a custom window, you would change the Window property for a given Contents item as shown in Figure 31.38.

FIGURE 31.38.

Setting the Window property of a Content item to display the information in a custom window.

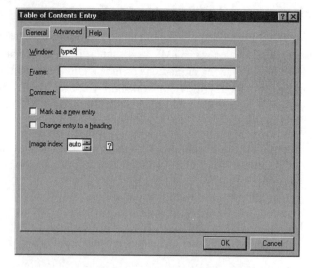

Linking to the Internet

Many of the newer applications, such as Microsoft Office 97, use jumps in their Help systems to take users to specific pages on the World Wide Web. When creating your Help system, you can also provide users with a way to locate your Web site or any other Internet Web site. This is now done by setting a URL address instead of a local Help file name.

Adding Multimedia

Another way to enhance your Help system is by adding video and sound clips to it. Video can be useful and fun to include in your Help system. Windows uses it in its *Online User's Guide*. Several topics include animation to explain how to perform a particular function. Adding any video or audio features to your Help system is done by using standard HTML tag commands. The following line of code will add a video to a topic page and will be played using the registered media player on the user's computer.

```
<A href="../Images/File.avi"> Click here to see a movie.</A>
```

Accessing Help from a Visual Basic Application

Besides using the Help system independently, your users will probably need to access it from within the Visual Basic application. Visual Basic provides several methods to access the WinHelp system. To learn how to use these methods, you'll create a small Visual Basic application and then add the different methods to the program. This application includes a single form with several objects on it. On this form, you add the different objects and program code to execute the various commands needed to display different topics from your Help file.

The Windows Common Dialog Control

The Common Dialog control provides a standard set of dialog boxes for operations such as opening and saving files. One function that it provides is the capability of displaying Help by using WinHelp. To see how to use the Common Dialog control, start Visual Basic and create a new project. Add controls to the default form and set their properties as shown in Table 31.8.

TABLE 31.8 ADDING CONTROLS TO THE FORM

Control	Property	Value
Command Button	Name	cmdClose
	Caption	Close
Command Button	Name	cmdHelp

continues

TABLE 31.8 CONTINUED

Control	Property	Value
Common Dialog	Name	CommonDialog
	HelpFile	*<path\filename>*

The Help Common Dialog control's properties can be changed by using the custom properties sheet (see Figure 31.39).

FIGURE 31.39.

The custom properties for the Help Common Dialog *control.*

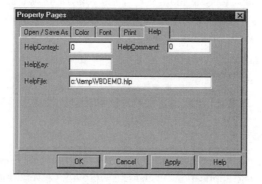

The Common Dialog control itself isn't visible when the application is executing. Only when you access this control in your application will the control be seen. When you've added these controls, the next step is to add the code to be executed when the command buttons are clicked. Copy Listing 31.5 into the general area of the forms code window.

LISTING 31.5   CH31CODE1.TXT—VISUAL BASIC CODE TO ACCESS THE HELP SYSTEM

```
Const HelpFinder = &h00B
Private Sub cmdClose_Click()
End
End Sub

Private Sub cmdHelp_Click()
CommonDlg.HelpCommand = HelpFinder
CommonDlg.ShowHelp
End Sub
```

This code calls the Help system and displays the Help Topics dialog box. Execute your application and click the Help command button to see your Help file.

> **CAUTION**
>
> Applications that have used the `HELP_CONTENTS` and `HELP_INDEX` commands to display the Contents topic and keyword index of the Help file will no longer work properly. These commands are no longer recommended. Instead, you should use the `HELP_FINDER` command.
>
> Visual Basic doesn't provide a `Common Dialog` control constant for the `HELP_FINDER` command. To access the Contents topic in a Help file, declare the WinHelp command as a constant in your applications general area as follows:
>
> ```
> Const HelpFinder = &h00B
> ```

You can use the same logic to display any topic by simply adding one line of code to the routine and changing the command. In the `cmdHelp_Click` routine, change the variable from `HelpFinder` to `cdlHelpContext`. Then add the following line of code to specify the topic you want to display:

```
CommandDlg.HelpContext = 3
```

> **NOTE**
>
> The preceding line of code will only work if you have previously defined a Mapped Topic ID with the value of 3.

This code line references the mapped value that you've already defined in the Help file project. Now when you execute the program and click the Help button, the specified topic is displayed.

Context-Sensitive Help

After you understand how to use the `Common Dialog` control, context-sensitive help is easy to implement. To see how it works, add a textbox to your form and name it `txtInput`. Each object that you can place on a form has two properties that enable you to set up context-sensitive help:

`HelpContextID`	When users press the F1 key, Visual Basic automatically calls Help and passes this value to display the specified Help topic.
`WhatsThisHelpID`	When users click the WhatsThis button and then click an object, this value is used to display the Help topic.

The WhatsThis button and the F1 key are mutually exclusive; only one can be active at one time on a form. To use this function, set WhatsThisHelpID to a topic value from your Help file. Then set the form's WhatsThisButton and WhatsThisHelp properties to True. The WhatsThisHelp property determines whether context-sensitive help uses the What's This pop-up provided by the Windows Help system. This property must be used with the WhatsThisButton property.

NOTE

The WhatsThisHelp property must be True for the WhatsThisButton property to be True. For these buttons to be shown on the form, the following properties must also be set as shown:

```
ControlBox property = True
BorderStyle property = Fixed Single or Sizable
MinButton and MaxButton = False
```

or

```
BorderStyle property = Fixed Dialog
```

Set these properties to True or set the forms border style to Fixed Dialog. Now when you run your application, you'll see a new button with a question mark in it at the top-right of the title bar. When you click this button, the mouse pointer changes (see Figure 31.40).

FIGURE 31.40.

The main application with the WhatsThisHelp *property being used.*

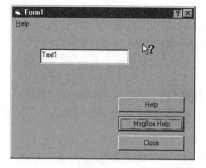

When you click an object that has WhatsThisHelpID set, the specified Help topic is displayed.

Summary

In this chapter, you learned how to use the Help Workshop to create a Help system that will complement your Visual Basic application. Also, you've seen how to add several of the available features to your Help system to enhance the overall look and feel of it. You also learned how to access the Internet and add multimedia to your Help system. In addition, you have taken a look at the new HTML Help system and Workshop to see how it differs from the Standard Help system. You also created a simple HTML Help system that can be used by the Visual Basic application. Finally, you explored how to connect the Help file to your Visual Basic applications by using properties and methods of several different controls and features included with Visual Basic.

Debugging and Testing Techniques

by Rob Thayer

IN THIS CHAPTER

- Starting at the Beginning   782
- Error Handling   783
- Avoiding Program Errors   783
- Debugging Programs in Visual Basic   784

Two of the most unpleasant phases of application development are debugging and testing. Unfortunately, there is no getting around them; they have to be done. Even the most accomplished programmer is likely to have bugs creep into his code now and then or fail to account for situations that might make his program act in unexpected ways.

Recent versions of Visual Basic have come a long way in preventing obvious coding errors. With features like Auto Syntax Check, Auto List Members, Auto Quick Info, and ToolTips, common programming mistakes such as syntax errors are often "nipped in the bud." On the other hand, problems such as logic errors are not so apparent and are far more difficult to find and debug. Hunting them down requires a firm grasp of debugging and testing techniques. This chapter details such techniques and how you can use some of VB's powerful program debugging features to your benefit.

Starting at the Beginning

The best way to take care of program errors is to prevent them from occurring in the first place. Easier said than done, of course, but there are some simple things you can do that will decrease the likelihood of a serious coding error.

The first and most important thing you can do to prevent errors is to design your program thoroughly before you write a single line of code. Many errors occur simply because not enough thought was given to how the program will work and how it will react to unusual situations. For example, a program that accepts some form of input from users might not take the proper precautions to ensure that the data entered is valid. The program might crash when an unexpected data value is encountered. The culprit behind the error is not poor coding but poor planning. If more attention had been paid during the program's design phase, it's likely that the potential of such a situation occurring would have been realized. The code would reflect this by trapping for such a situation.

Of course, there are times when even the most diligent design and planning efforts leave some circumstance unaccounted for, causing an error to pop up unexpectedly. It happens to everyone from time to time; no one is perfect. But proper design tenets should be followed to keep such errors at a minimum.

Object-oriented programming (OOP) techniques lend themselves to the prevention of errors. OOP makes it possible to write and thoroughly test code once and then reuse it again and again. Without having to "reinvent the wheel," the likelihood of errors occurring in reusable objects is reduced. OOP also enables you to create a class or utility object that handles errors. This component can then be used in any project, resulting in a consistent method of error handling.

Designing and object-oriented programming methods are beyond the scope of this chapter. However, you can find more information on those subjects in Chapter 10, "Object-Oriented Programming In Visual Basic."

Error Handling

In the old days of BASIC programming, lines of code were prefixed with numbers. Error messages would specify the number of the line of code that generated the error, so debugging was somewhat simplified. Unfortunately, Visual Basic is not nearly as specific when reporting errors. When an error does occur in a VB program, little information is provided as to its source or even in which module it occurred. To make things worse, error messages are often cryptic. The same error message may signify a variety of problems, leaving the programmer with only a vague idea of what the actual problem might be.

The fact that VB offers little in the way of error reporting makes the implementation of error trapping all the more important. By adding even simple error trapping code to all the routines in your programs, you can greatly enhance the information produced when an error occurs. You can also use the error trapper to take care of any last-minute chores that need to be completed before the program ends. For example, you might want to save any data that the user entered. Errors are never easy to take (especially for end users), but they're even worse when their effect is a loss in productivity.

When creating an error handling routine, try to design it in a way that will facilitate debugging efforts. Display as much information as possible as to where the error occurred, such as the name of the Sub or Function. A little thing like that can cut down substantially on your debugging time.

Avoiding Program Errors

Some of the most common program errors can be avoided by simply adding a few lines of code to your program modules. The Option Explicit and Option Base statements are two easy additions to your program code that might help you find errors.

The Option Explicit is used at module level (add it to your form or module's General Declarations section) and ensures that you do not use variables that have not been specifically declared. How many times have you mistyped the name of a variable somewhere in your code, resulting in a runtime error or, more often, a hard-to-find logic error? Under normal circumstances, Visual Basic assumes that any undeclared variable names are of the Variant type. So if you define the variable intCounter as an Integer but mistype the variable name in your code as `intCoutner`, Visual Basic will mistakenly assume that `intCoutner` is a new `Variant` variable.

Adding an `Option Explicit` statement to your code prevents errors like that. If the VB compiler detects an undeclared variable name, it generates an error and won't let the program run until you fix it.

The `Option Base` statement is useful for preventing errors pertaining to array variables. By default, arrays in Visual Basic are zero-based, meaning that their first (base) element is number 0. So if you define a string array as `strItems(25)`, the individual elements are numbered from 0 to 24. Being humans, we don't naturally tend to think that way. Instead, we think of `strItems(25)` as being an array of items from 1 to 25. Experienced programmers are more likely to remember that arrays are zero-based by default and compensate for that fact in their code. But even experienced programmers slip up once in a while and assume that an array is one-based instead of zero-based.

Adding an `Option Base 1` statement to your code changes the default for declared arrays from zero-based to the more natural one-based. If you find yourself consistently falling into the zero-based array trap, then use `Option Base` to change VB's default array attitude.

Perhaps a review of the `Option Explicit` and `Option Base` statements is elementary, but they are important tools in thwarting errors and improving the code's readability. Of course, they can't catch every error—if only it were that simple. In many cases, a solid understanding of debugging techniques is necessary for tracking down errors. The next section will tell you what you need to know to become an effective bug killer.

Debugging Programs in Visual Basic

Visual Basic programmers are fortunate. Many program debugging and testing features are included within VB's design environment, which means that programs can be fully debugged before they are compiled into executable code and distributed. Although you might have a basic understanding of debugging in Visual Basic, you might not be aware of all of VB's built-in debugging tools.

This section will introduce you to VB's debugging options and tools. These are split into two categories: those that let you control program flow by stepping through lines of code, and those that display information in special windows.

Stepping Through Code

When you need to flesh out a program bug, the best way is often to step through your code line by line. Fortunately, Visual Basic provides a way to do this while the program is running.

To begin, make sure that the Debug toolbar is displayed. Choose View I Toolbars to show which menus are currently being displayed. If there is no check mark next to the Debug option, then click Debug to highlight it. A toolbar like the one shown in Figure 32.1 will be added to VB's toolbar area. If you don't like its placement, you can grab its "handle" (the two vertical bars at the far left of the toolbar) and drag it to another part of the toolbar area, or you can make it free-floating by moving it away from the toolbar area.

FIGURE 32.1.

The Debug toolbar.

The Debug toolbar contains icons that enable you to perform certain debugging tasks, such as stepping through lines of code. It also enables you to display special windows that can be used to assist in your debugging efforts. Many of these icons have a corresponding hotkey, as shown in Table 32.1. The purpose of each icon (and its hotkey) will be discussed in a moment.

TABLE 32.1. THE ICONS ON THE DEBUG TOOLBAR AND THEIR CORRESPONDING HOTKEY, IF AVAILABLE.

Icon	Hotkey
Start	F5
Break	Ctrl+Break
End	
Toggle Breakpoint	F9
Clear All Breakpoints	
Step Into	F8
Step Over	Shift+F8
Step Out	Ctrl+Shift+F8
Next Statement	Ctrl+F9
Show Next Statement	
Locals Window	
Immediate Window	Ctrl+G

continues

TABLE 32.1. CONTINUED

Icon	Hotkey
Watch Window	
Quick Watch	Shift+F9
Call Stack	Ctrl+L

Other debug commands that can be found under the DEBUG menu include: Clear All Breakpoints, Set Next Statement (Ctrl+F9) and Show Next Statement.

All the debugging options (plus a few more) can also be found on VB's Debug, Run, and View menus. However, the icons and the hotkeys are usually the best way to go because they require fewer mouse clicks or keystrokes.

You're undoubtedly already aware of the Start, Break, and End icons because they are also displayed on VB's Standard toolbar. In fact, you probably use these icons to start and stop your programs. Therefore, there's little reason to talk about them other than to say that Start compiles and runs a program, Break halts program execution temporarily, and End terminates a program. These options are used to switch between a project's three modes: design time, runtime, and break mode. The current mode is always shown (enclosed in brackets) on VB's title bar.

You're probably also aware of the Toggle Breakpoint (F9) and Step Into (F8) options. Toggle Breakpoint lets you specify that program execution is to stop before a certain line of code is executed. To use it, you need only position the cursor on the line of code before which you want execution to stop and then click the icon or press F9. The line will be highlighted in reverse video (white on red), and a red dot will appear in the gray area to the left of the line of code. Certain lines, such as Dim statements, cannot be set as breakpoints. Visual Basic will let you know if you try to set an invalid breakpoint. To clear all breakpoints, press Ctrl+Shift+F9.

You can also have the program execute up to (but excluding) the line of code where the cursor is located without having to set a breakpoint. Choose Debug|Run to Cursor, or press Ctrl+F8.

The Step Into option lets you step through code line by line. A small yellow arrow appears to the left of the line of code that will be executed next. You can also change the code line that will be executed next by dragging the yellow icon to point to a new line.

When you're stepping through code using Step Into, you might come upon a line of code that calls a procedure, such as a Sub or Function. If you are sure that the procedure's code is working correctly, you can use the Step Over option. It will execute the entire procedure and then stop at the line of code immediately following the procedure call.

If you find yourself stepping through a procedure that you know is working properly, you can use the Step Out option to execute the rest of the procedure and then stop at the line immediately following the procedure call.

While you are stepping through program code, you can instantly find out the value of a variable by moving the cursor to a variable or property name. After about a second, the value of the variable or property will be displayed in a small "balloon."

Special Debugging Windows

Visual Basic also has several special windows that can be used specifically for debugging. They are the Locals, Immediate, and Watch windows.

The Immediate window is probably the best known of the three. It enables you to enter Visual Basic code to be executed immediately while the program is in break mode. Typically, the Immediate window is used to display the value of a variable or property. For example, the following line of code entered into the Immediate window would display the value of Form1's Width property:

```
print Form1.Width
```

Although the Immediate Window is used primarily to enter simple statements such as the preceding one, it can execute just about any valid line of Visual Basic code. You can also display results in the Immediate window by adding a line of code to your program, such as:

```
Debug.Print Form1.Width
```

You can also use the Immediate window to set the values of variables on-the-fly. For example, typing the following statement into the Immediate window will change the value of intCounter variable to 5:

```
IntCounter = 5
```

The Locals window (see Figure 32.2) shows a list of every property and variable within the scope of the current procedure. It also shows each property or variable's value and type.

FIGURE 32.2.

The Locals window shows all the variables and properties within the current procedure's scope.

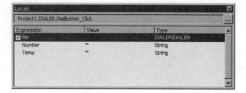

The Watches window (see Figure 32.3) can be used to monitor certain variables or properties. It can also be used to halt the program when a given expression becomes true.

FIGURE 32.3.

The Watches window can be used to monitor variables and properties or to break when expressions become true.

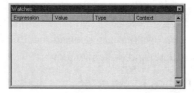

To add a new watch expression, right-click on the Watch window. From the pop-up menu, select the Add Watch option. You will then see the Add Watch dialog box shown in Figure 32.4.

FIGURE 32.4.

The Add Watch dialog box, where new or existing watch expressions are edited.

To monitor a variable or property, enter its name in the Add Watch dialog box's Expression text box; then set the Watch Type to either Watch Expression or Break When Value Changes. If you set the Watch Type to Watch Expression, the property or variable (and its value, type, and context) will be displayed in the Watch window. If you choose Break When Value Changes, the property or variable will still be displayed in the Watch window, but you can run the program and have execution stop automatically whenever the property or variable's value changes.

You can also enter any valid expression into the Expression text box and have its value displayed in the Watch window. For example, you might want to enter a formula, such as:

```
(intYearRate / 12) * 1.1
```

into the Expression text box and then choose the Watch Expression option. Then you will always see the value of that expression in the Watch window. Alternatively, you can choose the Break When Value Changes just as you would to monitor a property or variable. When the program runs, a change in the value of the `intYearRate` variable would cause the program to halt because that would affect the expression's value.

You can enter an expression and have program execution halt when the expression becomes True. For example, the expression:

```
(intYearRate / 12) * 1.1 > .05
```

could be specified, and the `Break When Value Is True` option selected. The program can then run and be automatically halted when the expression becomes `True`.

When you enter a Watch expression, you can also specify its context. You can have the Watch only performed within certain procedures, or you can specify that it be performed throughout the program. By being able to define an expression's scope, you can add Watch expressions for two variables that have the same name but exist in different procedures.

You can add as many Watch expressions as you like to the Watch window, but you should always try to keep it to the smallest number necessary. Otherwise, things become too complicated. To edit or delete a Watch expression, simply right-click the expression in the Watch window and choose Edit Watch or Delete Watch from the pop-up menu.

Another way to add a watch is to move the cursor to a variable or property name (or highlight an expression) and select the Quick Watch icon (or press Shift+F9). You will then see the Quick Watch dialog box (see Figure 32.5), which shows the variable, property, or expression's value and context. If you want to add the watch to the Watch window, click the Add button; otherwise, click Cancel.

FIGURE 32.5.

The Quick Watch dialog box, which can be used to view expressions or add them to the Watch window.

Another handy debugging tool is the Call Stack dialog box, which can be displayed by clicking the Call Stack icon or by pressing Ctrl+L. The Call Stack dialog box lists all the active procedure calls. Take, for example, the following section of code:

```
Private Sub Procedure1()

    Dim intValue As Integer
    intValue = Procedure2(5)

End Sub

Private Function Procedure2(intMult As Integer) As Integer

    Dim intProduct As Integer
    intProduct = intMult * intMult
    Procedure3(intProduct)

End Function

Private Sub Procedure3(intNumber As Integer)

    Dim intCalc As Integer
    intCalc = intNumber * 2

End Sub
```

Here you have three procedures, where each one calls another. The first procedure (`Procedure1`) is called when a command button is clicked. When debugging this kind of code, things can get confusing pretty quickly. If you were to place a breakpoint in the first line of code in `Procedure3`, you could then display the Call Stack dialog box to see which procedures have been called (see Figure 32.6).

FIGURE 32.6.

The Call Stack dialog box, which shows the procedures that have been called.

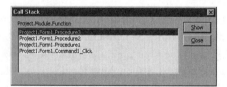

The current procedure is listed first, followed by the procedure that called it, then the one that called the second procedure, and finally the command button's `Click` event that called the first procedure. By displaying the Call Stack dialog box, you can see at a glance how the program's code arrived at the current procedure.

If you want to go directly to one of the procedures listed in the Call Stack, simply select the procedure name and click the Show button. You will then be taken to the last line of code that was executed in that procedure.

As you can see, Visual Basic has a host of tools and options that facilitate program testing and debugging from within its development environment. Knowing what they are and how to use them will make you much more efficient at combating bugs.

Summary

The best way to ease your debugging efforts is to prevent bugs from happening in the first place. There are several easy steps you can take toward this goal, though it is impossible to eliminate bugs altogether.

When more intensive debugging techniques are in order, Visual Basic has an arsenal of built-in tools for that phase of program development. They enable you to step through code and monitor important information concerning a running program.

This chapter introduces you to the tools you'll need to become a more effective program debugger. After you understand the tools, you're better equipped to handle comprehensive program testing and debugging.

32

DEBUGGING AND
TESTING
TECHNIQUES

Dynamic Control Creation and Indexing

by Rob Thayer

IN THIS CHAPTER

- **Creating Control Arrays**   794
- **Designing Event Handlers for Control Arrays**   800
- **Creating Controls Dynamically**   801
- **Instantiating Forms at Runtime**   803
- **Using Control Array Properties**   805
- **Creating** Data **Controls Dynamically**   807

The ability to add objects and controls to your Windows applications at runtime can be a very powerful tool, ultimately enabling programs to become truly dynamic in their design. Although most programs can be designed with a static, unchanging user interface, there are times when more flexibility is necessary. An extreme example of dynamic program design can be found in Visual Basic. After VB has been loaded, the user is free to add or remove controls to facilitate the creation of new programs. This flexibility allows programs of almost any kind to be designed. Your programs might not need to be as dynamic as Visual Basic, but there might be times when controls or objects need to be created on-the-fly at runtime instead of design time. The question of how to create objects programmatically will be answered in this chapter.

Another important aspect of control creation is the definition of control arrays. By grouping similar controls into an array (much like arrays that hold strings or some other data type), you can cut down on the amount of code in your program. Because all of the controls in the array share event handlers (for example, there is only one `Click` event for an array of `CommandButton` controls no matter how many controls are in the array), you do not have to duplicate event code for each individual control. As you'll see later in this chapter, the savings in terms of program code can be significant.

Combining dynamic controls with control arrays offers the best of both worlds. Dynamic controls enable your program to do a little jig in step with your end users' needs; the control array enables you to easily manage the pool of dynamically created controls. In this chapter, you will learn how to create and use dynamic controls and control arrays by reading and referring to the following topics:

- The mechanics of defining control arrays.
- Determining when a control array is best and how to maximize it.
- How to use control array properties and methods.
- Examples of creating forms on-the-fly.

If you have never created control arrays or dynamic controls, this chapter is a must-read. If you are an old hand at Visual Basic programming, you might find examples and demonstrations in this chapter that will help you hone your skills.

Creating Control Arrays

A control array, like any other array, groups together a number of like items. Some arrays group integer numbers, and some group strings. Control arrays group together controls. They can be `CommandButtons`, `ListBoxes`, or just about any kind of control in the Visual Basic toolbox. The controls in a control array do have to be like controls: all

`CommandButtons` or all `ListBoxes`, for example. You cannot have a control array that contains some `CommandButtons` and some `ListBoxes`, just like you can't have an array that contains some integers and some strings (unless, of course, it's an array of Variants).

You might have noticed that all controls in Visual Basic have an `Index` property. This property indicates the control's position in a control array. To add a control to a control array at design time, you need only set the `Name` property of one or more like controls to the same name. When you try to give the second control the same `Name` property as the first control, Visual Basic automatically asks you if you want to create a control array (see Figure 33.1). When it was created, the first control was assigned an `Index` number of 0. The second control, now part of the control array, is assigned an `Index` number of 1. If you add yet another control with the same `Name` property as the first two, it automatically becomes a part of the control array and is given the next sequential `Index` number (3).

FIGURE 33.1.

The Microsoft Visual Basic dialog box asks whether you want to create a control array.

Another way to create a control array quickly is to create one control, then copy it to the Clipboard by right-clicking on the control and choosing the Copy command from the pop-up menu (or Edit | Paste from VB's menu). Then choose Edit | Paste from VB's menu and you'll see the prompt shown in Figure 33.1. If you continue pasting controls onto your form, they will all become part of the control array.

Try this simple example. Start a new Standard EXE project in Visual Basic. Select View | Toolbox if the toolbox is not showing. Double-click on the `CommandButton` in the toolbox. While the newly-created `CommandButton` control is still selected—denoted by the solid squares surrounding the button—select Edit | Copy, followed by Edit | Paste. The dialog box shown in Figure 33.1 will be displayed. Clicking `Yes` will create a control array with two `CommandButtons` in the array.

Pros and Cons of Using Control Arrays

A control array can significantly reduce the amount of code you have to write if several controls of the same type utilize the same or similar code routines. For example, consider a slide viewer program that displays multiple thumbnail images (in Image controls) on-screen and enables the user to click an image to show it at full size. Without using a control array, the code for displaying each image in full size would have to be coded into each Image control's DblClick event. Putting all of the Image controls into a control array, however, requires coding only one Click event for the entire control array. Because the index number of the actual control that was clicked on is passed to the Click event, you can easily determine exactly which thumbnail image was selected and tailor your code to display that image in full size.

Determining whether or not the use of a control array makes sense is easy. If multiple objects share the same or similar function (such as in the example above), it would probably be worth creating a control array. However, if individual controls have different functions and you would have to make exceptions in your code for them, a control array probably is not a good idea.

> **TIP**
>
> If you find it necessary to add a significant amount of code to an event procedure because a single control in the array requires some exceptional processing, it's a good idea to place that code in a separate Function or Sub and call it from the event procedure. This will give your code a greater degree of modularity and readability.

When using control arrays, you can reduce the amount of code necessary by a factor of however many controls are in your array. For example, if there are a dozen controls in your array, you may reduce the amount of code in your program to roughly a twelfth of what it would have been if you had to add the code for each control separately. There might be some overhead in the way of determining which control in the array on which to act (by examining the control index), but that is usually minimal.

Using a Control Array

To illustrate how powerful the effective use of control arrays can be, let's go back to the slide show example that was mentioned in the previous section. Create a new project, then use Table 33.1 as a guide for adding controls and changing their properties.

TABLE 33.1. CONTROLS AND THEIR PROPERTIES FOR THE SLIDE SHOW EXAMPLE PROGRAM.

Control Type	Property	Value
Form	Name	frmSlideShow
	Caption	Control Array Example

Control Type	Property	Value
	Height	6630
	Width	6540
Image	Name	imgThumbnail
	BorderStyle	1 - Fixed Single
	Index	3
	Height	1305
	Left	4860
	Stretch	True
	Top	135
	Width	1485
Image	Name	imgThumbnail
	BorderStyle	1 - Fixed Single
	Index	2
	Height	1305
	Left	3285
	Stretch	True
	Top	135
	Width	1485
Image	Name	imgThumbnail
	BorderStyle	1 - Fixed Single
	Index	1
	Height	1305
	Left	1710
	Stretch	True
	Top	135
	Width	1485
Image	Name	imgThumbnail
	BorderStyle	1 - Fixed Single
	Index	0
	Height	1305
	Left	120
	Stretch	True
	Top	135
	Width	1485

continues

TABLE 33.1. CONTINUED

Control Type	Property	Value
Image	Name	imgFullSize
	BorderStyle	1 - Fixed Single
	Height	4575
	Left	120
	Stretch	True
	Top	1560
	Width	6240

For the `Picture` property of the `Image` controls in the `imgThumbnail` control array, use any bitmap images you have on your system. Because Visual Basic now supports .JPG and .GIF images as well as bitmaps, metafiles, and icons, finding some sample images shouldn't be too difficult—anything will do.

NOTE

In Table 33.1, the `Image` controls in the `imgThumbnail` array are given in reverse order so you are not prompted by Visual Basic as to whether or not you want to create a control array. When you add the first `Image` control and assign it an `Index` number of 3, Visual Basic knows the control is part of a control array.

This sample program is very straightforward. In fact, would you believe that it only has one line of code? It's true, and it's a testament to the power of using control arrays. Listing 33.1 shows the line of code that needs to be added to the `Click` event for the `imgThumbnail` control array. You can bring up the code window for this event by double-clicking on any of the `imgThumbnail` `Image` controls.

LISTING 33.1. CH33-01.TXT—A BITMAP SLIDE VIEWER USING ONE EVENT FOR AN ARBITRARY NUMBER OF BITMAPS.

```
Private Sub imgThumbnail_Click(Index As Integer)

    imgFullSize = imgThumbnail(Index)

End Sub
```

Listing 33.1 uses the `Index` argument of this event handler to distinguish which control in the array of `Images` was clicked and assigns that `Image` to the larger `imgFullSize` `Image`. It is evident that the amount of code saved is proportionate to the number of controls in the array.

When you're done adding the code, save the form as `CH3301.FRM` and the project as `CH3301.VBP`; then run the program. The program should look like the one in Figure 33.2.

FIGURE 33.2.

A bitmap slide viewer created with an Image *control array.*

33

DYNAMIC
CONTROL
CREATION &
INDEXING

Control arrays are powerful, but they have the potential of convoluting program code when used improperly. If some controls in the array have functions that are wildly different from the others, you have to make exceptions for those controls in your event procedure code. This can make your programs hard to decipher. Remember to group together only controls of similar or the same function and exclude those that require additional processing. The next section examines event handling for control arrays more closely.

NOTE

A good demo program illustrating the use of control arrays is included with Visual Basic and can be found in VB's Samples\VisData subdirectory. In the program, an array of `Toolbar` controls is used.

Designing Event Handlers for Control Arrays

Event handlers are generally associated with a single control. The importance of this is that when you are writing code for a control, the event handler provides the context. For example, there is clearly a distinction between the `Click` event for a form and one for a `PictureBox` control. The naming convention used—*controlname_eventname*—for event handlers also suggests the owner of the control. Hence, context determines which control originated the event. For control array events, the only way to determine the originator is by examining the `Index` argument. Consider the slight differences between a `Click` event handler for a `PictureBox` control and one for a `PictureBox` control array:

```
' Click for a PictureBox array
Private Sub Picture1_Click(Index As Integer)

End Sub


' Click for PictureBox that is not in an array
Private Sub Picture2_Click()

End Sub
```

The obvious distinction between the two events shown above is that in the `Picture1_Click` event, the argument `Index` (an integer value) is passed to the event. Only events for control arrays will have this argument. The Index argument is crucial for determining which control in the array actually raised the event.

The previous section contained an example of using the `Index` argument passed to the event procedure directly. The code for all of the controls in the array was identical, and the `Index` argument was used to refer to the control that generated the event. Event processing might not always be so cut and dry, however. In some cases, you will need to take different action based on which control generated the event. If the control array consists of two or three controls, you might decide to use an `If...Then` construct, such as in the following example:

```
Private Sub cmdEditOptions_Click(Index As Integer)

    If Index = 0 Then
        CutText
    ElseIf Index = 1 Then
        CopyText
    Else
        PasteText
    EndIf

End Sub
```

The code shown above tests the `Index` argument to see which subroutine should be called. If the first control in the `cmdEditOptions` control array raised the event (`Index =` 0), then the `CutText` subroutine is called. If the second control raised the event, the `CopyText` subroutine is called. In all other cases, the `PasteText` subroutine is called.

Using an `If...Then` construct is fine if you have a limited number of controls in your array, but a `Select...Case` construct is best for larger control arrays. In fact, because `Select...Case` statements are easier to read, you might opt to use them no matter how many controls are in the array. They also make it easier to code if you add additional controls to the array. Consider the following example:

```
Private Sub cmdEditOptions_Click(Index As Integer)

    Select Case Index
        Case 0
            CutText
        Case 1
            CopyText
        Case 2
            PasteText
        Case Else
            ' Do nothing
    End Select

End Sub
```

The `Select...Case` construct above does essentially the same thing as the previous example, but it's considerably easier to read and can be expanded with minimal effort. It also enables you to provide for an `Index` number that is unexpected with the `Case Else` statement.

When using a `Select...Case` construct, it's a good idea to keep the code under each `Case` statement to a minimum. If more than one or two lines of code are needed for processing the event for a given control, put the code into a `Function` or `Sub` and call it from the `Case` statement. The example above calls three Subs (`CutText`, `CopyText`, and `PasteText`) rather than include the code within the `Select...Case` construct.

You now know how to create control arrays at design time and associate event handlers with arrayed controls. In the next section, you will see examples that demonstrate how to create controls at runtime, reasons why you might want to do so, and how predefined event handlers are associated with dynamic control arrays.

Creating Controls Dynamically

There are two ways to create controls: at design time and at runtime. The former is by far the most commonly used. When you are designing a program in Visual Basic and select a control from the toolbox then add it to a form, you have created a design time instance of the control. Obviously, this is how most Visual Basic programs are conceived.

Runtime control creation, on the other hand, refers to adding a control to an existing form programmatically while the compiled program is running. This is seldom done, usually because a static user interface (with all controls added at design time) is all that is necessary. Some programs do need to be more flexible, however, and that is where runtime control creation comes in handy.

In some cases, you might want to add one or more additional controls to an existing control array dynamically. Visual Basic makes it extremely easy to do so. Listing 33.2 shows a Click event that dynamically adds a clone to a control (cmdTest) and adds it to a control array every time it is invoked. Note that the original control, cmdTest, must have its Index property set to 0 (indicating that it is part of a control array) before the event can work properly.

LISTING 33.2. CH33-02.TXT—ADDING CONTROLS ON-THE-FLY IS AS STRAIGHTFORWARD AS THIS EXAMPLE.

```
Private Sub cmdTest_Click(Index As Integer)

    Static intArrayPtr As Integer

    intArrayPtr = intArrayPtr + 1
    Load cmdTest(intArrayPtr)
    cmdTest(intArrayPtr).Left = cmdTest(intArrayPtr - 1).Left + 150
    cmdTest(intArrayPtr).Top = cmdTest(intArrayPtr - 1).Top + 150
    cmdTest(intArrayPtr).Caption = "Clone" & Str$(intArrayPtr)
    cmdTest(intArrayPtr).Visible = True
    cmdTest(intArrayPtr).ZOrder (0)

End Sub
```

The static variable intArrayPtr is used to keep track of the next available Index number for the control array and is incremented by one every time the event procedure is invoked. The Load statement is used to load (add) the new control into memory dynamically. The next four lines set the new control's Left, Top, Caption, and Visible properties. Figure 33.3 shows how a form might look if the event procedure in Listing 33.2 was triggered five times, causing five new CommandButton controls to be dynamically created.

FIGURE 33.3.

Command buttons added dynamically demonstrate the steps required to add controls.

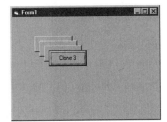

Instantiating Forms at Runtime

A special kind of control that can be created dynamically is the MDI (or multiple-document interface) style document. Software applications such as spreadsheets use MDI to share the code from one form among many instances. Consider Microsoft Excel's spreadsheet document. The cells and related code that make Excel work are the same among all worksheets, regardless of the number of worksheets in use. The only difference is the data in the sheets. Setting the MDIChild property of a form to True enables you to designate a child as a MDI document.

The implication is that you might have many copies of the same form open, and they will all behave similarly except for the data that is placed in them; that is, they will have the same layouts and controls but what the user does with the controls on each form may be vastly different. MDI child forms are ideal candidates for control arrays. The array structure enables you to manage the forms centrally, regardless of the number of forms in use.

A classic example of an MDI application is provided with Visual Basic in VB's Samples subdirectory. The sample project, MDINOTE.VBP, illustrates the dynamic creation of MDI child forms, as shown in Figure 33.4.

FIGURE 33.4.

The MDINote.vbp project provided with Visual Basic 5 demonstrates how to use a control array with MDI child forms.

Prior to MDI and Windows, text editors and word processors were designed to display one text document at a time. The MDINOTE.VBP example demonstrates how easy it is to use MDI and to manage MDI child documents using a control array. The MDI child itself is a form with a TextBox control (see Figure 33.5). In addition to the TextBox control, the form has its own menu, which, because it is an MDI child form, will be merged with the MDI form, or the parent form.

FIGURE 33.5.

notepad.frm *is the MDI child form that is capable of having multiple instances.*

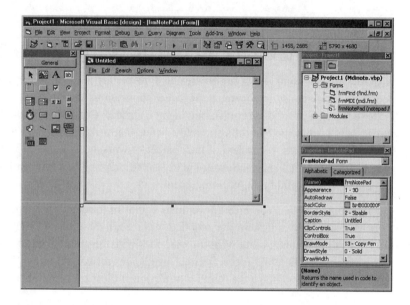

The module MDINote.bas contains the code that has the form array, which in turn manages all the child forms. The program looks simple, but there is a significant amount of code involved. That code would be greater if it were not for control arrays and MDI. Browse the brief fragment in Listing 33.3, which is followed by an explanation.

LISTING 33.3. CH33-03.TXT—MDINote.vbp DEMONSTRATES FORM CONTROL ARRAYS AND MDI DOCUMENT APPLICATIONS.

```
Public Document() As New frmNotePad      ' Array of child form objects

Sub FileNew()

   Dim fIndex As Integer

   ' Find the next available index and show the child form.
   fIndex = FindFreeIndex()
   Document(fIndex).Tag = fIndex
   Document(fIndex).Caption = "Untitled:" & fIndex
```

```
Document(fIndex).Show
' Make sure the toolbar edit buttons are visible.
frmMDI.imgCutButton.Visible = True
frmMDI.imgCopyButton.Visible = True
frmMDI.imgPasteButton.Visible = True

End Sub
```

The first line in Listing 33.3 declares a new control array of child forms called `Document`, which will have the characteristics of the previously-defined `frmNotePad` form. The subroutine, `FileNew`, contains the code to add a new instance of a form to the `Document` control array. Note that a form is considered to be a control and can be stored in a control array just like other controls can.

The `FileNew` subroutine uses the variable `fIndex` to indicate the index number of the form that will be added to the array. Instead of simply incrementing `fIndex` by one, the `FindFreeIndex` function is called. This function, which is also a part of the `MDINote.vbp` sample project, finds and returns the first available index number in a control array. Remember that a child form can be closed by the user, leaving gaps in the `Document` array. Therefore, simply incrementing the `fIndex` variable is not sufficient.

The next two lines in the `FileNew` subroutine set the properties for the dynamically-added form, `Document(fIndex)`. Then the new form's `Show` method is invoked so the form is displayed on the screen. Finally, the `Cut`, `Copy`, and `Paste` buttons on the parent MDI form are made visible.

Using Control Array Properties

Control arrays can access four properties that can be used in facilitating the processing of the array: `Count`, `Item`, `LBound`, and `UBound`. The `Count` property indicates the total number of controls in the array. The `Item` property is used to refer to specific controls in the array. The `LBound` and `UBound` properties are used to determine the lower and upper bounds of the array, respectively. All of these properties will be discussed in more detail in this section.

The `Count` Property

The `Count` property returns an integer number indicating the number of items that are in a control array. You can use the `Count` property for loop control. For example, the following code fragment demonstrates how you might iterate through all controls in a control array named `datTestDB`:

```
Dim intLoop As Integer
```

```
For intLoop = 0 to datTestDB.Count - 1

    ' Shows all record sets in the datTestDB control array
    MsgBox datTestDB(intLoop).RecordSet

Next intLoop
```

Note that the loop starts at zero and ends at the value returned by the `Count` property minus one. Remember that all control arrays are zero-based; that is, the first `Index` number in the array is always zero. You cannot change this, even if you include an `Option Base 1` statement in your code.

The `Item` Property

The `Item` property is the default property. `Item` enables you to refer to a specific item in the control array by specifying its index number. Since it is the default property, both

```
Command1.Item(number)
```

and

```
Command1(number)
```

refer to the same object. For all intents and purposes, these two lines of code are identical in their function.

The `LBound` and `UBound` Properties

The `LBound` and `UBound` properties—lower bound and upper bound, respectively—are included because you cannot use the functions with the same name to perform these tests. For example, given an array of integers

```
Dim intNumbers(10) As Integer
```

testing it with either `UBound` or `LBound` in the following manner

```
If LBound(intNumbers) < 0 Or UBound(intNumbers) > 10 Then
    ' Perform some action
End If
```

is syntactically correct. The same test cannot be performed on a control error. Hence this:

```
' The following section of code results in a syntax error.
If UBound(cmdOptions) > 5 Then
    ' Perform some action
End If
```

where `cmdOptions` is defined as a control array, is syntactically incorrect. The correct way to perform the equivalent test for either the lower or upper bound is

```
cmdOptions.LBound
```

or

```
cmdOptions.UBound
```

provided that `cmdOptions` is a control array. In this context, the control array name refers to all of the controls in an array. Note that because control arrays are always zero-based, the `LBound` property will always return 0.

Creating Data Controls Dynamically

You might write dynamic and extensible database programs by using what you have learned thus far and applying it to the `Data` control. The `Data` control can also be designated as a control array.

Dynamic `Data` controls have many applications. Suppose you want to manage several recordsets at once. A `Data` control array is a great way to do it. Consider the scenario where you want to queue any users' most frequent dynamic SQL queries. Combining a `Data` control array with a `DBGrid` control makes it a snap. Listing 33.4 shows a portion of a program that inserts a new `Data` control into a control array named `datCustomerDB`. Figure 33.6 shows how such a program might look onscreen.

LISTING 33.4. CH33-04.TXT—A DATA CONTROL ARRAY.

```
Public Sub AddNew()

    Const SQL = "Select CustomerID From Customers"
    Dim intDataPtr As Integer

    intDataPtr = datCustomerDB.Count
    dbgCustGrid.ClearFields
    Load datCustomerDB(intDataPtr)
    Set datCustomerDB(0).Recordset =
➥datCustomerDB(0).Database.OpenRecordset(SQL)
    dbgCustGrid.ReBind

End Sub

Private Sub AddDataSourceMenu_Click()

    Call AddNew

End Sub
```

FIGURE 33.6.

A short program demonstrating a control array of Data *controls.*

Listing 33.4 provides another example of a control array. Each time the user clicks Query | Add Datasource in the sample program, the same SQL statement is pushed to the front of the control array.

One important aspect of the code in Listing 33.4 is the Load statement. As with other control arrays, Load creates the control referred to by the index. On the following line, the 0th element is set to an open recordset; the statement used is roughly the same for any Data control whose recordset you want to change at runtime. For the sample program, DBGrid was used. The line dbgCustGrid.ClearFields resets the Microsoft Databound Grid Control to its default of two empty columns. The Set statement binds the fields in the current record, causing the correct number of columns to be displayed.

Summary

Using control arrays is a means by which you can share code among many like controls. You have learned that given an event handler for a control array, all controls in the array share the same code. Dynamic control creation also enables you easily to make your programs more flexible and extensible by offering your users a way to add controls during the execution and life cycle of their programs.

Implementing OLE Drag-and-Drop Capabilities

by Rob Thayer

IN THIS CHAPTER

- An Overview of OLE Drag and Drop 810

- What Is OLE Drag and Drop? 810

- How Does OLE Drag and Drop Work? 811

- Using Automatic OLE Drag and Drop 814

- Controlling the Manual Process 817

- Enhancing Visual Basic Applications with OLE Drag and Drop 826

An Overview of OLE Drag and Drop

Almost every Windows application on your PC has drag-and-drop functionality. Whether you are using a word processor to move (drag) a letter, word, or sentence to another location or using Explorer to copy a file to another folder, you are using drag and drop.

OLE drag and drop is an advanced version of the simple drag-and-drop functionality. Instead of dragging one object to another to invoke a section of code, you are moving *data* from one control or application to another. For example, dragging a text file from Windows Explorer into an open Notepad window uses OLE drag-and-drop operations.

In fact, when Microsoft developed the standards for Windows 95, it included OLE drag and drop as one of the features that defines a Windows 95–compliant product. These standards are used to determine whether a new product meets the requirements to be able to display the Windows 95 logo on its packaging and documentation.

In this chapter, you will see what OLE drag and drop is, how it works, and more important, how to use it in a Visual Basic application. You will see how to use OLE drag and drop for something that is useful in an actual application.

What Is OLE Drag and Drop?

OLE drag and drop is one of the most powerful and useful features available to a Visual Basic programmer. It adds the capability to drag text or graphics from one control to another, from a control to another Windows application, or from a Windows application to a control. With the information contained within this chapter, you'll be able to add this functionality to your own applications.

If you have been coding in Visual Basic for a while, you should be familiar with the standard drag-and-drop capabilities of the controls within a Windows application. All the concepts you learned to use the drag-and-drop functions still pertain to the newer OLE drag-and-drop functions. The difference is that the OLE drag-and-drop features open your Visual Basic application to any other application on the user's PC.

Most Visual Basic controls support OLE drag and drop in some fashion. Depending on the control, you can use OLE drag and drop without any code, or you might need to write some sections of code to support the function you need.

Controls that provide full support for the automatic OLE drag-and-drop capabilities include `Image`, `MaskEdBox`, `PictureBox`, `RichTextBox`, and `TextBox`. Other controls do not provide automatic drag and drop, but can still utilize manual drag-and-drop operations. This requires a bit more coding, but it's not very difficult. You'll see examples of both automatic and manual drag-and-drop operations in this chapter.

> **TIP**
>
> The easiest way to see what OLE drag-and-drop capabilities an ActiveX control has is to load the control and check the properties list. If OLEDragMode and OLEDropMode are listed, then the control supports automatic or manual processing.

How Does OLE Drag and Drop Work?

Certain events are triggered whenever an OLE drag-and-drop operation is performed. The events for the source control are always generated for both automatic and manual processing. However, events for the target control are only generated during a manual drop operation. Table 34.1 shows which events occur on the drag source and which occur on the drop target:

TABLE 34.1. OLE SOURCE AND TARGET EVENTS.

Source	Target
OLEStartDrag	OLEDragDrop
OLESetData	OLEDragOver
OLEGiveFeedback	
OLECompleteDrag	

Depending on how you want OLE drag and drop to perform, you generate code for only those events to which you want to respond. For example, you can create an application with a text box that enables the user to automatically drag data from another application into the text box. To do this, you simply set the text box's OLEDropMode property to Automatic. If you want to enable the user to drag the data from the text box control as well, you just set its OLEDragMode property to Automatic.

If you want to change the mouse cursors or perform different functions based on the button that was clicked or the Shift key that was pressed, you need to manually respond to the source and target events. Also, if you want to analyze or change the data before it's dropped into the control, you need to use manual OLE drag-and-drop operations. This gives you full control of the drag-and-drop process.

Because you can drag and drop data into many different Visual Basic controls and Windows applications, implementing OLE drag and drop can range in difficulty from straightforward to complex. The easiest method, of course, is dragging and dropping between two automatic objects, whether the object is a Word document or a control in your application that is set to Automatic.

NOTE

Even though many controls support OLE drag and drop, the examples used in this chapter use the TextBox control. The TextBox control is the simplest control with which to learn drag-and-drop concepts. You can apply what you learn here to other controls. For example, you could create an application with two list box controls where items can be dragged from one list box to another.

It is useful to know the terms for discussing OLE drag-and-drop operations. In a drag-and-drop operation, the object from which data is dragged is called the *source*. The object into which the data is dropped is called the *target*. Visual Basic provides the properties, events, and method to control and respond to actions effecting both the source and the target. Remember that the source and the target may be in different applications, in the same application, or even in the same control. Depending on your requirements, you might need to write code for either the source or target or both.

Beginning the Drag

A manual OLE drag-and-drop operation in your Visual Basic application starts when the user drags data from an OLE drag source (such as a TextBox control) by selecting and then holding down the left mouse button. The OLEStartDrag event is triggered, and you can then either store the data or simply specify the formats that the source supports. You also need to specify whether copying the data, moving the data, or both is allowed by the source.

Going Over the Target

As the user drags the data over the target, the target's OLEDragOver event is triggered. You can specify what the target will do if the data is dropped there. The three choices are copy, move, or refuse the data. The default is generally set to move, but it could just as easily be set to copy.

After the drop effect is set, the `OLEGiveFeedback` event is triggered. You use the `OLEGiveFeedback` event to give the user feedback on what action is taken when the data is dropped (that is, the mouse pointer changes to indicate a copy, move, or "no drop" action). Figure 34.1 shows the three different mouse pointer icons that come with Visual Basic.

Figure 34.1.

Default mouse icons for the OLE drag-and-drop process.

Completing the Drag

When the user drops the data onto the target, the target's `OLEDragDrop` event is triggered. The target checks the data from the source object to see whether it is the proper data type for the intended target. Depending on the outcome of that check, it either retrieves or rejects the data.

If the data was stored when the drag started, the `GetData` method retrieves the data. If the data wasn't stored when the drag started, the source's `OLESetData` event is triggered, and the `SetData` method retrieves the data.

When the data is accepted or rejected, the `OLECompleteDrag` event is triggered, and the source can then perform the necessary clean-up. If the data is accepted and a move was requested, the source deletes the data.

Automatic or Manual Processing?

Deciding whether to use automatic or manual OLE drag and drop really depends on the type of functionality you allow the user to perform with your application.

With automatic drag and drop, all operations are controlled by Windows and the internal Visual Basic process. You can drag text from one `TextBox` control to another by simply setting the `OLEDragMode` and `OLEDropMode` properties of these controls to `Automatic`. No code is required to respond to any of the OLE drag-and-drop events. When you drag a range of cells from Excel into a Word document, you perform an automatic drag-and-drop operation. Depending on how a given control or application supports OLE drag and drop and what type of data is dragged, automatically dragging and dropping data may be the best and simplest method.

When using manual drag and drop, you manually handle one or more of the OLE drag-and-drop events. Manual implementation of OLE drag and drop might be the better method when you need greater control over each step in the process or you need to provide the user with customized visual feedback. Manual implementation is the only option when a control does not support automatic drag and drop.

Using Automatic OLE Drag and Drop

If the controls you want to use support automatic drag and drop, you can activate the features by setting the control's OLEDragMode or OLEDropMode properties to Automatic. To see how this works, you are going to create a Visual Basic application that accepts text from a Word document and also enables you to drag text from the application into the Word document. To create this application, start a new Standard EXE project in Visual Basic. Then use Table 34.2 and Figure 34.2 as a guide for building the application's user interface.

TABLE 34.2. THE CONTROLS AND THEIR PROPERTIES FOR THE SAMPLE OLE DRAG-AND-DROP APPLICATION.

Control Type	Property	Value
Form	Name	frmDragDrop
	Caption	Automatic Drag-and-Drop
	Height	3735
	Width	4680
Label	Name	lblDrag
	Caption	Drag From Me
	Height	255
	Left	120
	Top	240
	Width	1095

Control Type	Property	Value
TextBox	Name	txtDrag
	Height	975
	Left	120
	MultiLine	True
	OLEDragMode	Automatic
	Text	" "
	Top	480
	Width	4215
Label	Name	lblDrop
	Caption	Drop On Me
	Height	255
	Left	120
	Top	1680
	Width	1095
TextBox	Name	txtDrop
	Height	975
	Left	120
	MultiLine	True
	OLEDropMode	Automatic
	Text	" "
	Top	1920
	Width	4215
CommandButton	Name	cmdQuit
	Caption	Quit
	Height	375
	Left	1800
	Top	3240
	Width	1215

34

IMPLEMENTING
OLE DRAG-AND-
DROP

Note that the txtDrag control's OLEDragMode property and the txtDrop control's OLEDropMode property have both been set to Automatic. This enables the two TextBox controls to provide automatic drag-and-drop capabilities.

FIGURE 34.2.

An automatic drag-and-drop form.

After the application's user interface has been designed, you only need to add code to the cmdQuit control's Click event so the program will end:

```
Private Sub cmdQuit_Click()

        End

    End Sub
```

Run the program, and then start Microsoft Word, Notepad, WordPad, or any other word processor or text editor that supports OLE drag and drop. Enter some text into the text editor, then select it and drag it to the Drop On Me text box in your VB program (see Figure 34.3). Next, try entering some text into the program's Drag From Me text box and dragging it to the text editor. Voila—automatic drag-and-drop capabilities without having to write code.

FIGURE 34.3.

An application after drag-and-drop operations.

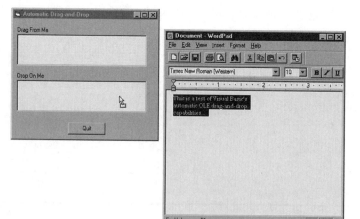

By default, when you drag text from the text box into a Word document, it is moved rather than copied into the document. To copy the text rather than move it, hold down the Ctrl key while you drag the text. This is the default behavior for all objects or applications that support OLE drag and drop. To change this default, you need to use the manual drag-and-drop techniques rather than the automatic process.

Automatic support does have some limitations, with many of them derived from the controls themselves. For example, if you move text from a Word document into a text box, all the rich text formatting in the Word document is stripped out because the standard text box control doesn't support this formatting. Similar limitations exist for most controls. The RichTextBox control is the correct control to use for this particular situation.

Modify the previous example by adding a RichTextBox control to the form and set its OLEDropMode property to Automatic. In the Word document, format some text and then drag it into both the standard text box and the RichTextBox. You'll see that the RichTextBox control retains the formatting properties of the text, but the TextBox control does not.

> **NOTE**
>
> When dragging data, you might notice that the mouse pointer shows whether the control it is currently on supports OLE drag and drop for the type of data you are dragging. If it does, the "drop" pointer is displayed; if it doesn't, a "no drop" pointer is displayed.

Controlling the Manual Process

If you want to specify which data formats or drop effects (copy, move, or no drop) are supported, or if the control you want to drag from doesn't support the automatic drag operation, you need to make your OLE drag operation manual.

Starting a manual drag-and-drop operation is done by calling the OLEDrag method. At that time, you can set the allowed drop effects and supported data formats, and if necessary, you can place data into the DataObject object.

You use the OLEDrag method to manually start the drag operation and the OLEStartDrag event to specify the allowed effects and the supported data formats.

Manual OLE drag and drop works the same way as the simple event-driven drag-and-drop manual operations. With OLE drag and drop, you're not dragging one control to another control to invoke some code; you're moving *data* from one control or application to another control or application. An example of this is when the user drags a range of cells from Excel into the DBGrid control in your application.

The `DataObject` Object

When working with the simple, event-driven drag and drop, you were always sure where the data came from. Because it was within the same application, the code could reference the `Source` variable in the event routine at runtime to access the information. However, when using OLE drag and drop, you do not always know where the data is coming from. The code process must work whether the data is within the same application or from another application, such as Word or Excel. To facilitate this process, Visual Basic provides an object to contain the data being moved, no matter where it comes from.

The `DataObject` object is the way Visual Basic moves data from the source to the target. It does this by providing the methods needed to store, retrieve, and analyze the data. Table 34.3 lists the property and methods used by the `DataObject` object.

TABLE 34.3. `DataObject` PROPERTIES AND METHODS.

Category	Item	Description
Property	Files	Holds the names of files dragged to or from the Windows Explorer.
Methods	Clear	Clears the content of the `DataObject` object.
	GetData	Retrieves data from the `DataObject` object.
	GetFormat	Determines whether a specified data format is available in the `DataObject` object.
	SetData	Places data into the `DataObject` object or sets a specified format.

These methods enable you to manage data in the `DataObject` object only for controls contained in your Visual Basic application. The `Clear` method enables you to empty the `DataObject` before setting the object with new information. The `Files` property enables you to send a list of filenames that can be dropped into a target.

Finally, the `SetData` and `GetData` methods use the `data` and `format` arguments to put or get data stored in the `DataObject` object.

> **NOTE**
>
> Visual Basic can detect only a few data types. If the data being dragged is a bitmap, metafile, enhanced metafile, or text, Visual Basic sets the format. All other formats must be specified explicitly, or an error will occur.

Table 34.4 outlines the constants used to specify the format of the data.

TABLE 34.4. DATA TYPE CONSTANTS.

Constant	Value	Meaning
vbCFText	1	Text
vbCFBitmap	2	Bitmap (.BMP)
vbCFMetafile	3	Metafile (.WMF)
vbCFEMetafile	14	Enhanced metafile (.EMF)
vbCFDIB	8	Device-independent bitmap (.DIB or .BMP)
vbCFPalette	9	Color palette
vbCFFiles	15	List of files
vbCFRTF	–16639	Rich text format (.RTF)

The SetData, GetData, and GetFormat methods use a *format* argument to specify the format that is desired or that is being used. The SetData method also has a *value* argument that is used to specify the data that will be assigned to the DataObject object. The GetData method passes the contents of the DataObject object as its return value.

In the following code, the selected text in the txtSource TextBox control (txtSource.SelText) is specified as the SetData method's *value* argument. Appropriately, the *format* argument is specified as text (vbCFText). This information is stored in the DataObject to allow the target control (wherever it might be) to retrieve the data:

```
Private Sub txtSource_OLEStartDrag(Data As DataObject, _
    AllowedEffects As Long)

    Data.SetData txtSource.SelText, vbCFText

End Sub
```

34

IMPLEMENTING
OLE DRAG-AND-
DROP

The OLEDrag Method

Just as in a simple drag and drop, the OLEDrag method is called from an object's MouseMove event when data is selected by clicking and holding down the left mouse button to drag the data.

The OLEDrag method's primary purpose is to initiate a manual drag and then allow the OLEStartDrag event to set the conditions of the drag operation.

You must set the `OLEDragMode` property to `Manual` and then use the `OLEDrag` method to have manual control over the drag operation. If the control supports manual but not automatic OLE drag, it will not have the `OLEDragMode` property; however, it will still support the `OLEDrag` method and the OLE drag-and-drop events.

The `OLEStartDrag` Event

When the `OLEDrag` method is called, the control's `OLEStartDrag` event is triggered. This event is used to specify what drop effects and data formats the source will support.

The `OLEStartDrag` event uses two arguments to set the supported data formats and indicate whether the data can be copied or moved when the data is dropped.

CAUTION

If no drop effects or data formats are specified in the `OLEStartDrag` event, the manual drag will not start.

The *allowedeffects* argument specifies which drop effects the drag source supports. The following code segment specifies that a move or a copy can be performed when the data is dragged. This argument can be checked in the target control's `OLEDragDrop` event, and the program can respond based on the settings.

To specify which data formats the source control supports, the `format` argument is set in the `OLEStartDrag` event. The `SetData` method is used to set the format of the data. The following code segment sets the *format* argument of the `DataObject` to both text and rich text data.

```
Private Sub rtbSource_OLEStartDrag(Data As _
    DataObject, AllowedEffects As Long)

    AllowedEffects = vbDropEffectMove Or vbDropEffectCopy
    Data.SetData , vbCFText
    Data.SetData , vbCFRTF

End Sub
```

Placing Data into the `DataObject` Object

Data is usually placed into the `DataObject` object when you begin a drag operation by using the `SetData` method in the `OLEStartDrag` event:

```
Private Sub txtSource_OLEStartDrag(Data As DataObject, _
    AllowedEffects As Long)

    Data.Clear
    Data.SetData txtSource.SelText, vbCFText

End Sub
```

The preceding code clears the default data formats from the DataObject, specifies the data format of the selected data, and also places that data into the DataObject object.

The OLEDragOver Event

The OLEDragOver event is triggered whenever data is dragged over a control. Two important arguments in the OLEDragOver event are the *effect* and *state* arguments. These inform the program of the exact properties and status of the data being dropped.

The *effect* argument of the OLEDragOver event is used to specify what action is taken if the object is dropped. Whenever the effect value is changed, the source's OLEGiveFeedback event is triggered. The OLEGiveFeedback event contains its own *effect* argument, which is used to provide visual feedback to the user; the mouse pointer is changed to indicate a copy, move, or "no drop" action. Table 34.5 shows the constants used by the *effect* argument of the OLEDragOver event.

TABLE 34.5. Effect CONSTANTS.

Constant	*Value*	*Meaning*
vbDropEffectNone	0	Drop target cannot accept the data
vbDropEffectCopy	1	Drop results in a copy. The original data is untouched by the drag source
VbDropEffectMove	2	Drag source removes the data
VbDropEffectScroll	&H80000000&	Scrolling is about to start or is currently occurring in the target

The *state* argument of the OLEDragOver event enables you to respond to the source data entering, passing over, and leaving the target control. For example, when the source data enters the target control, the *state* argument is set to vbEnter.

The *state* argument of the OLEDragOver event specifies when the data enters, passes over, and leaves the target control by using the constants in Table 34.6.

34

IMPLEMENTING
OLE DRAG-AND-
DROP

TABLE 34.6. State CONSTANTS.

Constant	Value	Meaning
vbEnter	0	Data was dragged within the range of a target.
vbLeave	1	Data was dragged out of the range of a target.
vbOver	2	Data is still within the range of a target, and either the mouse has moved, a mouse or keyboard button has changed, or a certain system-determined amount of time has elapsed.

The following code checks the DataObject object for a data format compatible with the target control. If the data is compatible, the *effect* argument tells the source that a move is requested if the data is dropped. If the data is not compatible, the source is informed, and a "no drop" mouse pointer is shown.

```
Private Sub txtTarget_OLEDragOver(Data As _
    DataObject, Effect As Long, Button As _
    Integer, Shift As Integer, X As Single, _
    Y As Single, State As Integer)

    If Data.GetFormat(vbCFText) Then
        Effect = vbDropEffectMove And Effect
    Else
        Effect = vbDropEffectNone
    End If

End Sub
```

Providing Customized Visual Feedback

To modify the default visual behavior of the mouse in an OLE drag-and-drop operation, you can insert code in the OLEDragOver event for the target or the OLEGiveFeedback event for the source.

OLE drag and drop provides automatic visual feedback during a drag-and-drop operation. For example, when you start a drag, the mouse pointer changes to indicate that a drag has been initiated. When you pass over objects that do not support OLE drop, the mouse pointer changes to the "no drop" cursor.

The OLEGiveFeedback Event

The source's OLEGiveFeedback event is triggered automatically whenever the *effect* argument of the OLEDragOver event is changed. In this event, you can change the default behavior of the mouse pointer based on the *effect* argument. The OLEGiveFeedback event contains the *effect* and the *defaultcursors* arguments. These enable you to check the effects allowed and then modify the default mouse pointers as needed.

The *effect* argument, like the other OLE drag-and-drop events, specifies whether data is to be copied, moved, or rejected. The purpose of this argument in the OLEGiveFeedback event is to enable you to provide customized feedback to the user by changing the mouse pointer to indicate these actions.

The *defaultcursors* argument specifies whether the default OLE cursor set is used. Setting this argument to False enables you to specify your own cursors using the Screen.MousePointer property of the Screen object.

> **TIP**
>
> Specifying custom mouse pointers is unnecessary because the default behavior of the mouse is handled by OLE.

> **CAUTION**
>
> If you decide to specify custom mouse pointers using the OLEGiveFeedback event, you need to account for every possible effect, including scrolling.

The following code example shows how to specify custom cursors (.ICO or .CUR files) for the copy, move, and scroll effects by setting the MousePointer and MouseIcon properties of the Screen object. The .ICO files that are used in this code come with Visual Basic. You will have to change the path names in the LoadPicture functions to reflect the directory in which the files are stored on your system.

```
Private Sub TxtSource_OLEGiveFeedback(Effect As Long, _
    DefaultCursors As Boolean)

    DefaultCursors = False
    If Effect = vbDropEffectNone Then
        Screen.MousePointer = vbNoDrop
    ElseIf Effect = vbDropEffectCopy Then
        Screen.MousePointer = vbCustom
        Screen.MouseIcon = _
            LoadPicture("c:\Program Files\devstudio\vb\icons\copy.ico")
    ElseIf Effect = (vbDropEffectCopy Or _
      vbDropEffectScroll) Then
        Screen.MousePointer = vbCustom
        Screen.MouseIcon = _
```

34

IMPLEMENTING
OLE DRAG-AND-
DROP

```
            LoadPicture("c:\Program Files\devstudio\vb\icons\copyscrl.ico")
    ElseIf Effect = vbDropEffectMove Then
        Screen.MousePointer = vbCustom
        Screen.MouseIcon = LoadPicture("c:\Program
            Files\devstudio\vb\icons\move.ico")
    ElseIf Effect = (vbDropEffectMove Or _
       vbDropEffectScroll) Then
        Screen.MousePointer = vbCustom
        Screen.MouseIcon = _
            LoadPicture("c:\Program Files\devstudio\vb\icons\movescrl.ico")
    Else
        DefaultCursors = True
    End If

End Sub
```

CAUTION

Always reset the mouse pointer in the OLECompleteDrag event if you specify a custom mouse pointer in the OLEGiveFeedback event.

The `OLEDragDrop` Event

The OLEDragDrop event is triggered whenever the user drops the data onto the target. If data was placed into the DataObject object, it can be retrieved when the OLEDragDrop event is triggered by using the GetData method. The following example retrieves data from the DataObject and places it into the target control. The dragged data is retrieved using the GetData method.

```
Private Sub txtTarget_OLEDragDrop(Data As _
    DataObject, Effect As Long, Button As _
    Integer, Shift As Integer, X As Single, _
    Y As Single)

    txtTarget.Text = Data.GetData(vbCFText)

End Sub
```

You might need to query the DataObject object for the data type that is dropped onto the target. You use the GetFormat method to check whether the data being dropped is compatible with the target. If it is, the drop action is completed.

The following code shows how to perform this action using an If...Then statement to choose which format to process:

```
Private Sub txtTarget_OLEDragDrop(Data As _
    DataObject, Effect As Long, Button As _
    Integer, Shift As Integer, X As Single, _
    Y As Single)

    If Data.GetFormat(vbCFText) Then
        txtTarget.Text = Data.GetData(vbCFText)
    End If

End Sub
```

If the data was not placed into the DataObject object when the OLEStartDrag event occurred, the OLESetData event is triggered when the target uses the GetData method to retrieve source data. The OLESetData event allows the source to respond to only one request for a given format of data.

The following code shows the OLESetData event responding only to text data:

```
Private Sub txtSource_OLESetData(Data As _
    DataObject, DataFormat As Integer)

    If DataFormat = vbCFText Then
        Data.SetData txtSource.SelText, vbCfText
    End If

End Sub
```

The *effect* argument of the OLEDragDrop event specifies how the data was moved to the target when the data was dropped. Whenever this argument is changed, the OLECompleteDrag event is triggered for the source control. The source control can then take the appropriate action in its event routine.

The OLECompleteDrag event is also triggered if the OLE drag-and-drop operation was canceled. The OLECompleteDrag is the last event in the drag-and-drop operation.

The OLECompleteDrag Event

The OLECompleteDrag event contains only one argument (*effect*), which is used to inform the source of the action that was taken when the data is dropped onto the target.

If a move is specified and the data is dropped into the target, the following code deletes the data from the source control and resets the default mouse pointer:

```
Private Sub txtSource_OLECompleteDrag(Effect As Long)

    If Effect = vbDropEffectMove Then
        txtSource.SelText = ""
    End If
```

34

IMPLEMENTING
OLE DRAG-AND-
DROP

```
          Screen.MousePointer = vbDefault

End Sub
```

The *button* and *shift* arguments can respond to the state of the mouse buttons and the Shift, Ctrl, and Alt keys. For example, when dragging data into a control, you can enable the user to specify a copy operation by pressing the Ctrl key when dragging the data.

In the following code, the *ctrl* argument of the OLEDragDrop event is used to determine whether the Ctrl key is pressed when the data is dropped. If it is, a copy is performed. If it is not, a move is performed.

```
Private Sub txtTarget_OLEDragDrop(Data As _
    DataObject, Effect As Long, Button As _
    Integer, Shift As Integer, X As Single, _
    Y As Single)

    If Shift And vbCtrlMask Then
        txtTarget.Text = Data.GetData(vbCFText)
        Effect = vbDropEffectCopy
    Else
        txtTarget.Text = Data.GetData(vbCFText)
        Effect = vbDropEffectMove
    End If

End Sub
```

You can use the *button* argument to respond to the various mouse button states. For instance, you might want to let the user move the data by clicking the right mouse button.

Enhancing Visual Basic Applications with OLE Drag and Drop

Now that you have seen what OLE drag and drop is and what it can do, you will create a small Visual Basic application that enables you to drag a text file from Windows Explorer into a text box.

The following application uses a TextBox control and the OLEDragOver and OLEDragDrop events to open a single text file using the Files property and the vbCFFiles data format of the DataObject object.

To create this application, first use Table 34.7 and Figure 34.4 as a guide for designing its user interface.

TABLE 34.7. THE CONTROLS AND THEIR PROPERTIES FOR THE MANUAL OLE DRAG-AND-DROP APPLICATION.

Control Type	*Property*	*Value*
Form	Name	frmManualDD
	Caption	Manual Drag-and-Drop
	Height	3735
	Width	4680
TextBox	Name	txtDragDrop
	Height	2895
	Left	120
	MultiLine	True
	OLEDragMode	Automatic
	OLEDropMode	Manual
	ScrollBars	Vertical
	Text	" "
	Top	240
	Width	4455
CommandButton	Name	cmdQuit
	Caption	Quit
	Height	375
	Left	1800
	Top	3240
	Width	1215

FIGURE 34.4.
The Manual Drag-and-Drop example program.

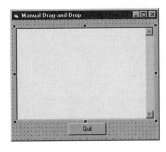

Add the following procedure to the application's code. The DropFile procedure opens the selected file and moves the text into the txtDragDrop TextBox control.

```
Sub DropFile(ByVal txtDragDrop As TextBox, ByVal strFilename As String)

    Dim intFile As Integer
    Dim strDataIn As String
    Dim strLineIn As String

    ' Open the filename that is passed to this
    ' routine in the strFilename argument, and
    ' read it in line by line.
    intFile = FreeFile
    Open strFilename For Input As #intFile
    While Not EOF(intFile) And Len(strDataIn) <= 32000
        Line Input #intFile, strLineIn
        If strDataIn <> "" Then
            strDataIn = strDataIn + vbCrLf
        End If
        strDataIn = strDataIn & strLineIn
    Wend
    Close #intFile
    ' Add the contents of the file just read in
    ' (stored in strDataIn) to the end of the
    ' TextBox passed as an argument to this
    ' routine (txtDropBox).
    txtDropBox.SelStart = Len(txtDropBox)
    txtDropBox.SelLength = 0
    txtDropBox.SelText = strDataIn

End Sub
```

Next, add the code for the txtDragDrop control's OLEDragOver event. It uses the DataObject's GetFormat method to test to see if it contains a compatible data format (vbCFFiles).

```
Private Sub txtDragDrop_OLEDragOver(Data As DataObject, Effect As Long, _
    Button As Integer, Shift As Integer, X As Single, Y As Single, _
    State As Integer)

    ' Check to see if the file to be dragged
    ' is in the right format. If it is, set the
    ' Effect to show that the file can be dropped.
    ' If the file is an invalid format, set the
    ' Effect to show no drop is possible.
    If Data.GetFormat(vbCFFiles) Then
        Effect = vbDropEffectCopy And Effect
    Else
        Effect = vbDropEffectNone
    End If

End Sub
```

Now add the code for the txtDragDrop control's OLEDragDrop event. When triggered, this event will test to see if the DataObject format is valid. If so, the DropFile procedure that was added earlier will be invoked so the file can be read.

```
Private Sub txtDragDrop_OLEDragDrop(Data As DataObject, Effect As Long, _
Button As Integer, Shift As Integer, X As Single, Y As Single)

    ' If the file format is acceptable, then
    ' pass its filename to the DropFile routine,
    ' which adds the file's contents to the
    ' txtDragDrop control.
    If Data.GetFormat(vbCFFiles) Then
        If Data.Files(1) <> "" Then
            DropFile txtDragDrop, Data.Files(1)
        End If
    End If

End Sub
```

Finally, add the following code to the Click event for the cmdQuit control:

```
    Private Sub cmdQuit_Click()

    ' End the program.
    End

End Sub
```

To test the application, open the Windows Explorer, highlight a text file, and drop it into the TextBox control. The final outcome should look like Figure 34.5.

FIGURE 34.5.

This text box application shows a dragged text file.

34

IMPLEMENTING OLE DRAG-AND-DROP

Summary

This chapter showed you how versatile OLE drag and drop really is. By using this feature of Visual Basic, you can use many different applications' data and enable your application to get data from and send data to anywhere.

You have seen that the OLE techniques are almost the same as the simple, event-driven techniques for drag and drop. The examples in this chapter have shown you only one useful way of using the OLE drag-and-drop features. By understanding how these examples work, you can take the techniques and extend them into your applications.

Tuning and Optimizing Your Application

by Rob Thayer

IN THIS CHAPTER

- Optimizing and Tuning with Visual Basic   832

- Creating and Using Templates to Perform Code Benchmarking   836

- Reviewing Performance Tips and Tricks   841

- Selecting the Proper Component Type   848

- Using the Visual Basic Code Profiler   850

Visual Basic has evolved into an extremely powerful programming language. The previous version of Visual Basic added many new language features as well as increased the performance of common tasks such as form displaying. Many tips and tricks required in earlier versions of Visual Basic are no longer required; however, with the many different application scenarios available to the Visual Basic 6.0 programmer, such as building ActiveX Internet components or distributed applications, optimizing and tuning is as important as ever.

In this chapter, you learn how to optimize and tune Visual Basic applications and components. This chapter shows you how to use several different utilities, such as the Visual Basic Code Profiler, to analyze existing applications. You also learn how to use various optimizing techniques and tricks and how to create and use a form template to perform simple code benchmarking.

Optimizing and Tuning with Visual Basic

Visual Basic presents many features and opportunities for optimizing and tuning applications and components. As of VB5, Visual Basic now includes a native code compiler to speed up application execution times. And because Visual Basic exists only in a 32-bit platform, you're dealing with an advanced 32-bit operating system such as Windows 95 or Windows NT, which offer improved performance and resource usage over Windows 3.*x*. This immediately raises the following questions:

- Do I still need to optimize and tune?
- Should I still worry about using up resources?

The answer to both questions is a resounding "yes," and in this chapter you learn that optimizing and tuning Visual Basic applications is more than telling end users to buy faster machines with more memory. Before getting into the finer points of optimizing and tuning Visual Basic applications, let's quickly review what optimizing and tuning is all about.

Understanding the Art of Optimizing and Tuning

Optimizing and tuning an application means doing one or more of the following:

- Increasing the execution speed of the application
- Effectively managing limited resources

- Decreasing the application size
- Increasing the display speed of an application
- Increasing the perceived speed of an application

You can tune an application for one or more of these definitions; however, it's difficult to tune an application for all of them because several of these definitions work against each other. For example, optimizing for speed often increases the size of the program; likewise, optimizing for size often decreases the speed of the application.

I've read many different books and articles and listened to several speakers at Visual Basic conferences refer to optimizing and tuning as an art form. Don't think of optimizing and tuning as an art form used excessively by Visual Basic gurus; rather, think of it as part of the software development cycle and obtainable by all programmers willing to put in a little extra time and effort. Consider some important optimizing and tuning points as you develop your application.

Using Proper Software Designs When Creating Applications

Back in the old days (that is, before Visual Basic), programming environments often required programmers and programming teams to use different methodologies to map out the application's functional and detail design specifications, as well as data dictionaries before a line of code was even written. Today, many C++ programmers use more modern object-oriented methodologies to generate program specifications before they ever sit down and write a line of code. Unfortunately, my experience has been that when working with many different clients, programming teams, and programmers, the Visual Basic community doesn't follow the same design methodologies. All too often, applications are prototyped and then quickly modified into the end product. These prototyped applications would benefit from a quick design session with object-oriented methodology or just some simple diagrams and brainstorming.

The first important lesson of optimizing and tuning is that they both start in the design phase (for example, when you're selecting the proper algorithms and defining the data structures and objects used by your application). Select the faster, more efficient algorithms or plan on benchmarking a few. When defining your data structures, avoid slow and inefficient data types (such as variants) in favor of faster data types (such as integers and strings).

35

TUNING AND
OPTIMIZING YOUR
APPLICATION

Testing on the Designated Platform or Environment

Too often developers test and develop on machines or in environments far superior to their application's actual production platform or environment. During the initial design phase, make sure that you take into account the production environment or platform in which your application will reside. For example, take into account platform parameters such as memory, disk space, communication speed, and processor power. If the platform is a 486 with 8MB of RAM, you don't want to deliver an application that uses Word 97 and Excel 97 via OLE Automation. The platform won't be able to support such functionality in a reasonable amount of time.

During the development phase, periodically test the application in the production environment to identify possible bottlenecks. By detecting bottlenecks early in the development cycle, you can resolve them before the application goes live and the situation becomes critical. You should always have the requirements of the program written down so that you can refer back to them during testing to ensure that those requirements are being met. A well thought-out plan for testing is also imperative.

> **TIP**
>
> One way of identifying bottlenecks in your applications is to develop a general-purpose metrics component that writes information (such as elapsed time) to a log file or the Windows NT event viewer. Code can be added to the program to call this component at specific times, such as before and after a procedure or operation is performed. You can then view the log file to identify the procedures or operations that are taking the greatest amount of time. Focus on optimizing those procedures and you'll be able to improve the efficiency of the application. By making the metrics component generic, you can use it for testing other applications as well.

Knowing What to Optimize

An important part of learning to tune and optimize Visual Basic applications is to understand what can be optimized, where to optimize, and what can't be optimized. You can optimize Visual Basic code, algorithms, and data access methods. You can't do anything to speed up your application if it's accessing files on a network, which is extremely slow.

A good example of knowing what and where to optimize is a client/server application that uses Microsoft SQL Server on the back end. The application is very fast except for one particular form that loads and displays very slowly. How should you approach optimizing and tuning for this application? There's no point tuning the forms that load quickly because you're happy with their performance. Instead, focus on the one form that loads and displays slowly. You can examine the data-access method used, although this probably isn't the problem because the other forms also use the same data-access method but run well. You can optimize and tune the form display time by trying to limit the number of repaints, but after you optimize the form display, the form is still slow. What now?

You've already determined that the data-access methods are the same on this particular form as they are on all the other forms and that you've done all you can to optimize the form display. At this point, it's time to stop trying to optimize the Visual Basic application and look more closely at the query used to populate the form. Is the query using indexes? Are the tables involved substantially larger than the tables used for the other forms?

It's the complexity of knowing what and where to optimize that has lead many to call optimizing and tuning an art. Optimize and tune things that you can change, such as Visual Basic code, algorithms, and display speed. Spend your time optimizing and tuning the poorly-performing parts of your application, not the parts that are already running fast. Understand the big picture of your application's environment and any outside resources with which your application interacts, such as the network, the database, and other components.

Testing Compiled Versions

When performing benchmark testing, test with compiled versions of Visual Basic. After all, you'll be distributing compiled versions, and you take out the oddities and overhead of testing in the Visual Basic development environment.

Optimizing and Tuning During the Entire Development Process

As stated earlier, optimizing and tuning is part of the development process, not something you do at the end. Tune and optimize your code throughout the development process. Especially when completing an ActiveX component or a frequently used function, make optimizing and tuning part of the debugging and initial test phases.

Avoiding Over-Optimizing

Avoid spending several hours rewriting code that works fine and isn't a bottleneck. For instance, avoid writing the fast sort routine when your current bubble sort routine works fine and you call the routine only once to sort 20 items. It's an entirely different story, however, if you're sorting many items, and the sort routine is called in a recursive routine and is now a bottleneck. Don't go crazy trying to optimize and tune each and every line. Write good, efficient code and spend your time fixing slow routines and bottlenecks.

Commenting Your Code Like a Maintenance Programmer

Too often, I have looked at well-written code from other consultants that performed well, but the consultants had failed to add a single line of comments! Comments *don't* increase the size of the application or hinder your application's performance. *Comment your code!* Comments are used to help you, as well as other programmers, maintain and enhance your application in the future. Programmers forced to maintain and enhance existing systems (for example, maintenance programmers) know all too well the difficulty of working with poorly commented code, and they learn not to be part of the problem by adding lots of comments. Make sure that you comment your code so that you, as well as individuals who might inherit your applications in the future, can easily determine what the code is doing and why.

Creating and Using Templates to Perform Code Benchmarking

What if you're busy developing an application and reach a critical coding point? Maybe you're about to create several forms that populate combo boxes from a database, and you're wondering what will be the fastest database access method to use or what's the fastest recordset type. You want to begin using the proper methods from the start so that you don't have to go back later and change the code to take advantage of a faster method. What do you do? What else but write some code and perform some benchmark testing?

Visual Basic offers a feature that enables you to quickly create benchmarking programs by using a form template. Included on the CD-ROM accompanying this book you'll find a Visual Basic form called FRMTIMER.FRM. Place this form in your Visual Basic home directory's \TEMPLATE\FORMS subdirectory. When you want to create a quick test program to benchmark some code, start a new Visual Basic project and select Project | Add Form from the main Visual Basic menu. The Add Form dialog box appears (see Figure 35.1).

Select the fRMTIMER form shown in Figure 35.1. The frmTimer template includes skeleton code to quickly test two different coding algorithms and compare them. Add the code you want to test to the CommandButton's Click event. Compile and execute the program by using the radio buttons to determine which algorithm you're testing. The amount of time required to execute each algorithm is displayed in a Label control. Two Label controls are used on the form, so after both tests are executed, you can easily compare the amount of time required to execute the algorithms. Listing 35.1 shows the code in frmTimer.

FIGURE 35.1.

The Add Form dialog box.

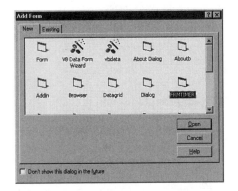

LISTING 35.1.   CH35-01.TXT—BENCHMARKING SKELETON CODE.

```
Private Sub cmdTest_Click()

    Dim Start, Finish, TotalTime

    If Option1.Value = True Then
        Start = Timer

        'Put the code you wish to time
        'here!

        'End of Code time test
        Finish = Timer
    Else
        'Option 2 selected
        Start = Timer

        'Put the code you wish to time
        'here!

        'End of Code time test
        Finish = Timer
```

continues

LISTING 35.1.   CONTINUED

```
End If

TotalTime = Finish - Start   ' Calculate total time.

'
'Set up display results
'
If Option1.Value = True Then
    'Option 1
    lblOpt1.Caption = "Total time to execute " & _
                      Option1.Caption & ": " & _
                      TotalTime
Else
    'Option 2
    lblOpt2.Caption = "Total time to execute " & _
                      Option2.Caption & ": " & _
                      TotalTime

End If

End Sub
```

The Visual Basic `Timer` function is used to perform benchmarking timing. Let's use the form template to benchmark a Visual Basic DAO performance tip. When you're modifying and adding database records with DAO, using the DAO object model methods (such as `Edit`, `AddNew`, and `Update`) is a common DAO programming practice. When you use these DAO methods to modify many records, performance can become an issue. A faster way to modify records when working with DAO is to replace the DAO methods with SQL statements and the DAO `Execute` method (for example, `AddNew` is replaced with a SQL `Insert` statement, the `Update` method is replaced with a SQL `Update` statement, and the `Delete` method is replaced with a SQL `Delete` statement). You can further increase the performance by placing the entire operation within a transaction. The code in Listing 35.2 demonstrates this performance tip. The benchmarking form is shown in Figure 35.2.

LISTING 35.2.   CH35-02.TXT—DAO PERFORMANCE-TIMING CODE.

```
Private Sub cmdTest_Click()

    Dim Start, Finish, TotalTime          'Timer Variables
    Dim rstPublishers As DAO.Recordset    'Holds the recordset used by
                                          'Option 2
    Dim strSQL As String                  'Update string for Option 2

    'With this timing example we just want to measure
    'the update time. All connections and recordsets
    'will be established prior to the timers starting.
```

```
'Open the recordset for Option 1
If Option1.Value = True Then
    'Open the Recordset object for the update
    'Only retrieve records from the state of CA
    '
    Set rstPublishers = _
        gdbBiblio.OpenRecordset("SELECT * FROM Publishers", _
        dbOpenDynaset)
Else
    strSQL = "UPDATE Publishers Set Comments = "
    strSQL = strSQL & "'Buy VB Development Unleashed'"

End If

'Begin the timing operation
If Option1.Value = True Then
    Start = Timer

    'DAO Update Timing Test - Note this is POOR
    'Performance - DO NOT UPDATE Several DATABASE
    'Records this way!
    With rstPublishers
        While Not .BOF And Not .EOF
            'Update the recordset comment field
            .Edit rstPublishers("Comments") = _
                "Buy VB Development Unleashed"
            .Update

            'Move to the next record
            .MoveNext
        Wend
    End With

    'End of Code time test
    Finish = Timer

    'Clean up
    rstPublishers.Close
    Set rstPublishers = Nothing
Else
    'Option 2 selected - SQL Updates and Transactions
    Start = Timer

    'Note: The following code performs much faster!
    'When updating, adding or deleting records using DAO
```

continues

35

TUNING AND
OPTIMIZING YOUR
APPLICATION

LISTING 35.2. CONTINUED

```
                'use transactions to speed up the operation.
                'When modifying or deleting a large number of records
                'use SQL statements
                gwksTest.BeginTrans
                gdbBiblio.Execute strSQL
                gwksTest.CommitTrans
                'End of Code time test
                Finish = Timer

        End If

        TotalTime = Finish - Start   ' Calculate total time.

        '
        'Set up display results
        '
        If Option1.Value = True Then
            'Option 1
            lblOpt1.Caption = "Total time to execute " & _
                            Option1.Caption & ": " & _
                            TotalTime
        Else
            'Option 2
            lblOpt2.Caption = "Total time to execute " & _
                            Option2.Caption & ": " & _
                            TotalTime
        End If

    End Sub
```

FIGURE 35.2.

The frmTimer *bench-marking record updating with DAO methods rather than SQL.*

> **NOTE**
>
> The code in Listing 35.2 uses the Visual Basic Microsoft Access database that ships with Visual Basic, BIBLIO.MDB. The code assumes that the database is in the same directory as the benchmarking application. Make the changes as necessary for your machine.

Reviewing Performance Tips and Tricks

Let's review some common Visual Basic optimization and tuning tricks.

Using the Visual Basic Compiler to Tune and Optimize

Visual Basic 5 was the first version of Visual Basic to include a native compiler as well as the p-code compiler available in previous versions. P-code is compiled to pseudocode that's interpreted to machine code at runtime. Native compiled code is compiled to machine code, so no interpretation is required at runtime. Native compiled code is typically faster than p-code applications; however, p-code applications are smaller than the same native compiled program. Again, there's the paradox of tuning for speed versus size, and vice versa. The native code compiler included with Visual Basic includes advanced tuning options to further optimize your compiled application (for example, you can select options such as ignoring overflow checks with integers).

Keep in mind that native code isn't the final answer to optimizing your applications. Native code improves performance greatly with mathematical code, complex algorithms, and looping code (see Table 35.1). If your application relies on graphical displays or database access, you might not notice huge performance gains between the native compiled code and the applications generated by p-code. Table 35.1 shows the benchmarks obtained by an application compiled with p-code, native, and native with all the advanced options selected.

TABLE 35.1. COMPILED APPLICATION BENCHMARK TEST (TIME IN SECONDS).

Test	P-Code	Native	Native with Options
Graphics	3.84	3.84	4.01
Variant Counter	12.85	10.77	10.38
Long Counter	2.74	.44	.05
Double Counter	4.95	1.98	1.60
Splash Screen	1.32	1.27	1.26
String Copy	.28	.27	.27

NOTE

The application used to obtain the various benchmark tests in Table 35.1 is the `OPTIMIZE.VBP` project that ships with Visual Basic in the `OPTIMIZE` subdirectory. The Optimizing application (see Figure 35.3) contains many good examples of common Visual Basic performance and optimization tips.

FIGURE 35.3.
The Visual Basic 6.0 Optimizing application.

NOTE

The compiled versions of the Optimizing application used to generate Table 35.3 are slightly larger than the application generated by p-code. The sizes of each compiled application are as follows:

- P-code: 483KB
- Native: 550KB
- Native with options: 532KB

Sorting Strings with a List Box

If you need to sort some data quickly and don't have a sort routine already written, use a Visual Basic ListBox control to sort the data. It makes no sense to spend time writing and optimizing a sort routine to sort a couple of items when you can use a Visual Basic ListBox control to perform the sort. Set the ListBox control's Sorted property to True and use the AddItem method to add each item to the list box. You can then read the items from the list box in sorted order. This trick might not provide you with the fastest possible sort routine, but it's not slow and will help you meet your project deadlines.

If using a ListBox to sort items is not feasible, you'll find some sorting algorithms in Chapter 36, "Algorithms For VB Programmers." Chapter 36 also contains code for an efficient Quick Sort routine.

Using the Windows API

For years, Visual Basic programmers have been taking advantage of the Windows API to improve application performance and add functionality that can't be accomplished by using Visual Basic alone. Entire books have been written about using the Windows API. You can use the API for simple speed-enhancing tricks, such as quickly finding a string in a list box, or for more complex tricks, such as creating a thread from a Visual Basic application with the Windows API. The Windows API is a great way to increase your application's performance. Wrap your favorite API calls into a Visual Basic class module to make them easier to use and modify.

Using Data Controls to Conserve SQL Server User Connections

Using bound data controls to populate a combo box or fill text boxes in a form is a great way to rapidly put together fully functional data-entry forms. Sometimes, several data controls are used on a single form to retrieve data and fill combo boxes. In a Microsoft or Sybase SQL Server environment, each data control uses a database connection (referred to as a *user connection*). A connection for each data control surprises many programmers when they learn that their simple data-entry form uses five simultaneous connections, they have only a ten-user license, and seven users need to use the application. Of course, you could resort to writing code to query the database and populate the combo boxes or form; however, you lose the speed and ease of use provided by the data control.

When populating combo boxes and list boxes with static-type recordsets, use code methods so that you don't waste several user connections populating list and combo boxes.

The code in Listing 35.3 shows how to use a data control to easily populate a data-bound grid or form while using only a single-connection global SQL Server connection.

Listing 35.3.   Сн35-03.тхт—Using a data control to populate a grid or form
with only one global SQL Server connection.

```
Dim gTest As New RDO.rdoConnection    'Global RDO connection used by all
                                      'the forms

Private Sub Form_Load()

Dim rsTest As RDO.rdoResultset        'Define a local RDO Resultset

'Set up the RDO connection parameters. These
'Will vary from one SQL Server to another.
With gTest
    .Connect = "uid=sa;pwd=;DSN=PubsDB;"
    .CursorDriver = rdUseOdbc
    .EstablishConnection rdDriverNoPrompt
End With

'Fill combo box
Set rsTest = gTest.OpenResultset("Select au_id from pubs..authors", _
    rdOpenStatic)

'Open the recordset using the global connection
Set rsTest = gTest.OpenResultset("Select * from pubs..authors", _
    rdOpenStatic)

'Set the data control resultset
'This data control could be bound to a grid or
'other controls, however it will not use a new
'user connection. Instead it will use the global connection.
Set MSRDC1.Resultset = rsTest

End Sub
```

Note

The code in Listing 35.3 uses RDO (Remote Data Objects), which is distributed only with the Enterprise Edition of Visual Basic and designed specifically for client/server databases such as Microsoft SQL Server and Oracle.

TIP

If the same set of static data is fetched from a remote database and is being used repeatedly throughout the application, you can boost performance by caching the recordset in a string array or other suitable data type. Subsequent access to the data is blazingly fast because the information is already in RAM and doesn't require a trip to the database to retrieve the resultset. As always, use caution when dealing with clients with low memory (8–12MB) and do not cache extremely large resultsets, as they will use up large amounts of memory.

Understanding Visual Basic's Limitations

Not only is it important to know what tips and tricks can be used to help tune and optimize your code, but it's also important to know that Visual Basic has some limitations and what those limitations are before you create an application that exceeds those limitations. Some Visual Basic limitations are as follows:

- Only 254 control names can be used per form (control arrays count once).

- A line of Visual Basic code can't exceed 1,023 bytes.

- A Visual Basic form, class, or module can't load more than 65,534 lines of code.

- The code in a procedure can't exceed 64KB, but you can have an unlimited number of procedures in a module.

- The maximum number of items a list box can store is 32KB, and each item can be up to 1K.

Reducing the Dots When Using Objects

I once helped a programmer use the Microsoft Excel `WorkSheets` object to read information from a Lotus Notes database and an RDBMS (relational database management system) database into an Excel spreadsheet by using a Visual Basic application. The routine took more than five minutes to complete. I looked at the code to try to speed up the process, and the first change I made to the code reduced the time to around 40 seconds. What was the change? I reduced the number of dots when referencing the Excel objects used in the code. For instance, Excel has a complex object model, and programmers often write code that references several objects to get to the object they want to use. The following code illustrates this example:

```
oApplication.oWorkbooks(0).WorkSheets(0)
```

Each dot used requires multiple calls to the object and OLE services; by reducing the number of dots, you greatly reduce the number of calls. To reduce the number of dots, get a reference to the object you want to use; this technique, called *aliasing*, can be used with ActiveX objects as well as objects created within your project.

The following example assigns the Excel `WorkSheet` object to a variable. The variable can then be used to execute the methods and properties of the worksheet object without the references to the Application or `Workbook` object, thus reducing the number of dots used:

```
Set oWorkSheet = oApplication.oWorkbooks(0).WorkSheets(0)
```

Using Method Parameters with Out-of-Process or Distributed Components

When calling out-of-process or distributed components, it's faster to pass parameters through a method call than to set several object properties and then invoke a method that uses the properties. Expensive cross-process calls are required for each property that's set, as well as for the method invoked. By using parameters with a method, the cross-process calls can be reduced to the method call. As an alternative, you can create a local object, set parameters on the local object, and then pass an object reference as a parameter to the remote object.

Increasing Perceived Speed with Splash Screens and Progress Indicators

If your application takes a long time to load, use a *splash screen* to give users something to look at during the load process. Splash screens improve the users' perception of the application's load time. If your application performs operations that take more than 5–7 seconds, display a progress indicator to aid the users' speed perception, as well as indicate that the program is still functioning. (Users have a terrible habit of giving up and hitting Ctrl+Alt+Delete.)

Using Early Object Binding Versus Late Binding

If you know the object type when using objects, use early binding. *Early binding* is when you declare the type of object that is to use the variable in your code. The following example declares a variable as an `Excel Application` object:

```
Dim oXl As Excel.Application
```

Early binding enables the compiler to check your code to make sure that the object actually supports the methods and properties you're using during compile time, as opposed to finding out at runtime. Visual Basic lets you use early binding for objects by selecting a reference to the object through Visual Basic's main menu (choose Project | References). Early binding is also much faster than *late binding*, when you declare objects as follows:

```
Dim oXl as Object
```

Use late binding only when the type of object you'll be using is unknown at runtime.

Optimizing Display Speed

The key to optimizing display speed is to try to minimize the number of repaints and the amount of memory consumed by graphics. Some standard optimization and performance tips are as follows:

- If you don't use graphical methods, turn off the ClipControls property (Forms and PictureBox control).
- For displaying images and bitmaps, use the Image control rather than the PictureBox control. The Image control uses substantially fewer resources than the PictureBox control.
- If you have many controls on a form, place them in a PictureBox control. When all the controls are set with the proper data, set the PictureBox control's Visible property to False while you load the controls on the form. Make the picture box visible to display the loaded form, thus reducing the number of repaints.

Optimizing Data Types

The following are useful tips when working with Visual Basic data types:

- Avoid using variants whenever possible.
- Use long integers or integers where possible.
- Never use floating-point data types (single, double, currency, and so on) for loop counters.

Optimizing File I/O Operations

To speed up file I/O, read file information into arrays. Also, rather than write a line at a time to a file, cache the information in a memory buffer (for example, a string variable) and then write the cache memory buffer to the file.

35

TUNING AND
OPTIMIZING YOUR
APPLICATION

Optimizing Memory

Here are some useful tips to help you reduce the amount of memory used by your application:

- Avoid variants, unless they have to be used, such as for certain aspects of OLE automation.
- Release memory used by objects (including forms) when you're done with them by setting them to `Nothing`.
- Unload unused forms.

Avoiding Calling Functions and Procedures in Different Modules

Visual Basic modules are loaded into memory on demand, not on application startup, which means that a module isn't loaded until a function or procedure in the module is called. During application startup, refrain from calling functions or procedures in many different modules. This slows application startup as each module is loaded into memory. Try to keep functions and procedures with similar functionality in the same module.

Selecting the Proper Component Type

Visual Basic 6 lets you create in-process (DLL) or out-of-process (EXE) ActiveX code components. Further complicating the type of component to create is the thread model you should select. Visual Basic lets you mark components as thread safe and generate components that support multiple threads or single threads.

For your applications, should you create an in-process (DLL) or out-of-process (EXE)? That depends on the application or service you're providing. An in-process component is faster when it's used on the same machine because it loads in the same address space as the application using the component. With DLLs, costly cross-process calls are avoided. In a distributed environment, however, out-of-process components deserve a second look because they provide asynchronous callback capabilities. By using asynchronous callbacks, a client can invoke a component method without *blocking* (that is, waiting for the component to finish). When the component completes the method, the client is notified. The Internet has been *the* hot technology area of the past few years; take a closer look at creating components for Web-based applications.

Optimizing Web-Based Components

You can use Microsoft's Web browser, Internet Explorer, to download ActiveX components and use them on a client machine. When creating ActiveX components to execute in a browser, create in-process components (DLLs) for the best performance. ActiveX components can also be used on the Web server side by Microsoft's Internet Information Server (IIS) and the Active Server Page framework. When creating Web-based server ActiveX components, create the component as an in-process component (that is, an ActiveX DLL).

Generating an ActiveX DLL provides better performance than out-of-process components because an in-process component runs in the same process space as the application that uses the component (that is, Internet Information Server). As such, the application can reference the component's properties and methods without making the costly cross-process calls required in out-of-process components. Out-of-process components do have some positive features not available to in-process components that can be used in a distributed computing or client/server environment, such as asynchronous callbacks or asynchronous notification events. In a Web-based environment, stick to using ActiveX DLLs.

Multithreaded or Single-Threaded Components

VB6 enables you to create either multithreaded (apartment model threaded) or single-threaded components. In most cases, you will probably use the latter. However, multithreaded clients such as Internet Information Server can take advantage of multithreaded ActiveX components by spawning separate threads of objects when creating objects from multithreaded components.

A *thread* is executing code; every application in a Windows environment has at least a single thread of execution. An application or component is said to be multithreaded if the application can create more than one thread of execution. Suppose that you have a financial database application and a computation that executes for a long time. If your application is multithreaded, you can start your computation by creating a thread to perform the computation and, while the computation thread is executing, begin to edit a database table by using another thread. Preemptive multitasking operating systems, such as Windows NT and Windows 95, allocate separate time slices for each thread that's to execute (that is, the computation thread and the edit table thread), giving the appearance of performing both tasks simultaneously.

When creating ActiveX components used in a Web or distributed environment, create multithreaded ActiveX components. Multithreaded ActiveX components are created at compile time by selecting the project option Unattended Execution. When the ActiveX DLL is compiled with the Unattended Execution check box selected, a DLL that supports multithreading is generated.

When creating multithreaded ActiveX components, keep in mind how Visual Basic DLLs use apartment-model threading. Remember also that ActiveX component automation uses serialization of requests to prevent multiple threads from executing a new operation before previous operations have completed.

Keeping component serialization intact is important because Visual Basic ActiveX components aren't re-entrant. *Re-entrancy* is the code's capability to be executed by a thread. Before the thread completes, it yields control of the processor to another thread to process the same code. When the second thread yields processor control, the variables and stack pointer are restored to the exact state before the processor yielded control to another thread. Because Visual Basic ActiveX components aren't re-entrant, when you create ActiveX components, don't do any of the following in your component, which might cause the processor to yield to another thread before completing the current operation:

- Call DoEvents
- Raise an event handled by an object on another thread or process
- Invoke a method or property of an object in another thread or process

NOTE

Multithreaded applications don't always equate to a faster application. In many cases, multithreaded applications let you manage the perception that an application is executing faster by not locking up the user interface during a lengthy process. Multithreaded applications and components make more sense when developing for server-side processing. Also keep in mind that Visual Basic doesn't currently support debugging multithreaded applications.

Using the Visual Basic Code Profiler

Visual Basic ships with a code-analyzing tool called the Visual Basic Code Profiler to help you optimize and tune your applications. You can use the Code Profiler to determine how many times a code line or function has been executed. This form of profiling is called *code coverage* and is useful for finding *dead code* (code that's never executed) in your programs. By pointing out what code is executed the most, code coverage is helpful in determining which functions or lines of code you might want to re-examine and tune.

The Code Profiler also can be used for performance optimizing by timing how long each line of code or function takes to execute. Using the Code Profiler for optimizing application performance is useful in helping you determine which functions or lines of code are possible application bottlenecks, as well as what parts of your application you might need to optimize.

Installing the Visual Basic Code Profiler

The Visual Basic Code Profiler isn't part of the Visual Basic installation. You can find the profiler on the Visual Basic CD-ROM in the \TOOLS\UNSUPPRT\VBCP directory. To install the code profiler, follow these steps:

1. Copy the VBCP.DLL file located on the Visual Basic 6 CD-ROM directory, \TOOLS\UNSUPPRT\VBCP, to a directory on your computer's hard drive (for example, the Visual Basic default directory).

2. To register the Code Profiler, use the Windows 95 or Windows NT 4.0 Explorer and the Registry utility, REGSVR32.EXE. Start the Explorer and locate REGSVR32.EXE on the Visual Basic CD-ROM in the \TOOLS\REGUTILS directory.

3. Start another copy of Explorer. Locate the VBCP.DLL file on you computer's hard drive. With the mouse, select VBCP.DLL, drag the file onto REGSRV32.EXE, and release. The Registry utility will register the Code Profiler DLL and display the successful Registry dialog box (see Figure 35.4).

FIGURE 35.4.

A successful Registry dialog box.

4. The following code is required in the Visual Basic Add-In initialization file, VBADDIN.INI, and is located in the Windows directory. Add the code if it doesn't exist:
```
[Add-Ins32]
VBCP.VBCPClass=0
```

5. From the Visual Basic Main Menu, select Add-Ins | Add-In Manager. The Add-In Manager dialog box appears (see Figure 35.5).

6. Check the VB Code Profiler and then click OK. The Visual Basic Code Profiler is now installed and ready to use.

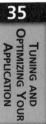

35

TUNING AND
OPTIMIZING YOUR
APPLICATION

FIGURE 35.5.

The Add-In Manager dialog box.

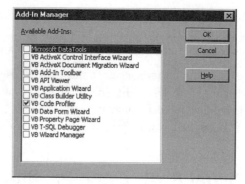

Using the Visual Basic Code Profiler

Using the Visual Basic Code Profiler is simple; before you open the project you want to profile, start the Code Profiler by selecting it from Visual Basic's Add-Ins menu. The Code Profiler dialog box appears (see Figure 35.6).

FIGURE 35.6.

The Visual Basic Code Profiler dialog box.

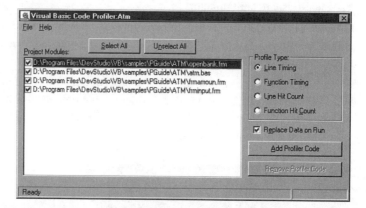

> **NOTE**
>
> The Code Profiler adds code to the project being analyzed and creates temporary files in your Visual Basic project. It's a good idea to back up your existing Visual Basic project before using the Code Profiler.

Follow these steps to profile your application:

1. In the Profile Type section, select the type of profile you want to run. The selections are as follows:

Line Timing	Amount of time required to execute each code line
Function Timing	Amount of time required to execute a function
Line Hit Count	Number of times a code line was executed during a run
Function Hit Count	Number of times a function was executed during a run

2. Mark the Replace Data on Run check box if you don't want to accumulate statistics from a previous test run. This cleans out the code profiler database and shows statistics for the current run.

3. You should mark this check box if you want to select a different type of profile. Mixing statistical information from different profile runs isn't recommended because the old data may not be valid with the newly selected profile.

4. Click the `Add Profiler Code` button.

TIP

If you see an error message that says `The Project or Component is dirty. Please save and try again`, you need to save the current Visual Basic project and then reopen it.

---

5. This step adds lines of code to your application used by the profiler and creates temporary Visual Basic files. Listing 35.4 shows an example of code the profiler adds during this step.

LISTING 35.4. CH35-04.TXT—EXAMPLE OF VISUAL BASIC CODE WITH CODE PROFILER LINES ADDED.

```
Select Case DoFlag
        Case True
    VBCP_Update 1, "cmdStartStop_Click", 2
            cmdStartStop.Caption = "Start Demo"
    VBCP_Update 1, "cmdStartStop_Click", 3
            DoFlag = False
    VBCP_Update 1, "cmdStartStop_Click", 4
            mnuOption.Enabled = True
```

continues

35

TUNING AND
OPTIMIZING YOUR
APPLICATION

LISTING 35.4. CONTINUED

```
VBCP_Update 1, "cmdStartStop_Click", 5
        If mnuCtlMoveDemo.Checked = True And _
            VBCP_UpdateIf(1, "cmdStartStop_Click", 6) Then
            ' Hide bouncing graphic again.
            picBall.Visible = False
VBCP_Update 1, "cmdStartStop_Click", 7
        ElseIf mnuLineDemo.Checked = True And _
            VBCP_UpdateIf(1, "cmdStartStop_Click", 8) Then
            ' Remove lines from the form.
            Cls
```

NOTE

The profiler code is designated with VBCP_.

---

6. Run the Visual Basic project you're profiling. The Code Profiler collects statistics while you're using the application.

7. After you test all your application features, you can review the statistics collected by the Code Profiler by selecting one of the following menu options located under the Code Profiler's File menu:

   • *View Results*—Shows the results of the selected test profile

   • *Export Results*—Exports the results to be used in other applications, such as Microsoft Excel

   • *Project Statistics*—Provides statistical information on the project being profiled

8. Choose File | View Results, and the Analysis window appears (see Figure 35.7).

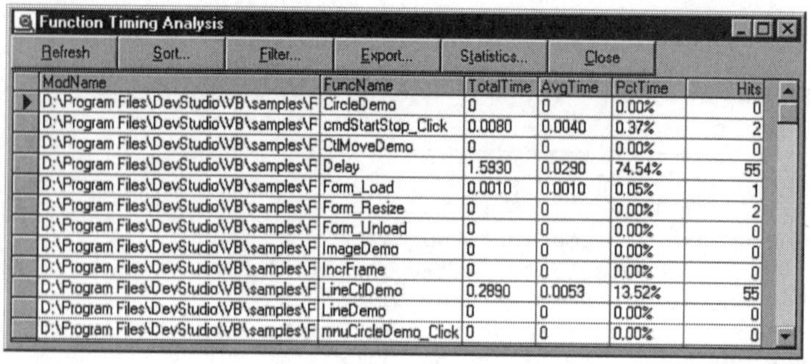

FIGURE 35.7.

The Visual Basic Code Profiler Analysis window.

ModName	FuncName	TotalTime	AvgTime	PctTime	Hits
D:\Program Files\DevStudio\VB\samples\F	CircleDemo	0	0	0.00%	0
D:\Program Files\DevStudio\VB\samples\F	cmdStartStop_Click	0.0080	0.0040	0.37%	2
D:\Program Files\DevStudio\VB\samples\F	CtlMoveDemo	0	0	0.00%	0
D:\Program Files\DevStudio\VB\samples\F	Delay	1.5930	0.0290	74.54%	55
D:\Program Files\DevStudio\VB\samples\F	Form_Load	0.0010	0.0010	0.05%	1
D:\Program Files\DevStudio\VB\samples\F	Form_Resize	0	0	0.00%	2
D:\Program Files\DevStudio\VB\samples\F	Form_Unload	0	0	0.00%	0
D:\Program Files\DevStudio\VB\samples\F	ImageDemo	0	0	0.00%	0
D:\Program Files\DevStudio\VB\samples\F	IncrFrame	0	0	0.00%	0
D:\Program Files\DevStudio\VB\samples\F	LineCtlDemo	0.2890	0.0053	13.52%	55
D:\Program Files\DevStudio\VB\samples\F	LineDemo	0	0	0.00%	0
D:\Program Files\DevStudio\VB\samples\F	mnuCircleDemo_Click	0	0	0.00%	0

The title bar of the Analysis window reflects the test performed. For Figure 35.7, the Function Timing profile was selected. For the Function Timing profile, the Analysis window displays the module name, the name of the function called, the total time spent executing the function, the average time for each execution of the function, and the number of times the function was executed (that is, hits). If lines are being profiled instead of functions, the line number is displayed in the Analysis window as well as the line of text being profiled instead of the function name. You can perform other functions with the Analysis window, such as apply filters to the results, export the results, or sort the results, as shown in the Visual Basic Code Profiler Sort dialog box in Figure 35.8.

FIGURE 35.8.

The Visual Basic Code Profiler Sort dialog box.

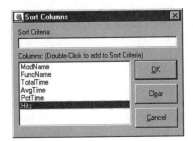

The Sort dialog box lets you sort by a specific column. This feature is useful when profiling a large project. For example, you can sort by the number of hits to quickly find the most used routines, or you can sort on the TotalTime, PctTime, or AvgTime to quickly locate possible bottlenecks.

> **NOTE**
>
> Setting the sort order requires double-clicking one of the columns to display another dialog box, which lets you sort the results in ascending or descending order.

Another feature of the Visual Basic Code Profiler is the project statistics information. Figure 35.9 shows a dialog box of project statistical information, such as the number of lines of code and functions in a project.

35

TUNING AND
OPTIMIZING YOUR
APPLICATION

FIGURE 35.9.

The Visual Basic Code Profiler Statistics dialog box.

Blanker Statistics

⚠ 1 Modules, 24 Functions Profiled, 287 Lines Profiled.

OK

NOTE

When you're finished profiling your project, don't forget to remove the profiling code that the Visual Basic Code Profiler adds. To remove the profiler code, click the `Remove Profiler Code` button shown in Figure 35.6.

Summary

In this chapter, you learned the many different factors and parameters you need to take into consideration to properly optimize and tune your Visual Basic applications. You learned some of the standard optimizing and tuning tricks, such as using Long integers rather than Variants whenever possible. Different tips and tricks were given to help you decide what to optimize and what not to optimize. The Visual Basic Code Profiler was discussed in detail as a tool to help you find dead code and to quickly locate functions and lines of code that require optimizing and tuning.

Algorithms for VB Programmers

by Rob Thayer

IN THIS CHAPTER

- Algorithms   858

Although Visual Basic has evolved into a serious tool for software development, the more complicated aspects of data processing are often left to other languages, such as C++. The VB programmer who goes looking for information on how to perform complex algorithms often comes up empty handed.

There is no good reason for this. Perhaps a few years ago, when Visual Basic was more limited and was considered to be a "toy" language, it could have been ignored as a competitor with other "real" development tools. However, that is no longer the case. It stands to reason that there would be information available specifically for VB programmers who want to delve into more advanced processing methods such as sorting, encryption, and compression. Unfortunately, that is not the case. While there is more of this kind of information available now than there was in the past, most books and articles that discuss advanced processing methods cater to C++ programmers rather than VB programmers.

This chapter will provide you, the VB programmer, with the basic knowledge you need to understand and use some of the data processing algorithms that have been reserved for other languages and development environments.

Algorithms

Most programs that you write in Visual Basic are simple. Few really need to manipulate data in ways that require complex algorithms. However, sometimes you might find yourself looking for just such an algorithm. You might need to sort data in some way, or encrypt it to secure it from prying eyes. Or, you might need to compress your data so that it will take up less space or so that it can be sent faster over a network connection.

Unfortunately, it might be difficult to find the algorithms you need to complete the task at hand. Don't worry, this chapter can help. It will introduce you to the basics of some of the more common algorithms in use today for sorting, data encryption, and data compression. It also provides you with sample code for each of those data processing tasks. You can adapt the code for your own use, or you can use the information provided about other algorithms as a start for learning more.

Sorting

One of the most common processing tasks that involves an algorithm is sorting. Many different algorithms have been devised to accomplish sorting. The Insertion, Bubble, Heap, Exchange, Shell, and Quick Sort methods are all viable ways of sorting items.

This section briefly describes these common sorting methods. It also provides an example Quick Sort routine, which is typically the fastest and most efficient of the different sorts.

The sort descriptions that follow operate on the premise that the data to be sorted is contained in an array. However, data can be sorted in formats other than arrays. For example, random files can be sorted just as easily as arrays, though the overhead of disk access will undoubtedly make the sorting less efficient.

Insertion Sort

The Insertion sort method loops through an array, evaluating each item in the array with all the preceding items. It then determines where the current item should be placed by moving backward through the array and inserts the current item into its new location. All the elements between the new location and the current item's old location are moved down to the next item to make space for the insertion.

Bubble Sort

The Bubble sort method is slightly more efficient than the Insertion sort method. It loops through an array of items and compares adjacent items to see whether they are out of order. If they are out of order, it switches them. It keeps looping through the array until no items are switched, indicating that the array has been sorted.

Heap Sort

The Heap sort method uses a binary tree (a "heap") to organize items in an array into nodes, with each parent node being greater in value than its child nodes. The heap is constantly being rebuilt and reorganized as the array is looped through and array items are moved up and down the tree.

Although the Heap sort is generally more efficient than the Insertion and Bubble sort methods, it is somewhat complicated and is not as efficient as some of the other sort methods yet to be discussed. The Exchange sort, for example, usually provides better results and is much easier to understand.

Exchange Sort

The Exchange sort method loops through each item in an array and compares it with the item that follows. If the following item is smaller than the current item, it is switched (exchanged) with the current item. The process then repeats for the next item in the array. When the last item in the array is reached, the array will have been sorted.

Shell Sort

The Shell sort method works similarly to the Bubble sort, but instead of comparing adjacent items in an array, it initially compares items that are halfway between the first and last items in the array. If the values are out of order, it switches them. It then determines the halfway point again and repeats the process. This halving of the array and comparing items continues until adjacent items are being compared. By then, most of the items in the array have been sorted. A final loop through the array works the same way as the Bubble sort and ensures that everything is in order.

Quick Sort

One of the fastest ways to sort items is by using the Quick Sort method. Quick Sort works by being passed a lower and upper boundary of an array of items. If the lower boundary is less than the upper boundary, then the boundaries are tested to see whether they are next to each other (upper boundary minus lower boundary equals one). If they are, and they are not in sorted order, then the two array items for the boundaries are switched. If the boundaries are not next to each other, then a random "pivot" item is selected that is somewhere between the lower and upper boundaries. The Quick Sort routine is called recursively with the new upper and lower boundaries representing each side of the two subdivisions created by the randomly selected pivot. This keeps happening until the array is sorted.

Because the Quick Sort routine is called recursively (that is, it calls itself within its own code), it can be difficult to grasp how it works. The QuickSort routine shown in Listing 36.1 should help you gain a better understanding of how such a sort might be coded.

LISTING 36.1. CH36-01.TXT—THE QUICKSORT ROUTINE, WHICH SORTS THE ITEMS IN THE GLOBALLY DEFINED strArray() ARRAY.

```
Public Sub QuickSort(lonLower, lonUpper)

Dim lonRandomPivot As Long
Dim lonTempLower As Long
Dim lonTempUpper As Long
Dim strLastItem As String
Dim strTempItem As String

Randomize Timer

' Only sort if the lower boundary is lesser
' than the upper boundary.
If lonLower < lonUpper Then
    If lonUpper - lonLower = 1 Then
        ' Switch the upper and lower array items
        ' if the lower is greater than the upper.
        If strArray(lonLower) > strArray(lonUpper) Then
            strTempItem = strArray(lonUpper)
            strArray(lonUpper) = strArray(lonLower)
            strArray(lonLower) = strTempItem
        End If
```

```
    Else
        ' Pick a random "pivot" item.
        lonRandomPivot = Int(Rnd _
            * (lonUpper - lonLower + 1)) + lonLower
        ' Switch the upper array item with the
        ' pivot item.
        strTempItem = strArray(lonUpper)
        strArray(lonUpper) = strArray(lonRandomPivot)
        strArray(lonRandomPivot) = strTempItem
        ' Store the upper array item.
        strLastItem = strArray(lonUpper)
        Do
            ' Define the temporary upper and
            ' lower boundaries.
            lonTempUpper = lonUpper
            lonTempLower = lonLower
            ' Move down towards the pivot item,
            ' looping until the pivot item is greater
            ' than or equal to the temporary
            ' lower boundary.
            Do While (lonTempLower < lonTempUpper) And _
                (strArray(lonTempLower) <= strLastItem)
                    lonTempLower = lonTempLower + 1
            Loop
            ' Move up towards the pivot item, looping
            ' until the pivot item is less than
            ' or equal to the temporary upper
            ' boundary.
            Do While (lonTempUpper > lonTempLower) And _
                (strArray(lonTempUpper) >= strLastItem)
                    lonTempUpper = lonTempUpper - 1
            Loop
            ' If the pivot item hasn't been
            ' reached, then two of the items on
            ' either side of the pivot are out
            ' of order. If so, then switch them.
            If lonTempLower < lonTempUpper Then
                strTempItem = strArray(lonTempUpper)
                strArray(lonTempUpper) = strArray(lonTempLower)
                strArray(lonTempLower) = strTempItem
            End If
        Loop While (lonTempLower < lonTempUpper)
        ' Switch the temporary lower boundary
        ' item with the original upper boundary
        ' item.
        strTempItem = strArray(lonTempLower)
        strArray(lonTempLower) = strArray(lonUpper)
        strArray(lonUpper) = strTempItem
        ' Call the QuickSort routine again
        ' recursively, using new upper and
        ' lower boundaries.
```

continues

LISTING 36.1. CONTINUED

```
        If (lonTempLower - lonLower) < (lonUpper - lonTempLower) Then
            QuickSort lonLower, lonTempLower - 1
            QuickSort lonTempLower + 1, lonUpper
        Else
            QuickSort lonTempLower + 1, lonUpper
            QuickSort lonLower, lonTempLower - 1
        End If
    End If
End If

End Sub
```

The routine shown in Listing 36.1 makes the assumption that a publicly defined array called strArray exists. It also assumes that the array is populated with data.

To try out the QuickSort procedure, you must define the strArray array in a code module. Another variable, lonArrayCount, should also be defined to keep track of the number of items in the array. The following code shows how strArray and lonArrayCount should be declared:

```
Public lonArrayCount As Long
Public strArray(1000) As String
```

Next, you must have a way of populating the array with data. The following subroutine can be used to read in the lines of a sequential file that will be stored in the array.

```
Public Sub ReadFile(strFileName As String)

Open strFileName For Input As #1
Do
    lonArrayCount = lonArrayCount + 1
    If (lonLineCount <= 1000) And (Not EOF(1)) Then
        Line Input #1, strArray(lonArrayCount)
    End If
Loop Until (EOF(1) Or lonArrayCount = 1000)
Close #1

End Sub
```

The argument that is passed to the ReadFile procedure, strFileName, should indicate the path and filename of a sequential file that contains data to be sorted. Note that a maximum of 1,000 lines of data will be read in because that is the number of elements that strArray can hold as it was defined.

After the array has been sorted, it should be written back out to another file. The following WriteFile routine can be used to accomplish that task. Again, the argument passed to the `WriteFile` routine should indicate the path and filename of the output file.

```
Public Sub WriteFile(strFileName As String)

Dim lonArrayPtr As Long

Open strFileName For Output As #1
For lonArrayPtr = 1 To lonArrayCount
    Print #1, strArray(lonArrayPtr)
Next lonArrayPtr
Close #1

End Sub
```

Finally, the `ReadFile`, `QuickSort`, and `WriteFile` routines should be called. You could add a CommandButton control to the form and put the following code in the control's `Click` event. Or, you could add it the `Form_Load` event so that it runs as soon as the program is executed.

```
ReadFile
QuickSort 1, lonArrayCount
WriteFile
```

Note that the initial values passed to the `QuickSort` routine are 1 and `lonArrayCount`, which represent the total number of items that have been read into `strArray`. These are the ultimate upper and lower boundaries of the items in the array. `QuickSort` will keep dividing the items between the upper and lower boundaries, determining new boundaries and calling itself recursively, until the array is sorted.

Data Encryption/Decryption

We are living in the Information Age. Computers thrive on information, with more and more data being obtained and processed every day. Data about you, your business, your bank account, your bills, and your credit is being processed every day. Information is a commodity that is sometimes valued more than gold and silver, and that's not likely to change any time soon.

Most information is freely accessible, available to anyone who wants it. The Internet is the world's largest source of information, an unlimited amount of data that is, for the most part, free for the asking.

But some information is not meant for public eyes and has to be secured, lest it fall into the wrong hands. Details of military operations, financial information, medical records, and some forms of communication are all types of information that need to be kept secret. This is where data encryption (also known as cryptography) comes in.

Data encryption is nothing new. It goes back to ancient civilizations that used hiero-glyphics to build messages. We're all familiar with the strange symbols used by the ancient Egyptians. These hieroglyphics were an early form of encryption, and a relatively good one. It wasn't until the Rosetta stone was found in recent times that these hiero-glyphics could be accurately deciphered. Although data encryption has always been important, never has it been as necessary and widespread as it is today.

A wide range of encryption techniques have been devised. Some are simple, whereas others are incredibly complex. Obviously, the simpler the encryption technique, the easier it is to "crack." Also, as computers get faster and more efficient, they become more capable of cracking existing encryption techniques. Therefore, newer and better methods of encrypting data are constantly being invented.

This section discusses some of the more common methods of encryption in use today. It also illustrates a simple but effective encryption method that can be used in your own programs.

Data Encryption Standard (DES)

DES was developed by the U.S. National Bureau of Standards in 1975 in an attempt to devise an encryption method that could be used in government applications. It has become one of the the world's most used encryption techniques.

DES encrypts data in 64-bit blocks of text, using a 56-bit key. Later versions of DES, such as 3-Round DES (Triple DES) and 6-Round DES, encrypt data multiple times using the same encryption method but different keys. A key is used in calculations when encoding and decoding data. The longer the key (that is, the more bits it uses) the more difficult it is to crack the encryption.

International Data Encryption Algorithm (IDEA)

IDEA was devised in 1990 as the replacement for DES. Again, 64-bit blocks of text are used, but they are split into four 16-bit blocks that are each encrypted separately. Also, a 128-bit key is used. A long sequence of calculations and bit operations are performed on the data and then the 16-bit blocks of encrypted data are combined together to once again form a 64-bit block.

IDEA is one of the most secure encryption methods ever devised, and it has not yet been broken. Of course, that might change in the near future, as new methods of cryptoanaly-sis are created.

Pretty Good Privacy (PGP)

PGP has come into vogue in the past few years as a widely available method of data encryption. It uses a public/private key encryption strategy, where two different keys are used for encryption and decryption. One key is made public, and one is kept secret. The public key is used for encryption, so anyone can encrypt data with that key. To decrypt the data, however, requires the private key. The private key cannot be obtained in any way from the public key, and vice versa. So why use two keys? That way, data can be transferred over unsecure channels, such as the Internet. You can give someone a public key and have him encrypt messages or data for you without having to know your private key. After you receive the encrypted data, you can then use your private key to decrypt it.

PGP has the capability of using large keys, up to 2,047 bits in size. Despite the fact that it is in widespread use by the masses instead of being used primarily by the government, PGP is one of the most secure methods of data encryption ever devised. That's probably why its creator, Phil Zimmermann, was for a time being closely investigated by the U.S. government as a possible violator of the International Traffic in Arms Regulations (ITAR).

PGP uses the IDEA method for its data encryption. It also uses elements of other encryption methods such as RSA (Rivest-Shamir-Adelman) and MD5 (Message Digest 5) to manage its keys as well as for data hashing and compression.

XOR Encryption

One simple way to encrypt and decrypt data is by using the XOR Encryption method. Basically, the characters in the data stream and those of a code key are XORed together to create an encrypted character. The process is exactly the same for data being encrypted as it is for data being decrypted.

The code key is a string made up of any alphanumeric characters you want to use. It can be any number of characters long, but the longer the key is, the more secure the encryption.

XOR Encryption is not a tight method of encryption, meaning that it can be broken relatively easily. However, if you want to encrypt messages or documents so that they cannot be viewed with a text editor or browser, then XOR Encryption offers a simple way to do so.

Listing 36.2 shows a function called XOREncryption that can be used to both encrypt and decrypt data. You need only pass it the code key (a string) and the data to be encrypted or decrypted.

LISTING 36.2. CH36-02.TXT—THE XOREncryption ROUTINE, WHICH BOTH ENCRYPTS AND DECRYPTS DATA WHEN PROVIDED WITH A CODE KEY AND THE DATA.

```
Public Function XOREncryption(strCodeKey As String, _
    strDataIn As String) As String

Dim lonDataPtr As Long
Dim intXORValue1 As Integer
Dim intXORValue2 As Integer
Dim strDataOut As String

For lonDataPtr = 1 To Len(strDataIn)
    ' The first value to XOR comes from the data to be
    ' encrypted.
    intXORValue1 = Asc(Mid$(strDataIn, lonDataPtr, 1))
    ' The second value to XOR comes from the code key.
    intXORValue2 = Asc(Mid$(strCodeKey, _
        ((lonDataPtr Mod Len(strCodeKey)) + 1), 1))
    ' The two values are XORed together to create a
    ' decrypted character.
    strDataOut = strDataOut + Chr(intXORValue1 Xor _
        intXORValue2)
Next lonDataPtr

' The XOREncryption function returns the encrypted (or
' decrypted) data.
XOREncryption = strDataOut

End Function
```

To try out the XOREncryption routine, you can add it to a form that has three TextBox controls (Text1, Text2, and Text3) and a CommandButton control. In the CommandButton's Click event, add the following code:

```
Dim strCodeKey As String
Dim strEncryptedText As String

strCodeKey = "Wxz19hgl3Kb2dSp"
strEncryptedText = XOREncryption(strCodeKey, Text1.Text)
Text2.Text = strEncryptedText
Text3.Text = XOREncryption(strCodeKey, strEncryptedText)
```

This will encrypt the contents of the Text1 control using the code key stored in the strCodeKey variable. It then places the results in Text2 and decrypts the encrypted data and places it into Text3.

You might be wondering why the strEncryptedText string is used to store the encrypted data instead of just placing it in Text2. The encrypted data is likely to contain strange characters, including nulls. The TextBox will truncate the encrypted string if it encounters a null, so it cannot be relied on to hold the entire string of encrypted data.

Data Compression/Decompression

Years ago, data compression was important because computer resources (memory and disk space) were limited. The more that could be fit into the same space, the better. Data compression started to become commonplace. Installation disks almost always contained compressed files, and no computer hobbyist could do without a copy of the latest file compression utility. Even the data on hard disks was compressed using programs like Stacker or DoubleSpace.

Data compression is still important today, if perhaps for different reasons. Programs are now typically distributed on CD-ROM, and compression is often not really a major concern because the disk can hold so much data (though CD-ROMs that are nowhere near being full usually have their data compressed anyway). Multi-gigabyte hard disks are now common, so the number of systems that use drive-compression utilities is dwindling. These days, the importance of data compression is no longer so much a matter of storage space, but of speed.

Telecommunications, in particular communication over the Internet, is more popular than ever before. And although efforts are being made to provide better and faster methods of telecommunications for the masses, many computers still connect to online services via dial-up connections that use relatively low-speed modems. This is where data compression becomes vitally important. Compressed data takes far less time to transfer than non-compressed data, meaning that accessing online services is faster. And the faster that information can be obtained, the better.

Data compression is still important; there's no doubt about that. Still, few programmers know how compression is achieved. There are two main reasons for this. The first is that there are several third-party controls and products that provide data compression and decompression services, so the programmer doesn't have to worry about how compression works, only that it does work. The second reason is perhaps more obvious: it's complicated. Data compression and decompression algorithms can be difficult to understand.

So why would you want to even fool around with trying to do data compression yourself? For one thing, there might be times when you can't find an ActiveX control that will do exactly what you want it to do. Most controls that offer compression/decompression services apply only to files. You might need to compress a data stream instead. Or you might not want the overhead that comes with an ActiveX control. Whatever the reason, it helps to know a little about how data compression can be achieved. This section discusses some standard methods used for data compression and details one of the simpler compression algorithms.

Code Table Optimization

One of the easiest methods for compressing data is to use a technique known as Code Table Optimization. Basically, Code Table Optimization works on a simple premise: instead of using 8 bits to store a character, you use less than that, say 5 or 6 bits. Using 5 bits enables you to store values between 0 and 31; 6 bits gives you double the range, with values between 0 and 63. The main drawback here is obvious: you can only store a limited number of ASCII characters using this method. However, it is relatively easy to code and gives you a 25 percent or 37.5 percent compression rate every time, depending on how many bits you use.

Huffman Compression

Huffman Compression uses a technique somewhat similar to Code Table Optimization. It also stores characters using a smaller number of bits, though it uses a more intelligent way of determining how the bits should be used. The Huffman Compression method scans a file (or data stream) and figures out which characters are used most often. This is usually accomplished using a binary tree, with the least-used characters being sifted to the bottom nodes of the tree. After each character's "weight," or number of times it occurs, has been established, it is assigned a binary code. The more common a character, the shorter the binary code. For example, the most frequently used characters might be assigned a two-digit (two-bit) binary code. The next most frequent characters would be assigned three-digit binary codes, and so on. The binary codes are combined and strung together, resulting in a compressed version of the original data. A table that defines the binary codes that were used is also included with the compressed data so that the seemingly random string of bits can be decoded and uncompressed.

Lemple-Ziv-Welch (LZW)

One of the more popular (and more efficient) compression methods is Lempel-Ziv-Welch or LZW Compression. LZW often provides the best results, but it is also more complicated than the other methods.

The LZW method creates a table of "shorthand" codes that stand for pieces of the data being compressed. The data is examined character by character. If a unique combination of characters is found, they are assigned a new code and are added to the shorthand table. When like character combinations are found, their shorthand code is written out instead of the characters themselves. This "tokenizing" of character phrases often results in a high compression rate.

Because LZW compression is so complicated, a more detailed discussion of how it works is beyond the scope of this chapter. Several documents on the Internet explain it, so do a few searches there for more information.

Run-Length Encoding (RLE)

Run-Length Encoding or RLE is a comparatively simple compression algorithm that yields high rates of compression for certain kinds of data, particularly graphics. RLE simply replaces subsequent characters that are repeated more than twice with two bytes: one to indicate how many times the character repeats (the "manager" byte), and one for the character itself. The manager byte is differentiated from other bytes because its uppermost bit is set. This allows the other seven bits of the byte to hold the number of characters that are repeated, a possible value of 0 through 127. Because no repeat character sequences of zero are possible, 1 can be added to the character count, giving an actual possible value range of 1 through 128.

If a character has its uppermost bit set, then it might be mistaken as a manager byte. To get around this, any character with its uppermost bit set is always assigned a manager byte that indicates a count of one.

This can be confusing, so let's look at an example. Take the following string of hexadecimal values that represent the string "AAABCCCCCCDDDD":

```
41h 41h 41h 42h 43h 43h 43h 43h 43h 43h 44h 44h 44h 44h
```

The first three bytes (41h 41h 41h) can be compressed down to two bytes, a manager byte indicating the count (3) and a byte for the character (41h). The result would be: 82h 41h. The 82h in binary is 10000010, a value (character count) of two with the uppermost bit set. Remember that the character count has 1 added to it, so a value of 2 actually represents 3. The compressed data (82h 41h) can be written out.

Moving along in the data, the next character (42h) only appears once. No compression can be done on that, so the character can be written out without modification.

Next in the data are six characters that have the same value, 43h. Again, this can be compressed down to two bytes, a manager byte and the character. The manager byte in this case will be 85h, which is 10000101 in binary. The last three bits (101) indicate that the count is 5, which will have 1 added to it, giving a count of 6. So the next two bytes written out are: 85h 43h.

The next four characters are also repeats, so they too will get summed up in two bytes: 83h and 44h. This gives us a complete output of:

```
82h 41h 42h 85h 43h 83h 44h
```

The original 14 bytes have been compressed down to 7, giving a 50 percent compression rate. Not too bad!

As mentioned earlier, if a character byte with its uppermost bit set is encountered, it gets assigned its own manager byte. Therefore, the character byte F5h would be written out as two bytes (80h and F5h). This is only if the character byte appears only once and is not repeated. If it is repeated, it gets counted just like any other character.

You might be wondering what happens when a character count is greater than 128, the largest value that can be stored in the manager byte. That's a good question that is easily answered. The first 128 occurrences of the character get the manager byte and the character byte, as usual. The remainder of the characters are then treated as if the first 128 bytes weren't even processed. If there are enough characters to be assigned a manager byte, then that's what happens. Otherwise, the characters are written out as is.

As you can imagine, Run-Length Encoding only works well on data that has many repeat character sequences. Text files seldom yield good results with RLE, but other data such as graphics usually do quite well.

To illustrate how the RLE Compression method can be coded, two sample functions have been included (see Listing 36.3). They each accept two arguments that specify the names of TextBox controls. The RLECompress& function compresses any data that is in the TextBox control indicated by its first argument and displays the compressed data in the TextBox indicated by its second argument. The RLEUncompress& function uncompresses the data in the TextBox indicated by its first argument and displays the uncompressed data in the TextBox indicated by its second argument.

LISTING 36.3.   CH36-03.TXT—THE RLECompress AND RLEUncompress ROUTINES, WHICH BOTH TAKE TWO TEXTBOX CONTROLS AS ARGUMENTS AND COMPRESS OR UNCOMPRESS THE CONTENTS OF ONE TEXTBOX AND PLACE THE RESULTS IN THE OTHER.

```
Public Sub RLECompress(txtDataIn As TextBox, _
    txtDataOut As TextBox)

Dim intCharCount As Integer
Dim intNewChar As Integer
Dim intLastChar As Integer
Dim intCharLoop As Integer
Dim lonCharPtr As Long
Dim lonCharStrLen As Long
Dim strCompressed As String
Dim bytMgrChar As Byte

intCharCount = -1
lonCharStrLen = Len(txtDataIn.Text)

' Loop through the contents of the TextBox
' character by character. The loop is executed
' an additional time to process the last
' character.
For lonCharPtr = 1 To (lonCharStrLen + 1)
```

```
' If this is not the last loop, then
' intNewChar is assigned the character that
' is read in. Otherwise, a -1 value indicates
' that it is the last loop.
If lonCharPtr < lonCharStrLen + 1 Then
    intNewChar = Asc(Mid(txtDataIn.Text, _
        lonCharPtr, 1))
Else
    intNewChar = -1
End If
' Add one to the character count.
intCharCount = intCharCount + 1
If lonCharPtr > 1 Then
    ' Same character as last time?
    If intNewChar = intLastChar Then
        ' Is the character's high bit set?
        If intCharCount = 128 Then
            ' If high bit is set, then the
            ' character will get its own
            ' manager byte. Assign the count
            ' to zero (count is always one
            ' less than actual).
            bytMgrChar = 128
            bytMgrChar = bytMgrChar Or 127
            ' Add the manager byte and the
            ' character to the output string.
            strCompressed = strCompressed _
                & Chr(bytMgrChar) & Chr(intLastChar)
            ' Set the character count to zero.
            intCharCount = 0
        End If
    Else
        ' The character read this time is
        ' different than the one read last time,
        ' so check to see if the character count
        ' is more than two.
        If intCharCount > 2 Then
            ' The character count is more than
            ' two, so this character sequence
            ' can get a manager byte. Set the
            ' count to one less than actual.
            bytMgrChar = 128
            bytMgrChar = bytMgrChar Or (intCharCount - 1)
            ' Add the manager byte and the
            ' character to the output string.
            strCompressed = strCompressed _
                & Chr(bytMgrChar) & Chr(intLastChar)
        Else
            ' Two of the same characters have
            ' been encountered, but that's not
            ' enough to warrant a manager byte.
```

continues

LISTING 36.3. CONTINUED

```
                    ' Add the two characters to the
                    ' output string.
                    For intCharLoop = 1 To intCharCount
                        ' Check to see if the character
                        ' has its high bit set. If
                        ' it does, it'll have to have a
                        ' manager byte.
                        If bytLastChar > 127 Then
                            bytOutChar = 128
                            bytOutChar = bytOutChar Or (intCharCount - 1)
                            strCompressed = strCompressed _
                                & Chr(bytMgrChar) & Chr(intLastChar)
                        Else
                            ' The character does not have
                            ' its high bits set, so it
                            ' can be added to the output.
                            strCompressed = strCompressed _
                                & Chr(intLastChar)
                        End If
                    Next intCharLoop
                End If
                ' Reset the character count.
                intCharCount = 0
            End If
        End If
        ' Make the most recently read character the
        ' last character so it can be checked in
        ' the next loop iteration.
        intLastChar = intNewChar
    Next lonCharPtr

    ' Assign the compressed string to the output
    ' TextBox.
    txtDataOut.Text = strCompressed

End Sub


Public Sub RLEUncompress(txtDataIn As TextBox, _
    txtDataOut As TextBox)

Dim bytNewChar As Byte
Dim intCharCount As Integer
Dim lonCharPtr As Long
Dim strUncompressed As String

lonCharPtr = 0
Do
    ' Increment the character pointer.
```

```
        lonCharPtr = lonCharPtr + 1
        ' Get the next character.
        bytNewChar = Asc(Mid(txtDataIn.Text, lonCharPtr, 1))
        ' Is the high bit set?
        If bytNewChar > 127 Then
            ' The high bit is set, so it must be a
            ' manager byte. Get the character count.
            intCharCount = (bytNewChar And 127) + 1
            ' Get the next character.
            lonCharPtr = lonCharPtr + 1
            bytNewChar = Asc(Mid(txtDataIn.Text, lonCharPtr, 1))
            ' Add the string of characters to the
            ' output string.
            strUncompressed = strUncompressed _
                & String(intCharCount, bytNewChar)
        Else
            ' This is a solo character (no manager
            ' byte), so add it to the output string.
            strUncompressed = strUncompressed _
                & Chr(bytNewChar)
        End If
    ' Keep looping until the last character has
    ' been processed.
    Loop Until (lonCharPtr >= Len(txtDataIn.Text))

    ' Assign the uncompressed string to the output
    ' TextBox.
    txtDataOut.Text = strUncompressed

End Sub
```

To try out these routines, you could create a simple form with two text boxes (txtDecrypted and txtEncrypted, for example) and two command buttons. When one button is pressed, you can pass the names of the text boxes (txtDecryped, txtEncrypted) to the RLECompress procedure. The string in the first text box will be encrypted and the results will be placed in the second text box. When the second button is pressed, you can pass the names of the text boxes (txtEncrypted, txtDecrypted) to the RLEUncompress procedure. The encrypted data in the first text box is decrypted and placed in the second text box.

Of course, you can modify these routines to compress and uncompress things other than the contents of a TextBox. Also, if you're going to be reading in data from a disk file, you wouldn't want to read it in a byte at a time. Instead, you would want to read in large chunks of the file into memory and then process the chunks byte by byte using the preceding routines.

Summary

Visual Basic is often ignored as a serious development platform, so it is often difficult for VB programmers to find information about common data processing tasks in a language they can understand. This chapter discusses some of the more commonly used algorithms in the areas of sorting, data encryption, and data compression. It also provides sample code for implementing sorts, encryption, and compression into your own programs.

Differences Between VBA and VB6

by Rob Thayer

IN THIS CHAPTER

- An Overview of VBA   *876*

An Overview of VBA

Visual Basic for Applications, or VBA, has come into vogue during the past few years. When Microsoft started integrating VBA into its popular Office suite of applications, VBA came into the limelight as the new standard for macro languages. By including VBA with applications such as Word, Excel, PowerPoint, and Project, Microsoft combined the flexibility and ease of programming that Visual Basic offers with the power of the application that hosts it.

Microsoft has also begun licensing Visual Basic to other software developers, meaning that VBA will be used in more applications than just the ones created by Microsoft. Visio and AutoCAD are just two examples of companies that have licensed VBA for use in their own applications.

Even though VBA parallels Visual Basic in many ways, VB developers might still be unfamiliar with the intricacies of the macro language. Indeed, the first question a VB programmer is likely to ask before trying to use VBA is, "What's the difference between the version of Visual Basic that I'm familiar with and VBA?" This chapter answers that important question.

As a Visual Basic programmer, you are no doubt aware of the possibilities (and limitations) inherent with VB; that is, you know what Visual Basic can do and what it cannot do. You've worked with VB extensively and have come to know all its little perks and quirks.

At face value, VBA is much like Visual Basic. The two development environments, or IDEs, look similar at first glance. But after a closer look, you'll see some minor differences.

VBA is also a lot like Visual Basic on the inside, but once again, there are differences. VBA is not as full-featured as Visual Basic, but that stands to reason. After all, VBA is not a full-fledged development environment; it is a macro language. This brings up an important point. Before VBA can be exploited, the role that it plays must be understood.

What VBA Is and Is Not

The first thing that differentiates VBA from Visual Basic is the fact that VBA is designed to function as a macro language, whereas Visual Basic is designed as a way of creating applications and program components. VBA cannot create compiled executable code like Visual Basic. VBA projects can only run within their host application. For example, if a VBA project is created to work with Excel (its host application), then it can only be executed within the Excel application.

So what can VBA do, and what is it used for? VBA is used to enhance or extend its host application in some way, such as adding new functions to Excel or changing Word's menu structure by adding new options or removing the ones you don't want to see. VBA can also be used to facilitate communication and interoperability between applications that support VBA. For example, you could use VBA to read an Access database and transfer that information to a Word document. The possibilities are endless.

The VBA Development Environment

One area of difference between VBA and Visual Basic is in the development environment, or IDE. Compare the IDE for VBA (see Figure 37.1) with that of Visual Basic (see Figure 37.2). You'll notice several things right away.

FIGURE 37.1.

The VBA develop-ment environment, or IDE.

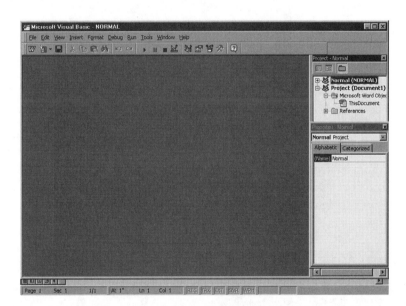

> **NOTE**
>
> The VBA environment depicted in Figure 37.1 and in the rest of this chapter shows the Project and Properties windows on the right side of the screen. However, when you use VBA for the first time, they might be on the left side of the screen. Like Visual Basic, VBA also enables you to determine where your windows will be placed. You can move them to the right side if that is more familiar to you.

FIGURE 37.2.
VB6's development environment.

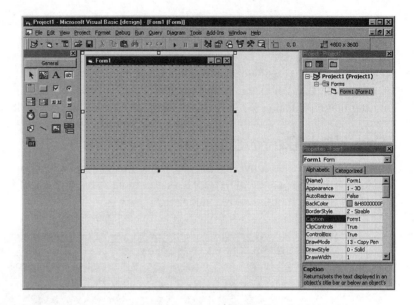

For one thing, VBA does not provide a blank Form or container object right away like most Visual Basic projects do. Instead, you have to add a Form yourself (although in VBA, forms are called UserForms, which will be discussed later).

Also, you'll notice that the Toolbox is missing. VBA does have a Toolbox (see Figure 37.3), but it does not appear until a UserForm object has been added to the project. VBA's Toolbox is not dockable, like VB's Toolbox is. Instead, it exists in a floating window.

FIGURE 37.3.
VBA's floating Toolbox, which is not visible until a UserForm object has been added to the project.

The controls included in VBA's Toolbox are different from those in Visual Basic, as you can see. The controls in the VBA Toolbox come from the Microsoft Forms 2.0 control library, which includes versions of many of VB's standard controls: Label, TextBox, ComboBox, ListBox, OptionButton, Frame, CommandButton, and Image. It also includes one of the VB Professional controls (TabStrip). The HScrollBar and VScrollBar controls used in Visual Basic have been combined into a single ScrollBar control, and the ToggleButton, Multipage, and SpinButton controls have been added.

As in Visual Basic, VBA's Toolbox can be modified by adding and removing controls. However, VBA does not support all ActiveX controls.

Another difference between the development environments for VBA and Visual Basic is in their menu bars. VB's Project menu has been replaced with the Insert menu in VBA. Both provide similar services, enabling you to insert new objects such as `Forms` (`UserForms` in VBA) and Class Modules into the current project. However, VB's Project menu has many more insertable objects than VBA.

Missing from VBA's menu bar is the Add-Ins menu item. There's a good reason for this: VBA does not support the same kind of Add-Ins that are supported in Visual Basic. In VBA, the AddIn object is a member of the AddIns collection. This collection contains all of the Add-Ins available to the host application, whether they're currently loaded or not. The AddIns collection includes global templates or Word Add-In Libraries (WLLs). These Add-Ins are displayed in the Templates and Add-Ins dialog box that can be accessed from VBA's Tools menu.

The VBA and VB menu bars differ in other ways too. For example, VBA's File menu is quite different from the File menu in Visual Basic. VBA files and projects themselves cannot be saved or loaded, so there are no options to facilitate this. VBA projects are saved with their host document or document template and do not exist separately. The only way to share VBA forms and modules with other VBA projects is by importing and exporting them. Options for Import and Export are included in VBA's File menu.

The toolbars of Visual Basic and VBA are different too. VBA adds a few new icons, such as the one that switches back to the host application. In Figure 37.1, this is the leftmost icon on the toolbar, which shows a Microsoft Word logo. Other icons are missing from VBA's Toolbar. For example, the Menu Editor icon is not on the VBA Toolbar because that tool is not included in VBA.

You can see that there are many differences between the Visual Basic and VBA design environments. Some are apparent right away, but others are hidden.

Programming Differences

Probably the best way to illustrate how Visual Basic and VBA differ in the way they are programmed is to create two separate but similar projects, one using Visual Basic and one using VBA. The first project will be created in Visual Basic. It will be so simple that you probably won't even want to try it out.

The VB program uses a `TextBox` control and a `CommandButton` control. When the `CommandButton` is clicked, the text in the TextBox is parsed (separated into words) and reversed. For example, if the phrase *Let the fun begin* was entered, it would be changed to *begin fun the Let*. Not the most useful program, to be sure, but it will serve to illustrate the differences between a VB and a VBA program.

> **NOTE**
>
> In this text, VBA projects are often referred to as *programs*. However, in VBA they are usually called *macros*. In this context, you can think of a macro and a program as being synonymous.

The interface for the VB program will look like the one in Figure 37.4 and as stated earlier it will use one TextBox control (txtInputArea) and one CommandButton control (cmdReverse). Listing 37.1 shows all the code for the program:

FIGURE 37.4.

The user interface for the Visual Basic version of the Reverse Text program.

LISTING 37.1. CH37-01.TXT—THE CODE FOR THE VISUAL BASIC VERSION OF THE REVERSE TEXT PROGRAM.

```
Private Sub cmdReverse_Click()

Dim intSpacePos As Integer
Dim intLastPos As Integer
Dim strNewWord As String
Dim strNewText As String

' You can set this value depending on your preferences.
' If you want to have this routine strip out any non-
' alphanumeric characters (A-Z, a-z, 0-9, Space), then
' set it to True. Otherwise, set it to False.
booAlphanumericOnly = True

' If there's nothing in the text box, exit the routine.
If txtInputArea.Text = "" Then Exit Sub

' Add a space to the end of the text so it can parse
' the last word.
txtInputArea.Text = txtInputArea.Text & Chr(32)

' Parse the contents of the text box (txtInputArea).
Do
```

```
        intSpacePos = InStr(intLastPos + 1, _
            txtInputArea.Text, Chr(32))
    If intSpacePos Then
        strNewWord = Mid(txtInputArea.Text, _
            intLastPos + 1, intSpacePos - intLastPos)
        ' Strip out non-alphanumeric characters?
        If booAlphanumericOnly Then
            strNewWord = StripPunctuation(strNewWord)
        End If
        ' Add the new word to the front of the string,
        ' so the string of words becomes reversed.
        strNewText = strNewWord & strNewText
    End If
    intLastPos = intSpacePos
Loop Until (intSpacePos = 0)

' Assign the new string (which should be reversed) back
' to the text box.
txtInputArea.Text = strNewText

End Sub


Function StripPunctuation(strWordIn) As String

Dim bytChar As Byte
Dim intCharPos As Integer
Dim strNoPuncWord As String

strNoPuncWord = ""

' Loop through the current word and discard anything
' that isn't alphanumeric or a space.
For intCharPos = 1 To Len(strWordIn)
    bytChar = Asc(Mid(strWordIn, intCharPos, 1))
    Select Case bytChar
        Case 32:
            ' Add spaces (ASCII 32).
            strNoPuncWord = strNoPuncWord & Chr(32)
        Case 48 To 57:
            ' Add characters 0-9 (ASCII 48-57).
            strNoPuncWord = strNoPuncWord & Chr(bytChar)
        Case 65 To 90:
            ' Add characters A-Z (ASCII 65-90).
            strNoPuncWord = strNoPuncWord & Chr(bytChar)
        Case 97 To 122:
            ' Add characters a-z (ASCII 97-122).
            strNoPuncWord = strNoPuncWord & Chr(bytChar)
    End Select
Next intCharPos
```

continues

LISTING 37.1. CONTINUED

```
StripPunctuation = strNoPuncWord

End Function
```

Although the code is somewhat lengthy, the program is still simple. It loops through the text in the text box (`txtInputArea`) looking for spaces (also known as *parsing*). When it finds a space, it extracts a word and adds it to the beginning of a string (`strNewText`). When the loop is done, `strNewText` contains all the words in the text box, except reversed.

A Boolean variable (`booAlphanumericOnly`) is used to determine whether nonalphanumeric characters should be stripped out of the string. If alphanumeric characters, such as punctuation, are left in, then the text string, *This is a test.* would be reversed to *test. a is This*. Stripping out the nonalphanumeric characters fixes this and results in *test a is This*. If `booAlphanumericOnly` is set to `True`, then the function `StripPunctuation` is called during the parsing loop. It strips out any unwanted characters.

If you want to try out the Visual Basic program, go ahead. Just remember to call the `TextBox` control `txtInputArea` and the `CommandButton` control `cmdReverse`.

Next, a similar program will be created using VBA. Instead of using text entered into a `TextBox`, however, the VBA program will use any currently selected text. The host application will be Microsoft Word, so you can select any text you want reversed in a document and then invoke the program and have it do its thing.

To implement the reverse text processing code in VBA, start up the host application, which in this case will be Microsoft Word. Choose Tools | Macro and then select Macro from the pop-up window (or press the shortcut key, Alt+F8). This will display the Macros dialog box (see Figure 37.5), which lists all the macros available for the current document. Unless the document that you are using was generated from a template that included macros or you have been fooling around with VBA on your own, the list of macros should be empty.

To create a new macro, type in a name (*ReverseText* is suggested) and click the `Create` button. After a few moments, Word brings you directly to the VBA environment. It also provides you with an empty Sub procedure for your new macro as well as comment lines that indicate when the macro was created (see Figure 37.6).

FIGURE 37.5.

The Macro dialog box, which lists all the macros available to the current document.

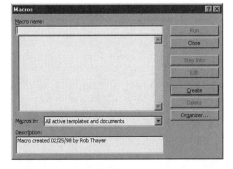

FIGURE 37.6.

When you add a new macro, the VBA environment is called up and an empty Sub *procedure is added for you.*

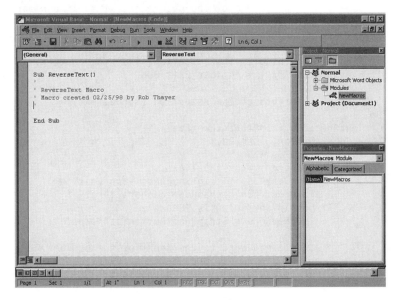

You can now add the code for the ReverseText Sub procedure (see Listing 37.2). This is essentially the same code that was used with the VB version of the program, but with a few minor—but important—changes.

LISTING 37.2. CH37-02.TXT—THE CODE FOR THE ReverseText SUB PROCEDURE, A MICROSOFT WORD MACRO.

```
Sub ReverseText()
'
' ReverseText Macro
' Macro created 02/25/98 by Rob Thayer
'
Dim intSpacePos As Integer
```

continues

LISTING 37.2. CONTINUED

```
Dim intLastPos As Integer
Dim strNewWord As String
Dim strNewText As String
Dim strSelText As String

' You can set this value depending on your preferences.
' If you want to have this routine strip out any non-
' alphanumeric characters (A-Z, a-z, 0-9, Space), then
' set it to True. Otherwise, set it to False.
booAlphanumericOnly = True

' Add a space to the end of the selected text so it can parse
' the last word.
strSelText = Word.Selection & Chr(32)

' If there's nothing in the selection, exit the routine.
If RTrim(strSelText) = "" Then Exit Sub

' Parse the contents of the selection (strSelText).
Do
    intSpacePos = InStr(intLastPos + 1, _
        strSelText, Chr(32))
    If intSpacePos Then
        strNewWord = Mid(strSelText, _
            intLastPos + 1, intSpacePos - intLastPos)
        ' Strip out non-alphanumeric characters?
        If booAlphanumericOnly Then
            strNewWord = StripPunctuation(strNewWord)
        End If
        ' Add the new word to the front of the string,
        ' so the string of words becomes reversed.
        strNewText = strNewWord & strNewText
    End If
    intLastPos = intSpacePos
Loop Until (intSpacePos = 0)

' Assign the new string (which should be reversed) back
' to the selection.
Word.Selection = strNewText

End Sub
```

The biggest difference here is that the txtInputArea control is no longer used to provide the text to be processed. Instead, a new string (strSelText) is used. It gets its value from another object, Word.Selection. This is important, and it merits further discussion.

In VBA, you often utilize objects and classes from the host application (in this case, Word). All the Office97 applications use a wide variety of different objects. In Word, there is a `Documents` collection, a `Document` object, an `ActiveDocument` object, and many others. There is also a `Selection` object, which is being used here. The `Selection` object contains any text currently selected. These objects make up the application's object model, which can be used to interact with the application from within other OLE programs.

The VBA macro you are constructing here is applied to the current selection. However, it could just as easily be applied to the entire document if, instead of assigning `strSelText` the value of `Word.Selection`, it was assigned the value of `Word.ActiveDocument.Content`, which refers to the entire content of the active document. Using the current selection, however, makes more sense.

To become fluent in using VBA, you must be familiar with the various objects and classes implemented in the host application or applications for which you want to create macros. This is a key point. You wouldn't be able to use Visual Basic effectively if you did not have an understanding of VB's objects (forms, text boxes, command buttons, and so on). Likewise, you cannot use VBA effectively if you do not understand the objects available to it. A discussion of Office97 objects and classes is beyond the scope of this chapter. Consult a book on VBA programming for more information (*Using Visual Basic for Applications Special Edition* by Que Publishing is recommended).

To continue with the VBA project, the `StripPunctuation` function needs to be added next (see Listing 37.3). This is identical to the function used in the Visual Basic project created earlier.

LISTING 37.3. CH37-03.TXT—THE `StripPunctuation` FUNCTION, WHICH IS USED BY THE `ReverseText` SUB PROCEDURE (A WORD MACRO).

```
Function StripPunctuation(strWordIn) As String

Dim bytChar As Byte
Dim intCharPos As Integer
Dim strNoPuncWord As String

strNoPuncWord = ""

' Loop through the current word and discard anything
' that isn't alphanumeric or a space.
For intCharPos = 1 To Len(strWordIn)
    bytChar = Asc(Mid(strWordIn, intCharPos, 1))
    Select Case bytChar
        Case 32:
            ' Add spaces (ASCII 32).
            strNoPuncWord = strNoPuncWord & Chr(32)
        Case 48 To 57:
```

continues

LISTING 37.3. CONTINUED

```
               ' Add characters 0-9 (ASCII 48-57).
               strNoPuncWord = strNoPuncWord & Chr(bytChar)
          Case 65 To 90:
               ' Add characters A-Z (ASCII 65-90).
               strNoPuncWord = strNoPuncWord & Chr(bytChar)
          Case 97 To 122:
               ' Add characters a-z (ASCII 97-122).
               strNoPuncWord = strNoPuncWord & Chr(bytChar)
     End Select
Next intCharPos

StripPunctuation = strNoPuncWord

End Function
```

To try out the macro, exit VBA (don't worry; you won't lose your work) and go back to the Word document. Type in some text and then select it (see Figure 37.7). Press Alt+F8 to display the Macro dialog box. Note that the ReverseText macro is now listed.

FIGURE 37.7.

Selected text in Microsoft Word, which will be processed by the ReverseText macro.

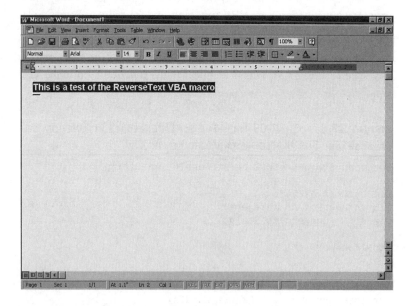

With the ReverseText macro selected, click the Run button. The ReverseText procedure will then be executed, and the selected text will be reversed (see Figure 37.8).

FIGURE 37.8.

The selected text is reversed using the ReverseText *macro.)*

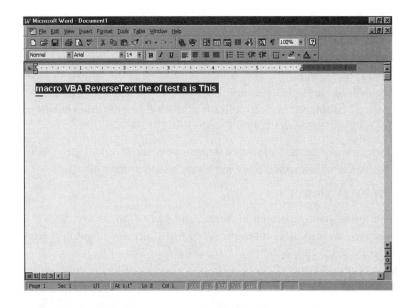

> **NOTE**
>
> The ReverseText macro is somewhat limited in that it is only designed to work with single lines of selected text. Modifications to facilitate the handling of multiple lines of text can be made relatively easily, but were not included originally in an attempt to keep the code as simple as possible.

As you can see, the VBA macro and the VB program created earlier do basically the same thing; they are just implemented differently. To review, note the differences between the VB and VBA projects:

- The VB program uses the contents of a TextBox control for the text to be processed. The VBA macro uses the Word object Word.Selection. With VBA, a user interface like the one in VB could have also been constructed using a form and a text box. However, it is often more desirable to perform the necessary operation without requiring any additional user intervention; thus, the operation is directly performed on the selected text in the example.

- In the VB program, the main processing code is contained in a command button's Click event. In the VBA macro, the code is contained in a Sub procedure.

- The VB program uses a form with controls for its user interface. The VBA macro works from within its host application (Microsoft Word). Essentially, Word is utilized as its user interface.

Consider the last difference pointed out in the preceding list. The VBA macro has no user interface. Instead, it uses Microsoft Word and works "behind the scenes." Of course, this is not always the case. There might be times when you want a user interface to be displayed, perhaps to enable the user to select different options or customize the macro that will be performed. Because VBA works with a host application, a form is not automatically displayed by default like it is in a VB program. So how do you implement a form-like interface in VBA?

First, you design the form—that much is obvious. In VBA, a form is called a UserForm. To display it, you would use a line of code such as the following:

```
UserForm1.Show
```

This code would be placed in the Sub procedure of the macro. So if it were to display a form for the ReverseText macro, the ReverseText Sub might look like this:

```
Sub ReverseText()

    UserForm1.Show

End Sub
```

The form (UserForm1) could contain controls that in turn call other procedures or respond to events, just like they do in Visual Basic. After forms are used, VBA becomes easier to understand to VB programmers.

As you get into VBA and start developing more complex macros, you'll find other differences from Visual Basic. But by using what you've learned in this chapter, you should have an understanding of how VBA works. Your skills as a VB programmer will take you the rest of the way.

Summary

Visual Basic and VBA are development environments that are both similar and different. Because VBA is a macro language and relies on a host application (such as Microsoft Word or Excel), the concept of a standalone executable program is not feasible in VBA.

VBA has some differences that might at first be confusing to VB programmers. However, after a few sample VBA macros are constructed, Visual Basic developers should have no problem adapting to VBA.

This chapter is designed to introduce VB programmers to VBA. It presents two similar programs, one created in Visual Basic and the other as a VBA macro, to illustrate how the two environments differ.

Programming for Microsoft Transaction Server

by Loren Eidahl

IN THIS CHAPTER

- **Understanding Distributed Transaction Processing   890**

- **Introducing Microsoft Transaction Server   893**

- **Integrating Visual Basic Classes with Transaction Server 896**

- **Calling Transaction Server Objects from Visual Basic 908**

It seems like the only topic that is discussed more than the Internet is client/server applications using n-tier technology. Applications that use n-tier architecture can be divided into at least three separate and distinct parts. These parts typically include separate interface, logic, and database functions. The main reason for developing applications that use this architecture is scalability and the ease in which the application can be upgraded. As a result, client/server applications provide a much higher level of performance than non-client/server applications. The traditional client/server model only supported two tiers, the client and the server. Now, with the advent of n-tier client/server architecture, we can develop applications that more closely follow the object-oriented paradigm. The n-tier is a superior application architecture because of the following:

- Scalability—The capability of an application architecture to scale up to hundreds of simultaneous users.

- Manageability—The ease with which problems can be isolated, updates distributed, and configurations managed.

- Transparency—The capability to switch server processing from one particular computer to another, as dictated by scheduled or unexpected system outages.

In this chapter, you take a look at Microsoft's Transaction Server and find out how you can use it to build applications. You will also learn how the Transaction Server and Visual Basic 6 can be used to build large, robust, distributed applications.

Understanding Distributed Transaction Processing

One of the key differences between traditional, or two-tier, client/server models and second generation, or n-tier (where *n* is any number greater than two) client/server architectures is in the use of what is known as middleware. Some of the most popular kinds of middleware are Transaction Monitors and Object Request Brokers (ORB). Microsoft's Transaction Server is a combination of these two technologies, providing you with a flexible and powerful middleware component that can be used to build very large-scale distributed processing applications with minimal coding and configuration effort on your part. The typical three-tier architecture is composed of the following three tiers:

- The presentation tier—This tier consists primarily of the user-interface and runs on the desktop computer.

- The business-logic tier—This tier consists of shared application processing logic modules and runs on one or more application servers. Each of these application servers is connected to multiple desktop computers. This middle tier also contains the data services implemented by data objects that facilitate the connection between the business objects and the third tier, the database server.

- The data server tier—This is also known as the database server. There is usually one database server serving multiple application servers. If there are multiple database servers, they are normally spread out over a large geographical area with the common data replicated between them.

Before we begin, let's take a look at a common scenario that applies to a large number of businesses today. Imagine that your company has several independent database systems: one for maintaining the current inventory in the company warehouse, one for maintaining all items that have been requisitioned and should be arriving on the receiving dock, and a third database for maintaining customer orders and shipping information.

In this company, when an order comes in, the order is entered into the order entry system, which produces a shipping order. This order is then taken to the warehouse, where each item in the order is removed and taken to the shipping dock to be packaged and sent to the customer. While at the warehouse, the employee filling the order finds that one or two items are out of stock. The employee then takes the order to the requisition department and back-orders the missing items for later shipping.

At each of these points, the individual systems have to be updated. Even the Shipping Dock system has to be updated to produce an accurate shipping bill-of-lading, which correctly reflects the back-ordered items.

This seems like a lot of wasted and duplicated effort. Wouldn't it make a lot more sense to connect all of these systems so that they could all exchange the necessary information to perform most of these tasks themselves? If you put a network in place and connect all of these systems to the network, the potential for these systems to exchange the appropriate information can be realized.

Unfortunately, anyone who has attempted to connect separate systems in this way knows that after you have all of the systems on a network, the work is just beginning. Enabling all of these systems to work together is what middleware is all about.

Transaction Monitors

The original idea behind the client/server computing model was to split the application processing between two computers, the client and the server. The server portion of the application tended to handle the database-centric tasks, whereas the client portion of the application handled the everyday processing of the transactions. The split of the application performed reasonably well until a situation arose that allowed more data to be returned from the server than the client could process. The failure by the client to adequately process this data would cause the server to slow down and possibly crash. Computers today are less prone to the memory and hard drive restrictions of their distant pre-Pentium cousins.

As the number of active users of these early client/server systems increases, the workload on the database increases. A normal application maintains an open connection to the database server during the entire time the application is running. This requires that the database server have additional processing power to service all of those open connections, even if they are sitting idle. This also increases the cost associated with the database itself, as most traditional database license prices are based on the number of users that can be connected to the database simultaneously.

As the number of databases with which an application needs to interact increases, the number of open connections that the application must maintain also increases. This adds to the processing load on the client computer, as well as the network management and configuration. The total number of connections that must be maintained can be calculated as the number of clients multiplied by the number of database servers to which the client connects.

This is a lot of configuration information that has to be maintained for each client computer. If one of the databases that an application uses has to be taken offline and the backup database brought online, the configuration of each and every client that connects to the database has to be updated to reflect the new database server (with care taken not to update the wrong database server information).

This is one of the primary problems that Transaction Monitors were designed to solve. A Transaction Monitor goes between the client systems and the database servers. Each of the clients maintains a single connection to the Transaction Monitor instead of the database servers. Likewise, the Transaction Monitor maintains connections to each of the database servers. This enables the Transaction Monitor to act as a traffic cop, passing each database query or update to the appropriate database, and to maintain only as many open database connections as are currently required, which enables the database servers to run more efficiently.

Object Request Brokers

Object Request Brokers (ORBs) fall into a different category of middleware from Transaction Monitors. ORBs provide location transparency to application modules and services. *Location transparency* occurs when an application needs to interact with a server process; the application does not need to know where that specific server process is located on the network. The only process of which the application knows the location is the ORB client stub, located on the same machine as the application.

The ORB knows where all server processes are running, or on which machines the server processes can be run. If a particular server process is not running when an application requests access to it, the ORB starts the server process on one of the machines for which the process is configured to run. The client application does not know on which server the requested process is running, or if the server process is even running. The ORB keeps track of all server processes for the client applications. The ORB can even perform load balancing between two or more servers running the same process, so that each of the servers is servicing about the same number of requests.

Taking another look at the catalog sales company, it is reasonable to expect that the order entry system would make use of various services that could be located on a series of servers on the company network. One of these services could be a sales tax engine, which calculates the tax for each of the customer orders. It makes sense to keep this set of calculations on a server because tax laws have a tendency to change. By keeping this processing module on the server, it would be a lot easier to update in this one location every time the tax laws changed, as opposed to having to update every order entry work-station in the company.

Additional services might include a business rules system. The business rules system would perform basic calculations such as inventory adjustments, minimum purchase requirements, and shipping-related costs. By keeping the systems on their own servers, you have the flexibility to perform updates when the business rules change.

Considering that the functions provided by these server modules are critical to the core business of your catalog sales company, it's important to make sure that these modules are always available for the order entry systems. To make sure that these systems have high availability, they should be mirrored onto more than one system. If the order entry application made direct accesses to these services, then each copy of the application would have to know which machines each of these services are running on at all times. By using an ORB, the individual copies of the order entry application don't know and don't care on which servers any of these services are running. The ORB takes care of making the connections and passing the results back to the order entry application.

Introducing Microsoft Transaction Server

Microsoft's Transaction Server is somewhat of a cross between a Transaction Monitor and an ORB, although it tends to lean more towards the ORB set of functionality. If you are running an application on a Windows NT system that has Transaction Server installed and you are using ODBC to access a database, Transaction Server transparently inserts itself between your application and the database to manage that connection (as well as all of the other open connections to the same database). Transaction Server also allows application functionality to be built as a series of ActiveX DLLs and distributed across a network.

The latest of version of MTS can be found on the distribution CDs that come with Visual Basic 6. The Transaction Server is installed when you install the NT option pack 4 upgrade. The Microsoft Transaction Server (MTS) version 2.0 contains a number of new features designed to aid in the deployment of robust and scalable Internet and intranet applications. It is beyond the scope of this chapter to detail every feature of MTS; however, the following might pique your desire to read the online documentation that comes with MTS v. 2.0.

- Integration with Internet Information Server (IIS) version 4.0.
- Support for Transactional Active Server Pages—Scripts in Active Server Pages can now execute within an MTS-managed transaction.
- Crash Protection for IIS Applications—IIS Web applications can now execute within their own MTS package, providing process isolation and crash protection for Web applications.
- Transactional Events—Developers can embed commands into scripts on Active Server Pages, enabling customization of Web application response based on transaction outcome.
- Microsoft Cluster Server Support—MTS 2.0 supports Microsoft Cluster Server (MSCS), which enables automatic failover of MTS packages in a cluster.
- Support for the XA transaction protocol, including native support for Oracle.

Managing Database Connections

When an application is using the ODBC interface to access a database, Transaction Server takes control of the database connection to provide more consistent access, a quicker connection, and transaction control. By placing itself between the application and the database, Transaction Server can open its own connection to the database and provide the application with a connection to Transaction Server instead of the database. This enables Transaction Server to limit the actual number of database connections to only as many as are necessary to service all of the application requests. This relieves the work of maintaining all of those connections from the database, enabling the database to perform better and be more responsive.

When an application closes its connection to the database, Transaction Server maintains the open database connection so that the connection can be reused either by the application that closed the connection, or by another application (or client) that needs the same connection to the database. This enables application modules to be written in such a way that they only maintain open connections to a database for those periods of time that the application really needs to have the connection open. The performance penalty for closing and reopening a database connection is removed, making it more attractive to write applications that release the associated resources when they are not needed.

> **NOTE**
>
> By combining Transaction Server with OLEISAPI2 applications, the remaining bit of overhead that you want to eliminate by using a SAPI interface is removed by enabling the OLEISAPI2 application to disconnect each time it finishes servicing a client call, and to reopen the database connection with each new call.

Managing Distributed Objects

Transaction Server provides a framework in which to build distributed applications. This framework enables you to build functionality into any number of ActiveX server DLLs, and then distribute them across your network. The Transaction Server is used to track each of these DLLs and provides the means of communication between them and the parent applications. In this way, the individual DLLs can be routed to the area of the network that has the most resources to serve the individual components. This method of routing or load balancing is based on load requirements for each DLL as it responds to the service request from the application. The Transaction Server also allows for redundant load balancing by allowing multiple copies of the same DLL to reside on multiple computers.

In addition to the various load balancing methods that the Transaction Server provides, you also have the ability to have DLLs from multiple languages reside on the same computer. This gives you great flexibility in development languages including Visual Basic 6, Visual C++, Visual J++, and Delphi. This flexibility means that you can create DLLs with a specific function in the language that is best suited for the particular operation.

Transaction Coordination

One of the many beneficial features of Transaction Server is its capability to provide coordinated transaction control through many objects and over multiple databases. Transaction Server accomplishes this by using the Microsoft Distributed Transaction Coordinator (DTC). The DTC was first released as part of SQL Server 6.5 and is

38

PROGRAMMING FOR TRANSACTION SERVER

included with Transaction Server. It provides a low-level infrastructure for distributed transactions, controlling and guaranteeing the outcome (either commit or rollback) across multiple databases, and database connections. The DTC uses a two-phase commit protocol to ensure the outcome of these transactions.

> ## TWO-PHASE COMMIT
>
> A two-phase commit is where a data change (insert, update, or delete) to two or more databases absolutely has to be successful in all, or unsuccessful in all. If the situation dictates that the changes to the data cannot be committed in one of the databases without being committed in the others, then two-phase commit is necessary.

Integrating Visual Basic Classes with Transaction Server

When building server objects for use with Transaction Server, there are a couple of basic details that have to be taken into consideration. These details affect the design of your objects and add a small amount of Transaction Server-specific code. You will look at each of these aspects as you build a simple server object. You'll add on to this object with additional objects a little later.

Initializing the Visual Basic Project

All server objects for use with Transaction Server have to be built as ActiveX DLLs, regardless of which programming language is used. After you have started a new Visual Basic 6 ActiveX DLL project, you need to include a reference to the Microsoft Transaction Server Type library by choosing Project | References, as seen in Figure 38.1.

FIGURE 38.1.

You need to include a reference to the Transaction Server Type library.

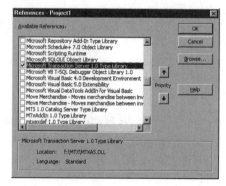

The sample object that you will be building is a warehouse inventory adjuster object for a catalog order company. To start with, only two tables will be needed. These tables are the Products table, shown in Table 38.1, and the Inventory table, shown in Table 38.2. You'll be adding additional tables as you expand the scope of this system later in this chapter.

TABLE 38.1. THE PRODUCTS TABLE

Column Name	Data Type	Size
Prd_ID	int	
Prd_Name	char	8
Prd_Desc	varchar	40
Prd_StandardStock	smallint	

> **NOTE**
>
> The int and smallint data types in SQL Server are a fixed size and therefore, do not require a column size to be specified. An int data type is defined as four bytes, and a smallint is defined as two bytes. The available number range that can be stored in each of these data types is completely dependent on what range of numbers can be represented by each of these storage allocations.

TABLE 38.2. THE INVENTORY TABLE

Column Name	Data Type	Size
Prd_ID	int	
Inv_Count	smallint	

To wrap up your project initialization, you name your project InvMaint and give the project a description to remind yourself what this module does at a later time. You'll also mark this module for unattended execution, so that it can run in a multi-threaded environment. There is a single class in this project that you should name InvMnt.

> **TIP**
>
> It a good idea to provide a project description for the modules that you are building in this and the following chapters. You will be building several DLLs and including references to DLLs that you have already built. By including a description, the project description will show up in the Project References dialog box. If you don't provide project descriptions, then only the project name will show up in the References dialog box.

Stateless Objects

One of the keys to designing and building well-performing components for use with Transaction Server is to design the objects and methods to be stateless. This means that there are no variables and conditions that are held within the object; all variables are received as parameters to the methods that are exposed; and all results are returned either as the result of the method or through method parameters that were passed by reference.

The primary reason for building stateless objects is because the same method can be called as part of several different applications. These calls can happen simultaneously or sequentially; regardless, it is a high likelihood the same method could be called from different applications. Keep in mind that this is the same approach that you need to take when building thread-safe objects. It is possible to build stateful objects for use with Transaction Server, but these objects entail a lot more overhead and will not perform as well when the system is under load.

There are a few exceptions to the rule of building stateless objects. These exceptions consist primarily of information that the object will be using across all processes, such as the database connection information. To build your server object in a stateless manner, your declarations are limited to the database connect string and the error number that you will be raising in the event of an error. This gives us the class declaration section found in Listing 38.1.

LISTING 38.1.   INVMNT.CLS—ERROR NUMBER AND DATABASE CONNECTION INFORMATION

```
Option Explicit
'We always return the same error number
Private Const ERROR_NUMBER = vbObjectError + 0
'The database connect string
Private Const strConnect = "DSN=InvMntDB;UID=TxsVB;PWD=vbtxs;"
```

Transaction Context

When an object is running with Transaction Server, it is running in the context of a transaction. There is a transaction attribute that controls how the objects interact with the current transaction within their context. This transaction attribute can have any one of four values, as seen in Table 38.3.

TABLE 38.3. THE TRANSACTION ATTRIBUTE VALUES

Value	*Description*
Requires a transaction	Objects with this transaction attribute must execute within the scope of a transaction. If the object that called this object was executing within a transaction, then this object executes within the scope of the same transaction as the calling object. If the calling object is not executing within a transaction, then this object starts (and completes) a new transaction.
Requires a new transaction	Objects with this transaction attribute always begin (and complete) a new transaction, regardless of whether the calling object was running within a transaction or not.
Supports transactions	Objects with this transaction attribute execute within the scope of the transaction of the calling object, if that object was executing within a transaction. If the calling object was not executing within a transaction, then this object executes without a transaction.
Does not support transactions	Objects with this transaction attribute always execute outside the scope of any transactions, regardless of the transaction state of the calling object.

38

PROGRAMMING
FOR TRANSACTION
SERVER

Using the transaction attribute on all objects running within Transaction Server, you can configure an extensive transaction model, separating objects into distinct transactions that are executed within the midst of other transactions.

For example, take the collection of objects in Figure 38.2. In this model, Object A calls Object B, which calls Object C. All three of these objects have their transaction attributes set to Requires a transaction. The transaction in which all three of these objects are executing will commit the changes made by these objects only if all three objects execute successfully. If any one of the three has an error, the entire transaction is rolled back.

FIGURE 38.2.

The transaction attribute enables you to define separate transactions within other transactions.

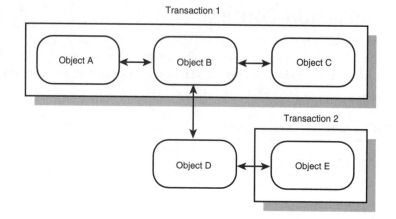

Notice that Object D is also called by Object B; only Object D has its transaction attribute set to `Does not support transactions`. This means that Object D does not affect the transaction within which Objects A, B, and C are executing. Object E, which is called by Object D, might have its transaction attribute set to either `Requires a transaction` or `Requires a new transaction`. Because Object D does not support transactions, Object E always starts a new transaction, which is completely independent of the transaction of Objects A, B, and C. If Object E is set to `Requires a transaction`, and Object D is set to `Requires a new transaction`, then the transaction of A, B, and C would continue to be independent of the transaction of D and E.

Being able to tell Transaction Server whether an object was successful—or that it ran into problems—requires a few lines of code. The first task is to get a reference to the transaction context object, which is the transaction context within which the object is executing. This is done with the `GetObjectContext()` function, as in the following code:

```
Dim ctxObject As ObjectContext
Set ctxObject = GetObjectContext()
```

After you have the transaction context, you can use the context object's two methods, `SetComplete` and `SetAbort`, to tell Transaction Server whether the object was successful or not. If your object executed without any problems, you use the following call to tell Transaction Server that you are finished and that the transaction can be committed:

```
ctxObject.SetComplete
```

If your object ran into problems, you can use the `SetAbort` method to tell Transaction Server that the transaction should be rolled back, as follows:

```
ctxObject.SetAbort
```

> **NOTE**
>
> The context object (ctxObject) does more than control the transaction. It also controls the objects and the resources that those objects are consuming. When an object calls SetComplete or SetAbort, the object is informing Transaction Server that the object is finished processing and it can be deactivated, and all of the system resources being used by the object can be reallocated to other objects. If SetComplete or SetAbort are not called, Transaction Server does not know when it can release those resources for use by other objects. This eventually bogs down the system performance.

You can take this understanding of how to use the context object to build your first object, which will maintain the current inventory of a particular product in the warehouse. You name your method ChangeInv, and you pass it a product identification number and the number of the product that you want to move. A positive number adds inventory to the warehouse, and a negative number removes inventory from the warehouse. You also have this object tell us how many of the product remain in stock after your request, and (in the case of a negative number) how many need to be back-ordered to fulfill your request. You can do this with the code in Listing 38.2.

38

PROGRAMMING FOR TRANSACTION SERVER

LISTING 38.2. INVMNT.CLS— ADDING AND REMOVING INVENTORY FROM THE WAREHOUSE WITH THE ChangeInv METHOD

```
Public Function ChangeInv(aiPrdID As Long,
➥aiChange As Integer, _
                                ByRef aiBackOrder
➥As Integer, _
                                ByRef aiStockRemain As Integer
➥) As Integer
    Dim ctxObject As ObjectContext
    Dim rdoConn As rdoConnection
    Dim strSQL As String
    Dim rdoRS As rdoResultset

    'Get our object context
    Set ctxObject = GetObjectContext()

    'Set up error handling
    On Error GoTo ErrorHandler

    'Obtain the RDO environment and connection
    Set rdoConn = rdoEngine.rdoEnvironments(0).
➥OpenConnection("", _

➥rdDriverNoPrompt, False, strConnect)
```

continues

LISTING 38.2   CONTINUED

```
    'Update the Inventory
    strSQL = "UPDATE Inventory SET Inv_Count =
➥Inv_Count + " _
                + Str$(aiChange) + " WHERE Prd_ID =
➥" + Str$(aiPrdID)
    rdoConn.Execute strSQL, rdExecDirect
    'Get resulting inventory which may have been further
    'updated via triggers
    strSQL = "SELECT Inv_Count FROM Inventory WHERE
➥Prd_ID = " _

➥                        + Str$(aiPrdID)
    Set rdoRS = rdoConn.OpenResultset(strSQL,
➥rdOpenForwardOnly, _
                            rdConcurReadOnly,
➥rdExecDirect)
    'Did we retrieve anything?
    If rdoRS.EOF <> True Then
        'Yes, get the current inventory count
        aiStockRemain = rdoRS.rdoColumns("Inv_Count")
        'Check if the inventory is overdrawn
        If aiChange < 0 And aiStockRemain < 0 Then
            'Set the number of items that are backordered
            aiBackOrder = 0 - aiStockRemain
            'Update the inventory count
            strSQL = "UPDATE Inventory SET Inv_Count = 0
➥WHERE Prd_ID = " _

➥+ Str$(aiPrdID)
            rdoConn.Execute strSQL, rdExecDirect
            aiStockRemain = 0
        Else
            'We are not overdrawn, so we don't need to back
➥order anything
            aiBackOrder = 0
        End If
    Else
        'No, there is a problem as no product inventory
➥record was found
        Err.Raise ERROR_NUMBER, "Could not find product
➥inventory record."
    End If

    'Close the database connection
    rdoConn.Close
```

```
       'Tell Transaction Server that we have successfully
➥completed our task
       ctxObject.SetComplete

       'Return a 0 to signal that we were successful
       ChangeInv = 0

 Exit Function
ErrorHandler:
       'Have we connected to the database yet?
       If Not rdoConn Is Nothing Then
           'If so, then close the connection
           rdoConn.Close
       End If

       'Tell Transaction Server that we had problems
       ctxObject.SetAbort
       'Indicate that an error occured
       ChangeInv = -1
End Function
```

Registering Visual Basic DLLs with Transaction Server

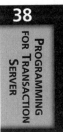

After you create your ActiveX DLL project, you need to register it with Transaction Server before it can be used. You do this through the Transaction Server Explorer. After you have started up the Transaction Server Explorer, you need to make sure that the DTC is running. If the DTC is not running, click the Computer icon for your computer, and then choose Tools | MS DTC | Start.

Creating Packages

Before you can start registering components in Transaction Server, you must have a package into which you are going to install the components. *Packages* are logical groupings of objects that are generally used as a unit. As a general rule, you will want to create one package for each set of applications that makes use of Transaction Server. You can create a package by following these steps:

1. Select the Packages Installed folder.
2. Choose File | New from the main menu.
3. On the first screen of the Package Wizard, choose Create an Empty Package, as seen in Figure 38.3.

FIGURE 38.3.

For registering components that you have built, you need to create an empty package into which the components will be installed.

4. Type in a name for the package, as shown in Figure 38.4. For your catalog sales company package, call it **Inventory**. Then click the Next button.

FIGURE 38.4.

Provide the package with a name that reflects the functionality, or family of applications, that the components in the package will be providing.

5. If the objects in the package need to run under a specific login account, select the This User radio button and provide the username and password. Otherwise, leave the default radio button selected, as in Figure 38.5, which runs all of the objects in the package under the account of the users using the applications that use the objects in this package. (This can affect the availability of resources for the process components, depending on how the access privileges are configured in the system security.)

6. Click the Finish button to complete the process.

FIGURE 38.5.

If you need the components in the package to execute as a specific user login, you need to specify the user login and password for resource access purposes.

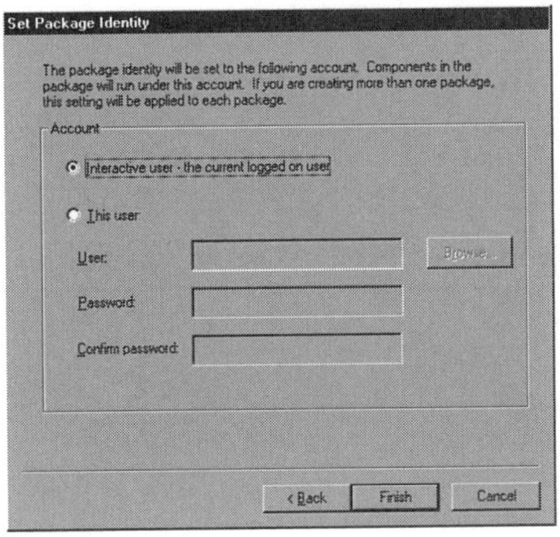

Installing Components

After you have a package, you can begin installing components into it. This is where you register the ActiveX DLLs that you have and will be creating with Visual Basic 6. You can install your components by following these steps:

1. Select the Components folder in the package into which you want to install the components, as seen in Figure 38.6.

FIGURE 38.6.

Select the Components folder in the package that you have created to install the newly created Inventory package.

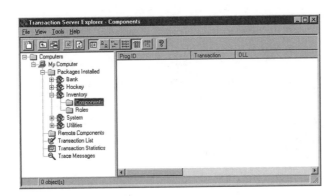

2. Click the Install New Component(s) button, as seen in Figure 38.7.

FIGURE 38.7.

If you are installing components that you have built, you need to select the Install New Components option.

3. Click the Add Files button and select the ActiveX DLL that you want to install, as seen in Figure 38.8.

FIGURE 38.8.

You need to select the DLL containing the components that you are installing.

4. When you return to the Install Components dialog box, the upper list box should show the DLL that you are installing, and the lower list box should show all of the visible classes within the DLL, as in Figure 38.9.

5. Click the Finish button, and the components are installed in Transaction Server, as seen in Figure 38.10.

6. Select the components you just installed, one at a time, and right-click the mouse. Select Properties from the pop-up menu. On the component Properties Editor, select the Transaction tab, and select the transaction attribute desired for the currently selected component, as in Figure 38.11.

FIGURE 38.9.

The Install Components dialog box displays all of the components found in the specified DLL.

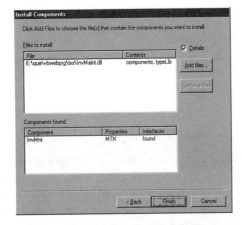

FIGURE 38.10.

After you have installed the components, they show up in the Transaction Server Explorer.

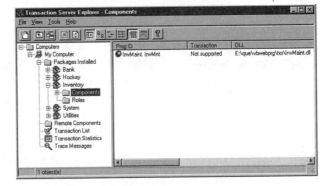

FIGURE 38.11.

You need to open up the Properties dialog box for the installed component to specify the transaction attribute setting.

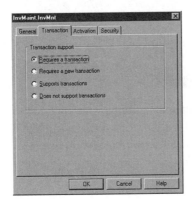

Whenever you recompile any ActiveX DLL built in Visual Basic 6, you need to refresh the component information in Transaction Server. This can be easily done by deleting the component from the Transaction Server Explorer and reinstalling the component by following the same steps as were followed to install the component originally. Another way of refreshing the component information in Transaction Server is by choosing Tools | Refresh All Components.

> **NOTE**
>
> To maintain the same GUID in the system registry, it is a good idea to set the version compatibility of the VB project to binary compatibility before you compile it into the DLL that will be installed in MTS. This will eliminate the unnecessary hassle of unregistering previous versions of the DLL.

> **MTS v 1.0 ODDITIES**
>
> In working with Transaction Server 1.0, the Refresh All Components menu option often scrambles the component names in the package with which you were working. You end up with what looks like two or three copies of the same component in the package, and some components appear to be missing. You might not notice any problems when attempting to run the applications that used these components, but usually end up deleting all of the components from the package and reinstalling them.

Calling Transaction Server Objects from Visual Basic

Now that you have a component built and registered with Transaction Server, how do you call the method in this object from a Visual Basic application? First, the Visual Basic application has to get a reference to the Transaction Server object. After the reference has been acquired, the object's methods can be called. There are three ways that a reference to a Transaction Server object can be acquired:

- Using the CreateObject function
- Using the GetObject function
- Using the New keyword

> **NOTE**
>
> There is a fourth method for acquiring a reference to a Transaction Server object by another Transaction Server object; that is through the use of the Context Object's `CreateInstance` method, which creates the object reference in the same transaction context of the current object (depending on the new object's transaction attribute). You see this method in use in the following chapters.

From a Visual Basic application, you can create your reference to your Inventory Maintenance object with the following code:

```
Dim obj As Object
Set obj = CreateObject("InvMaint.InvMnt")
```

> **NOTE**
>
> The same Transaction Server object could have been created using the New keyword by using the following code:
>
> ```
> Dim obj As New InvMaint.InvMnt
> ```
>
> As a general rule, all Transaction Server components can be referenced in the same way as all other ActiveX server objects. Transaction Server works with the operating system to make sure that when Transaction Server components are requested, they are created and called within Transaction Server.

From here, you can call the object methods by referencing them via the object you have just created, as so:

```
obj.ChangeInv(iiProductID, CLng(txtCount.Text), iBackOrder, iCurInventory)
```

If you build a simple little applet using the Remote Data Control and the Data Bound Combo Box, you can call your object and see how Transaction Server works. The first thing you need to do is to add the Remote Data Control and the Data Bound List Controls to your Toolbox. You do this by choosing Project | Components, as seen in Figure 38.12.

FIGURE 38.12.

You have to include the Data Bound List Controls and the Remote Data Control into your Visual Basic project before you can use them.

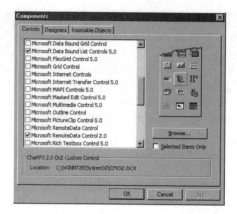

With these two controls, you can build a simple form that provides a drop-down list box, containing the product descriptions from the Products table in the database. You accomplish this by binding the Remote Data Control to the ODBC configuration you have set up for your database, providing the username and password that you have configured, and using the following SQL to populate the Remote Data Control:

```
SELECT * FROM Products
```

Next, specify the Remote Data Control as the row source for the Data Bound Combo Box and specify the `Prd_Desc` column as the `ListField`, `DataField`, and `BoundColumn`. Add a text box in which the user can enter the number to add or remove from the inventory, and you have the form seen in Figure 38.13.

FIGURE 38.13.

Use a very simple form to call the method in the object you registered with Transaction Server.

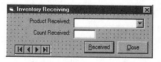

Setting the Product ID

When the user selects a product, you need to have a variable into which to place the selected product ID, so declare a variable in the form declarations using the code in Listing 38.3.

LISTING 38.3. RECVNG.FRM—DECLARING A VARIABLE FOR HOLDING THE SELECTED PRODUCT ID

```
Option Explicit
'We always return the same error number
Private Const ERROR_NUMBER = vbObjectError + 0
'The currently selected product ID
Dim iiProductID As Long
```

You set the product ID into this variable whenever the user selects a product from the list by navigating in the Remote Data Control to the currently selected row, and then getting the Prd_ID column from that row, as in Listing 38.4.

LISTING 38.4. RECVNG.FRM—GRABBING THE PRODUCT ID FROM THE REMOTE DATA CONTROL WHEN THE USER SELECTS A PRODUCT

```
Private Sub dbcProduct_Click(Area As Integer)
    Dim varCurRecord As Variant

    'What is the currently selected item?
    varCurRecord = dbcProduct.SelectedItem
    'Move to the selected record in the result set
    MSRDC1.Resultset.Move 0, varCurRecord
    'Grab the product ID
    iiProductID = MSRDC1.Resultset!Prd_ID.Value
End Sub
```

38

PROGRAMMING FOR TRANSACTION SERVER

> **CAUTION**
>
> The code that you are using to grab the selected product ID is dependent on the Remote Data Control being used for the ListField, DataField, and BoundColumn. If you use the Remote Data Control for just the ListField, the dbcProduct_Click method will error out with an invalid bookmark error when you click it to select a product. This is due to the fact that the control starts out with the selected item of 0, which the Remote Data Control interprets as an invalid row. It is after you have selected a row that the control has a valid row number, but you cannot get to that point.

NOTE

You could easily wait until the user clicks the Received button when calling the Transaction Server object to determine the selected item. Calling the object in this way requires additional code in the specific method isolated by using the method that you have. This is not really better, but it does isolate the functionality, enabling you to focus on the core functionality that you are implementing in each method.

Calling the Transaction Server Object

When the user clicks the Received button, you can create a reference to the Transaction Server object that you created by using the earlier code snippets, and you can display for the user the resulting stock and back-order amounts with the code in Listing 38.5.

LISTING 38.5. RECVNG.FRM—CREATING A REFERENCE TO YOUR TRANSACTION SERVER OBJECT AND CALLING THE METHOD THAT YOU CREATED IN THE OBJECT

```
Private Sub cmdReceived_Click()
    Dim iBackOrder As Integer
    Dim iCurInventory As Integer
    Dim ProgID As String
    Dim obj As Object

    'Set up the error handling
    On Error GoTo ErrorHandler

    'Decide which component to use
    ProgID = "InvMaint.InvMnt"

    'Create the appropriate object
    Set obj = CreateObject(ProgID)
    'Were we able to create the object?
    If obj Is Nothing Then
        MsgBox "Create object " + ProgID + "failed."
        Exit Sub
    End If
    'Call the object method
    If obj.ChangeInv(iiProductID, CLng(txtCount.Text), iBackOrder, _
                        iCurInventory) = -1 Then
        Err.Raise ERROR_NUMBER
    End If

    'Release the object
    Set obj = Nothing
```

```
        'Display for the user what the current inventory is
        MsgBox "New Inventory received, current backorder count = " _
                + Str$(iBackOrder) + " and current inventory = " _
                + Str$(iCurInventory)
        Exit Sub

ErrorHandler:
        'Show the user the error message
        MsgBox "Error " + Str$(Err.Number) + " : " + Err.Description
        Exit Sub
End Sub
```

Before you run your form, let's change the view in the Transaction Server Explorer to show the status of your object. You do this by selecting the Components folder in the package you have created. Next, choose View | Status. The right side of the Explorer now shows the activity status of your object. If you run the form with the Transaction Server Explorer where it can be seen, you can watch as the object that you created earlier is instantiated and executed, as seen in Figure 38.14.

FIGURE 38.14.

When the form that you have created calls the object that you registered in Transaction Server, you can watch as the object is created and run.

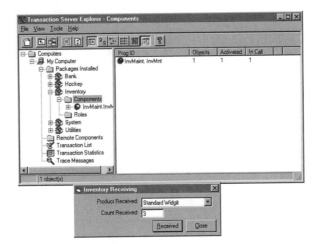

Summary

Using Visual Basic with Transaction Server provides you with an opportunity to create applications that are truly distributed applications. The Transaction Server enables you to reuse basic applications components and control the communication process between the applications components and the server. In this way, you can create applications that are scalable and manageable.

Visual SourceSafe: A Necessity for Serious Developers

by Loren Eidahl

IN THIS CHAPTER

- Understanding Source Control   916
- Introducing Visual SourceSafe   917
- Understanding Project-Oriented Programming   922
- Using Visual SourceSafe from Visual Basic 6   927

The concept of tracking changes made to a software project is not a new one; its roots were actually found back in the days of the mainframe. Back then, large numbers of developers would use a single computer to develop their applications. As the need for more sophisticated applications increased, so did the need for a method of controlling and tracking the changes made to any given software project. The process of tracking the changes made by each of the developers on a project was known as *Change control*.

With the advent of the personal computer, developers once again had to deal with the requirements of tracking software changes made to an application. Initially this level of tracking was quite small due mainly to the size of the applications that were being developed at the time. As time and technology progressed, so did the need for a comprehensive application that could handle the myriad of developers working applications that spanned multiple versions and the multitude of support files.

Microsoft Visual SourceSafe 6.0 (VSS) is the latest installment of Microsoft's answer to the challenges of managing source code for projects of any size. VSS enables you to track the changes made to single or multiple file software projects and keeps each iteration securely stored in a database for later retrieval. VSS is easy enough to be used by individual developers and robust enough to handle a large team of developers working on multiple projects.

> **NOTE**
>
> VSS is included with the Enterprise Edition of Visual Basic 6 and with Visual Studio 98. It can also be purchased individually.

Understanding Source Control

Understanding the concept of source control is the first step toward knowing why you need to do source control if you are or plan to be a serious Windows application developer. If you've ever done any programming, you know the problems that occur when trying to protect your source code. What would you do if you realized that the changes you just saved to the file are wrong, and you have to go back to an earlier version of the code? Without source control, you would need to save or back up the files to several different locations so that you could always go back to a previous copy of a file.

With a tool such as VSS, you no longer need to worry about making multiple copies of your files. The tool also keeps track of your program changes. Source control enables you to create components that can be compiled into many different applications. This *sharing* of components keeps you from having to deal with the question, "Which version of the component am I using here?" If you don't know which version is which, you might compile an application that doesn't work correctly. VSS is the tool that lets you design and program your Windows application in Visual Basic without worrying about any of these problems.

Introducing Visual SourceSafe

VSS is a project-oriented version-control system for individual or team development of software applications, as well as any other work that benefits from using source control. It stores and tracks changes to files of any type—text or binary. VSS supports team application development by enabling team members to share files, modify them independently, and later merge the changes into a single copy of the file. Team members can review a file's history and recover to an earlier version of a file. VSS is flexible enough to support any project size and any number of users.

Unlike other version-control programs, VSS provides these features in a project-oriented system that keeps track of relationships among files so that developers don't have to. Version 6 is a 32-bit compatible application that comes with Visual Basic 6 (Enterprise Edition only) or can be purchased separately. You can use VSS directly with any of the Microsoft Visual development tools, including Visual Basic 6. The most commonly used commands are available from within the Visual Basic 6 environment. The rest of the VSS command set is always available from the VSS Explorer interface.

Understanding How VSS Can Help You

A typical software development team can include many programmers, writers, testers, and designers, or it can be a single programmer working in the comfort of his or her own home. Any development effort also should have the following functions performed to protect the application:

- Check files in and out, keep them where they belong, and store important documents.
- Record all file activity.
- Make sure that files go only to those with the proper security.
- Keep track of utilities and keep things running smoothly.

Rather than rely on programmers to keep track of the changes they make or worry about changes made by others, you can have VSS take control of these changes. This way, one programmer can be prevented from changing a section of code that another programmer is already modifying.

The most important feature of VSS is what the name says—keeping your source files safe. Using VSS with your applications is like checking books in and out of a library; the only difference is that these "books" can't get lost. The advantages of using VSS are as follows:

- The ability of two or more programmers to check out files at the same time
- Sharing common code files between projects without needing separate copies
- Checking files in and out easily and adding comments to describe the changes made
- Preventing program files from accidental deletion

VSS is a history service that keeps the records for your application project. By knowing the history of any given program file, you can tell what the changes were, who made them, and when they were made. This way, you can choose the correct version of the program file to use with your application. Also, by using passwords on the VSS user definitions, you can prevent unwanted usage of any program file that's included in the VSS project.

Installing the VSS Server

The first step in installing VSS is the Server Setup, the VSS administrator that creates the SourceSafe database to which all users have access. Also, each user might want to take a second step and do a personal setup. The Server Setup step improves performance and reduces network traffic but—more importantly—registers VSS for direct integration into Visual Basic 6, both Enterprise and Professional Editions. For single developers, the setup is done by using the standalone PC as the network server.

To set up the VSS Administrator, you will need to run the SETUP.EXE program located in the \\VSS_SS folder on the Visual Studio or Visual Basic distribution disks. This will create the necessary VSS database and the SRCSAFE.INI file. After you have done this, you can select the VSS Administrator from the Microsoft VSS Server program group. To allow VSS to integrate with VB6 you will need to run the SSINT.EXE program located in the \\VSS_SS\VSS\WIN32 folder. Running this will allow VSS to be fully integrated with VB 6.

> **NOTE**
>
> VSS integration into the Visual Basic environment won't work until you've done a network or client setup. Also, you must select the Integration option when you are installing VSS, or it won't be able to integrate with VB.
>
> If you try to run VSS without setting up the server, you will get an error message asking you to supply the location of the srcsafe.ini file. This file is only created after the server is initialized.

When VSS is installed, an empty VSS database is created for you. The next step is to run the VSS Administrator's program and add all your users to the VSS user list.

> **NOTE**
>
> The number of users that you can legally add to this list is based on the number of VSS licenses you've purchased.

Administering the VSS Environment

The administrator of the SourceSafe environment is responsible for maintaining the user list and the associated working parameters for each user. The administrator also keeps the database working smoothly, backing it up and fixing any problems that might occur.

The VSS database is where all program file master copies, file history, and project structures are stored. A project is always contained within one database, but you can store multiple projects in one database or multiple projects in multiple databases.

When you start the VSS Administrator, you'll see the Administrator's visual interface, which lists the users defined in the SourceSafe database (see Figure 39.1).

The user list shows every user who has access rights to the VSS environment. Any user who doesn't appear in this list can't access the database. Additional users can be added by selecting the Users | Add User option from the menu. By default, when you install VSS, this list has only two entries: Admin and Guest. These users are defined as follows:

- *Admin:* There can be only one Admin user. This user can't be deleted or have its username changed. The Admin user has full access rights and has the right to undo the checkout of a file that another user has checked. Finally, Admin is the only user who can run the VSS Administrator and modify the user list.

39

VISUAL SOURCESAFE

FIGURE 39.1.

The VSS Administrator displays users defined in the database.

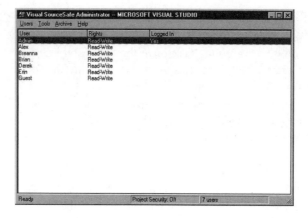

- *Guest:* The Guest user is a default template that you can use to create other users. It's also used to provide access to the VSS database for occasional or first-time users. You can delete the Guest user and can also change its access rights.

Select a user from the list and then choose Tools | Options from the menu to bring up the SourceSafe Options dialog box (see Figure 39.2).

NOTE

The admin password when you install the server side of VSS is usually (VSS). This should be changed as soon as VSS is installed to prevent unauthorized access.

FIGURE 39. 2.

The SourceSafe Options dialog box for a user.

The pages in this dialog box cover several different areas of the VSS environment for each user:

- *The General page*. This page includes settings that affect all the users defined in the user list. This is where information about the default database and log files is stored.

- *The Project Security page*. This page controls whether security is on or off for a project. If security is on, you can then set default access rights for the users. This page affects security on a global level; it has nothing to do with the actual security applied to individual files.

- *The Shadow Folders page*. This page is used to set the shadow folder for a particular project. A shadow folder is a central folder that contains current versions of all files in a project.

- *The Web Projects page*. This page sets the information that applies to a single Web project. This information includes the URL and specific deployment information.

- *The Web tabbed page*. This page sets options for all Web projects at once rather than for an individual Web project. Information such as default filenames and proxy information is stored here.

- *The File Types page*. This page sets the types of files users can store in VSS. This is a handy page in a multiple-developer environment where you want to limit the type of files that are accessed.

After you have completed the install and set up your users, I would recommend that you back up your VSS database. Thereafter, regular VSS database backups will ensure that your database is always the most current. Make sure that these backups are full backups, not incremental or differential.

It's also recommended that you run the ANALYZE program to check your VSS database for corruption. If any corruption is found, the ANALYZE program can often be used to repair the problem.

The Analyze.exe utility can be found in the c:\Program Files\Microsoft Visual Studio\VSS\win32\ folder. The Analyze.exe utility should only be run after all of the users are locked out of the VSS database. The Analyze utility can either be run from the command line or as part of a script that gets initiated at some later time.

39

VISUAL
SOURCESAFE

TIP

Updates to the ANALYZE program are periodically posted to the VSS Web site at www.microsoft.com/ssafe. You should check this site every so often to keep this utility updated.

With the administration setup completed, you can now work with VSS, including any projects for which you want to track the history and changes.

Understanding Project-Oriented Programming

If you have been using Visual Basic for any length of time, you have most likely been exposed to the concepts of project-oriented programming. During the process of program development, you are typically only modifying a few of the modules or classes in a project at any given time. In applications that contain multiple file types, it is easier to group these files together in a project that can be compiled into the desired application. VSS is designed to enable you to check out the various file types that make up a project, make the required changes, and then check them back into VSS again. This ability enables you to work on a very large project without having to check out the entire project. In situations where a number of developers are working on a single project, this feature saves a great deal of time and a lot of confusion.

Using Projects in Visual SourceSafe

Because VSS is a project-oriented tool, you must have a project in which to place the files before you can do anything with them. When you begin working with VSS, the first thing to do is create a project for your application. The organization of projects is similar to the organization of folders on your PC. Projects contain subprojects in the same way that folders contain subfolders.

When you're designing projects, it's always a good idea to mirror the directory structure you created in your project in the project structure in VSS. For example, if your files are in one folder with four subfolders, you should create a project in VSS with four subprojects. The VSS Explorer provides the graphical representation of the relationships of projects and subprojects (see Figure 39.3).

You can access the VSS Explorer by selecting the Microsoft VSS 6.0 menu option from the Microsoft Visual Studio 6.0 program group. The VSS Explorer is the main user interface; you use it to navigate your project tree, select files, and execute the commands that act on those projects and files. The files in your project are stored in the VSS database. You'll never work with the master copy of any program file that's stored in VSS, except occasionally to compare another copy to it. VSS provides each user with a copy of the file to read or change. Each time someone checks in a file, VSS stores not only the changed file, but also the history of the changes as well.

FIGURE 39.3.

The VSS Explorer interface shows you the control project directory layout that should match the application's directory structure on the hard drive.

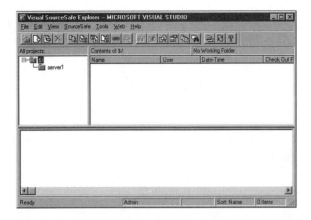

> **NOTE**
>
> As long as you back up the VSS database and perform the required routine maintenance, the changes you store in VSS are never lost.

When using VSS, you need to have several other folders defined on your PC. You use these folders to work with your application program files. You need shadow folders and working folders.

VSS uses shadow folders to hold the current versions of all the files in a single project. These folders don't contain the master copy of a file or the local copy of a file. They do, however, provide a central location from which to look at the overall structure of the project with which you're working. They also serve as a good place from which to build or compile the project.

When you use VSS to control your programming projects, you can't actually work with a file within VSS. When you want to work on a file, you must obtain a copy of the file from VSS, and then have a place to put it. That place is your *working folder*. VSS attaches a separate working folder on your PC for every project it controls. This working folder is your personal workspace for a given project.

Your working folder is a directory on your hard disk that you use to work on files you've obtained from VSS. You can use an existing folder on your hard disk drive as your working folder, create a new one from within VSS, or use Windows 95 Explorer.

39

VISUAL
SOURCESAFE

> **NOTE**
>
> You must set a working folder *before* you start working on any files stored in VSS projects.

To retrieve a file from VSS, you request to check out the file from the SourceSafe project. It's then copied into your working folder for that project, thus providing you with a local copy with which to work. If you haven't yet specified a working folder for the project, VSS prompts you to do so. After you make changes to the file, you check the file into VSS, which copies it from your working folder into your current project.

> **NOTE**
>
> Working folders are associated with projects, not with individual files. You can't choose a different working folder for each file in a project. However, each individual user can, and should, have a separate working folder for each project.

VSS has made checking out a file from its associated project easy. Start VSS and log in with the username that has access to the project with which you're working. The file list for the project appears (see Figure 39.4).

FIGURE 39. 4.

Opening VSS for a specific project lists all the available files in the project and also shows whether any are already checked out by a user.

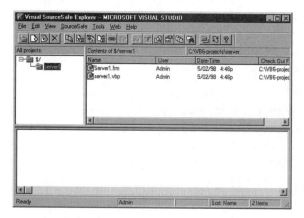

Then, from the list of files available in the project, select the files you want to use and choose SourceSafe | Check Out from the menu to have the files copied to your working folder. You're now ready to work with these files.

Another VSS feature is its capability to mark a file or files as *shared*, thus enabling that file to be part of two or more projects at the same time. The master copy of the file resides in the VSS database, but the file is accessible from all projects that share it. When someone makes a change to a shared file in any project, the change is immediately made to all projects sharing the file. Sharing files saves time and resources by avoiding duplication of effort and storage.

Checking the Files Back Into Visual SourceSafe

After you finish making the needed changes to a file in your working folder, you should return the file to the VSS project it came from. The SourceSafe | Check In command is used to replace the file into the project. The Check In dialog box gives you several options when returning the file to the project (see Figure 39.5):

- Keep the file checked out to continue working on it after you check in your changes.

- Remove the copy of the file from your working folder after the check in is complete. By default, a read-only copy of the file is left in your working folder.

- Display differences between the version of the file you're checking in and the version you checked out.

- Browse folders in search of other files you've checked out that you would like to check in.

FIGURE 39.5.

When checking a file into the project, you can choose between two actions.

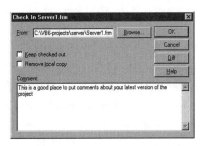

39

VISUAL
SOURCESAFE

In addition to these settings, you also can enter a comment that describes the changes you've made to the file. When you're working in a team environment with shared files, make it a practice to list the differences and history of the file before checking it back in to the SourceSafe project. This way, you can see whether anyone else worked with the file while you were working with it; if someone did, you can then check for differences. This list will let you see whether your changes will be affected by changes made by another programmer.

Adding Files to the SourceSafe Project

When you create a project in VSS, you need to add the files you want to track to the SourceSafe project. You can add these files to the project by using the Add File dialog box (see Figure 39.6) or by dragging and dropping from the Windows Explorer to the SourceSafe Explorer. If you have an entire folder that you want to put in the project, you can add it the same way you would add a single file to the project.

FIGURE 39.6.

Adding files or folders to the SourceSafe project is as easy as saving a file to your hard disk.

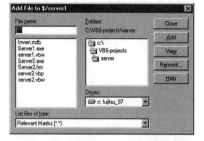

Tracking Different Versions of Your Project

If you're working with an application that will grow over time, as Microsoft Word has grown and changed from version to version, you need to use version tracking to keep the changes straight. You'll see version tracking in almost every application that runs on a PC. When an application goes from version 1 to version 2, someone must keep track of what changes were made for the new version. Also, the older version must still be kept around for users who don't upgrade to the newer version. VSS has three methods of tracking the different versions of files and projects with which you're working:

- *Version numbers*. These internal numbers are maintained by VSS. You have no control over these numbers. Every version of every file and project in VSS has a version number. The version number is always a whole number and always increases.

- *Labels*. You can apply to any version of a project or file. A label is a freeform string of up to 31 characters. The following are all valid labels: "1.0", "2.01b", and "Field Test 3".

- *Date/time*. These strings tell when a file that was modified was checked in. VSS supports 12-hour format (with an a or p suffix) and 24-hour format.

The best of these methods is to allow VSS to control the versioning itself. Letting SourceSafe do the version numbering keeps you from forgetting to change the version label or mislabeling a file. To use this method, you do absolutely nothing—version numbering is automatic.

Using Visual SourceSafe from Visual Basic 6

Now that you've seen what VSS is and what it can do, look at how Visual Basic works with it. When using Visual Basic 6 with VSS, you get all the features of SourceSafe, but they're fully integrated into the Visual Basic development environment. Whether you're working with an existing Visual Basic project or starting a new project, VSS is present to make sure that the project will be controlled, if you want it to be.

To use VSS, it must be registered properly on your system. To register VSS, select Add-Ins; then click the Add-In Manager. You will see a dialog box showing a list of the available Add-Ins. Highlight the Source Code Control Add-In option and select the Load on Startup and the Loaded/Unloaded option, as show in Figure 39.7.

FIGURE 39.7

The Visual Basic Add-In Manager enables you to add a number of different Add-Ins to your development environment.

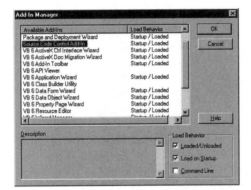

VSS Options

After you have registered VSS into your system, a SourceSafe menu option is added to the Tools menu in Visual Basic.

When you select the SourceSafe menu option, a secondary menu will appear. This secondary menu has the following four options:

- Create Project from SourceSafe
- Add Project to SourceSafe
- Run SourceSafe
- Options

When you select the Options item, the Source Code Control Options dialog box displays, as shown in Figure 39.8.

FIGURE 39.8.

Setting the options to control how SourceSafe performs.

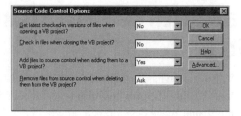

This dialog box enables you to control the interaction between VSS and VB6. The questions on this form are fairly straightforward and require that you answer with either a Yes or No response. Although the questions themselves are simple, how you answer them will have profound effects on how you use VSS with Visual Basic. In most cases the default settings are adequate. If you desire more control over VSS, the Advanced button will display an additional dialog box with more detailed options (see Figure 39.9).

FIGURE 39. 9.

SourceSafe options can be set on the tabbed Options dialog box.

This dialog box enables you to modify many of the settings that VSS uses to communicate with Visual Basic. The following list details the information on each tab of the dialog box:

Tab	Description
General	Enables the user to modify general configuration settings.
Local Files	The user can change how the files in the working folder are handled.
Integration	Displays integration information about your project and the related Visual SourceSafe project.

The remaining choices on the SourceSafe submenu enable you to check files in and out, display a form's history, and even add new files to the project.

Using an Existing Visual Basic Project

When you start Visual Basic and open an existing project, the first thing that happens (if VSS is installed on your PC) is that SourceSafe recognizes that the project isn't in the SourceSafe database and asks whether you want to add the project. If you say that you want to add it, you're then prompted to log in to SourceSafe (see Figure 39.10).

FIGURE 39.10.

Logging in to SourceSafe is required whenever interacting with SourceSafe.

Enter your SourceSafe username and password (if any), and then click OK. Next, you're prompted to select the SourceSafe folder where you want to add this project (see Figure 39.11). The new project folder can be added to the root level of the database or created as a subfolder of an existing project folder.

FIGURE 39.11.

Adding the project folder is the first step in protecting your work.

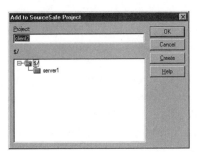

If the folder you want to use doesn't exist, click the Create button to add the new folder to the database. When you have the folder you need, click OK to continue. Now that the project folder exists, you're shown a list of files that are in the Visual Basic project (see Figure. 39.12). Select the files that you want to add to the SourceSafe project and click OK.

FIGURE 39.12.

Choose the files to include in the SourceSafe project.

After you select the files, VSS finishes the process by actually adding these files to the project and copying them to the shadow folder that the administrator of SourceSafe created for you. While this is happening, a status box onscreen shows SourceSafe at work. Don't expect to be able to start programming yet. Display a form in Visual Basic, and you'll see something new in the title bar (see Figure 39.13).

FIGURE 39.13.

The newly protected files in a project are read-only, preventing any changes from being made.

The label (Read Only) means just that. You must check out a form or module file before you can make any changes to it. To work with VSS, choose Tools SourceSafe from the menu to display the appropriate dialog box. If you want to check out files, choose Check Out from the menu to get the Check Out dialog box (see Figure 39.14).

Select the files you need and click OK. If you need to check out only a single file, you can simply right-click the file in the project window to display a pop-up menu (see Figure 39.15) and select the Check Out option. All the other VSS functions are available from this menu.

FIGURE 39.14

Using the SourceSafe Check Out dialog box to select several files to work with at the same time.

FIGURE 39.15

Using the SourceSafe options from the Visual Basic pop-up menu.

Creating New Visual Basic Projects

When you're creating a new Visual Basic application, SourceSafe will not prompt you until you're ready to save the project the first time. VSS prompts you for all required information to create the SourceSafe project from your new Visual Basic application.

If you're joining a project team that's already using SourceSafe, you'll have to create the working project on your PC. To do this, choose Tools | SourceSafe | Create Project from SourceSafe from the menu. This will display the project folders from the SourceSafe database. After you select a project folder, you're prompted for the local directory in which to create the project. When you click OK, this directory and the Visual Basic project are created on your PC. To make any modifications to this project, you will need to check it out because the project is read-only.

39

VISUAL
SOURCESAFE

NOTE

Remember, when you're finished making changes to a file, check it back in to the SourceSafe project to protect those changes.

Summary

This chapter only briefly showed you how VSS and Visual Basic can be used together. Using Visual Basic and VSS is a surefire combination to guaranteeing that your source code will always be protected from those unexpected disasters that can ruin an otherwise good day.

An added benefit of using VSS to track all of your development activity is the ability for you to support older versions of your applications with ease. No longer do you have to require that all of your users use the latest version of your software. By having all of your changes stored in VSS, you can gradually update your older versions of applications with ease and peace of mind. Probably one of the more attractive reasons to use VSS is the ability to create code libraries that contain all of the modules and classes that you have built. This way you can quickly locate and reuse a section of code, saving you time in the development and testing process of new applications.

INDEX

A

About boxes, adding to
   ActiveX controls, 142-144
abstract classes, 217
abstractions (OOP), 216
Accept method, 544
accessing
   databases
      ADO, 263-264
      controls, 266
      DAO, 261-262
      Data Environment,
         264-266, 311-314
      methods, 260-264
      RDO, 262-263
   documents, 530-531
   files
      Internet Transfer Control,
         530-531
      Windows API, 692-697
   System Registry
      INI files, 718-720
      Windows API, 720
   WinHelp system, 775-778
Accessing the Help system
   listing, 776
AccessType property, 522
Activate method, 634
active threads, 203
ActiveX controls, 75-77, 83,
   87-89
   assembling, 93-95
   automation, 74
   About boxes, adding, 142-144
   adding to Web pages, 155
   bindable, 192
   .CAB files
      advantages, 155-156
      deploying, 156-157
      testing, 156-157
   ComboBox, 33
   Common Dialog, 775
   compiling, 150-155
      conditional arguments,
         152
      debug information, 154
      documentation, 152
      file sizes, 153
      optimization, 153-154
      P-code, 152
      version numbers, 151
   constituent controls, 76, 85-87
   containers, 89-90
   Coolbar control, 20-32
   creating, 83-86

data consumers, 77, 176,
   192-193
data sources, 77
   creating, 176-192
   functionality, 186-190
   methods, 190-191
   properties, 180-185
DataCombo, 361-363
DataGrid, 363-374
   appearance, 367-368
   binding data, 366
   Column object, 371-373
   methods, 368-369
   navigation, 366-367
   properties, 364-368
   Split objects, 373-374
DataList, 358-360
DDE, 68-69
deploying, 150
design
   importance of, 82-83
   interfaces, 90-92
   standardization, 83
Dictation, 629
DLLs, 436
DTPicker control, 43-46
dynamic, 801-802
enhanced controls, 16
events, 88
   adding, 131-132, 135
   creating, 135-138
   custom, 135-138
   defaults, 138-139
   naming, 138
   sequences, 115
EXEs, 436
FlatScrollbar control, 46-47
history, 68-69, 72-79
HScrollBar control, 46
ImageCombo control, 32-37
ImageList control, 27, 33
instances
   design-time, 112-113
   runtime, 114
interfaces, 90-93
Internet, downloading,
   432-434
licensing issues, 86-87
LightButton control, 92
   constituent, 95-96
   global code module, 97
   initializing, 97-98
   interface elements,
      130-131
   naming, 94
   properties, 95

resizing, 100
run mode, 103
saving, 100
sizing, 94
test form, 101-103
testing, 103-104, 111-112,
   127-128
Timer event, 98-100
troubleshooting, 104-108
localized controls, 90
MAPI, 488-492
   MAPIMessages, 488-492
   MAPISession, 488-492
MDI, 803-805
methods, 89, 139-141
MonthView control, 37-42
MSHFlexGrid, 374-388
multithreaded components,
   198
new features, 16-17
OLE, 68-69, 561-569
   drag and drop, 810
   methods, 568-569
   properties, 568-569
optimizing applications, 843
planning, 83-85
projects, 77-79
properties
   adding, 116-121
   ambient, 90
   BackColor, 88, 121
   BackStyle, 88
   BorderStyle, 88, 122
   ButtonMode, 122
   Caption, 88
   descriptions, 145-147
   Enabled, 88, 128-130
   Font, 88, 122
   ForeColor, 88, 123
   grouping, 144-145
   Height, 88
   initializing, 124-125
   Left, 88
   Name, 88
   passing, 87
   Picture, 123
   property bag, 109-111
   reading, 124-127
   SelColor, 124
   SelPicture, 124
   Text, 88
   Top, 88
   Visible, 88
   Width, 88
   writing, 124-127
resizing, 104

Setup Wizard, 155
sited, 106
standardization, 83
TAPI, 622
Text-to-Speech control, 638
threads, 197
toolbox icons, changing, 147
user-drawn 76, 86
Voice Text control, 629
VScrollBar control, 46
Web applications, 115-116,
  155
Winsock, 539-547
ActiveX Data Objects, *see*
  ADO
**ActiveX Document Migration
  Wizard, 448-451**
ActiveX documents
adding, 445-447
advantages, 429
AsyncRead method, 432-433
AsyncReadComplete event,
  433-434
CancelAsyncRead method,
  433
coding, 440-441
compiling, 441-442
creating, 437-442
forms, 445-447
Hyperlink object, 434-435
interfaces, 439
Internet Explorer, 447-448
menu design, 442-444
Migration Wizard, 448-451
starting new, 438
testing, 441
understanding, 428-430
UserDocument, 430-435
activity log (MAPI), 502
actors
classes, 219
problem statements, 242
**Add File dialog box (VSS),
  926**
**Add Module command
  (Project menu), 96**
Add Module dialog box, 96
**Add Procedure command
  (Tools menu), 116**
**Add Project command (File
  menu), 101**
Add Project dialog box, 101
Add Watch dialog box, 788
Add-In code listing, 657
Add-In Designer, 14
**Add-In Management
  Package, 652-654**

add-ins
compiling, 659
example, 655
see also EOM
adding
About box, 142
ActiveX documents, 445-447
Data Environment, 317-321
events, 131-135
forms, 445-447
functions, 877
keywords (Help Index),
  756-757
multimedia, 761-762
properties, 116-124
VSS files, 926
**Adding controls on-the-fly
  listing, 802**
**Address Book button's Click
  event listing, 515**
**address book providers
  (MAPI), 486-487**
**addressing MAPI messages,
  502**
**administrating VSS environ-
  ment, 919**
**ADO (ActiveX Data Objects),
  263-264, 270**
Command object, 311
data controls, 176, 279-294
  advanced, 358
  events, 280
Data Form Wizard, 349
databases
  accessing, 263-264
  *front ends, creating,
    292-294*
  OLE DB datasource, 290
  RDBMS, 270
  *relational databases,
    270-276*
HTML, 278
libraries, 178, 279-294
object model, 280-289
recordsets, 295-296
remoting, 295-296
advanced data controls
DataCombo, 361-363
DataGrid, 363-374
DataList, 358-360
aggregates (SQL), 402-403
aggregations
collections, 227-228
threads, 201-203

algorithms, 858
compression
  *Code Table Optimization,
    868*
  data, 867-873
  *Huffman Compression,
    868*
  LZW, 868
  RLE, 869-873
decompression, 867-873
decryption
  data, 863-864, 867
  DES, 864
  IDEA, 864
  PGP, 865
  XOR, 865
encryption
  data, 863-864, 867
  DES, 864
  IDEA, 864
  PGP, 865
  XOR, 865
sorting, 858-863
  Bubble, 859
  Exchange, 859
  Heap, 859
  Insertion, 859
  Quick, 860
  Shell, 859
aliasing, 846
All object, 458
**altering data definition state-
  ments, 409-411**
Ambient object, 90
ambient properties, 90
analysis
class model, 253-254
methods, 234-235
**Analysis window (Code
  Profiler), 855**
analysts (OOA), 236
ANALYZE program (VSS), 921
**apartment-model threading,
  198-203**
events, recording, 208
reentrancy, 200
serializing, 201
thread safety, 203
API Viewer, 50-51
**APIs (Application
  Programming Interface),
  598**
arguments, passing, 585-586
child processes, 608-612
functions, 592-593
  display functions, 599-607
  system functions, 607-615

images, 599-607
    BitBlt, 599
    copying, 599-602
    drawing, 603-604
    StretchBlt, 599
text
    rotating, 604-606
    Text Viewer, 589-591
    window captions, 606-607
Windows
    callbacks, 594-595
    declaring functions,
      583-585
    library files, 580-583
Appearance property, 47
Applets object, 458
Application Wizard, 14
application-centric, 69
applications
    Code Profiler, installing, 851
    compiler, optimizing, 841
    debugging, 784-791
      breakpoints, 786
      error handling, 783
      special windows, 787-791
      stepping through code,
        785-787
    designing, 833
    DHTML, 455-456
      compiling, 474-475
      debugging, 474
      deploying, 476-477
      implementing, 473-481
    multi-tiered client/server, 277
    optimizing, 832-835
      commenting code, 836
      sorting strings, 843
    preventing errors in, 782-784
    speech recognition, creating,
      629-630, 633-635
    subsystems, 229-230
    TAPI, 620-625
    testing, 834-835
    tuning, 832-833
    two-tiered client/server, 277
    Windows API, optimizing,
      843
    see also listings
architects (OOA), 238-239
arguments
    data types, 586-588
    drag-and-drop OLE, 821
    overwrite, 333
    reference, passing by, 585-586
    showdialog, 333
    value, passing by, 585-586

arrays
    controls
      attributes, 795-796
      creating, 794-798
      properties, 796-798,
        805-807
    event handlers, designing,
      800-801
assembling controls, 93-95
AsycReadComplete event,
430
asynchronous downloads,
432-434
AsyncRead method, 432-433
AsyncReadComplete event,
433-434
AttachmentNameproperties
property, 504
attributes, *see* properties
Auto Increment box, 151
automation (OLE), 569-577,
814-815
avoiding program errors,
783-784

B

BackColor property (ActiveX
controls), 88, 121
BackStyle property (ActiveX
controls), 88
Band object, 21-23
BandBorders property, 23
Bands collection, 21-23
base classes, 217
Basic Telephony (TAPI), 619
batch queries, 417
behaviors, 217
Benchmarking skeleton code
listing, 837
binding
    control properties, 192
    data, DataGrid control, 366
    early, 846
BitBlt API function, 599-602
Bitmap slide viewer listing,
798
blocking reboot command,
613-614
Boolean variables, 882
BorderStyle property
(ActiveX controls), 88, 122
bottlenecks, 834
breakpoints

applications, debugging, 786
    T-SQL Debugger, 419-421
Bubble sort method, 859
building
    classes, 221-226
    Help system, 738-747
      Help Contents files,
        752-755
      Help Topics files, 739-743
    wizards, 666
Building a Help system list-
ing, 743
business-logic tier (distrib-
uted transaction process-
ing), 890
ButtonMode property
(ActiveX controls), 122
BytesReceived property, 541

C

.CAB files, 15
    advantages, 155
    deploying, 157
    testing, 156-157
calculated columns, 400
CalendarForeColor property,
43
Call Stack dialog box, 790
callbacks, Windows API,
594-595
CallByName function, 10
calling objects, 908-913
Cancel method, 525
CancelAsyncRead method,
433
candidates, problem state-
ments, 240
Caption property (ActiveX
controls), 88
cardinality (OOA), 254
CGI (Common Gateway
Interface), 214
Change control, 916
Change event, 34
Check Out dialog box (VSS),
930
checking out VSS files, 924
Child command properties
dialog box, 309
child commands, 308-309,
311
child processes, 608-612

Class members for the class CheckingAccount listing, 219
class models, 253-254
class utilities, 651
classes, 217-220
abstract, 217
actor, 219
base, 217
Class Builder, 221-226
menus, 223-224
creating, 220-221
development processes, 220
example, 219
externally creatable, 207-208
instantiating, 217
persistence, 230
SingleUse, 211
states, 220
Transaction Server, integrating, 896-908
Click event, 88
client/server programming
clients
creating, 547-549
thick clients, 278
thin clients, 278
design, 276-278
multi-tiered applications, 277
two-tiered applications, 277
Winsock
example, 547-555
programming, 538
clients
creating, 547-549
thick clients, 278
thin clients, 278
Close event, 54
Close method, 544
CloseSubkey function listing, 729
cmdExit_Click event listing, 32
cmdExport_Click Event listing, 333
cmdFirst_Click event, 190
cmdLast_Click event, 190
cmdLaunch_Click event - OLE automation listing, 574
cmdLogIn's Click event listing, 497
cmdLogOut's Click event listing, 498
cmdSave_Click event OLE listing, 565

cmdSendLogNow's Click event listing, 499
code
benchmarking, 836-839
commenting, 836
conventions, 497
debugging, 784-791
breakpoints, 786
error handling, 783
special windows, 787-791
stepping through code, 785-787
FTP servers, 531
LightButton example, 96-104
Re-entrancy, 850
see also listings
code coverage, 851
Code for wizard template listing, 676
Code Manipulation package, 653
Code Profiler
Analysis window, 855
installing, 851
using, 850-855
Code Profiler dialog box, 852
Code Profiler Sort dialog box, 855
Code Profiler Statistics dialog box, 856
Code required to load cookies listing, 473
Code Table Optimization, compression algorithms, 868
CodeModule object, 653
CodePane object, 652
CodePanes collection, 648
coding ActiveX documents, 440-441
collections
aggregations, 227-228
Bands, 21-23
CodePanes, 648
Command object, 282-283
CommandBars, 649
Connection object, 283-284
DataBindings, 193
Error object, 284
ExportFormats, 332
Field object, 285
Parameters, 286
Property, 287
VBProjects, 646
Windows, 647
Column object, 371-373

columns
calculated, 400
SQL, adding/deleting, 410-411
COM (component object model), 69
DCOM, 73
GUIDs, 73
OLE, 69-74
ComboBox control, 33
ComboItem object, 33-34
Command button INI file listing, 714
Command Line Arguments box, 152
Command collection, 282-283
Command object, 282-283
CommandBar object, 651
CommandBars collection, 649
commands
child commands, 308, 311
File menu, Add Project, 101
Project menu, Add Module, 96
Query menu, Run, 307
Tools menu
Add Procedure, 116
Procedure Attributes, 129
comments, 836
Common Dialog control, 775
common keys (SQL), 401
Compile a Help File dialog box, 748
Compile tab (Project Properties dialog box), 152
compiling
ActiveX controls, 150
conditional arguments, 152
debug information, 154
documentation, 152
file sizes, 153
optimization, 153-154
P-code, 152
version numbers, 151
ActiveX documents, 441-442
Add-Ins, 659
DHTML applications, 474-475
optimizing applications, 841
component concurrency, 197-198
components, 69
in-process, debugging, 209
multithreaded, 196-198, 849
ActiveX, 198
concurrency, 197-198
multithreaded development, 198-203

new features, 18
OLE automation, 573
out-of-process, debugging,
    209
proper types, selecting,
    848-850
publishing, 61
sharing, 917
single-threaded, 849
Transaction Server, installing,
    905-906
Web-based, selecting, 849
see also controls
Components dialog box, 520
Compose method, 511
compound documents, 74
compression algorithms,
867-873
    Code Table Optimization, 868
    Huffman Compression, 868
    LZW, 868
    RLE, 869-873
ComputeControlSize method,
40
concrete objects, 217
concurrency, multithreaded
components, 197-198
Connect event, 545
Connect method, 545
Connection collection,
283-284
Connection object, 264,
283-284, 301
Connection1 Properties dia-
log box, 318
ConnectionRequest event,
546
ConnectionString property,
188
constituent controls
(ActiveX), 76, 85-87
    creating, 86-87
    events, exposing, 132
    properties, passing, 87
consumer data, creating,
192-193
containers, 74, 89-90, 112,
560
Contents files (Help systems),
752-755
context-sensitive Help, 777-
778
control arrays
    creating, 794-798
    event handlers, 800-801

properties
    creating, 795-798
    using, 805-807
Control Selection dialog box,
352
ControlContainer property,
90
controlling threads, 203
controlname_eventname
event handler, 800
controls, see ActiveX controls
conventions (coding), 497
cookie cutter classes, 217
cookies, 472
Coolbar control, 20-32
    events, 24
    properties, 23-24
Copy button's Click event
listing, 514
copying images, 599-602
Core Objects, EOM, 645-646,
650
    Add-In Management Package,
        652-654
    Event Response Package, 652
    Form Manipulation Package,
        651-652
    IDTExtensibility object,
        649-650
    instance variable, 651
    VBProjects, 646
    Windows collection, 647-649
Count property, 805
CountEngines property, 638
CountOfLines property, 653
Create Object dialog box,
347
CreateFontIndirect& API
function, 604
CreateProcess& API function
    arguments, 609
    constants, 611
    declaration, 608
CreateToolWindow method,
648
creating
    ActiveX controls, 83-85
        constituent controls, 86-87
        data controls, 347-348,
        807-808
        dynamic controls, 801-802
        methods of, 85-86
    ActiveX documents, 437-442
    ADO database front end,
        292-294

classes, 220-221, 342-346
clients, 547-549
control arrays, 794-798
    attributes, 795-796
    properties, 796-798
data consumers, 192-193
data sources, 176-192
    functionality, 186-190
    methods, 190-191
    properties, 180-185
DHTML pages, 464-468
editors
    INI files, 697-715
    System Registry, 725-735
Help projects, 747-762
mail-enabled applications,
    494-504
MAPI programs, 493-514,
    517-518
    e-mail applications,
    506-518
objects, 342, 345-348
OCX files, 150-154
packages, 903-904
queries, 415-417
reports, 316-334
speech recognition applica-
    tions, 629-630, 633-635
SQL tables, 409-410
TAPI applications, 620-625
templates, 836-839
user-drawn controls, 86
wizards, 662-665
CriticalError routine listing,
509
cross-thread marshaling, 198
Crystal Reports, 334
CurrentMode property, 638
custom events, creating,
135-138
custom marshaling, 74
CustomFormat property, 44

D

DAO (Data Access Objects),
261-262
data
    bindable, 192
    binding, 366
    compression, 867-873
    decompression, 867-873
    decryption, 863-864, 867

encryption, 863-864, 867
normalization, 272
SQL
  deleting, 405
  inserting, 403-405
  limiting selections,
    397-400
  retrieving, 394-403
  selecting, 395-397
  updating, 406-407
data consumers, 77, 192-193
Data control array listing,
  807
data controls, 279-294
  advanced
    DataCombo, 361-363
    DataGrid, 363-374
    Datalist, 358-360
  custom, creating, 347-348
  dynamic, creating, 807-808
  events, 280
  optimizing applications, 843
data definition statements,
  409-411
Data Environment, 300
  adding, 317-321
  child commands, 308, 311
  connections, defining,
    301-303
  Data Report Utility, 316
  databases, accessing, 311-314
data Environment (OLE DB),
  302
Data Environment designer,
  264-266
Data Form Wizard, 13,
  349-354
Data Link dialog box, 317
Data Link properties dialog
  box, 302
Data Object Generator
  Wizard, 13
Data Object Wizard, 342,
  345-348
Data Report Utility, 316
  creating reports, 316-334
  designing reports, 321-327
  report sections, 322
data server tier (distributed
  transaction processing), 891
data sources
  ActiveX controls, 77
    creating, 176-192
    functionality, 186-190
    methods, 190-191
    properties, 180-185
  Recordset objects, 184

data types, 847
Data View window, 264,
  338-339
data-centric, 69
DataArrival event, 546
database engines (SQL), 392
Database Environment, SQL
  Query designer, 304-305
databases
  accessing
    ADO, 263-264
    DAO, 261-262
    Data Environment
      designer, 264-266
    methods, 260-264
    RDO, 262-263
  connections
    Data Environment, 318
    Transaction Server, 894
  controls, 266
  data definition statements,
    409-411
  Data Environment, accessing,
    311-314
  data sources, 186-190
  Data View window, 338
  fields, 396
  front end (ADO), creating,
    292-294
  management, 237
  relational
    ADO, 270-276
    data normalization, 272
    foreign keys, 273-275
    indices, 275
    primary keys, 271-272
    referential integrity, 275
    tables, 271
    views, 276
  reports
    Crystal Reports, 334
    exporting, 332-334
  SQL Editor, 339-341
DataBindings collection, 193
DataCombo control, 361-363
DataGrid control, 363-374
  appearance, 367-368
  binding data, 366
  Column object, 371-373
  current cell, 368
  events, 370
  methods, 368-369
  navigation, 366-367
  properties, 364-368
  record selectors, 367
  Split objects, 373-374

DataList control, 358-360
DataMember property, 358
DataObject object, 820
DataSource property, 358
date/time (VSS), 926
DateTimePicker control,
  43-46
  events, 43
  formats, 42
  properties, 43
DblClick event, 88
DCOM (distributed compo-
  nent object model), 69, 73
DDE, 68-69
dead code, 851
Debug toolbar, 785
debugging applications,
  784-791
  breakpoints, 786
  DHTML applications, 474
  error handling, 783
  Immediate window, 787
  in-process components, 209
  Locals window, 787
  multithreaded systems,
    208-210
  out-of-process components,
    209
  program errors, avoiding,
    782-784
  queries, 419-421
  stepping through code,
    785-787
  T-SQL Debugger, 414-418,
    421
  windows
    special, 787-791
    Watches window, 788
Declaration for the
  StretchBlt& function listing,
  602
Declare statement, 586-588
declaring Windows API func-
  tions, 583-585
decompression, 867-873
decryption
  data, 863-864, 867
  DES, 864
  IDEA, 864
  PGP, 865
  XOR, 865
defining connections,
  301-303
definition statements,
  409-411

Delete button's Click event listing, 514
DeleteSetting statement, 720
deleting
    SQL columns, 410-411
    SQL data, 405
    SQL indexes, 410-411
    SQL tables, 411
deploying
    ActiveX controls, 150
    ActiveX documents, 447-448
    .CAB files, 156-157
    DHTML applications,
      476-477
DES (Data Encryption
    Standard), 864
design
    ActiveX controls
      Ambient objects, 90
      constituent controls, 85-87
      containers, 89-90
      events, 88
      interfaces, 90-92
      licensing issues, 86-87
      methods, 89
      planning, 83-85
      properties, 87-88
      user-drawn, 86
    applications, 833
    client/server, 276-278
    DHTML pages, 464-468
    event handlers, 800-801
    importance of, 82-83
    menus, 442-444
    reports, 321-327
    standardization, 83
    wizards, 662
design time, 112-116
Detail reports, 322
developing
    multithreaded components,
      198-203
    source control, 916-917
    VSS, 917-922
development environment,
    877-879
development processes, 220
DHTML (Dynamic HTML), 17
    applications, 455-456
      compiling, 474-475
      debugging, 474
      deploying, 476-477
      implementing, 473-481
    code security, 456
    converting HTML pages, 465

    cookies, 472
    dynamic interaction, 456
    events, 459-463
      form events, 462
      keyboard events, 459
      Mouse event, 460
      selection events, 461
    faster response time, 456
    object model, 457-463
    objects, 457-459
    offline capability, 456
    Package and Deployment
      Wizard, 476
    page designer, 464, 467-468
    pages
      creating, 464-468
      events, 461
    project type, 463-473
    server load reduction, 456
    state maintainence, 456,
      470-473
DHTML Properties dialog
    box, 465
dialog boxes
    Add File (VSS), 926
    Add Module, 96
    Add Project, 101
    Add Watch, 788
    Call Stack, 790
    Check Out (VSS), 930
    Child command properties,
      309
    Code Profiler Sort, 855
    Code Profiler Statistics, 856
    Compile a Help File, 748
    Connection1 Properties, 318
    Control Selection, 352
    Create Object, 347
    Data Link, 317
    Data Link properties, 302
    DHTML Properties, 465
    File Source, 480
    Footnote and Endnote, 745
    Help Topics, 751
    Include Files, 479
    Insert Object, 563
    Macro, 883
    Make Project, 150-151
    Package Folder, 479
    Package Type, 478
    Packaging Report, 481
    Procedure Attributes, 130,
      138, 144
    Profiler dialog, 852
    Project File Name selection,
      747

    Project Properties, 199
      Compile tab, 152
      Make tab, 151-152
    Quick Watch, 789
    Safety Settings, 480
    Select User Control Type, 347
    Source Code Control Options,
      927
    SourceSafe Options, 920
    Windows Properties, 759
Dictation control, 629
Direct Speech control, 631,
    634
Disable reboot listing, 614
display speed, optimizing,
    847
Display text upside down
    listing, 606
DisplayAboutBox procedure,
    143
distributed transaction pro-
    cessing, 890-893
    business-logic tier, 890
    data server tier, 891
    Object Request Brokers,
      892-893
    transaction monitors, 891-892
distribution lists (MAPI), 486
DLLs (Dynamic Link
    Libraries), 580
    ActiveX, 436
    API
      USER32.DLL, 581-582
      Windows, 580-583
    extensions, 583
    GDI32.DLL, 582
    KERNEL32.DLL, 582-583
    Transaction Server, register-
      ing, 903-906
Document property, 522
documents (ActiveX)
    adding, 445-447
    advantages, 429
    AsyncRead method, 432-433
    AsyncReadComplete event,
      433-434
    CancelAsyncRead method,
      433
    coding, 440-441
    compiling, 441-442
    creating, 437-442
    forms, 445-447
    Hyperlink object, 434-435
    interfaces, 439
    Internet Explorer, 447-448

menu design, 442-444
Migration Wizard, 448-451
starting new, 438
testing, 441
understanding, 428-430
UserDocument, 430-435
Download and Register an ActiveX Document listing, 448
downloading ActiveX controls, 432-434
DownLoadMail property, 501
drag and drop (OLE)
arguments, 821
automatic, 814-815
controls, 810
DataObject Object, 820
drag operation, 812
enchancing VB, 826-829
functionality, 811-814
manual process, 817, 820-822, 826
OLECompleteDrag event, 825
OLEDrag method, 819
OLEDragDrop event, 824
OLEDragOver event, 821
OLEGiveFeedback event, 822
OLEStartDrag method, 820
processing, 813-814
target event, 812
visual behavior, 822
drawing images, 603-604
DSN (Data Source Name), 415
DTPicker control, 43-46
events, 43
formats, 42
properties, 43
DTPicker property, 44-46
dynamic controls, creating, 801-802, 807-808
Dynamic HTML, *see* **DHTML**
dynamic identification variable, 651

E

early binding, 846
early bound objects, 106
editors
INI files, creating, 697-715
System Registry, creating, 725-735
e-mail applications, see MAPI embedding (OLE), 68, 566

Enabled property, 88, 128-130
Enabled property listing, 129
encryption algorithms
data, 863-864, 867
DES, 864
IDEA, 864
PGP, 865
XOR, 865
engines, scripting, 172
enhancing
Help files, 758
VB, drag and drop OLE, 826-829
EnterFocus event, 430
entering Help text, 741-743
EOM (Extensibility Object Model), 644
Core Objects, 645-646, 650
Add-In Management Package, 652-654
Event Response Package, 652
Form Manipulation Package, 651-652
IDTExtensibility object, 649-650
instance variable, 651
VBProjects, 646
Windows collection, 647-649
implementing, 654-661
packages, 645
Error collection, 284
Error event, 547
error handling, debugging applications, 783
Error object, 284
establishing MAPI sessions, 500-501
Event Builder, 227
event handlers, designing control arrays, 800-801
Event object, 458
Event Response Package, 652
event trace diagram, see sequence diagram
events
ActiveX controls, event sequences, 115
adding to ActiveX controls, 131-132, 135
ADO Data Control, 280
apartment, recording, 208
AsycReadComplete, 430
AsyncReadComplete, 433-434

Change, 34
Click, 88
Close, 545
cmdFirst_Click, 190
cmdLast_Click, 190
Connect, 545
ConnectionRequest, 546
Coolbar, 24
creating, 135-138
DataArrival, 546
DataGrid, 370
DblClick, 88
defaults, setting, 138-139
DHTML, 459-463
DTPicker, 43
EnterFocus, 430
Error, 547
ExitFocus, 430
exposing, 132
GetDayBold, 42
Hide, 430
ImageCombo, 34
InitProperties, 184-185, 430
Internet Transfer Control, 528-529
KeyDown, 88
KeyPress, 88
KeyUp, 88
MonthView, 42
Mouse, 460
MouseDown, 88
MouseMove, 88
MouseUp, 88
MSHFlexGrid, 385-386
naming, 138
OLE, source, 811
OLECompleteDrag, 825
OLEDrag, 820
OLEDragDrop, 813, 824
OLEDragOver, 812, 821
OLEGiveFeedback, 813, 822
OLESetData, 813
onhelp, 460
onkeydown, 459
passing along, 87
ReadProperties, 184, 431
Scroll, 431
SendComplete, 546
SendProgess, 546
Show, 431
StateChanged, 528
Validate, 34
Winsock, TCP/IP, 545-547
WriteProperties, 184, 431

Events pane, Class Builder, 224

exception handing, providing, 678-680

Exchange sort method, 859

Execute method, 525-527, 531-533

executing queries, T-SQL Debugger, 417-419

EXEs, ActiveX, 436

Exit button's Click event listing, 516

ExitFocus event, 430

ExitWindowsEx& API function, 612-613

ExportFormats collection, 332

exporting reports, 332-334

ExportReport method, 332

exposing events, 132

Extended MAPI, 486

Extended Telephony, TAPI, 619

extensibility, 644

extension DLLs, 583

external systems (OOA), 250

externally creatable classes, instantiating, 207-208

Extracting the value from cookies listing, 473

F

features, VB6
   components, 18
   controls, 16-17
   Internet, 17
   language, 9-13
   new, 9-18
   wizards, 13-16

Fetch method, 510

FetchMessages routine listing, 509

FetchMessages subroutine, 508

field names (databases), 396

Field object, 285

Field object collection, 285

fields (databases), 396

file I/O operations, optimizing applications, 847

File menu commands, Add Project, 101

File Source dialog box, 480

filename argument, 332

files
   .CAB, 15
      advantages, 155
      testing, 156-157
   Internet Transfer Control, accessing, 530-531
   VSS
      adding, 926
      checking out, 924
      returning, 925

Filter function, 11

Find (Help), setting up, 757-758

FixedBackground property, 22

FixSectionName function listing, 711

Flash method, 139-141

flashing window captions, APIs, 606-607

FlashWindow API function, 599

FlashWindow& API function, 606

FlatScrollbar control, 46-47

FlatScrollbar properties, 47

focus of control bar, sequences, 252

Font property, 88, 122

Footnote and Endnote dialog box, 745

ForeColor property, 88, 123

foriegn keys, relational database, 273-275

Form Load event lising, 27

Form Manipulation package, 651-652

Format property, DTPicker, 44-46

FormatCurrency function, 11

FormatDateTime function, 11

FormatNumber function, 11

FormatPercent function, 11

formats, Help windows, 759-760

forms (runtime), instantiating, 803-805

Forms object, 458

Forward button's Click event listing, 513

Frames object, 458

friend classes, 218

FTP (File Transfer Protocol), 520
   proxy servers, 529
   servers
      code, 531
      Internet Transfer Control, 531-533
   TCP/IP, 536

functionality
   databases, data sources, 186-190
   MAPI, 488-492
   OLE, drag and drop, 811-814
   VSS, 917-918

functions
   API
      GetPrivateProfileInt, 695
      GetPrivateProfileSection, 694
      GetProfileInt, 695
      GetProfileSection, 694
      WritePrivateProfileSection, 696
      WritePrivateProfileString, 697
      WriteProfileSection, 696
      WriteProfileString, 697
   argument, 332
   CallByName, 10
   Filter, 11
   FormatCurrency, 11
   FormatDateTime, 11
   FormatNumber, 11
   FormatPercent, 11
   GetAllSettings, 720
   GetSetting, 719
   INIAdd, 704
   INIRetrieve, 706
   InstrRev, 12
   Join, 12
   MonthName, 12
   new, 10-13
   RegAdd, 704
   Replace, 12
   Round, 12
   Split, 12
   StrReverse, 13
   VBA, adding, 877
   VBScript, 167-173
      conversions, 172
      scripting engines, 172
      testing, 172
   WeekdayName, 13
   Windows API
      applications, 592-593
      declaring, 583-585

G

GDI32.DLL API, 582
Gender property, 639
Generated code to maintain state listing, 470
gerunds, problem statements, 240
GetAllSettings function, 720
GetData method, 544
GetDataMember event listing, 186
GetDayBold event, 42
GetFirstVisible method, 34
GetHeader method, 527
GetKeyHandle function listing, 726
GetPrivateProfileInt API function, 695
GetPrivateProfileSection API function, 694
GetProfileInt API function, 695
GetProfileSection API function, 694
GetSetting function, 719
GetSystemDirectory& API functions, 614-615
GetWindowsDirectory& API functions, 614-615
Grabbing the Product ID listing, 911
GrammarFromString method, 634
graphics APIs, 599-607
Group Footer (reports), 322
Group Header (reports), 322
grouping
    properties, 144-147
    SQL statements, transactions, 407-409
GUIDs, COM, 73

H

Heap sort method, 859
Height property (ActiveX controls), 88
Help
    building, 738-747
    Contents file, building, 752-755
    context-sensitive, 777-778

    enhancing standard files, 758
    Find, setting up, 757
    HTML, 762-775
        advanced features, 773-774
        Internet linking, 774
    HTML Workshop, 765-772
    hypertext links, 740
    Index, adding keywords, 756-757
    Internet links, 761
    multimedia, adding, 761-762
    projects, creating, 747-762
    text, entering, 741-743
    topic ID, 744-747
        mapping, 750
    topics
        building, 739-743
        labeling, 744-747
    window formats, 759-760
    WinHelp system, accessing, 775-778
    Workshop, HTML Index, 771-772
Help Connecting to the Internet listing, 743
Help Table of Contents text listing, 742
Help Topics dialog box, 751
Help Workshop listing, 743
HelpContextID object, 777
Hide event, 430
Hierarchical FlexGrid Control, *see* MSHFlexGrid control
hInternet property, 522
history, ActiveX, 68-69, 72-79
History object, 459
HitTest method, 41
hsbRecScroll_Change event listing, 188
HScrollBar control, 46
HTML (Hypertext Markup Language)
    ADO, 278
    cookies, 472
    DHTML, converting, 465
    Help, 762-775
        advanced features, 773-774
        linking to Internet, 774
    Help Workshop, 765-772
    page designer, 464
    ActiveX, 428
HTTP (Hypertext Transfer Protocol), 520
    proxy servers, 529
    TCP/IP, 536

Huffman Compression (compression algorithms), 868
Hyperlink object, 434-435
Hyperlink to the ActiveX Documen listingt, 448
hypertext, Help links, 740

I

icons, changing, 147
IDEA, encryption algorithms, 864
identifying bottlenecks, 834
IDTExtensibility object, 650
Image property, 22
ImageCombo control, 32-37
    events, 34
    methods, 34
    properties, 34-35
ImageCombo control imcCountry listing, 36
ImageList control, 27, 33
ImageList property, 23
images, APIs
    copying, 599-602
    drawing, 603-604
Images object, 458
Immediate window, debugging, 787
implementing
    DHTML applications, 473-481
    EOM, 654-661
    multithreaded systems, 205-206
in-process components, 77
Include Files dialog box, 479
Indentation property, 33
indexes, SQL
    adding, 410-411
    deleting, 410-411
indices
    Help
        adding keywords, 756-757
        HTML Workshop, 771-772
    relational database, 275
INI (initialization) files, 690
    contents, 691
    editors, creating, 697-715
    sequential, 692
    System Registry, 715-717
        accessing, 718-720

System Registry Editor program controls, 697-701
Windows API, 692-697
INIAdd function, 704
INIAdd function listing, 703
INIDelete function listing, 708
INIEdit module listing, 702, 725
INIRetrieve function, 706
INIRetrieve function listing, 705
initializing properties, 124-127
Initializing the speech engine listing, 637
InitProperties event, 184-185, 430
INIUpdate function listing, 707
Insert Object dialog box, 563
inserting SQL data, 403-405
Insertion sort method, 859
installing
Code Profiler, 851
components, Transaction Server, 905-906
Package and Deployment Wizard, 477
T-SQL Debugger, 412
VSS server, 918
instantiating
classes, 217
externally creatable classes, 207-208
forms, runtime, 803-805
InstrRev function, 12
integrating VB classes, Transaction Servers, 896-908
interaction diagram, *see* **sequence diagrams**
interfaces
ActiveX documents, 439
controls, 90-93
objects, 228-229
Internet
Help links, 761
new features, 17
Internet Explorer, deploying ActiveX documents, 447-448
Internet Transfer Control, 520-529
documents, accessing, 530-531
events, 528-529

Execute method, 531-533
files, accessing, 530-531
FTP, 521-529
servers, accessing, 531-533
HTTP, 521-529
methods, 524-528
OpenURL method, 530
properties, 521-523
proxy servers, 529-530
IP addresses (TCP/IP), Winsock, 538
ISDN, telephony, 619
ISQL (Interactive Structured Query Language), 393
Item property, 806

J-K

Join function, 12
joins (SQL), 352
setting up, 400-402

KERNEL32.DLL API, 582-583
KeyDown event, 88
KeyPress event, 88
keys, System Registry, 719
KeyUp event, 88
keywords
Help Index, adding, 756-757
Private, 219
Public, 218

L

labeling Help topics, 744-747
labels, VSS, 926
languages
localization, 53-56
strings, 54
LargeChange property, 47
late bound objects, 106
LBound property, 806
LCID (locale ID), 52, 90
identifiers, 53-56
Left property (ActiveX controls), 88
libraries, ADO, 279-294
licensing controls, 86-87
LightButton control, 92
About box, 142-144
adding to Web pages, 155
.CAB files

advantages, 155
testing, 156-157
compiling, 150
debug information, 154
documentation, 152
file sizes, 153
optimization, 153-154
P-code, 152
version numbers, 151
constituent controls, 95-96
event sequences, 115
events, 130-131
adding, 131-132, 135
creating, 135-138
defaults, 138-139
naming, 138
initializing, 97-98
instances
design-time, 112-113
runtime, 114
methods, 130-131
adding, 139
Flash( ), 139-141
Refresh( ), 139
naming, 94
properties, 95
adding, 116-121
BackColor, 121
BorderStyle, 122
ButtonMode, 122
descriptions, 145-147
Enabled, 128-130
Font, 122
ForeColor, 123
grouping, 144-145
initializing, 124-125
Picture, 123
property bag, 109-111
reading, 124-127
SelColor, 124
SelPicture, 124
writing, 124-127
resizing, 100
run mode, 103
saving, 100
sizing, 94
testing, 103-104, 111-112, 127-128
test form, 101-103
Timer event, 98-100
toolbox icon, changing, 147
troubleshooting, 104-108
Web applications, 115-116
LightButton example, 94
code, 96-104

LightButton's General Declarations listing, 132
LightButton's Refresh method listing, 139
limitations (Visual Basic), 845
limiting data selections (SQL), 397-400
line devices (telephony), 619
links, Help, 740, 761
Links object, 458
LipType property, 640
Listen method, 544
listings
  About box, 142
  Accessing the Help system, 776
  Add-In code, 657
  Adding controls on-the-fly, 802
  Address Book button's Click event, 515
  Benchmarking skeleton code, 837
  Bitmap slide viewer, 798
  Building a Help system, 743
  Class members for the class CheckingAccount, 219
  Client and Winsock control, 548
  CloseSubkey function, 729
  cmdExit_Click event, 32
  cmdExport_Click Event, 333
  cmdLaunch_Click event - OLE automation, 574
  cmdLogIn's Click event, 497
  cmdLogOut's Click event, 498
  cmdSave_Click event OLE, 565
  cmdSendLogNow's Click event, 499
  Code for wizard template, 676
  Code Profiler, 853
  Code required to load cookies, 473
  Command button INI file, 714
  Copy button's Click event, 514
  Copying images with API, 601
  CreateProcess& function declaration, 608
  CriticalError routine, 509
  Data control array, 807
  declaration for the StretchBlt& function, 602
  Delete button's Click event, 514

Disable reboot, 614
Display text upside down, 606
Download and Register an ActiveX Document, 448
Enabled property, 129
Exit button's Click event, 516
Extracting the value from cookies, 473
FetchMessages routine, 509
FixSectionName function, 711
Form Load event, 27
Forward button's Click event, 513
Generated code to maintain state, 470
GetDataMember event, 186
GetKeyHandle function, 726
Grabbing the Product ID, 911
Help Connecting to the Internet, 743
Help Table of Contents text, 742
Help Workshop, 743
hsbRecScroll_Change event, 188
Hyperlink to the ActiveX Document, 448
ImageCombo control imcCountry, 36
INIAdd function, 703
INIDelete function, 708
INIEdit module, 702, 725
INIRetrieve function, 705
Initialize the speech engine, 637
INIUpdate function, 707
LightButton control
  About box, 143
  Caption property, 107
  custom events, 136-137
  Enabled property, 129
  event procedures, 133-134
  exposing events, 132
  Flash( ) method, 140
  Initialize event, 98
  Property procedures, 117-121
  RaiseEvent command, 137-138
  Refresh( ) method, 139
  Resize event, 100
  Timer event, 98-99
LightButton's General Declarations, 132
LightButton's Refresh method, 139

LOGFONT type, 604
lstFileContents_Click, 712
lstMessages's Click event, 515
MDINote.vbp, 804
Modifications to LightButton control, 105
Modified SendActivityLog subroutine, 504
Module1's General Declarations section code, 97
Multiple SQL statements in transaction, 408
Navigate to the Requested .vbd File, 448
Navigating the database, 313
OLE automation Click events, 575
optType_Click event, 734
Product ID, 911
Properties of the ADO Control, 294
Property Get procedure returns the Recordset, 184
Property Let and Property Get procedures, 182
Property variable and default value declarations, 181
QuickSort routine, 860
ReadFile function, 710
ReadFile procedure, 710
RegDelete function, 731
RegRetrieve function, 730
Reply button's Click event, 512
ReplyAll button's Click event, 512
Reverse Text program, 880
ReverseText Sub procedure, 883
RLEUncompress routines, 870
Rounded corner rectangle, 603
Selecting specific voice type, 637
SendActivityLog subroutine, 499
speech recognition code, 633
STARTUPINFO declarations, 610
StripPunctuation function, 885
TAPI sample program, 623
TAPIStatus Sub procedure, 624
tbrEdit_ButtonClick event, 29
tbrFile_ButtonClick event, 30

tmrChkStatus's Timer event, 98

tmrChkStatus_Timer event code, 126

UserControl's Resize event, 100

UserControl_Resize event, 180

ValidateUserInput routine, 679

VBScript code in HTML document, 163-164

Windows caption flasher, 607

Wizard source code Resource File, 685

Wizard template, 677

XOREncryption routine, 866

LocaleID, 90

LocalHostName property, 541

LocalIP property, 541

localization, language strings, 53-56

localized controls, 90

LocalPort property, 541

Locals window, debugging, 787

location, transparency, 73

Location object, 459

location transparency, 73

LOGFONT type listing, 604

low-level, 237

lpReturnedString argument, 694

lstFileContents_Click listing, 712

lstMessages's Click event listing, 515

LZW (Lemple-Ziv-Welch), compression algorithms, 868

M

Macro dialog box, 883

macros, VBA, 880

Mail Application Programming Interface, *see* **MAPI**

maintaining states, DHTML, 470-473

Make Project dialog box, 150-151

Make tab, 152

command line arguments, 152

conditional compilation arguments, 152

documentation, 152

managing

database connections, Transaction Servers, 894

distributed objects, Transaction Servers, 895

manual drag and drop OLE process, 817, 820-822, 826

MAPI (Mail Application Programming Interface)

activity log, 502

address book providers, 486-487

controls, 488-492

creating e-mail applications, 506-518

distribution lists, 486

e-mail applications, creating, 506-518

functionality, 488-492

mail-enabled applications, 494-504

messages

addressing, 502

sending, 502

passwords, 501

programs, creating, 493-514, 517-518

service providers, 484-488

sessions, establishing, 500-501

SMTP, 485

specification, 484-488

Spooler, 488

transport providers, 487

MAPIMessages control, 488-492

MAPISession control, 488-492

mapping topic IDs, 750

marshaling, customing, 74

MDI (multiple-document interface) controls, 803-805

MDIChild property, 803

MDINote.vbp listing, 804

memory, optimizing, 848

menu bars, VBA, 879

menus

ActiveX documents, designing, 442-444

Class Builder, 223-224

message sets, 510

message store providers, MAPI, 487

messages, MAPI

addressing, 502

sending, 502

Method Builder, 226

method parameters, 846

methodology, analysis, 235

methods

Accept, 544

Activate, 634

adding to ActiveX controls, 139

AsyncRead, 432-433

Cancel, 525

CancelAsyncRead, 433

Close, 544

Compose, 511

ComputeControlSize, 40

Connect, 545

CreateToolWindow, 648

data sources, 190-191

databases, accessing, 260-264

DataGrid, 368-369

Execute, 525-527, 531-533

ExportReport, 332

Fetch, 510

Flash, 139-141

GetData, 544

GetFirstVisible, 34

GetHeader, 527

GrammarFromString, 634

HitTest, 41

ImageCombo, 34

Internet Transfer Control, 524-528

Listen, 544

MonthView, 40-41

Move, 89

MoveFirst, 190

MoveLast, 190

MoveToRecord, 190

MSHFlexGrid, 384-385

NavigateTo, 436

OLE controls, 568-569

OLEDrag, 819

OpenURL, 528-530

passing along, 87

PeekData, 544

ReadProperty, 110

ReBind, 373

Refresh, 89, 139

Send, 512

SendData, 544

SetFirstVisible, 34

Speak, 641

Winsock, TCP/IP, 543-545

WriteProperty, 109-110

Methods pane, Class Builder, 224
Microphone Setup Wizard, 630
microphones (speech recognition), setting up, 630
Microsoft Voice Text control, 635
Microsoft Word, embedding objects, 566
ModeName property, 640
Modifications to LightButton control listing, 105
modified SendActivityLog subroutine listing, 504
MonthName function, 12
MonthView control, 37-42
MonthView events, 42
MonthView methods, 40-41
MonthView properties, 38-40
Mouse event, 460
MouseDown event, 88
MouseMove event, 88
MouseUp event, 88
Move method, 89
MoveFirst method, 190
MoveLast method, 190
MoveToRecord method, 190
MSHFlexGrid control, 374-388
    parent Command, 387
    properties, 376-384
    unpopulated space, 375
MSHFlexGrid event, 385-386
MSHFlexGrid methods, 384-385
multi-tiered client/server applications, 277
multimedia, adding Help, 761-762
Multiple SQL statements in transaction listing, 408
multithreaded components, 196-198, 849
    active threads, 203
    ActiveX, 198
    apartment models, 198-203
    concurrency, 197-198
    control, 203
    cross-thread marshaling, 198
    development, 198-203
    reentrancy, 200
    round-robin model, 203
    serialization, 201
    single-use objects, 210-211
    thread aggregation, 201-203

threads, safety, 203
unattended execution, 199
multithreaded systems
    debugging, 208-210
    implementing, 205-206

N

n-tier servers, 890
Name property (ActiveX controls), 88
naming
    ActiveX controls, 94
    events, 138
Navigate to the Requested .vbd File listing, 448
NavigateTo method, 436
Navigating the database listing, 313
navigation, DataGrid control, 366-367
Navigator object, 459
nested queries, 407
non-deterministic threads, 203
normal scenario sequences, 247

O

object collections, 227-228
object concurrency, 198
object model
    DHTML, 457-463
object models, ADO, 280-289
object-oriented programming, see OOP
Object Request Brokers (ORB), 890-893
Object-Oriented Analysis, see OOA
objects
    All, 458
    Ambient, 90
    Applets, 458
    Band, 21-23
    CodeModule, 653
    CodePane, 652
    Column, DataGrid control, 371-373
    ComboItem, 33-34
    Command, 282-283
    CommandBar, 651

component objects, 69
concrete, 217
Connection, 264, 283-284, 301
Data Object Wizard, creating, 342, 345-348
DataObject, 820
DHTML, 457-459
distributed, Transaction Server, 895
early bound, 106
Error, 284
Event, 458
Field, 285
Forms, 458
Frames, 458
HelpContextID, 777
History, 459
Hyperlink, 434-435
IDTExtensibility, 650
Images, 458
interfaces, 228-229
late bound, 106
Links, 458
Location, 459
Navigator, 459
Parameter, 286
Property, 287
protocols, 228-229
Recordset, 264, 287
reducing dots, 845-846
Scripts, 458
Selection, 458
single-use multithreaded, 210-211
Split, DataGrid control, 373-374
stateless, Transaction Server, 898
Stylesheets, 458
Transaction Server, calling, 908-913
UserControl, properties, 431-432
UserDocument, 430-435, 449
VBScript, 161-162
verbs, 568
WhatsThisHelpID, 777
OCX files, 75
    compiling, 150
        conditional arguments, 152
        debug information, 154
        documentation, 152
        file sizes, 153
        optimization, 153-154

P-code, 152
version numbers, 151
creating, 150-154
Office 97, OLE, 560-561
OLE (Object Linking and Embedding), 68, 560
ActiveX, 68-69
automation, 74, 569-577
COM, 69-74
compound document, 74
controls, 561-569
methods, 568-569
properties, 568-569
DB datasource, ADO, 290
drag and drop
automatic, 814-815
controls, 810
DataObject Object, 820
drag completion, 813
drag operation, 812
enhancing VB, 826-829
functionality, 811-814
manual process, 817, 820-822, 826
OLECompleteDrag event, 825
OLEDrag method, 819
OLEDragDrop event, 824
OLEDragOver Event, 821
OLEGiveFeedback event, 822
OLEStartDrag method, 820
operation, 812
processing, 813-814
target event, 812
visual behavior, 822
drag-and-drop, 74
events, source, 811
Microsoft Word, embedding, 566
Office 97, Visual Basic, 560-561
Structured Storage, 74
OLE automation, components, 573
OLE automation Click events listing, 575
OLECompleteDrag event, 825
OLEDrag event, 820
OLEDrag method, 819
OLEDragDrop event, 813, 824
OLEDragMode property, 814
OLEDragOver event, 812, 821
OLEDropMode property, 814
OLEGiveFeedback event, 813, 822

OLESetData event, 813
on-the-fly programming (OTFP), 215-216
onhelp event, 460
onkeydown event, 459
OOA (Object-Oriented Analysis), 235
analysts, 236
architects, 238-239
cardinality, 254
external systems, 250
foundations, 235-239
sequence diagrams, 247-252
use-case methodology, 239-254
problem statement, 240-245
use-case model, 245-246
OOP (object-oriented programming), 214
abstractions, 216
programming, 216-217
OpenURL method, 528-530
OpenURL property, 524
operators, VBScript, 167
optimizing
applications, 832-835
compiler, 841
data controls, 843
data types, 847
file I/O operations, 847
memory, 848
Windows API, 843
Code Profiler, 850-855
commenting code, 836
display speed, 847
overkill, 835
Option Explicit statements, debugging, 784
options
T-SQL Debugger, 421
VSS, 927
optType_Click event listing, 734
ORB (Object Request Brokers), 890-893
ordinal numbers, function names, 588
Orientation property, 23
OTFP (On-the-fly programming), 215-217
out-of-process components, 78
debugging, 209
overwrite argument, 333

P

Package and Deployment Wizard, 13-15, 156, 442
DHTML, 476
installing, 477
operating, 477-481
Package Folder dialog box, 479
package Type dialog box, 478
packages
EOM, 645
Transaction Server, creating, 903-904
Packaging Report dialog box, 481
page designer, DHTML pages, 464
creating, 467-468
Page Footer (reports), 322
Page Header (reports), 322
pages (DHTML), creating, 464-468
Parameter object, 286
parameters, methods, 846
parent Command, MSHFlexGrid control, 387
parsing, 882
passing arguments
reference, 585-586
value, 585-586
passing along properties, 87
Password property, 524
passwords, MAPI programs, 501
PeekData method, 544
persistence, 237
classes, 230
PGP (Pretty Good Privacy) encryption algorithms, 865
phone devices (TAPI), 619
Picture property, 23, 123
planning application design, 833
ports, TCP/IP, 539
POTS (telephony), 619
presentation tier, distributed transaction processing, 890
previewing reports, 328-330
primary keys, 271-272
printing reports, 331-332
private classes, 218
private keyword classes, 219
problem statement (use-case methodology), 240-245

Procedure Attributes command (Tools menu), 129
Procedure Attributes dialog box, 130, 144
procedures
  Property Set, 108
  stored, SQL Editor, 339-340
  VBScript, 162
Procedures Attribute dialog box, 138
processes, 196
processing OLE drag and drop, 813-814
PROCESS_INFORMATION structure, API system functions, 610
product ID (Transaction Server), 910-911
Product ID listings, 911
program errors, avoiding, 783-784
programming
  by chaos, 236
  client/server, Winsock, 538
  on-the-fly, 215
  OOP, OTFP, 216-217
  spaghetti code, 216
  VBA, differences, 879-888
programs
  MAPI, creating, 493-514, 517-518
  VBA, 880
Project and Component Manipulation Package, 653
Project File Name selection dialog box, 747
Project menu command, Add Module, 96
Project Properties dialog box, 151, 199
  Compile tab, 152
project type, DHTML, 463-473
project-oriented programming, VSS, 922-926
projects
  ActiveX, 77-79
  Help, creating, 747-762
  new VB6 with VSS, 931
  VB, VSS, 929-931
  versions, tracking, 926
  VSS, using, 922-925
properties, 217
  AccessType, 522
  ActiveX controls, 88
    adding to, 116-124
    descriptions, 145-147
    grouping, 144-145

ambient, 90
Appearance, 47
BackColor, 88, 121
BackStyle, 88
Band object, 21
BandBorders, 23
BorderStyle, 88, 122
ButtonMode, 122
BytesReceived, 541
CalendarForeColor, 43
Caption, 88
categories, 145
ConnectionString, 188
control arrays, 805-807
Coolbar, 23-24
Count, 805
CountEngines, 638
CountOfLines, 653
CurrentMode, 638
CustomFormat, 44
data sources, 180-185
DataMember, 358
DataSource, 358
descriptions, 144-147
Document, 522
DownLoadMail, 501
DTPicker, 43
Enabled, 88, 128-130
FixedBackground, 22
FlatScrollbar, 47
Font, 88, 122
ForeColor, 88, 123
Format, 44-46
Gender, 639
grouping, 144-147
Height, 88
hInternet, 522
Image, 22
ImageCombo, 34-35
ImageList, 23
Indentation, 33
initializing, 124-127
Internet Transfer Control, 521-523
Item, 806
LargeChange, 47
LBound, 806
Left, 88
LipType, 640
LocalHostName, 541
LocalIP, 541
LocalPort, 541
MDIChild, 803
ModeName, 640
MonthView, 38-40
Name, 88

OLE controls, 568-569
OLEDragMode, 814
OLEDropMode, 814
OpenURL, 524
Orientation, 23
passing along, 87
passing from constituent controls, 87
Password, 524
Picture, 23, 123
property bag, 109-111
Protocol, 522, 542
Proxy, 523
reading, 124-127
RemoteHost, 523, 542
RemotePort, 523, 542
RequestTimeout, 523
ResponseCode, 523
ResponseInfo, 523
RowMember, 358
RowSource, 358
SelColor, 124
SelectedItem, 34
SelPicture, 124
SelText, 34
SmallChange, 47
State, 543
StillExecuting, 523
TAPI, 622
Text, 88
ThreadID, 198
Top, 88
Transaction Server, 899
UBound, 806
UseCoolbarColors, 22
UseCoolbarPicture, 22
UserControl object, 431-432
UserName, 524
VariantHeight, 24
Visible, 88
Width, 88
Winsock, TCP/IP, 541-542
writing, 124-127
Properties of the ADO Control listing, 294
Properties pane
  Class Builder, 224
property bag, 109-111
Property Builder, 226
Property Get procedure returns the Recordset listing, 184
Property Let and Property Get procedures listing, 182
Property Let procedures, 108

Property object, 287
Property Set procedures, 108
Property variable and default value declarations listing, 181
Protocol property, 522, 542
protocol stacks (TCP/IP), 536
protocols, objects, 228-229
providing exception handing, 678-680
Proxy property, 523
proxy servers
   FTP, 529
   HTTP, 529
   Internet Transfer Control, 529-530
public classes, 218
public keyword classes, 218
Publish Wizard, 62
publishing components, 61

Q-R

queries
   batch, 417
   nested, 407
   SQL Query designer, 304-305
   T-SQL Debugger
      creating, 415-417
      debugging, 419-421
      executing, 417-419
Query Designer, 341
Query menu commands, Run, 307
Quick sort method, sorting algorithms, 860
Quick Watch dialog box, 789
QuickSort procedure, 862
QuickSort routine listing, 860

RaiseEvent command, 137
RaiseEvent statement, 87
RDBMS (ADO), 270
RDO (Remote Data Objects), 262-263
   databases, accessing, 262-263
RDS (Remote Data Service), 295
ReadFile function listings, 710
ReadFile procedure listing, 710
reading properties, 124-127
ReadProperties event, 184, 431

ReadProperty method, 110
ReBind method, 373
reboot, blocking, 613-614
record selectors, DataGrid control, 367
recording apartment events, 208
Recordset object, 264, 287
   data sources, 184
rectangles, drawing rounded corners, 603-604
reducing dots (objects), 845-846
re-entrancy, multithreaded components, 200
reference counting, 71-73
Reference to your Transaction Server Object listing, 912
references, 561
   arguments, passing, 585-586
referential integrity, relational database, 275
Refresh( ) method, 89, 139
RegAdd function, 704
RegCloseKey API function, 723
RegDelete function listings, 731
RegDeleteKey API function, 723
RegEdit
   backing up, 718
   System Registry, INI files, 715
registering DLLs, Transaction Server, 903-906
RegOpenKeyEx API function, 722
RegRetrieve function listing, 730
relational databases
   ADO, 270-276
   data normalization, 272
   foreign keys, 273-275
   indices, 275
   primary keys, 271-272
   referential integrity, 275
   tables, 271
   views, 276
relationships, joining, 352
RemoteHost property, 523, 542
RemotePort property, 523, 542
remoting, ADO, 295-296

Replace function, 12
Reply button's Click event listing, 512
ReplyAll button's Click event listing, 512
Report Footer, 322
Report Header, 322
reports
   Crystal Reports, 334
   Data Report Utility, 316
      creating, 316-334
   designing, 321-327
   exporting, 332-334
   previewing, 328-330
   printing, 331-332
   sections, Data Report Utility, 322
   viewing, 328-330
RequestTimeout property, 523
Resize event, LightButton control, 100
resizing controls, 100, 104
Resource Compiler, wizards, 686
Resource Editor, 52-56
resource files, wizards, 683-687
ResponseCode property, 523
ResponseInfo property, 523
retrieving data (SQL), 394-403
returning VSS files, 925
reverse engineering, Visual Modeler, 59
Reverse Text program listing, 880
ReverseText Sub procedure listing, 883
RLE (Run-Length Encoding) compression algorithms, 869-873
RLEUncompress routines listing, 870
rotating text, APIs, 604-606
Round function, 12
round-robin threading model, 202-203
round-trip engineering, 59
Rounded corner rectangle listing, 603
RoundRect& API function, 599, 603-604
RowMember property, 358
RowSource property, 358
Run command (Query menu),

307
running VSS from VB6,
  927-930
runtime, 112-116
  instantiating forms, 803-805
runtime mode (ActiveX controls), 114

S

Safety Settings dialog box,
  480
SAPI (Speech Application
  Programming Interface),
  628
  applications, creating,
    629-630, 633-635
  introduction, 628-629
  Text-to-Speech, 628
  voice recognition, 628
SaveSetting statement
  (Registry), 719
Scripts object, 458
Scroll event, 431
secondary windows (Help),
  759
sections (reports), Data
  Report Utility, 322
SECURITY_ATTRIBUTES structure, API system functions,
  609
SelColor property, 124
Select User Control Type
  dialog box, 347
SelectedItem property, 34
selecting
  component types, 848-850
    Web-based, 849
  data, SQL, 395-397
selecting specific voice type
  listing, 637
Selection object, 458
SelPicture property, 124
SelText property, 34
Send method, 512
SendActivityLog subroutine
  listing, 499
SendComplete event, 546
SendData method, 544
sending MAPI messages, 502
SendProgess event, 546
sequence diagrams, OOA,
  247-252
sequential INI files, 692

serializing calls, 201
server-side VBScript, 161
servers
  distributed transaction processing, 890
    business-logic tier, 890
    data server tier, 891
    *Object Request Brokers,
      892-893*
    *transaction monitors,
      891-892*
  n-tier, 890
  proxy, Internet Transfer
    Control, 529-530
  Transaction Servers, 890-893
    business-logic tier, 890
    data server tier, 891
    *integrating VB classes,
      896-908*
    introduction, 893-895
    managing database connections, 894
    *managing distributed
      objects, 895*
    *Object Request Brokers,
      892-893*
    *transaction coordination,
      895*
    *transaction monitors,
      891-892*
service providers, MAPI, 484
SetFirstVisible method, 34
setting
  product ID, Transaction
    Server, 910-911
  triggers, SQL Editor, 340-341
setting up
  Data Environment, 317-321
  Find (Help), 757-758
  joins, SQL, 400-402
  microphones, speech recognition, 630
Setup Wizard, 155, 661-662
sharing components, 917
Shell command, API system
  functions, 608
Shell sort method, sorting
  algorithms, 859
Show event, 431
showdialog argument, 333
Simple MAPI, 486
single-threaded components,
  849
single-use objects, multithreaded, 210-211
SingleUse class, 211

sited controls, 106
sizing ActiveX controls, 94
  LightButton example, 100
SmallChange property, 47
SMTP, MAPI, 485
sorting
  algorithms, 858-863
    Bubble, 859
    Exchange, 859
    Heap, 859
    Insertion, 859
    Quick, 860
    Shell, 859
  strings, list boxes, 843
Source Code Control Options
  dialog box, 927
source control, developing,
  916-917
source events, OLE, 811
source files, safety, 918
sources (data)
  creating, 176-192
  functionality, 186-190
  methods, 190-191
  properties, 180-185
SourceSafe Options dialog
  box, 920
spaghetti code, 216
Speak method, 641
Speech Application
  Programming Interface, *see*
  SAPI
speech recognition
  applications, creating,
    629-630, 633-635
  microphones, setting up, 630
speech recognition code
  listing, 633
Speech SDK, building applications, 630
splash screens, 846
Split function, 12
Split object, DataGrid control, 373-374
Spooler, MAPI, 488
SQL (Structured Query
  Language), 392
  aggregates, 402-403
  columns, 410-411
  data
    deleting, 405
    inserting, 403-405
    *limiting selections,
      397-400*
    retrieving, 394-403

selecting, *395-397*
updating, *406-407*
database engines, 392
indexes, 410-411
ISQL, 393
joins, setting up, 400-402
queries, 308, 311
SQL Datasheet, 393
statements, 305
grouping, *407-409*
Query Designer, *304-305,
341*
SELECT, *394*
tables
creating, *409-410*
deleting, *411*
working with, 392-396,
399-411
SQL Editor
databases, 339-341
triggers, setting, 340-341
SQL Query designer, 341
Database Environment,
304-305
**STARTUPINFO declaration
listing, 610**
State property, 543
StateChanged event, 528
**stateless objects, Transaction
Server, 898**
statements
DeleteSetting, 720
RaiseEvent, 87
SQL, 305
grouping, *407-409*
VBScript, 173-174
states
classes, 220
DHTML, maintainence,
470-473
Step Into option, 786
**stepping through code,
debugging, 785-787**
StillExecuting property, 523
storages, 74
**stored procedures, SQL
Editor, 339**
streams, 74
StretchBlt (API funtion), 599
**StretchBlt& (API function),
599-602**
**strings, sorting (list boxes),
843**
**StripPunctuation function
listing, 885**
StrReverse function, 13

strSubkeys array, 728
strTempKeys array, 728
Stylesheets object, 458
subclasses, 220
**subkeys, System Registry,
719**
subprojects, VSS, 922
subsystem brokers, 230
subsystems, 229-230
**Supplementary Telephony,
TAPI, 619**
**system functions, APIs,
607-615**
System Registry
editors, creating, 725-735
INI files, 715-717
accessing, *718-720*
keys, 719
RegEdit, 715
subkeys, 719
Windows API, accessing, 720
system scheduler, 196

T

T-SQL Debugger, 392, 412
breakpoints, 419-421
installing, 412
Options, 421
queries
creating, *415-417*
debugging, *419-421*
executing, *417-419*
using, 414-415, 418-421
tables
relational database, 271
SQL
creating, *409-410*
deleting, *411*
**TAPI (Telephony Applications
Programmer Interface), 618**
applications, creating, 620-625
Basic Telephony, 619
controls, 622
Extended Telephony, 619
ISDN, 619
line devices, 619
needed materials, 621
phone devices, 619
POTS, 619
properties, 622
sample program, 621-625
Supplementary Telephony,
619
TAPI21.EXE, 621

telephony, 619-620
**TAPI function declaration list-
ing, 623**
**TAPI sample program listing,
623**
**tapiRequestMakeCall TAPI
function, 625**
**TAPIStatus Sub procedure
listing, 624**
target events (OLE), 811-812
**tbrEdit_ButtonClick event
listing, 29**
**tbrFile_ButtonClick event list-
ing, 30**
TCP, Winsock, 540
**TCP/IP (Transmission Control
Protocol/Internet Protocol),
536**
protocol stacks, 536
Winsock
controls, *539-547*
events, *545-547*
introduction, *536-539*
IP addresses, *538*
methods, *543-545*
operating modes, *540*
ports, *539*
properties, *541-542*
TCP, *540*
UDP, *540*
telephony, 618
Basic Telephony, 619
Extended Telephony, 619
ISDN, 619
line devices, 619
POTS, 619
Supplementary Telephony,
619
TAPI, 619-620
Template Manager, 62-64
templates
code benchmarking, creating,
836-839
Template Manager, 62
wizards, building, 668
testing
ActiveX controls, 127-128
LightButton example,
103-104
test forms, *101-103*
ActiveX documents, 441
applications, 834
compiled versions, 835
multithreaded systems,
208-210
text

APIs, rotating, 604-606
Help, entering, 741-743
Text property (ActiveX controls), 88
Text-to-Speech control, 638
Text-to-Speech, SAPI, 628
thick clients, 547
client/server, 278
thin clients, 547
ThreadID property, 198
threads, 196-197
active, 203
ActiveX components, 197
aggregation, 201-203
control, 203
non-deterministic, 203
round-robin, 202-203
safety, 203
Three-Tiered Service Model, 57
Timer event, 99
LightButton control, 98-99
tmrChkStatus's Timer event listing, 98
tmrChkStatus_Timer event (LightButton control), 126-127
Toolbar Wizard, 16
toolbars, bands, 20-21
toolbox, changing icons, 147
Toolbox, VBA, 878
Tools menu commands
Add Procedure, 116
Procedure Attributes, 129
Top property (ActiveX controls), 88
topic IDs
Help, 744-747
mapping, 750
topics, Help
building, 739-743
labeling, 744-747
tracking project versions, 926
transaction context (Transaction Server), 899-903
transaction coordination (Transaction Server), 895
Transaction Monitors, 890
distributed transaction processing, 891-892
Transaction Server
components, installing, 905-906
database connections, managing, 894
distributed objects, managing, 895

DLLs, registering, 903-906
introduction, 893-895
objects, calling, 908-913
packages, creating, 903-904
product ID, setting, 910-911
stateless objects, 898
transaction attributes, 899
transaction context, 899-903
transaction coordination, 895
VB classes, integrating, 896-908
Transaction Server Explorer, 903
Transaction Servers, 890
transactions
context, Transaction Server, 899-903
SQL statements, grouping, 407-409
use-case, 245
transport providers, MAPI, 487
triggers, setting (SQL Editor), 340-341
tuning applications, 832-833
compiler, 841
two-tiered client/server applications, 277

U

UBound property, 806
UDP, Winsock, 540
unattended execution, multi-threaded components, 199
Universal Naming Convention, 445
unpopulated space, MSHFlexGrid control, 375
updating SQL data, 406-407
use-case methodology, OOA, 239-254
problem statement, 240-245
use-case transactions, 245
use-case model, OOA, 245-246
UseCoolbarColors property, 22
UseCoolbarPicture property, 22
user connections, 843
user-drawn controls (ActiveX), 76, 86
USER32.DLL API, 581-582
UserControl object, 94

properties, 431-432
UserControl's Resize event listing, 100
UserControl_Resize event listing, 180
UserDocument object, 430-435, 449
UserName property, 524
utilities
API Viewer, 50-51
RegEdit, 715
Resource Editor, 52-56
Template Manager, 62-64
Visual Component Manager, 59-62
Visual Modeler, 56-59

V

Validate event, 34
ValidateUserInput routine listing, 679
values, passing arguments, 585-586
variables, Boolean, 882
VariantHeight property, 24
VBA (Visual Basic for Applications), 876
development environment, 877-879
functions, adding, 877
macros, 880
menu bars, 879
programming differences, 879-888
programs, 880
Toolbox, 878
VBE object, 645
VBProjects collection, 646
VBScript, 160-174
client-side scripting, 161
example script, 163
functions, 167-173
conversions, 172
scripting engines, 172
testing, 172
objects, 161-162
operators, 167
procedures, 162
server-side, 161
statements, 173-174

VBScript code in HTML document listing, 163-164
VBX, 75
verbs, objects, 568
versioning, 72
versions
 numbers, VSS, 926
 projects, tracking, 926
views, relational database, 276
Visible property (ActiveX controls), 88
visual behavior, drag and drop OLE, 822
Visual Component Manager, 59-62
Visual Data Tools, 338-341
Visual Modeler, 56-59
voice recognition, SAPI, 628
Voice Text control, 629
VScrollBar control, 46
VSS (Visual SourceSafe)
 Admin user, 919
 administrating, 919
 Administrator, 918
 ANALYZE program, 921
 date/time, 926
 developing, 917-922
 explorer, 922
 File Types page, 921
 files
  adding, 926
  checking out, 924
  returning, 925
 functionality, 917-918
 General page, 921
 Guest user, 920
 labels, 926
 options, 927
 Project Security page, 921
 projects
  existing VB6, 929-931
  new VB6, 931
  using, 922-925
 server, installing, 918
 Shadow Folders page, 921
 subprojects, 922
 VB6, running, 927-930
 version numbers, 926
 Web Projects page, 921
 Web tabbed page, 921
 working folder, 923

W-Z

waiting, child processes, 608-612
Watch Expression option, 789
Watches window (debugging), 788
Web components, optimizing, 849
Web pages, controls, 155
WeekdayName function, 13
WhatsThisHelpID object, 777
Width property (ActiveX controls), 88
Win APIs
 display functions, 599-607
 graphics functions, 599-607
 system functions, 607-615
WIN.INI, INI files, 693
Windows arguments, passing, 585-586
windows
 captions, flashing, 606-607
 debugging, 787-791
 Help formats, 759-760
Windows API
 applications, 592-593
  optimizing, 843
 argument data types, 586-588
 callbacks, 594-595
 functions
  declaring, 583-585
  private INI files, 693
  WIN.INI, 692
 INI files, accessing, 692-697
 library files, 580-583
 System Registry
  accessing, 720
  functions, 721
Windows caption flasher listing, 607
Windows collection, 647
Windows Properties dialog box, 759
WinHelp system, 775-778
Winsock (Windows Sockets), 537
 client/server example, 547-555
 controls
  events, 545-547
  methods, 543-545
  operating modes, 540
  properties, 541-542
  TCP, 540

TCP/IP, 538, 539-547
 UDP, 540
TCP/IP
 introduction, 536-539
 IP addresses, 538
 ports, 539
Wizard Manager, 665-666, 671-675
Wizard source code Resource File listing, 685
Wizard template listing, 677
wizards
 ActiveX Document Migration, 448-451
 Add-In Designer, 14
 Application, 14
 building, 666
 creating, 662-665
 Data Form, 13, 349-354
 Data Object, 342, 345-348
 Data Object Generator, 13
 designing, 662
 Manger, 665-666, 671-675
 Microphone Setup, 630
 new features, 13-16
 Package and Deployment, 13-15, 156
  installing, 477
  operating, 477-481
 Publish, 62
 Resource Compiler, 686
 resource files, 683-687
 Setup, 13, 155, 661-662
 templates, building, 668
 Toolbar, 16
working folder, VSS, 923
WritePrivateProfileSection API function, 696
WritePrivateProfileString API function, 697
WriteProfileSection API function, 696
WriteProfileString API function, 697
WriteProperties event, 184, 431
WriteProperty method, 109-110
writing properties, 124-127

XOR encryption algorithms, 865
XOREncryption routine listing, 866

Sams Teach Yourself Database Programming With Visual Basic 6 in 21 Days

Curtis Smith and Mike Amundsen

Sams Teach Yourself Database Programming with Visual Basic 6 in 21 Days is a tutorial that allows the reader to learn about working with databases in a set amount of time. The book presents the reader with a step-by-step approach to learning what can be a critical topic for developing applications. Each week focuses on a different aspect of database programming with Visual Basic. Week 1—Data Controls and Microsoft Access Databases. Learn about issues related to building simple database applications using the extensive collection of data controls available with VB. Week 2—Programming with the Microsoft Jet Engine. Concentrate on techniques for creating database applications using Visual Basic code. Week Three—Programming with ODBC Interface and SQL. Study advanced topics such as SQL data definition and manipulation language, and issues for multiuser applications such as locking schemes, database integrity, and application-level security.

$45.00 US/$64.95 CDN
0-672-31308-1

1000 pp.
Sams

Sams Teach Yourself OOP With Visual Basic in 21 Days

John D. Conley III

In just 21 days, you'll have all the skills you need to get up and running efficiently. With this complete tutorial, you'll master the basics and then move on to the more advanced features and concepts. Understand the fundamentals of object-oriented programming with Visual Basic. Master all of the new and advanced features that object-oriented programming with Visual Basic offers. Learn how to effectively use the latest tools and features of topic by following practical, real-world examples. Get expert tips from a leading authority on implementing object-oriented programming with Visual Basic in the corporate environment. This book is designed for the way you learn. Go chapter by chapter through the warranted, step-by-step lessons, or just choose those lessons that interest you the most.

$39.99 US/$56.95 CDN
0-672-31299-9

600 pp.
Sams

Dan Appleman's Visual Basic 5.0 Programmer's Guide to the Win32 API

Daniel Appleman

No other book on the market can compete with this complete guide to the Win32 API. It is already being hailed as the definitive reference for Visual Basic programmers as it contains a wealth of background information on how Windows works. It includes the API Toolkit and Desaware API Class Library. The CD-ROM contains video annotations by the author in the full text, searchable edition of the book and source code examples.

$59.99 US/$84.95 CDN
1-56276-446-2
CD-ROM

Beginning - Advanced
1,584 pp.
Sams

Sams Teach Yourself More Visual Basic 6 in 21 Days

Lowell Mauer

Provides comprehensive, self-taught coverage of the most sought-after topics in Visual Basic programming. This book uses the step-by-step approach of the best-selling Sams Teach Yourself series to continue more detailed coverage of the latest version of Visual Basic. Not only does this book cover a wide array of topics, but it also goes into each topic to a level that the reader can apply to their own programs. In addition, this book includes various tips and tricks of Visual Basic programming that will help the more inexperienced programmer. Topics include: enhanced controls, collections, loops, and other things; procedures, functions, and logic; MDI and SDI window types; database processing and designing a database application; data bound controls, Data Form Wizard, and OLE Drag and Drop; Internet programming and ActiveX Documents and building Online Help and using Crystal Reports. It includes complete coverage of database applications and uses real-world applications to demonstrate specialized programming. It teaches the user how to incorporate Crystal Reports into their applications.

$29.99 US/$42.95CDN
0-672-31307-3

Beginner-Intermediate
700 pp.
Sams

Add to Your Sams Library Today with the Best Books for Programming, Operating Systems, and New Technologies

To order, visit our Web site at www.mcp.com or fax us at

1-800-835-3202

ISBN	Quantity	Description of Item	Unit Cost	Total Cost
0-672-31308-1		Sams Teach Yourself Database Programming with Visual Basic 6 in 21 Days	$45.00	
0-672-31299-9		Sams Teach Yourself OOP with Visual Basic in 21 Days	$39.99	
1-56276-446-2		Dan Appleman's Visual Basic 5.0 Programmer's Guide to the Win32 API	$59.99	
0-672-31307-3		Sams Teach Yourself More Visual Basic 6 in 21 Days	$29.99	
		Shipping and Handling: See information below.		
		TOTAL		

Shipping and Handling

Standard	$5.00
2nd Day	$10.00
Next Day	$17.50
International	$40.00

201 W. 103rd Street, Indianapolis, Indiana 46290   1-800-835-3202 — FAX

Book ISBN 0-672-31309-X

What's on the CD-ROM

The companion CD-ROM contains all of the authors' source code and samples from the book and many third-party software products.

Windows 95/98/NT4 Installation Instructions

1. Insert the CD-ROM disc into your CD-ROM drive.
2. From the Windows 95 desktop, double-click the My Computer icon.
3. Double-click the icon representing your CD-ROM drive.
4. Double-click the icon titled SETUP.EXE to run the installation program.
5. Installation creates a program group named "VB6 Unleashed." This group will contain icons to browse the CD-ROM.

NOTE

If Windows 95 is installed on your computer and you have the AutoPlay feature enabled, the disc starts automatically whenever you insert the disc into your CD-ROM drive.